IMMIGRATION

Public Legislation and Private Bills

Bernadette Maguire

University Press of America, Inc.
Lanham • New York • Oxford

University Press of America,® Inc.
4720 Boston Way
Lanham, Maryland 20706

12 Hid's Copse Rd.
Cummor Hill, Oxford OX2 9JJ

Printed in the United States of America
British Library Cataloguing in Publication Information Available

Library of Congress Cataloging-in-Publication Data

Maguire, Bernadette
Immigration : public legislation and private bills / Bernadette Maguire.
p: cm.
Includes bibliographical references and index.
1. Emigration and immigration law--United States. 2. United States.
Congress--Private bills I. Title.
KF4829.M34 1997 342.73'082--dc21 97-24848 CIP

ISBN 0-7618-0791-8 (cloth: alk. ppr.)

∞™ The paper used in this publication meets the minimum requirements of American National Standard for information Sciences—Permanence of Paper for Printed Library Materials, ANSI Z39.48—1984

To ALP

CHAPTER 3

CHAPTER 4

CHAPTER 5

List of Figures

Foreword

The unique characteristics of private immigration bills command special recognition. "Immigration: Public Legislation and Private Bills" accomplishes that by revealing for the first time the drama of these individual cases. By doing so, the author exposes the human toll and the unintended consequences that our immigration laws can have on individuals.

I congratulate Bernadette Maguire on the breadth and scope of this project. The sheer unwieldiness and complexity of the immigration law does not lend itself easily to case by case analysis. By using her special expertise of the legislative process and immigration laws, she explains how a constituent's letter describing an extraordinary set of circumstances immediately compels his Member of Congress to seek special redress from the parameters of the general law. These are cases which usually would not come before Congress but for their particularly unique and compassionate nature.

For instance, a private bill allowed immigration benefits on behalf of Mishleen Earle, the widow of a Navy Corpsman whose tragic death in the 1983 bombing of Marine Headquarters in Beirut left her grieving and bereft of support. The special legislation recognized his sacrifice by allowing her to join his family in the United States. Another case involved Jacob Gross, a two-year old child who survived his family's airplane crash in Czechoslovakia in 1949. The bill allowed the grandparents to rescue the child from the prospects of an orphanage by bringing him to the United States.

In addition, the particular situation of defectors such as Viktor Belenko who flew his Soviet Mig-25 Foxbat interceptor to northern Japan in 1976 is among those cases where Congress recognized the special contribution of those who shared sensitive intelligence with this country, often at great peril to their own personal safety. These are some of the unique cases which demanded attention of the Congress, and which demonstrated some of the critical decisions which Congress confronts when it makes an exception to the general law.

Private bills serve another purpose, they portend changes in the general law. By tracing the enactment of private immigration bills on behalf of orphans from war-torn Europe and families separated due to medical conditions, this book shows how these humanitarian acts paved the way for remedial legislation. Trends in the number of private bill cases brought to the attention of Congress on behalf of spouses of United States citizens afflicted with tuberculosis and mental or physical impairments such as epilepsy are other examples. These cases starkly highlighted the need to change the general law in 1961 and 1965 to reunite the families and alleviate their suffering. It is a challenging story of how one person can change the law for many individuals.

It is also a history of how the integrity of the process is maintained through close legislative oversight, and reform of the rules which guide private immigration bills. The author does this by outlining the development of Rules of Procedure for fair and expeditious treatment of cases.

I commend Bernadette Maguire for providing this valuable resource for immigration experts and scholars of the legislative process. It is the seminal work in this area. Its history and precedents will help understand the role of Congress as a "court of equity" when special circumstances warrant relief from the general law.

PETER W. RODINO, JR.*

**Former Chairman, Committee on the Judiciary (D-NJ), U.S. House of Representatives (1973-1988)*

Preface

In 1974 I joined the staff of the Committee on the Judiciary of the House of Representatives, and from then on I became intrigued with the legislative process. Steeped in the history of Congress and immigration law through the succeeding years by my mentors Jim Cline, Fran Christy, and Skip Endres, no law or case went unresearched. That is what started this book, the need to bring together all the history and cases which oftentimes were the foundation of amendments to the general law. Private bills became my life. Many times the Chairman of the Judiciary Committee, Peter W. Rodino, Jr., asked for the precedents of a particular case, and Jim or Skip asked "have we done this before?" I trekked into the archives of private bills to find support for, or ammunition against, a particular case. Forever in the committee archives, and later in the National Archives researching this book, I soldiered onward to finally review over 7,000 private laws.

How do you say thanks to these special people for getting me started on the way? Bringing it all together in this book is my way of saying thanks to all of them, for bringing me on staff, and for their support throughout my career. As "Mr. Immigration," Congressman Rodino, stated in the foreword, the story of private bills starts with the constituent, but as the legislation goes through Congress, there are many people who guide it along the way. Among those are the staff cultivating the facts and the precedents, and the Members of Congress making the tough decisions striving to maintain integrity in the process. I am honored to be among those who participated in this process.

From the beginning, the task was daunting. As I reviewed the legislative history of each private law, the uniqueness of each case became evident. This made the decision as to which cases to choose for precedents more difficult. In reviewing them, some cases have been chosen because of their unique aspects, particularly the individual or family hardship encountered. Other cases have been selected because they represented a trend in a particular area leading to changes in the general law.

In researching why an exception to the law was necessary, I had to understand the historical perspective of the changes in the general law. My frame of reference became such tomes on immigration law as Edward P. Hutchinson's *Legislative History of American Immigration Policy* and John Higham's *Send These To Me*. As that second phase of the historical research progressed, the links between private bills and public legislation became even more apparent.

The third stage then evolved, demonstrating through private law cases and statistical analysis the relationship between private bills and public legislation. But, once this was accomplished, the purpose of the book still did not yield the complete results, and that left the fourth and final stage of the book, to enlighten the public on the private bill process. To do this, the journey of the private bill from constituent to law had to take place. This involved explaining the rules and process for private bills.

The book is organized for academic pursuits as a supplement to books on the political process. It demonstrates how legislation for one person is as much a part of the democratic process as making laws for the general public. The information on Congress's internal checks and balances, and Executive Branch checks on the system offer insights to important parts of the process.

The book is also structured, however, to meet the needs of historians and immigration experts. The precedents are arranged for use as a resource for public officials and private citizens to determine whether a case may be the subject of a private bill. Case summaries are listed by type of private law rather than solely citations.

Since there are a wide variety of books on immigration, this book focuses primarily on those laws where private bills had the most impact. For that reason, the historical perspective is a necessary prelude to the precedents. For instance, the National Origins Quota Act of 1921 was the principal immigration law determining the numbers and countries from which immigration flowed until 1965. To understand why Congress enacted so many private laws for occupations such as sheepherders from Spain and nuns from Italy, and at the same time excluded aliens from Japan and China, the basic law at that time must be understood. In addition, a historical setting provides a context for societal changes which are reflected in the changes to the immigration laws as well as the private laws. Extensive use of endnotes has been made to provide the researcher with more information as to why a private law was not covered already in the general law.

I have presented the three major areas of immigration law separately, that is, quota, exclusion, and naturalization. In this way, the specific trends and statistical analyses are identified as clearly as possible. These distinct categories also enhance the book's use as a reference tool.

In the sections on the legislative process, a basic guide to following legislation is the brochure "How Our Laws Are Made." For this purpose I did not go into specific details on the intricacies of Congress. The book's emphasis lies on those portions of the legislative process, such as the House Private Calendar, which play a significant role in the processing of private immigration bills. Also, my tenure with the Committee ended with the 100th Congress, thus this book completes its cycle at that point.

There are four lessons learned from this book. First, as Fran Christy has stated, the more equitable the general immigration laws become, the less there is a need for private bills. Second, when Congress enacts changes to the general law without adequate mechanisms to take care of hardship situations, the need for private bills is triggered. Third, precedents showing the controversial aspects of some of the general laws, such as the high volume of private bills waiving exclusion of those "ineligible due to race," can be a lesson in the results of discriminatory laws. Fourth, checks and balances within the Congress, and leadership from the Executive Branch, best serve the public in processing private legislation as well as in the general laws.

This book would not have been possible without Fran Christy's institutional memory of the voluminous cases which made precedents. Her reputation for knowledge of the immigration law, and her compassion in many cases brought before the Congress, were the foundation for my learning experience as her successor on the Judiciary Committee staff. As I came before the Subcommittee meetings to present the private bills for action, her words of advice "know your cases" were always with me.

One of the most important influences in immigration legislation to whom this book owes its start was Jim Cline. Although Jim died before the book was finished, he regaled me with many stories of some of the cases which started me on my mission. Like Fran, he had words of advice to me which I brought to each case, "be objective."

Many more people helped along the way, or inspired me to acquaint the public with this special legislative vehicle. Skip Endres,

Immigration Subcommittee Counsel, made sure private bills were handled with the same importance as other legislation. Others whose technical advice during my tenure with the Subcommittee laid the foundation upon which I could make this contribution on private bills were: Neil Leary with the INS, Dick Scully with the Department of State, Joyce Vialet with the Library of Congress, and Ed Grossman with the Office of Legislative Counsel, House of Representatives.

But it is also the Members of Congress who met the challenge of reviewing these cases to whom I am also thankful. Members such as Romano L. Mazzoli (D-KY), Hamilton Fish, Jr. (R-NY), Daniel Lungren (R-CA), F. James Sensenbrenner (R-WI), Barney Frank (D-MA), Sen. Edward M. Kennedy (D-MA), and Sen. Alan K. Simpson (R-WY). Giants in the immigration field like Francis E. Walter (D-PA) and Emanuel Celler (D-NY) are mentioned often in this book and their knowledge of the rules on private bills established precedents upheld by succeeding Congresses.

But most of all, the insistence of "Mr. Immigration," Peter W. Rodino, Jr. (D-NJ), on knowledge of the law and fairness to the beneficiary, and to those whose cases did not reach Congress, made my job of processing private bills so rewarding.

Much gratitude goes to Juan Osuna, my editor, whose questions and expertise in the immigration law kept the book focused. When I haven't adhered to his suggestions, I'll shoulder any criticism as a result. I also thank my sister, Mary, who worked on the precedents, along with her team of experts. We shared many hard decisions on which cases needed to be eliminated to bring the book into a manageable size and useable format. Mary died shortly before this book went to press, after bravely fighting an acute illness. Veronica Woo also helped with assuring the accuracy of the precedents. My friend, Lynn Jacquez, was the first to get me started as she embarked on her own career. And, finally, I thank Cheryl Barnes who rescued the book from potential software disasters and developed the camera-ready copy.

Chapter 1

What Is A Private Bill?

Private bills derive from the English system of government whose origins were "as assemblies for the redress of wrongs and the remedy of abuses."[1] Petitions from individuals requesting relief from the law had been filed with Parliament and became known as private legislation.[2]

Congress and the courts have accepted the right of petition by means of a private bill.[3] The use of private bills as a function of Congress originally met with opposition. John Quincy Adams, for example, viewed private bills as inconsistent with the separation of powers principle:

> There ought to be no private bills before Congress...There is a great defect in our institutions by want of a court of Exchequer or Chambers of Accounts * * * A deliberative assembly is the worst of all tribunals for the administration of justice.[4]

Despite these concerns, nine private bills became law in the First Congress.[5] The first of these resulted from a petition filed by Baron de Glaubeck to allow payment of wages as a captain in the United States Army. At that time the authority for the enactment of private bills was unclear.[6] Although the right to petition Congress under the First Amendment has been held by some as the basis for Congressional enactment of private bills,[7] that Amendment was not ratified until December 15, 1791, two years after enactment of the first law on behalf of Baron de Glaubeck.[8]

The First Amendment to the Constitution of the United States states:

> Congress shall make no law respecting an establishment of religion, or prohibiting the free exercise thereof; or abridging the freedom of speech, or of the press; or the right of the people peaceably to assemble, *and to petition the Government for a redress of grievances.*[9]

It is the last phrase of the First Amendment that has been cited as authority for private bills. The introduction of a bill or petitioning of Congress does not, however, guarantee the enactment of a private law.[10] Power to enact private laws is solely within the authority granted to Congress under Article I relating to the responsibilities of the legislature to pay the debts of the United States which the courts have interpreted to include moral or even honorary debts.[11] The authority of Congress to enact immigration laws, under the commerce clause of the same Article, may also be interpreted as entitlement of Congress to enact private immigration bills.[12]

The underlying principle of any private bill is to correct an injustice which cannot be remedied under the general law. As the United States Supreme Court noted in 1896 in *United States v. Realty Co*, private bills act as the nation's conscience:

> It is conceded and indeed it cannot be questioned that the debts are not limited to those which are evidenced by some written obligation or to those which are otherwise of a strictly legal character. The term 'debts' includes those debts or claims which rest upon a merely equitable or honorary obligation, and which would not be recoverable in a court of law if existing against an individual. The nation, speaking broadly, owes a 'debt' to an individual when his claim grows out of general principles of right and justice; when, in other words, it is based upon considerations of a moral or merely honorary nature, such as are binding on the conscience or the honor of an individual, although the debt could obtain no recognition in a court of law.[13]

Other constitutional aspects of the private bill, however, have been questioned. Scholars have discussed possible objections such as the "equal protection" clause when an individual with almost identical facts may be denied relief, and the separation of powers doctrine recognizing the private bills as an "inherently judicial" act, or as a bill of attainder. But, as scholars have noted, the long held acceptance of the private bill leaves many of these objections as "largely speculative" since their "justiciability is severely limited."[14]

The difference between private bills and public bills has been outlined in the House of Representatives:

A private bill is a bill for the relief of one or several specified persons, corporations, institutions, etc., and is distinguished from a public bill, which relates to public matters and deals with individuals only by classes.[15]

Although the Senate Rules contain no such definition, precedents conform to that rule. Because of the difficulty at times of distinguishing between public bills and private bills, the final determination lies with the Speaker of the House or the President Pro-tempore of the Senate who reviews its details and determines whether the bill relates to an individual or a class.[16]

At the time when private bills became a frequent vehicle for redress after the Civil War, most cases related to debts of the nation to soldiers, widows, and children who had been victimized by war. Among other things, these claims against the Government paid pensions, resolved military status, and occasionally resolved patent disputes on behalf of individuals.[17] Immigration bills were very few in the early days of Congress. The first private immigration law on behalf of Dr. John Campbell White on February 13, 1839 corrected court records admitting him to citizenship.[18] By the 75th Congress (1937-1938), however, the number of immigration bills introduced and enacted began to occur with regularity.

Factors To Consider

Hardship is the principle determining factor in private immigration bills. The case must be extraordinary in circumstance to justify an exception to the general law. House Committee on the Judiciary Chairman Peter W. Rodino, Jr. (D-NJ), explained in 1971:

> A private immigration bill is an extraordinary remedy available to assist aliens with unusual problems resulting in unusual hardship. The private immigration bill is, in essence, an exception to the general law and should be viewed as such and not as a method to circumvent the general law.[19]

In addition to the threshold hardship criteria, the second element of major significance for a private law is Congressional precedents. When confronted with a particular case, the Congress looks to past action to determine whether a bill should be enacted into law. In some cases, Executive Branch opposition, veto by the President, or failure of passage in the House of Representatives or the Senate of similar bills strongly indicate potential failure to become law. Conversely, the large number of precedent cases showing strong relationships to United States citizen relatives indicate possible favorable disposition to a similar case.

While hardship is of necessity a subjective standard, the precedents of Congress indicate that historically the same general criteria have been used. Factors such as the beneficiary's relationship to a United States citizen, a lack of remedy under existing law, mental or physical ailments, and the United States national interest are considered. Two precedents illustrate the hardship criteria. One involved a 13-month old child from Germany who had been adopted by United States citizens. The adoptive parents had lost two infant children to a liver disease. The second case admitted the widow of a United States citizen killed in a terrorist act against the United States in Turkey.[20]

Precedents are important not only for Immigration Subcommittee consideration but also for the processing through Congress and final enactment. Precedents can help or hinder a case, can guide a bill through Congress, or kill it upon introduction.

The precedents provided later in this book illustrate the types of cases which have become law. These precedents have developed over 100 Congresses and reflect the hardship situations prompting private immigration bills. They have developed in some instances as a result of Executive Branch recommendations on the merits, or where a veto is likely.

The selected precedents represent unique types of private bills. They also have been chosen as representative of trends in private bills which demonstrate their relationship to public legislation. Some cases highlight the position of the Executive Branch.

Immigration Subcommittee Rules also illustrate the precedents and indicate where favorable action is unlikely due to lack of precedents. Two such areas are cases involving draft dodgers and aliens convicted of criminal offenses. Also, the Rules indicate the difficulty of waiving the citizenship laws in specific private bills. On the other hand, the Rules can be a positive factor in adoption cases, where the guidelines indicate generally favorable consideration.

In many respects, the precedents act as case law when reviewing private bill cases for possible action. As House Immigration Subcommittee Chairman Romano L. Mazzoli (D-KY), stated in a letter to House Members in 1983, "while the Subcommittee is not bound by precedent...it rarely deviates from precedent when handling private immigration bills."[21]

Public Legislation

Private bills serve another purpose; that is, they are a harbinger of changes to the general immigration law. Three areas of immigration law demonstrate this relationship: quota chargeability (allocation of permanent visas according to the country where an alien is born); grounds of exclusion (which bar admission to the United States); and requirements for citizenship.

The history of immigration to the United States is replete with diametrically opposed temperaments. Welcoming arms have been extended when building the country and filling certain needs for special skills as well as humanitarian impulses in times of war. These attitudes alternated with limitations on numbers during economic downturns or perceptions of harmful influences. In each case, special legislation, including private bills, pointed out the need for moderate and humane laws which accommodate close family relationships yet do not raise angst among the general population.

Briefly, the immigration system initially encouraged immigration with incentives such as land ownership and employment prospects. But the high volume of immigrants resulted in a demand for limits on immigration. The National Origins Act of 1921 limited the number and countries of origin of immigrants. That Act allocated each country a specific *quota* based on the number of natives of that country in the United States. This law greatly reduced immigration from southwestern European countries such as Italy and Greece. It applied to relatives of United States citizens as well as those who sought immigration for economic reasons.

Gradual restrictions preceded the quota laws through screening the types of aliens to enter the country. The screening measures, *exclusions*, barred admission to the United States of paupers, criminals, and insane aliens. Again, these exclusions barred any immigrant from entering the country, including relatives of citizens or permanent resident aliens.

At the same time, *naturalization* laws by 1907 came into disrepute. Various acts broadened the circumstances under which a United States citizen could lose citizenship, and sometimes tightened the process for an alien to acquire citizenship.

Many of these laws continued, particularly supported at times by economic conditions such as the Great Depression. Gradually, however, legislation broadened the ability of refugees to enter the United States outside the quotas, and provided special visas for orphans, spouses of United States citizens, and those with skills.

By the 1960's, the era of civil rights reforms, the immigration laws became more moderate, stressing family reunification, allowing certain categories of skills admissions, and setting a ceiling on overall immigration from all countries. Exclusions also became more flexible reflecting medical advances and allowing waivers for family members afflicted with epilepsy and insanity. International travel and the role of the United States engaged in commerce resulted in the pliability of the naturalization statutes for residence and eliminating most expatriating acts. Private bills were a significant factor in each of these developments.

Quota chargeability is the first area where private bills had a prominent role. Private bills sought to ameliorate the harsh results of the strict admission quota laws under the National Origins Quota Act of 1921. By narrowing the admissions policy, cases came to the attention of Congress seeking exemption from the law for those individuals from countries adversely affected by the 1921 Act, or for families separated due to birth in another country. These exceptions, embodied in private bills introduced by Members of Congress, helped pave the way to repeal of the national origins system of immigration in 1965. The 1965 legislation expanded the number of visas available to countries other than northwestern Europe.

In addition, private bills became the only means to achieve legal status for many individuals who entered the United States illegally or overstayed their visas. The majority of these people established long periods of residence in the United States, and some had United States citizen children. The high volume of bills for this group presaged remedial action in 1940 allowing such individuals permanent residence.

The second area paralleling the relationship between private bills and public legislation is the grounds for excluding aliens from the United States, especially in cases where the individual had a health condition or committed a minor criminal violation. In many cases citizen relatives sought the admission of these individuals by contacting a Member of Congress and asking for a private bill. The number of private bills increased to such a proportion that Congress felt the need to address the problem with more generic legislation in 1954 and 1957 allowing the Attorney General the discretion to waive those excludable offenses where appropriate to promote family reunification.

Naturalization statutes is the third category reflecting the relationship between private bills and public legislation. For example, private bills highlighted the unequal treatment of men and women under certain naturalization laws, resulting in efforts to make these laws more uniform. Special acts addressing expatriation through voting in foreign elections and prolonged residence abroad were the forerunners of laws to change loss of citizenship provisions in 1951 and 1959. Private bills also recognized that increased international travel and movement of people impacted on the ability of aliens to meet certain residence requirements for naturalization. In 1952 the law addressed these restrictions by allowing waivers of some of the residence requirements.

The impact of the increases in private bills and subsequent changes to the general law are revealed in the statistics. As a result of the 1952 and 1965 Acts, as well as House Subcommittee rules changes in 1969, the number of private bills introduced decreased to 2,866 in 1972 from an all time high of 7,293 in the 90th Congress (1967-1968). Senate and House Subcommittee Rules changes through 1981 resulted in further reductions in bills introduced as well as laws enacted, so that in the 100th Congress (1987-1988) the number of private bills introduced totaled 194, and 21 were enacted into law (See Fig. 4.1).

Chapter 2

Rules Governing Private Bills

There are two bodies of rules which govern private bills. The rules of the House of Representatives and the Senate guide consideration of all legislation in Congress. Specifically, the rules relate to debate on legislation by all Members of Congress on the Floor of the House of Representatives or the Senate which is reported from the Committees of jurisdiction. The respective Committees on the Judiciary in each House have jurisdiction over private bills, including private immigration bills. However, the Subcommittees within each Committee actually initiate any action on legislation through hearings and by preparing background reports. Therefore, the "Rules of Procedure" are adopted by the Subcommittees on Immigration and then affirmed by the Committees on the Judiciary.

Both rules are important in two respects. The Subcommittee rules impact initial action and whether legislation can move to consideration in the Committee and onward to the full House or Senate for debate and possible enactment. The Rules of the House and the Senate operate to endorse the action or defeat the legislation. This chapter outlines the history of both of these rules and how they help or hinder the ability to enact a bill on behalf of one individual.

Early Congressional Action

In the early years of the nation, Congress enacted relatively few private laws. Only nine of the 118 laws approved by the first Congress were private laws.[1] These nine laws related primarily to claims against the United States government. The number increased dramatically after the Civil War because no administrative mechanism existed for granting pensions, and war veterans and their widows sought redress from Congress. The number of private laws exceeded public laws in the 49th Congress (1885-1887), 1,031 to 434 respectively.[2] In the 59th Congress (1905-1907) the number increased dramatically, 6,249 private laws to 775 public laws. The private laws comprised 89% of the total, and most concerned pensions.[3]

After the enactment of general laws in the latter 1800s that allowed certain claims against the government to be handled administratively,[4] the number of private laws subsided; in the 60th Congress (1907-1909) private laws comprised only 36% of all laws enacted.[5] At that time private immigration bills were sparsely introduced and enacted into law. From the first private immigration bill in 1839, until 1938 Congress enacted 41 private immigration laws. In the 76th Congress (1939-1940), the number of private laws in that Congress alone totaled 35 which climbed steadily to 507 in the 81st Congress (1949-1950). Legislative efforts in 1940 and 1948 granted authority to the Attorney General to consider cases previously the subject of private immigration bills. Yet the numbers continued to rise.[6] By the 84th Congress (1955-1956), they peaked at 1,634 primarily due to the war years and the inability of contemporary immigration laws to deal with displaced persons from Europe seeking immigration.

The numbers of laws may appear high, but when compared to the number of private immigration bills and private claims bills *introduced*, the numbers demonstrate the effectiveness of close scrutiny. For instance, in the 76th Congress (1939-1940) the number of immigration bills which were introduced totaled 601 of which 35 became law, and in the 81st Congress (1949-1950) the number of private immigration bills introduced totaled 2,811 of which 507 became law. Private claims bills also follow this pattern. In the 81st Congress, the number of claims bills introduced totaled 1,980 of which 1,103 became law.[7]

The Congress spent a lot of time considering these private bill measures. As a result, Members of Congress sought to relieve their workload by refining the rules governing the consideration by making the process as orderly as possible, while continuing to carefully scrutinize each piece of legislation.

Congress instituted several in-house policing efforts to accommodate the time necessary for the other legislative business. In 1932 and 1935 the House private bill process limited debate time on private bills, and Members were appointed to screen bills prior to Floor action.

One of the final acts in organizing the manner of handling private bills was incorporated into the Legislative Reorganization Act of 1946.[8] That Act primarily reshuffled committee jurisdiction in the House and Senate because of previously overlapping functions. It also decreased the number of those committees as well as prohibited acts of Congress to correct military records, settle certain tort claims and provide for pensions.[9] In addressing private bills, the Senate Committee noted in its report on the legislation the inordinate amount of time taken for these cases:

> Private claims bills and inconsequential legislation dealing with local affairs and matters only slightly related to national policy take an excessive amount of congressional time from consideration of national affairs...Congress should jealously guard its time for ample debate and consideration of matters of national and international importance.[10]

Because the Reorganization Act eliminated the Committees on Immigration and entrusted the Committees on the Judiciary of each House with that jurisdiction, the Committees expected "several hundred more bills involving immigration and naturalization."[11]

The Senate and the House of Representatives differ greatly in their procedures for legislation. As the House of the "people," with 435 Members, the governing of that body is best achieved with a comprehensive set of rules. But in the Senate, the country's "deliberative" body of 100 Senators, there are few rules guiding legislative scheduling. These major differences are reflected in the following discussion on procedures on private immigration bills for the House and the Senate.

Rules of the House Of Representatives

The processing of private bill legislation in the House of Representatives is first guided by the House Rules and precedents of the House of Representatives.[12] These rules and precedents cover the legislative process in Committees and their jurisdiction, and debate on legislation after the particular Subcommittee and Committee which are assigned jurisdiction have acted upon a particular bill. In the case of immigration, the Committee on the Judiciary and its Subcommittee on Immigration have jurisdiction in this area. Once a bill is acted upon by these Committees, the legislation is scheduled for debate on the Floor of the House of Representatives.

The rules relating to debate on the House Floor concern such matters as the scheduling of bills for consideration, how long a piece of legislation can be debated, and the recognition of members for purposes of debate. The Rules of the House on private bills differ from other legislation because the time limits for consideration are narrower, and there are special screening mechanisms prior to consideration on the House Floor.

The Rules of the House of Representatives covering debate on the House Floor were significantly changed in 1932 and 1935 regarding the timeframe for consideration and screening for action. The rules provide a calendar to which all private bills are referred after action by the Committee; and they furnish a schedule for consideration of bills placed on the Calendar for debate.

> Rule XIII, clause 1: There shall be three calendars of business reported from committees, namely: First. A calendar of the Committee of the Whole House on the State of the Union to which shall be referred bills raising revenue, general appropriation bills, and bills of a public character, directly or indirectly appropriating money or property; Second. A House Calendar to which shall be referred all bills of a public character not raising revenue nor directly or indirectly appropriating money or property; and Third. A *calendar of the Committee on the Whole House, to which shall be referred all bills of a private character.*

> Rule XXIV, clause 6: On the first *Tuesday of each month after disposal of such business on the Speaker's table as requires reference only, the Speaker shall direct the Clerk to call the bills and resolutions on the Private Calendar*. Should objection be made by two or more Members to the consideration of any bill or resolution so called, it shall be recommitted to the committee which reported the bill or resolution, and no reservation of objection shall be entertained by the Speaker. Such bills and resolutions, if considered, shall be considered in the House as in the Committee of the Whole. No other business shall be in order on this day unless the House by two-thirds vote on motion to dispense therewith, shall otherwise determine...On the third Tuesday of each month...preference [shall] be given to omnibus bills.[13]

Although the first rule existed since 1839,[14] "most of the time "special orders" were used to consider private bills on the House Floor";[15] that is, requests by the Committee for certain periods of time to discuss private bills. By circumventing the Private Calendar, the Committee could request action on private bills without waiting for the particular date set aside to discuss such matters. This practice continued even with the major changes in 1932.[16]

Since 1810, the second rule specifying the date and time of consideration set aside Friday for consideration of private bills. Changes in 1935 moved the date to Tuesday, where it remains today. The bills are given priority consideration early in the day before other legislative items can interrupt action on them.[17]

Two major points of controversy recurred throughout the rules changes for private bills in the House: the lengthy time consumed in reviewing the bills, including the ability of members to use parliamentary maneuvers to conduct protracted debate on unrelated matters; and the role of "objectors" in screening bills. Proposing limitations on debate, by its very nature, may exclude some Members of Congress who may wish to speak to the merits of the legislation. For this reason, narrowing the democratic nature of the debate was controversial. On the other hand, the time consumed with these matters also excluded consideration of other legislation. In essence, limitations were seen as punitive in both cases.

1932 Rules Changes

The contentious nature of these arguments became evident in 1932, when Rule XXIV instituted limitations on debate time and special screening procedures. Because so many claims bills involved the payment of Government funds to beneficiaries, the bills and rules changes provoked much animosity. One member who opposed some of the claims measures was described by his colleague, Mr. Paul Shafer (R-IO), as "the self-styled Member who stands alone as guardian over the taxpayers' Treasury." In addition to placing a ten minute time limit on debate of private bills so that debate did not occur ad infinitum, the changes also provided for the appointment of certain House members to screen private bills after reaching the House Floor. This meant that the full House did not have to examine the bills. These members could halt the legislative process by voicing an "objection," thus they became known as the "Official Objectors."[18]

These changes provided more order to the process, but at the same time allowed one or two Members of Congress to withhold action on any private legislation. The latter continues to be one of the most controversial aspects of the legislative processing of private bills. A private bill can be denied consideration by the full House, thus negating the action of the Committee which reported the measure for action to the House. In some cases, a bill may be denied Floor action for an entire Congress. From a policy perspective, however, where some private bills lack sufficient precedent or merit, this can be a positive aspect of the Rules, as illustrated later in a review of the bills halted by the objectors.

At the time of the proposed rules, the debate indicated 30 pages of private bills for persons seeking redress. The centralization of power in a few Members resulted in a certain amount of distrust. Mr. Robert Luce (R-MA), a supporter of the change allowing a few Members to review the bills, stated, "This jury of 40 or 50 is likely to reach just as accurate and wise conclusions as if the 435 were present."[19] Among the opponents, Mr. Arthur H. Greenwood (D-IN), argued that a few Members would impose their own standards on the merits of private bills and effectively halt them forever.

> There have been those who believe that when a committee considers a bill...there ought to be an opportunity for such bills to be heard on their merits at some time and that no one man or group of three men ought to have the power to dislodge that bill, strike it from the calendar, and send it to a place where it can never again receive a hearing or be considered on its merits.[20]

Mr. James G. Strong (R-KN) defended the role of the objectors as not one simply of arbitrariness or capriciousness but one of gathering information:

> A man now passed from us, who spent a great deal of time going into this Private Calendar, used to rise, reserve the right to object, then cross-examine the man who had the bill in charge. If after that cross-examination he thought the bill was good, he withdrew his objection.[21]

Thus, in order to halt action completely on a private bill, one of the objectors needed to be recognized on the House Floor and then the Member would voice an objection to the bill. As a result, the bill would remain on the Private Calendar for each date that it was called until the end of the Congress. The objector had to voice an objection at each call of the Private Calendar to halt any consideration by the full House.

A different means of expressing concern with a particular private bill allowed an objector to express a "reservation of objection." This allowed the objector an opportunity to question the supporter of the bill or the Committee regarding some of the provisions. After the explanation, the objector could allow the bill to pass or object to the measure.

The last means available to the objectors under the rules of the Private Calendar occurred when three objectors voiced opposition. As a result, the legislation would not be passed, but would be placed on a "deferred" list for another call of the Private Calendar. At that time a specified period of debate time was divided between supporters and opponents, with further time for other participants. This allowed some of the controversial bills involving substantial claims against the government, or nonmeritorious immigration bills to be debated fully. Bills not approved were sent back to their originating Committee, and this ended any further action on these "recommitted" bills for the remainder of the Congress. Approved bills would be forwarded to the Senate.

1935 Rules Changes

In 1935 the rules addressed legislative filibustering which occurred in the use of the mechanism of "reservation of objection." Members charged that under this provision some of their colleagues made speeches for "consumption back home," and unrelated to the legislation being discussed even in the course of debate on a private bill. Eliminating the "reservation of objection" to seek responses to questions on cases, considerably reduced the time used for private bills.[22] In addition, the rules reduced the number of objectors needed to recommit a private bill back to the originating Committee from three to two; and instituted a new form of "omnibus" private bill for handling controversial matters.

When confronted with charges that the objectors thwarted the will of the Committees by logjamming private bills regardless of merit, one of the objectors, Mr. Thomas L. Blanton (D-TX), defended his role. He indicated that he was not predisposed to any bills, but the Speaker appointed him to watch for "bad bills," and he did so, and when the next Speaker resigned, he continued his watch. He also noted that it should lie on the "shoulders of every one of the 435 members of the House equally to stop bad bills." Mr. Marion A. Zioncheck (D-WA), another supporter of the need for reform, complained that sometimes the objectors did not perform their role properly, thus forcing the President to act as the final objector.[23] Mr. Clifford Hope (R-KN), one of the opponents of limiting debate on private bills, responded by arguing that there would be "nothing in the record to show why the

Member who made the objection did so. The committee to which the bill is recommitted should have the benefit of that information."[24]

As a balance to the new restrictions, the rules permitted debate in a different forum. For the first time, omnibus bills existed to deal with controversial measures. An omnibus bill could be only one controversial private claims or immigration bill, or it could include several private bills. The newly designated omnibus bill was one which had been presented to the House of Representatives previously, but it had been recommitted to the originating Committee due to lack of merit or other reasons. In order for the recommittted bills to be considered a second time by the House, they had to be transformed into a different legislative vehicle, an omnibus measure. By designating the bills as omnibus measures, also, the Calendar notified Members that these measures required careful scrutiny.

The compromise omnibus bill allowed bills which had been the subject of adverse action by the objectors a "day in court," with sufficient time set aside for discussion. This approach, however, raised questions as to merit. "Every bill that goes into an omnibus bill will be a questionable bill. So if we pass an omnibus bill we pass bad bills by the wholesale," Mr. Clarence E. Hancock (R-NY) argued. In addition, some Members feared that many bills with little or no merit would pass as part of an omnibus measure because almost every Member of the House had a bill included in such measures.[25]

Immigration bills appeared in omnibus form in 1937-1938. During hearings by the Senate Immigration Committee on deportation matters, Mr. Lindsay C. Warren (D-NC) voiced some of the same criticisms levied against the 1935 changes:

> The extreme hardship cases that we know of have been before Congress for at least 3 years, and no solution has yet been found that is acceptable to the majority.[26]

Policy considerations played a prominent role in the view of one of the appointed objectors to the House Private Calendar. As Mr. John M. Costello (D-CA) noted during the House Floor debate on some of the private immigration bills:

> The reason those bills were referred back to the committee was because we, as objectors, did not feel we should set ourselves up as a group that would definitely commit this Congress to a policy concerning immigration...Personally, I did not object to any of the first bills...I do feel that the Congress, as a body, should express its opinion on whether

> the Congress desires to extend to these hardship cases the hand of sympathy and allow these immigrants to remain in this country, and in each particular instance abrogate the laws now in existence. I do not think the duty rests upon a half a dozen of us here, acting as unofficial objectors, to set ourselves up as judges and definitely determine, by reason of the fact we let one bill go through, what is going to be the law to be followed by this Congress...This was not done in an effort to overrule the committee but simply to preserve in the Congress the rights of this body, when these bills come up in an omnibus measure, to discuss them and by a vote of the House determine what shall be its policy.[27]

Since that time there has been little need to resort to the omnibus method because the Committees have established rules and guidelines on the types of cases presented to the House. As a result, the majority of such cases are not precedent-setting. In fact, in cases when objections occur the Committees very rarely bring the cases back to the full House for consideration. In 1956, one bill considered under the omnibus method related to Boris Kowerda, a 47-year old native of Poland, who murdered a Soviet diplomat in Poland.[28] The Russian diplomat had allegedly participated in the assassination of the last Czar of Russia and his family, Nicholas II. The bill had been previously recommitted by the House, therefore, the only means of reconsideration was through an omnibus vehicle. As a policy matter, also, the passage of legislation involving such a serious offense, required more attention since Congress had not acted favorably on any cases of a similar nature.

The term "omnibus" bill can sometimes have a different meaning. For instance, in the 1950's Congress incorporated many bills involving benefits of a similar nature into one piece of legislation to save legislative processing time, and time for the President in signing such bills. For instance, one resolution included 70 beneficiaries excluded due to tuberculosis and another resolution included 26 orphans.[29]

Agreements Between Official Objectors

After the 1946 Legislative Reorganization Act and the other major rules changes, the Committees of jurisdiction primarily disposed of private bills. However, the objectors continued to screen bills for precedents and policy reasons. The Speaker of the House delegates appointment of the Official Objectors to the Majority Leader and Minority Leader.[30] They each appoint three objectors. In exercising their role, objectors can "object to any private bill which they feel is objectionable for any reason."[31]

In 1958 the objectors entered into an "agreement" between them which set certain ground rules for consideration of private bills once placed on the Private Calendar after Committee action.[32] The agreement required seven days to allow the objectors sufficient time to review a case, after reported from the Committee and placed on the House Private Calendar. The agreement is reaffirmed and placed in the *Congressional Record* from time to time, usually at the beginning of the Congress.[33]

In addition, the objectors developed a means of allowing bills to remain on the Private Calendar when there may be future resolution of a case. In these situations, any one objector can be recognized and ask that the bill be "passed over without prejudice." It then comes before the House on each call of the Private Calendar until the end of that particular Congress.

Although six Official Objectors are appointed, this does not prevent any other Member of the House from voicing opposition to a particular private bill, or two Members of the House recommitting a private bill. This rarely occurs, however, because the Official Objectors are consulted to take appropriate action if a bill is objectionable.

The designation of the objectors and their role continues to be an arduous one, arousing the animosity of colleagues: "The job of being one of the six designated objectors to private bills in the House certainly doesn't help to make friends," Mr. James I. Dolliver (R-IO) said in 1951.[34]

Precedents

Among those precedents where the objectors have recommitted bills to the Committee, due to precedents or lack of equities, are citizenship and fraud cases. In addition, other cases involved those which have received unfavorable Executive Branch recommendations. As with all legislation before Congress, the Executive Branch views are requested prior to action on legislation. These "reports" are discussed in more detail later in this Chapter, but generally they involve comments on the merits of a bill.

For example, one recommitted bill involved a citizenship case on behalf of a Hindu precluded from obtaining citizenship benefits due to a United States Supreme Court ruling. The Committee supported the measure, having stated "ample justification" existed for the temporary waiver of the strict racial limitations in the uniform naturalization laws.[35] Another recommitted case involved restoring citizenship for voting in an election in Italy.[36] Other cases included a United States citizen expatriating through armed service with another country;[37]Martina Navratilova, who sought expeditious United States citizenship to compete in the international tennis tournaments;[38]Milos Forman, a movie director seeking expedited citizenship;[39] Ivan Lendl, another tennis competitor requesting expedited citizenship;[40] and a former United States citizen who had renounced United States citizenship and sought reinstatement. He operated a business worth two million dollars.[41] Criminal and fraud cases recommitted included a case relating to obtaining false documents,[42] and convictions for bankruptcy,[43] indecency,[44] and narcotics.[45] Other cases involved mental illness,[46] and another related to a cancer specialist awaiting a visa..[47]

Cases passed over but not recommitted in a particular Congress included bills where aliens sought waivers of exclusion such as a fraud case,[48] a questionable marriage,[49]a narcotic violator,[50]and immigration status for "heroes" who assisted the United States abroad.[51] In these cases, only one objector halted action on the bills.

On occasion, bills have been rejected or passed over by the House but become law in a subsequent Congress.[52] Various reasons such as further information brought to the attention of the House Objectors or simply a new Congress with different views can contribute to the changes in action.

Senate

There are few rules guiding the Senate on private bills. As with the House of Representatives, jurisdiction for immigration matters rests with the Committee on the Judiciary and the respective Subcommittee on Immigration. When bills are considered in the Senate, after Committee action, they are placed on a "Calendar of Business" along with public legislation listed under "General Orders." The bills are generally taken up by unanimous consent on the Senate Floor at a time convenient to the Majority Leader, without designation of days or time limits.[53]

Although debate on private bills is not prohibited in the Senate, there are few occasions when it occurs. The counterpart to the House Objector system is the ability of one Senator to place a "hold" on any legislation, which prevents its consideration on the Floor.[54] This hold can be placed anonymously and may extend throughout the entire Congress. In addition, if a private bill is controversial, it may become the subject of delaying tactics, such as a filibuster, thus defeating the bill.

Until 1969 the staff often handled the introduction of private bills, but after a controversy involving bills introduced on behalf of Chinese crewmen, the Majority Leader of the Senate, Michael J. Mansfield (D-MT), and the Minority Leader, Hugh D. Scott (R-PA), wrote to the Secretary of the Senate requiring that private bills delivered to the Senate desk be "signed by and delivered at the desk, in person, by the Senator introducing them."[55]

Committees

There are three factors in the processing of private bills through the House and Senate Judiciary Committees. First, Committee Agreements with the Immigration and Naturalization Service (INS) and Rules of Procedure stem the high volume of private bills introduced as a means for staying deportation of aliens in the United States. The Agreement commenced in 1947, after the House and Senate acted upon various measures to "stay the deportation" of aliens in the United States who needed special relief. The Rules of Procedure followed in 1954 with major changes in 1969, 1979 and 1981.

Second, precedents of the Congress adhered to by the Committees are a major factor in determining which private bills should become law. These are expressed through policies adopted by the Subcommittees, and by a review of the types of cases which become law or which are defeated at various stages of the legislative process.

Third, public legislation can provide possible relief in an individual case; alternatively, trends in private bills can demonstrate on an individual basis the need for changes to the general law.

Precedents and trends in public legislation and private bills are more fully discussed in Chapter 4.

1930s INS Stays of Deportation

Initially the House Committee handled private bills through frequent hearings with voluminous testimony from the authors, beneficiaries, and representatives of the Executive Branch.[56] While the first cases involved citizenship matters, as the general laws changed and immigration levels rose many cases involved aliens who had entered the United States illegally, or who had overstayed their visas, with no way to become legal residents under the existing immigration structure.

Early immigration laws left no discretion to the INS[57] (formerly within the Department of Labor) to withhold deportation of aliens who resided illegally in the United States. Thus, when INS apprehended such aliens for deportation, many of whom had been in the United States over long periods of time, their departure presented hardships to those relatives remaining in the United States, some of whom already held United States citizenship. Occasionally, the INS administratively withheld final orders of deportation in compassionate cases. It was this procedure which called attention to the need either for statutory discretion to allow these people to remain in the United States or consideration of individual private bills.

The administrative stay of deportation initiated by the Executive Branch became the foundation for recommendations for public legislation to take care of these cases. The stay process also served as the precedent for "stays of deportation" in private bill cases, and that precedent continues to the present time.

1934 House Committee Resolution - The first stay of deportation that Congress supported for these "classes" of aliens occurred through a resolution by the House Committee on Immigration in the 73rd Congress (1933-1934). The numerous private bill requests to Congress for withholding of deportation in the interests of family reunification prompted the Committee to pass a two-year resolution that "the proper officials of the Immigration and Naturalization Service, upon the approval of the Secretary of Labor, should further suspend deportation proceedings" where such action had been undertaken by the Executive Branch. The resolution included cases where:

> deportation would operate a distinct hardship by separation of a family circle, including citizens of the United States by birth or naturalization...the separation thus effected would have the effect of placing those members of the family circle left behind subjects for public or private charitable relief...[58]

It is notable, however, that the Great Depression and restrictionist sentiments in Congress blocked efforts of the Executive Branch for more general legislation which would have allowed the granting of permanent resident status on a discretionary basis in individual cases.

1935 House Resolution 350 - Administrative action continued to be supported by Congress during the 74th Congress (1935-1936). In light of 60 private bills introduced during that Congress, the Immigration Committee reported, and the House passed, a similar resolution to continue the stay of deportation of eligible aliens through March 1, 1936. Among those opposing the resolution and any liberalizing provisions of the immigration law, Mr. Thomas A. Jenkins (R-OH) stated that the measure offered:

> nothing more than a blind behind which the Secretary of Labor is seeking to shield herself from the just criticism that would be directed at her if the facts were known. Why did she not deport those who should be deported and spare those whose cases excite sympathy?...Do not be carried away by this sob stuff that we have been hearing for years about breaking up families...None of these people will be deported.[59]

The Chairman of the House Immigration Committee, Samuel Dickstein (D-NY), appealed to a sense of justice for some of the compassionate cases:

> What do the restrictionists on this committee want? I am trying to reach an agreement with them. They want me to introduce 2,600 individual bills--one for every immigrant. That is an impossible procedure to follow, for the reason that you would have to stay here for 5 years to carry through the program.[60]

In the 75th Congress (1937-1938) the number of private immigration bills introduced (293) increased dramatically from the previous Congress. The volume highlighted rising tensions and the need for a solution to the problem of separated families. In fact, when an attempt was made to overcome opposition to the bills, the private bills were rolled into omnibus measures to assure full debate, but these bills also failed to pass.[61]

1938 House and Senate Resolution (H.J. Res. 714)[62]- In view of the continued difficulties of the public legislation and the failure to pass private legislation, a third and final resolution endorsing stays of deportation gained the support of both Houses of Congress.[63] It differed from previous measures because of its narrow scope and the lack of a role for the Secretary of Labor. Rather, the 75th Congress stay required a link to the introduction of a private *bill* in Congress. The resolution suspended deportation for "any alien whose relief from deportation is provided for by any bill which has been favorably acted on by either the Senate Committee on Immigration or the House Committee on Immigration and Naturalization."[64] The stay under the resolution expired with the adjournment of the first session of the 76th Congress (1939-1940). The legislation encompassed 150 cases within the various omnibus measures which had been blocked from consideration on the House Floor. Mr. Samuel Dickstein (D-NY), Chairman of the Immigration Committee, defended the measure, stating:

> We have been deprived of our day in court. The bills concerning these cases about which we are speaking, which affect only a limited number of people, have been unanimously reported. I am sure if the facts were presented to the House, these bills would pass the House unanimously.[65]

Mr. William T. Schulte (D-IN), a Member of the Immigration Committee, said that the Committee had acted unfavorably on "hundreds of cases that we thought were not justified."[66]

A substantial increase in the number of private bills introduced (601) occurred in the next Congress, the 76th (1939-1940).[67] The increase reflected the lack of a resolution of the public legislation issue and steadfast refusal of the Executive Branch to further stay deportations without promises of action on its more general proposal, which had been under discussion for six years. Thus, the only alternative, private bills, became the vehicle for addressing such cases.

Rather than confront another deluge of private bills, Congress finally acquiesced to passage of public legislation granting the Executive Branch discretion on many of the subject cases. This legislation became one of the first instances, as indicated above, when private bills pointed to the need for remedial legislation. The Alien Registration Act of 1940 Act relieved the Congress and the Executive Branch of the many cases which had required attention,[68] and resolved the issue by requiring both branches of Government to share responsibility. Decisionmaking on individual cases reposed in the hands of the Executive Branch, but the cases subsequently had to be submitted to Congress for approval or rejection by either the House or Senate. The compromise ended the stalemate and provided relief in many cases, until declared unconstitutional in 1983 when the Supreme Court held that one house of Congress alone could not negate Executive Branch action.[69]

1947 Agreements with INS

A need remained for classes of bills not covered by the 1940 legislation. The unique process whereby Congress had previously supported stays of deportation by the Executive Branch provided the foundation for a more formalized "Agreement" between the Judiciary

Committee and the INS for beneficiaries of private bills (See Appendix B for Agreement with INS).

In the 80th Congress (1947-1948), immigration and nationality matters became part of the jurisdiction of the Committee on the Judiciary. One of the Committee's first orders of business was to address the stay of deportation issue. The number of private bills introduced in the 80th Congress rose to 1,141, reflecting the start of high post-war immigration, when many aliens entered the United States seeking refuge illegally or overstayed their visas. Private bills sought to allow them to stay in the United States on a permanent basis.

The House Committee requested that the stay of deportation issue and its relationship to private bills filed in Congress be studied by its Immigration Subcommittee.[70] Because of the "embarrassment and expense" of this practice, on February 27, 1947 the House Committee adopted a policy negating any automatic stay of deportation upon introduction of a private bill unless the Committee addressed a communication to INS concerning the bill.

In a letter to Attorney General Tom C. Clark on that date, Committee Chairman Earl C. Michener (R-MI) instructed that "unless the Committee addresses some formal communication to you after the introduction of any such bill...you may feel free to disregard the practice of staying deportation proceedings."[71] Although not legally binding,[72] the exchange of correspondence between Attorney General Clark and Chairman Michener set the first Committee policy on private bills and their relationship to stays of deportation, which is reaffirmed by almost every Congress throughout the 100th.[73]

The Senate entered into a similar agreement with the Executive Branch which is reaffirmed in most Congresses. The Senate, however, required an affirmative stay of deportation pending adverse action by the Committee. This meant that the introduction of a bill itself stayed deportation unless adverse action occurred.[74] Another difference in the Senate policy involved the documentation required by the INS. In the Senate, the sponsor furnished the information to the INS, whereas in the House the Chairman of the Committee requested the report by providing appropriate documentation. The Agreement addressed to Senate Subcommittee Chairman Chapman Revercomb (R-WV) from INS Commissioner Watson B. Miller June 18, 1948 stated:

> In the case of any alien concerning whom a private bill is pending in the Senate, but concerning which bill *unfavorable action shall not have been taken*...deportation should be stayed.[75]

In the Senate, this process (whereby introduction of a private bill automatically stayed deportation) complicated Congressional policy vis-a-vis House procedures. In 1947, the House Committee directed its Chairman to confer with the Senate Committee on the Judiciary to "arrive at some common understanding relative to the treatment of bills ordering a stay of deportation in certain cases."[76] The House Committee continued to strive for consistency of procedures in each body, and again in the 81st Congress (1949-1950), the Committee sought a "uniform rule for both Houses."[77] These efforts to have parallel procedures in both Houses did not bear fruit until 30 years later.[78] In 1979 (96th Congress), changes to the Senate Committee rules required that the Committee had to request a report rather than the sponsor. This occurred only after a determination of hardship when the alien was in the United States.[79]

The report requested from the INS by the Committee involved an investigation by the INS of the beneficiary of the private bill. This included verification of the individual, check of police records, fingerprinting, and other items. The Commissioner of INS then forwarded a summary of the case to the Committee on the Judiciary. The INS report was also included in the legislative history of legislation which accompanied a bill to be considered on the House or Senate Floor.

Today, the main points of the INS' agreements with Congress are that: (1) no stays of deportation are put in place unless the Committee requests a report from the INS; (2) the INS may disregard any action taken by the Committee in clearly adverse circumstances; and (3) stays of deportation are only operative until final action in Congress takes place. Although the Agreements have essentially remained the same, the Rules of Procedure have from time to time narrowed the scope of those eligible for private bill consideration and attempted to close loopholes which could be abused.

1954-1988 Rules of Procedure and Policies

Three major changes occurred in the Rules of Procedure for both the House and the Senate. The first involved the establishment of the House Subcommittee Rules in the 83rd Congress (1953-1954) at which time the Senate Committee also outlined its policies on private immigration bills. The second major change in the House occurred in the 91st Congress (1969-1970) when the Subcommittee tightened its

Rules and expedited procedures established to consider the bills. The third major change occurred in the 96th Congress and 97th Congress (1979-1982) at which time the House and Senate outlined their revised procedures on private bills (See Appendix A for chronology of Committee on the Judiciary Rules of Procedure).

1954 Establishment of House Rules of Procedure, and Senate Policies - From 1947 until January 1954, when the House Committee first adopted Rules of Procedure formalizing existing practices governing private bills, the House Committee requested a report from INS on any bills where the author wrote to the Subcommittee for action. Under the 1947 Agreement, the Committee request for report automatically stayed deportation if the alien was in the United States. In the Senate, generally, the introduction of a bill continued to stay deportation.

A high volume of private bills precipitated the need for Rules of Procedure. The number of private bills introduced increased from 1,141 in the 80th Congress (1947-1948) to 2,811 in the 81st Congress (1949-1950). This continued to be a major concern of the Congress because of their intervention in the deportation of aliens by legislative fiat. During a House Judiciary Committee meeting, a discussion of bills on behalf of aliens transiting the United States (changing airplanes but not staying in the country), resulted in the Committee prompting the Department of Justice to "proceed with the enforcement of existing laws and regulations and also to find out through proper investigation, whether or not fraud is involved in this attempt to keep in this country such a large number of aliens through the introduction of private immigration bills."[80]

In 1952 in order to dispose of nonmeritorious cases and resolve the stigma associated with the volume of private bills introduced to stay deportation, the Chairman of the House Immigration Subcommittee, Francis E. Walter (D-PA), cleared a backlogged docket of private bills, thus giving the go-ahead for deportation of the aliens involved.[81]

In the 83rd Congress (1953-1954), after being "faced with an unprecedented influx of private bills" (2,001 introduced in the first session of the 83rd Congress), the House Immigration Subcommittee adopted Rules of Procedure for private bills.[82] The rules became necessary to deal with the large number of bills relating to people illegally in the United States, many of which "should never have been introduced."[83] The rules followed an investigation in 1953 by the House and Senate Judiciary Committees into the Department of Justice's role in the stays of deportation. During hearings on the investigation, Chairman of the House Judiciary Committee, Mr. Michener, alleged that slow Department of Justice procedures assisted stays of deportation in private bill cases and had a "serious effect upon the administration of our laws relating to deportation."[84] The Committee reprimanded INS for not expeditiously enforcing the deportation of aliens whose bills had been denied.

The Committee also urged INS to promptly submit reports on private bills, since the delay in review by the Committee contributed to stays in deportation. In addition, the Senate expressed its concern with the delays.[85] A notice inserted into the *Congressional Record* advised Members of the House about the the new rules and the requirements for certain identifying information which had to be submitted prior to consideration of any measure.[86]

The most important change in the process involved the stays of deportation. The 1954 rules stated that the Subcommittee would not request a report from the Attorney General, thus staying deportation, on behalf of those aliens who entered the United States as "stowaways, or deserting seamen, or by surreptitiously entering without inspection through land or sea borders of the United States" unless the Subcommittee found that the purpose of the bills involved "uniting or preventing *separation of families*." This became the Subcommittee's "Rule 4," to be overcome only by a presentation of hardship.

Another change of policy under the 1954 rules, again to reduce the volume of bills, required that all administrative avenues be pursued prior to Subcommittee action and that "mere inconvenience" would not warrant special legislation. Other administrative procedures included a stipulation that the consideration of private bills had to be chronological and that no bill would be deferred for a hearing due to nonappearance of the author. The Subcommittee also would not reconsider cases unless some of the facts changed substantially.[87]

In addition to notice in the *Congressional Record*, Chairman of the House Judiciary Committee, Chauncey W. Reed (R-ILL), distributed a "Dear Colleague" letter to all House Members, providing an updated report on the Committee's policy.[88] The Chairman included the exchange of correspondence between the Committee and the INS. He stated in the letter that a backlog existed of 4,000 private bills involving 6,000 aliens, and that the House denied 1,100 of those cases and approved 600. INS, in response, reiterated that it would continue to allow a certain period of time for the beneficiaries of pending bills to remain in the United States to accommodate the "meritorious" cases. However, INS reserved the right for some discretion in nonmeritorious bills when deportation or other action would be appropriate. The Committee agreed with that policy.[89]

The 1954 Rules of Procedure remained substantially intact through the 100th Congress (1987-1988). Changes primarily consisted of tightening the rules regarding the hardship criteria necessary for the Committee's consideration of bills, as well as guidelines on precedents to which the Committee would adhere.

Although the Senate did not adopt formal rules or procedures, and the process on stays of deportation operated more liberally, the actual disposition of cases by the Senate Committee on various types of bills closely followed that of the House Committee. In a policy statement in the 83rd Congress (1953-1954), the Senate Committee outlined various precedents on bills and types of cases subject to unfavorable action. The guidelines indicated that the Committee should indefinitely postpone (deny) most cases, especially those involving "serious criminal acts or exchange visitors." In addition, the Senate Committee noted that factors such as the special needs of the United States citizen or permanent resident relative in the United States and relatives abroad provided situations for favorable action.[90]

The policy also had a national interest component, in that it recognized the need for certain skills in the United States economy. "Judicial notice should be taken of the fact that there is a need for doctors and scientific men and women," the Committee said. Exclusions relating to petty theft which involved spouses of citizens also generally received a favorable waiver, as well as those on behalf of individuals with mental or physical defects when based on the "ability of relatives in this country to take care of such aliens and to furnish bond if required."

But under the Senate policy, the cases involving exchange visitors received particularly stringent consideration. "Exchange students are here for a particular purpose and are specifically denied any administrative relief under the law...As a general policy, they have been postponed," the Committee noted. Other cases considered unfavorably included those where administrative relief was available.[91] The Senate Committee also required certain documentation to be filed on each case by the sponsor.

The House, through its Rules of Procedure in 1954, operated under similar guidelines relating to hardship criteria, and precedents of the House indicated analogous policies.[92] The Senate formally adopted guidelines in 1979 closely paralleling those of the House with respect to identifying hardship criteria prior to requesting a report resulting in a stay of deportation.[93]

The Agreements with the INS and the Committee Rules of Procedure operate in tandem. Members of Congress have been advised of the rules and procedures through Dear Colleagues, as well as notices in the *Congressional Record* from time to time.[94]

1950s and 1960s Experience with the Rules - Even with the new rules, the numbers of bills introduced continued to climb. The lack of general legislation to cure the limited visas available under the National Origins Quota Act had a significant impact on the increase, but it was also evident that the rules required further tightening. The first House restrictions relating to changes in the rules occurred in the 84th Congress (1955-1956) during which Members introduced 4,474 bills, of which 1,634 became law. The House Immigration Subcommittee imposed an "extreme hardship" criteria to Rule 4 cases (bills on behalf of aliens already in the United States). The Rules also sought to coordinate action with the Senate by precluding reconsideration of a bill which had been adversely acted upon by the Senate.[95]

The Senate Judiciary Committee also took steps to address the volume of bills in 1955 by concurring with the INS policy that cases where the file "lacks essential merit" would be subject to deportation unless the sponsor presented "unusual equities."[96] The Senate reaffirmed its position on certain cases where the beneficiaries of private bills had remedies under the existing law. In its report on activities in the 84th Congress, the Senate Judiciary Committee stated: "the Committee has a general policy of disapproving private bills in cases in which an administrative remedy appears available."[97]

Other measures to address the volume included the addition of aliens in transit to the Rule 4 cases, thus requiring a waiver prior to consideration; and the initiation of omnibus measures to assist in workload problems in processing groups of bills for enactment.[98]

1969 House Rules Changes - Following the highest number of private bills introduced (7,293) in the 90th Congress (1967-1968), the House Immigration Subcomittee again, in the 91st Congress (1969-1970) expanded the prohibited category for private bills to include visitors, exchange visitors, and students.[99]

In supporting the 1969 rule change initiated by Mr. Rodino of the Immigration Subcommittee, Mr. William T. Cahill (R-NJ), the Ranking Minority Member of the Subcommittee indicated the necessity of the changes because of the increased number of private bills "obviously lacking in merit and introduced merely to stay deportation." He noted that 85 percent of the private bills introduced in the last Congress related to visitors, exchange visitors, and students. In many cases aliens entered the country and immediately thereafter exerted pressure on Members of Congress to introduce private legislation to stay their deportation. Mr. Cahill explained that

> dilatory private bills sacrifices valuable time of the subcommittee...the delay in deportation that a private bill might have given to a visitor who has violated the terms of his admission is not justified by the great expense both in time and money.[100]

Additionally, he noted that the Subcommittee looked unfavorably upon bills which

> would benefit those who violate the law over aliens who apply for immigrant status in the home country under the general law and patiently wait their turn for admittance.[101]

The new and expanded Rule 4 of the Rules of Procedure provided:

> The Subcommittee shall not address to the Attorney General communications designed to defer deportation of beneficiaries of private bills who have entered the United States as *visitors, exchange visitors, students, stowaways, in transit, or deserting seamen, or by surreptitiously entering without inspection through the land or sea borders of the United States.*
>
> Exemption from this rule may be granted by the Subcommittee in cases where the bill is designed to prevent extreme hardship. However, no such exemption may be granted unless the author has secured and filed with the Subcommittee full and complete documentary evidence in support of his request to waive this rule.[102]

In the 92nd Congress (1971-1972) the Immigration Subcommittee refined the rules. Under the revised Rule 4, all nonimmigrants (aliens entering the United States on any temporary visa) required a hardship waiver before a private bill could be considered. At that time, the newly elected Chairman of the Immigration Subcommittee, Mr. Rodino, noted the general purpose of private bills. He said that private bills address hardships which the general law cannot alleviate, and that they were not a panacea for all cases, particularly where administrative relief may be available.[103]

The backlog of cases prior to 1969 had contributed to increased stays of deportation. As noted previously, if a report from the INS had been requested by the Committee, INS stayed the deportation of the alien until the Committee took any adverse action. Thus, as long as the Committee's agenda remained backlogged, the aliens continued to reside in the United States. This situation caused much concern to Subcommittee Chairman Rodino. He expressed his desire to eliminate the long waiting period between introduction and consideration of private bills.

Among the steps Chairman Rodino initiated to reduce the backlog involved the requirement that the staff of the Immigration Subcommittee make recommendations for proposed action on the private bills. In cases of unanimous favorable or unfavorable recommendations between staff of both Democratic and Republican Subcommittee members, the Subcommittee adopted those recommendations quickly. In the cases where the staff could not agree, the Members of the Subcommittee heard testimony from the authors of the legislation.

With the 92nd Congress rule and frequent meetings, the number of backlogged private bills awaiting action by the Subcommittee decreased substantially. By 1973 the Subcommittee achieved a current docket of private bills.[104] In addition, the number of bills introduced was reduced from 7,293 in the 90th Congress (1967-1968) to 2,866 in the 92nd Congress (1971-1972), of which 62 became law.

1979-1981 Senate Rules of Procedure and Policies - The Senate, in the 96th Congress (1979-1980), for the first time formally adopted guidelines to "bring a greater measure of order and fairness to the processing of private immigration bills." The Judiciary Committee's report of activities for the 96th Congress noted that the Chairman, Edward M. Kennedy (D-MA), who also had responsibility for the Subcommittee handling immigration matters, directed the staff to

> treat all private bills on a first-come, first-served basis, strictly on their merits, and with a view of acting compassionately on deserving cases.[105]

The Committee also noted that while those bills exhibiting equity and some "humanitarian need" would be expedited, bills where administrative relief existed would not be favorably reported unless compelling circumstances existed.

The new guidelines implicitly abolished the practice of staying deportation merely as a result of the introduction of a bill and request for a report from the sponsor. In addition, the policy specifically prohibited consideration of private bills for medical doctors who had not passed the required medical competency tests for immigration.

The Immigration Subcommittee met more frequently to prevent backlogs, and the Chairman gave the staff of both Democrat and Republican members of the Committee wider authority for purposes of screening bills in order to determine which cases merited a request for report. The final action on reporting legislation, however, remained with the members of the Immigration Subcommittee. The most significant difference between the House and the Senate remained the more formalized hearing structure of the House for purposes of voting on a request for a report from the INS.

The policies regarding the types of cases considered and the applicable precedents remained similar to guidelines in the 83rd Congress (1953-1954) and paralleled House action.

Discussion of the guidelines between Sen. Howard Metzenbaum (D-OH) and Chairman Kennedy, during a meeting of the Committee on the Judiciary in 1979, indicated that many Senators had not been aware of the criteria for action on private bills:

> Sen. Metzenbaum: I'm not certain what the criteria is that we use in these matters, and frankly, when people come to me and ask me to sponsor special bills, I'm not even positive when I should and when I shouldn't.
>
> Sen. Kennedy: Well, Senator, we have circularized the [guidelines], it's rather subjective--based upon humanitarian needs...it is reviewed case by case. We have also circularized--which is the first time that this Committee ever has---the individual fact situation to hopefully every member of the staff....basically it is a subjective kind of test. The ones that I say we have recommended here quite frankly...I think have been of value."106

The Rules of Procedure in the 97th Congress (1981-1982) incorporated the policies outlined above, with the support of Committee on the Judiciary Chairman Strom Thurmond (R-SC).[107] The new Immigration Subcommittee Chairman Alan K. Simpson (R-WY) explained:

> The historical aspects of this have been that where a stay occurs through the filing of a bill, that has caused us a great deal of concern, at least in the Subcommittee. We passed some changes unanimously in the Subcommittee in regard to a private bill simply because I think perhaps

the Abscam caper caused a great deal of attention to lie upon the apparent abuses of private bills. What we proposed, and what was passed unanimously by the Subcommittee, is that the author of the bill present to us the reason a bill has merit, why existing administrative and judicial procedures are not available and the inequities which support this rather extraordinary relief.

We would do what the House already has done in change its procedures, and we could certainly reduce a stay for nonmeritorious cases in private bills, and we would reduce the wasteful effort which is extended when the report goes on up, comes back, and we have nothing later to deal with. It puts an extra burden on the Subcommittee but we are ready to accept it, and about once a month in half an hour we can process the bills with the criteria we have.[108]

Additionally, in 1981 Immigration Subcommittee Chairman Simpson presented the rules to the Committee members in the form of a "Dear Colleague" letter noting that the policy would reduce the "likelihood that a stay of deportation will be immediately granted for non-meritorious cases." The letter also stated that the rules would eliminate the "wasted effort expended in preparation of a formal Executive Branch report for cases which would not pass an initial screening by the Subcommittee."[109]

With the formal adoption of the rules, the number of private immigration bills introduced in Congress substantially decreased from 728 in the 97th Congress (1981-1982) to 194 in the 100th Congress (1987-1988). The precipitous decline paralleled that in the House when rules changes became effective in 1969. Immigration Subcommittee Chairman Kennedy and Ranking Member, Sen. Simpson, jointly distributed another "Dear Colleague" in 1987 reenforcing the adopted rules. The letter reiterated the "extraordinary" nature of a private bill and the fact that the introduction of a bill does not stay deportation.[110] The Chairman of the Judiciary Committee, Joseph R. Biden, Jr. (D-DE) also supported the changes. With the adoption of the Senate rules both Houses had the same guidelines operating with respect to private bills.

Committee Precedents

As a major consideration by the Committees in processing private bills, precedents have developed on the basis of the legislative reports which accompany legislation which has become law. These are explored more fully in Chapter 4. However, at various times the Immigration Subcommittees have published with the Rules or through

Dear Colleagues to Members of the House or Senate, an outline of various types of expected action on private immigration bills.

One of the first occasions that the House Immigration Subcommittee circulated its policies occurred in the 97th Congress (1981-1982). The Subcommittee sent a Dear Colleague to all members of the House and inserted the letter into the *Congressional Record.* It outlined the new rules for private legislation relating to doctors entering the United States for medical training (foreign medical graduates or FMGs).[111]

In the letter the Subcommittee noted the role of precedents as an important factor "because a decision on one private bill to benefit a single FMG may set a precedent for thousands of other FMGs."[112] Certain criteria for considering these bills was adopted requiring doctors to pass medical exams establishing competence and obtain a waiver of the two year return-home requirement, which was an obligation of most doctors entering the U.S. under the "exchange visitor" program visa. The Subcommittee noted that its policy was established to reduce the reliance of United States medical facilities on FMGs, and to deter other FMGs from pursuing such legislation.

The FMG exchange visitor policy continued the practice of both the House and Senate to deny private bill relief for aliens who entered the United States under the special terms of the exchange visitor visa. The exchange visitor policy had been re-enforced in 1955 when President Eisenhower vetoed a bill for an exchange visitor.[113]

In the 98th Congress (1983-1984), another notice was inserted into the *Congressional Record* outlining the revised Rules of Procedure for that Congress, and the Immigration Subcommittee's policies and precedents.[114] An advisory sent to Members of the House with the Rules stated:

> In fairness to those immigrants who are awaiting legal immigration, it is the policy of the Subcommittee generally to act favorably on only those private bills which meet certain precedents.[115]

The broad categories of favorable precedents included adoption cases where there was a bona fide family relationship. In all other categories--doctors and nurses, individuals with drug or criminal histories, individuals with medical conditions, deferred action cases, investors, waivers of exclusion and naturalization--little likelihood existed for favorable action unless the case met the strict requirements. Even with the threshhold criteria met, the Subcommittee indicated that processing would be extremely difficult. The Rules closely adhered to internal guidelines which the House and Senate Committees had previously recognized at least since the 83rd Congress (1953-1954).[116]

In the 99th Congress (1985-1986), to re-enforce the need to adhere to precedents, the House Subcommittee on Immigration amended its Rules of Procedure to require a two-thirds favorable vote to even schedule a bill in certain categories for consideration.[117] These cases included bills where the beneficiaries sought medical treatment, FMGs, and bills to waive the naturalization laws. Added to this list in the 100th Congress (1987-1988) were bills on behalf of relatives of legalized aliens. A new law, passed in 1986 to "legalize" aliens who had been in the United States since 1982, had the potential of family members seeking relief through the private bill route. The Subcommittee noted that

> legalized beneficiaries may exercise the same petitioning rights as all other immigrants upon granting of permanent residence...Congress did not provide derivative benefits to accrue outside normal immigration levels.[118]

The House and the Senate have addressed other policy areas jointly to stem unfavorable precedents. For instance, both Immigration Subcommittees had been confronted with several private bills in the previous Congress requesting expedited citizenship for athletes who wished to participate as United States citizens in the 1988 Olympic Games. In 1987, the Subcommittees addressed letters to the U.S. Olympic Committee concerning the undesirability of precedents relating to granting of citizenship on behalf of Olympic athletes.[119] These cases were also added to the two-thirds rule of the House Immigration Subcommittee in the 100th Congress.

Role of the Executive Branch

The Executive Branch has very little influence on the private bill process. Its role primarily involves three areas: 1) stays of deportation and investigations upon request for a report from the Subcommittee after a finding of "hardship"; 2) recommendations on situations when public legislation may be an alternative; and 3) the Presidential veto. Prior to 1953, the Executive Branch had a greater role in the process. At that time, the Executive Branch often took positions on private bills, endorsing or opposing individual cases. Since that time, because of the lengthy processing for bills and the pressures placed upon the

Department of Justice by sponsors of the bills, the Executive Branch has rarely taken positions on private bills and has shown very little interest in their disposition.

An Exception to the Law or Equity for All

The relationship between Congress and the Executive Branch with respect to private bills has always been contentious. As an exception to the general law, the Executive Branch views private relief as a unique remedy and is reluctant to see one alien benefit through special privileges when the general population may have equally or more meritorious claims. In fact, in 1947 the Executive Branch boldly proposed legislation prohibiting their introduction. "We do not like the principle of private bills," said Edward J. Shaughnessy with INS.[120] The injustice of some of the private bills was argued by Attorney General Tom C. Clark at the time:

> Now, there are people who are deserving of some action, many of them; but, on the other hand, there are hundreds of cases of people who do not know anyone and are not able to get to you. I don't mean by that that they know you personally, but they are unable to get action. In other words, for all those who are able to have their cases called to your attention there are hundreds who are unable to do so...and so what you are doing is permitting those who do have some connection, or who do know how to go about writing you or something like that, to have, you might say, a preference in that they do get some attention by the Congress.[121]

INS Stays of Deportation

It is the stay of deportation aspect of private bills, however, that results in the most antagonism between the Executive Branch and the Congress. Ironically, the Executive Branch initiated the first stays of deportation, when it became evident that many aliens who had entered the United States had no legal status, primarily because they had overstayed their visas or entered without proper documents. Also, in some cases documentation at the time of entry had been inadequate. The argument as to the means for providing relief for that population--that is, through public legislation or private immigration bills--was the focus of both branches of Government during hearings in 1934,[122] and for the next 20 years until ultimately resolved by public legislation in 1940[123] and 1952.[124]

The Executive Branch, through the Department of Labor, had administratively stayed the deportation of some aliens in hardship cases involving the possible separation of families. As the number of these aliens increased, and the lack of support for more generic legislation became evident, the schism between the Executive and Congress began to widen. While the House Committee had originally endorsed the stays of deportation through a resolution in 1934,[125] the Great Depression and immigration restrictionists in Congress created an unhealthy environment for passage of general legislation. Administrative stays of deportation by the INS were to be curtailed in 1935 unless Congress acted in a more generic fashion. INS Commissioner, D.W. MacCormack, testified at that time:

> ...I wish to make it entirely clear that, unless this Congress gives us a mandate which is clear and unmistakable, as to what we shall do, I must and will proceed with the deportation of these cases...
>
> There is no reason in the world why Congress should depart and I be left behind to take the burden of doing this thing--this abominable thing, that should not be done. The responsibility is yours, gentlemen, and you have got to carry it.[126]

In requesting statutory changes, the Commissioner pointed to 2,355 cases which had been presented to him and argued that the ad hoc means of addressing the hardship situations was problemmatic. Many Members of Congress, however, suspected that the discretion of the Department of Labor had already been used too frequently, and feared that statutory authority might be exercised so broadly as to virtually nullify any existing immigration law.[127] The unwillingness of Congress to relinquish any of its authority to act on individual cases resulted in the refusal of the Executive Branch to continue administrative stays of deportation.

INS Commissioner D.W. MacCormack tried forcing the hand of Congress on the need for more generic legislation:

> If the Congress passes a law, be the law a good one or a bad one, it should be enforced. If it is, in the opinion of the enforcing officer, a bad law, he should courageously present his opinion to the Congress which enacted it, and ask the Congress to change it. Rather than continue the policy that had existed for years of handling these cases by indirection, the extralegal means, I made up my mind that we were going to enforce the law as it is, and let the Congress decide, and take the responsibility for its decision.[128]

Even with resolutions in 1935 and 1938[129] setting forth congressional demands to stay deportation, the number of private bills introduced continued to escalate from 60 in the 74th Congress (1935-1936) of which 4 became law to 601 in the 76th Congress (1939-1940) of which 35 became law. In 1939 and 1940[130] the efforts of the Executive Branch bore fruit when Congress enacted laws to provide relief. First, aliens who established residence in the United States prior to 1924 could register as permanent immigrants. Secondly, aliens in the United States for five years and who could prove "serious economic detriment" to a citizen or permanent resident spouse, parent or child could apply to the Attorney General for suspension of deportation resulting in permanent status. The alien could not have a criminal record, however. These cases had to be reported to Congress which could disapprove action. In 1947 the number of private bills again rose, but the House Committee primarily addressed the stays of deportation through internal changes, and public legislation in 1948 accommodated most needs for relief.[131]

Workload and Enforcement Problems

Another factor in the Executive Branch's workload with respect to private bills is the number of reports requested by Congress, since lengthy investigations are conducted and deportation is not carried out during this time-consuming process. The workload was one factor leading to Attorney General Tom C. Clark's recommendation for general legislation in 1947. During hearings before the House Judiciary Committee, he noted that nonmeritorious bills received requests for reports, as well as those with equities:

> And, of course, whenever a bill is introduced up here, we immediately, if we already haven't had it under consideration, take it under consideration. So you waste a lot of time of Congress and you also waste a lot of time of the Attorney General because I cannot do anything about it anyway...[132]

In 1950, INS noted in its *Annual Report* the impact of the introduction of 2,811 bills (507 became law):

> While comparatively few, (less than ten percent) of the private bills are enacted into laws, the increase in the number of such bills introduced is becoming an exacting tax on the investigative force of the Service...These cases are given top priority in field investigations.[133]

The INS also indicated in its 1951 *Annual Report* that many aliens learned that stays of deportation accompanied many private bills, and therefore apply for a private bill shortly after arrested.[134]

It wasn't only the Executive Branch which exhibited concern about the stays of deportation. In 1953, in conjunction with an investigation, a Special Subcommittee to Investigate the Department of Justice queried the INS about the lax enforcement response to denied private bill cases. Mr. Kenneth B. Keating (R-NY), Chairman of the Special Committee, cited the "somewhat delicate" problem whereby private bills which were introduced stayed deportation, even though the cases had been previously denied. He said such deportation delays jeopardized the integrity of the private bill process.

INS Commissioner Argyle R. Mackey indicated during the 1953 hearings that even when private bills were pending, "We go ahead with the proceedings, up to an order of deportation, and defer execution of the order pending passage of the bill." The Commissioner added that deportation was stayed in many cases because the beneficiaries still had administrative remedies or legal appeals to pursue. Although investigations of cases took considerable time, the Commissioner stated that most Members of Congress preferred background checks because usually they received only "one side of the story, from the alien himself, or the alien's counsel."[135]

It was after this investigation that the Department of Justice delegated the processing of reports on private immigration bills to INS. Since that time, the reports have been submitted to Congress by INS without any recommendation as to support or opposition to a measure.

In Congress, the response to the high number of stays of deportation and problems with the Executive Branch was the adoption of formal Rules of Procedure. The new rules governed the initiation of requests by the Committee so that a waiver by the Subcommittee was required prior to a request for Executive Branch reports when an alien was in the United States.[136] Although there continued to be a high volume of private bills introduced, the internal corrective measures narrowed the potential for abuse. This rule change, in addition to the enactment of general legislation which had been adopted in 1952, solved many problems highlighted by the House Committee investigation.

In 1955, although recommendations by the Executive Branch on private bills had stopped, the House Judiciary Committee encountered intervention by the Office of Management and Budget (OMB), formerly the Bureau of the Budget. Prior to the President's signature, OMB is the office which coordinates the views of the various Cabinet offices on whether legislation should be signed into law or vetoed. In this particular case, instead of making recommendations on legislation as had been done previously by the Executive Branch, OMB had begun to contact Members of Congress about the merits of their bills after the House and Senate passed the measures and they were enrolled for signature by the President. Immigration Subcommittee Chairman Mr. Walter, wrote to Deputy Assistant to the President, General Wilton B. Persons that:

> It seems that at least three officers of the Bureau of the Budget have undertaken to contact authors of private immigration bills and Committee staff members, with the request to *justify* the passage of certain private immigration bills...I am quite certain that I do not have to tell you how I feel about this unprecedented procedure...[this] seems to me not only highly inappropriate, but also violative of our constitutional processes.[137]

General Persons replied that in many cases such inquiries resolved conflicts in some of the facts, but that he would be pleased to discuss the matter with the Chairman.

Since that time, there have been few occasions of controversy or cooperation with Congress by the Executive Branch. One occasion, however, was evident during a 1981 hearing on legislation relating to FMGs. House Immigration Subcommittee Chairman Romano L. Mazzoli (D-KY) and the Acting Commissioner of INS, Doris Meissner discussed INS action on private bills which the Subcommittee denied:

> Mr. Mazzoli: I'm curious about the record of deportation. Our committee, of course, wrestles with private bills. We have this incredible wrestling match with our colleagues, and a lot of times we rise to the occasion and resist the issuance of a waiver of rule 4 of our subcommittee rules. But that's the last we ever see of it. That's just like the tree in the forest; is there any sound when nobody is around? If I gave you the names of those cases...could you tell us whether those people have been deported?...I just have the eerie feeling that we're in the middle of a futile exercise here, and I want to make sure this is not futility to the 20th power.
>
> Ms. Meissner: I think it's quite an interesting exercise because I suspect a large proportion of those people were not deported because of other equities they developed over the period of time during which the private bill was pending.

Mr. Mazzoli: I'm saying the private bill isn't an automatic block to deportation.

Ms. Meissner: The whole period the private bill is pending we are prevented from doing anything, and that is usually a 2- or 3-year period.[138]

Although the Executive Branch relinquished its responsibilities in 1953 on taking positions on legislation, that did not dramatically impact precedents of the Congress relating to private bills. Many cases before and after have closely paralleled precedents and internal Rules of the Committees, but after 1953 the pressures which the Executive Branch could not handle shifted solely to the Congress which then had no secondary source of support for denying or approving relief. The President's veto remained the only real Executive Branch authority left.

Recommendations on Legislation

Before 1953, in the reports forwarded to the House and Senate Judiciary Committees, three principle reasons existed for which the Executive opposed private legislation: (1) the unavailability of administrative relief, (2) establishment of an unfavorable precedent, or (3) the preference for more generic legislation.

Administrative relief - The Department of Justice cited the reason of administrative relief for not enacting a private bill when aliens sought private legislation to overcome oversubscribed quotas. In one case of a displaced person who sought special relief, the Department of Justice noted the alien's case was not unlike

> those of many other aliens who desire to enter this country for permanent residence, but are unable to do so because of the oversubscribed condition of the quotas to which they are chargeable. The considerations presented do not appear sufficient to justify the enactment of special legislation granting him a preference.[139]

Precedent - Opposition based on adverse precedent generally included waiver of exclusion categories. One such case involved a request for waiver of epilepsy which was opposed because the health exclusions were enacted by Congress "for the protection of the American public."[140]

In the 1950s, faced with an increasing number of medical cases on behalf of relatives who had tuberculosis, the Department of Health,

Education and Welfare expessed its reluctance to wholeheartedly support such measures.[141]

Another case where endorsement was withheld due to possible adverse precedent involved an alleged "hero" who assisted United States forces in World War II. The Department of Justice noted the record failed to justify

> granting her a preference denied to other aliens, including many who, in performing their patriotic duty to their own country, also rendered valuable service to the Allied cause.[142]

In related cases, the Executive Branch has always been adamantly opposed to granting relief in the form of permanent residence or citizenship to draft dodgers. In one case, the Attorney General noted that while an alien was within his rights to avoid military service, the enactment of a special law

> would be in direct conflict with the express policy of the Congress in barring from citizenship those subjects of neutral countries who declined to assist the United States in time of war.[143]

Generic legislation as a solution - One case where the Executive Branch opposed relief because more generic legislation was preferable involved the lack of support for a citizenship bill relating to expatriation:

> The problem of preserving the nationality of such naturalized citizens is a general one and should be resolved by general legislation.[144]

In some cases the Executive Branch took no position but stated, as in the case of an alien ineligible for admission due to race, that the decision to waive the general requirements of the law "presents a question of legislative policy concerning which this Department prefers not to make any recommendation."[145] In many other cases the Executive Branch simply noted without embellishment that it was "unable to recommend enactment of the bill" and let stand only the facts with the decision a matter of legislative prerogative.[146]

More recently, in attempting to solicit a position from the Department of Health and Human Services (HHS) on private bills relating to FMGs 198l, the Chairman of the House Immigration Subcommittee, Mr. Mazzoli, asked HHS for assistance in reviewing the merits of private legislation:

We might need to deal humanely with the problems of inner cities and rural areas and other medically underserved districts in the Nation by way of a private bill at times. We may not elect to go that route, but, again, your information could be helpful to us, without breaching the clear distinctions between branches of government.[147]

While HHS responded that there was a certain reticence on its part in advising Congress on private bills, Dr. Robert Graham placed the burden squarely back on the Members of Congress to "just say no" to them. He said:

I think that you can't ever, as a constitutional matter, keep a Member of Congress from filing a bill; but, of course, if it's spread in the record that you don't think any private bills ought to be agreed to--and you may not be able to say such a thing--but I think it should say that doctors who come here for training for 7 years, even if there are changes in government or whatever, ought to go back home after that training.[148]

While the Executive Branch since 1953 has withheld input on private bills, there were many occasions when bills were passed notwithstanding strong objections. This development, along with the pressures brought to bear by sponsors and constituents, left the Executive with little alternative than as a bystander in the process. On the other hand, the Executive's infrequent use of the veto power in recent private bill cases may indicate a lack of leadership in establishing parameters in some of these cases.

Problemsolving Cases Through Public Legislation

Although the powers of Congress are primarily to make the laws, Executive Branch leadership has been undervalued and infrequently exercised, particularly in offering initiatives for generic solutions to individual cases. In the past, both the Executive Branch and Congress sought to eliminate or reduce the volume of private bills through proposals for generic legislation. For example, public legislation, often initiated by the Executive Branch, resulted in major legislation in 1940, 1948, 1952, and 1965 which alleviated the necessity for many private bills.

However, the issue of vesting discretion with the Executive Branch over individual cases is a matter with which Congress has always grappled. Not only does Congress jealously guard its prerogatives in its ability to enact private bills, but at various points Congress has argued that the Executive does not use its discretionary authority as wisely as Congress when reviewing individual cases. In 1934, during one of the earliest discussions on proposals vesting authority in the Executive Branch for relief for aliens in particular hardship situations, Mr. Martin Dies (D-TX) stated:

> assuming we make this matter discretionary, we never know from time to time the temperament or the views of the particular administrator that comes into power...One administrator we may know who is not in sympathy with them but is heartily and sincerely for restrictive laws, but that administrator may be subject to tremendous political influences and here comes a Congressman down on him and Senators who say, 'Look here, we have a fellow here and they are about to deport him and we do not want you to do it.' Would not that be a terrific problem or task that the administrator would face?...why cannot we frame legislation that will not throw this burden upon the administrator, this constant pressure that comes and will come, not only from the alien himself, but all of his friends and organizations that apply to Congressmen and Senators, political leaders, and so forth?[149]

D. W. MacCormack, INS Commissioner, explained how the INS' proposal had been created:

> I approached most reluctantly even the thought of exercising discretion. I know the pressure that is brought to bear upon administrative officers...I finally, however, came to the conclusion that unless these cruel and unnecessary hardships were to continue, and to continue indefinitely, to disgrace, I may say, the good name of the United States, that discretion must be vested somewhere in order to avoid it.[150]

The Commissioner noted that the Service had reviewed all deportation cases and found that 5% (465 cases) would qualify under the hardship criteria for remedial legislation. The Committee intimated that clear statutory language without discretionary factors served a better purpose so long as the standards were concise. "We like to see those things set out so that not only the alien but everyone else will then know precisely what their rights are," said Mr. Everett Dirksen (R-IL).[151]

In House Judiciary Committee hearings in 1947 on legislation allowing waivers for minor excludable offenses, Attorney General Tom C. Clark again emphasized the need for discretionary authority to cover the types of cases represented by private bills. He said:

> We have a general immigration law, so my thought in regard to that was, why should we not have a yardstick, a pattern that we might go by, that would lodge in the Attorney General some discretion in these cases.[152]

The Attorney General noted that the cases involved people who had been in the United States for 25 or 30 years and had proven themselves in their communities.[153] At the same time, the Executive Branch had proposed the elimination of all private immigration bills which was the ultimate generic solution to Congressional involvement on case-by-case immigration cases.[154]

Public legislation was also recommended in 1953 by an independent Commission requested to review the immigration laws. The Commission noted:

> The increase in the number of private immigration bills introduced into, and passed, by the Congress is itself evidence that something is wrong with our immigration laws.[155]

It stated that the hardship presented by private bills would be better and more fairly corrected through discretionary authority with agency officials. The Commission regarded the provisions of the law granting permanent residence after seven years in the United States, suspension of deportation, superfluous in the reporting requirements to Congress. The Commission further stated:

> The failure of the Congress to follow the constitutional pattern is obstructive of good government and destructive of fundamental principles...The exercise of discretion according to standards fixed by Congress is peculiarly an executive function. The legislature is not equipped, and not intended to be equipped, to handle the details of administration...It is no more the function of Congress to pass upon individual cases involving suspension of deportation than it would be to pass upon the issuance of individual visas, or for that matter upon the custom inspection of an individual alien's baggage.[156]

In 1965 when Congress debated whether to allow the Executive Branch discretion to waiver further medical exclusions, the Members noted that private bills were reviewed carefully and it was sympathetic to such cases; there was no need to delegate that authority to someone else.[157]

On the other hand, occasionally the Executive Branch cooperated with Congress when enactment of public legislation appeared imminent and which related to pending private immigration bills. As indicated previously, from the 84th through the 86th Congress (1955-1960) the House and Senate initiated omnibus measures, as they had done in the 75th Congress (1937-1938), but this time there were no policy reasons for doing so. Instead, the purpose of the bills was to alleviate the workload in processing adoption and health waiver cases. In 1955, the Chairman of the Immigration Subcommittee of the House, Mr. Walter, proposed to Attorney General Herbert Brownell, Jr.:

> I wish to advise you that having for quite some time realized how burdensome is the task of the President in signing several hundred private immigration bills enacted in each session of Congresss, I have, back in May of this year, instructed our staff to examine the possibilities of such procedural changes as could possibly permit us to act on "omnibus resolutions" instead of individual bills.[158]

In fact, the Chairman indicated that he preferred omnibus measures in lieu of efforts for public legislation because he did not believe the Committee would support the latter.[159] Deputy Attorney General William P. Rogers replied: "It is very important to do something to give the President some relief."[160]

Also, in order to accommodate some of the meritorious private bills during the consideration of some of the pending public legislation, the Executive Branch and the Committees coordinated efforts in assuring consistency of approach. In a report on a private immigration bill in 1951 relating to tuberculosis, the Department of Health, Education and Welfare had outlined terms and conditions with respect to care, hospitalization, and maintenance which would adhere in the extraordinary cases where Congress determined a private bill would be enacted.[161] Further, in 1955, for example, there was an agreement between the Department of State and the House Judiciary Committee requiring that all cases involving waivers of tuberculosis "should be submitted by the Department to the Committee for a determination by the Congress as to enactment of private legislation."[162]

Additionally, during 1955 the Senate Committee advised the INS that it was withholding action on some private bills relating to processing under "pre-examination" guidelines (obtaining visas in Canada rather than returning to the home country) because of possible administrative remedies.[163] At that time, because of restrictions by the 1952 Act, the pre-examination process was reinstituted.

The following year, 1956, when establishing a policy on the consideration of bills on behalf of foreign students, House Subcommittee Chairman Walter noted that although the Subcommittee had "consistently refused to adjust the status of alien students to that of permanent residents," occasionally private legislation was necessary. The Subcommittee sought assistance from the Commissioner of INS to allow students to complete studies when a private bill was pending.[164]

The INS noted in 1956, after a comprehensive analysis of private legislation that led to the introduction of public bills for waivers of exclusion and orphans, that more than 85% of the private immigration bills enacted during 1955 would have been unnecessary, if the recommended legislative proposals had been law.[165] Soon thereafter, Congress enacted a law to eliminate some of the problems associated with these types of private bills.[166]

In 1957, again there was cooperation when House Immigration Subcommittee Chairman Walter asked the Commissioner of INS, J. M. Swing, to review private bill cases where beneficiaries claimed relief due to fear of persecution:

> In my opinion, this entire problem requires a survey and possibly legislative action...It is quite possible that by submitting to our attention the cases which I have in mind...your Service could convince us that the matter could be solved by the enactment of an 'omnibus bill' in the nature of private legislation.[167]

In 1960, House Committee Chairman Emanuel Celler agreed upon a policy initiated by the White House with respect to consideration of immigration bills regarding individuals with mental afflictions. Citing concerns about "public charges," that is, the possibility that government funds would be needed for medical treatment, David W. Kendall, Special Counsel to President Dwight D. Eisenhower advised:

> The President feels that the enactment of measures waiving these grounds of inadmissibility is not in the best interests of the United States nor of the individual States...should the Congress continue to pass private legislation of this nature, others will undoubtedly continue to be encouraged to immigrate to the United States with full knowledge that an afflicted member of their family cannot meet the requirements of our laws, but with the expectation that they may thereafter obtain special privileges via private legislation for that purpose.[168]

Chairman Walter of the House Immigration Subcommittee responded by noting that "we find ourselves in basic agreement with the President's policy stated therein. Consequently, we intend to act favorably on private legislation of this type only in the most impelling cases."[169] The Senate also agreed on the general policy.[170]

That policy was re-iterated in the Administration of President John F. Kennedy in 1963. However, according to Mr. Myer Feldman, Counsel to the President, the President desired to be "somewhat more flexible in this kind of case because of his strong views that immigration policy should, wherever possible, facilitate the reuniting of families," but that generally there would be a presumption against their admission.[171]

In another area, INS Commissioner J.M. Swing had responded favorably to a review of private bills in 1960 relating to Army enlistees so that action would be withheld until a determination of availability of relief could be made.[172]

The Presidential Veto

Ultimately, the Executive Branch has the last word by way of the President's veto power on any legislation, particularly in view of the fact that few bills are overriden by Congress. There have been 28 vetoes (including 7 pocket vetoes) of private bills based on three general policies: precedent, character, and administrative remedy. President Franklin D. Roosevelt vetoed eleven, President Harry S. Truman vetoed nine, and six vetoes took place under President Dwight D. Eisenhower, one by President John F. Kennedy, and one by President Ronald Reagan.

The few vetoes since the 1950s may reflect an accommodation between Congress and the Executive on the merits of such legislation, as well as cooperation with respect to passage of public legislation eliminating the need for the majority of private cases. On the other hand, as noted previously, it may reflect the weakened role of the Executive Branch in the private bill area.

There have been only three cases which have become law without Presidential endorsement. The fact that there have been few private bills which are the subject of an override, principally involves the lack of general interest needed to muster opposition to the President's stand, particularly since private bills are unique to the interests of only one Member's constituent.[173] On the other hand, there is no prohibition on introducing another bill for the same person in a subsequent Congress.

A veto also assists Congress in subsequently determining which cases should be sent forward for enactment. In many of the veto cases, subsequent action on similar cases by Congress is diminished.

Precedent - The bills vetoed based on potential problems of precedent vary. The cases included a native-born United States citizen who expatriated in order to engage in business for which Canadian citizenship was required, and who later wished to regain United States citizenship. The President noted "No reason is discernable why a special dispensation should be accorded to him from compliance with all of the requirements of the naturalization laws."[174] Another case involved a 34-year old native of Poland who was a deserting crewman and who had spent two years in the Polish underground fighting against the Nazis. The President noted that although a sympathetic case, the situation was

> not unlike thousands of others throughout the world who are seeking a haven in the United States...[granting special priviliges to him] would postpone the entry of some other hopeful Polish person rightfully awaiting the opportunity to enjoy the blessings of a new life in this country.[175]

Other vetoes on the basis of adverse precedents included a 32-year old native and citizen of Denmark whose mother and sister were permanent residents;[176] a 43-year old native-born United States citizen and her 11-year old Romanian-born son, where the mother had lost citizenship by becoming a naturalized citizen of Italy in order to marry her husband, an employee of the Italian consular service;[177] a 53-year old native and citizen of Spain who possessed exceptional skills as a designer of furs and was chosen as one of the 10 best fur designers in the United States;[178] a 28-year old native of Czechoslovakia and citizen of Austria and metallurgical engineer who had entered the United States as an exchange student;[179]and a case of natives of Germany and the Netherlands who owned interests in an exporting and importing business in their homeland was vetoed because it was too broad and allowed no administrative discretion from other applicable immigration laws.[180]

Two bills that the President pocket vetoed included those of a 53-year old native of Turkey and citizen of Greece who was an attache of the Greek Embassy and whose two children married United States citizens;[181] and of 35- and 24-year old natives of Iran and Russia who entered the United States as exchange students from the World Health

Organization, with twin United States citizen children, but who violated his student status through employment.[182]

Character of Beneficiaries - The President often vetoed private bills based on the character of the beneficiaries. Examples included a veto of a bill on behalf of 26- and 22-year old natives of Germany who were fugitives from Germany and one beneficiary who had been sentenced to death for avoiding the draft under Hitler. The President noted that the aliens had criminal proceedings pending against them for "fraud and civil claims for the recovery of property."[183] Another case involved a 45-year old native and citizen of Germany who was in the United States for 13 years and did not seek to regularize his status, but in fact sought repatriation to Germany during the war. The President stated that he "showed his allegiance time and again as that of a German national."[184]

Other vetoes involved 61- and 30-year old natives and citizens of Germany who entered the United States as visitors shortly before Hitler's rise and had invested in various industrial corporations controlled by the German Government.[185] Another veto involved a 51-year old native-born United States citizen who lost citizenship by acquiring French citizenship during the war and who made disparaging statements about the United States.[186] That private bill later became law. Other veto cases included a bill on behalf of a 43-year old native of Sweden who claimed exemption from military service;[187] and a 43-year old native and citizen of Canada who had maintained a "bawdyhouse" in Canada and had been married four times.[188] The same case later became law without the President's approval.

Although use of the pocket veto does not generally provide an explanation of why enactment is denied, several cases can be surmized to be related to character problems. One case involved a 47-year old native and citizen of Greece who entered the United States in 1921 and later was convicted and imprisoned for issuing bad checks. He subsequently married a United States citizen and had a seven-year old child. The bill was opposed by the Department of Justice because of his "disregard for the laws and principles of the United States."[189] Another pocket veto involved a 24-year old native and citizen of Sierra Leone and student who falsified an application for a student loan.[190]

Administrative Remedy - Vetoes where administrative action could be taken involved a deserting crewman and spouse of a permanent resident alien with a citizen child who was eligible to apply for permanent residence under a new law;[191] and a 40-year old native of Germany and spouse of a United States citizen who had resided in the United States for 14 years and had administrative relief available under newly enacted legislation.[192] One bill was rejected on behalf of natives of Lithuania who had resided in the United States for 14 years and where the relief afforded by the legislation canceled deportation proceedings. In his veto message to Congress, the President expressed concern that the status afforded no permanency in the United States stating that it is "highly questionable whether it is in the best interests of the United States to place persons living in this country in such a peculiar status."[193]

Another case involved a 27-year old native and citizen of China residing in Hong Kong who was registered on the quota list for immigration by virtue of a petition filed by United States citizen adoptive parents. She had resided with her adoptive parents 12 years prior to marriage and was married with six children. The adoptive father suffered paralysis. The President noted that the law which had been cited in the private bill presented to him had been repealed and therefore no purpose would be served.[194]

Laws without Presidential Approval - Bills which became law without Presidential approval included two relating to character and one involving a possible adverse precedent. The two former included a 41-year old native and citizen of Italy who entered the United States as a minister of religion but was found deportable for having procured a visa by fraudulently claiming to be a priest.[195] The other case, as noted above, was a bill on behalf of a 43-year old native and citizen of Canada who had maintained a "bawdy house." That bill was vetoed and later became law without the President's approval.[196] The third case involved a possible adverse precedent on behalf of a 71-year old native-born United States citizen taken to Germany by her father at the age of eight and who lost her citizenship through marriage to a German citizen. She also voted in a German election.[197]

Chapter 3

The Process

Private bills follow the same legislative course as public bills--they require action by both Houses of Congress and signature by the President. It is the prerogative of each Member of Congress to decide which legislation to sponsor. Many Members have a general policy of not introducing private bills because they believe that if a particular case poses hardship, generic legislation should be considered, instead of private legislation granting one individual an exception. On the other hand, some Members believe that any person who seeks redress is entitled to a hearing from Congress. Still other Members feel that an exceptional case may sometimes warrant a special act of Congress.

The role of the Judiciary Committee in each House is very different than that of the Member who introduces the private bill. It is a dual role: the Committee functions as a reviewing organ of the equities based on hardship criteria and precedents, and acts as the procedural vehicle for guiding the legislation through Congress. While the Member's role is constituent-oriented, the Committee's role is institutional, and its responsibilities lie with preserving the integrity of the process.

Introduction

The private bill process usually starts when a constituent writes to his or her Member of Congress requesting assistance with an immigration problem. This could also be a letter addressed from a relative or friend of the individual. Other means of bringing a case to a Member's attention include letters from organizations, such as church or civic groups on behalf of the individual.

The Member's office then reviews the correspondence to see whether the particular problem could be solved administratively. That is, perhaps the law already provides a remedy for the situation. If no relief is available under the law, that Member may decide to approach informally or by a letter the Subcommittee on Immigration of either the House or the Senate which has jurisdiction over private bills and to ask whether any relief exists under the law, or if a private bill is the only solution. If a private bill is the only remedy, the Subcommittee Chairman or staff reviews the threshhold hardship criteria, the basic principle for any private bill, and the Committee Rules of Procedure and precedents relating to the types of private bills which can be considered.

The Member is then advised of the result either informally or through a letter from the Chairman of the Subcommittee. These "advisory opinions" by the Subcommittee assist Members in determining the need for a private bill and possible prospects for passage.

It is not mandatory that a Member seek advice from the Subcommittee prior to introduction, but it is in both the Member's and constituent's best interests to know its prospects. Paperwork, research and interrogatories are usually handled by the Subcommittee staff until a formal meeting on private bills is scheduled for voting purposes.

If a Member chooses not to introduce a bill because of the Subcommittee's adverse recommendation, or because administrative relief is available, the constituent is so advised by the Member. If the Member decides to introduce a bill, whether or not the Subcommittee recommended favorably, that Member lets the constituent know, and seeks further advice on the documentation the Subcommittee would need under its Rules to initiate the process.

The Member's office may draft the legislation, or request a draft from the Office of Legislative Counsel in the House or the Senate, which advises Members of Congress on legislation in Congress. The bill would be drafted in a way to overcome the particular provision of law that would prevent the constituent's relative immigration to the United States.[1] Types of relief sought include adoption, waivers of certain grounds of exclusion, and permanent residence or naturalization.

When the bill is drafted, it is signed by the Member and dropped in the "hopper" of the House (where bills are introduced); or in the Senate, they are taken to the Clerk of the Senate for introduction. In either case, the Clerk assigns a number and the bill is referred by the Speaker of the House or President Pro-Tempore of the Senate to the appropriate committee (the Committee on the Judiciary) which exercises jurisdiction over immigration matters.[2] After the Government Printing Office prints the bill, it is sent to the Judiciary Committee which then refers it to the Immigration Subcommittee.

As soon as a bill is received in the Subcommittee, a file is created for any correspondence on the case. It is the bill sponsor's responsibility to submit information to the Subcommittee on the legislation. If a Member does not wish to aggressively pursue a bill to indicate his or her support of the case, no communications from the Member are sent to the Subcommittee and no stays of deportation apply. The bill remains pending in the Subcommittee with no action anticipated and dies like other legislation when the two-year period of a Congress ends, to be possibly reintroduced in the succeeding Congress.

If the Member is seriously interested in acting on behalf of the legislation after it is introduced, under the House and Senate Subcommittee rules, a letter is addressed to the Chairman of the Subcommittee on Immigration supplying identifying information on the beneficiary of the bill and the bill's interested party (usually the relative or family of the beneficiary). Additionally an outline of the hardship factors is included in the letter. The record is based solely on the facts submitted by the bill's sponsor, and although oftentimes petitions may be submitted by interested parties or lawyers, the Committees focuses its attention primarily on the information provided directly by the sponsor. This channel is appropriate in order to make sure that all the information available is authorized by the sponsor.

Upon receipt of the letter from the Member on a private bill, the Subcommittee Chairman or staff first reviews the case for any possible alternative relief and for the adequacy of documentation, as well as for conformity with Subcommittee rules and guidelines. For instance, the House Subcommittee Rules require that all bills on behalf of doctors indicate that the beneficiary passed certain medical exams, that private bills involving drug cases include character affidavits in the file, and that bills involving adoptions include adoption decrees.

In cases clearly outside the scope of the Subcommittee Rules, the sponsor is advised that the bill does not comply with the rules and will not be scheduled. Alternatively, the Subcommittee Chairman may inform the Member that the bill may be scheduled, but that due to Subcommittee Rules or Congressional precedents, passage would be difficult, if not impossible. In addition, the Subcommittee may recommend alternative language in the bill which would better clarify the relief sought. Generally, legislation is considered only on a very narrow basis, so that the beneficiary must meet all other applicable laws. There have been only a few cases also where a temporary status has been granted.[3] Where documentation is lacking or questions arise, the sponsor is requested to respond to the Subcommittee's inquiries.

Executive Branch Reports

The second step involves deciding whether Executive Branch reports should be requested. Executive Branch reports include comments on the legislation related to the drafting and purpose of the bill, and are similar to those presented for public legislation. In the area of private bills, the report is usually requested from the INS and from the State Department. These are requested by the Chairman of the full Judiciary Committees in the House or the Senate because of the high degree of importance which the Agreements attach to this action. The House and Senate Rules require that the reports be received prior to any action.[4] In most cases, an interview is conducted with the beneficiary and interested parties, and a review conducted of any previous agency files, in addition to FBI checks and medical exams for the beneficiaries. Also, an examination is made as to whether there are any other immigration provisions which may apply to the case.

Initiation of request for report - In both Houses the request for an Executive Branch report, which commences the administrative handling of cases, is guided by whether the beneficiary is in the United States (Rule 4 of the Subcommittee Rules of Procedure) or outside the United States.[5] When a person is in the United States, the requesting of a report triggers a stay of deportation under an agreement with the Congressional Committees and the INS Commissioner.[6] The Rules of the House and Senate state that the Subcommittee will not *automatically* request reports from the Executive Branch when a person is in the United States, and that a showing of "hardship" must be made on the case.[7]

In the House the request for a report on a beneficiary inside the United States is subject to a formal meeting of the Subcommittee, at which time the bill's sponsor must present compelling reasons for the private bill. A vote is required on the threshhold hardship criteria, which would initiate Executive Branch comments, thus staying deportation, or deny the request. By contrast, the Senate reviews the cases informally as to hardship and as to whether Executive Branch comments should be requested.

In cases where the beneficiary is outside the United States, Executive Branch comments are automatically requested as soon as the information is received from the sponsor. Upon receipt of the Executive Branch comments, a copy is forwarded to the author and the bill is then placed on the Subcommittee's agenda for action at its next meeting on private bills. This distinction between bills for aliens in the United States and outside the United States is important not only because of the stay of deportation, but because the delay in a request for report results in a longer timeframe for processing, since the reports take about three months to complete.

INS and State processing of reports - The processing of reports in the Executive Branch are guided by the Operating Instructions of INS and the Foreign Affairs Manual of the Department of State.[8] According to INS instructions, upon receipt of a "request for a report" by the Chairman of the House or Senate Judiciary Committee, a stay of deportation is initiated if the alien is in the United States:

> a stay of deportation or voluntary departure shall not be authorized solely to permit the introduction of a private bill or in anticipation of receiving a congressional committee request for a report on such a bill.

The information in the request for a report must include the name and address of the beneficiaries, the date and place of birth and other relevant information. Based on this information, the INS Commissioner directs the Private Bill Control Unit within INS to notify by cable the District Office of the Service where the beneficiary resides that a stay of deportation is initiated. Under the INS Agreement with the Committees, however, the Commissioner still retains discretion to deport the alien in notorious cases. While the bill's beneficiary must continue through any administrative proceedings, final deportation does not take place unless adverse action is taken. If the alien is in a legal temporary status, the permanent status of the bill can alter that status.

The stay of deportation operates until February 1 of the next odd-numbered year, but could be for less time if the alien's "continued presence here would be contrary to the best interests of the United States." Other cases, not necessarily involving deportation, such as citizenship or adoptions, are referred for investigation to the relevant branches of the INS and are not impacted by the Committee Agreements relating to deportation.

The investigation of the beneficiary by the local INS office involves a review of any INS files, FBI fingerprint checks, police checks, interviews of the beneficiaries and interested parties, and, in adoption cases, verification of adoption. In criminal cases, the investigation involves a review of conviction records.

As noted previously, prior to 1953 routing of cases was through the Department of Justice, which formalized a statement of support or opposition to the legislation. Additionally, the INS structure has changed from time to time, involving which office held responsibility for the preparation of reports. Since 1955 a special private bill unit has been in the INS Enforcement division, as part of a reorganization for "coordinating all Service functions relative to private legislation from the introduction of the bill to adjustment of the alien's status following enactment, or enforcement of departure following adverse action."[9]

Upon completion of the review of the report, the INS Commissioner sends the report to the Chairman of the Senate or House Judiciary Committee, where it is forwarded to the Subcommittee. At that time, the sponsor of the bill receives a copy of the report from the Subcommittee. In addition, the reports are also included in the House and Senate reports filed as legislative history accompanying bills in the Congress. Reports are also shared between INS and the State Department which assists in the corroboration of information.

Reports for persons outside the United States are usually requested from the Department of State. In these cases, reports from the State Department are coordinated with the relevant Embassies or consulates abroad where the beneficiaries or interested parties reside.

The Department of State instructions to the Embassies state that upon receipt of a request for a report from the Committee to the Secretary of State in Washington, the Visa Office transmits a cable with identifying information to the appropriate Embassy requesting that the post review the file on the beneficiary. In most cases, an interview includes police checks, medical examinations, copies of any conviction records if applicable, and in adoption cases, verification of the legality of the adoption. The State Department notes in its instructions that:

> A fully documented backround investigation would not only alert these Members to any relevant facts which may surface subsequent to completion of the bill proceedings but would also substantiate the necessity of passage of the private bill.[10]

If there is an interested party in the United States, then the INS interviews those individuals also.

Fig. 3.1: The Private Immigration Bill Process

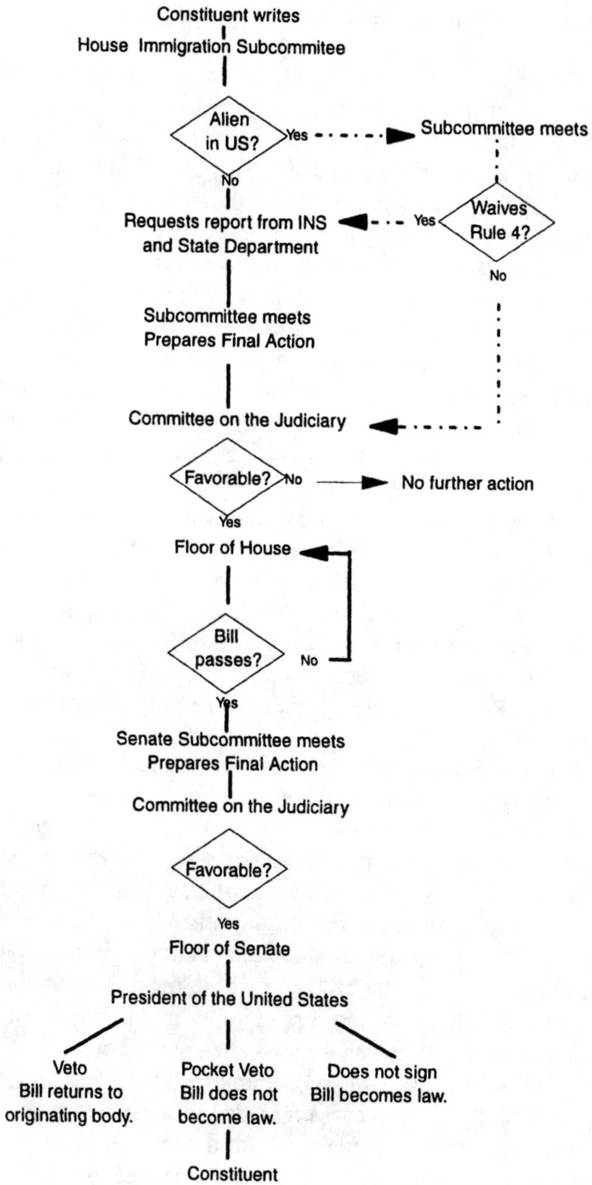

Subcommittee Meetings

Subcommittee meetings on private bills are within the discretion of the Chairman. As soon as a meeting date is set, agendas are submitted to the Chairman for review and possible scheduling. It has been the practice of the House and the Senate Subcommittees to schedule a meeting for consideration of a full agenda of private bills rather than meeting on an ad hoc basis on individual bills. This takes less time from the general legislative business as well as avoids colleagues importuning the Subcommittee to "hurry-up" and meet to stay the deportation of an alien through a waiver of Rule 4.

Bills which are docketed must first be reviewed by the Committee staff for completeness of the file, including Executive Branch reports and consistencies between information submitted by the author and the reports. Adoption documents, conviction records, and any other pertinent laws are also reviewed.

Subcommittee meetings consider two types of issues. First are Rule 4 cases, which must undergo the initial hardship test to decide whether Executive Branch reports will be requested. In the House, this decision is made at the formal meeting of the Subcommittee and the sponsor must come forward to explain the hardship on behalf of the Rule 4 case. No other witnesses, such as the beneficiary or lawyers, are allowed to testify. Representatives of the INS and the Department of State attend the meetings.

In the Senate, the decisions are made informally by the staff at intermittent meetings without recourse to testimony or representatives of the Executive Branch. If favorable action is taken by the House or the Senate Subcommittee on a Rule 4 case, the request for a report is forwarded from the Chairman of the Judiciary Committee to the INS, thus staying deportation. On the other hand, unfavorable action halts any further processing by the Subcommittee. In the House, unfavorable action means that the bill is tabled; in the Senate the bill is indefinitely postponed. This is the first hurdle in the processing of a private immigration bill on behalf of an alien in the United States.

The second type of Subcommittee action involves final actions on private bills. These cases include those for which reports had already been requested and received from the Executive Branch (including previously acted upon Rule 4 cases where reports have been received). For final action bills, both the House and the Senate Subcommittees meet formally for disposition. The fact that Rule 4 was waived previously on a bill does not necessarily mean that the bill will be favorably considered when reviewed again for final action.

Favorably acted upon legislation is forwarded--as with public legislation--to the full Judiciary Committee for processing. It is at this point also that any amendments to the original legislation would be considered, if the bill was improperly drafted or if the Subcommittee wanted to restrict the relief or provide alternative relief. For instance, some bills have been amended to require that relief is sought within two years of enactment,[11] and in some physician cases the physician must practice medicine in the area for which relief is sought for a period of time.[12]

Cases which are tabled or indefinitely postponed are forwarded to the full Committee with that recommendation. Denial may be for a variety of reasons, including lack of merit, the availability of administrative relief, and death of the beneficiary.

The agendas for the meeting prepared by staff, oftentimes at the request of the Chairman, include recommendations for action based on precedents which are generally adopted by the Subcommittee. In cases in which there are no firm guidelines or precedents, the Subcommittee debates more extensively.

Full Committee

Consideration at the Full Committee is at the discretion of the Chairman of the Judiciary Committee, but it usually occurs soon after Subcommittee action. The full Committee generally adopts the recommendations of the Subcommittee with little debate. However, there have been occasions where controversial bills not within the Subcommittee's guidelines or precedents cause acrimonious discussion.[13]

Once the full Committee has voted favorably on a bill, as with public legislation, the measure is "reported" on to the Floor of the House or Senate. A report by the Committee is prepared and printed by the Government Printing Office, and which becomes part of the official legislative history of the bill as it proceeds through Congress.[14] The report outlines the facts of the case and includes a copy of the Executive Branch comments, any substantiating documents, a statement by the sponsor of the bill, and a statement of the need for Congressional action.

In the tabled or indefinitely postponed cases (denied), a letter is addressed to the INS and the Department of State by the Chairman of the Judiciary Committee informing them of the action.

House and Senate Floor

After the full Committee action and the filing of the report, consideration of the private bill in the House and Senate differ procedurally. In the House, private bills are listed on the Private Calendar and can only be considered on the Floor of the House on the first and third Tuesdays of the month. Additionally, there is a layover period of seven days after the reporting by the full Committee before the Calendar bills can be considered.

There is a Committee of six Official Objectors (three Democrats and three Republicans) appointed by the Majority and Minority Leaders to watch over the Private Calendar, acting as guardians of the House so that the full membership need not review each individual case coming before it. Under the House Rules there is no debate allowed on private bills, and votes on individual cases are very rare. The House Membership and the Objectors place a large degree of trust in the work of the Subcommittee and full Committee, and most private bills reported from Committee are passed in the House.

Controversial cases, however, including drug-related offenses, criminal acts, questionable adoptions, and grants of citizenship, are sometimes stopped by the Official Objectors. Although there are no special guidelines for objecting to bills, the reasons for halting passage are usually on the basis of precedents, lack of information, or inequities. If the bill is called by the Speaker on the day of the Private Calendar and no objection is made, the bill passes the House without any further action.

On the other hand, if one of the Official Objectors asks that the bill be passed over without prejudice the bill remains on the Private Calendar until the problems are resolved. That may continue until Congress adjourns at the end of each two year period. If the bill is a particularly grievous case, two Official Objectors may rise in opposition, thereby recommiting the bill by sending it back to the originating Committee, where it is not allowed to be considered again that Congress, except under extraordinary circumstances.

In the Senate once a bill has been reported out of the full Committee for three days, the Senate Majority Leader determines when the private bills are to be brought to the Floor of the Senate for consideration. The scheduling is usually done in a timely manner by unanimous consent (the manner in which many noncontroversial matters are considered), depending on any other legislative business in the Senate. There is no comparable Official Objector system as the House, although the Senate Leadership does have a general policy--as in public legislation--that when an objection is heard to bringing any bill up for consideration, including public legislation, that objection ("hold") can stop any further processing until the problems are resolved. As in the House, there is very rarely any debate; and the Senate passes the measure with the knowledge that the Committee has already scrutinized the cases.

Once a private bill has been passed by either the House or Senate, it is very likely that the other body will adopt the bill. It is not, however, a *rubber-stamp* approval. There may be differences of policy between the Subcommittees, or the Membership may find the case without sufficient hardship. Additional information may also be needed, and such information is requested from the sponsor of the legislation. The sponsors of the bill have the primary responsibility to respond to any inquiries about the case, and the Committee is the procedural organ for the processing of the legislation.

The Committee's legislative report accompanying the bill is primarily the basis for the other body's review. After the bill has been referred to the Subcommitee and action taken on the legislation, the bill is routed through the Committee structure in the other respective body and then to the Senate or House Floor. In some cases, there may be amendments by the respective Committees, or on a rare occasion there may be a conference between the House and the Senate to resolve differences on a particular bill. The latter is infrequent because the Committees generally work together to resolve any major differences during deliberations.

Upon passage by both Houses, the private bill is returned to the originating body and enrolled for forwarding to the President.

Presidential Signature

Upon receipt by the President, the relevant federal agencies prepare comments as to whether the President should sign the bill. As indicated previously, the Office of Management and Budget (OMB) coordinates these comments and submits the legislation with a recommendation for signature or veto to the President. This procedure is identical to that of public legislation. In the private bill cases, however, INS and State usually perform another perfunctory check with the local office to assure that there has been no change of facts before submitting their report to OMB. After the President signs the bill, the National Archives assigns the bill a law number, and it is printed by the Government Printing Office.

The President also, however, can veto the bill or withhold signature at the end of the Congress as a pocket veto. The President can refuse to sign the bill while Congress is in session which would allow the bill become law without approval.

After signature, the beneficiaries and/or interested parties are alerted to the new law by the INS or the Department of State. The beneficiary is scheduled for an appointment and interview for whatever action is necessary to implement the terms of the private law. For instance, in an adoption case, the adoptive parents are interviewed and requested to file appropriate forms with the INS for the adopted child who is the beneficiary of the bill. In the case of a person outside the United States, the Department of State interviews the person.

The approximate timeframe for enactment of a private immigration bill is at least two years. In rare cases, a private bill may be repealed for various reasons, such as a public law which overtook events and already provided relief. In addition, there may be amendments to private laws.[15]

The Private Bill Process: "Real Life" Examples

The following are examples of how the private bill process works, from the initial request by a constituent for a private bill to enactment.

Administrative Remedy: No Subcommittee action.

John Doe has written his Congressman about his brother, Jack, who is in Germany and would like to immigrate permanently to the United States. The Congressman reviews the letter and finds that the immigration law has a provision that allows brothers or sisters of United States citizens to immigrate, but there is a five-year waiting period. Because Jack is divorced and has just lost his job, the Congressman believes there are extenuating circumstances which may warrant a private bill. The Subcommittee advises that there is an administrative remedy for Jack, and that he must wait in line for immigration. The "hardship" factor is not met. Additionally, the Subcommittee notes there are few precedents for such a case. The Congressman then advises the constituent that the bill would not receive favorable action and advises the constituent to pursue the administrative remedy by filing a petition for his brother.

"Rule 4 Hardship"- Alien in the United States

Subcommittee adverse action - Susan and Dan Johnson and their two-year old citizen child entered the United States as visitors and bought a motel in order to remain in the United States. They write their Congressman asking for a special bill for permanent immigration. The Congressman seeks the advice of the Immigration Subcommittee which indicates the policy toward "investors" is negative. However, the Congressman decides because of community interest to introduce the bill anyway.

After the bill is referred to the Subcommittee, the Chairman advises the sponsor again that there are few precedents and that the bill may not be scheduled because of the lack of favorable action. The Chairman reiterates that there will be no intervention by the Subcommittee in any deportation proceedings in the interim. At the time of a meeting of the Subcommittee, the Members of the Subcommittee decide no hardship exists and they adhere to their policy of acting unfavorably on such cases; therefore no stay of deportation results. The bill is forwarded to the full Committee with an adverse recommendation, which ends all legislative action.

In the Senate, the staff of the Subcommittee meets and finds no extenuating circumstances, and advises the Senator that a report will not be requested on the case, thus no staying of deportation. The bill is then forwarded to full Committee as indefinitely postponed.

Subcommittee favorable within precedents - Widower John Doe, who has six citizen children, entered the United States to attend the funeral of his citizen wife, and contacted his Congessman asking what relief might be available to him under the immigration laws to remain in the United States. The Congressman finds no remedy under the law and, after receiving a favorable advisory opinion from the Subcommittee indicating that precedents for such a case exist, the Congressman introduces a bill and addresses a letter to the Immigration Subcommittee Chairman with the documentation required by the Subcommittee's Rules. The Chairman advises that the bill will be scheduled when a meeting is held on private bills, but that there will be no intervention in any deportation proceedings until the Subcommittee votes to waive Rule 4. When the meeting is held, the Subcommittee's favorable action results in the request for a report from the INS, by the

Chairman of the full Committee which stays deportation. The bill is considered again at another meeting for final action after the reports have been received, and the bill is then forwarded to the full Committee for further processing.

In the Senate, similar processing occurs, except that the determination as to the "hardship" Rule 4 waiver occurs at an informal staff meeting. If favorable action, the report would be requested by the Chairman of the full Committee, and a stay of deportation occurs on the basis of favorable action. Final action, as in the House, occurs after receipt of the reports. After the final action vote by the Subcommittee, the legislation is forwarded to the full Committee for final processing.

Alien Outside the United States

Mary and John Smith, employed as missionaries overseas, took into their home a three-year old child who resided with them for 16 years. When the Smith family sought to return to the United States, they realized that the child could not come with them because no legal adoption took place. A letter is addressed to their Congressman, who seeks advice from the Subcommittee about any possible relief. The Immigration Subcommittee Chairman advises that under immigration law the child had to be adopted under the age of 16 and that a private bill would be necessary, but that no assurances of favorable action could be made. The Smith family is required to document their support of the child and the reasons why the child was not adopted. The Congressman reviews the necessary documentation and then decides to introduce a bill and to write a letter to the Subcommittee with the relevant facts.

Because the Smith family is outside the United States, the Subcommittee immediately requests a report from the State Department and, if needed, INS comments. Later that year the reports are received, and when a meeting of the Subcommittee is scheduled the case is docketed for consideration. At the meeting, the Subcommittee acts favorably and reports the bill to the full Committee. If the Subcommitte acted adversely, the bill is forwarded to full Committee with an adverse recommendation.

Full Committee

At the full Judiciary Committee meeting, the Chairman of the Immigration Subcommittee explains the bills, and the Committee acts favorably and reports the bill to the full House or Senate. Alternatively, the Committee tables the bill or indefinitely postpones the bill, which halts any further action. A letter is then addressed by the Chairman of the Committee to the INS and State Department advising of the final action on unfavorable bills, so that any stay of deportation is lifted and proceedings for removal from the country resumed.

Floor Action in the House and Senate

When the Private Calendar is called in the House, and there is no objection, the private bill is passed. In the case of the adoption bill there may be discrepancies in the adoption documents, and an Official Objector halts its consideration in the House by passing the bill over "without prejudice" until the discrepancies are resolved. Alternatively, two objectors may recommit the bill, which results in returning the legislation to the originating Committee. After passage, the bill goes to the other Body (Senate or House) for Subcommittee and Committee processing. Thereafter, the bill is enrolled by the clerk of the originating body and submitted to the President.

Enactment

Prior to signature, the Executive Branch Departments submit their views at the request of OMB for presentation to the President. Upon signature by the President, in the adoption case, the INS receives a copy of the printed law and the parents are interviewed. The parents are requested to file appropriate forms for declaring the child eligible for benefits under the new law, and the child is admitted to the United States for permanent residence. In the widower case, the father is called for an interview by the INS and processed for his permanent resident card. On the other hand, if unanticipated problems have developed, or derogatory records revealed at the last minute, the President can veto the case, use the pocket veto, or let the bill become law without approval.

Chapter 4

Public Legislation and Private Bills

Over the years private bills have influenced public legislation on immigration, especially in the three areas discussed below. This chapter outlines the relationship between private immigration bills and public legislation.

An historical perspective precedes each analysis of the relationship of individual bills to the general law. Also included is a statistical summary and a description of precedents established during each Congress which have become law. A key to the categories is provided in Appendix D3, and statistical notes at the end of the book provide further information. For purposes of discussion, the term "quota" is used throughout the 100 Congresses, even though the 1965 Act replaced the country quotas with per country ceilings on immigration. Because of the low number of private laws through the 79th Congress (1945-1946), early precedents are summarized. In the succeeding Congresses, each Congress is discussed separately.

The first major impact of private bills occurred in the area of immigration quotas allotted to each country under the Quota Act of 1921, which continued until 1965. Throughout the years of immigration based on national origins, a high volume of private bills existed. This is primarily because natives of countries who did not have a large number of visas allocated to them had no recourse for entry to the United States other than a private bill. These cases led Congress to recognize the need for revision of that quota system.

The second area demonstrating the relationship between private bills and public legislation is in the grounds of exclusion, which prohibited

Fig. 4.1 Impact of Private Bills on Public Legislation

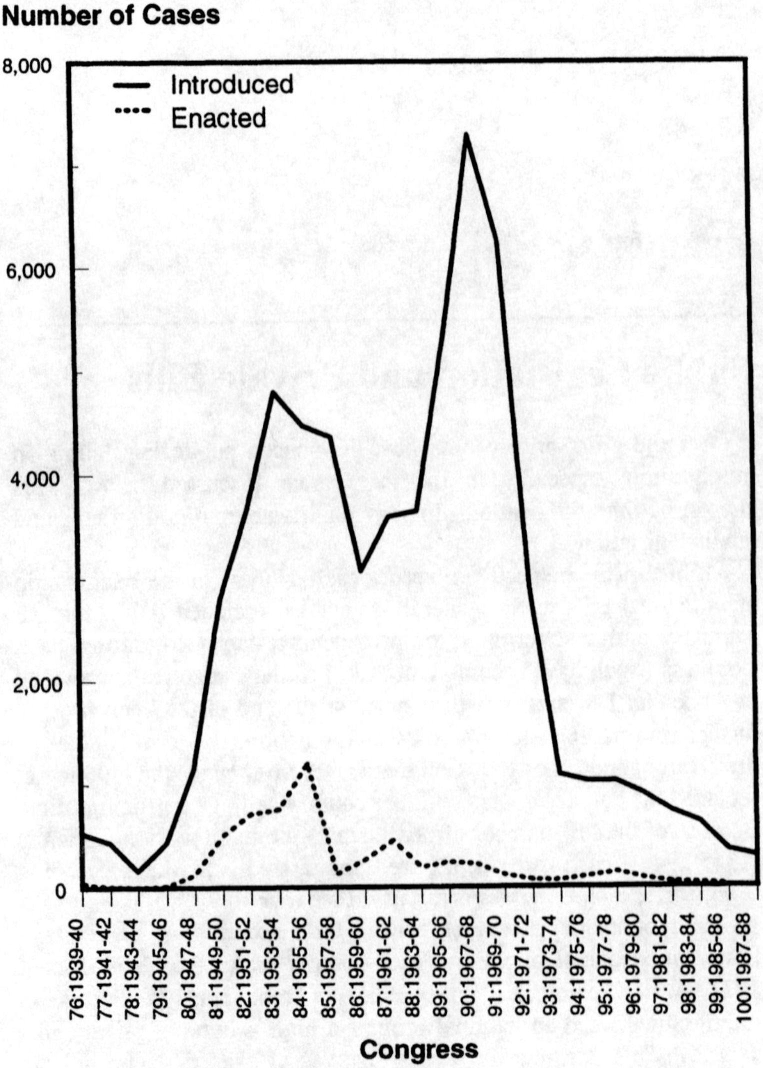

Public legislation in 1952, 1957, 1961, 1965 and 1981 and rules changes in 1969 and 1979 greatly reduced the number of private bills introduced and enacted.

the entry of individuals for a variety of reasons, including health grounds and criminal activity. The large volume of bills on behalf of close relatives of United States citizens and permanent residents in 1957 and 1961 set the stage for remedial legislation in this area.

The third type of legislation impacted by private bills is in the naturalization area, where increased numbers of private bills revealed inequities in the naturalization law due to expatriating acts through long periods of residence abroad.

Private bills were not the sole basis for major immigration law changes. Certainly, a combination of humanitarian responses in wartime, and social and political changes resulted in major legislation. Private bills, however, brought individual cases to the attention of the Congress which mirrored the human tragedy of separated families under the law, and thrust into the debate the need to assist more individuals.

QUOTAS

Historical Perspective

Country quotas did not begin until 1921. Strict levels of immigration and national origins have been used to limit immigrants from certain parts of the world and to respond to humanitarian impulses in the aftermath of war. While family and occupational patterns alternatively have been principal considerations in establishing criteria for entry, the quotas, together with exclusions of classes of aliens, kept limits on overall immigration. Liberalization of the immigration laws did not occur until the late 50's and 60's, when social changes steered Congress toward more progressive attitudes.

The Early Years

In the early years of the republic, individuals immigrated not only for religious freedom and other democratic principles brought about by the American Revolution, but also for the lure of economic benefits.[1] Improved transportation, augmented by a population crisis in Europe and the rural breakdown of European economic systems, made the new country more accessible and desirable to even larger numbers of immigrants than had been anticipated.[2] Immigration from 1820-1924 differed from the earlier first waves of Protestant Anglo-Saxons in the 1700s, however. It was a "Babel of tongues" and complexions from southern and eastern Europe and primarily Catholic.[3] This second wave of immigrants motivated the Congress toward restrictions on levels of immigration, which took the form of a quota system allocating each country a certain number of visas per year.

The forerunner of the quota system, however, related to action taken at the end of the Nineteenth Century to impede the flow of Chinese and Japanese laborers. The floating pools of labor on the West Coast, resulting from the Gold Rush and the building of the railroads (1849-1870), aroused cultural and racial antagonisms against the Chinese, and later fueled anti-Japanese sentiment in 1900.[4] Public opinion against the influx of Chinese forced President Chester A. Arthur to take steps to renege on a previously entered into agreement with China which had allowed the entry of laborers. A new 1881 treaty barred Chinese nationals from entry, and that policy continued through various acts until 1943.[5]

Likewise, the immigration of Japanese to the West Coast and their settlement in farming areas pressed President Theodore Roosevelt to restrict the volume of Japanese laborers entering the United States in 1907.[6] By 1917, the issue of race increasingly became intertwined with immigration policy. The remaining group excluded from citizenship and immigration included Asians other than Japanese or Chinese. The 1917 Act,[7] which established grounds of exclusion, sought to bar Hindus from entry by prohibiting immigration from the so-called "Barred Zone," which included Siam, part of Afghanistan, Malay, India, and Burma. The majority of the racial exclusions remained in the law until 1952,[8] when eliminated as a basis for limiting immigration and naturalization.[9]

World War I brought latent immigrant antagonisms to a head. There was a fear expressed that "millions of wartorn Europeans would descend on the United States--in a veritable flood which would completely subvert the traditional American way of life."[10] These fears, combined with the prior high levels of immigration from southern and eastern Europe in 1880-1890, invoked a sense of urgency in establishing a national immigration policy.[11] In addition, concerns of postwar unemployment, housing, and labor shortages contributed to a new awareness of the immigrant.[12] New labor "flocked to centers where their compatriots had already congregated," and not to farmlands where previous streams of immigrants had gone and where demand was great.[13] Finally, the war years stimulated a newly-awakened sense of American nationalism, which urged the need for assimilation and uniformity as a nation.[14] The second wave immigrant from southern and eastern Europe, who appeared to be unassimilable groups, became the scapegoat of the anti-immigrant feelings.[15]

Proposals to thwart the impending tide of immigrants followed two Congressional Committee investigations which centered around the types of immigrants who presented problems, such as paupers and convicts, as well as the economic aspects of immigration. In 1889, the Ford Committee (Melbourne H. Ford, D-MI), recommended various exclusion laws to prevent undesirables from entering the country. In 1911 the Dillingham Commission, named after Senator William P. Dillingham (R-VT), published its 11-volume study centering around the economic aspects of immigration, recommending further immigration limits.[16]

There was also ample theoretical justification to restrict the new wave of immigrants. Eugenics, the heredity study propounded by Sir Francis Galton, taught that mankind would benefit by breeding from the "best" and restricting the offspring of the "worst." This gave intellectual credence for a selection policy which favored those from current United States "stock" and disfavored intending immigrants from southeastern Europe.[17]

The first quota act, in 1921,[18] followed restrictions on the type of immigrants to be admitted in 1917. The new quota act, stated in the scientific theoretical terms of Galton, reflected alien indigestion and the weakened faith in assimilation.[19] It created a system where a formula determined the admissions level based on percentages of the "foreign-born" population in the 1910 census. Under the formula, the number of immigrants allowed from each country was comparable to 3% of the number of foreign-born natives of that country in the United States in 1910. After the first year of the 1921 Act, immigration totaled 309,556, mostly from northern and western Europe, compared with 805,228 in 1921, thus maintaining the status quo in terms of immigrant ethnicity.[20]

The quota law charged immigrant admissions to the immigrant's country of birth and set forth two basic categories of admissions. Nonquota, those persons who did not count against the immigration levels, consisted of the following: 1) those entering temporarily, 2) Western Hemisphere natives who had resided in that Hemisphere one year, 3) children of United States citizens, and 4) persons entering for business or pleasure. Western Hemisphere natives remained outside general quotas until 1965 because of labor needs and the special relationship of Western Hemisphere countries with the United States.[21] Quota immigrants, on the other hand, were subject to the 3% limitations.

Special "provisos" guided immigration of the fourth group which primarily related to entry on the basis of skills: one proviso allowed the admission of certain professionals and domestic servants, and another proviso granted "preference" to citizen relatives and relatives of immigrants who had applied for citizenship (wives, parents, children, brothers and sisters, and fiancees).[22] United States citizen women could not confer these benefits on relatives until 1928, and they waited until 1952 for full petitioning rights.[23]

Having set the cornerstone of immigration policy, advocates of maintaining an Anglo-Saxon heritage further sought to advance their goals as fears of the expiration of the two-year 1921 Act grew. In discussing legislative proposals for a new quota law in 1924, the tensions between immigrant groups became more blatant and racial overtones prevailed in arguments to retain migration from the preferred stock of the earlier immigrants.[24]

Proponents of change sought movement of the 1910 census date of the foreign-born population to an earlier date of 1890 which would have favored the first waves of immigrants from northern Europe of Anglo-Saxon heritage. Others, who favored increasing immigration from southern and eastern Europe, preferred a later census date such as 1920 which incorporated greater numbers of their fellow countrymen who had immigrated after 1890. In its report on the legislation, the House Immigration Committee explained the preference for the earlier date favoring northwestern European countries:

> We owe impartial justice to all those who have established themselves in our midst. They are entitled to share in our prosperity...Late arrivals are, in all fairness, not entitled to special privilege over those who have arrived at an earlier date and thereby contributed more to the advancement of the nation.[25]

The final bill combined both approaches through a compromize. The 1924 Quota Act[26] changed the census date to the latter of 1920, but the applicable population base included not just the foreign-born but individuals whose *national origins* were from a particular country. This meant that the base population represented more individuals from northwestern Europe since their national origin descendants entered into the statistical mix. The quota formula for admissions of a country under the 1924 Act had to be the "same ratio to 150,000 as the number of inhabitants in the United States in 1920 having that *national origin*...bears to the number of inhabitants in the United States in 1920."

For instance, under the national origins formula, England had a total population in the United States in 1920 of 39,216,333 compared to a total United States population of 94,820,915. As a result England received 65,721 of the 150,000 quota visas. On the other hand, for a country such as Greece whose total population in the United States in 1920 totaled 182,936, the number of visas allotted totaled 307.[27] Nonquota immigrants continued to be exempt from the levels established.

The 1924 Quota Act was hailed as arresting "the tendency toward a change in fundamental composition of the American stock." Others, however, declared the legislation a "clumsy instrument of selection which bars individuals by discrimination against nations instead of considering personal qualifications of immigrants..." overlooking the differences of individuals among groups.[28]

The new law, which became effective July 1, 1929, also redefined the nonquota and quota groups, and prioritized certain immigrant categories within the quota classes.[29] The law contained the following definitions:

> **Nonquota** - Wives and unmarried minor children under 18 of United States citizens, returning residents, ministers and professors, their wives and children, natives of the Western Hemisphere and students at least 15 years of age.
> **Quota** - First preference - parents of adult citizens, unmarried children under 21, and spouses of United States citizens.
> **Second preference** - Persons skilled in agriculture and their wives and children. Fifty percent of the quota of each nationality was available for the first two classes without priority between them. Regulations established other priorities.[30]

Immigration in 1924 had been 707,000; and it dropped in 1929 to 280,000 which included quota and nonquota immigrants.[31] The 1930s, however, reflected low levels of immigration, primarily because of the Great Depression. The low levels of immigration continued during World War II, with the exception of encouraged immigration from Mexico under an agricultural agreement to fill the needs of farms and industry for laborers.[32]

From 1924 until 1965, the most significant change in the basic quota system for admission to the United States occurred in 1952 when the priorities for immigrating under the quota laws changed. In the interim, however, many laws were enacted to relieve some of the hardships of the immigration law. Initial efforts centered on granting permanent status to those already inside the United States for long periods of time. Later, humanitarian responses to wartime measures impacted immigration, and these laws primarily benefited spouses and fiancees of United States citizens who married overseas during World War II, war orphans, and refugees. Finally, incremental clearing of quota backlogs led to modifications to the priority and selective criteria of admissions within the quota system, resulting in the 1952 changes and ultimately repeal of the national origins system.

Granting Permanent Status to Long-term Residents (1929-1940)

Two major initiatives addressed relief for long-term residents of the United States who did not possess adequate admission documentation, or overstayed their visas. Those included the "registry" provisions which allowed permanent residence immediately if the alien had entered the United States prior to a particular date. The other involved the "suspension of deportation" provisions of the law which allowed permanent residence based on longevity in the country.

The Registry Act, in 1929, provided a record of permanent residence for those who had entered the United States prior to June 3, 1921, the date of the initial quota law. The cut-off date was later advanced to 1924, 1940, 1948 and lastly to 1972.[33] The initial need for the registry provision stemmed from the fact that many aliens had lost their records of admission or had improperly entered the United States, and could not avail themselves of citizenship.[34]

Suspension of deportation provisions had been advocated since 1934. The "Alien Registration Act of 1940,"[35] in addition to requiring registration of aliens, provided for suspending deportation and subsequently granting permanent residence in certain cases. Eligibility criteria required that the aliens have no criminal record, demonstrate good moral character for the preceding five years, and whose deportation would result in "serious economic detriment" to a United States citizen or resident alien who was the spouse, parent or minor child. Aliens ineligible for immigration due to race were prohibited from making an application for relief. All such cases required submission to the Congress for review after INS approval.

The suspension of deportation provision responded to a stringent law which had been exposed as cruel by imposing "unbearable hardships" on families and serious financial charges upon the United States in medical cases.[36]

Amendments to the 1940 law in 1948[37] allowed relief regardless of family ties, changed the residence period to seven years as of the date of enactment, and allowed relief for those ineligible due to race. Although changes in 1952[38] tightened some of the eligibility requirements, and allowed criminals the ability to apply for relief after a ten year residence, by 1965 the suspension of deportation provisions became an avenue of permanent residence for many hardship cases.[39] Requirements included a showing of "extreme hardship," good moral character, and seven years residence for those without close relatives in the United States; and for those with criminal backgrounds, "exceptional and extremely unusual hardship," good moral character, and ten years residence. The reporting requirements to Congress for review, however, were declared unconstitutional in 1983 (*INS v. Chadha*).[40]

Wartime Legislation (1940s and 1950s)

The rumblings of war in Europe stirred many to advocate liberalizing the immigration laws to assist persons subject to persecution. Those efforts drew more support with the rise of Hitler and the increasing unavailability of quotas to benefit displaced persons in European countries.[41]

Among the first postwar measures, the so-called GI-War Brides Act in 1945 allowed nonquota admissions of wives of veterans for a three-year period.[42] Two years later, racially ineligible spouses and children of United States citizens in the Armed Forces became eligible for the same benefits. Natives of Japan and Korea were thus admitted in this manner.[43] Legislation in 1946, referred to as the GI-Fiancee bill, granted admission for fiancees until 1948.[44] Another wartime measure, in 1949, included the allotment of 100 visas annually for the Central Intelligence Agency's use for aliens "essential to the furtherance of the national intelligence mission."[45]

The second major group to benefit from wartime legislation, for which support could be mustered without enraging the restrictionists, were orphans. The Displaced Persons Act of 1948[46] allowed the admission of 3,000 orphans. Five years later, under the Refugee Relief Act of 1953,[47] another 4,000 orphans entered the United States, but were subject to a limit of two adopted children per family. After various temporary extensions providing additional admissions of adopted children, in 1961 adoption provisions became a part of the permanent immigration law.[48]

The third and most numerous group impacted by wartime relief legislation were refugees from Eastern Europe. In the first aberration of the quota laws the Displaced Persons Act of 1948 allowed up to 205,000 displaced persons to enter the United States for two years. Subsequently, that Act was extended and expanded, thereby allowing 415,744 additional admissions.[49] In taking care of displaced persons, Secretary of State Marshall stated: "The tasks that are imposed by a declaration of war are not completed when the guns cease fire. This is one of the tasks which we have not completed."[50]

The Displaced Persons Act provided for the mortgaging of quota numbers where the ceiling for a particular country had been reached. This meant that the visas for a particular year would be charged to the future quota allotment. In some cases, this chargeability could be mortgaged ten years to the future. The law also established a priority for the issuance of these visas. First preference provided for those engaged in agricultural pursuits. Second preference related to those in clothing and garment occupations, as well as persons with special educational or other professional qualifications. The third preference included blood relatives of United States citizens and permanent residents. Priorities established within preferences included veterans and those in displaced persons camps as of January 1, 1948.[51]

In 1953, another breach of the quota controls arose because of the previous law's inequities. Rising overpopulation in Europe, due to the refugee exodus, acted as a catalyst to permit 214,000 aliens immigration based on persecution under the Refugee Relief Act of 1953.[52] The provisions differed from previous legislation by acknowledging the flaws of the Displaced Persons Act relating to mortgaging of visas, and, instead, allowed visa allotments outside normal quotas.

Other refugee legislation included Refugee-Escapee legislation in 1957[53] which also defined a refugee as those escaping from Communism or a country in the Middle East, and the so-called Refugee Fair Share Act in 1960[54] which allowed the Attorney General to use his parole power (entry to the United States without normal visa documentation) to admit refugees, and provided for their adjustment of status to permanent status after two years. That act also enabled the United States to participate in the resettlement of refugees through the auspices of the United Nations High Commissioner for Refugees. Both the definition and many of the refugee provisions remained substantially unaltered, and incorporated into the 1965 Act,[55] until changed in 1980.[56]

Prelude to Quota Relief: 1952 Act Preference System

The third and most significant pre-1965 change occurred with the codification of sweeping immigration changes in 1952, enacted over President Harry S. Truman's veto.[57] The McCarran-Walter Act, named after its Senate and House sponsors (Sen. Pat McCarran, D-NV and Mr. Francis E. Walter, D-PA), followed a comprehensive study of the immigration system and adopted most of the Senate investigating committee's recommendations.[58]

Paradoxical in nature, the 1952 Act was generous to some, but contained protectionist elements reflecting the cold war atmosphere after World War II. One of the authors, Sen. McCarran, explained the need for protecting American institutions and traditions when he stated that immigrants should be viewed as

> a stream of humanity [which] flows into the fabric of our society...If that stream is healthy, the impact on our society is salutary; but if that stream is polluted, our institutions and our way of life become infected.[59]

Mr. Hugh J. Addonizio (D-NJ), one of the advocates of a more open immigration policy, claimed that

> immigration legislation should be based on the assumption that the infusion of fresh new blood, of a selected stream of immigration, is good for the economic, spiritual, and cultural growth of our country.[60]

Although the 1952 Act did not change substantially the formula for the quota system,[61] the allocation of visas within the quotas of each country changed to grant greater preference to skilled aliens and less to the relatives of United States citizens or permanent residents. In addition, nonquota continued for the spouse and child of United States citizens and permanent resident aliens. This preference structure was reversed again in 1965 in favor of family reunification. The 1952 preferences are shown below:

First preference - Aliens whose services are needed urgently in the United States because of education, training, experience or ability (50% of quota)- plus visas not used under second and third preferences).
Second preference - Parents of United States citizens 21 years of age or over (30% of quota)- plus visas not used under first and third preference).
Third preference - Spouses and children of permanent resident aliens (20% of quota)- plus visas not used under first and second preferences).

Fourth preference - Brothers, sisters and sons or daughters of United States citizens (25% of quota)-plus visas not used under first, second and third preferences).
Nonpreference - Other immigrants - unused visas from the above preferences.[62]

In the 1952 Act, the Asia Pacific Triangle received an overall quota of 2,000 per year. However, the new law established ancestry as a basis for chargeability for that area.[63]

Western Hemisphere immigration continued to exist without regard to quotas until 1965, and absent the preference system which was in place for the Eastern Hemisphere. Therefore registration of immigrants from the Western Hemisphere occurred chronologically, requiring only a demonstration that the immigrant would not adversely impact the labor market. Parents, spouses, and children of United States citizens and permanent residents were exempt from the labor test, however.

Other provisions enacted in 1952 included authority for the use of parole as a basis for discretionary waivers, new refugee definitions and residence periods, and "withholding of deportation" for fear of return to the home country. For the first time, immigration law instituted a labor test for those admitted based on skills.

A new procedure in the 1952 Act authorized processing for immigrant visas within the United States. This replaced the "pre-examination" procedure established in 1935.[64] Processing of visas in Canada had been allowed in lieu of returning to the country of origin, for close relatives of citizens and permanent residents as well as in cases of veterans and aged persons where "exceptional merit" and good moral character were present, as long as there had been a certain residence period in the United States.[65] The new provision of the law, "adjustment of status," allowed this process to occur inside the United States, for any alien who entered the United States on a temporary visa and maintained lawful status.

In his veto message to Congress on the 1952 Act, President Harry S. Truman argued against the continuation of the national origins system:

> The basis of this quota system was false and unworthy in 1924. It is even worse now. At the present time this quota system keeps out the very people we want to bring in. It is incredible to me that, in this year of 1952, we should again be enacting into law such a slur on the patriotism, the capacity, and the decency of a large part of our citizenry.

> Today, we are 'protecting' ourselves as we were in 1924, against being flooded by immigrants from Eastern Europe...We do not need to be protected against immigrants from these countries--on the contrary we want to stretch out a helping hand, to save those who have managed to flee into western Europe...
>
> In no other realm of our national life are we so hampered and stultified by the dead hand of the past, as we are in this field of immigration...[66]

In 1952, 265,520 immigrants entered the United States, and in 1953, 170,434 entered the country, according to INS.

Incremental Quota Relief (1952-1965)

Between 1952 and 1965 various laws cleared some of the backlogs for oversubscribed countries and further refined the 1952 Act preferences. In 1957[67] the mortgaging of quotas imposed under the Displaced Persons Act of 1948 was removed. The 1957 legislation also provided nonquota status for illegitimate children under certain circumstances, continued special provisions for admission of adopted children, and provided immigrant status for certain diplomats. In addition, it granted nonquota immigrant status to aliens in the first three preferences (family- and skills-based) on whose behalf a petition for preferred status had been approved prior to July 1, 1957. Amendments in 1958, 1959, 1961 and 1962 granted similar status for certain preferences (family- and skills-based).[68]

In 1959[69] Congress reclassified the preferences by broadening many of the categories relating to family preferences: the second preference included unmarried sons and daughters of United States citizens, which had been previously limited to parents of United States citizens; the third preference included unmarried sons and daughters of permanent resident aliens, which had been previously composed of spouses and minor children; fourth preference included married sons and daughters of United States citizens in addition to brothers and sisters of United States citizens, along with an increase in the number of visas allocated.

In 1961[70] immigration amendments placed nonquota status for orphans into the permanent law. Also, in 1961 a new exchange visitor visa modified procedures for the exchange of aliens with skills between countries. Restrictions on adjusting their status to permanent residence or changing to other nonimmigrant categories were continued.[71]

Other special legislation at this time included relief on behalf of 250 sheepherders "whose services were needed" in many Northwestern states in 1950, and for whom additional visas were granted in subsequent legislation in 1952 and 1954.[72] In addition, in 1963 the Bracero farm labor program for agricultural workers received its last extension, to 1964.[73]

National Origins System Repeal: The 1965 Act

A milestone in immigration law, the Act of 1965,[74] came in an era of domestic civil rights battles which sought to break down racial barriers.[75] The 1965 Act removed the last vestiges of discrimination in immigration law--the national origins system. A hemispheric system of immigration replaced the system of quotas for each country based on that country's origins in the United States. Immigration definitions reflected these changes, so that "ceilings" replaced "quota" allocation. In addition, spouses, children, and for the first time parents of United States citizens were defined as "immediate relatives" rather than "nonquota." This also meant, however, that this specific group of close relatives continued to be exempted from numerical limits. The priority for admission to the United States in favor of labor market needs changed to emphasis on family reunification.

In the first instance, the new act set two hemispheric ceilings for immigration. Prior to 1965 the national origins system immigration levels had been 158,561 visas for Eastern Hemisphere countries, while the Western Hemisphere was nonquota, that is, without restriction. It had become apparent under the national origins system that in addition to favoring certain countries, many large quota countries did not use their allotted visas, and the unused visas could not be transferred to other countries. Countries such as the United Kingdom and Ireland had insufficient immigrants to meet its quota, while countries such as Italy had a waiting list far exceeding their country quota.[76]

Under the 1965 Act, the Eastern Hemisphere had a ceiling of 170,000, with per country ceilings of 20,000 (except immediate relatives), and a new preference structure. Western Hemisphere immigration for the first time had a limited ceiling of 120,000, with no country ceilings or priority system for preferences according to family or skills. Immigration from the Western Hemisphere, therefore, was on a first-come, first-served basis, with a labor test, except immediate relatives who immigrated outside the ceiling.[77]

The ceiling on Western Hemisphere immigration reflected a longstanding concern that the "human tide" of illegal aliens from Mexico had severe economic and social repercussions.[78] Commenting on the need for a limit on immigration at that time, the House Judiciary Committee reported that it had become "increasingly concerned with the unrestricted flow of immigration from the nonquota countries" and that special treatment of Western Hemisphere natives remained the last vestige of immigration based on national origins.[79]

The second important change related to the priority of admissions in the preference categories under the new Eastern Hemisphere ceiling. Allocation of visas under the ceiling shifted in emphasis from attracting needed professional and skilled labor to reuniting families. The preference system is outlined below:

First preference - Unmarried sons and daughters of United States citizens (20% of the ceiling)-34,000.

Second preference - Spouses and unmarried sons and daughters of aliens lawfully admitted for permanent residence (20% of the ceiling)-34,000 plus unused first preference visas.

Third preference - Members of the professions and sciences, or aliens of exceptional ability in the arts (10% of the ceiling)-17,000.

Fourth preference - Married sons and daughters of United States citizens (10% of the ceiling)-17,000 plus unused visas from above.

Fifth preference - Brothers and sisters of United States citizens (24% of the ceiling) -40,800 plus unused visas in the above preferences.

Sixth preference - Skilled and unskilled workers in occupations for which labor is in short supply in the United States (10% of the ceiling)-17,000.

Seventh preference - Refugees (6% of the ceiling)-10,200.

Nonpreference - Other immigrants - unused visas from the above preferences.

The third major change included a protection for United States workers for employment-based immigration. Previously, foreign workers entered the country unless the Department of Labor ruled otherwise. The 1965 law required an affirmative Department of Labor certification prior to entry, so that no United States workers would be displaced.

Other changes included the elimination of the Asia Pacific Triangle and any chargeability based on ancestry. Adjustment of status provisions relating to the processing for visas within the United States prohibited Western Hemisphere natives that visa processing privilege. The 1965 Act also incorporated refugee definitions similar to those in the Refugee-Escapee legislation in 1957, and the Refugee Fair Share Act of 1960, with a two-year conditional status.

Toward a Worldwide Immigration System: 1970s

The last major changes to the immigration structure occurred in 1976 and 1978. The 1976 Act[80] extended the seven-category preference system, the 20,000 per-country limit, and the provisions for adjustment of status for Eastern Hemisphere countries to the Western Hemisphere. The previous overall ceiling of 120,000 for the Western Hemisphere was retained, however. The purpose of the preference change, to prevent disparate treatment of immigrants, was explained by the House Judiciary Committee in its report on the legislation. The Committee noted that under the Eastern Hemisphere system, the 22-year old British citizen daughter of a United States citizen received preferential treatment, but the 22-year old Brazilian daughter of a United States citizen in the Western Hemisphere had to take a place in line with other intending immigrants, and wait more than two years for a visa.[81]

In 1978[82] the last step involving the total eradication of the quota laws from 1921 and the development of one system of immigration wordwide was accomplished. The combining of both the Eastern and Western Hemispheres established a worldwide ceiling of 290,000, except immediate relatives. As the House Judiciary Committee noted in its report on the legislation:

> The worldwide ceiling provided for in this bill represents the third and final step in the elimination from our immigration law of discrimination on the basis of place or origin.[83]

The number of immigrants entering the country after the 1978 Act was 460,348, according to INS.[84]

Other changes in the 1970s included provisions for the admission of fiancees of United States citizens who had been previously admitted under temporary programs after World War II.[85] In addition, amendments to the adoption laws in 1975[86] and 1978[87] allowed single parents to adopt a foreign born child, and removed the two-petition limitation for immigration of adopted children.

One of the other changes where Congress gave special attention in 1976, was the health professions. Three major concerns developed: the heavy reliance of the United States on foreign medical professionals, the quality of health care provided by the foreign medical graduate (FMG), and the "brain drain" from developing countries. The 1976[88] set forth qualitative guidelines for the practice of medicine for FMGs by requiring the passage of a medical exam prior to entering the United States temporarily for training or for permanent residence. It also tightened requirements relating to return-home provisions for purposes of excluding the FMGs from future admission to the country.[89]

During the debate on the 1976 amendments, Sen. J. Glenn Beall (R-MD) referred to a statement by the American Association of Medical Schools that "FMGs undermine the process of quality medical education in this country and ultimately pose a threat to the quality of care delivered to the people..." Senator Edward M. Kennedy (D-MA) also noted:

> An equally serious concern exists that the United States the wealthiest nation in the world, is in the position of obtaining nearly one-fourth of the free world's foreign medical graduates. Since some foreign nations are actively opposing emigration of large numbers of their physicians...it is desirable that the practice cease.[90]

Refugees, Illegal Immigration, and Other Legislation - 1980s

Refugee matters received a high degree of attention in 1980 as a result of the exodus of Cuban and Haitian boat people. A comprehensive bill, the Refugee Act of 1980,[91] adopted the United Nations definition of refugee, which meant an alien had to prove a "well-founded fear of persecution," rather than primarily based on association with Communist regimes. The Act also set forth a structure for determining annual admissions of refugees. In addition, the law required an application process for asylees, as well as levels for the number of asylees who could obtain permanent residence. The 1980 Act also reduced the two year conditional residence period to one year prior to adjusting status to permanent residence.

The "Immigration Reform and Control Act of 1986,"[92] a result of fifteen years of attempts at passage, addressed the problem of illegal immigration. The law penalized employers who hired illegal aliens, and provided amnesty to aliens who entered the United States prior to 1982. A Select Commission on Immigration and Refugee Policy, established in 1978,[93] had recommended many of the changes provided in the law.

The 1986 Act also moved the registry date for granting permanent residence on behalf of those already in the United States from 1948 to 1972. Other provisions allowed the father of an illegitimate child petitioning rights. The bill also provided 5,000 visas for countries "adversely affected" by the 1965 Act. This was one of the first attempts to provide diversity in the immigrant flow, recognizing that although repeal of the system based on national origins was important, it left many second generation relatives of immigrants without access to the "chain" for bringing to the United States distant relatives. In many respects, however, it represented a return to immigration based on national origins.

Other legislation in the 1980s included legislation which increased the adoption age limit from 14 to 16 in 1981[94] and legislation in 1986[95] which clarified the two-year residence period for adoption of nonorphans. Also in 1981,[96] doctors who already resided in the United States prior to the 1976 amendments restricting their entry were granted permanent residence. In addition, legislation in 1982 provided for special immigration visas on behalf of "Amerasians"; that is, children fathered by United States citizens in Asia, primarily Vietnam and Korea.[97]

Public Legislation and Private Bills

Private bills relating to quotas have been the largest category of private immigration laws enacted, primarily due to the small quota allocation in some countries under the national origins system. Private bills sought relief for particular individuals from low quota countries such as Italy and Greece. Other private bills sought relief from the priorities of the preference system. For example, some bills sought relief for persons disadvantaged by the emphasis on particular skills. Private bills addressing these preference classifications revealed their inadequacies.

Quota legislation and private bills, like other areas, demonstrated the restrictive nature of immigration policy in the early years of the republic, and the liberalization after World War II. In addition, the humanitarian response to the flow of displaced persons included increased refugee admissions; and the large numbers of servicemen and Americans residing abroad forced an internationalization of immigration policy towards adoptive children and warbrides. Much of this liberalizing was seen through the private bill process. After the 1965 Act, immigration laws continued to be refined to address family unity and economic needs.

The major parallels of the quota laws demonstrating the relationship between private bills and general legislation were the 1952 and 1965 Acts relating to the preference structure for admission of immigrants and establishment of levels for immigration. Other major public laws that illustrated the relationship included suspension of deportation under the 1940 Act, war efforts allowing the admission of displaced persons in 1948, quota relief through reduction of backlogs from 1957 to 1962, the registry provisions of the Act of 1958, elimination of race as a bar to admission in 1952, and adoption legislation in 1961 and 1981.

Of the 7,266 private bills enacted into law in the 100 Congresses, those relating to quotas totaled 4,728 (65%), the largest category of relief. The majority of quota private laws occurred in the 84th Congress (1955-1956) when 932 were enacted. In the next Congress there were 606 private quota laws. The number of private quota laws subsided to a total of 66 in the 91st Congress (1969-1970), when the 1965 Act became fully operative. For the remainder of the Congresses, adoption cases became the predominant types of bills to be considered. By the 100th Congress (1987-1988) there were only 15 private laws enacted relating to quotas of an overall level of 21 private immigration laws.

Trends in Public Legislation and Private Bills for Quota Relief

As indicated above, the major trend in private bills preceded the 1965 Act and involved overcoming the low quotas. The fact that the number of laws for beneficiaries from oversubscribed countries totaled 3,805 during the period between the 81st Congress and the 87th Congress (1949-1962) clearly illustrates that trend. This period represented 52% of all private laws enacted throughout the 100 Congresses.

Oversubscription of visas also had a major impact on those within occupational preferences. Although the 1952 legislation granted a higher priority for individuals with skills, the small quotas continued to impede visa issuance. The only relief for this group prior to the 1965 Act other than private bills were temporary measures clearing backlogs 1957-1962. The latter period reflected not only the lack of visas for occupational reasons but many hardship situations for families due to lack of quota availability.

Another trend in the quota area related to aliens ineligible for a visa due to race, and fiancees. During the 81st and 82nd Congresses (1949-1952), there were 344 private laws to overcome the bar to immigration due to race. With the enactment of the 1952 law eliminating race, no further need for private bills remained. Also, from the 83rd Congress through the 85th Congress (1953-1958), there were 118 private laws on behalf of fiancees, which was reduced dramatically.

Adoption cases was another area of trends, particularly prior to the 1961 amendments to provide special visas for adoption. From the 84th

Congress through the 87th Congress (1955-1962) there were 481 adoption bills. In addition, with legislation eliminating the two-petition limitation for adoptive children and allowing single persons to adopt, these cases were reduced by the 97th Congress (1981-1982) to 18.

Categories of Quota Relief

Of the 4,728 private laws in the quota area during the 100 Congresses, the cases are represented by six major categories. The first involved conferring immediate relative status (formerly "nonquota") on behalf of spouses, children (including adopted children and those born out of wedlock), parents and other close relatives. These types of cases totaled 1,664 (35% of the total quota laws). The purpose of these bills was to eliminate lengthy visa waiting periods, overcome age and residence requirements, or avoid problems with the petitioning process.

The second category of cases related to establishing a preference for relatives or for those with certain skills, as well as conferring status on returning permanent residents. These cases totaled 351 (7% of the total quota laws). These bills generally bypassed oversubscribed quotas or an inadequate priority system for either skills or family.

The third category covered those ineligible for a visa due to race, including fiancees, and this total was 380 (8% of the total quota laws). This group needed to overcome the exclusions of the 1924 Act which prohibited entry of persons from most parts of Asia.

The fourth category involved fiancees, and in many cases the fiancees needed waivers for health or criminal reasons. Fiancee cases totaled 165 (3% of the total quota laws). These cases covered a short period of time after World War II when servicemen seeking marriage to a foreign national needed private bills in the absence of public legislation.

The fifth group included generally oversubscribed bills of a miscellaneous nature, such as occupational reasons or instances of separated families of citizens or permanent residents. These totaled 2,168 (46% of the total quota laws). In most cases the miscellaneous group included occupations and other purposes because the private law did not specify a particular preference, and the major reason for enactment involved low country quotas. Other groups in the miscellaneous category included those for medical reasons, military service, persons whose actions were deemed in the national interest, and refugees.

Historical Parallels: Registry and Suspension of Deportation (1940's)

The first indications of the relationship between public legislation and private bills occurred even before major generic legislation in 1940, when there had been 894 private bills introduced in the 75th and 76th Congresses (95 became law), many of which sought to address inequities of the quota system. Other bills related to those who had entered the United States and became subject to deportation, although they had resided in the United States for lengthy periods of time.

The only statutory means of addressing the hardship cases included the Secretary of Labor's authority under the Act of 1917, which allowed voluntary departure for the alien to remain in the United States for a finite period of time, and through the registry date provisions which allowed creation of records for those who entered the United States prior to 1924. The increase in private bills, and the limited ability to alleviate the separation of families, led to many personal appeals to the Congress. As early as 1934 the Executive Branch had urged an accommodation of the harshness of the law through legislative changes, as INS Commissioner D.W. MacCormack testified:

> There has been wide-spread criticism by the press, social agencies, the courts, and I may say Members of both Houses of Congress of certain deportations, mandatory under the present law. It is difficult for Americans generally to realize and to understand why the law should make inevitable such hardships as the breaking up of homes or the separation of children from their parents. Such, however, is now the case...The very nature of the immigration laws necessitate hardship in their enforcement. Experience has shown, however, that in some individual cases the interests of the United States would not be affected adversely if relief could be had from the unyielding mandate of a statute. Laws which deal directly with human beings should leave room for human and humane considerations. The recommendations which we have made to permit the exercise of discretion have been most severely limited...[98]

Congress, however, was not ready to address the issue and expressed its recalcitrance by criticizing the Executive Branch for being too lenient in allowing illegal aliens to remain in the United States. On the other hand, Congress realized that elimination of discretionary power would lead to an avalanche of private bills. Mr. Martin Dies (D-TX) commented on this fact during those hearings:

> Supposed we open up this committee for private bills in the cases of families, there would be 10,000 private bills filed in this committee inside of 30 days, and whenever could we undertake them.[99]

The antagonism between the Congress and the Executive Branch did not end until six years later when the sudden influx of private bills increased pressures on both branches of Government for a solution. The total number of bills introduced in the 76th Congress (601) exceeded the total introduced in the 75th Congress by 308 bills. The end result was a sharing of power combining Executive Branch discretion with Congressional review.[100] The 1940 Act allowed the Attorney General to suspend deportation and grant permanent residence on behalf of aliens where there would be economic hardship to relatives of United States citizens and permanent residents. With the enactment of this discretionary authority, the introduction of private bills subsided to 430 in the 77th Congress (1941-42) and then to 163 in the 78th Congress (1943-44).

In 1948 changes to the suspension of deportation provisions allowed those who did not have relatives to obtain permanent residence. The Senate Judiciary Committee, in its report on the legislation, stated:

> The committee has already considered and recommended the enactment of private bills to adjust the immigration status of certain deportable aliens who are in this general category. It is only just that other persons in this category who have not been favored by the introduction of private bills should have their cases considered for relief.[101]

The 1948 Act also allowed aliens who were racially ineligible for citizenship to qualify for suspension of deportation since "the only relief available to these people would be private bills."[102] As indicated previously, during this period, the Executive Branch presented a proposal to eliminate private bills completely, but which failed of enactment.[103]

Further amendments to the suspension of deportation provisions, which allowed additional aliens to benefit, relieved many individuals from seeking private relief bills.[104]

Wartime Relief (1940s and 1950s)

The rigidity of the quotas during the war years brought forth additional demands for redress, thus evidencing the relationship between private bills and public legislation. The areas needing reform included orphans, refugees and families of servicemen stationed abroad who did not fit into the narrow quota laws or preferences. The total number of private bills introduced rose from 429 in the 79th Congress (1945-46) to 4,797 in the 83rd Congress (1953-54). The number of private laws enacted steadily climbed from 15 in the 79th Congress (1945-1946) to 117 in the 80th Congress (1947-48), 507 in the 81st Congress (1949-50), 733 in the 82nd Congress (1951-52), and 750 in the 83rd Congress (1953-54). Between 1945 and 1954, the number of private laws totaled 2,122, of which the majority related to oversubscription for occupations and family.

It became obvious that private bills and other piecemeal legislative efforts, such as the Displaced Persons Act of 1948, could not possibly accommodate the continued numbers of persons fleeing Europe after World War II. Their inadequacy was discussed by Chairman Celler during joint House and Senate Judiciary Committee hearings in 1951 on proposals to change the quota laws.

> It would undoubtedly reduce the number of bills that we have...And you are going to get more and more private bills as we clog up the quotas, by virtue of mortgaging the quotas to permit the DP's to come into the country. You will see that you will have more and more efforts made to offer private bills, to reach out over Europe and bring them in.[105]

1952 Act

Another major corollary between private bills and public legislation occurred in 1952, when Congress reordered the preferences for family and employment-based immigration. In response to a Congressional override of his veto, President Harry S. Truman commissioned a report on the need for changes to the immigration system, and in that report, "Whom We Shall Welcome," the Commission chided Congress for

> ignoring the national origins system through special legislation, such as the displaced persons and the war fiancee programs, and private bills, which together admitted almost half a million people since the war.[106]

The report also noted the hardship presented by the restrictive nature of 1952 changes to suspension of deportation standards and recommended that more discretion be vested in the Executive Branch to reduce the need for Congressional review.[107]

Although the preferences under the 1952 Act established priorities for immigration, low quotas remained the stumbling block for any immigration for occupational purposes from those countries. Prior to the 1952 Act, 153 private quota laws related directly to occupational needs. During the period 1952 and 1965 Act, a total of 160 private quota laws related to occupations.

The 1952 Act also provided another parallel between public legislation and private bills when racial ineligibility was eliminated as a bar to admission to the United States. There had been 344 (33% of the total) of the quota laws relating to ineligibility due to race enacted during the period just prior to the 1952 Act (81st and 82nd Congresses).

Between the 1952 Act and the 1965 Act various temporary measures brought some relief to quotas and the use of private bills, but a dramatic reduction in private bill laws did not occur due to the underlying problem of low country quotas. In fact, the increased use of omnibus measures highlighted for the Executive Branch and Congress the need for repeal of the national origins legislation.

Adoption Relief (1957-1961)

Adoption is a significant area where private bills greatly impacted public legislation, and this mostly occurred during the period between the 1952 Act and the 1965 Act. These laws included the Displaced Persons Act of 1948, allowing the immigration of orphans, the Refugee Relief Act of 1953, admitting additional orphans, and the 1957 law granting nonquota status to nonorphan adopted children. During debate on the 1957 legislation the Chairman of the House Judiciary Committee, Mr. Celler, noted that many Members of Congress had "received hundreds and hundreds of beseeching letters requesting the enactment of private bills" on behalf of adopted children and other areas.[108] Mr. Walter, the Chairman of the House Immigration Subcommittee outlined the role of private bills during debate on legislation in 1961 for permanent provisions in the law for adopted children:

> [It is] the rather exacting work which the Judiciary Committee has before it continuously in connection with private relief legislation. These...served to test the effect of this type of legislation upon the individuals affected and upon the national interest...The effects of these enactments--I can assure the House--were carefully observed, reviewed, and investigated by the committee.[109]

While that act eliminated many of the needs for adoption cases, this group remained prominent for private bill purposes due to age limitations, petitioning requirements, and definitions.

Backlog Relief (1957-1962)

In addition, prior to the 1965 amendments, another area demonstrating the relationship between public legislation and private bills related to backlog clearance legislation for family and skills-based in 1957, 1958, 1959 and 1962. The rigidity of the quota laws for countries such as China, Greece, Egypt, India, Japan, Spain and Turkey was noted in the House Judiciary Committee's report on legislation in 1957:

> The Committee believes that there is an inconsistency in conceding on the one hand that the services of certain foreign scientists, physicians, skilled nurses, etc., are urgently needed in this country, while at the same time acknowledge the lack of available visas for this highly desirable class of immigrants and forcing them to depart or to remain in this country by sufferance.[110]

Adjustment of Status Relief (1955-1958)

Private bills also pointed to a need for change in the process for allowing aliens to adjust their temporary status to that of permanent immigrants. Prior pre-examination provisions, and amendments in 1952, had addressed some of the hardship cases which forced travel outside the country for a visa. However, the continued use of private bills indicated that the law still did not fully address some of the cases. In 1955 a special report by the House Judiciary Committee on the administration of the laws noted:

> The analysis of private laws enacted in the 83rd Congress, as well as a continuously conducted close scrutiny of the general trend of pending private legislation...appears to warrant the conclusion that sections 244 and 245 of the act, are inadequate to meet the realities.[111]

More than half of the private bills enacted in the 83rd Congress (1953-1954) related to pre-examination. Through those bills, the beneficiaries were allowed to remain in the United States to adjust status.[112] In 1958 amendments to the adjustment of status provisions allowed those who overstayed their visa the privilege of remaining in the United States for processing. The House Judiciary Committee noted in its report on the legislation:

> the review of a considerable number of private relief immigration bills seeking adjustment of status of nonimmigrants has further demonstrated

to the Committee the desirability of general amendatory legislation on this subject.[113]

Sheepherders (1957)

Private bills provided relief from 1949 to 1957 for sheepherders in the western states. This led to public legislation in 1957 and revision of Department of Labor policies in the admission of temporary workers in this area. During debate on legislation in 1954, Judiciary Committee Chairman Celler noted that three public bills had been enacted as well as 80 private sheepherder bills, totalling 1,155 sheepherders. He expressed frustration with the problems encountered with preferential treatment of sheepherders:

> I do not know where all these sheepherders are going. I do not know why there is always an insistence that if you need sheepherders, you have to have Basque or Spanish sheepherders...There are many well-deserving, God-fearing Spaniards who desire to come to this country. They would make good citizens. They are not shepherds, but they have no friends who are Members of either the House or the Senate, and therefore they cannot importune this body through such friends and receive preference to enable them to come to this country. We need many nurses, we need doctors, we need engineers...but, somehow or other, sheepherders are in an exalted position...We are either going to enforce the McCarran-Walter Act with its restrictions or we are not. Every time you pass a bill admitting immigrants you circumvent and bypass the McCarran-Walter Act...These subterfuges are used constantly, making exceptions to the statute, to bring groups in as nonquota. It is time to call a stop to this practice. Amend the basic act.[114]

A later investigation into some sheepherder practices by the Judiciary Committee found that in many cases the sheepherders were found at work in "restaurants, in the dairy industry, in the mining industry, or have accepted employment as domestic servants."[115]

Registry Provisions (1958)

The registry provisions provided another parallel of public legislation and private bills prior to the 1965 amendments. In 1958, the registry date, which had been 1924, was liberalized to allow those who had entered the United States prior to 1940 to obtain permanent residence. The Senate Judiciary Committee, in its report on the legislation, stated:

> The growing concern of the Congress with numbers of private bills proposing the granting of permanent residence to aliens who have had long periods of residence has necessitated a reappraisal of the existing provisions of section 249 of the INA relating to the creation of a record of lawful admission for permanent residence for certain aliens.[116]

In summary, while various temporary and permanent laws were enacted to address the shortcomings of the quota system, private bills remained one of the principal vehicles for overcoming these restrictions.

The use of private bills, for instance, is particularly highlighted in the occupational categories for natives of Italy, Japan and Greece. In addition, relatives of United States citizens experienced delays, even with backlog reduction. The major emphasis on relationship to United States citizens also led to a higher priority for this group in the 1965 amendments.

1965 Act

Finally, in 1965, Congress repealed the national origins system. During hearings in 1964 on the legislation, Mr. Celler, Chairman of the House Judiciary Committee, explained the hard work of the Members in handling the many private bills necessary to overcome low country quotas:

> And you, gentlemen, know best how much time, effort, blood and sweat you, yourselves, put into the patchwork repair job of our immigration laws when you sit each week, almost day after day, and examine thousands of private bills, all, or in most instances, disregarding the national origin theory, never reaching the bottom of the barrel.[117]

The Committee's report on the legislation, prior to its consideration on the House Floor, noted the aberrations from the general law through use of private bills and other temporary measures:

> The performance of the Congress in the field of immigration in the postwar period has been far more generous and sympathetic than adherence to the national origins system alone would allow. The failure of that system is noted by the continual changes that special legislation have made on the matter of immigration over the years.[118]

After enactment of the 1965 law, the number of private immigration laws declined substantially. Compared to the period from 1955 to 1962 (84th Congress through 87th Congress) when private bills enacted totaled 2,227, the period after the 1965 Act reflected the reduction in the need for private bills. The 89th Congress (1965-1966) had a total of 117 private quota bills enacted of a total across all categories of 246. In the 90th Congress (1967-1968) there were 54 quota laws. During the post 1965 Act period, oversubscription continued to be a problem for such countries as the Philippines and China, for which private bills often became the last resort.

The decades following repeal of the national origins involved further liberalizing changes to the immigration laws in the quota area for adoptions, doctors, and investors.

Post 1965 Parallels: Adoption, FMGs, and IRCA

The private bill mechanism continued to reveal strengths and weaknesses of the general law. Adoption laws in particular increased due to international travel and the large number of members of the Armed Forces overseas who wanted to adopt children. Two areas illustrated the public legislation and private bill relationship.

In the first major legislation since the 1961 law incorporating orphans into the immigration laws, legislation in 1975 allowed single citizens the ability to adopt foreign-born children. The number of private bills in this area totaled 19 from 1960-1975. The House Judiciary Committee noted in its report on the legislation that

> existing law has created undue hardship and inconvenience of single United States citizens, who are attempting to bring in children whom they have adopted abroad.[119]

Also, the Committee indicated that a trend of state legislatures allowed single persons to adopt children, and that many cases involved "unmarried aunts of the orphan child and widows, who are desirous of adopting orphans, are unable to satisfy the statutory requirements."[120]

Previous limitations on adoption of only two foreign born children were removed in 1978. This, too, had been prompted by private bills. As the House Judiciary Committee noted in its report on the legislation:

> the subcommittee has also addressed this issue during its consideration of private bills to waive the two petition limitation. The Subcommittee, the Committee on the Judiciary and the full House have consistently approved such legislation. The purpose served by private bills is to demonstrate and identify the need for public legislative reform in a particular area. This need has long since been demonstrated in this

> area...The committee believes it is now more timely, equitable, and efficient to enact public legislation on this subject.[121]

From 1975-1978 (94th and 95th Congresses), the total number of private laws for this purpose totaled 35.

Private bills were cited in 1981 as demonstrating again the need for remedial legislation when Congress addressed amendments to the law in the areas of adoption, and status for doctors and investors.

> Over the years, private immigration bills have provided an extraordinary form of relief in cases where no administrative relief is available under existing law and equitable considerations justify the enactment of special legislation.[122]

The 95th through the 97th Congress (1977-1982) had witnessed the largest increase in adoption cases since the 1960s when a total of 143 cases related to adoption. After the 1981 law, which raised the age of adoption from 14 to 16, the number of private laws for adoption decreased to 4 in the 98th Congress (1983-1984).

In the area of FMGs, legislative restrictions in 1976 were supported by a review of private bills. A survey of FMG private bills indicated that when the physician received permanent residence oftentimes full licensure had not been obtained, and the medical needs of the local community were not met. The legislation required certain medical exams prior to admission to the United States, as well as expanded certain prohibitions on obtaining permanent residence.[123]

Again, during consideration of amendments relating to FMGs in 1981, private bills were highlighted. In that Congress, a total of 40 private bills which were introduced related to FMGs, reflecting a further need to respond to the health care issues presented by those bills. During hearings on FMG legislation, the House Immigration Subcommittee noted its concern with the increased number of private bills for doctors who served in health manpower shortage areas. The Subcommittee reviewed anticipated difficulties if the law were narrowed:

> Mr. Daniel Lungren (R-CA): In other words, what I'm trying to get at is if we get rid of this [waiver], are we going to have 36 private bills coming before this panel...
>
> Dr. Robert Graham, Department of Health and Human Services: Given the way the system works and given the ability of anybody to introduce a

private bill, yes, I would expect that the House would experience private bills.[124]

In addition, the long period of residence in the United States was a concern to the Subcommittee Chairman, Romano L. Mazzoli (D-KY), "The kids start wearing snoopy T-shirts and pretty soon they are American kids...then their own home becomes a foreign country."[125]

In considering the same legislation in 1981 for permanent immigration status for some investors whose visas were curtailed due to changes in the worldwide ceiling law of 1978, the Committee noted 10 private bills for investors had been under consideration.[126] After the 1981 Act, the private quota laws steadily declined from 36 in the 97th Congress (1981-1982) to 15 in the 100th Congress (1987-1988), out of an overall number of 21 private laws enacted.

Provisions of the "Immigration Reform and Control Act of 1986"[127] providing legalization of aliens in the United States since 1982, permanent residence for those registering residence since 1972, eligibility for putative fathers to confer immigration benefits without legitimation, and increase of colonial visas to 5,000 also resulted in a decrease in private bills.

Precedents

There were few precedents in the early Congresses relating to bills introduced to overcome the quota laws. For that reason, a summary of the precedents is provided for the 75th through the 79th Congress (1937-1946). After that period of time, each Congress is analyzed separately.

The cases are selected to represent various trends of the quota area as well as some of the unique circumstances of some of the cases. In addition, some cases highlight the opposition of the Executive Branch to some of the special bills.

As indicated previously, there are generally four categories in the quota area. The first group conferred immediate relative status on the beneficiary. These type of cases involve widows of United States citizens, adoption cases, and others where there is a close relationship to a United States citizen.

The second group, conferring preference status, established a priority for immigration. These cases include occupational preference, other relatives such as brothers and sisters of United States citizens, and returning lawful permanent residents.

In the third group, the quota law provided a means to overcome the bar to immigration for those ineligible to immigrate based on race.

The fourth group provided quota relief on the basis of a wide variety of reasons. In many cases, the private law granted permanent residence without specific reference to the particular statutory prohibition. For this reason, they are grouped as miscellaneous cases. The cases involved granting special exemption from the quota based on heroic deeds, medical hardship cases, overcoming certain displaced persons laws, and military service. In addition, in some cases, there were close United States citizen relatives or a major reason for relief appeared to be occupation-related.

In the quota area, relief included such means as cancelling deportation in the case of aged persons for whom full relief was not warranted, deeming a person born in another country to overcome the quota, specifying the particular preference category, as well as other reasons.

Particular points of note include the fact that the early years reflected a need to overcome the quota ineligibility for race. In addition, prior to the 1965 Act the majority of cases involved occupational needs of the country. Many precedents involve a wide range of occupations such as sheepherders, engineers, doctors, and teachers from low quota countries. In addition, many cases involved beneficiaries who performed various deeds benefiting this country. After the 1965 Act the focus is primarily relationship to United States citizen.

Early Congresses through the 79th Congress (1945-1946) - The number of quota laws during this period totaled 59 of a total of 122 private laws (48%). The quota precedents are in the following categories: two laws conferring immediate relative status (one adoption, and one widow of a United States citizen), two granting preference status, 11 removing the bar to immigration for aliens ineligible to citizenship, and 44 of a miscellaneous nature.

Precedents relating to those *ineligible due to race* included a bill on behalf of an 11-year old native of the Malay States, who was half-Chinese and inadmissible to immigrate because of his birth in the so-called barred zone. His mother was widowed and a United States citizen.[128] Another bill related to a 17-year old native of Singapore and subject of Great Britain who was an orphan and who had been taken into the custody of a United States citizen. He had been imprisoned for six months during the Japanese capture of Hong Kong, and then he came to the United States with 1500 American prisoners.[129]

In the *miscellaneous-occupation* area one precedent involved a Brother of the religious Order of St. Benedict who entered the United States without a visa.[130] Another bill included 11 beneficiaries, natives of Spain (Basque), who entered the United States at various times as seamen or visitors and then obtained employment in Utah and Nevada as sheepherders. In receiving favorable action, it was stated they were "practically indispensable to the war food program in that they make excellent shepherds."[131] Yet another bill involved natives of Greece who were involved in deep-sea sponge diving because "American divers would not take the hazard" of that occupation.[132]

Precedents in the *miscellaneous-general* category included a 36-year old native of Ireland who entered the United States illegally and enlisted in the United States Army and served over 12 years.[133] Others included a bill on behalf of a family, natives of Poland and Russia, who entered the United States to attend the wedding of a relative and who resided here for 15 years thereafter. They had one citizen child. It was noted that all beneficiaries except the father would be able to obtain immigrant visas because of the oversubscribed quota for Poland. The Committee report noted, "To require his departure for the purpose of adjustment or regularization of status...would be a distinct hardship."[134] Another bill related to a native of Romania who entered the United States as a seaman and resided here for 15 years. He married a widow with three children, one of whom was an invalid of infantile paralysis.[135]

80th Congress (1947-1948) - In this Congress quota laws totaled 80 out of 117 private laws (68%). Of those, 6 related to immediate relatives (3 adoption cases), one preference case, 12 cases pertaining to individuals ineligible for visas due to race, and 61 miscellaneous bills (18 relating to occupations and others due to special deeds).

In the category relating to *immediate relative-adoption*, one precedent involved a 29-year old native and citizen of the Philippines adopted by a United States citizen, and who provided assistance to interned prisoners.[136] An *immediate relative-widow* case involved the spouse and a daughter, 47- and 14-year old natives and citizens of the Philippines. The mother who had been a United States citizen was killed by the Japanese for refusing to assist them during the war.[137]

Precedents for those *ineligible due to race* included a 38-year old native and citizen of Japan married to a United States permanent resident with two United States citizen children.[138] Another involved a beneficiary married to a United States citizen and veteran of World War I with four United States citizen children. Two daughters had been interned by the Japanese with the father and two boys were permitted to remain with the mother. In order to prevent the boys from being taken into the Japanese Army, the mother trekked into China for five months, where she became bedridden due to the hardships experienced on the journey. The Committee report stated that "A mother born Japanese who was so loyal to her husband's country that she risked her own life and the lives of her sons to prevent them from taking up arms against it can hardly be regarded as an undesirable alien."[139]

Another precedent involved a husband, wife and minor son, who were natives and citizens of Japan. The elder beneficiary had been employed by the Office of Strategic Services. Some persons believed them to be inclined towards communism, but others stated they were of good moral character. The male beneficiary wrote a book entitled "The New Sun" and published in several magazines. He was also a "well-known Japanese artist in this country."[140]

In the *miscellaneous-occupation* category eight Basque sheepherders of Spain employed in Nevada obtained relief. The Attorney General stated that "Their continued residence in the United States has proved advantageous to the sheep-raising industry."[141] Another precedent related to a 54-year old native and citizen of Poland, employed as a domestic by the United States Ambassador to Poland who paid her passage to the United States. The beneficiary later obtained employment with the President of General Mills.[142]

Among the cases in the *miscellaneous-due to deeds* category was a 55-year old native and citizen of Estonia who, while serving aboard an Estonian vessel in 1941, refused to comply with the orders of a member of the Russian consulate who had boarded the vessel and told him to raise the Russian flag. He later joined the United States Merchant Marines, served for three years, and was the recipient of three awards from the Warshipping Administration.[143] Another precedent involved a family, natives of Russia and France, who, while in the French Basque region, facilitated the entry and departure through that area of "persons friendly to the American cause" and "laid the groundwork for such activities by enlisting the aid of the French clergy, school authorities, and farmers." It was also reported, however, that several persons who knew one of the beneficiaries said that he was engaged in smuggling and black-market activities and was not trustworthy.[144]

Another case involved natives of Hungary, a family, who allowed their home to serve as a "haven for Allied fliers and parachutists who were dropped into Hungary."[145] Another beneficiary, a 51-year old native of Australia, had previously been in the United States during

World War II on official business for the British Air Commission and had been a fighter pilot in the Royal Air Force during World War I. He organized a commercial flying service in Australia and later founded the Percival Aircraft Company, which became the "second largest manufacturer of purely civil aircraft in Great Britain." During World War II his factory assisted the war effort by building motors for the fighter bombers.[146]

Other precedents of a *miscellaneous-general* nature included a 19-year old native of Russia who had been taken prisoner by the Germans during the invasion of Russia and who later worked in various United States Army camps in Germany.[147] Another bill involved a 46-year old native of Turkey and subject of Greece who was the brother of George Dilboy, a veteran of World War I who had been awarded the Congressional Medal of Honor.[148] Another beneficiary, a 10-year old native and citizen of Poland, was orphaned at the age of five when his parents were shot before his eyes by the Germans. His only remaining relative, his uncle, learned of his plight while in a United Nations refugee camp and brought him to the United States.[149]

Still another precedent related to a 60-year old native and citizen of Japan who had been a permanent resident for 19 years when he returned to Japan to marry, and then returned to the United States as a treaty merchant and remained for 40 years. He had six United States citizen children.[150] One case related to a 27-year old native and citizen of Poland who had previously been in the Polish Army during World War II and who served in the African campaign and Italy. The case had been opposed by the Attorney General as "unfair to those who are waiting their turn from oversubscribed countries."[151] Finally, another case involved a 27-year old native of Poland who entered the United States as a stowaway. She was incapacitated because of a leg injury in the war.[152]

81st Congress (1949-1950) - This Congress witnessed one of the most dramatic increases in quota laws, from 80 in the previous Congress to 423, of a total of 507 private laws (83%). This reflected the trend whereby private bills responded to wartime emigration. Displaced Persons legislation in 1948 had allowed the admission for a period of time of orphans, but there still remained the need for private bills relating to adoption for those who could not meet the residence or age requirements for quota purposes. Additionally, although legislation allowed the admission of war brides from 1945-1951, private bills addressed lack of visas for those ineligible for a visa due to race as well as the temporary nature of some of the general laws. In the 81st

Congress there were 58 immediate relative laws (44 adoption cases), 18 relating to preferences, 169 related to ineligibility because of race (78 of whom were also fiancees), five fiancees because of country quotas, and 173 were miscellaneous cases (58 occupation cases, and others due to special deeds and questions of citizenship).

Among the early precedents in the area of *immediate relative-adoption* cases was a bill for the relief of a four-year old beneficiary whose future adoptive parents were visiting Denmark with their five-year old child. The five-year old child was attacked by a mad dog and rushed to a hospital, but died in surgery. The parents then sought to adopt the beneficiary.[153]

One of the first bills on behalf of a child born out of wedlock related to a 20-year old native of Portugal, adopted by the United States citizen natural parent, who had contributed to her support since birth.[154] Other beneficiaries included a six-year old orphan who was rescued from extermination in Poland by the Catholic Church, and then he was brought to Germany in a convoy. Later, he was placed in an orphanage in Paris.[155]

A case involving an *immediate relative-widow of citizen* pertained to a native and citizen of Czechoslovakia with three United States citizen children whose husband had been making arrangements to move the family to the United States when he was taken by Soviet authorities to Russia, where he later died in a prison camp.[156] Another bill related to a 62-year old native of Hong Kong, and mother of three United States citizen children, who had returned to China after 19 years, but whose citizen spouse had died.[157] A similar case involved a widow and daughter, natives and citizens of Germany, who were relatives of a deceased United States citizen. The citizen drowned on furlough to the United States.[158] Another involved a widow whose husband was a Yugoslav flyer serving in the United States Armed Forces who was killed during World War II. Her three brothers were also killed during the war.[159]

Immediate relative-miscellaneous cases included children who were natives of China, and who did not derive United States citizenship because the citizen parent had not met requirements to confer citizenship. A petition was filed on behalf of the spouses as immediate relatives; however, since the minor children were Chinese, their visas were oversubscribed.[160] Another case pertained to a five-year old beneficiary, a native of Greece and stepchild of a United States citizen who had accepted employment with the American Mission in Greece.[161]

In the *preference* category, one of the cases involved a native and citizen of China, whose sister and mother were lawful permanent residents. The sister worked for Rev. Msgr. Fulton J. Sheen. The beneficiary had been unable to immigrate with the family to the United States because he had attained the age of 21.[162]

A *returning permanent resident* precedent related to a 74-year old native of Hungary and former permanent resident for 50 years who moved to Canada to take care of her ailing married sister, and then sought return to the United States 10 years later. The Attorney General opposed the bill as not sufficiently meritorious to justify granting preference over other aliens.[163] A similar case involved a 71-year old native and citizen of Japan and lawful permanent resident who had been in the United States for 37 years, but returned to Japan because of the illness of her husband. She thus lost her permanent status because of her extended absence from the United States. She had three United States citizen children.[164]

Among the cases granting relief on behalf of those *ineligible due to race* were four-year old twin natives of Japan and stepdaughters of a United States citizen veteran, who were adopted by their grandparents because the natural parents had not been married. The natural parents later wished to have them enter the United States.[165] Another case involved a 37-year old ethnic Chinese native of Jamaica married to a United States citizen with four minor children. It was stated that unless the beneficiary could join his wife she would have to work and board her children.[166]

Other precedents included a 44-year old native and citizen of Korea who was employed by the Voice of America and was an ordained minister;[167] and a family, natives of Korea and China, where the three siblings were United States citizens, one of whom served in the Army reserves. Two other members of the family were naturalized, the eldest had been recognized because of bravery in China as a representative of the Supreme Allied Command.[168]

In the *miscellaneous-occupation* area one precedent involved beneficiaries, natives and citizens of the Netherlands (ages 39, 32, 9, 6), who entered the United States to inspect a rice mill owned by Rickert Rice Mills, Incorporated. The adult male beneficiary had been employed by that company 17 years and was hired in the United States due to the ill health of one of the managers. The Department of Justice opposed the bill because it placed the beneficiary ahead of others in similar situations who must await a visa.[169]

Other precedents involved several laws on behalf of nuns from Italy who conducted educational and charitable work in New York,[170] performed sewing and cooking at Marymount,[171] taught the mentally retarded and physically handicapped persons in Chicago,[172] educated boys for the priesthood,[173] and taught "black and white" children in an orphanage in Louisiana.[174]

Further occupational precedents involved a 41-year old native and citizen of Greece who became a partner in a large textile organization, Pee Dee Mills in North Carolina. He resolved many serious labor and modernizing problems of the mills, thereby benefiting the local area.[175] Other beneficiaries included a 29-year old native and citizen of Greece, the son of a United States citizen, who was employed as a stage director with the Metropolitan Opera in New York;[176] a 28-year old native and citizen of the Philippines who had "rendered highly meritorious service" during World War II;[177] and a 46-year old native and citizen of Italy, a "highly skilled violin repairman" employed by Kagan and Gaines Company, manufacturers and distributors of band and orchestra instruments.[178]

A group that was granted relief solely due to their occupation involved seven Spanish physicians residing in Puerto Rico and practicing surgery, psychiatry and other medical specialties. The Attorney General opposed the bill because it would "encourage other aliens to circumvent our immigrant laws by entering the United States allegedly as visitors, then remaining here...due to oversubscribed conditions."[179] Further precedents involved sheepherders, 48 natives and citizens of Spain, employed in Nevada whose services were deemed to be "urgently needed in the sheep-raising industry;"[180] and 152 sheepherders in Nevada and Idaho.[181]

Other precedents on the basis of occupational skills involved a native of Turkey, a research technician in the manufacture of candies whose technical knowledge was "necessary to the development of an infant American industry;"[182] a family, natives and citizens of Iraq and Great Britain, who established a textile mill in Massachusetts whose exports and imports totaled a quarter of a million dollars per year;[183] a 57-year old native and citizen of Italy and cheese bacteriologist employed by Concord Cheese Corporation;[184] and a 38-year old native and citizen of Italy engaged in supervising a State-sponsored agricultural project including breeding of cattle and other livestock.[185]

Further cases included a 27-year old native and citizen of Turkey, and graduate of Harvard Medical School employed at Children's Hospital in Boston, and regarded as "one of the most promising investigators in medical research in this country;"[186] a 46-year old native and citizen of Italy and silversmith employed by Da Prato Statuary Company to "bring new ideas into the manufacture of religious articles";[187] natives of Latvia required to operate a textile mill in Rhode Island;[188] and 48- and 40-year old natives of Poland and citizens of Canada, one of whom was employed as an organizer and business agent for the International Ladies Garment Workers' Union.[189]

There was one precedent in the category of *miscellaneous-Displaced Persons Act* relating to a family of Polish refugees sent to Siberia at the time of the partitioning of Poland and released to Iran, and subsequently to India, by direction of the Polish government. The parent's husband and siblings had been killed in Poland.[190]

Among those granted relief in the *miscellaneous-due to deeds* category was a native of Italy who "risked his life by crossing the German lines in Athens, Greece to join the British Army...giving them valuable information about the German Navy and land positions." The case had been supported by Admiral Nimitz.[191] Other precedents involved a 21-year old native of France who became attached to the United States Army as a mascot after American troops invaded Africa and later went to Anzio;[192] and a 55-year old native and citizen of Poland commissioned in the Army of Czar Nicholas II who, at the outbreak of the Russian Revolution, joined with other Poles to liberate that country from Germany and was awarded the Legion of Merit by the United States Government.[193]

Another beneficiary, a citizen of India and subject of Great Britain, and spouse of the actress Deborah Kerr, was one of a few surviving Royal Air Force fighter pilots during the Battle of Britain decorated twice with the Distinguished Flying Cross. He had participated in the Battle of Dunkerque and in the North Africa and South Pacific campaigns.[194]

Also benefiting from private relief was a 40-year old native and citizen of China who during the war performed "valuable service on the highly secret Manhattan project";[195] and a 31-year old native and citizen of China who was the sole survivor of the British freighter *Ben Lomand* when it was torpedoed in 1942, and who spent 133 days adrift. He received the British Empire Medal. The Attorney General commented on his "fortitude and ingenuity in overcoming perils of the sea...," and found no objection to enactment because of his experience in devising equipment for the use of survivors of torpedoed vessels.[196]

In addition, two nurses, natives and citizens of Burma, were also granted permanent residence after having performed "distinguished service in behalf of the United States Armed Forces in the Far East." They received the Bronze Star Medal as well as a citation from President Roosevelt. In 1942 they had set up a hospital for the care of American and Chinese forces in India. When the reinvasion of Burma occurred, they accompanied forces during raids and scouting expeditions. They later accompanied the Stillwell group on their trek out of Burma.[197]

Another bill involved natives and citizens of Italy, one of whom held the position of Italian vice consul to Freiburg, Germany during World War II. In that capacity he established contact with the British consul through the underground to communicate with his brother-in-law. His relative had crossed the lines to join the government which had overthrown Mussolini in Salerno. Because those secret communications were intercepted, he was arrested by the German Gestapo and imprisoned for treason. The Committee report noted he would have been executed "except for the intervention of the papal nuncio."[198]

Miscellaneous-general precedents included beneficiaries, natives of China and the Philippines, whose father had been a Chinese consul in Manila and executed by the Japanese.[199] Another beneficiary, a 35-year old native and citizen of Italy, worked as a secretary and translator for the Allied and Military Government in Rome. His mother was a United States citizen.[200] Another precedent involved a 28-year old native and citizen of Germany who entered the United States as the fiancee of a United States citizen, but because of religious differences did not marry. She was later employed as a maid for the vice president of Bethlehem Steel Corporation. The legislation was opposed by the Attorney General.[201]

Another beneficiary, a 72-year old native of Turkey and former permanent resident who abandoned status to live in France for 27 years, working at various charitable purposes among Armenians with a trust fund established by her husband.[202] Other beneficiaries included a family, natives and citizens of Greece, who owned three ships worth one million dollars. The bill was opposed by the Attorney General. The ships had been engaged in delivering cargo under the Marshall Plan.[203]

Further precedents included a 27-year old native and citizen of Yugoslavia who did various farm chores and who was under sponsorship by a Member of Congress.[204] In addition, there was a 21-year old ordained minister, who was a native and citizen of the Netherlands employed by the Salvation Army.[205] Both cases were opposed by the Attorney General.

Other cases included a 38-year old native of Hungary and citizen of France who served as a lieutenant in the French Army Feminine Auxiliary Ground Forces during World War II;[206] natives of Poland who were in-laws to the president of the Switlik Parachute Company "the leading supplier of parachutes to our armed forces";[207] a 26-year old native and citizen of the Netherlands and caretaker for numerous graves of American soldiers, among them the grave of Mr. and Mrs. Ridenhour's son;[208] and natives and citizens of Bulgaria and Romania who had served in various posts with the Romanian government and left Romania with King Mihai when he abdicated his crown.[209]

For the first time, a bill was enacted granting nonimmigrant status. The bill related to Sister Elizabeth Kenny who founded the Sister Kenny Foundation in Minneapolis.[210] She was a native and citizen of Australia who had evolved a treatment for infantile paralysis.

82nd Congress (1951-1952) **-** In this Congress the number of laws enacted in the quota area increased substantially for a total of 613, the second largest number in the 100 Congresses and representing 84% of all laws during the 82nd Congress (733). The major increase was due to adoption cases, granting status for those ineligible to immigrate based on race, and oversubscribed country cases. The adoption cases increased almost twofold from 44 in the last Congress to 82. Several cases continued to be necessary for displaced persons for reasons such as inability to meet requisite residence periods. Those ineligible because of race remained a category for private bills in spite of legislation which had allowed warbrides from those countries to benefit. These were needed in some cases because of the temporary nature of the general law.

In the immediate relative category there were 139 laws (82 adoption cases); 20 relating to preference (6 returning permanent residents); 175 to ineligibility due to race (33 of which were on behalf of fiancees), 13 to fiancees; and 266 miscellaneous cases (95 occupational, 64 Displaced Persons, 54 refugees, and other cases relating to special deeds, citizenship, and medical conditions).

Precedents in this Congress included in the *immediate relative-adoption* area a 20-year old native of Germany, born out of wedlock, whose United States citizen putative father sought adoption but was unable to immigrate due to the oversubscribed visas for Germany.[211] Further precedents included two sisters (ages 5, 3) adopted by a citizen employed by the World Health Organization in China. The Attorney General noted that there were many war orphans desirous of immigrating and that this case did not present sufficient equity for relief. The other case involved a native of Norway adopted by Cong. and Mrs. Bentsen when a visa wait for that country would have entailed several years.[212] Also, other cases included a 19-year old native and citizen of Italy adopted by his citizen uncle;[213] an 18-year old native and citizen of Lebanon, whose citizen aunt filed a petition for adoption;[214] and beneficiaries, natives of Greece, adopted by United States citizens.[215]

Other *immediate relatives-miscellaneous* cases included that of a native and citizen of Greece, who was a spouse of a United States citizen unable to obtain a visa due to oversubscription because the petition which had been filed was not processed in a timely fashion.[216]

In the area of those granted *preference status* through private bills, there was a bill for the relief of a native of Turkey who served in the American Embassy in Uruguay for 20 years and who held the position of special assistant to the commercial attache, but who could not obtain a visa due to oversubscription of the country quota.[217] Another beneficiary, a 55-year old native of Turkey and citizen of Germany who lost her mother and three sisters during World War II, wished to join her three brothers who resided in the United States and supported her.[218]

A *returning permanent resident* precedent related to a 63-year old native and citizen of Japan who resided in the United States for 28 years and returned to Japan. After becoming widowed she sought reentry, but due to World War II she was unable to obtain appropriate documents. She had eight United States citizen children, four of whom served in the United States Army and one of whom was killed in action.[219]

Among those cases involving *ineligibility due to race* was that of a native of Japan and orphan, whose father was a United States serviceman and whose Japanese mother was institutionalized for having a child born out of wedlock.[220] Another related to natives and citizens of China whose father was deceased and whose United States citizen mother died before taking them to the United States. It was stated the beneficiaries were heir to their mother's interest in a Chinese restaurant in San Francisco.[221] Another case involved a native of Japan adopted by United States citizens;[222] a 10-year old native of China and son of a United States citizen who did not derive citizenship because of insufficient residence in the United States, yet whose other three siblings were citizens;[223] and a native and citizen of Japan whose parents were married through a nonlegal family ceremony, one of whom was a United States citizen who was killed in action.[224] Other beneficiaries included a 57-year old native and citizen of Japan and mother of eight United States citizen children. Four of the children served in the United States Armed Forces during World War II, and one of whom was killed.[225]

Further cases involved the widow and children of a United States serviceman;[226] a four-year old native of Japan whose mother was a permanent resident and whose father had already entered the United States;[227] a native and citizen of Japan whose spouse and seven children were United States citizens who had resided in the United States for 45 years and desired to return to Japan to visit an ill brother, but could not obtain a return visa due to excludability;[228] a native and citizen of Japan, and spouse of a United States citizen with two citizen children, whose wife had gone to China and started an orphan asylum for Chinese children;[229] a native of Japan and stepchild of a United States citizen employed with the United States Army in a civilian capacity;[230] and a native and citizen of Japan born out of wedlock and released to United States citizens who were missionaries and who adopted her.[231]

Among those granted relief in the *miscellaneous-occupational* category was a family of beneficiaries, natives of Austria, Russia, and Germany, who were employed by Ringling Brothers and Barnum & Bailey Circus, and one of whom was represented as being the only man in the world who could balance himself on one finger.[232] Another beneficiary, a 41-year old native and citizen of Australia associated with the Medical Arts School of Johns Hopkins University, was recommended as a "highly skilled technician" who had "rendered meritorious services to the United States in constructing bombing target maps."[233] Other beneficiaries included, 62- and 53-year old natives and citizens of Austria, one of whom was employed as a trainer of Lippizaner horses in Kansas and who graduated from the Spanish Riding Academy.[234]

Other cases included a 64-year old native and citizen of Germany who was an "expert designer and builder of tricot machines" employed by Vanity Fair Mills, Incorporated and who had been previously affiliated with the Nazi party for business purposes;[235] natives and citizens of Italy employed in the granite and marble industry in Vermont whose services were "vitally needed" in such industries in New England;[236] and a 25-year old native and citizen of India and trainer of circus elephants.[237]

Further occupational precedents included a native and citizen of Lebanon who was an Arabic instructor for Berlitz Schools and who contracted with the Department of State and the military;[238] a 36-year old native of Romania who was a violinist with the Palestinian Orchestra, and who was giving concerts in the United States on behalf of the United Jewish Appeal;[239] natives of Hungary and Israel whose blind son was a well-known concert violinist.[240]a 41-year old native and citizen of Italy and sculptor and former assistant at the Department of Sculpture in the Royal Academy of Fine Arts in Rome;[241] and a 28-year old native and citizen of Turkey who entered the United States to obtain an artificial leg, and who later became employed with an Artificial Limb Company whose "skills in this particular field are needed because of the shortage of such labor and [because of] the increasing number of amputees."[242]

Religious occupations benefited from private bills for Italian priests doing missionary work in Ohio,[243] Spanish nuns attending to crippled and mentally disabled children at the Joseph P. Kennedy Memorial Hospital,[244]and Spanish nuns engaged in the treatment of mental diseases in Puerto Rico primarily involving Army veterans.[245]

Other beneficiaries included a 35-year old native of Fiji Island and Chinese citizen of Great Britain who was a doctor in New York;[246] and a 45-year old native and citizen of Finland and maid for Mr. Lamont DuPont, Jr.[247]

One interesting case involved a native of Russia, Baron Fred Alexander D'Osten-Sacken, engaged in training thoroughbred horses in Kentucky. The beneficiary was internationally known after having won the Warsaw Derby in 1921 with Barbara Belle and managed the stables of Marcel Boussac. Toward the end of the war he rescued the stallion Pharis and later won other Derbies. It was stated he was instrumental in introducing to the United States the French stallion Ardan as a new breed of stock from France.[248]

A number of interesting precedents involved in the *miscellaneous-Displaced Persons Act* category included children who were natives of Poland and who were denied relief under the Displaced Persons Act because they could not show they were unable to return to their last place of residence. It was noted they were "active in giving aid and comfort to American prisoners held by the Japanese in the Philippines, doing so with great danger to their lives."[249]

Other bills related to 55- and 54-year old natives and citizens of Poland, one of whom entered the United States as a minister of religion, but it was later discovered he did not have the credentials to be a minister. They had two sons, one of whom served in the United States Army.[250] Another bill related to natives of Czechoslovakia and citizens of Austria, one of whom was a successful "journalist, publisher and manufacturer" prior to the war and whose aunt was a United States citizen and opera singer, Madam Maria Jeritza. Their applications for relief under the Displaced Persons Act were denied because they could not return to their home country for a visa. The male beneficiary was engaged in the United States organizing an umbrella company.[251]

One case included 64- and 53-year old natives and citizens of Czechoslovakia, one of whom was formerly the Czechoslovakian Minister in Iraq and Iran.[252] Another precedent involved natives of Russia, France and Mexico, a family, who escaped Germany and entered France where they were later seized by the Germans. They traveled to Spain, Cuba, and then proceeded to Mexico, where they established a business in drapery materials. They returned to France, where the male beneficiary acquired United States patent rights to a "catalytic agent for water treatment" and set up that business in the United States.[253] Another bill involved natives of Poland, one of whom joined the Polish Armed Forces under British command. In the United States they were employed as a butler and cook for the Embassy of Saudi Arabia. Enactment was opposed by the Attorney General in that it would "encourage others to circumvent our immigration laws by entering the United States in the guise of visitors and then attempting to adjust their status to permanent residence..."[254]

Other Displaced Persons precedents involved a former Czechoslovakian Ambassador to France who was later employed by the National Committee for Free Europe at the Library of Congress.[255] One bill related to a 74-year old native and citizen of the Netherlands and a 34-year old native of China and citizen of the Netherlands, one of whom was associated with financial companies and went to China to assist as a financial adviser for the New Chinese Republic at the request of Sun Yat Sen. He remained there engaging in various other businesses.[256] Another case related to a 25-year old native of Czechoslovakia and former member of the Czech Olympic hockey team who defected in Sweden. He had been befriended by United States hockey team members who invited him to play local hockey in the United States and to attend school.[257]

Two other bills involved beneficiaries, 36- and 13-year old natives of Poland and France, who were supported by a United States citizen uncle. It was noted they were the "sole survivors of a family of approximately 60 people in Europe, lost either in the war or in the pogrom in Poland."[258] Another case involved beneficiaries, natives of Austria, one of whose spouse was formerly the manager of the House of

Rothschild. Their remaining family died in Europe but whose applications for relief were denied.[259]

One bill, among the first involving a group of individuals, was on behalf of 386 natives of Estonia, Latvia, Finland, Sweden, Poland and Russia who sought refuge from Communism in Sweden. They then purchased sloops and schooners and arrived on the United States eastern seaboard in 1945 and 1950. The Attorney General paroled them into the United States.[260] The Department of Justice opposed the legislation due to possible "undesirable precedent."

Those cases in the *miscellaneous-due to deeds* category included that of a native and citizen of Russia who was employed in the Russian consulate and taught students of Russian diplomats in New York City. She received much publicity because of her "kidnapping" by Soviet officials in 1948 as a result of her seeking asylum in the United States. She subsequently escaped by leaping from the third floor window of the Soviet consulate. She then published a book entitled "Leap to Freedom."[261] Status was also granted to a family whose father was employed by Chiang Kai-shek and who later was political adviser to the United States Ambassador in China for five years. Two daughters were married to United States citizens.[262]

Another case involved a 20-year old native and citizen of Greece whose United States citizen uncle intended to make the beneficiary his heir. He was granted status because it was noted that there was "confidential information that the presence in the United States of the beneficiary of the bill would be beneficial to the security interests of this country."[263]

A number of interesting precedents involved in the *miscellaneous-general* category included one bill relating to a 36-year old native and citizen of the Netherlands, who entered the United States at the invitation of the Gold Star Mothers whose sons had been billeted in her home in the Netherlands during the war.[264] Another bill, on behalf of natives and citizens of Germany (ages 53, 44, 19), involved one of whom had been employed by United States Lines Company, and who had been drafted into the German Army in 1944. He participated in an uprising against Hitler for which he was imprisoned and reduced to the rank of private.[265]

One bill related to a seven-year old native and citizen of Italy who had erroneously entered the United States as a United States citizen.[266] Another beneficiary, a 49-year old native of China and former manager of the Bank of China in London, had that position terminated upon recognition of the Peoples Government of China by the British

Government.[267] Another case related to a native of Italy, who was admitted for permanent residence based on a petition by his United States citizen spouse; but it was later discovered the spouse had not derived United States citizenship and therefore his immigration status was under question.[268]

83rd Congress (1953-1954) - Private quota bills totaled 542 this Congress. This was 72% of all private laws in the 83rd Congress (750), but was somewhat less than the previous Congress (613) because one of the provisions of the 1952 Act eliminated the prohibition of immigration due to race. Ancestry, however, remained an obstacle for some immigrants from Asia. The 1952 Act also restructured the preference system so that skills were a higher priority, but because of oversubscribed countries visa waits remained lengthy, and private bills remained the only vehicle for circumventing that ceiling. Again, the Displaced Persons Act and the Refugee Relief Act of 1953 allowed many orphan admissions, but private bills for adoption continued because of age limits, residence requirements, or visa unavailability. The number of adoption laws was one of the highest in all Congresses.

Among the categories, there were 139 immediate relative bills (118 adoption cases), 22 preference (seven returning permanent residents), 59 fiancees, 322 miscellaneous (115 occupations, and others relating to purposes such as medical, citizenship, military and those due to deeds).

Precedents in the *immediate relative-adoption* area included a case of a 14-year old native of China adopted by a United States citizen. When the natural mother died, the child was left in the care of the United States citizen who was a missionary at that time.[269] Another case involved a four-year old native of New Zealand adopted by a former United States citizen who served eight years with the United States Marines. The former citizen desired that the child immigrate with his family.[270]

Other adoption cases included two beneficiaries (ages 9, 8), natives and citizens of Australia, adopted by United States citizens. They were taken away from their adoptive mother in the United States and placed in prospective adoptive care because of the adoptive mother's drinking problems. The husband had been placed in incarceration in Australia. Other United States citizens desired to adopt the beneficiaries.[271] Another precedent involved a 24-year old native and citizen of Italy who intended to marry a United States citizen, but the marriage failed to materialize. She had been adopted prior to entry to the United States by her aunt and uncle, but they disowned her because she refused to marry their selected husband.[272]

Precedents granting status as *immediate relative-widows of United States citizens* included a 44-year old native and citizen of Finland whose husband lost his life serving in the Merchant Marine when the vessel was torpedoed.[273] Another case involved a 58-year old native and citizen of Albania who had been admitted for permanent residence as the spouse of a United States citizen. It was later learned the citizen died two months prior to her entry.[274] One *immediate relative-miscellaneous* case involved a nine-year old native and citizen of Italy, and stepson of a United States citizen, who was unable to immigrate because he was born out of wedlock.[275]

Among those precedents granting *preference* status despite the quotas was a native of Greece who was unable to qualify as a displaced person at the same time as his parents and four siblings because he was in the Greek Army.[276] Thirteen- and 12-year old natives and citizens of Holland whose parents died in a concentration camp, and whose aunt and uncle were eligible to enter the United States for immigration, were granted relief.[277] One precedent involved a 36-year old native and citizen of Panama chargeable to the oversubscribed quota for China because of her father's ancestry. She was unable to immigrate immediately with her permanent resident spouse and their children.[278] Another case related to a native of Yugoslavia unable to immigrate with her parents because she had attained the age of 21. The delay in obtaining a visa was caused by difficulties attaining exit permits from the Yugoslav Government.[279]

In the area of granting *returning lawful permanent resident status*, one case involved 67- and 65-year old natives of Poland and citizens of Mexico who had previously held United States citizenship. They returned to Mexico to attend to the husband's business and lost their United States citizenship as a result of protracted residence abroad.[280] Another precedent in this category involved a 41-year old native of Turkey who had been granted permanent residence by private legislation, but had been unable to travel because he did not have the requisite seven year consecutive residence to qualify for a waiver of excludability for draft exemption.[281]

In the *miscellaneous-occupations* category, there was a bill relating to 63- and 57-year old natives of Hungary, one of whom was an author and widow of the famous dancer, Nijinsky. The male beneficiary assisted in the production of a motion picture on the dancer. The daughter of Mrs. Nijinsky was a permanent resident.[282] Another case involved a native of Iran employed as a sulfur geologist.[283]

There were several nuns from Italy benefiting from relief teaching children in Alabama,[284] caring for chapels and altars at the LaSalette Shrine in Massachusetts,[285] and engaged in nursing work at the Joseph P. Kennedy Memorial Hospital for mentally disabled children.[286]

Another case involved 41- and 46-year old natives and citizens of the Philippines, a husband and wife, employed as physicians at Harlem Hospital in New York, where their services were "extremely necessary because of the shortage of doctors."[287]

One precedent involved a 22-year old native of Poland studying at a Rabbinical Academy in New York.[288] Another case involved a 43-year old native and citizen of Spain who was a musician and a known authority on Basque music and traditions.[289] Another bill involved a 55-year old native and citizen of Estonia, reputed to be an outstanding icon painter, who was invited to the United States by various officials of the Western Orthodox Church in connection with work to be done for the churches and monasteries.[290]

Other precedents related to 57- and 53-year old natives of Russia and Poland, one of whom was a pilot and aeronautical engineering consultant to his brother Maj. Alexander P. de Seversky;[291] a 59-year old native of Yugoslavia who was a cabinet maker;[292] a 34-year old native and citizen of China and dental trainee;[293] a 23-year old native and citizen of Greece whose uncle was the publisher of a periodical, Harrison's reviews;[294] a family, natives and citizens of Egypt, one of whom was an expert in the cotton exchange and was employed by James Lawrence & Company, where he advised on materials for parachutes, uniforms, and army shoelaces;[295] and 68- and 69-year old natives and citizens of the Netherlands employed in the raising and sorting of tulip bulbs.[296]

Another case involved natives and citizens of China, one of whom had been employed as President of an export and import company, and who had been involved in several trading companies in China. Among his activities in China, he was chairman of the Yunnan Economic Council for two years and later adviser to Gen. R.B. McClure with the American ground forces in China in 1945.[297]

In the *miscellaneous-due to deeds* category those aliens granted relief included a 34-year old native and citizen of Finland who was part of the Finnish resistance against Russia and "one of the few living holders of the highest Finnish war decoration, the Knight of the Mannerheim Cross."[298] Another involved Joseph Cerny, a 69-year old native and citizen of Czechoslovakia and former member of the Czechoslovak Parliament and Minister of Interior, who was jailed by the Communists for two years before fleeing that country.[299] Natives of Austria and Czechoslovakia who overpowered the Communist crew of a Czech airplane in flight to Frankfurt were also granted relief,[300] as were 50- and 44-year old natives of Russia and Estonia who "cooperated with various congressional committees in their investigations of communism."[301] Another case involved natives of Russia who had been assigned to the Russian Embassy and who wrote several anti-Soviet articles.[302]

Further precedents included a 36-year old native of Greece whose ship joined the British Fleet when Germany invaded Greece, and who was awarded the Distinguished Service Cross.[303] In an interesting case, Alice Masaryk, the daughter of Thomas Masaryk, the first President of the Republic of Czechoslovakia and sister of Jan Masaryk, the Prime Minister of the Czechoslovakian Government-in-exile during World War II, was the subject of a private bill.[304] Another case involved a native of Hungary and member of the Hungarian armed forces engaged in underground activity. He was an aide-de-camp to General Nagy and was cited by the Hungarian Government for his anti-Nazi role. The French Government decorated him with the Silver Medal of the Gratitude of France.[305]

In the *miscellaneous-general* category precedents included a 65-year old native and citizen of China who resided in the United States seven years and was formerly the Chinese Ambassador to Mexico and Brazil, and whose sons were United States citizens.[306] Another case involved a 63-year old native and citizen of Italy who had resided in the United States for 17 years and who had made trips to Italy upon the death of her parents.[307] One precedent involved 46- and 35-year old natives and citizens of Poland who served in the Polish underground during World War II counterfeiting passports.[308] Another case involved a 25-year old native of Germany, and a permanent resident, who was found deportable because her stepmother misstated the beneficiary's place of birth when she entered the United States. She was employed by Life magazine and resided in the United States for 13 years.[309]

Other precedents involved a Chinese native of the Philippines who had been employed in an American Officers' Club in Manila and was befriended by a group of American officers;[310] a 27-year old native and citizen of Greece who entered the United States as a fiancee, and later married a different man solely for the purpose of remaining in the United States;[311] a 23-year old native and citizen of Korea whose parents and three siblings were permanent residents, but who was ineligible to immigrate at the time because he reached his 18th birthday;[312] a seven-year old native and citizen of Italy who was granted relief under the care of his grandparents, after it was discovered he had not derived citizenship because the father had already been married and the mother remarried;[313] a 76-year old native of Russia who was a blind widow and whose permanent resident son sought to support her;[314] and a 30-year old native of Saudi Arabia and national of Israel whose spouse, a United States citizen, was blind and had received a law degree.[315]

Other precedents related to: a native of Spain who entered the United States for plastic surgery after being struck by a bomb fragment;[316] a 33-year old native of Hungary who fled from the Communists because of his position as head of the Peasants Alliance in Hungary, and in the United States he operated a dairy farm owned by Ferenc Nagy, former Hungarian Premier;[317] brothers (ages 30, 28), natives of the Netherlands East Indies, whose parents were permanent residents and whose father was an ordained minister of the Seventh Day Adventist Church;[318] a 27-year old native and citizen of Germany who was married to a disabled United States citizen veteran;[319] a native of China who claimed United States citizenship which had been denied in a court action, and whose father had died declaring him his heir and next of kin.[320]

Further cases involved a 35-year old native of Poland who served in the Polish Army and was with the Anders Army in England, and whose mother and brother were admitted to the United States as displaced persons but his documents were not processed because he was at sea;[321] and 54- and 45-year old natives of Yugoslavia, one of whom was a former Yugoslav diplomat serving with the Foreign Office and who had been the first secretary of the Yugoslav Embassy in Romania, Italy, and England, and was private secretary to ex-King Peter in 1948.[322]

***84th Congress (1955-1956)* -** In this Congress the number of bills on behalf of quota beneficiaries increased dramatically from 542 in the previous Congress to 932. This was 57% of all bills enacted this Congress. It was also the highest number of quota laws in the 100 Congresses. For the first time omnibus measures were used in cooperation with the Executive Branch to reduce the processing times in both branches of the government. Immediate relative cases increased, while adoption remained about the same as in the last Congress. There were 170 immediate relative laws (139 adoption cases), 43 preference (22 returning permanent residents), 12 ineligible for immigration due to race, 28 fiancee, and 679 miscellaneous (27 occupation, 160 refugees, and others because of deeds, military, citizenship, and related matters).

A precedent involving the *immediate relative-adoption* category related to 15- and 12-year old natives of Russia whose parents were separated during World War II, and who, while in a refugee camp with their mother, were befriended by members of the Mennonite Church who assisted them in relocating in Paraguay until the death of the mother. Two United States citizens, who had three other adoptive children, sought to bring them to the United States as adopted children without regard to the lengthy visa wait.[323] Another precedent involved a 10 year old native and citizen of Austria and stepchild of a United States citizen. She had been an illegitimate child and was to be adopted by a United States citizen.[324]

In the *immediate relative-widow of citizen* category one precedent involved a 30-year old native of Austria and widow of a United States citizen serviceman who wished to accompany her two citizen children to the United States and reside with her in-laws.[325] Another case involved the 60-year old spouse of a United States citizen and native of Turkey whose husband died one year after marriage.[326]

Other *immediate relative-miscellaneous* cases included an 18-year old native and citizen of Italy whose father was a citizen and disabled veteran who lost citizenship by returning to Italy. The son wanted to reside in the United States with his aunt and uncle.[327] A 22-year old native and citizen of the Philippines, unable to immigrate with her six siblings because she had attained the age of 21, was also granted relief. Her father was a United States citizen and 30-year veteran of the United States Army.[328]

Precedents in the *preference* category included the case of a 24-year old native and citizen of Italy who sought to join her mother and father, a lawful permanent resident and citizen, who were self-employed as voice teachers and opera singers "highly regarded in their profession." It was stated the beneficiary could become one of the greatest sopranos of the opera stage, but she had been unable to immigrate immediately because she was over the age of 21.[329]

Another precedent involved a 32-year old native and citizen of Spain and daughter of United States permanent residents whose husband was employed as a medical artist. The bill was supported by the Department of State which noted that enactment would "serve as a recognition of the contribution to this country of the services of her father…the greatest expert on the physical structure of the eye for special surgery."[330] Another involved natives of Italy whose visas were invalid because the spouse had been killed on the day of visa issuance by a relative of the fiance of his oldest daughter, who did not believe that she would return to Italy to marry.[331]

In the *returning permanent resident* category, several precedents are cited. One case involved a three-year old native of Germany adopted by United States citizens, one of whom was employed with the United States Information Service in Saigon. They sought to allow the child to enter the United States as a permanent resident in order to acquire sufficient time to qualify for naturalization.[332] Another case involved 68- and 66-year old natives and citizens of Japan who were the parents of five children, four of whom were United States citizens and three of whom served in World War II. One parent had been lawfully admitted for permanent residence, and the spouse was discovered not to have been entitled to permanent resident status. They both resided in Japan after 15 years residence in the United States.[333]

In the *miscellaneous-occupational* category, one case involved a native of Portugal employed as a houseboy for United States Foreign Service citizens.[334] Another case involved a 58-year old native and citizen of Korea who worked as radio lecturer with the American military and traveled and lectured in the United States. She was the author of the book "September Monkey."[335] One bill involved a family, natives of the Philippines, whose father was employed with the United States Department of Agriculture as a veterinary meat inspector. The Committee report noted that there was an "insufficient number of veterinarians to properly conduct Federal meat inspection activities."[336]

Among those granted status in the category *miscellaneous-due to deeds* was a case involving Dr. and Mrs. Ivan Pernar (ages 56 and 55), one of whom served as a senator and undersecretary of the Interior for the Kingdom of Yugoslavia, and who fled that country when the Communists took over.[337] Another precedent involved a 34-year old native and citizen of Nicaragua orphaned at an early age and who was placed in a boys home. He later went to China, where he became an interpreter for the United States Army in China and a guerrilla warfare expert. He was later employed with General Chennault's Air Transport Association in Formosa.[338] Another bill was for the relief of a 21-year old native of Czechoslovakia who escaped to West Germany Christmas Day 1951.[339]

In the *miscellaneous-general* category one case involved a native of Belgium who had been a Major General in the Chinese Nationalist Army and had served as liaison for Chiang Kai-Shek. The family had visas available under the Refugee Relief Act, but the beneficiary had been ineligible because he was born in Belgium.[340]

Other cases involved a 20-year old native and citizen of Korea whose United States citizen sponsor wanted to educate him in the United States in memory of their son who was killed in action;[341] a 25-year old native of Egypt who played a role in the rescue of the steamship *Greenville* by the *Ile de France* in 1953;[342] a 29-year old native and citizen of Poland whose brother was killed in an auto accident, and the mother and two siblings were permanent residents and dependent upon him for support;[343] a family, natives of Turkey and France, one of whom was engaged in producing motion pictures in Europe and the United States;[344] and a native of Greece whose husband was employed with the United Nations and who was told by her husband upon arrival that he divorced her and remarried. An investigation determined it was a bigamous relationship.[345]

Another case involved a 27-year old native of Hungary and citizen of Israel whose parents and five siblings died in Auschwitz and his two surviving brothers, United States citizens, resided in the United States.[346]

85th Congress (1957-1958) **-** There were a total of 606 private laws enacted in the quota area in this Congress, of which 386 were within omnibus measures. The number was substantially less than in the previous Congress (932), due to temporary legislation allowing backlog reductions for admission of those with family connections and skills. These temporary measures were a trend which continued the decline through 1962. The 606 laws represented 53% of all laws enacted in this Congress (1,141). Adoption cases continued notwithstanding the enactment of legislation in 1957 allowing nonquota status for adopted children under the age of 14. Private bills remained necessary, however, for reasons such as age, residence, and visa waiting periods. There were 243 immediate relative laws (175 adoption), 57 preference (six returning permanent residents), one ineligible due to race, 31 fiancees, 274 miscellaneous (including three occupations, and others involving those granted status due to deeds, citizenship, and military service).

In the *immediate relative-widow of United States citizen* category one bill involved a 37-year old native of Poland and spouse of a United States citizen unable to adjust status because her citizen husband disappeared.[347] In the *immediate relative-miscellaneous* category, a precedent involved an 81-year old native of Austria-Hungary and citizen of Hungary who sought to immigrate with his spouse, the beneficiary of her stepdaughter's petition.[348]

Precedents conferring *preference* status included a 54-year old native of Malta and citizen of Great Britain with a hearing deficiency who wished to enter the United States with her sister on whom she was entirely dependent. She also had a United States citizen brother.[349]

In the *returning permanent resident* category, one precedent involved a 52-year old native and citizen of Italy who had resided in the United States for 22 years but was found deportable due to convictions for larceny and burglary. The alien was later pardoned by the Governor, and he had four citizen siblings residing in the United States.[350]

The *ineligible due to race* category involved only one case as a precedent: a three-year old native and citizen of Canada who was adopted by United States citizens. She was unable to obtain a visa because she was 50 percent Japanese, and visas for that country were oversubscribed.[351]

Precedents involving the *miscellaneous-due to deeds* category included the case of a 31-year old native and citizen of China whose father was Governor of Yunnan Province from 1924-1945 and who later served as a puppet figure in Communist China. His father and Chiang Kai-shek became disassociated with each other and he moved to Hong Kong, later returning to China. He served as liaison between the Chinese Nationalist Army and the United States for two years. The beneficiary also owned the well-known Peking Palace Restaurant in Washington, D.C.[352] Another case involved H.H. Haidostian who rendered "valuable services" to a United States Government Agency.[353] Another precedent involved a family, natives and citizens of Czechoslovakia, who escaped from that country in a homemade tank made from an old British command car, which took three years to build.[354]

The *miscellaneous-general* category included a family, natives of Turkey, Egypt and Greece (ages 64, 27, 68), who owned a department store in Cairo. They could not safely return to that country because of their Jewish faith.[355] Another case involved a 46-year old native and citizen of the Philippines inducted into the United States Army. The beneficiary served five years and attained the rank of Colonel. He was awarded the Legion of Merit and the Presidential Unit Citation with two clusters. It was learned later that the awards were granted erroneously because the officer who inducted him did not have the authority to induct or grant such commissions. The beneficiary was later employed with the Metropolitan Club in Washington, D.C. as a waiter.[356] Another case related to Michael Romanoff, a spouse of a United States citizen, who entered the United States after the age of nine and was placed in a Juvenile Asylum for lack of guardianship. He was deportable due to a lack of admission documentation. He and his spouse were owners of Romanoff's Restaurant in California.[357]

86th Congress (1959-1960) - The private quota bills totaled 383 this Congress, of which 236 were included in omnibus measures. These represented 76% of all private bills enacted in the 86th Congress (504). This number was less than in previous Congresses, however. The two-petition limit for the immigration of adopted children continued to result in private bills to overcome that restriction. In the 86th Congress, backlogs for low quota countries were reduced through temporary measures for family and skills.

Also, in 1958 registry provisions extending permanent status to aliens in the United States prior to 1940 benefited many potential beneficiaries of private bills. In addition, in 1958 adjustment of status provisions became available to everyone except contiguous countries.

There were 192 immediate relative bills (167 adoption cases), 34 preference (including four returning permanent residents), 12 fiancee, and 145 miscellaneous (seven occupation, and others which included medical cases, military services, and citizenship issues).

In the *immediate relative-adoption* category there was one case, on behalf of children who were natives and citizens of Canada, adopted by United States citizens. The adoptive parents were visiting a cousin in Canada and found the beneficiaries living in an abandoned truck with their parents without heat, electricity or water. They suffered from malnutrition which resulted in one of the children having a deformity.[358] An *immediate relative-miscellaneous* case involved a 25-year old native and citizen of Italy eligible for admission to the United States under the Refugee Relief Act of 1953, but whose visa was erroneously allocated to another person.[359]

Several precedents are cited in the *preference* category. One case involved 21- and 19-year old natives of Okinawa and citizens of Japan, as well as sisters, who sought to enter the United States to join their mother, a permanent resident. The parents had been divorced and the mother had immigrated believing that she could file a petition for her children, but the preference category became oversubscribed.[360] Another case involved a 25-year old native and citizen of Japan born out of wedlock to a United States citizen. The Japanese mother was the beneficiary of a previous private law but the citizen father had died prior to filing a petition on behalf of his son. It was indicated he was heir to a substantial trust fund.[361]

Another bill related to a 39-year old native of China and citizen of Germany who sought admission to the United States to join his lawful permanent resident spouse, whose mother was disabled as a result of an amputated leg. The beneficiary indicated that he would assume responsibility for support of his wife's mother.[362] Another precedent involved a 38-year old native and citizen of Yugoslavia and widow whose husband had been accorded status through his mother but he died of cancer prior to visa issuance.[363] A further case involved Hsiao-li Lindsay, a "universally recognized" critic of China who was bestowed in Australia with the title of Lord Lindsay of Birker and was on the staff of American University.[364]

A bill enacted relating to *returning permanent resident status* was on behalf of a 74-year old native and citizen of Japan admitted for permanent residence for 30 years who left to obtain a divorce in Japan, and who during World War II was unable to return to the United States. Her citizen adopted daughter supported her.[365]

A case in the *miscellaneous-general* category involved a unique bill for a group of 18 individuals comprising two households who were members of the family of the Patriarch of the Church of the East, a United States citizen. They were natives of Turkey, Iran, Israel, Cyprus and Lebanon. It was stated that the Church of the East was one of the oldest Christian churches in the world whose ancient home was Turkey until driven from that country in 1915. The Patriarch had held his position with the church 39 years.[366] One case involved a 27-year old native of the British West Indies who was inducted into the United States Army and while performing guard duty in Korea was accidentally shot by another member of the Armed Forces and paralyzed.[367]

87th Congress (1961-1962) - In this Congress there were 306 quota bills enacted, out of 443 total private laws (69%). This represented a slight decrease from the previous Congress (383). The 87th Congress was the last Congress where there was a significant number of quota laws. There were 164 immediate relative laws enacted (135 adoption), 36 preference cases (including six returning permanent residents), 8 fiancee, and 98 miscellaneous (eight occupations, and others relating to citizenship issues and military services).

The number of adoption cases represented the highest number of adoption laws in the 100 Congresses. These were reduced substantially, however, in the succeeding Congresses after legislation in 1961 made adoption provisions a permanent part of the immigration law. Over the next two decades the number of quota bills enacted each Congress averaged approximately 80.

Other impacts on the reduction of private laws included the fact that the cut-off date for obtaining permanent residence based on suspension of deportation was eliminated in 1962 and the 2000 Asia-Pacific Triangle numerical limitation was removed in 1961. The 87th Congress was the last Congress where paralleling backlog reduction occurred in 1962 preceding the 1965 Act. Another impact included the further broadening of adjustment of status in 1960.

Precedents in the *immediate relative-adoption* category included a case involving one-year old quadruplets and citizens of Korea whose mother died at birth, and whose prospective United States citizen parents were confronted with the two-petition limitation on immigration of adopted children.[368] Another case involved a 15-year old native and citizen of Greece adopted by United States citizens who had already adopted the beneficiary's 13-year old twin sisters.[369] A precedent in the *immediate relative-widow of United States citizen* category included a 26-year old native and citizen of Korea and widow of a United States citizen whose husband served 15 years in the Armed Forces, and who died from leukemia. They had two citizen children.[370] Other *immediate relative-miscellaneous* cases included a 16-year old native of Jamaica and illegitimate child of a United States citizen who was supported by his putative father and resided with his ailing grandmother.[371]

In the *preference* category, a few precedents are cited. One involved a 53-year old widow of a United States citizen and her 22- and 19-year old daughters, natives of Jamaica and subjects of Great Britain, whose father was naturalized but who died before completing plans to bring his family to the United States. He had been cited by the British and French Governments for intelligence work during World War II.[372] Another case involved a 54-year old native and citizen of Italy who sought to join her eight United States siblings. Her brother filed a petition but the visas were oversubscribed.[373]

Other precedents involved a 39-year old native and citizen of China and doctor married to a lawful permanent resident who immigrated based on his employment by the Kentucky State Department of Mental Health in Louisville. The beneficiary had been unable to join him because of the oversubscription of visas in that category.[374] Another bill involved a family, natives of Hong Kong, one of whom was a physician employed as a lecturer and whose medical specialty was diseases of the heart and circulatory system. He was the author or coauthor of 15 related publications and the recipient of a grant from the United States Public Health Service for a study of arteriosclerosis.[375]

In the *former permanent residents* category, several cases are cited. One involved a 52-year old native and citizen of Italy and former United States citizen who lost citizenship by returning to Italy after residing in the United States for 17 years. Her mother and five siblings were United States citizens. Her spouse was convicted of murder in Italy and was serving a lengthy prison sentence. She had three children whom she wished to bring to the United States.[376] Another case involved a 39-year old native of China who entered the United States misrepresenting himself as a United States citizen, after having derived citizenship through his father. It was later discovered, however, that his relative was an uncle, and not his father. The beneficiary had resided in the United States for 16 years.[377] Another case involved 55-year and four-year old natives and citizens of Italy who resided in the United States seven years and returned to Italy. The elder beneficiary was married to a United States citizen, but had been granted a divorce. She had three United States citizen siblings in the United States.[378]

In the *miscellaneous-general* category precedents cited include a 40-year old native and citizen of China who was a crewman aboard British and Chinese Nationalist vessels and whose case under the Refugee Relief Act was not approved by Congress.[379] Another case involved a 30-year old native and citizen of the Philippines serving with the Coast Guard and who was injured on active duty during a fall from a gymnastic bar. He was confined to a wheelchair as a quadriplegic and retired from service.[380]

88th Congress (1963-1964) - In this Congress the number of bills enacted in the quota area (112) decreased substantially from the previous Congress (306), primarily due to the 1961 adoption legislation and prospects for repeal of the national origins system. The 112 quota laws represented 60% of all private laws enacted this Congress (187).

There were 71 immediate relative laws (65 adoption cases), 19 preference (three returning permanent residents), 3 fiancee, and 19 miscellaneous (including those due to deeds and military cases).

Precedents in the *immediate relative-adoption* category included a case involving a six-year old native and citizen of Korea who was adopted by a United States citizen employed by the United States Government. The citizen had been unable to bring the child to the United States because she was single.[381] Another case involved one-year old twin sisters, natives and citizens of Greece, whose parents were living but were unable to financially care for them. Two United States citizens wished to adopt them in the United States.[382]

The bills enacted in the *preference* category included a 38-year old native and citizen of Greece found ineligible for a visa due to a violation of nonimmigrant status following repeated entries into the United States as a seaman, which canceled his priority date for visa issuance.[383] Another bill related to 29- and 31-year old natives and citizens of China, one of whom was employed by Boeing Company, which needed his services in connection with research involving defense contracts.[384]

One precedent in the area of granting status to *lawful returning residents* category involved a 71-year old native of Yugoslavia and citizen of West Germany who resided in the United States for 10 years as a permanent resident, and who returned to Yugoslavia for 25 years. Her close relatives were deceased and her remaining relatives resided in the United States.[385]

Among the precedents in the *miscellaneous-general* category was one granting relief to a 22-year old native and citizen of the Philippines who did not derive United States citizenship at birth due to the invalid marriage of her father, deemed bigamous, and who was unaware that she was not a United States citizen until she tried to obtain a United States passport.[386] Another bill related to an 80-year old widow and native of the British West Indies who was ineligible to adjust status in the United States due to ill health, and who could not travel abroad for a visa.[387]

One case involved a 34-year old native and citizen of China who entered the United States by falsely claiming United States citizenship, and whose father was a citizen, and mother and brother were permanent residents. The beneficiary was ineligible for suspension of deportation due to an absence from the United States.[388] Another precedent involved the very unique provision of granting status as parolee on behalf of a 42-year old native of Poland and citizen of Germany who had served in the German Navy and was held as a prisoner of war by the Russians 8 years until he escaped to Italy.[389]

89th Congress (1965-1966) - The total number of quota laws in this Congress (117) was about the same as in the previous Congress (112) which represented 48% of all private laws enacted in the 89th Congress (246). The low levels continued to reflect the 1965 Act, which became fully operative in 1969. Other areas which changed and which impacted private bills related to the imposition of per country limits of 20,000, thus raising the levels of immigration from a particular country, or in previously large quota countries, lowering the visas. There were 92 immediate relative bills (83 adoption cases), 11 preference (one returning permanent resident), 3 fiancee, and 11 miscellaneous (including citizenship issues and military cases).

Precedents in the *immediate relative-adopted children* category included a 10-year old native and citizen of Korea who had polio, and whose United States citizen adoptive parents sought her admission to the United States. They had previously adopted two other children and required a waiver of the two-petition limitation.[390] Another case involved a one-year old child adopted by a single parent who was a United States citizen. The parent was a foreign correspondent, producer for National Educational Television and a researcher for "David Brinkley's Journal."[391]

A five-year old native and citizen of Korea adopted by United States citizens who had previously adopted eight Korean orphans was also granted relief. Five of the previous orphans had been destined for other families when they entered the United States, but they were placed with the adoptive parents because they were neglected or mistreated.[392]

In the *immediate relative-widow of citizen* category one case involved a 44-year old native and citizen of the Philippines who was the widow of a United States citizen killed in action at Bataan. She had entered the United States to testify in behalf of the United States Government in litigation pending before the Court of Claims, and then returned to the Philippines to care for her father.[393]

In the *miscellaneous-general* category, precedents included a 35-year old native of Canada brought to the United States at the age of six months by his United States adoptive parents and for whom there was no record of admission.[394] Still another precedent involved a 32-year old native and citizen of China employed in a restaurant who was ineligible for suspension of deportation due to brief trips outside the United States.[395]

90th Congress (1967-1968) - Quota laws totaled 54 this Congress, which represented 25% of all private bills enacted during this Congress (216). This was less than half of the number enacted in the previous Congress (117), reflecting the impact of the 1965 Act. Adoption bills continued to be one of the most used categories, because of the failure of beneficiaries to meet some of the requirements of the law. There were 48 immediate relative laws (44 adoption cases), 4 preference, one fiancee, and one miscellaneous. Special relief on behalf of Cuban nationals in 1966 also ameliorated the need for permanent residence or naturalization for this group.

Precedents in this Congress in the area of allowing *immediate relative-adopted children* admission to the United States included a 10-year old native and citizen of Italy who had been placed in the care of his aunt when he was eight-months old, and who later was adopted by the aunt. Because the aunt's husband died prior to the issuance of the adoption decree, a waiver of the single parent prohibition of filing a petition was required.[396]

Another case involved a two-year old native and citizen of Korea to be adopted by United States citizens who had previously adopted three Korean orphans, one of whom had died. The parents had journeyed to the orphanage where their deceased child had been found and learned of the beneficiary.[397] A further precedent involved a four-month old native and citizen of Korea to be adopted by United States citizens who had previously adopted two Korean orphans, one of whom died within 13 hours of arrival in the United States.[398]

In the *immediate relative-miscellaneous* category one case involved a 65-year old native of Spain and citizen of Venezuela who resided with her adopted daughter, for whom she had custody since the age of two. The daughter, who was not formally adopted until the age of 17, later became a citizen after marriage to a United States citizen and sought to have her adoptive mother remain with her in the United States.[399]

Enactment of private quota laws in the ***91st through 94th Congress (1969-1976)*** remained fairly consistent in the quota area averaging about 60 each Congress, with a grand total of 235.

91st Congress (1969-1970) - In this Congress there were 66 private quota laws enacted, out of a total of 112 private laws this Congress (59%). With the 1969 effective date of the 1965 legislation, this Congress ended the major decline in all laws enacted. Of the 66 laws enacted in the 91st Congress, 40 were immediate relatives (32 adoption cases), 21 preference, two fiancee, and three miscellaneous.

Several precedents are cited, including an *immediate relative-adoption* case on behalf of a one-year old native and citizen of South Vietnam who was adopted by a single United States citizen nurse employee of the United States Agency for International Development.[400]

Another case in the category *immediate relative-widow of citizen* involved a 22-year old native and citizen of China, whose spouse had been killed while serving with the United States Air Force in Vietnam.[401] In that same category, there was a 63-year old native and citizen of Russia and widow of a United States citizen, who was separated from her spouse when he was forcibly taken from Russia to

Germany as a laborer. The spouse later became a United States citizen, but the beneficiary was not granted permission to leave Russia until six years later. The spouse died shortly after her arrival.[402]

In the *returning permanent resident* category one case involved a 32-year old native and citizen of Italy who was a United States permanent resident and returned to Italy due to the illness of her father. She then entered the United States six years later as a stenographer.[403]

Among those precedents in the *miscellaneous-general* category included the case of three family members, natives of Greece and Australia (ages 17, 22, 13), who resided with their United States citizen aunt and uncle for several months after their father killed their mother and committed suicide.[404]

92nd Congress (1971-1972) - The number of quota laws this Congress totaled 42, of 62 private laws (68%). There were 27 immediate relative laws (20 adoption cases), nine preference (two returning permanent residents), and six miscellaneous cases. Definitions of "orphans" and other adoption provisions left some need for bills in this category.

In the *immediate relative-adoption* category one case involved a 19-year old native and citizen of Greece coming to the United States for adoption by his United States citizen uncle and aunt, who had also been previous sponsors of private legislation for two other nephews.[405]

A precedent on behalf of an *immediate relative-widow of citizen* involved a 22-year old native and citizen of Mexico whose spouse was murdered six years after her entry to the United States. They had three citizen children.[406] In the *immediate relative-miscellaneous* category one bill was on behalf of a two-year old native and citizen of Italy born out of wedlock. His natural father, a United States citizen serving in the Air Force, was unable to legitimate him. His mother had been killed in an accident.[407]

The precedents in the *miscellaneous-general* category included that of a 41-year old native and citizen of Italy and spouse of a United States citizen whose marriage was later discovered to be bigamous, because her husband had not terminated his previous marriage. It was learned that he had been declared mentally incompetent when discharged from the Army which apparently "explained his failure to disclose the prior marriage."[408]

Another precedent involved a 70-year old native and citizen of the Philippines and widow of a veteran of guerrilla forces who served with the American troops in the Philippines World War II.[409]

93rd Congress (1973-1974) - Quota laws in this Congress totaled 49, slightly more than in the previous Congress. This was 80% of the total number of private laws enacted this Congress (61). There were 30 immediate relatives laws (21 adoption cases), 15 preference (four returning permanent residents), and four miscellaneous including a medical case.

Among the precedents granting *immediate relative-adoption* status were a case involving a 23-year old native and citizen of Mexico adopted by United States citizens who were missionaries in Mexico and who resided with them for 16 years.[410] Another case involved a 19-year old native of British Guiana and citizen of Guyana adopted by United States citizen parents who was raised by them from infancy. The adoptive father was deceased and had founded British Guiana Airways. He died while preparing for his return to the United States. He had been awarded the Order of the British Empire and the King's Medal for Service in the Cause of Freedom for his service during World War II. They had previously adopted two children.[411]

In the *preference* category, one case involved a 27-year old widow and her seven- and three-year old children. The oldest was a native and citizen of Italy, and the youngest was a native of the United States born in diplomatic status. They had entered the United States as members of a diplomatic mission, and the spouse was the beneficiary of a petition filed by his sister. While the family was in the process of adjusting to immigrant status in the United States, the 27-year old's spouse died and they were no longer entitled to immigrant visas.[412] Another case involved a 28-year old native and citizen of Colombia whose United States citizen aunt and uncle wanted to adopt her, but she remained in her native country to care for her ill mother and younger brothers. Her mother was later placed in a mental institution and her father died.[413]

Another precedent involved a 56-year old native and citizen of China whose spouse and child were beneficiaries of a petition filed by her United States citizen sister. His spouse and child died in a traffic accident, and the beneficiary was ineligible for a visa because his name was not included on the immigrant petition.[414] One case involved a 22-year old native and citizen of the Philippines who was adopted at the age of 21 by a retired United States citizen Air Force sergeant. He had served as a houseboy for one and a half years with the adoptive father.[415] Another case involved a 25-year old native and citizen of Poland married to a lawful permanent resident who filed a petition on her behalf, but who died of a gun shot wound prior to visa issuance.[416]

Among those precedents granting *returning permanent resident* status was the case of a 39-year old native and citizen of Great Britain who resided in the United States for 20 years and did not obtain a re-entry permit when she left the United States due to marital difficulties. She and her husband were later divorced with two United States citizen children, one of whom had a rare speech defect resulting in an inability to talk since birth.[417]

In the *miscellaneous-general* category, one case included a 20-year old native and citizen of Mexico whose mother was a permanent resident prior to death and whose father was unknown.[418]

94th Congress (1975-1976) - There was a slight increase in the number of private quota laws enacted in this Congress primarily because of an increase in adoption bills. Quota laws totaled 78, compared to 49 in the previous Congress. The total private laws this Congress was 99. In the adoption area legislation was enacted in 1975 eliminating the bar to adoption by single persons, one area in which private bills had been enacted. On the other hand, due to the two-petition limitation, an increasing number of adoption bills were enacted to overcome that provision, as well as the 14-year age limit and definition. There were 62 immediate relative bills (54 adoption cases), 9 preference, and 7 miscellaneous cases.

Several precedents are cited in the *immediate relative-adoption* category. Three laws involved natives and citizens of Korea who resided in a leper colony in Korea, and whose adoption was sought by United States citizens. Because their natural parents were living, the children did not qualify as orphans.[419] Another case involved seven beneficiaries, ages five through 13 who were natives and citizens of Ecuador, and who were adopted by United States citizens who had already adopted other children. The eldest beneficiary was blind and two others suffered from cerebral palsy.[420] One precedent involved an 18-year old native and citizen of Mexico adopted by his permanent resident sister and her citizen spouse at the age of 16. His natural mother was ill and unable to care for him, and the father deceased.[421]

In the *preference* category, one case involved a 20-year old native and citizen of Jamaica adopted by a permanent resident with whom he had resided from infancy.[422] Another case involved a 41-year old widow with four sons and daughters, natives and citizens of Lebanon, who were beneficiaries of a petition filed on behalf of the husband, who was killed by sniper fire in Lebanon. The United States citizen brother assumed full financial responsibility for the beneficiaries.[423]

Another precedent involved six siblings, natives and citizens of the Philippines, aged 10 through 27, who were the children of a United States citizen killed by her husband, who then committed suicide. Their citizen mother had filed petitions on their behalf prior to her death. A United States citizen brother had also filed petitions on their behalf, but visas in that category were oversubscribed.[424]

In the *miscellaneous-general* category there was a bill on behalf of a 44-year old native and citizen of the Netherlands, and spouse of a United States citizen with two citizen children, who was deserted by her spouse seven years after marriage.[425] Another case involved a 47-year old native and citizen of the Philippines who entered the United States to care for the three children of her sister who was suffering from terminal cancer. She was later appointed the children's legal guardian.[426]

95th Congress (1977-1978) - Quota laws totaled 106 this Congress, the majority of which continued to reflect an increase in adoption cases. This represented 76% of the total number of private laws in this Congress (139). There were 80 immediate relative cases (71 adoption), 16 preference (two returning permanent resident cases), and ten miscellaneous (including military and medical cases).

Among the *immediate relative-adoption* precedents in this Congress was that of a three-year old native and citizen of the Philippines who was adopted by lawful permanent residents, one of whom was an aunt, and whose natural parents and five siblings remained in the Philippines.[427] Another case involved a 19-year old native and citizen of Guyana adopted by United States citizens at the age of 17. At the age of three she had been given to her grandmother for caring, but had gone to live with a cousin when the grandmother had difficulty supporting her and three sisters. The cousin died three years later; and the adoptive parents, ages 81 and 70, sought to bring her to the United States.[428]

Another precedent involved a three-year old native and citizen of Korea to be adopted by a United States citizen who had already petitioned for two adopted children, one of whom died at the age of three in a drowning accident.[429] An interesting case involved Andre Previn, an internationally recognized symphony conductor, and his spouse, actress Mia Farrow, who adopted a seven-year old native of Korea.[430]

In the *immediate relative-miscellaneous* category one case involved a 21-year old native and citizen of Colombia for whom United States citizen godmothers cared since infancy. When the godmothers immigrated to the United States, the natural father refused to execute documents allowing the beneficiary's immigration and forced her to reside with an aunt and uncle.[431] Another case involved a 67-year old native and citizen of Korea who was the natural father of a United States citizen. Because there was no marriage between her parents, the daughter's petition for him was denied, but the mother and sister's petitions were approved.[432]

In the *preference* category several precedents are cited. One bill involved a 24-year old deaf-mute native and citizen of Morocco, adopted by a United States citizen, the president of American Express.[433] Another precedent involved a 27-year old native and citizen of the Philippines who was adopted by a United States citizen Roman Catholic priest who intended to retire in eight years and wished the beneficiary to "care for him during his retirement years."[434] A further case involved a 22-year old native and citizen of Mexico adopted by United States citizen missionaries at the age of 14. He had been found guilty of petty larceny and been given one year of probation at the age of 21.[435]

One bill involved a 33-year old native and citizen of Italy who sought to immigrate as the sister of a United States citizen. She was raised in the household of her natural father and was not aware she and the petitioner were not sisters until the petition was denied.[436] Another precedent involved a widow and three children, natives and citizens of Korea, ages 39, 16, 13, and 9, who were in the process of obtaining immigrant visas when the father died of cancer and the petition by his United States citizen father became invalid.[437]

In the *returning lawful resident* category, one case involved a 37-year old native and citizen of France who had been married to a United States citizen for seven years and then divorced. She had custody of their two citizen children, had married and divorced again, and wished to return to the United States.[438]

In the *miscellaneous-general* category, one case pertained to a 34-year old native and citizen of the Philippines who served for 25 years with the United States Navy, until it was learned that he suffered from a hearing loss and retired on disability. He resided with his United States citizen brother.[439]

96th Congress (1979-1980) - The number of private laws in the quota area decreased substantially, due to the 1978 amendments which eliminated restrictions on petitioning for adopted children. The quota private laws totaled 73 compared to 106 in the previous Congress. Private laws in this Congress across all categories totaled 82, of which quota bills enacted represented 89%. There were 57 cases of immediate relatives (55 adoption cases), 3 preference, and 13 miscellaneous (including a military case).

Among the precedents relating to the *immediate relative-adoption* category was that of a mother and child (ages 21 and 3), natives and citizens of Jamaica, who were coming to the United States to reside with the mother's adoptive mother, a United States citizen who adopted her at the age of 17. Although the grandmother had not known of the adoptive child's daughter, she indicated that she would welcome her.[440] Another precedent involved a 21-year old native and citizen of India adopted by United States citizens, aged 76 and 78, which involved a dispute as to the legality of the adoption. The matter was resolved by requiring the child be readopted in the United States.[441]

Another case involved a 22-year old native and citizen of Indonesia, adopted at the age of 19 by United States citizens who had previously employed her for six months as a domestic. It was noted that there was a "true parent-child relationship" and that the parents would provide a valid home for the beneficiary.[442] Another precedent involved a 15-year old native and citizen of India orphaned at an early age who was the victim of polio which had paralyzed both legs. She was to be adopted by United States citizens who had nine other adopted children.[443]

A further case related to a one-year old native and citizen of China adopted by United States citizens, whose adoptive mother resided with the child for six months but could not comply with the two year residence requirement for nonorphans.[444]

In the *miscellaneous-due to deeds* category, one case involved a family, natives of the Philippines, one of whom served one year in the United States Navy and was discharged after an accident aboard a United States vessel while on combat duty in the Tonkin Gulf resulted in amputation of his leg.[445]

In the *miscellaneous-general* category one bill related to 21- and 18-year old natives and citizens of Jamaica whose mother died when they were ages three and two days respectively and whose United States citizen grandmother became their legal guardian. The daughter of the grandmother sought to care for the beneficiaries.[446]

Another case, one of only a few in all Congresses, involved a group of 653 members of the Mennonite Church who had entered the United States from Mexico and Canada, allegedly under a claim that they could purchase land and live in the United States permanently without submission of any further immigration papers. They settled in Texas and Oklahoma and later learned there was little water in the area.[447]

97th Congress (1981-1982) - Quota laws totaled 36 this Congress which was approximately half of those enacted in the previous Congress (73). A total of 40 private bills were enacted in the 97th Congress, of which quota laws were 90%. The decrease was primarily a result of 1981 amendments in the adoption area. That law increased the age at which children could be adopted prior to entering the United States from 14 to 16. In subsequent Congresses the total adoption cases would continue this downward trend. In addition to the change in the adoption law, provisions were made for special visas on behalf of investors and FMGs, which eliminated the need for private bills in those categories.

Of the quota laws this Congress, there were 22 immediate relative laws (18 adoption cases), four preference, and 10 miscellaneous cases (including three occupational cases and a medical case).

There were four precedents relating to the *immediate relative-adopted children* category. One involved a 21-year old native and citizen of Korea to be adopted by United States citizens who was the "Amerasian" offspring of an American soldier and Korean woman."[448] Another case involved a six-year old native and citizen of Brazil adopted by a United States citizen parent and lawful permanent resident at the age of four, and whose adoptive mother attempted to comply with the two year residence period but was taken ill.[449]

Another case was a 17-year old native and citizen of Haiti adopted at the age of 15 by United States citizens whom she met while on a visit to the United States with a church group.[450] One bill involved a 19-year old native and citizen of Japan born illegitimately and given to the maternal grandmother 30 days after her birth for adoption. The natural mother left the child to reside in the United States but later returned to reclaim the child.[451]

A further precedent in the *immediate relative-miscellaneous* category involved an 81-year old native and citizen of France on whose behalf the United States citizen adoptive daughter sought entry to the United States.[452]

The *miscellaneous-occupational* category included a physician and his family, natives and citizens of the Philippines, specializing in colon rectal surgery.[453] For the first time, Congress required that the doctor serve two years as a physician in the geographic area where he was employed prior to granting permanent residence.

In the *miscellaneous-general* category, one case involved a 23-year old native and citizen of Ecuador who was befriended by a United States citizen doctor during a visit to a missionary hospital in that country, where the beneficiary was treated for malnutrition and polio. He had been born one of seven illegitimate children, and had been sold to a restaurant, where he remained until he met the doctor. He was then placed with foster parents in the United States.[454]

98th Congress (1983-1984) - There were 23 private quota bills enacted in this Congress continuing the decline from the 95th Congress. This represented 66% of the total number of laws in this Congress (35). There were 6 immediate relative cases (4 adoption cases), three preference, and 14 miscellaneous (including medical, military, deeds, and refugee cases). The need for legislation on behalf of "Amerasians" was eliminated with legislation in 1982 providing special immigration benefits.

In the *miscellaneous-occupation* category there was a case involving natives of Hong Kong employed in the hi-tech industry and who received labor certification for their employment, but due to oversubscribed visas, they were unable to immigrate.[455]

In the *miscellaneous-due to deeds* category, one case involved a 48-year old native and citizen of the Philippines who assisted American prisoners of war at the age of six during World War II.[456]

One precedent in the *miscellaneous-general* category was on behalf of a 19-year old native of Scotland and citizen of Great Britain who had been a ward of the Government of Scotland since birth, because his father was in prison and his mother could not provide for him. He had been placed in foster homes since the age of 12. When he accompanied a foster parent to the United States the relationship broke down, and he was placed in a different foster home.[457]

99th Congress (1985-1986) - Private laws for quotas totaled 13 this Congress, out of 15 enacted across all categories this Congress. This was the lowest number of laws enacted since the 79th Congress (1945-1946) when there were 14 quota laws. Legislation in 1986 which granted amnesty to those in the United States since 1982, eliminated the need to resort to private bills for some cases. In addition, the legislation moved the registry date provisions for permanent residence to 1972. Other provisions allowing putative fathers to confer immigration benefits without legitimation eliminated those private bills. There were 8 immediate relative bills in this Congress (five adoption cases), and five miscellaneous cases.

A bill which was an *immediate relative-adoption* case involved 21- and 18-year old natives and citizens of Bolivia who were the nephew and niece of the adoptive United States citizens. Their natural mother died in March 1981 of cancer, and the father died in September of that same year.[458]

Among those precedents included in the *miscellaneous-general* area was one bill on behalf of a 45-year old native of Korea who was the victim of spousal abuse and had entered the United States on an exchange visa. She had custody of two citizen children.[459] Another case involved a family, natives of Ireland (ages 39, 39, 13), who entered the United States as treaty traders employed with an Irish airline, but who changed employers and were no longer entitled to the special visa for treaty countries. This was one of very few bills granting temporary status by allowing the beneficiaries to remain in nonimmigrant treaty trader status.[460]

Another precedent involved two 24- and 20-year old natives of Korea, whose parents and two brothers died aboard Korean Airlines Flight 007, shot down by Soviet jets in 1983.[461]

100th Congress (1987-1988) - Private quota laws totaled 15 in this Congress, out of 21 for all categories this Congress. There were eight immediate relatives (five adoption cases), four preference, and three miscellaneous.

One case in the *immediate relative-widow of citizen* category involved a 27-year old native of Honduras who entered the United States on a diplomatic visa, but whose husband committed suicide. They had a four-year old citizen child.[462] An interesting case related to Gillian Sackler, the widow of a United States citizen. Her spouse had endowed the Sackler Art Gallery in Washington, D.C.[463]

Precedents in the *preference* category included a 23-year old native of Hong Kong who was over the age of 21 when the family obtained permanent residence, and thus could not be included in their immigrant petition.[464]

A precedent in the *miscellaneous-general* category was a medical case involving a family whose eight-year old child, a native of Chile, had a birth defect involving the bladder.[465]

EXCLUSION

Historical Perspective

Exclusion laws have been primarily reactionary, first in relation to the health and background character of the new immigrants and later in response to wartime sentiments. During heavy immigrant waves the exclusions also have been used to achieve quota balance by restricting entry on the basis of race and literacy, or as barriers during the Great Depression through narrowing of public charge interpretations. At the same time, however, liberalizing provisions have been adopted in response to postwar humanitarian impulses, including the need to accommodate the entry of relatives of large contingents of United States servicemen overseas. Liberalizations also were a result of favorable economic and social changes in the 1960s.

The Early Years

In the early years, federal control of immigration closely paralleled the laws and concerns of the various states.[466] The thrust of the exclusion rules of the states related to the control of the entry of destitutes, particularly those who would be a financial burden, and restrictions aimed at criminal elements who posed a threat to community harmony. Increasingly, there was a "strong suspicion at the time that Europe was deliberately exporting its human liabilities."[467] Congress initially expressed its displeasure in 1866 through a resolution concerning the undesirable elements entering the country, when President Andrew Johnson signed a joint resolution protesting against pardons by foreign governments of persons convicted of "infamous offenses" if they would immigrate to the United States.[468]

The first Federal legislation designating excludable classes of aliens was the Act of March 3, 1875,[469] which prohibited the admission of those convicted of certain crimes and outlawed the importing of women for prostitution.[470] It was largely responsive to information gathered by Congress on the landing in the United States of "convicts...paupers, idiots, insane persons" and others incapable of supporting themselves.[471] The same data reported on the involuntary importation of Chinese labor, particularly Chinese women, who had been "brought for shameful purposes, to the disgrace of the communities where they settled and to the great demoralization of the youth of those localities."[472] The 1875 Act exempted political crimes on the basis that the United States had always been heralded as a safe haven for persons convicted of purely political offenses.[473]

The next Act in 1882[474] addressed the same issues--burdens on the states of the new immigrants--by expanding the excludable classes from two to four, adding mental defectives (lunatics and idiots) and potential public charges.[475] The statute also responded to a United States Supreme Court case holding unconstitutional, in violation of the commerce clause, a New York law imposing taxes and bonds on incoming immigrants.[476] This ended funding for many immigrants entering through New York and resulted in lobbying for federal control.[477] At the same time, worries of the impact of Chinese laborers on the west coast led to the Chinese Exclusion Act of May 6, 1882.[478] Allegedly to protect domestic labor from foreign competition, it was more intentionally aimed at the cultural traits of the laborers.[479] That Act received various extensions until its final repeal on December 17, 1943.[480]

Another labor-related law, the first of the alien contract labor laws, enacted in 1885[481] and continued until 1952, prohibited the importation under contract of most foreign labor unless the skills were not found in the United States. This occurred at a time of significant economic trouble when immigrants were seen as fermenting strikes and reducing the wages of citizens, particularly in the coal fields.[482]

With high levels of immigration causing more and more consternation, particularly as immigrant admissions shifted from Northern and Western Europe to Southern and Eastern Europe, a Select Committee on Investigation of Foreign Immigration was established in 1888 to investigate charges that the exclusion laws were being evaded, and that inadequate enforcement measures existed.[483] The Ford Committee, as mentioned previously, concluded that large numbers of people entered the country in disregard of the law.[484] This conclusion paralleled earlier Congressional findings prefacing the first Federal Act in 1875, but went further in that it reflected new fears of the composition of the second wave of immigrants from southeast Europe.

In 1891[485] Congress expanded the list of excludable aliens to include insane persons, polygamists, and those with a "dangerous contagious disease." This last exclusion ground was due to fear of epidemics in Europe. The 1891 Act introduced to the statute exclusions for persons convicted of crimes involving "moral turpitude."[486] It kept open the door to immigrants who came to the New World to better themselves but barred those who were "involuntarily" inflicted upon the New World.[487]

Following the 1901 assassination of President William McKinley by Leon Czolgosz, described as "an anarchist of American birth but obviously foreign extraction," exclusion laws turned towards barring entry of political activists.[488] Referred to as the "Alien and Sedition Laws," the 1903 law[489] enlarged the list of excludables to include anarchists and prohibited the entry of those who believed in or "advocate the overthrow by force of violence of the Government of the United States or of all governments or of all forms of law, or the assassination of public officials."[490]

The 1903 Act also addressed health concerns, as a result of an investigation conducted by the Industrial Commission in the 55th Congress (1897-1898) focusing on the burdens that immigrants placed on states and on the need to exert controls for their fitness and adaptability in the United States. In response to the "solicitation of some of the States whose asylums for treatment of the insane have become overcrowded with aliens...,"[491] the health exclusions added the following: "professional beggars," "epileptics," previously insane persons, and those who accompanied an alien rejected due to illness to ensure safe return.[492] Also, for the first time, the law provided a limited waiver for persons afflicted with a "loathsome or dangerous contagious disease" in cases where the waiver would benefit wives or children of immigrants who filed for citizenship.[493]

The Act of February 20, 1907[494] reaffirmed the desirability of maintaining limits on some characteristics of the immigrant population through an expansion of the excludable classes. Presidential messages raised concerns about the increasing level of immigration, which reached its highest levels during the first decade of the 20th century.[495] President Theodore Roosevelt told the 58th Congress (1903-1904) that "we cannot have too much immigration of the right kind, and we should have none at all of the wrong kind."[496] Expanding the exclusion of criminal elements, the 1907 law barred not only those who had a conviction for a crime involving moral turpitude but also aliens who admitted committing such an offense, and barred those persons practicing polygamy.

In the health area the 1907 Act continued mental and physical exclusions by also excluding: "imbeciles," "feeble-minded persons," those afflicted with tuberculosis, and those having mental or physical "defects" which would impact on their ability to earn a living. The Act also established a Joint Commission on Immigration to investigate the subject of immigration. That Commission, named after its Chairman,

Senator William P. Dillingham (R-VT), published a 42-volume report in 1911 centering on the economic aspects of immigration.

The Act of February 5, 1917[497] addressed further the health of incoming immigrants, and for the first time used exclusion grounds as a means of filtering the ethnic composition of the "new" immigrants from the "old."[498] The exclusion grounds were expanded to include illiteracy, for those over the age of 16, thus imposing de facto numerical limitations on the second wave of immigrants from southeastern Europe. This blatantly ethnic attack had caused previous similar legislation to be vetoed, once by President Grover Cleveland, once by President William H. Taft, and the last two by President Woodrow Wilson. The last veto of President Wilson, however, was overriden resulting in the final expansion and codification of the exclusion law.

Mr. Augustus P. Gardner (R-MA) expressed concerns as to assimilation and numbers of immigrants during debate on the restrictive measures:

> We restrictionists believe that altogether too many able-bodied persons are coming into this country, whether their characters are good, bad, or indifferent. We believe that immigrants are coming too fast to be assimilated, and we believe that the low wages which they are willing to accept are a menace to our high standard of living.[499]

The Dillingham Commission had also recommended exclusion of the less desirable new immigration from Eastern and Southern Europe in preference to the old, from Northern and Western Europe. As Sen. Dillingham stated on the Senate floor in 1916:

> We took the nations from which this immigration comes so largely, the eastern and southern nations of Europe, and ascertained what the literacy percentage was among the people of those nations. We saw at once that if we adopted the educational test, it would substantially decrease the volume of that stream 30 percent. . .[500]

This laid the groundwork for major legislation enacted in 1921 and 1924 establishing quotas to assure that only the most desirable immigrants entered the country.

The 1917 Act also enlarged health prohibitions so that "persons of constitutional psychopathic inferiority" and persons with chronic alcoholism were excluded. The former included those with congenital defects related to mental activity resulting in an inability to adapt to society.[501] The exclusion of persons with physical defects was clarified to prevent only those who could not earn a living. The bar on those mentally defective was explained as necessary in order to prevent "strains of mental defect that may continue and multiply through succeeding generations..."[502] Another bar to entry related to the exclusion of vagrants, stowaways, and aliens who had been deported and thereafter sought readmission due to their practice of immediately attempting re-entry after expulsion.[503] The Act also established the so-called "barred zone," excluding aliens from many parts of Asia. This was later incorporated into the 1924 Quota Act.

In response to wartime measures in 1918, legislation prohibiting the entry of anarchists, subversives and others dangerous to national security were recodified.[504] Further attention was also given to prohibiting the entry of those engaged in sabotage, or those engaged in writing, publishing, and otherwise advocating proscribed activities. Also excluded were aliens who were members of associations involved in the circulation of such material.[505]

The Act of May 26, 1924,[506] although primarily re-establishing numerical limits in the form of the national origins quota system, excluded those who were ineligible for citizenship. As the House Immigration Committee explained in its report on the legislation:

> All must agree that nothing can be gained by permitting to be built up in the United States colonies of those who can not, under the law, become naturalized citizens, and must therefore owe allegiance to another government.[507]

For a long period of time the exclusion grounds remained the same, except for minor exceptions, including permission for re-entry of previously excludable aliens[508] and expansion of the ability to exclude based on documentary requirements.[509]

The War Years and Its Aftermath (1940-1960)

It was not until 1940 that the exclusion and deportation grounds were revisited, arising out of hostilities with Germany. The first major Act in 1940 reflected the threats of Nazism and other political forces which could threaten the stability of the United States. From 1940 through 1965 legislation often addressed these fears, but at the same time some laws responded in a humane fashion to the refugee exodus through the establishment of various refugee programs.

The 1940 Act expanded the 1917 grounds of exclusion relating to threats to the nation of subversive elements by broadening the bar against those who were members of certain proscribed organizations to include past affiliation with such groups. This was in response to a strict Supreme Court ruling in 1939 narrowly holding the exclusion to present membership (*Kessler v. Strecker*).[510] It also required fingerprinting and registration of aliens in the United States. Other legislation provided the United States government with the authority to deny a visa and admission to those who sought to enter the United States to engage in activities which might "endanger the public safety of the United States."[511]

The second major act relating to national security, the "Internal Security Act" of September 23, 1950,[512] codified security grounds and added a bar to entry against those who would be likely to engage in subversive activities *after* entry, including espionage, sabotage, and public disorder. The Internal Security Act for the first time mentioned the Communist Party, and provided three new categories of exclusion involving membership in the party or its affiliates. Amendments to the Act in 1951 waived the prohibition of affiliation with proscribed organizations in cases of involuntary association.[513]

Other legislation in the wartime era included codification, in 1944, of previous Selective Service laws barring from entry those who departed the United States to evade training or service in the armed forces during wartime,[514] and providing, in 1948, for the exclusion of those who sought to gain admission by fraudulent means. This was a response to persons seeking admission as refugees with inappropriate documentation.[515]

The third major act seeking to exclude aliens on security grounds related specifically to efforts in the postwar period and cold war era against Communism. The McCarran-Walter Act in 1952,[516] named after its Senate and House sponsors, Sen. Pat McCarran (D-NV) and Mr. Francis E. Walter (D-PA), revised and codified all existing immigration law. It was preceded by a study of the Senate Judiciary Special Subcommittee to Investigate Immigration and Naturalization in the 80th Congress (1947-48), which found that

> our present laws are shot through with weaknesses and loopholes, and...criminals, Communists, and subversives of all descriptions are even now gaining admission into this country like water through a sieve...[517]

The 1952 Act lengthened and strengthened the grounds for exclusion, primarily by codifying the previously enacted Internal

Security Act of 1950. Despite President Harry S. Truman's veto, based on the fact that the legislation did not repeal the national origins system and posed an unwarranted paranoia of national security, the bill became law when Congress overrode the veto.

The 1952 Act also, in a major way, addressed the character of incoming immigrants and refined the health grounds of exclusion. The legislation also tried to address the impact of immigration on the United States labor market. The Act rendered excludable those with criminal records, narcotic violators and addicts, those coming to engage in immoral sexual acts, and smugglers.[518] In the health area, the McCarran-Walter Act eliminated the reference to idiots and imbeciles, but retained the reference to feeble-minded persons since it was "an inclusive generic term represented by subclasses of idiots, imbeciles, morons, and persons of border-line intelligence." The 1952 Act also changed the terminology from excluding "persons of constitutional psychopathic inferiority" to "aliens afflicted with psychopathic personality" due to problems of defining the former term. The Public Health Service noted that a psychopathic personality was "characterized by developmental defects...in the personality manifest by lifelong patterns of action or behavior, rather than by mental or emotional symptoms." The term "mental defect" was added as a ground of exclusion to cover those with hereditary disturbances which did not fit into other categories.[519]

The third major exclusion provision of the 1952 Act required labor tests in lieu of the contract labor provisions, which allowed entry to the United States for employment unless the Department of Labor certified it would be harmful to the domestic labor market.

Other provisions of the 1952 Act included a bar to admission on the basis of fraudulent acts which had been provided in the Displaced Persons Act of 1948. For only the second time in immigration law, the 1952 Act allowed a waiver of a ground of exclusion, for aliens with physical defects if they could affirmatively show that the ground was inapplicable. The waiver for illiteracy was also codified. Another provision provided status to so-called "defectors" who had been members of the Communist Party and demonstrated rehabilitation over a period of time.

After the 1952 Act there were many liberalizing features to the immigration law, culminating in the 1965 repeal of the national origins system. Most of the statutes involved alleviating hardships in the separation of families due to exclusions, and these reflected changing attitudes of the United States towards immigrants.

In 1954 an exemption of the criminal exclusion was carved out for those whose only bar was commission of a petty offense, as a means of reunifying families whose principal had been excluded due a minor offense.[520] Waivers of both criminal and health grounds were provided in 1957.[521] The 1957 Act provided for waivers of crimes involving moral turpitude and prostitution on behalf of parents, spouses, and children of citizens and permanent residents. It also provided similar temporary waivers of exclusion for tuberculosis and misrepresentation.

In 1961 the criminal waiver mechanisms became permanent, and the tuberculosis waiver was expanded to include unmarried sons and daughters of United States citizens and permanent resident aliens.[522] The legislation eliminated tuberculosis as a separate ground of exclusion but set forth a broad category into which tuberculosis could be subsumed. That is, aliens "afflicted with any contagious disease" became excludable, the purpose of which was to define through regulation those diseases which would pose a threat to national welfare. Leprosy was also eliminated as a specific exclusion, but was to be covered through regulation as a contagious disease.

Liberalizing Changes (1960s)

In 1961 the exchange visitor program was also reviewed. Since its inception in 1948 under the Smith-Mundt Act,[523] which encouraged exchange programs, the obligation to return home for those who had entered on exchange visas had been tightened in 1956,[524] to require a two-year foreign residence prior to seeking permanent status or changing to another temporary visa. A waiver was allowed, however, if the United States Government determined the alien's stay in the United States would be in the public interest. In 1961 a second waiver was added to address hardship situations.[525] Later amendments in 1970 and 1976 provided further waivers for persecution or when the home country voiced "no objection" to nonreturn, but restricted the latter in cases of FMGs.

The Act of October 3, 1965,[526] although most commonly known as the act which eliminated the national origins basis for selective immigration, further liberalized the health exclusions. The changes primarily reflected medical advances. The term "mentally retarded" was substituted for "feeble-minded," in order to conform with modern medical terminology. The bar on admission of epileptics was eliminated, since "medical advances have brought this condition under control." For the first time, waivers of those excluded due to mental retardation and of those who had a previous attack of insanity were made available in a similar fashion to the waivers for tuberculosis. Specifically, the parent, spouse, son or daughter of a United States citizen or permanent resident or immigrant could benefit from a waiver. The only narrowing of exclusion grounds related to homosexuals. In response to a 1962 Court of Appeals decision in *Fleuti v. Rosenberg*, which held that the term "psychopathic personality" did not encompass homosexuals, Congress added the term "sex deviant" to the exclusion grounds to resolve any doubt that homosexuals were to be prohibited from entry.[527]

Exclusions Revisited (1980s)

The exclusion laws remained substantially intact until 1981 when legislation designed to streamline the administration of the law provided a discretionary waiver of the narcotics exclusion for a single offense of 30 grams or less of simple possession of marijuana, if the waiver was on behalf of the spouse, child or parent of a United States citizen or permanent resident.[528] In addition, in 1986 marriage fraud was addressed by tightening immigration provisions based on marriage to a United States citizen or permanent resident.[529] A limited waiver was provided in cases of extreme hardship.

Public Legislation and Private Bills

Waivers of exclusion grounds on behalf of those seeking admission to the United States were another area which illustrated the parallels between public bills and private legislation. The high volume in the exclusion area, while less than in the quota area, can be explained in terms of family reunification. The majority of waivers sought to alleviate the separation of spouses and other members of the family. Exclusion laws were most harsh in times of war, when large numbers of United States servicemen were overseas, and when refugees sought alternative homelands. The intermingling of United States forces with persons from other countries, and the plight of refugees, led to high numbers of immigrants seeking to enter the United States either to join their family or to seek refuge. However, many could not immigrate due to ineligibility on the basis of health conditions, criminal offenses, or document fraud. In response, waivers for exclusions for these groups of people were obtained through private bills and later under the general law.

The major parallels between private bills and public legislation in the exclusion area included the Act of 1954 and the 1957 Act, the result of a steady increase of private bills waiving minor criminal offenses for close family members; the 1961 and 1965 Acts which allowed health waivers; and the 1981 legislation providing limited waivers for drug offenses. Because of the restrictive nature of exclusion laws, most remedial legislation allowed discretion to lie with the Attorney General to waive certain exclusion grounds, rather than to repeal entirely the particular prohibition for entry.

In the 100 Congresses, a total of 1,843 private laws waived the various exclusion laws. This was 25% of the total number of private laws in the same time period. The exclusion laws were enacted sporadically, with a total of only 63 until the 81st Congress (1949-1950), when 51 were signed into law. They increased in the 82nd Congress (1951-1952) to 75. The highest number of exclusion laws enacted occurred in the 83rd through the 85th Congresses (1953-1958) when 1,355 were enacted (74% of the waiver laws in all the Congresses). The majority waived criminal and health exclusions for which the general law had no remedy.

The aftermath of war and the need to address the admission of spouses of servicemen excludable for various reasons contributed to a steady increase in private bills. Because of the high volume, omnibus measures incorporated many groups of individuals where circumstances for relief were similar.

Trends in Public Legislation and Private Bills for Exclusion

There were three major trends in private bills and resulting responses by means of more generic legislation. The 83rd Congress (1953-1954) established the first major trend when 190 laws were enacted waiving grounds of exclusion. One hundred fifty-seven of these related to criminal grounds. This trend continued during the 84th and 85th Congresses (1955-1958), when the number of waivers substantially increased, primarily in the criminal and health areas. Of the 1,355 waivers enacted during this trend (1953-1958), 700 were due to criminal offenses, and 578 were health related. This period accounted for 71% of the waivers for criminal grounds and 77% of health waivers during the 100 Congresses.

Legislation in 1957 granted discretionary authority to the Attorney General to waive the exclusions based on moral turpitude and prostitution in cases of family reunification as well as fraud waivers. The 1957 legislation reduced the number of exclusion bills for all of those categories from 360 in the 84th Congress (1955-1956) to 183 in the 85th Congress (1957-1958) to 23 in the 86th Congress (1959-1960).

The waiver of these grounds represented 47% of all exclusion laws in these Congresses and 20% of the total number of private laws across all categories for these Congresses.

The second trend demonstrating the relationship between private legislation and public laws involved bills waiving health grounds. Legislation in 1957 allowing discretionary authority for the Attorney General to waive the tuberculosis exclusion for close relatives of citizens or permanent residents resulted in the reduction of private bills for this purpose from 186 in the 85th Congress (1957-1958) to 13 in the 86th Congress (1959-1960). During the high period of bills waiving tuberculosis (84th Congress and 85th Congress: 1955-1958) when there were 397 private laws, these cases represented 22% of all waiver bills and 14% of all private laws enacted in those Congresses. In 1965 the same waiver authority was extended on behalf of mental retardation for close relatives of citizens or permanent residents. In the period of the 84th through the 88th Congress (1955-1964), there were 244 waiver bills for mental health conditions on behalf of relatives of citizens or permanent residents. This represented 13% of the total waiver laws, and 6% of all laws enacted during that time. After the 1965 Act there were only seven private bills for exclusion in the 89th Congress (1965-1966).

The third illustration of private bills resulting in public legislation occurred in 1981, after a surge of private bills relating to drug waivers in the 94th and 95th Congresses (1975-1978). During that time, 29 private bills for drug exclusions were enacted into law which represented 73% of the exclusion laws during that timeperiod. After the 1981 Act, there were only three private laws for drug violations through the 100th Congress (1987-1988).

Categories of Exclusion Relief

The private bills for exclusions involved primarily three broad categories on behalf of close relatives of United States citizens or permanent residents: waivers of the criminal offenses, waivers of the health grounds, and "special exemption" waivers. Of the 1,843 exclusion waiver laws in the 100 Congresses, there were 982 (53%) which related to criminal grounds on behalf of close relatives of United States citizens or permanent residents, and within that category 712 laws (74%) involved moral turpitude and other related crimes, 66 laws (7%) involved drugs, 186 laws (19%) involved fraud, and 18 (2%) involved smuggling.

In the second category, health waivers, there were 750 laws (41%) of which 308 (41%) were for waivers for mental retardation and 442 laws (59%) for tuberculosis.

The third category involved special exemption waivers which totaled 88 laws (5%) and those included 42 waivers for draft evasion, 35 Communist Party membership, and 11 for illiteracy. Other miscellaneous bills included 23 cases.

Historical Parallels: The War Years and Their Aftermath (1940-1960)

When private bills began to increase in the 80th Congress (1947-1948), one of the first areas illustrating the relationship between public legislation and private bills occurred during deliberations on proposals on Communist Party membership exclusions when mention was made of private bills on behalf of Arthur Koestler and Victor Kravchenko. The latter was the author of a book entitled "I Chose Freedom," and both were Communists for many years and were excludable under law. As Mr. Frank Chelf (D-KY) stated during Joint House and Senate Judiciary Committee hearings on the legislation in 1951:

> The Committee has recognized what you have to say about that particular type of people and I am sure you are familiar with the fact that Victor Kravchenko had a private bill passed and there is one pending now also on the other person you mentioned, Koestler.[530]

The 1951 legislation provided a waiver of the Communist exclusion for involuntary membership.

In 1954 amendments to waive the exclusion of a "petty offense" impacted many wives of servicemen. As Chairman of the Immigration Subcommittee, Mr. Walter noted in the House debate on the measure:

> it has become apparent to the Committee on the Judiciary that American consular officers are excluding entirely too many aliens on very technical grounds. Case after case has been brought before us under private legislation, in which visas are being denied to persons who committed such petty crime as theft of a loaf of bread during the famine days of 1946 in Germany, or for failure to return a ration card...or for killing and roasting a duck while on an outing, and so forth.[531]

Private bills also pointed to a need for more general legislation in 1956, when Congress tightened the requirements relating to exchange visitors in order to eliminate the use of that channel as a means of permanent immigration.[532] The 1956 legislation was enacted shortly after a veto of a private bill passed by Congress on behalf of an exchange visitor from Czechoslovakia who sought to remain in the United States employed as a metallurgical engineer. In vetoing the measure in 1955, President Dwight D. Eisenhower noted that although Congress had previously passed private bills on behalf of exchange visitors when compelling circumstances were demonstrated, the instant legislation not only undermined the program but established a bad precedent:

> I feel it is my duty to disapprove this bill and at the same time to recommend enactment by Congress of a clear statutory requirement that exchange personnel return home and remain there for a minimum period before being eligible to reenter the United States for permanent residence. Such provisions of law will protect the purposes of the exchange program, will prevent unjustifiable evasion of immigration procedures, and will establish legislative policy to guide the committees of Congress in taking action on future private bills which would set aside the general law.[533]

The 1956 legislation was widely recognized as a tool to "reduce the burden on the committees in considering private bills."[534] Commenting on Congressional action on private bills for exchange visitors in 1959, Immigration Subcommittee Chairman Walter stated:

> Both before and after the enactment of the act of June 4, 1956, the Committee on the Judiciary has not looked with favor upon private relief legislation affecting EX visitors. Its detrimental effect on the international educational exchange program was, of course, quite obvious to us...Soon after [the] veto message was received, three Senators served notice that in an effort to protect the international education exchange program, they intend to object on the Floor of the Senate to every private bill under which an EX visitor would obtain permanent residence in the United States...I believe that it is my duty to inform my colleagues in the House that under this policy, private legislation affecting the immigrant status of exchange personnel will not be favorably reported to the parent committee.[535]

Private bills relating to health hardships also demonstrated a need for general discretionary authority. In 1957 Congress enacted a temporary waiver of tuberculosis for close relatives of citizens and permanent residents. The House Judiciary Committee, in its report on the legislation, noted:

> The language of this section follows closely the language used in several hundred cases where private legislation was acted upon favorably by the Congress in cases certified to the Congress by the Department of State... It is believed that enactment of this section under which families of United States citizens and of aliens lawfully residing in the United States would be given an opportunity to be reunited is not contrary to the public interest, while it will greatly contribute to the stability of the homelife of many American and immigrant families directly affected.[536]

As a result of these amendments, the number of private bills enacted in the health area decreased, particularly those for tuberculosis which had been the largest category. The number of private law health waivers was reduced from 273 in the 85th Congress (1957-1958) to 46 in the 86th Congress (1959-1960). During the period of the 84th through the 86th Congress (1955-1960) 69% of the health waivers were for tuberculosis.

In 1965 epilepsy was removed as an exclusion ground and waivers were provided for mental retardation and previous attacks of insanity. As usual, the waivers had to be on behalf of parents, spouses, and children of United States citizens and permanent residents. In discussion of the proposal, the House Judiciary Committee indicated its reluctance to give authority for case-by-case review to the Executive, particularly because such cases presented no undue burden on Congress. As Mr. Frank Chelf (D-KY) stated during the hearings on the legislation:

> I am really not convinced that we need this sort of an approach in the law; because this committee has been, in my opinion, very, very, fair and very decent and very sympathetic...we have never turned a case down.[537]

However, the Executive Branch noted that many cases did not come to the attention of Congress through private bills, and a listing of cases denied was submitted in support of liberalizing the statute.[538] With this additional health-related legislation in 1965, there was virtually no need for health waivers on behalf of most close relatives. Health waivers only totaled 13 in the remaining Congresses.

Fraud also revealed the relationship of public legislation and private bills. In 1957 the first enactment of public legislation waiving fraud for the parents, spouses and children of United States citizens and permanent residents was passed after being highlighted through private bills, as noted by the House Judiciary Committee in its report on the legislation:

> The Committees on the Judiciary of the House and the Senate have a considerable number of private bills before them under which the conduct of such aliens, considering their family situation, would be condoned. A great number of such private bills passed the Congress and were enacted into law during the last few years. It appears to the committee that it is unfair and improper to extend the benefit of legislative relief solely to a few selected individuals who are in a position to reach the Congress for redress of their grievances. It is felt that that humanitarian approach should be extended to an entire defined class of aliens rather than to selected individuals.[539]

Private law waivers relating to fraud decreased from 73 in the 84th Congress (1955-1956) to 39 in the 85th Congress (1957-1958) and to eight in the 86th Congress (1959-1960).

This same legislation in 1957 also addressed waivers for crimes involving moral turpitude and prostitution on behalf of the parent, spouse, or child of a United States citizen or permanent resident alien. The need for waivers was evident through the large number of private bills, the majority of which reflected postwar immigration of the spouses of servicemen in Korea, Japan, and Germany ineligible for immigration due to minor offenses. In enacting the waivers for minor criminal offenses, Sen. Arthur V. Watkins (R-UT) noted during debate on the legislation that many of the cases had previously been the subject of a great deal of private legislation to accommodate the separation of families.[540] Prior to enactment of the 1957 law 360 of 674 private exclusion laws enacted in the 84th Congress (1955-1956) waived criminal offenses. In the 85th Congress (1957-1958) there were 183 of 491 exclusions related to criminal offenses. That number was reduced to 23 in the 86th Congress (1959-1960).

The three public laws relating to health waivers, criminal activities, and fraud virtually eliminated the need for private bills, while providing general relief for the larger population. The total exclusion laws decreased from a high in the 84th Congress (1955-1956) of 674 to 491 in the 85th Congress (1957-1958) to 77 in the 86th Congress (1959-1960). In the entire post 1965 period there were only 87 laws enacted relating to waiver exclusions. Yet, because the laws provided waivers only for family members, private bills were intermittently sought for those who did not qualify for waivers because they were not family members.

Exchange Visitor Visa Problems Revisited (1960s)

In 1969 the repercussions of the restrictions on the immigration of exchange visitors in 1956, mentioned above, led to 500 pending private immigration bills. As Immigration Subcommittee Chairman Michael A. Feighan (D-OH), noted during hearings on the subject:

> The inability of the act to function effectively appears to be most prevalent where medical personnel are concerned. Presently, this subcommittee has some 500 private immigration bills introduced in behalf of exchange doctors pending before it. Furthermore, members of the Judiciary Committee are approached almost daily to intercede in behalf of a community or hospital which wishes to retain exchange doctors who have completed their exchange program, but nevertheless are greatly needed in the United States.[541]

The cumbersome processing and concommitant pressures on Congress for such bills resulted in an added waiver mechanism to the prior public interest waiver of the two-year residence requirement. In 1961 a hardship waiver was added, and in 1970 new waivers included the basis of possible persecution, or "no objection" letters from the home government, as well as a skills list for admission of certain exchange visitors.[542] The no objection waiver became unavailable as a grounds for waiver for FMGs in 1976.

Drug Exclusion Hardships (1970s)

In the 95th Congress (1977-1978) the number of private bills waiving drug violations increased. Twenty-one of 28 exclusion waivers were in this category. The trend and need to address waivers in hardship cases in terms of generic legislation resulted in amendments in 1981 to vest discretionary waiver authority with the Attorney General for the spouse, child or parents of a United States citizen or permanent resident. As noted by the House Judiciary Committee report on the legislation:

> The private bills have demonstrated to the Committee that this ground of exclusion has resulted in undue hardship to many U.S. citizens...In the past 10 years the Committee has approved 34 private bills for spouses or children of United States citizens who had been convicted of a minor drug violation and had since demonstrated their rehabilitation[543]

The Committee noted that the cases which were brought to the attention of the Immigration Subcommittee related to possession of small amounts of marijuana for one's own use and, in some cases, the conviction records had been expunged. Further, it was the Committee's judgment that the denial of waiver authority for these offenses was "unreasonable and illogical, particularly when one considers that the Attorney General can currently exercise such authority for serious and even violent criminal offenders."[544]

Precedents

The exclusion precedents which are cited, as noted previously, fall into three major categories: health exclusions, criminal and/or fraud exclusions, and waivers of exclusion based on special exemptions. The latter category includes such precedents as waivers of Communist Party membership, illiteracy, and draft dodgers.

The types of relief which a private law in the exclusion group provided included such means as cancelling deportation if the person resided in the United States, requiring posting of a bond in the case of some of the health exclusions, and waiving a particular provision of law such as draft dodgers, but at the same time denying that individual any citizenship benefits.

Some of the points to note in exclusions include the generous waivers provided for spouses of United States citizens, the minor types of offenses in most cases which are waived, and the few precedents in areas such as draft dodgers, smuggling activities, and Communist Party membership waivers. In some of these areas, the limited number of bills in some categories reflected the opposition of the Executive Branch as well as reflected strong opposition of Congress to those who would place the country in jeopardy.

Other factors which are significant include the age of the alien, length of residence in the United States, and association with Armed Forces personnel. In criminal cases, the period of time since the offense and age at the time of conviction, as well as rehabilitation, are a major factor in determinations. In addition, in the health area, age and non reappearance of a particular condition, were significant factors in determining the passage of the law.

Early Congresses through the 79th Congress (1945-1946) - Exclusion bills totaled 38 during this period compared to a total of 122 private bills enacted in these Congresses (31%). The 38 laws were comprised of five waivers in the health area, 31 in the criminal/fraud group, and one special exemption (Communist Party membership case), and one miscellaneous bill. The first bill waiving a ground of exclusion on behalf of a person seeking immigration was in the 74th Congress, and related to a 28-year old native of Romania who was married to a United States citizen and had been excluded based on false statements on claims to citizenship.[545]

In the *health category* there was one case which involved a 21-year old native of Cuba who entered the United States for medical treatment as an "imbecile," and resided here for 10 years with her mother and nine siblings. It was noted "this alien could not be deported in her present condition and even if she could she has no relatives to take care of her in Cuba..."[546]

Another bill involved a 53-year old native of Italy and permanent resident who was deportable as likely to become a public charge. She had resided in the United States for 12 years and returned after a temporary visit. Seven years later she was hospitalized for psychosis with cerebral arteriosclerosis. Her husband and seven children resided legally in the United States, three of whom were native-born United States citizens. It was stated that deportation would not be easily accomplished and that although her family could not always support her "it was better to let her remain in the United States even though there was no possibility of recovering and her health condition was progressively worse."[547]

Another precedent involved a family, where the father was a former United States citizen with five children and a wife. The father had become ill and returned to the United States for a temporary visit from Canada, but failed to recover enough to return to Canada. Because he was paralyzed and could neither move nor speak, and because he had been absent from Canada for 14 years, it was unlikely that Canada would accept him or his family.[548] Another beneficiary, a 32-year old native of Iran was admitted for permanent residence but found deportable due to institutionalization for dementia and public charge concerns, since her relatives could not pay the costs. Her only relatives, a mother and two siblings, resided in the United States; and it was noted "that if there ever was a hardship case this is one."[549]

Among those bills requiring waivers due to *criminal and/or fraud* grounds was a bill for the relief of a 35-year old native of Italy under deportation based on a rape conviction in Italy at the age of 17. That rape had involved a wager between two women, that one of them could not seduce a young man, 11 years her junior. After the seduction she charged him with rape. The beneficiary was married to a lawful permanent resident with five children. It was noted that he was never arrested and not present at the time of the trial, and that separation would inflict "great hardship on the wife and five children and they would be compelled to rely on relief or be taken care of by charitable institutions."[550]

Another beneficiary, a 37-year old native of Germany, was excludable due to an arrest at the age of 18 for taking leather from a factory. After entry to the United States, the beneficiary had assisted in the arrest of persons who had stolen household goods and other property. It was noted the beneficiary did not conceal his arrest in Germany, and that the persons who testified on his behalf presented a good image of the beneficiary.[551]

A further precedent cited involved a native of England who resided with his spouse and two children and who was employed with the same company for 13 years. He was found deportable due to false statements at the time of entering the United States. His parents had been separated when he was a child and he was later adopted, but always thought of the United States as his country of birth. In acting favorably, it was noted that "while the statement that he was born in Canada was false, it is not of such a nature as to constitute a serious offense, and because of his wife, children, and position, it would be unjust hardship to deport him."[552]

Another case involved a 31-year old native of Canada and spouse of a United States citizen who was deportable due to illegal entry and who pled guilty to possession of alcohol in Canada, where he had been committed to a boys' reformatory. It was noted that during his residence in the United States he worked continuously, paid his debts and supported his family, and that deportation would thus be a "severe hardship on his wife and baby."[553]

Other beneficiaries included a family, natives of Yugoslavia and derivative United States citizens by birth, who entered the United States as sons of a United States citizen without knowledge that their father's citizenship had been canceled. The father paid to arrange a visa for his family's entry to the United States when the family members were ages 14, 16, and 19. They later went into the oyster business their father had established in New Orleans. It was noted that the beneficiaries were unaware of their illegal status, nor did it appear that they knew that their father had paid a sum of money to secure fraudulent visas.[554]

Another bill involved a native and citizen of Italy who entered the United States as a visitor and who was married a short time after arrival in the United States. There were two citizen children involved. While the law granted permanent residence, it prohibited the alien from ever becoming eligible for citizenship.[555] Another beneficiary, a 35-year old native of Italy, had deserted the ship on which he served. He was married to a United States citizen with one citizen child and served five years in the United States Army. He was ineligible for a visa due to false statements made when registering as an immigrant.[556]

In the *special exemption* category one case related to a 45-year old native of England and former member of the Communist Party who had been a candidate of that party in a London Council election. She was employed as an economic adviser in the United States and denounced affiliation with the Communist Party in a book entitled "The Dream We Lost" and several articles.[557]

80th Congress (1947-1948) - There were 25 private exclusion bills, representing 21% of the total number of bills which became law this Congress (117). Six laws were health-related and 19 involved criminal/fraud cases.

The two precedents cited on behalf of those in the *criminal and/or fraud* category included 54- and 45-year old natives and citizens of Italy, and parents of five United States citizen children, three of whom served in the United States military. They were found deportable due to their connection with a house of prostitution.[558] Another precedent related to a 42-year old native and citizen of Luxembourg married to a United States citizen who was found excludable due to theft of a piece of lead weighing 100 pounds, for which he was convicted for petty larceny.[559]

81st Congress (1949-1950) - The number of private exclusion laws began to increase this Congress. Waivers of exclusion totaled 51 this Congress, which was 10% of the total private laws this Congress (507). This included six health waivers, 38 criminal/fraud cases, six special exemptions (draft cases, Communist Party and an illiteracy case), and one miscellaneous bill.

In the *health* area, one precedent related to a 23-year old native and citizen of Britain whose mother was a United States citizen and who had been brought to the United States. The beneficiary had been drafted into the Army and served as a medical technician in China, Burma and India, and while abroad received medical treatment for epilepsy. After discharge, he left the United States to visit his father in England, but was excluded when attempting re-entry due to his affliction with epilepsy.[560] Another precedent involved a 38-year old native and citizen of Italy and spouse of a United States citizen, with a citizen child, who entered the United States for permanent residence and resided here for four years. She was later diagnosed with paranoia, the result of her first-born child dying of pneumonia.[561]

A 43-year old native of Russia and spouse of a permanent resident alien was also excluded for health reasons. The spouse had entered the United States as an immigrant and had been convicted with his wife for smuggling diamonds with a value of $8,500. The permanent resident spouse received an unconditional pardon from the President, but the beneficiary remained excluded for mental illness. Her United States citizen parents and minor child, as well as other sibling relatives, resided in the United States.[562] Another case pertained to an eight-year old native and citizen of France whose United States citizen mother and stepfather accompanied him to the United States for medical treatment for tuberculosis.[563]

Precedents for exclusion bills for those committing *criminal acts and/or fraud* included the case of a 24-year old native and citizen of Australia, and spouse of a United States citizen and war veteran, who was excluded due to theft of a pair of shoes, one handkerchief and other small articles; and the case of a 23-year old native and citizen of Germany, and spouse of a United States citizen veteran, as well as mother of two United States citizen children, who was excluded due to a conviction for breaking into a chicken coop and stealing two chickens.[564]

Other precedents involved a 33-year old native and citizen of Canada, and spouse of a lawful permanent resident, who was excluded due to a conviction for mail fraud in Canada.[565] Another was on behalf of a 24-year old native and citizen of Germany and son of United States citizen parents who was excludable for a conviction of food theft. His parents had immigrated to the United States and intended to return to Germany and bring the beneficiary to the United States, but could not travel due to the outbreak of World War II. They later learned that the beneficiary lost a leg in Russia while in the German Army.[566]

In another case, a 28-year old native and citizen of Mexico, and spouse of a United States citizen with two United States citizen children, had been deemed ineligible for a visa due to his committing perjury in attempting to immigrate. It was stated that his spouse was on relief and was in "serious need of support from her husband for herself and children."[567]

An interesting case involved a citizen of Austria and spouse of a United States citizen, who claimed a relationship to George Washington, the first American President, through his half-brother. It was noted, however, that there was "no documentary evidence to support this claim of relationship . . .[and] the alien has made many conflicting statements concerning his origin and his present and past activities." He had been found excludable due to a conviction of a felony for passport alterations.[568]

Another beneficiary, a 36-year old native of Canada whose brother was a United States citizen, was ineligible for a visa due to a conviction for illegally trespassing at the age of 16 while looking for empty bottles.[569] Similarly, another case involved a 78-year old native and citizen of Spain who had been a permanent resident of the United States since the age of 30, and who had resided in the United States and Spain intermittently. He had been convicted one year after entry for selling liquor without a state license.[570]

A further precedent involved a 44-year old native of Portugal, who resided in the United States 25 years and was the spouse of a permanent resident. He was found ineligible for a visa due to perjury in connection with his visa. In providing relief, the House Committee noted that he "reared seven stepchildren, [and] has a reputation of being a good workman, a good familyman, hardworking, a good provider, devoted to his wife and stepchildren."[571]

In the *special exemption* category, the first precedent relating to exclusion due to illiteracy involved a 49-year old who had four United States citizen children, and who had resided in the United States for 12 years. She had traveled to Bermuda during the Great Depression where her husband later found employment. Her two sons had served in the United States military.[572]

82nd Congress (1951-1952) - In this Congress the number of waiver bills enacted continued to increase, from 51 in the previous Congress to 75 which represented 10% of all private laws enacted this Congress (733). A total of 48 related to the criminal/fraud category, 24 health, two special exemptions (one draft case, and one illiteracy bill), and one bill was in the miscellaneous category.

Precedents waiving the grounds of exclusions in the *health* category included the case of a native of the Netherlands and spouse of a United States citizen ineligible for entry due to previous attacks of insanity, for which she was institutionalized eight years. She had been in good health until her two children died. One death occurred when she was washing clothes and the child fell into a tub of boiling water, and the second death occurred when the child swallowed a piece of copper money. It was stated she did not show any mental disturbances after treatment, and that she had two other children.[573]

Another precedent, although opposed by the Attorney General in favor of more generic legislation, related to a waiver of exclusion on behalf of a 60-year old native of Spain and widow who had experienced previous attacks of insanity. She had two United States citizen children and four United States citizen siblings in the United States. The Attorney General noted, "While the case admittedly has appealing elements, the excluding provisions of the immigration laws nevertheless were enacted for the protection of the citizenry of this country as a whole."[574]

A further case related to a mother and child of a United States citizen, ages 28 and five, natives of Britain and China, who were barred from entry due to the mother's infection with tuberculosis.[575] Another case included a 35-year old native and citizen of Germany who suffered a nervous breakdown when separated from her family who had immigrated to the United States and later became citizens. She spent eight years in a hospital in England and at the end of which she was deemed cured.[576] Also, a native of Switzerland and son of United States citizens, was ineligible for a visa because at the age of 6 weeks he was given improper medication, resulting in brain damage.[577]

Precedents involving exclusion based on commission of *criminal and/or fraudulent* acts included that of a 33-year old native and citizen of Great Britain and spouse of a United States citizen, with a citizen child, who was convicted for crimes of theft, forgery, and fraud in Canada. He served in the Canadian Army from 1941 to 1945. The Attorney General noted that insufficient facts appeared to warrant enactment.[578] Another precedent involved a 28-year old native of Germany and spouse of a United States citizen with a citizen child who was excludable due to a conviction for selling flour and sugar on the black market.[579] Another case related to a 26-year old native and citizen of France and spouse of a United States citizen serving in the United States Armed Forces. She was found ineligible for a visa because she had previously been married under bigamous circumstances. They had three citizen children.[580]

Other precedents included: a native of Wales and citizen of England, and spouse of a United States citizen, who had been deported on the basis of a conviction of assault resulting from a fight with three other persons;[581] a 39-year old native and citizen of Italy, and spouse of a United States citizen, who had been admitted for permanent residence and who resided in the United States for 20 years, but whose citizenship had been canceled due to management of a house of prostitution;[582] a 43-year old native of Poland and permanent resident, and spouse of a United States citizen, who had been involved in prostitution but who took care of two of her sister's children and had "effected a complete reformation and rehabilitation";[583] and a 40-year old native and citizen of Greece and spouse of a citizen who was ineligible to obtain a permanent visa because of a conviction for theft of a letter containing funds which amounted to 0.006 cents in the United States.[584]

A case in the *special exemption* category included a waiver of Communist Party membership on behalf of a 46-year old native of Hungary and citizen of Great Britain who was an author, and who "used his experiences as a Communist for the exposure of Communist methods and had continued a relentless fight against the Communist menace."[585]

***83rd Congress (1953-1954)* -** The number of private exclusion laws enacted in this Congress surged to 190, as the aftermath of war brought the need to reunify families, separated in many cases by an exclusion for minor theft. This number represented 25% of all private laws enacted in this Congress (750). The criminal/fraud category totaled 157, 29 in the health category, and three special exemptions (Communist Party membership cases), and one miscellaneous bill.

In the category of *health* exclusion private laws, one beneficiary, a 23-year old native and citizen of Belgium, was excluded from entry with his parents and siblings due to a mental defect from a childhood injury when he fell from a table at the age of three months. He could perform simple duties, but was unable to read or write adequately.[586] Another case involved a 49-year old native and citizen of Italy, and spouse of a United States citizen with two citizen children, who was ineligible for a visa due to paranoia, although he had no disturbances for 20 years.[587] Another precedent related to a three-year old son of a United States citizen who was a member of the Armed Forces. The beneficiary was ineligible for a visa due to mental retardation, and was unable to walk or speak.[588]

Precedents in the category of *criminal and/or fraudulent* acts included a 37-year old native and citizen of Italy and spouse of a citizen who was ineligible to immigrate due to a conviction for attempted homicide, when she fired shots at a young man who refused to marry her after a suit brought against him by her parents for rape was dismissed.[589] Another case involved a native and citizen of Germany, and spouse of a United States citizen, who was ineligible for a visa due to a conviction for theft when her sister climbed a walnut tree and tried to shake some nuts from the tree and fell. The beneficiary accompanied her to the police for questioning and was also charged.[590]

Exclusion grounds were waived on behalf of a 28-year old native and citizen of Canada and spouse of a United States citizen. The beneficiary had been excluded due to four different convictions for minor thefts and possession of stolen goods. The United States citizen spouse was a licensed pilot and instructor with the Civilian Air Patrol until she was injured in a crash, which resulted in the loss of a leg. They had one citizen child.[591]

Another beneficiary, a 77-year old native and citizen of Italy and former United States citizen who lost citizenship due to residence abroad, had been deemed ineligible for a visa due to theft of wheat at the age of 16. He had resided in the United States for 23 years and his spouse was a permanent resident with one citizen child.[592] Another precedent involved a 48-year old native and citizen of Italy, and spouse of a United States citizen, who was ineligible for a visa due to aiding and abetting in the theft of a chain used to hook up horse plows. Their six children and spouse were admitted for permanent residence but he was excluded.[593]

One of the first exclusion private bills to be enacted in Congress waiving ineligibility due to prostitution related to a 22-year old native and citizen of Cuba and spouse of a United States citizen.[594] Another beneficiary, excluded due to fraud, was a 33-year old native of Latvia and spouse of a permanent resident, who was refused a visa due to concealing his membership in the Baltic Legion when applying for admission as a Displaced Person.[595] Another case involved a 33-year old native of Germany and spouse of a United States citizen in the Armed Forces who was ineligible for a visa due to a conviction for abortion.[596]

Other precedents included a 43-year old native and citizen of Italy and former permanent resident who had resided in the United States for 20 years. On a visit to Canada he was convicted for armed robbery and deported to the United States where he resided another 15 years with his United States citizen father, before being ordered deported to Italy due to the robbery conviction.[597] Another case involved a family, natives of Romania, Czechoslovakia, and Germany (ages 47, 40, 13, 9, 7), who entered the United States as Displaced Persons, but it was later learned that the husband had been previously deported and had misrepresented that fact.[598]

A 46-year old native and citizen of Holland and former permanent resident was excluded due to entry without documents after a trip to Holland. He was the president of a textile mill in Massachusetts and had one United States citizen child.[599] Another case involved a 57-year old native and citizen of France and former permanent resident deportable based on fraudulent statements in connection with visa applications. The statements were made because of a conviction in absentia by a political court in France for collaboration with the enemy. She had been a member of the twin council at Versaille and adhered to the Vichy Government. She was taken into custody because of that association by the Free French Forces.[600]

A private law in the *special exemption* waiver category related to a waiver for Communist Party membership. This involved a 21-year old native and citizen of Poland who escaped in a Soviet MIG 15 fighterplane and landed on the Danish island of Bornholm, "giving the technicians of the free world their first opportunity to examine an undamaged aircraft of that type."[601]

84th Congress (1955-1956) - The largest number of bills providing for waivers of exclusion occurred during this Congress when 674 bills were enacted into law of which 488 were omnibus measures. This represented 41% of the total private laws this Congress (1634). In order to address the spiraling volume of bills many cases relating to a particular waiver were rolled into omnibus measures which saved time for both Congress and the Executive Branch. The number of bills relating to tuberculosis showed a large increase from the total of 16 in the 83rd Congress to a total of 211, and the number of cases involving fraud increased from 20 in the previous Congress to 73. There were 276 bills enacted in the health category, 360 in the criminal/fraud category, 33 in the special exemption category (draft cases, and 27 Communist Party membership cases), as well as five miscellaneous cases.

In the *health* area, one precedent involved a 48-year old native of Germany, and sister of a lawful permanent resident, excluded due to a previous attack of insanity for which she was institutionalized for two years. Her brother, a United States citizen, was employed as a scientist by the United States Air Force and was her sole support.[602] An eight-year old native of Hungary was found ineligible for a visa due to a glandular disturbance which resulted in a deformed condition. His father had divorced the mother because she would not leave the child to come to the United States, and later they were remarried and both became permanent residents.[603]

Another case involved a 37-year old native and citizen of Italy who had an eye disease and whose parents were United States citizens. When discharged from medical treatment and eligible for a visa, he was over 21 and unable to immigrate as a child.[604] Another precedent involved a 65-year old native of Latvia with a mental defect who was excluded for previous mental illness. He was employed with the Latvian Evangelical Lutheran Church.[605]

Other precedents involved a 32-year old native of Germany and daughter of a United States citizen who was denied a visa due to mental retardation, and who was left behind when the family immigrated;[606] and a 20-year old native and citizen of Ireland, with 10 citizen siblings, excluded for mental deficiency, who had derived United States citizenship at birth but had been unable to meet the retention requirements.[607] Another case involved a 25-year old native and citizen of Portugal inducted into the United States Army, and who served in Korea where he received the Purple Heart. He was ineligible for a visa due to tuberculosis and could not receive permanent residence based on military service because he did not reside in the United States for one year prior to induction.[608]

Precedents for waivers in the category of *criminal and/or fraudulent* acts included those of a 79-year old native and citizen of Italy, and father of three United States citizen, who was ineligible for a visa due to a conviction at the age of 22 for assault with a dangerous weapon;[609] and a 44-year old native and citizen of Italy and spouse of a United States citizen convicted of attempted murder. The offense occurred after a promise of marriage did not take place. Her citizen spouse was employed by the New York, New Haven and Hartford Railroad for 40 years and had been injured on the job and disabled.[610]

Another precedent involved a 49-year old native and citizen of Italy, and spouse of a United States citizen, ineligible for a visa due to convictions at the age of 19 for theft of grass and fruit from an orchard. The marriage had produced five children, three of whom were citizens.[611] Another case related to a 24-year old native and citizen of Germany, and spouse of a United States citizen in the Armed Forces with one child, who was excluded due to a conviction for prostitution.[612]

Other cases included a 59-year old native and citizen of Italy who had been excluded as a result of threatening his wife's lover with a knife. He had a United States citizen brother in the United States. Another involved a 47-year old native and citizen of Italy whose spouse had three children, two of whom were United States citizens, who had been convicted at the age of 18 for exchanging gunshots in an argument concerning the affections of a girl.[613] Another precedent involved a 69-year old native and citizen of England and father of a United States citizen who had been convicted of embezzlement. He had been an officer of the British Red Cross for seven years.[614]

Another case involved a former United States citizen who had her naturalization revoked based on misrepresenting herself as one of her relatives when being admitted to the United States.[615] Another precedent involved a spouse of a United States citizen who resided in the United States for 29 years, and who had been excluded due to a conviction of embezzlement prior to entering the United States.[616] Further cases involved a 32-year old native and citizen of France who was denounced as a German collaborator in France and imprisoned, but later released and condemned to death in absentia. He returned to France and was exonerated. His spouse and three children were United States citizens.[617] Another precedent involved a 27-year old native and citizen of Mexico who was deported three times for illegal entry and who was married to a United States citizen with two citizen children.[618]

Other cases included a 42-year old native and citizen of Mexico and spouse of a permanent resident with seven children, five of whom were United States citizens, who was excluded due to fraudulently claiming United States citizenship;[619] a 29-year old native and citizen of Mexico and spouse of a United States citizen with two citizen children who had obtained a visa after fraudulently claiming United States citizenship;[620] and a native of Italy who entered the United States as a minister of religion and had been excluded because he fraudulently claimed his membership in a church where he was no longer a member.[621]

Special exemptions included those who claimed exemption from the draft or evaded military service. One case involved a native of Turkey and spouse of a United States citizen who claimed exemption from military service as a neutral alien,[622] and a 44-year old native of Spain and permanent resident of the United States for 28 years who claimed exemption but later withdrew the request.[623] In some of these cases, the Committee noted its reluctance to approve the bill but granted relief in the form of cancelling deportation proceedings rather than admit the alien to "the privilege and benefits of United States citizenship."

Also, the waivers of the ground of exclusion relating to membership in certain proscribed organizations included a 56-year old native of Poland, and father of citizens of the United States, who fraudulently attempted to impersonate his brother-in-law in obtaining an immigrant visa. The beneficiary had been imprisoned by the Nazi Government in Poland six years and was later released with the stipulation that he repatriate to countries under Soviet domination and join organizations championing their cause. It was noted in support of the bill that "liberated victims of Nazi camps cannot be made--as a rule--responsible for their short-lived membership in those organizations."[624] Another waiver for membership in an organization involved a 34-year old native of the Soviet Union who defected upon refusing an assignment to kill a Russian resistance leader in Germany.[625]

A further special exemption involved a 25-year old native of Czechoslovakia who was one of a group of Czechoslovaks who commandeered a passenger airplane and used it to escape to the West Zone of Germany.[626] In another precedent, there were 60- and 52-year old natives of Russia who had been admitted to the United States as diplomats. The male beneficiary was a former counterintelligence officer who broke with the Communist Party. He published several articles and a book entitled "The Secret History of Stalin's Crimes."[627]

85th Congress (1957-1958) - This Congress saw a substantial decrease in exclusion laws enacted, from 674 in the previous Congress to 491, which represented 43% of all laws enacted this Congress (1141). Of the 491 bills enacted, 404 were omnibus measures. The decrease in exclusion laws reflected the impact of 1957 amendments providing for a waiver of fraud, moral turpitude and prostitution excludability for the spouse, child and parents of United States citizens or permanent residents. The decreases in the area of criminal and/or fraud cases went from 360 in the 84th Congress to 183 in the 85th Congress. Also, 1954 amendments eliminating petty offenses from the criminal exclusions impacted bills in this category.

The 1957 amendment to allow a temporary waiver of tuberculosis for the same close relatives reduced the number of health exclusions for tuberculosis.

A total of 273 bills were enacted in the health area. Special exemption bills totaled 21 (draft evasion cases, Communist Party membership cases, and illiteracy bills), and 14 miscellaneous cases.

In the *health* area, the precedents primarily involved those excluded from admission based on tubercular conditions. All cases required the posting of a bond in order to overcome possible public charge aspects. One such case related to a 54-year old native and citizen of Switzerland, sponsored for admission to the United States by a priest in Colorado. The beneficiary, also a priest, was to assist the pastor, due to the "critical shortage of Catholic clergy men in the United States."[628] Another beneficiary, a 59-year old native and citizen of Russia, desired to immigrate with her parents, who were 83- and 78-years old. The father was blind and the mother was also afflicted with tuberculosis. The mother was able to obtain a waiver as the parent of a United States citizen. It was stated that because of the parents' advanced ages, the beneficiary would be able to assist them in the United States.[629]

Precedents involving waiver of exclusionary grounds involving *criminal and/or fraudulent* acts included the case of a 52-year old native and citizen of Germany convicted of embezzlement of property. A writer-producer for Warner Brothers sponsored her as an office worker.[630] Another case involved a 22-year old native and citizen of Germany and spouse of a United States citizen in the Armed Forces. They had one-month old twins and two other children. The beneficiary had been excluded due to convictions for petty larceny.[631]

Another precedent involved a family, natives and citizens of Denmark with a three-year old United States citizen child. One of the beneficiaries' occupation was acrobatics. They were denied immigrant visas due to fraudulently presenting an erroneous birthdate so that a member of the troupe could join them as acrobats in the United States.[632] Precedents also included a native and citizen of Mexico and father of six United States citizen children who was convicted of rape, and one year later married the woman who became a United States citizen.[633]

In the *special exemption* category, one case involved a waiver of exclusion for claiming exemption from military service on behalf of a 54-year old native and citizen of Finland who was married to a United States citizen. The beneficiary had four citizen brothers, two of whom served in the Armed Forces.[634]

86th Congress (1959-1960) - Private exclusion laws totaled only 77 in this Congress. The low number reflected the continuing decline of the need for exclusion legislation as a result of the 1957 waivers for criminal and health grounds. This number was 15% of all private immigration bills enacted this Congress (504). It was the last Congress that resorted to omnibus bills for private measures, with only 29 bills of this kind. The remaining basis for most of the health waivers after the 1957 amendments related to the exclusion for mental afflictions, until the 1965 generic legislation allowed waiver discretion to lie with the Attorney General, and repeal of certain health exclusions. There were 46 health related bills which became law, as well as 23 criminal/fraud bills, and eight special exemptions (draft evasion cases).

In the category of bills relating to waivers of grounds of exclusion due to *health* conditions, one precedent involved a 30-year old native and citizen of Italy who resided in the United States illegally for four years and was deported to Italy. He had been institutionalized in a mental hospital. His spouse and child were United States citizens.[635] Another case involved a 23-year old native and citizen of Ireland, and spouse of a United States citizen with two United States citizen children, who was found excludable due to an affliction with epilepsy. It was stated that she suffered the illness from childhood which had been "well controlled by drugs."[636]

Two other precedents involved beneficiaries immigrating under occupational preferences. One was on behalf of a 36-year old native and citizen of Great Britain who was ineligible for a visa due to two previous attacks of epilepsy. He had been offered employment with Bendix Corporation on patents relating to guided missiles, and had no medical problems for 10 years.[637] The other beneficiary was a 29-year old native and citizen of Poland excluded due to a tubercular condition. He had an approved petition filed on his behalf by a firm of architects, and his father was a United States citizen and his mother a lawful permanent resident.[638]

Precedents in the category of *criminal and/or fraud* waivers included a 55 year old native and citizen of Italy ineligible due to a conviction for assault with a dangerous weapon, a pitchfork, and who had a United States citizen brother residing in the United States.[639] A similar precedent related to a 33-year old native and citizen of Italy and beneficiary of a petition as an ironwork specialist. He had been convicted of rape in Italy, but was later pardoned. His parents and sister were permanent residents and another sister was a United States citizen.[640] Another case pertained to a 47-year old native-born United States citizen who expatriated himself by service in the Canadian armed forces, and who later sought reinstatement to citizenship. He was found ineligible for a visa due to convictions of setting fire to a truck and theft of an automobile battery. He had two siblings residing in the United States.[641]

A *special exemption* case involved a 35-year old native and citizen of Mexico, and former permanent resident of the United States for 14 years, who departed the United States during time of war to evade service in the Armed Forces.[642] He was married to a United States citizen with four citizen children. The Committee noted its reluctance to approve the case, but canceled deportation solely based on the hardship of the family who received public assistance.

87th Congress (1961-1962) - Laws on behalf of exclusion waivers in this Congress remained approximately the same, with a slight decrease from 77 to 69, although at this time the waiver for tuberculosis was permanently placed into law for close relatives of citizens and permanent residents and expanded to include unmarried sons and daughters of citizens. Legislation in 1961 which added waivers for exchange visitors to change to permanent status reduced the need for private bills in that category. The number of laws represented 16% of the total private laws enacted this Congress (443). There were 36 health-related laws, 27 criminal/fraud laws, and six special exemptions (draft evasion cases, Communist Party membership bills and illiteracy cases).

In the category of *health waivers,* one precedent involved a 63-year old native and citizen of Portugal and former permanent resident alien for 10 years who was found deportable due to hospitalization for dementia. Her husband had deserted her 19 days after returning to their home in the Azores, and she returned to the United States to obtain a divorce. She had two United States citizen children who served in the Armed Forces, one of whom filed a petition on her behalf. Although 30 years had elapsed since her previous attacks of insanity, she remained excludable.[643]

Another case involved a 25-year old native and citizen of China who was excluded due to feeblemindedness. Her citizen mother was formerly chief of the Anesthesia Department at the Peiping Union Medical College Hospital in China and was employed in the United States at a Veterans' Administration hospital. The Committee noted that it did not wish to deviate from the general policy of disapproving bills for feeblemindedness, but that she had few relatives in China.[644]

Another precedent involved a 24-year old native and citizen of Hungary paroled into the United States as a Hungarian refugee who was ineligible for adjustment to permanent status because he was afflicted with tuberculosis.[645]

Precedents in the category of waivers for *criminal and/or fraud* activity included one of the first waivers involving drug offenses. The beneficiary, a 53-year old native and citizen of Italy, entered the United States for permanent residence at the age of two and had resided here for 30 years, but was found deportable due to sale of morphine. His spouse and three children had been lawfully admitted for permanent residence.[646]

A case on behalf of a beneficiary excluded due to a crime involving moral turpitude involved a 32-year old native of Yugoslavia and citizen of Germany convicted of demolishing a barracks for wood, and for stealing tobacco and onions from a farm. His father was a United States citizen and his mother and sister were lawfully admitted for permanent residence.[647] A similar precedent in this area involved a 23-year old native of Yugoslavia and citizen of Italy desiring to join his permanent resident mother and twin sister in the United States. He was denied a visa due to a conviction for aggravated assault with a knife involving an attempt to protect his mother who had been attacked.[648]

One case waiving the ground of exclusion relating to visa fraud involved a 31-year old native and citizen of Greece who entered the United States based on marriage to a citizen, but it was later discovered that the marriage was annulled and he was not entitled to a visa. The beneficiary had served in the Royal Hellenic Air Force for five years and was employed by the University of Wisconsin, which filed a petition on his behalf.[649]

In the *special exemption* category one case involved a waiver of exclusion grounds due to membership in a proscribed organization on behalf of a 26-year old native of Czechoslovakia and citizen of Germany found ineligible for a visa due to membership in the Socialist Unity Party for three years. She was married to a United States citizen with a citizen child. Her spouse had served in the United States Armed Forces and continued employment as a civilian. It was stated that she had been a member of the Party in order to receive training for her employment. Although she severed her ties with the organization when leaving East Germany, she was unable to accumulate the residence period necessary to qualify for an administrative waiver.[650]

Another special exemption case involved a 47-year old native of Mexico and permanent resident convicted of burglary, and who claimed exemption from military service.[651] His spouse and eight children were permanent residents, and the Committee noted deportation proceedings were canceled based on the hardship of the family who would be deprived of his support. The Committee denied any naturalization benefits.

One case involved waiver of the literacy requirement. That law related to a 67-year old native and citizen of Turkey and widow supported by her brother. The beneficiary had been left in the care of a religious order when the family had been admitted to the United States for permanent residence.[652]

88th Congress (1963-1964) - The exclusion waivers decreased slightly this Congress, from 69 to 44, representing 24% of all private laws enacted this Congress (187). There were 29 health related cases, and 15 criminal/fraud cases.

With regard to the *health* category, a 35-year old native of England and spouse of a permanent resident, was found ineligible due to prior attacks of insanity. Because the attacks were connected to pregnancy-related depression, she had been sterilized, and had not had any attacks for 15 years. Her husband was engaged in research with Purdue

University working under grants from the National Science Foundation and the National Institutes of Health.[653]

Among those bills in the category waiving exclusion relating to *criminal and/or fraudulent* acts was a bill for the relief of a 31-year old native and citizen of Austria, and spouse of a United States citizen veteran with two citizen children, who had been convicted for fraud, theft, larceny, embezzlement and prostitution. A discretionary waiver was denied because "the beneficiary had not demonstrated any substantial reformation." He had previously been the beneficiary of a private law, but at the time of earlier enactment the INS and the Department of State had no previous knowledge of the offenses which presented obstacles to benefits.[654] Another bill related to a 25-year old native and citizen of Yugoslavia, whose mother and stepfather were United States citizens, who was excludable due to a conviction of assault with a dangerous weapon when he was involved in a brawl, attempting involvement with some ladies.[655]

One case waiving exclusion due to fraud involved a 55-year old native and citizen of Hungary who was ineligible for a visa as a minister of religion due to fraudulent certification of his credentials as a rabbi. Although he was educated as a rabbi he had lost his certificate and had another prepared by unauthorized authorities. A United States citizen brother resided in the United States.[656] Another case involved a 32-year old native and citizen of Mexico and spouse of a United States citizen with three citizen children, including one child who was mentally retarded and handicapped. He was excluded due to entering the country by falsely claiming citizenship. He served for one year in the United States Army and had been unable to proceed to Mexico for a visa due to financial difficulties.[657]

89th Congress (1965-1966) - Laws in the exclusion area during this Congress decreased substantially from 44 in the previous Congress to 22, which represented 9% of all private laws enacted this Congress (246). This reflected the impact of the 1965 amendments, which enacted general waiver authority for health exclusions for mental retardation and insanity on behalf of spouses, parents and children of citizens and permanent residents, and eliminated epilepsy as a bar to admission. The number of health exclusions went from 29 in the previous Congress to seven, and there were 15 criminal and/or fraud cases. The number of private laws enacted continued to decline through the 100th Congress, with the numbers never reaching above the total for the 89th Congress, except for the 95th Congress (1977-1978), when enactment of drug waivers brought the total of exclusion laws to

28. Moreover, the 1960's reflected changing social norms regarding drugs, and private bills became the means of overcoming the exclusion, until general legislation provided a limited waiver in 1981.

There were two exclusion precedents in the *health* category. One beneficiary was a 20-year old native and citizen of Italy ineligible for a visa due to feeblemindedness and whose father was a citizen, and mother and seven siblings were permanent residents. The beneficiary resided in Italy with her aunt and 77-year old grandmother, and was supported by her parents.[658] Another beneficiary was a 48-year old native of Poland and citizen of France who had a prior attack of insanity. She was the only survivor of her immediate family who suffered persecution during World War II and had experienced severe depression as a result. Her prognosis for recovery was good. Her spouse was the beneficiary of a petition along with their two children.[659]

Precedents relating to the category of *criminal and/or fraud* waivers included a 66-year old native and citizen of Mexico, and spouse of a United States citizen with six United States citizen children, who was arrested for possession of 50 grains of cocaine and had been deported to Mexico. His spouse had been convicted of alien smuggling and served five months in jail.[660] A similar precedent involving narcotics related to a 63-year old native of Poland and citizen of Colombia convicted of illegally dealing in drugs for which he was deported. His spouse and four children were lawful permanent residents, and they had a citizen child.[661]

Another case involved a previous fraudulent marriage for visa purposes involving a 31-year old native and citizen of Greece whose spouse and daughter were United States citizens.[662] A smuggling case related to a 36-year old native and citizen of Mexico who entered the United States for permanent residence, and was later convicted along with her husband for importing aliens for prostitution and assisting contract laborers to enter the United States.[663] Another case involved a 31-year old native and citizen of China who falsely entered the United States as the son of a United States citizen due to misinterpretations of the immigration laws relating to Hawaii.[664]

90th Congress (1967-1968) - The number of bills waiving exclusion grounds continued to decline in this Congress, reflecting amendments to the general law in 1965. Waivers laws totaled 10, which was 5% of all private laws enacted this Congress (216). There were nine criminal/fraud-related cases, and one special exemption relating to illiteracy. A number of cases involved smuggling, but these primarily addressed families where the principal alien was the sole provider for the family.

One precedent in the category of waiving *criminal and/or fraudulent* activity related to a beneficiary who was a 35-year old native and citizen of Great Britain employed by a pharmaceutical manufacturing company. He was an "internationally known and widely respected scientist" and was formerly married to a United States citizen. He had been excluded due to evasion of duty on a watch.[665] Another beneficiary, a 42-year old native and citizen of Mexico, was refused an immigrant visa because he had smuggled aliens into the United States. He and his spouse resided in Mexico with four children, and their fifth was a permanent resident alien.[666] A precedent involving drug possession involved a 34-year old native and citizen of Japan, and spouse of a United States citizen in the Armed Forces, who had been convicted for larceny and had a narcotics violation involving 0.0192 grains of heroin.[667]

The *special exemption* category included a waiver of illiteracy on behalf of a 67-year old native and citizen of Greece and widow, whose only close relative was a United States citizen who had contributed to her support for 30 years.[668]

***91st Congress (1969-1970)* -** This Congress had 13 laws on behalf of beneficiaries seeking waivers of exclusion, which was 12% of all private laws enacted this Congress (112). There were three health-related cases, seven criminal/fraud cases, and three special exemptions for illiteracy.

In the *health* category illiteracy was waived on behalf of a 54-year old native and citizen of Portugal who was afflicted with spinal meningitis at the age of three, and which left her a deaf mute. She was supported by four siblings, three of whom were United States citizens.[669]

The precedents for waivers in the category of *criminal and/or fraudulent* acts included that of a 42-year old native and citizen of Austria who resided in the United States for 12 years as a ski instructor and was excluded due to theft of a drill and other tools.[670]

92nd Congress (1971-1972) - Few exclusion bills were enacted in this Congress. Only 9 bills became law, which represented 15% of the total number of private laws enacted this Congress (62). There were two health waiver laws, six criminal/fraud cases, and one special exemption for illiteracy.

In the category of *health* exclusion, one case also waived illiteracy on behalf of a 54-year old native and citizen of Italy who was denied a visa due to mental retardation resulting from spinal meningitis. Her United States citizen sister and brother supported her.[671]

Among the precedents due to *criminal and/or fraud* activity was the case of a 49-year old native and citizen of Hungary employed as a physician who had been convicted 12 years previously for forging a false prescription for narcotics (morphine).[672] Another precedent involved a 23-year old native and citizen of Canada and spouse of a United States citizen, with two citizen children, who was deported from the United States for a conviction of possession of marijuana for which he was later pardoned.[673]

Another case involved a 30-year old native and citizen of China, convicted of two counts of armed robbery at the age of 16 and whose parents were a United States citizen and a permanent resident. He had four siblings, three of whom were lawful permanent residents and one of whom was a United States citizen.[674] Still another bill related to smuggling, and that was on behalf of a 61-year old native and citizen of Mexico with a United States citizen spouse and five children.[675]

93rd Congress (1973-1974) - In this Congress there were only four bills enacted involving exclusion waivers which represented 7% of the total number of laws enacted this Congress (61). There was one case related to health and three related to criminal and/or fraud.

One precedent in the category of *criminal and/or fraud* was that of a 53-year old native of Germany and citizen of Canada and former permanent resident alien who was deported for engaging in prostitution. She resided in the United States with her United States citizen mother, who suffered from hypertension and arthritis.[676]

94th Congress (1975-1976) - There were 12 bills which became law in this Congress waiving exclusionary grounds. This was 12% of all laws enacted this Congress (99). There were 10 criminal/fraud cases, one health case, and one special exemption (draft evasion case). Cases providing waivers on behalf of drug cases continued to increase from eight in this Congress to 21 in the next Congress, until generic legislation was enacted providing a limited waiver for drug offenses.

In the *health* category, one case involved two waivers, one due to mental retardation as well as illiteracy, on behalf of a 53-year old native and citizen of Italy who resided with her United States citizen sister. Her father was a United States citizen and died 10 days after the beneficiary's arrival in the United States.[677]

Among those precedents relating to exclusion on behalf of persons involved in *criminal and/or fraud* activity, primarily in the drug area, was that of a 24-year old native and citizen of Great Britain who was admitted for permanent residence and subsequently returned to England. In seeking re-entry to the United States she was found ineligible for a visa due to drug possession. She had suffered injuries in a car accident in the United States, which had contributed to her involvement with marijuana and had led to theft to support her habit. Her father was a United States citizen and she was married to a citizen with a citizen child.[678] Another drug-related precedent involved a 47-year old native and citizen of England and spouse of a citizen convicted at the age of 23 for possession of three grains of cocaine, 161 4/5 grains of heroin and morphine.[679]

Other drug-related precedents included a 46-year old native and citizen of Great Britain and spouse of a United States citizen who entered the United States for permanent residence, and who was found deportable 11 years later for possession of marijuana which record was later expunged.[680] A 32-year old native and citizen of England and spouse of a citizen was also found excludable due to a conviction for possession of 19.8 grains of marijuana. The beneficiary's spouse desired to return to the United States because of the illness of both parents, one of whom was undergoing treatment for cancer and the other suffered from Parkinsons disease.[681]

Another bill related to exclusion based on an attempt to immigrate on the basis of a fraudulent marriage. The beneficiary was a 27-year old native and citizen of Portugal and spouse of a United States citizen with a citizen child. It was noted that "The Committee does not wish to condone such reprehensible behavior but believes that the bill should be approved solely on the basis of hardship which is being caused to the beneficiary's second wife and child."[682]

In the *special exemption* category, one of the first over a long period of time, waived the ground of exclusion relating to those who sought to evade military service. The law was on behalf of a 55-year old native of the United States and citizen of Peru who was born in the United States to diplomat parents. He was admitted for permanent residence, lived in the United States for three years, and then was employed by Rubber Development Corporation, an agency of the United States Government. He subsequently applied for relief from United States military service. He then remained in the United States for 30 years in diplomatic service, after having relinquished permanent residence, until the termination of his diplomatic position when he requested political asylum. He was married to a United States citizen for 25 years and had four citizen children.[683]

95th Congress (1977-1978) - There was a substantial increase in the number of bills waiving exclusionary grounds in this Congress. They rose from 12 in the 94th Congress to 28 in this Congress. The most dramatic increase involved 21 bills waiving drug offenses. The total of 28 bills represented 20% of all private laws enacted this Congress (139). There were two health related waiver cases, 24 criminal/fraud waivers, and two special exemptions for illiteracy.

Two precedents are cited involving waiver of *health* conditions. One involved a 31-year old native and citizen of Italy who was inadmissible due to mental retardation and whose United States citizen sister contributed $100 per month for support. His parents, a United States citizen and lawful permanent resident, had died.[684] Another case related to a 43-year old native and citizen of Ireland excluded due to mental retardation and illiteracy. He had been employed previously for 21 years as a bookbinder and had no relatives in Ireland. He had three United States citizen sisters and one permanent resident brother in the United States who wished him to join them.[685]

Among the precedents in the category involving *criminal and/or fraudulent* activity was a bill for the relief of a 29-year old native and citizen of Korea and spouse of a United States citizen serving in the Army, who had been excluded due to a conviction six years previously for possession of 120 grains of marijuana.[686] Other drug-related precedents involved a 27 year old native and citizen of Australia and spouse of a United States citizen with two convictions for possession of cannabis and Indian hemp seeds; and a 22-year old native and citizen of Korea and spouse of a United States citizen serving in the Army convicted of giving two individuals 69 tablets of valium.[687]

Another bill related to a 32-year old native and citizen of Germany, and spouse of a United States citizen serving in the United States Air Force. She had been found ineligible for a visa due to a conviction at the age of 23 for trafficking in narcotics (hashish), fraud, forgery and tax evasion. The beneficiary had received probation because of "extenuating circumstances" relating to her assistance in the investigation of the principals in the case.[688]

In other areas of *criminal/fraud* exclusions, one beneficiary, a 28-year old native and citizen of Mexico and spouse of a citizen with a citizen child, was excluded due to smuggling aliens into the United States, an offense for which he had been deported.[689] Another precedent involved a 46-year old native and citizen of Italy, and beneficiary of a petition filed by her sister, who had two convictions for theft of firewood.[690]

Two bills in the *special exemption* category related to waivers of inadmissibility due to illiteracy. One beneficiary was a 80-year old native and citizen of Italy whose United States citizen friend cared for her since the death of the beneficiary's mother.[691] Another bill related to a 79-year old native and citizen of China who resided with her United States citizen godson for 16 years after the death of the godson's mother.[692]

96th Congress (1979-1980) - The number of exclusion laws decreased substantially from the previous Congress. The number of waiver laws totaled three, out of a total of 82 private laws enacted this Congress. There was one health-related law and two involving criminal/fraud activity.

97th Congress (1981-1982) - There was one law waivering exclusion relating to criminal/fraud, of 40 bills enacted this Congress. The number of drug-related bills was curbed substantially due to 1981 amendments which allowed a waiver for 30 grams or less of marijuana on behalf of the spouse, child, or parent of a United States citizen or permanent resident.

A bill considered a precedent in the *criminal and/or fraudulent* category related to a 35-year old native and citizen of Germany excluded due to two counts of assault with a deadly weapon during a jealous rage at the age of 25. He was supported by his United States citizen mother until joining the German Navy at the age of 17, and she desired to have him with her in the United States.[693]

98th Congress (1983-1984) - Private waiver laws totaled two this Congress, of a total 35 private laws. One waiver involved health exclusions and one involved criminal/fraud activity.

99th Congress (1985-1986) - In this Congress there was only one private exclusion law, a health-related case, out of 15 private laws this Congress.

100th Congress (1987-1988) - Four laws were enacted for waivers in this Congress out of a total of 21 laws. There were was one health related case, and three related to criminal and/or fraud activity.

One case in the *criminal/fraud* category related to a 37-year old native and citizen of Korea and widow of a United States citizen.[694] She had been convicted of possession of 50 grains of marijuana ten years previously. There were two United States citizen children. For the first time, the Congress suspended deportation for two years requiring establishment of good moral character and rehabilitation prior to granting relief. In an interesting case related to the stepson of Senator John Warner (R-VA), and the natural son of his spouse, actress

Elizabeth Taylor, stepson Michael Wilding, a native and citizen of Great Britain, had been convicted of possession of 13.6 milligrams of cannibas when he was 21.[695]

NATURALIZATION

Historical Perspective

The naturalization statutes primarily address the uniformity of the naturalization process, the transmission of citizenship to those born abroad, and accommodation of international travel needs of employees working for the United States Government or other United States businesses. These laws have also been responsive to wartime measures through narrowing or liberalizing provisions. Additionally, they have been used to reward those who have performed military service for the United States. The bestowing of citizenship has been based on two concepts: the granting of a benefit through special exemptions and the responsibilities of this country to protect those who have acquired United States citizenship.

The Early Years

As with other laws, United States laws concerning citizenship are derived from British law. The first principle adopted, that of *jus soli* -- whereupon a person's nationality is determined by his place of birth-- emerged from common law, which had been particularly suited to isolated English society. As the decline of feudalism and increased trade led to travel overseas, English law then set forth conditions from the Romans for the transmission of citizenship to children of English parentage who were born abroad. This was the principle of *jus sanguini*, the "right of blood" or parentage through descent. The founding fathers generally accepted this means of providing a homogeneous nation without the necessity of specificity in the Constitution until after the Civil War.[696] The Fourteenth Amendment resolved many of the questions of the citizenship of freed black slaves.[697] Treaties also were effected ruling on the naturalization in other countries.[698]

Among the first concerns of the settlers to America involved the King's attitude toward the colonies. The Declaration of Independence charged that the King had "endeavored to prevent the population of these States; for that purpose obstructing the Laws for Naturalization of Foreigners."[699] At that time, England adhered to the principle that the colonists remained British subjects.[700] Moreover, the Articles of Confederation in 1778 held that citizens of each state were citizens of every other state.[701] Absent federal laws, this meant that each state had its own rules on immigration which in essence encouraged the entry of newcomers.[702] Naturalization standards of the individual states also varied, and this situation became unwieldy when some states granted citizenship to immigrants, thereby forcing others to accept them,[703] leading to "the intrusion of obnoxious aliens through other states."[704]

When the Constitution became effective in 1789 all citizens of the 13 original states were held to be United States citizens.[705] The principle of *jus soli* continued. Additionally, Article I of the Constitution granted Congress the power to "establish an uniform Rule of Naturalization"[706] throughout the United States.

One of the first acts of Congress in 1790[707] addressed the Article I uniform rule. It provided for the naturalization of "any alien, being a free white person." It set a uniform residence requirement for naturalization at two years, at least one of which had to be within the state; provided for the oath of allegiance calling for "support of the constitution;" and required that the applicants possess "good character." Power to naturalize was vested in common law courts. One of the major concerns addressed in the legislation related to *jus sanguinus*: "The case of children of American parents born abroad ought to be provided for, as was done in the case of English parents, in the 12th year of William III."[708] Accordingly, the Act of 1790 provided for transmission of citizenship to children born abroad to American citizens, but limited the conferral rights to fathers who had previously resided in the United States.[709] These requirements, allowing transmission of citizenship through only the father, remained in place until 1934.[710] The 1790 Act also provided that the children of naturalized citizens under the age of 21 at the time of naturalization and dwelling in the United States were to be citizens.

Five years later, Congress raised the residence requirements for naturalization to five years, and also required that the applicants declare an intention to seek citizenship.[711] An applicant for naturalization also had to renounce forever "all allegiance and fidelity to any foreign prince, potentate, state or sovereignty" where the alien may be a citizen or subject. Barred from citizenship were those convicted of joining the army of Great Britain during the War of Independence.

During an era of anti-alien sentiment, and when relations with France during the French Revolution were strained, Congress sought new limits on naturalization.[712] In 1798 the residence requirement was raised to 14 years, with five years in a state.[713] Various other acts passed by Congress attempted to rid the nation of persons who could be dangerous to it.[714] As sentiment toward immigration became more relaxed, the residence requirements were returned to five years in 1802.[715]

The first statutes involving the ability of married women to obtain citizenship were enacted and patterned after British law in 1855.[716] Although these laws never involved single women,[717] the nationality of married women had been held to conform to that of the husband for purposes of political unity.[718] The law provided for the automatic United States citizenship of an alien woman upon marriage to a United States citizen. Similarly, a United States citizen woman was deemed to have expatriated herself upon marriage to an alien.[719] Gender remained an obstacle to naturalization of women until 1922, after the suffrage movement and successful ratification of the Nineteenth amendment.[720]

The citizenship status of some native-born persons such as Indians, "Negroes, and Orientals" remained questionable particularly after the Civil War. After the Civil War, in 1866,[721] Congress provided that all persons born in the United States, excluding Indians, were declared to be citizens. Two years later the Fourteenth Amendment, indicated below, declared all persons born in the United States as citizens:

> All persons born or naturalized in the United States and subject to the jurisdiction thereof, are citizens of the United States and of the State wherein they reside.[722]

African natives became eligible for naturalization laws in 1870.[723] The heavy influx of Chinese nationals, whose "undesirable qualities" were declared a menace to immigration, diminished chances for revision of the naturalization laws for them and other nationalities.[724] Subsequent immigration laws, in fact, became more restrictive toward the Chinese as well as other Asians, making them statutorily ineligible to citizenship and excluding them from immigration.

Towards the end of the 19th century, the process of naturalization as well as the protection of citizens abroad was the focal point of concern. For example, President Ulysses S. Grant's message at the beginning of the Congress in 1869 pointed out a high incidence of fraudulent naturalizations, and concerns about those who became citizens solely to avoid military service or taxes in their own country.[725] United States diplomats were instructed to examine claims for protection abroad of United States citizens who sought to use their status as Americans as a deterrent for carrying out some of those obligations in their native country.[726] The expatriation of citizens who resided abroad for long periods of time and subsequently sought protection from the United States for themselves and their children also continued to raise concerns.[727]

As indicated above, by 1882, the steady immigration of Chinese led to prohibitions on their admission to the United States, as well as citizenship from 1882 through 1943.[728]

The lack of uniformity in the role of the Federal and state courts in performing naturalization, in addition to widespread fraud, resulted in the appointment of a Commission on Naturalization in 1905.[729] Many courts, in fact, naturalized large groups of aliens on the eve of political elections regardless of whether the aliens met statutory requirements.[730] Varying evidentiary documents, forms, and records also reflected a need for consistency.[731] The Act of June 29, 1906[732] vested administrative supervision of naturalization in a Federal agency, while the courts retained power for final grant or denial of citizenship. Uniform forms and fees were required and knowledge of the English language. The applicant had to provide two witnesses who could testify to their character. The Act also provided for penalties for those persons who committed fraud in the acquisition of United States citizenship and barred from naturalization any person who was opposed to organized government or affiliated with any such organization advocating the overthrow of such government.

In 1907, as a result of recommendations by the Citizenship Board of the Department of State to correct "embarrassing questions" concerning citizens abroad and their protection by the United States Government, Congress enacted several expatriating provisions.[733] The first basis for expatriation was naturalization in a foreign state. Another basis was residence by a naturalized person for two years in the country from which he came, or for five years in any other country. Such loss of citizenship, however, could be overcome upon evidence of the temporary nature of the abode abroad. The new law also held that no United States citizen could be allowed to expatriate in time of war.

As already mentioned, the 1907 Act's fourth basis for expatriation involved women who married aliens, who were held to have taken the nationality of the husband.[734] Most of these expatriating provisions remained in the statutes throughout the 20th century, until overturned by the United States Supreme Court 71 years later and repealed by Congress.[735]

Another area that the 1907 Act addressed involved the issue of protection of children born abroad to a United States citizen and an alien parent. It retained provisions for derivative citizenship upon naturalization of the parent, but required the child to be residing permanently in the United States. Children who acquired citizenship at birth through the father were required to declare their allegiance before a consular officer before the age of 18.

In 1873 Secretary of State Hamilton Fish had described the "cloak of citizenship":

> the Congress did not contemplate the conferring of the full rights of citizenship upon the subject of a foreign nation who had not come within our territory, so as to interfere with the just rights of such nation...[736]

With the onset of war, and the increased presence of the United States overseas for both military purposes and business ventures, many of the subsequent naturalization statutes related to special exemptions from the residence requirements.

World War I brought about special exemptions from the naturalization residence requirements on behalf of many noncitizens who had served in the Armed Forces. Aliens who had served prior to 1900 were provided waivers of residence. Also, aliens who served during World War I, and those honorably discharged before the war's end were relieved from the residence requirements for naturalization. Seamen exemptions from the naturalization laws covered those who served three years on board United States vessels, whether public or private.[737]

The Act of 1924[738] rendered ineligible to citizenship aliens who had previously been excluded in 1917. That group, therefore, was forever barred from both entry and citizenship. It included the Chinese and Japanese nationals who had been the subject of previous legislation,[739] as well as those from the barred zone defined in the Act: Burmese, Koreans, Malayans, Polynesians, Tahitians, and Samoans. The prohibitions remained substantially intact until repealed in 1952, except for ancestry.[740]

In 1934[741] American mothers were extended equal rights to transmit citizenship by descent to their children born abroad, a right which previously allowed only by the American fathers. A child born of two United States citizen parents was conferred citizenship if either had resided in the United States. In addressing concerns that a child who derived citizenship through the marriage of a citizen parent and alien might be born into a home of divided allegiance, the statute held that in order to retain such citizenship the child had to return to the United States for five years immediately prior to the 18th birthday, and take an oath of allegiance within six months after the 21st birthday in order to retain citizenship.[742] The only restrictive element in the 1934 Act related to increasing the period of residence for citizenship for spouses of United States citizens from one to three years.[743]

In 1936 Congress added special exemptions from the residence requirements of the naturalization law on behalf of persons engaged in "advancing American interests abroad."[744] Aliens who traveled abroad as employees of the United States Government, or under contracts engaging in foreign trade and commerce of the United States, or aliens conducting research for an American institution, could obtain a waiver of part of the residence period. Reinstatement to citizenship was also granted in 1936 to women who had lost citizenship due to marriage prior to 1922.[745] Clergy received special waivers of the residence requirement by the Act of August 9, 1939.[746]

Uniform Rules and Expatriating Provisions (1940s)

The first major codification of the naturalization laws occurred in 1940,[747] following a five-year study by a Cabinet Committee whose task involved making recommendations so that the statutes would be uniform and "facilitate the naturalization of worthy candidates, while protecting the United States against adding to its body of citizens persons who would be a potential liability rather than an asset."[748] The Act outlined which classes of individuals were deemed to be citizens of the United States, specified who could become citizens by naturalization, set forth the procedure by which a person could become naturalized, and outlined the circumstances under which citizenship could be lost or regained. The major areas which the law changed related to stricter requirements for derivative citizenship, and an expansion of the expatriating grounds.

The first area of significant policy change involved conferring derivative citizenship automatically to children born abroad, as well as upon naturalization of the parents. The 1940 Act set forth stringent residence requirements for transmission of citizenship in the case of children born abroad to one citizen parent and an alien parent. The citizen parent was required to have resided in the United States 10 years, at least five of which occurred after attaining the age of 16 prior to conferring citizenship. In imposing these strict residence requirements preceding the ability to confer citizenship, the Senate Immigration Committee report on the legislation stated that the 1940 Act sought to:

> prevent the perpetuation of United States citizenship by citizens born abroad who remained there, or who may have been born in the United States but who go abroad as infants and do not return to this country. Neither these persons nor their foreign-born children would have a real American background or any interest except that of being protected by the United States while in foreign countries.[749]

In addition, according to a letter to President Franklin D. Roosevelt from the Secretary of State, the Attorney General, and the Secretary of Labor in 1938, the 1940 Act was justified in light of:

> there were important reasons for ending United States citizenship when persons have resided abroad long periods of time, virtually abandoning the United States...it will prevent them from transmitting American nationality to their foreign born children having little or no connection with the United States, and embroiling this Government in controversies which they may have with the governments of foreign countries in which they reside.[750]

The retention of citizenship requirements for children born abroad of different nationalities changed slightly so that return to the United States for five years was required between the ages of 13 and 21, and that residence had to be established prior to age 16. Exemptions included children whose parents were employed regularly abroad with the United States Government, or with American organizations.[751]

The 1940 Act also modified derivative naturalization provisions. The Act required that the child must have been permanently residing in the United States. Also, the age before which the child had to return to the United States was lowered to 18 from 21.

The 1940 Act also provided for the first time adopted children with certain citizenship benefits which accrued to natural children, by allowing their naturalization upon petition of the citizen parent if the child was under the age of 18 and residing permanently in the United States two years.[752] The provisions for out of wedlock children were narrowed from the previous law, where citizenship was derived through the mother or father if there had been a residence in the United States. The 1940 statute provided that unless paternity was established through legitimation before the age of 21, only the mother would be able to transmit citizenship.[753]

The second area related to exemptions from naturalization requirements for spouses of United States citizens. For example, various two or three-year residence requirements were imposed for those whose marriages occurred prior to certain effective dates of previous laws.[754] In addition, spouses of citizens who were regularly stationed abroad with the United States Government, American businesses, or certain institutions received benefits waiving the residence requirements.

Armed Forces personnel serving in peacetime received similar benefits as those who had served in World War I, except that a specified aggregate period of three years was required prior to eligibility for a waiver of the residence requirements.[755] In addition, the provisions for residence waivers for religious occupations encompassed nuns.

Also, the 1940 Act modified the laws relating to expatriation, the third area of policy change, by adding new grounds for loss of citizenship to include voting in a foreign election, formal renunciation of citizenship in a foreign state, military service in another country, and employment by a foreign government.[756] Prolonged absences abroad was retained as an expatriating act. In the letter to President Franklin D. Roosevelt in 1938 from the Secretary of State, Attorney General, and Secretary of Labor, the Cabinet officials explained the basis for keeping the grounds for expatriation:

> when a naturalized citizen abandons his residence in the United States and takes up residence in the state of which he was formerly a national, definite termination of his American citizenship should follow.[757]

Most of these remained in the law until declared unconstitutional and repealed in 1978.[758]

The War Years and Their Aftermath (1940-1952)

Between 1940 and 1952 there were several liberalizing measures. In 1943 the Chinese were removed from the category of those ineligible for citizenship, thus also allowing immigration under established quotas,[759] and in 1946 Indians and Filipinos were allowed admission and naturalization.[760]

Special exemptions were continued for members of the Armed Forces through new waiver mechanisms in 1946 that allowed service in

World War II to fulfill the 10 year residence requirement for transmitting citizenship to children born abroad.[761] In 1942 and 1948 expeditious naturalization was allowed for those who had served during World War II.[762] Moreover service with allied armies was eliminated as an expatriating act in 1942.[763] On the other hand, provisions of the Selective Service Act of 1948[764] forever barred from naturalization aliens who claimed exemption from training and service and who applied for such relief.

Other postwar acts related to the ability to regain citizenship by those who had lost it through voting in elections in Italy from 1946-1948 and those who voted in Japan between 1945 and 1952, the period of occupation by the American military.[765]

The Internal Security Act of 1950,[766] enacted at a time when "considerations of national security and international conflict took precedence over all other aspects of the immigration question,"[767] addressed membership in various associations as well as the screening process for citizenship applicants. It expanded the 1906 prohibitions on citizenship for ideological reasons by extending the bar to citizenship to those affiliated with the Communist Party or who advocated its principles, unless they had resided in the United States 10 years prior to seeking naturalization. It also tightened the English language requirements so that applicants also had to be able to read and write English as well as demonstrate a knowledge of United States history and government. However, an exemption was made for permanent residents age 50 who had been in the United States 20 years on the date of enactment.

The bill was the subject of a Congressional override after vetoed by President Harry S. Truman on the basis that its provisions denying naturalization to those associated with Communist organizations were "so vague and ill-defined that no one can tell what it may mean or how it may be applied. The result might be to weaken our naturalization laws rather than strengthen them."[768]

The 1952 Act

The first significant area of change in the naturalization laws after 1940 followed a study of the entire immigration law, conducted because of the enormous number of displaced persons after World War II. Although many of the provisions of the 1952[769] law were punitive, some of the quota and naturalization provisions were liberalizing in nature. One of those was the repeal of the prohibitions to citizenship based on race. In 1950, the Senate Judiciary Committee reported after a comprehensive review of the immigration laws that racial prejudices had decreased and the "hysteria and fears of the war years" had slackened. The Committee stated:

> The time [has] come to erase from our statute books any discrimination against a person desiring to immigrate to this country or to become a naturalized citizen, if such discrimination is based solely on race.[770]

Natives of Japan and Korea were primarily involved, and the Senate Committee noted that most had been in the United States long periods of time, and that many had sons who had served in the armed forces.

> Granting them the privilege of citizenship will give recognition to their loyalty to our country, and will remove the stigma which they and their children feel as being branded as belonging to a race ineligible to become naturalized citizens.[771]

The second generous provisions in the 1952 Act related to conferral of citizenship to children born abroad. Out-of-wedlock children who were legitimated by the citizen father were not required to go through court jurisdiction. In addition, the transmission requirements for children born to a citizen and alien parent were expanded to allow half of the 10-year residence period of the citizen prior to the birth of the child to accrue after the age of 14, rather than the age of 16. On the other hand, children born out of wedlock were held to acquire citizenship if the United States mother was physically present in the United States for a continuous period of one year.

Retention requirements were also broadened so that children born abroad who acquired citizenship through birth of a citizen parent and alien parent could fulfill the five-year residence period between the ages of 14 and 28, but they had to establish residence prior to age 23. However, the special exemption from the retention requirements for children born abroad to citizens employed with the United States Government or other organizations regularly stationed overseas was eliminated.[772]

The third area providing further exemptions of the physical presence requirement related to benefits for those who were employed abroad with a public international organization. Also, expedited naturalization in certain circumstances was allowed for those employed with the Central Intelligence Agency.

The fourth area of the 1952 Act was restrictive in some respects, and related to special exemptions for residence on behalf of spouses of

United States citizens. The residence requirement for purposes of naturalization based on marriage to a United States citizen was established at three years. Prior to 1952, the number of years that a spouse had to reside in the United States prior to submitting an application for naturalization was between one and three years, dependent upon the year of marriage. The Senate Judiciary Committee indicated in its study that a uniform requirement was necessary because the prior varying waivers were prone to fraud.[773]

Also, prior waivers of residence for those performing religious duties abroad were restricted in the 1952 Act. As the Senate Judiciary Committee stated in its report:

> The Subcommittee feels that all persons in this class should be physically present in the United States for at least a year prior to leaving, even in such a professional capacity.[774]

At the same time, however, missionaries were added to the group of religious functionaries allowed to take advantage of the residence waivers.

The availability of waivers of residence on behalf of seamen continued restrictions in the 1952 Act to those who had obtained permanent residence, in order to deter shipjumping. Additionally, the declaration of intention as a prerequisite for making an application for naturalization was eliminated.[775]

Responding to International Demands and Supreme Court Decisions (1950-1990)

After the 1952 codification, special exemptions to the naturalization requirements were sporadic, and usually in response to military service, increased overseas travel, and employment of United States citizens and their families either in Government or American business abroad. Also, as noted previously, Supreme Court decisions led to modifications and repeal of certain expatriating statutes.

Special exemptions from residence periods included the Act of September 11, 1957,[776] which provided expeditious naturalization of adopted children of citizens regularly stationed abroad with the United States Government and international organizations. In 1958[777] spouses and adopted children of clergy were provided residence waivers. In 1967[778] residence periods were also waived on behalf of certain employees of United States organizations abroad involved in disseminating information. Radio Free Europe was an example of such an organization. During the 1960's exemptions from the residence periods were also accorded those who served honorably in the Armed Forces during the Korean War,[779] those who served in the Vietnam War or other hostilities declared by the President,[780] and the surviving spouses of United States citizens who died in active duty status in the Armed Forces.[781]

In 1956 transmission and retention requirements were broadened. Members of the Armed Forces who served between 1946 and 1952 were held to comply with the 10 year residence period for transmitting citizenship to children born abroad of an alien parent and citizen parent.[782] The provision was later expanded in 1966 to cover all periods of Armed Forces duty as well as employment abroad with the United States Government and certain international organizations.[783] In 1972[784] the retention requirements involving return to the United States of children born abroad of one citizen and an alien parent were reduced from five years to two between the ages of 14 and 28, and finally repealed in 1978,[785] although the Supreme Court had upheld its constitutionality in 1971 (*Rogers v. Bellei*).[786] There were allegations that its repeal would create the possibility of generations of citizens residing abroad with little, or no connection with the United States. In response, The House Judiciary Committee, in its report on the legislation, noted that such an occurrence was precluded by the transmission provisions under the act where a citizen who desired to transmit citizenship was required to have resided in the United States for 10 years prior to being eligible to confer citizenship.[787] This provision was itself changed in 1986[788] to five years of residence, of which two years were required to have been physically in the United States after the age of 14.

Provisions relating to loss of citizenship, particularly with regard to naturalized citizens whose citizenship was in jeopardy through prolonged periods abroad, were liberalized in 1959. The 1959[789] Act provided that parents of United States citizens residing abroad were exempt from the loss of citizenship provisions. Also excused were naturalized citizens who had resided in the United States for not less than 15 years before traveling abroad, as well as those who had resided in the United States for 15 years prior to age 21.

Supreme Court decisions also impacted interpretations of loss of citizenship. The Court held in 1958 that Congress could not revoke citizenship for desertion (*Trop v. Dulles*).[790] Likewise, the Court declared unconstitutional loss of citizenship by a naturalized citizen through residence abroad in 1964 (*Schneider v. Rusk*),[791] and in 1967 the Court held that United States citizenship once acquired could only be lost through voluntary relinquishment (*Afroyim v. Rusk*).[792] In 1978[793] Congress repealed many of the remaining provisions regarding loss of citizenship of naturalized aliens through residence or other voluntary acts.

The Cuban Adjustment Act of 1966[794] addressed the problem of 153,000 Cubans who had escaped from the Castro regime to the United States by granting permanent residence to that group outside the normal immigration ceilings. The retroactive nature of the legislation provided expedited naturalization for many of the beneficiaries.

In the next two decades there were various provisions relating to waivers and providing expeditious naturalization. An expanded exemption of the English language requirement was provided in 1978[795] which removed the limiting effective date provisions of the 1950 Act[796] to allow any alien 50 years of age and who had been living in the United States for periods totaling 20 years subsequent to acquiring permanent residence to take advantage of the provisions.

Other amendments in 1978[797] included the elimination of the two-year residence requirement in the United States for adopted children prior to the United States citizen petitioning for the child's citizenship. For the first time, adopted children were granted derivative naturalization upon the naturalization of an alien parent, and the age for automatically acquiring citizenship through those provisions was raised from 16 to 18. In addition, in 1981[798] expedited naturalization was provided for adopted children of United States citizen parents employed abroad. Other amendments of the 1981 Act allowed the spouse and dependent son or daughter who were members of the household of a citizen employed with the United States Government, or certain other institutions, to have part of the residence periods waived.

In 1985[799] special provisions were set forth for the expeditious naturalization of former Communist Party members, primarily defectors who had assisted the United States Government, by allowing five residence waivers per year after a minimum one year residence requirement in lieu of the 10-year prohibition. The 1985 legislation also limited the number of persons eligible for the waiver to five per year.

In 1986[800] the provisions for acquisition of United States citizenship on behalf of illegitimate children were liberalized so that the father could confer citizenship through establishing paternity. That law also provided for administrative naturalization for adopted children by allowing the issuance of certificates of naturalization.

Public Legislation and Private Bills

Although private bills relating to naturalization were the first type of private legislation to be considered by the Congress, beginning in 1839, the total number of bills enacted into law in this category is the lowest of the three groups of private bills. One reason for this is the higher standard generally applied to citizenship cases.[801] The few laws also reflect the fact that the naturalization statutes, unlike the quota laws, remained substantially the same, not requiring much deviation through special legislation. The changes in law primarily related to accommodating international travel through waivers of the residence requirement and retention provisions.

The first major area demonstrating the relationship between private bills and general legislation was reinstatement of citizenship through private bills due to voluntary loss such as voting in foreign elections. This prohibition was repealed in 1951[802] for Italy and 1954 for Japan.[803] Another area involved loss of citizenship because of residence abroad by naturalized citizens. This area was the subject of a large number of private bills, resolved through a Supreme Court decision in 1964[804] declaring it unconstitutional, as well as legislation in 1978[805] repealing the statute.

Another area involved the granting of retroactive permanent residence, thereby expediting citizenship, in the aftermath of the Cuban exodus, so that barriers to occupations requiring citizenship could be overcome. Those private bills culminated in 1966 with legislation granting permanent status to Cubans.[806]

The final area involved expansion in 1972,[807] 1978,[808] and 1986[809] of the retention and transmission requirements for children born abroad to United States citizens. This too was an area where private bills pointed to a need for reform.

In the 100 Congresses there were 695 bills relating to naturalization, which represented 10% of the total 7,266 private laws enacted. Although naturalization laws were the first types of bills Congress enacted, the numbers have never been substantial in comparison to other areas, which were given considerable weight because of the hardship of separated families. In addition, the bestowing of citizenship through a private bill became a highly privileged act, as reflected by the infrequent occasions and the highly contentious debate surrounding their process.[810]

The highest number of naturalization private laws occurred in the 90th Congress (1967-1968) when 152 were enacted. By the 93rd

Congress (1973-1974), private naturalization laws totaled less than 10 in each subsequent Congress.

Trends in Public Legislation and Private Bills for Naturalization

The majority of citizenship bills which were enacted waived the residence requirements. These types of bills were most frequent during the 89th and 90th Congresses (1965-1968). Most of these bills granted retroactive permanent residence on behalf of Cuban nationals seeking citizenship to enter various occupations, where citizenship was a prerequisite under state laws. During that period there were 259 private citizenship laws (37%) enacted, of which 128 waived the residence requirement. The second highest area of bills in the naturalization category occurred from the 85th to the 87th Congresses (1957-1962), when 154 bills were enacted. This represented 22% of all naturalization bills. During this period the largest number of bills related to residence waivers (52), and 42 related to retention of citizenship. These two periods accounted for 413 of the 695 bills enacted in the naturalization area (59%).

These trends illustrate the manner in which private bills pointed the way toward enactment of generic legislation. As already noted, as a result of the many bills enacted to retroactively grant permanent residence for Cuban nationals, legislation was enacted in 1966 to provide permanent status. Subsequently, the total number of private bills for citizenship decreased to 33 in the 91st Congress (1969-1970) from 152 in the 90th Congress (1967-1968).

Likewise, the 154 bills enacted due to residence waivers and retention of citizenship difficulties during the 85th through the 87th Congresses (1957-1962) decreased substantially to 31 in the 88th Congress (1963-1964). The decrease in retention of citizenship bills was the result of legislation in 1959 allowing persons with long residences in the United States and parents of United States citizens the ability to reside abroad without jeopardizing citizenship, as well as a Supreme Court decision in 1964 declaring the law unconstitutional.[811] For the remainder of the 100 Congresses, there were only five laws enacted for retention of citizenship.

Categories of Naturalization Relief

There were four broad categories relating to naturalization bills: loss of citizenship because of voluntary acts, the inability to confer or derive citizenship, failure to retain citizenship once gained, and the inability to meet the residence requirements for naturalization purposes.

The first category, that of loss of citizenship due to voluntary acts, included waiving the provisions of law when a person lost citizenship due to marriage to a foreign national, voting in foreign elections, or actual renunciations of citizenship. There were 89 of these cases in the 100 Congresses, totalling 13% of all citizenship private bills.

The second category related to the inability of a person to confer citizenship upon children or derive citizenship through parents because of insufficient residence periods in the United States. These cases totalled 43 (6%).

The third group involved failure to retain citizenship, which included those who lost citizenship due to travel abroad to their home country or another country for prolonged periods of time after naturalization, as well as children born abroad to a United States citizen and alien, who were required to return to the United States for a period of time to retain citizenship. There were 93 (13%) bills in this category.

The fourth area related to the failure to meet the residence requirement in the United States prior to submitting an application for naturalization. There were 364 (52%) private bills in this category.

Special exemptions of naturalization laws totaled 68 (10%). This group included draft dodger cases, Communist Party members, United States government and English requirement cases. Miscellaneous waivers of naturalization statutes totaled 38 (5)%.

Historical Parallels: Equalization for Women (1924-1934)

Some of the early indications of the impact of private bills on public legislation related to remedial legislation eliminating the loss of citizenship provisions for women who married aliens, and conversely, the gaining of citizenship of women who married American men. During hearings by the House Committee on Immigration in 1924, a discussion of private bill cases and testimony from the spouse of a woman who lost citizenship in her home country when she married a United States citizen, drew sympathy from the Committee. The United States citizen spouse noted the difficulties he and his wife encountered would "recur time without number, unless an amendment to the present act is enacted."[812] The history of the initial cases brought before Congress was described in 1933 during hearings of the Senate Immigration Committee:

> Many meritorious cases came before the committee, demonstrating clearly the inadequacy and unfairness of the laws then governing the citizenship of married women...In time the need of general remedial

legislation became apparent, and the individual cases which came before the committee finally led to the enactment of the married women's independent citizenship act of September 22, 1922.[813]

As a result of some of these cases and other legislative efforts, in 1934 American mothers were allowed to confer citizenship to their children born abroad.[814]

Through the 79th Congress (1945-1946) there were few private laws relating to citizenship. The majority of the 25 which were enacted were in two areas: voluntary loss of citizenship (7 bills) and inability to confer or derive United States citizenship (7 bills). The 1940 Act, which tightened the transmission requirements of children born abroad to United States citizens, caused a number of bills to be enacted in this area.

Expatriation and Retention of Citizenship (1950s)

In addition to the expatriating measures of 1907,[815] through which loss of citizenship often occurred as a result of residence abroad, the 1940[816] Act added voting in foreign elections as an act resulting in loss of citizenship. As a result of these provisions, the number of private citizenship laws increased slightly from 33 in the 81st Congress (1949-1950) to 45 in the 82nd Congress (1951-1952), and only subsided with special legislation reinstating citizenship for natives of Italy (1951) and Japan (1954) who had voted in foreign elections.[817] The Chairman of the House Immigration Subcommittee, Mr. Walter, explained the review of private bills for some of the expatriating acts during hearings in 1951:

> The Subcommittee of the House felt that...we could perhaps determine better whether or not people were actually renouncing allegiance through voting by considering private bills, because there are not many of them. And we felt that through that medium we could learn more about them, and whether or not they did intend to become citizens of another country...[818]

Private bills relating to inability to retain citizenship because of lengthy residence in the native country gradually decreased in number as a result of legislation in 1959 exempting parents of citizens from loss of citizenship due to residence abroad. Another exemption of the 1959 law benefited those who had resided in the United States long periods of time prior to returning abroad.[819] As indicated before, the Supreme Court decision in 1964 (*Schneider v. Rusk*)[820] and 1967 (*Afroyim v.*

Rusk)[821] also led to decline so that after that time private bills to alleviate loss of citizenship through voluntary acts or inability to retain subsided from 113 during the period of the 84th through 89th Congress (1955-1966) to four in both categories for the 90th through the 100th Congress.

Other legislation in 1952[822] allowed certain conferral of citizenship benefits, but because of the increased travel of United States citizens, private bills to waive these provisions increased from three in the 82nd Congress (1951-1952), to a total of 27 from the 83rd through the 89th Congress (1953-1966). Legislation in 1956, 1966, 1972, and 1978 virtually eliminated the need for any bills relating to conferral or deriving citizenship.[823]

National Security (1950s)

The ten-year prohibition on naturalization of members of the Communist Party which was imposed in 1950 with the Internal Security Act, resulted in a need for private legislation in some important defector cases. Even though the 1952 legislation provided waivers in some cases,[824] from 1952 through 1974, there were 15 bills waiving the naturalization laws for those who did not meet the waiver requirements.

In addition, stricter English language requirements, and the institution of a test on knowledge of the United States Government in 1950, prompted a few private bills in this area.

More recently, because of the inflexibility of the citizenship laws, in 1985 Congress provided five discretionary waivers for use by the Executive Branch for national security cases.[825] In the Conference report of the House and the Senate on that legislation, the Conferees noted:

> this authority will be used to reward those aliens who for a significant time have maintained a relationship with the United States. Only in rare instances should expedited citizenship be afforded to defectors with no previous relationship with the United States, and only after careful scrutiny should the promise of expedited citizenship be offered as an inducement for future services.
>
> The conferees emphasize that private immigration legislation remains the preferred method for processing exceptions to the Immigration and Nationality Act provisions, because it allows full Congressional consideration of the merits of individual cases...The waiver authority is meant for special kinds of situations, and it should not normally be used

as an alternative to be employed when efforts to enact private immigration legislation are unsuccessful.[826]

Cuban Adjustment of Status and Retroactive Naturalization (1960s)

Even with the substantial decrease in the number of private bills as a result of statutory changes and court decisions, the number of private citizenship cases rose from 31 in the 88th Congress (1963-1964) to a total of 107 in the 89th Congress (1965-1966) to a total of 152 in the 90th Congress (1967-1968) which was the highest number in all Congresses of naturalization laws.

The increase in private naturalization laws was primarily due to waivers of the residence requirements on behalf of Cuban nationals. The waivers of residence represented 88% of all private citizenship laws in those two Congresses, and were 33% of the total laws enacted in the naturalization area throughout the 100 Congresses. With the Cuban Adjustment Act of 1966, however, which provided permanent status for all Cubans who entered the United States in the 1960s, there was no need to resort to private bills.

The House Judiciary Committee report on the 1966 legislation outlined the problems which private bills had also highlighted:

> The Cubans' lack of permanent residence status prevents them, under the law, from accumulating the necessary residence in the United States, which is presently a prerequisite to naturalization as a United States citizen. The result is that many skilled and professionally trained individuals who would be a credit to this country are prevented from obtaining gainful employment here, either because of conditions imposed independently by employers, or because of restrictive statutes in many States which prevent the practice of one's profession, for example, as a dentist, lawyer, physician, or teacher, by one who has not acquired full citizenship or has not filed a declaration of intention.[827]

After 1968, the need for waiver of any of the citizenship laws diminished greatly.

Responding to Global Dynamics (1970s)

The remaining citizenship retention requirements were liberalized and finally repealed in 1978[828] and transmission requirements were reduced in 1986.[829] Enactment of naturalization laws from 1968 throughout the remaining 100 Congresses was sporadic, totalling only 88 bills, and mostly involving waiver of residence requirements due to international travel. Half of the bills fell in this category. The only aberration was in the 91st Congress (1969-1970) when 11 cases were enacted bestowing posthumous citizenship on behalf of Vietnam veterans. In addition, in 1978,[830] as an amendment to a private immigration bill, a waiver of the English language requirement for aliens 50 years old with 20 years residence in the United States obviated the need for some laws in that area.

Precedents

As noted previously, naturalization waivers are the lowest number of private laws enacted because of the high regard for maintaining the standards of citizenship.

The precedents in these cases involve four groups: voluntary loss of citizenship, conferring or retaining citizenship, waiver of residence requirements, special exemptions, and miscellaneous cases. The special exemptions category includes such cases as draft dodgers, English language and history tests, and Communist Party membership.

In the majority of cases, residence in the United States was already achieved, but not in the particular order which satisfied the naturalization laws. For example, some of the naturalization laws require half of the residence period prior to applying for naturalization to be "physical" presence in the United States, while the other half of the timeperiod requires "continuous" presence. Some private laws were sought to overcome either one of these requirements.

There are many other types of relief which can be provided to overcome the particular naturalization statutes needed. Some of these include retroactive permanent residence as was done in the case of many Cuban nationals; allowing the first entry to the United States to establish admission for permanent residence for purposes of residence requirements; reinstatement of United States citizenship which was lost, as well as other means of overcoming the naturalization statutes.

Some of the points to observe are that in the early years the expatriating provisions were among the most frequent to overcome, and in the later years residence requirements for parents and children due to international travel in particular occupations became more frequent. It is significant to note that in many cases there is a national interest component, the fact that the beneficiary was working in an occupation reflecting on United States interests. In addition, the lack of frequency of naturalization laws in some areas such as draft dodgers and waiver of English language or government knowledge reflects the opposition of the Executive Branch, and strong views of Congress in withholding citizenship as the most fundamental concept of the responsibilities of citizenship.

Early Congresses through the 79th Congress (1945-1946) - During this period there were few private bills relating to nationality. There were a total of 25 during this period which was 20% of all of those enacted across categories (122). There were seven involving the reinstatement of citizenship which had been voluntarily relinquished, seven relating to the inability to confer or derive citizenship benefits, one concerning the inability to retain citizenship once obtained, two waiving the residence period, one waiving special prohibitions (draft evasion), and seven involving miscellaneous provisions.

The first private laws enacted related to naturalization. In fact, it was not until 1915 that non-naturalization laws were considered by the Congress. On February 13, 1839 a private law was enacted on behalf of Dr. John Campbell White,[831] thus creating the first precedent for private relief. He had been admitted to citizenship but due to a clerical error the surname was omitted. Because the district court refused to correct the tardy notice of record, Congress declared "it is right and just that the misprision or mistake of the clerk in the entry of the said record should be corrected . .."

The second Act of Congress, again relating to naturalization, provided that the renunciation of United States citizenship in writing by Frederick Hinkel was to be accepted by the President as "equivalent in effect to the residence of two years in his former country without intent to return to the United States provided for in the fourth article of the treaty...between the United States and the North German Confederation."[832] The Congress in another early act, that of May 18, 1898, reinstated United States citizenship on behalf of Nellie Grant Sartoris, the widowed daughter of General Ulysses S. Grant who was born in the United States, and married a subject of Great Britain and immigrated to that country.[833] The statute provided that since Ms. Sartoris had returned to the United States to reside she should be unconditionally readmitted to citizenship "in accordance with the provisions of Article III of the convention relative to naturalization between the United States and Great Britain."

In the *voluntary loss* category, some of the bills dealt with reinstatement of citizenship on behalf of women who had married aliens, thereby losing United States citizenship. One case reinstated United States citizenship to Marguerite Mathilde Slidell De'Erlanger, a 75-year old native of the United States who lost her citizenship by marriage to a German Baron. She resided abroad with her husband until his death and then sought return to her relatives in the United States, which included Admirals in the United States Navy. The Congress noted in its action, "It is unnecessary to be reminded of the distinguished place in American public life her father, the Hon. John Slidell, held, being for a time a Member of the House of Representatives of the United States and a Senator of the United States."[834]

Another bill allowing citizenship to be regained was on behalf of a native-born United States citizen woman who married a native of Germany. He was the owner of a business in France, where they resided until World War I and then left for Germany to avoid internment. Although it was alleged that she was in jeopardy in Germany, she had not taken up the nationality of any country during her absence from the United States.[835]

Reinstatement of citizenship also was allowed on behalf of Augusta Louise De Haven-Alten, who had married a native of Germany. She had previously resided in the United States, until the death of her mother, after which the father took the family to Switzerland. She later separated from her husband and sought to return to the United States. Her father had served during the Civil War, and her mother's father was Admiral Bigelow, who distinguished himself with 45 years in the Navy. The House Committee report noted: "The record of the hearings in this case not only shows a family record of truest Americanism, but shows a record of the highest patriotism displayed by herself from the moment the United States entered the war."[836]

Another precedent involved a native-born United States citizen who had lost her citizenship by taking an oath of allegiance in Italy after her marriage to an Italian diplomat.[837]

In the category of *conferring or deriving citizenship*, the first private law enacted related to the citizenship of a child born abroad to a United States citizen residing in Russia, and who had not acquired citizenship through his father because he was over 21.[838] The second bill declaring a person a United States citizen related to the son of a United States citizen, aged 44 and a native of England, whose family had moved to the United States when he was 15 and who thought he derived citizenship upon his father's naturalization. He subsequently registered as a citizen and voted in elections in the United States but discovered that he was not a citizen when he applied for a passport.[839]

Another bill conferring citizenship related to a 50-year old native of England who entered the United States with his family at the age of four. As an adult, he was appointed a missionary and resided in China for 15 years, but did not learn of his lack of citizenship until he applied for a United States passport in China.[840]

Other precedents included that of a 55-year old native of Ireland who believed that he had derived citizenship from his father's naturalization but later learned he was not a minor and therefore did not acquire citizenship. It was stated that the beneficiary was employed by the W.P.A. and the father of eight children who may "lose his employment unless he qualified for citizenship."[841] Another precedent related to a 55-year old native of the Soviet Union who entered the United States at an early age and was unaware that he was not a United States citizen through his father's naturalization because he was overage. He had served for 30 years in the United States Navy and had been a Deputy United States Marshal in Shanghai, and later was employed with United States tobacco firms in China.[842]

Another case involved a 31-year old native and citizen of Canada who was born to a naturalized United States citizen, but did not derive citizenship because there was no record of his entry to the United States. He had served for four years in the United States Marine Corps and married a United States citizen.[843]

In the category of *special exemptions*, one beneficiary, a former native-born United States citizen, deserted from the United States Navy after having been in the United States Naval Academy and having served for three years. He was tried and found guilty of desertion, and was then pardoned by the President four days after court-martial. He had resided in the United States for 22 years and was later employed in construction work with the Navy.[844]

In the *miscellaneous* category, one case involved the cancellation of a Certificate of Citizenship on behalf of a Hindu.[845] That bill related to a descendant of a family who ruled India for "thousands of years and still rules the State of Gherwal." The beneficiary had been granted United States citizenship by a court over the objection of the Naturalization Service because he was a Hindu and not a "free, white person" entitled to citizenship under the statutes at that time. Although he had exercised his citizenship rights for two years and served in the military during the war, a complaint was filed by the Government to cancel his citizenship. When he sought to file a court action, he found that he was unable to sue the Government without a special Act of Congress permitting him to do so. The law conferred jurisdiction on a district court to hear his case.

Another case involved a 37-year old native and citizen of Ireland who entered the United States with her citizen mother. She had traveled erroneously on her mother's passport and was unaware she had not automatically acquired citizenship upon the naturalization of her parent, until she was requested to furnish proof of citizenship for employment purposes.[846] Another precedent, relating to performance of military service, was a case on behalf of a 28-year old native of Germany who enlisted in the United States Army in China and who served as a mechanic and crew chief training Chinese personnel. He desired a commission, but because he had not enlisted in the United States he could not take advantage of expeditious naturalization provisions.[847]

80th Congress (1947-1948) **-** Naturalization waivers in this Congress totaled 12, which represented 10% of the total private laws enacted this Congress (117). There was one case relating to failure to retain citizenship, five involving residence waivers, two relating to special exemptions (a posthumous citizenship case and waiver of Communist Party membership case), and four miscellaneous cases.

Among the precedents in the category for those *unable to retain* citizenship once gained, one case allowed reinstatement of citizenship on behalf of a native of South Africa and naturalized United States citizen who lost citizenship by prolonged absence abroad, claiming his inability to travel to the United States.[848]

In the *waiver of residence* category, one precedent involved a 34-year old native and citizen of Germany admitted for permanent residence, who desired retroactive status to apply for naturalization. His family was engaged in insurance and he was owner of a large amount of shares in Rheingruppe companies. The Swiss Government was anxious to divest the beneficiary of his ownership in light of his German origin. Because of laws in Switzerland and Holland he was unable to administer, transfer or sell his holdings. He sought citizenship as a means of reinstating his business abroad. It was noted that the beneficiary had said that he would be unwilling to fight against Germany. The Attorney General indicated that "Congress has theretofore been reluctant to make exception in the naturalization process through the medium of private legislation except in the most meritorious cases. There appear to be no circumstances in the instant case which would warrant enactment . . ."[849]

In the *special exemption* category, a bill granting posthumous citizenship involved a native of Romania who had entered the United States at the age of three without proper documents. He enlisted in the Army and was killed in action in Normandy. The Attorney General reported that while it appeared to be an "idle gesture to confer citizenship upon a deceased person, I am not wholly unsympathetic to the feelings of the boy's mother."[850]

In the *miscellaneous* category a bill providing expeditious naturalization due to military service benefited seven Yugoslav fliers who were trained B-24 crews deserving of special benefits because of gallant service with the Army Air Corps 367th Bombardment Group. The detachment "attacked vital enemy installations in their home country of Yugoslavia as the destruction of those objectives was of utmost importance in the Allied offensive."[851]

Another case related to a 72-year old former native-born United States citizen and naturalized citizen of Czechoslovakia who resided in the United States until the age of 12, when taken by his parents to Czechoslovakia. During World War I he served as sugar commissioner for the Food Administrator in the Czechoslovakian government. He later retired in the United States as a businessman.[852] Another precedent involved beneficiaries, natives of Canada, who entered the United States illegally from Canada. The father became a naturalized citizen but his certificate had been canceled because of the illegal entry.[853]

81st Congress (1949-1950) - The number of private naturalization laws began to increase in this Congress, as those who were abroad during the war sought relief from the expatriating and retention provisions. The number of laws totaled 33. This was 7% of all private naturalization laws enacted this Congress (507). There were ten relating to persons who had lost United States citizenship voluntarily, four relating to those who were unable to retain citizenship due to residence abroad; six pertaining to persons who failed to meet the residence requirements for purposes of submitting an application for citizenship; seven special exemptions (Communist Party membership cases and exemption from the draft cases); and six miscellaneous cases laws.

In the category of *voluntary loss* of citizenship for voting in a foreign election, one case pertained to a 73-year old native-born United States citizen who married a native of England, and while residing in that country voted in elections until the husband's death. She had kept contacts in the United States with two United States citizen siblings and had filed income tax returns.[854] A similar case, although opposed by the Executive Branch as failing to present sufficient considerations for enactment, involved a 49-year old native United States citizen who was a nurse residing in Newfoundland and who voted in elections in that country.[855] Another bill related to a 26-year old native and citizen of

Italy who had derived citizenship through his father but later expatriated himself by voting in an Italian election. The Attorney General noted the bill failed to "present consideration sufficient to justify the enactment of special legislation." The Attorney General preferred to resolve the issue by general legislation if necessary.[856]

A bill on behalf of a beneficiary who *failed to retain* due to protracted residence abroad involved a native of Germany who acquired citizenship through her mother, but departed the United States for Germany in order to take care of some inheritance money, and had been unable to return due to her mother's illness.[857] Another bill related to a 62-year old native and citizen of Luxembourg and naturalized citizen, who lost citizenship when he returned to his home country after 18 years in order to be with his mother who had suffered a stroke.[858]

Waivers of residence prior to submission of an application for naturalization included that of a 40-year old native and citizen of Canada employed as a surgeon in Montana, who sought citizenship for state licensure.[859]

In the *special exemption* category, one case provided a waiver of former Communist membership on behalf of a 41-year old native of the Soviet Union, Viktor Kravchenko, author of a publication entitled "I Chose Freedom," which was highly critical of the communist system.[860] Another case involved a permanent resident of the United States who applied for exemption from military service.[861] The Committee noted that after applying for citizenship "he became engaged in a confidential capacity by the Government of the United States" and deferred his naturalization, and then claimed exemption from service.

In the *miscellaneous* category, one precedent related to a 24-year old native and citizen of Poland who enlisted in the United States Army and served for three years, but was ineligible to apply for naturalization because he had not enlisted while in the United States nor had he been lawfully admitted for permanent residence.[862] Another related to a 27-year old native of India of a British father and an American mother who did not derive citizenship at birth, because her mother lost citizenship upon marriage to her husband. The mother was later naturalized. The beneficiary did not benefit since she had not been lawfully admitted for permanent residence, due to the fact that her father's employment required extensive travel abroad and the Indian quota was oversubscribed.[863]

Another case involved a 38-year old native of France admitted for permanent residence who desired expeditious naturalization. He had been awarded the Medal of Freedom for meritorious service during

World War II for organizing and operating an "extensive intelligence net throughout French Indochina." He had abandoned successful business enterprises to perform such activities.[864]

Another beneficiary was an 86-year old native and citizen of Canada who believed herself to be a citizen by virtue of marriage but learned that her husband had not derived citizenship, and thus she had no claim. The daughter of the beneficiary was a United States citizen.[865] Another case involved a 59-year old native and citizen of the Philippines who lived in China for 26 years providing "an extremely valuable contribution to the cause of the United States...," and was imprisoned by the Japanese twice and was decorated with the Medal of Freedom.[866]

82nd Congress (1951-1952) - Citizenship laws this Congress totaled 45, of a total of all private bills enacted this Congress of 733 (6%). This was a slight increase from the previous Congress (33 private laws). As the individuals sought to return to the United States after the war, increased private bills pointed to the fact that many naturalized aliens lost citizenship due to protracted residences abroad. There were 11 bills on behalf of persons who voluntarily lost United States citizenship, three related to inability to confer or derive citizenship, 13 concerned retention requirements, eight involved waiver of residence requirements, four for special exemptions (posthumous citizenship cases, and Communist Party membership bills), and six miscellaneous laws.

Among those precedents restoring citizenship on behalf of beneficiaries due to *voluntarily loss* was one for the relief of Priscilla Ogden Dickerson Gillson de la Fregonniere, a 47-year old native-born United States citizen who renounced her citizenship and voted in British elections, but who returned to the United States in 1947 and purchased an estate in Middleburg, Virginia. The Executive Branch opposed relief indicating it was "inexpedient" since her act was performed as an adult. Congress acted favorably citing the fact that her grandfather had been the Secretary of the Navy under President Andrew Jackson and her uncle had been a Governor of New Jersey.[867]

Another native-born United States citizen desiring reinstatement of citizenship after voluntary loss due to voting in foreign elections was a 27-year old member of the United States Women's Army Corps, who married an Australian Air Force pilot and had moved to Australia.[868] A further precedent involved a 71-year old native-born United States citizen who lost citizenship through marriage to a German national, and subsequently regained citizenship. She then lost it again due to voting in foreign elections.[869]

In the category of those unable to *confer or derive* citizenship was a bill on behalf of Dulcie Ann Steinhardt Sherlock, a 27-year old native born United States citizen who resided abroad with her father, a United States Ambassador. Because of the extensive absence from the United States, she did not have the requisite 10-year period of residence to transmit citizenship to her child born abroad. In this case the Executive Branch recommended favorable action, noting that she had been obliged to reside abroad with her family while her father was in the Foreign Service.[870] Another case included a seven-year old native of Japan and daughter of a United States citizen who did not acquire citizenship from her mother because she did not have the requisite period of residence in the United States.[871]

Another bill related to a family, one of whom was a former United States citizen who left the United States to study in Japan. When she tried to return to the United States, the ship was attacked near Pearl Harbor and returned to Japan. Her five brothers and sisters were United States citizens. She had lost her citizenship by voting in a Japanese election. Her child did not derive citizenship because she had not accumulated sufficient residence to confer citizenship.[872]

Among the precedents reinstating citizenship due to *failure to retain* because of prolonged absence abroad was a bill involving two natives of Norway who were naturalized citizens and skilled craftsmen in plumbing and heating, and who had been sent to Venezuela by a United States firm to help with construction projects in that country. Although it was noted that their contributions to the country of Venezuela were "beneficial to the United States in that they further amicable relations...and also promote American trade and commerce," the Executive Branch noted its preference for generic legislation to remedy such hardships, rather than enactment of a special bill.[873] Another beneficiary who was provided an opportunity to regain citizenship was a 65-year old native of Germany and naturalized citizen who lost his citizenship due to protracted residence abroad as a professor under contract with the University of Bonn.[874]

Another case involved 38- and 36-year old natives of Italy whose citizenship was in jeopardy due to residence abroad. They were brothers who had served in the United States Army and returned to Italy to settle the family estate.[875] A further precedent involved a 63-year old native of Australia who acquired citizenship on the basis of marriage to a United States citizen and who resided in the United States for 30 years. She then traveled to Peru with her husband, where he died. She was unable to retain citizenship because she did not return to the United

States due to a lawsuit in the Peruvian courts.[876] Another case involved a native of China and former United States citizen who derived citizenship through his father, but who lost entitlement because he did not return before his 16th birthday. He had been unable to obtain exit permission from China.[877]

Precedents on behalf of those who were unable to meet the *residence* requirements of the law prior to applying for naturalization included that of two adopted children of United States citizens (ages 13, 5), who were natives of Germany and Austria, and one of whose parents was employed abroad by United Press International for 21 years. The children were unable to comply with the two-year residence requirement for adopted children.[878]

Two cases involving waiver of the residence requirements on behalf of persons who were employed with the United States Government are included. One bill related to a person who taught in a Displaced Persons Camp and another to an individual who was employed with the Department of State in France and other posts for 20 years, but who did not have the one year physical presence in the United States required to take advantage of special expeditious naturalization provisions for employees of the United States Government.[879] Although in the first case the Executive Branch found no compelling reasons for granting relief over others who rendered valuable assistance in the war effort, the latter bill was supported by the Executive Branch.

Two other precedents waiving the residence provisions are cited. One case, opposed by the Executive Branch, involved the 20-year old stepson of a United States citizen, a Brigadier General of the Air Force, who desired citizenship to accept an appointment in the United States Military Academy. Also, a bill waiving residence requirements on behalf of an athlete for participation in the Olympic Games was approved on behalf of Eliana Meulenkamp, an 18-year old native of the Netherlands who sought to compete in swimming competition.[880]

Another beneficiary, a native of England and citizen of Greece and spouse of shipping magnet Aristotle Socrates Onassis, was unable to petition for citizenship due to absences abroad.[881] Another case involved a 41-year old native of Greece who was a doctor employed in research under a Rockefeller Fellowship at the National Cancer Institute in hepatitis and who desired expeditious naturalization. The Attorney General indicated that his services were "invaluable to the United States and to all humanity."[882]

In the *miscellaneous* category there were two cases. The first related to a 49-year old native and citizen of Greece, and seaman on United

States vessels for 10 years, who was unable to file for naturalization because special naturalization provisions had expired.[883] The other pertained to a 34- year old native and citizen of the Philippines who served in the Philippine Scouts and later with the United States Air Force for four years. He had been unable to petition for expeditious naturalization because he did not enlist in the United States.[884] Another bill related to a 56-year old native of China who entered the United States claiming citizenship, but was unable to establish his claim and had allegedly been in the United States for 30 years. He was the owner of a restaurant.[885]

83rd Congress (1953-1954) - Private citizenship laws declined substantially from the previous Congress, from 45 to 18. This represented only a small percentage of the total private laws this Congress (750). There were six laws reinstating citizenship on behalf of those who lost due to voluntary acts, seven bills relating to failure to retain citizenship, three involving residence, and two special exemptions (draft evasion and posthumous citizenship cases). Two general laws in 1951 and 1954 repealing the loss of citizenship for naturalized United States citizens who voted in Italian and Japanese elections decreased some of the need for private laws in this area.

One precedent in the category of persons who were *unable to retain* citizenship once gained, which was supported by the Executive Branch, related to a 35-year old native of France and naturalized United States citizen who was in jeopardy of losing citizenship through residence abroad, due to her husband's employment as an interpreter at the Court of International Justice at the Hague.[886] Another precedent involved a 64-year old native of Italy and naturalized citizen who divested himself of citizenship by continuous residence abroad while performing services for the Vatican.[887] An interesting case related to Karl Ullstein, a 61-year old native of Germany, who was a member of the famous family of Germany known as the House of Ullstein, a large publishing firm. The Department of State noted "it would be against the interests of the United States if the beneficiary was forced to discontinue his activities in Germany where he employed 4,000 persons."[888]

In the category of *waiver of residence* requirements, one case related to a family, natives and citizens of Greece, in which the husband was chief of the Commercial Unit of the Economic Section at the American Embassy in Greece, where he was employed over 27 years. The family was found entitled to nonquota visas but could not meet the one-year residence requirement allowing expeditious naturalization of United States Government employees.[889]

In the category of *special exemptions*, one precedent involved a waiver of the prohibition for naturalization against draft dodgers. A native of Spain who entered the United States for permanent residence requested military exemption on the basis of alienage. He was later married to a United States citizen with a child. One of the reasons cited for granting relief was his three year service in the United States Army after World War II.[890]

84th Congress (1955-1956) - Private citizenship laws totaled 28 in this Congress, including omnibus measures, which was a relatively small portion of the 1,634 private laws this Congress. There were eight laws which reinstated citizenship on behalf of those who lost citizenship due to voluntary acts, one relating to conferring or deriving citizenship, 14 relating to failure to comply with retention requirements, four relating to residence provisions, and one miscellaneous in nature.

In the category of those who *voluntarily lost* citizenship, one case involved a 26-year old native-born United States citizen who served in the Israeli Army for two years.[891] Other precedents relating to regaining citizenship included that of a 50-year old citizen who voted in a Swedish election and who resided with her husband, a career diplomat, in Portugal.[892]

Another case involved a former United States citizen who lost citizenship by acquiring Italian citizenship. She had resided in the United States 40 years and then left for Italy, where she lived for seven years. Her parents and four siblings were United States citizens, and her father was a sculptor who constructed the architectural model for the Metropolitan Museum of Art in New York and the State seals in the House of Representatives' Chamber.[893] Another precedent involved a 45-year old native of Poland and former United States citizen taken to Poland at the age of 11, where he remained for 24 years and accepted employment with a British concern. As a condition of employment, he had been advised to obtain Polish citizenship.[894]

The *waiver of residence* category included the case of a 51-year old native of the Philippines and permanent resident who was employed with the United States Army in Japan but had not obtained the necessary approval for an absence from the United States of over one year, thus jeopardizing his eligibility for naturalization.[895] Another precedent involving waiver of naturalization requirements related to a 20-year old native of Germany who was an Olympic athlete who was considered a top-ranking bicyclist, and who was one month short of being eligible for filing a petition for naturalization.[896]

In the *miscellaneous* category, expeditious naturalization was granted on behalf of a crewman who was a 53-year old native and citizen of Estonia employed on a United States vessel for five years. He was ineligible for expeditious naturalization due to two years of shore duty in the United States, which interrupted his cumulative time towards special residence waivers for naturalization for those serving on board United States vessels.[897]

85th Congress (1957-1958) - In this Congress the number of naturalization laws enacted sharply increased, to almost twice that of the previous Congress (28), for a total of 44. This was 4% of all private laws enacted this Congress (1,141). Two omnibus measures were included in this Congress. There were 16 relating to voluntary loss of citizenship, three to an inability to confer or derive citizenship, 19 involving those who failed to retain citizenship, five pertaining to those who were unable to meet the residence requirements, and one in the special exemption category (draft evasion case).

One precedent involving *voluntary loss* of citizenship and subsequent reinstatement through an Act of Congress involved a 44-year old citizen who married a permanent resident of the United States and traveled to India with him where he was employed until he had to be evacuated from India during wartime. When her husband was transferred to South Africa, she was denied a United States passport to accompany him because it was determined that his travel was not essential, and she thereafter renounced her citizenship to accompany him. Her parents resided in the United States, and her father was a Member of Congress.[898]

Another case involved a 35-year old former United States citizen who lost citizenship by serving in the Mexican Army and accepting employment with the Mexican Police Force. He had been taken to Mexico at the age of eight and resided in that country until entering the United States at the age of 35.[899] Another precedent involved a 53-year old native-born United States citizen who accompanied her parents to Italy at the age of six and voted in Italian elections. She was dependent on her citizen siblings for support.[900] One case involved a 37-year old native-born United States citizen who expatriated based on service in the Israeli Air Force Reserves, but he had also served in the United States Army Air Corps three years.[901]

Precedents involving *conferring or deriving* citizenship included a 34-year old native of England and citizen who resided abroad with her father, a career Foreign Service Officer and who then married a British subject. Upon her husband's death she sought return to the United

States with her child as a United States citizen. Another case related to a 37-year old native-born United States citizen whose family resided in China, where her father served as District Attorney to the United States Court for China. Upon returning from China with her parents, she traveled to Cuba and married a Cuban citizen involved in advertising, and associated with the Columbia Broadcasting System. In both of the above cases, Congress deemed the beneficiary to be in compliance with the 10-year residence period in the United States, thereby allowing transmission of citizenship to the children.[902]

Derivative citizenship was sought in the case of a 55-year old native and citizen of Portugal unable to acquire citizenship from her father's naturalization because she did not enter the United States when she was a minor. She was married to a United States citizen for 17 years and then divorced. She remained in Portugal during her adult years to care for her ill mother. Her four United States citizen brothers contributed to her support. It was noted that Congress was reluctant to grant full restoration of citizenship, but that there was "sufficient equity to warrant placing her in a position to enter the United States for permanent residence, thereby giving her an opportunity to regain United States citizenship through the naturalization process."[903]

In the category relating to reinstatement of citizenship on behalf of those who *failed to retain* citizenship after naturalization was a case involving a 48-year old native of Canada and former member of the United States Marine Corps. He returned to his home country after World War II to pursue his career as a professor, but continued to be active in the Marine Corps Reserve.[904] A case of citizenship in jeopardy due to prolonged absence from the United States for employment purposes related to Wolfgang Stresemann, a 54-year old native of Germany and naturalized United States citizen who was the chief official of the Radio Symphony Orchestra in Berlin where his work was considered of "direct and substantial benefit to the interests of the United States." He had been formerly on assignment in Germany as a historical advisor for a motion picture based on the life of his father, the former Chancellor of Germany, Gustav Stresemann.[905]

Another case involving reinstatement of citizenship related to a 46-year old native of England and naturalized citizen who was married to Hubert Scott-Paine, the pioneer of PT boats. Upon his death, the spouse returned to England to settle the estate and married an English native. She later desired to retire in the United States. The Department of State indicated that: "There have been compelling reasons for her residence in England . . . She has kept her money and property in this country..."[906] Another case involved a 27-year old native of Czechoslovakia who had derived citizenship through her mother upon entry to the United States, where she had resided for 21 years. She then departed to attend school in England.[907]

In the category of *waiving residence* there was the case of a 27-year old native and citizen of China who sought employment with General Dynamics Corporation in the production planning of submarine construction work. That industry was stated to be "vital to the United States Government."[908]

A *special exemption* case involved a native and citizen of France and permanent resident of the United States who requested relief from military service as a neutral alien and later enlisted in the Free French Forces for two years.[909]

In the *miscellaneous* category one precedent involved a 24-year old native of Canada who entered the United States as a citizen, but who during college training discovered he was not a citizen. He served for four years with the United States Air Force.[910]

86th Congress (1959-1960) - This Congress also had a substantial number of private laws enacted relating to naturalization. There were 44 laws, which represented 9% of all private laws enacted across categories this Congress (504). There were seven relating to voluntary loss of citizenship, six to the inability to confer or derive citizenship, 10 involved failure to retain United States citizenship, 16 involving the failure to meet the residence requirements, and five on behalf of special exemptions (Communist Party membership cases, a draft case, and English language cases). Congress enacted a bill on behalf of a person who was unable to meet the English language requirements of the naturalization statutes. Also, after a lengthy period without waivers for Communist Party membership, there were two bills relating to waiving the prohibitions on Communist Party membership for naturalization.

Four bills are included as precedents in the category of bills concerning the ability to *confer or derive* United States citizenship abroad. One related to a 31-year old native of Latvia who was unable to derive citizenship through her father's naturalization because she had reached the age of 18 four months prior to his becoming a citizen. She was later employed with the United States Army for 12 years and was unable to petition through the regular process because the absence would jeopardize her civil service status.[911]

Another case involved a 34-year old native of Latvia born abroad while his father was with the Foreign Service and who married a Swedish national, but who was unable to transmit citizenship to their child without the requisite 10 year period of residence in the United States.[912]

The third case involved a native-born citizen who resided abroad with her father, who was assigned as Deputy for Defense Efforts to the United States special representative in Europe and later married a French national employed with Singer Sewing Machines. She was unable to transmit citizenship to her son without the requisite residence in the United States.[913] Another precedent related to a 22-year old native of Germany who desired expeditious citizenship for a commission in the Air Force Reserve.[914]

Among the precedents relating to *failure to retain* citizenship once gained due to residence abroad was a case involving a 38-year old native of the Netherlands and his spouse and three United States citizen children, who accepted a position in his home country with N.V. Leo de Winter Company, which manufactured and marketed processed milk. The firm was wholly owned by United States citizens, and the beneficiary was responsible for looking after the interests of the stockholders.[915]

Other bills involved a 50-year old native of England who was employed by the United States Government in the Panama Canal Zone for 14 years and operated a poultry ranch supplying military dependents;[916] a 66-year old native of Canada employed for nine years with a United States railroad and whose employment was transferred to the Canadian National Railways;[917] and a 33-year old native of France who resided in the United States 10 years but returned to her home country with her mother, whose spouse was assigned to NATO as Vice Chief of Staff for the French Army.[918]

Another case cited involved a 40-year old United States citizen who lost citizenship through the naturalization of her father in Lebanon and did not return to the United States within the timeframe set by law. Two brothers of the beneficiary were United States citizens.[919]

In the category of *waiver of residence* requirements, there were two cases as precedents: one bill filed on behalf of a native of Great Britain employed with the World Health Organization, and another on behalf of a native of China, who was the recipient of grants by the Ford Foundation to pursue Far East studies at Harvard and the Massachusetts Institute of Technology.[920] Other residence cases included a 45-year old native and citizen of Portugal and permanent resident who desired expeditious naturalization so that he could be admitted to practice law.[921] One case involved a 36-year old native of Italy and permanent resident whose marriage to a United States citizen was terminated, and she was thus unable to apply for expeditious naturalization.[922]

Another case involved C.C. Wei, a 45-year old native and citizen of China whose application for permanent residence had been previously denied. For 10 years he was an officer of a subsidiary of companies of the China International Foundation. Along with other officers, in 1953 he was indicted for having a vessel chartered to a person not a United States citizen. A fine of $2 million was imposed. The Ingalls-Taiwan Shipbuilding and Dry Dock Company was anxious for him to become a citizen because of various contracts with Government agencies. Also, the Department of the Navy indicated that "in the event of increased activity in the Taiwan Straits, the Ingalls-Taiwan yards would be required for the repair and dry docking of United States vessels."[923]

Another case involved a 54-year old native and citizen of Korea employed as an instructor in the Korean language by the National Security Agency, and later by the United States Army for 12 years in Japan.[924] In addition, the residence requirements were waived on behalf of Jack Kent Cooke, a native of Canada, who owned the Canadian Mapleleaf hockey team and who desired United States citizenship to purchase broadcasting stations in the United States.[925]

Special exemptions included a bill relating to draft evasion on behalf of a native and citizen of Ireland who claimed exemption from military service, but later served in the United States Army for three years.[926] A bill waiving naturalization prohibitions on behalf of former Communist Party members involved a 38-year old native of the Soviet Union and former Lt. Colonel in the Army, who defected through West Berlin in 1953 and who was cited as having "unalterably" changed his loyalty away from the Soviet Union.[927]

Yet another special waiver related to the English language requirements for naturalization and involved a 63-year old native of Hong Kong who resided in the United States for 12 years and was the manager of the New China Daily Press in Hawaii. He also had three citizen children.[928]

87th Congress (1961-1962) - Congress again increasingly acted favorably on private legislation waiving the naturalization laws in this Congress. Sixty-eight such laws were enacted, with the majority relating to the failure to retain citizenship and inability to comply with the residence period. This reflected the realities of the growing global economy and international trade. There were a total of 443 private laws enacted this Congress, of which 15% related to naturalization. Nine of those were on behalf of persons who voluntarily lost citizenship, four involved those who were unable to confer or derive citizenship, 15 concerning failure to retain, 31 waiving the residence period, five special exemptions (draft evasion cases, English language cases and Communist Party membership), and four miscellaneous cases.

Two precedents in the area of those who *voluntarily lost* citizenship by expatriating acts are cited. One involved a 22-year old native of the United States who was taken to Canada at the age of 13 and lost citizenship through service in the Canadian military reserve. His entire family, including 10 siblings, resided in the United States.[929] Another law related to a 28-year old native of the United States who lost citizenship after he accepted employment as a customs officer in the British West Indies where his parents had taken him at the age of five.[930]

In the category of those ineligible to *confer or derive* citizenship, one case involved a 30-year old native-born United States citizen who married a native of Cuba and moved to that country. Three children derived citizenship at birth through the mother, but the fourth child did not acquire citizenship due to changes in the residence transmission period.[931]

Among the laws involving *failure to retain* citizenship were three cases where protracted residence abroad jeopardized status. The first two involved a 32-year old native of Egypt and a 55-year old native of Germany, one of whom was employed abroad with United States associated companies, and the other who was employed overseas as a special assistant to the U.N. High Commissioner for Refugees.[932] A precedent relating to other retention requirements included that of a 23-year old native of Brazil who acquired citizenship at birth, but who was unable to meet retention requirements requiring return to the United States prior to age 23. He desired to enter Air Force Officers' Candidate School.[933]

There were several precedents relating to *waiver of residence* requirements prior to an application for citizenship. One bill pertained to a 46-year old native of Hungary employed abroad for 12 years with the United Nations in various capacities; and another bill related to a 46-year old native of Ireland employed with the New York Times.[934] Other cases in the same category involved a 35-year old native of Italy and widow of a United States citizen who served in the Armed Forces eight years. He also had five United States citizen children.[935] Another bill involved a 24-year old native of Brazil and citizen of Cuba who desired United States citizenship to qualify as an aviation cadet in the United States Navy.[936] A further case involved a native of Germany and doctor of Medicine who desired United States citizenship for a regular commission in the Air Force.[937]

Other precedents included a 69-year old native of Germany who immigrated to American Samoa and was married three times to United States nationals, and had five children. It was stated that he was a highly respected resident and was a person of "considerable influence in support of our Government."[938] Another case involved a 31-year old native and citizen of China who subsequently discovered that he was not a citizen upon his father's confession and who desired citizenship to continue his employment with the New York City Transit Authority.[939] Also, a 37-year old native of Germany employed with Von Kohorn Corporation which erected plants and machinery for manmade fibers was granted a waiver.[940]

Other cases involved two Boeing Airplane Company employees. One was a 35-year old native and citizen of China who worked on defense contracts in thermodynamics and heat transfer fluid mechanic research sponsored by the Atomic Energy Commission. He was also involved in research for the Air Force in the aerodynamics and heat transfer of parachutes at supersonic speed;[941] the other employee was a 32-year old native and citizen of China who desired proper security clearance for government contracts in defense and missile programs.[942]

In the *special exemptions* category there was a bill relating to a 66-year old native of Sweden and spouse of a United States citizen who served for several months in the United States Army during World War I, and two days before the armistice applied for exemption from service. He was later naturalized, but his citizenship was revoked in view of his exemption application. In enacting the legislation, it was noted that Congress did not "look with favor upon bills which would remove ineligibility to citizenship," however, in view of the fact that the beneficiary's Army unit had been disbanded prior to any action on his application for exemption, relief was justified.[943]

Another bill providing special relief related to a waiver of the bar to naturalization for Communist Party members, and involved a 37-year old native of Czechoslovakia who defected to the United States. He was formerly attached to his country's Embassy. It was noted that he had "cooperated with our Government."[944] A different case related to waiver of the English language requirement for purposes of naturalization, and that law involved a 65-year old native of China who had resided in the United States for 22 years as a permanent resident. His spouse and four children were United States citizens.[945]

Other cases as precedents in the *miscellaneous* category involved naturalization of adopted children. One bill was on behalf of a 12-year old native of Italy adopted by citizens who were unable to petition for the child due to prolonged absence abroad while one of the parents was employed with Time magazine. The mother was a foreign correspondent and had previously been married for five years to Ernest Hemingway.[946] The other adoption case involved a 20-year old native of Germany unable to fulfill residence requirements because the adoptive mother had been assigned overseas with the Armed Forces as a nurse.[947]

88th Congress (1963-1964) - The number of private naturalization bills enacted decreased from the previous Congress (68) to 31. This number represented 17% of all private laws this Congress (187). The number of bills relating to loss of citizenship had begun to decrease due to 1959 amendments removing some of the requirements for retention of citizenship through protracted residence abroad. In addition, in 1964, as a result of a Supreme Court decision (*Schneider v. Rusk*),[948] those retention provisions were declared unconstitutional. There were seven which related to voluntary loss of citizenship, five involved inability to confer or derive citizenship, four were on behalf of those who failed to retain citizenship once achieved, 12 involved failure to meet the residence requirements, and three special exemptions (one relating to a Communist Party membership case).

One bill in the category relating to failure to *confer or derive* citizenship involved a 35-year old native United States citizen who lost citizenship by voting in a foreign election. Although four children derived citizenship prior to the mother's act of expatriation, the fifth child did not do so.[949]

In the category relating to *failure to retain* citizenship, a 57-year old native of England and permanent resident of the United States for 10 years, who also held United States citizenship for 20 years, was in jeopardy of losing citizenship because his employment in the movie industry required him to remain abroad as producer working with Dina DeLaurentus. In approving the bill, it was noted that his work was of "valuable service to the United States...in presenting the best possible image of our country to others abroad."[950]

A waiver of *residence* precedent involved a 70-year old native and citizen of the Philippines who served in the Philippine Scouts six months and in the United States Navy for 20 years. He was also a prisoner of war for three years.[951]

In the *special* exemption category, a precedent cited involved a 40-year old native of Poland who defected from that country in 1958 and was later employed by the United States Government. It was noted his services to the United States Government "rates as truly significant."[952]

89th Congress (1965-1966) - The number of private citizenship laws enacted in this Congress increased dramatically to a level of 107, which was 43% of all laws this Congress (246). Waivers of residence remained one of the reasons for private bills. There were six bills on behalf of those who had voluntarily lost citizenship; eight relating to the inability to confer or derive; three in the inability to retain category; 88 relating to waivers of residence, due primarily to Cuban nationals who sought expeditious naturalization to enter certain professions; and two special exemptions relating to Communist Party membership.

Among those bills involving the *inability to confer or derive* citizenship was that of a 47-year old native United States citizen whose parents were born in Belgium and who took him abroad during childhood. He later served with the United States Armed Forces and was employed with the American Embassy in Paris, and subsequently the Economic Cooperation Administration abroad for seven years. Due to the extended absence, he was unable to meet the 10 year residence requirement for transmission of United States citizenship to his child.[953]

Another precedent involved a 28-year old native United States citizen and daughter of Ambassador Douglas MacArthur II, who spent most of her life abroad and married a native of Belgium. She was unable to transmit citizenship to her child without the requisite residence in the United States.[954]

A third precedent in this area involved a 20-year old native of Canada whose father was a United States citizen who served in the Royal Canadian Air Force for two years. The father had also served in the United States Air Force until his death in action in Normandy. The father had expatriated due to taking an oath of allegiance to the British Crown, and as a result could not transmit citizenship to his child.[955]

There are three cases cited as precedents for *waivers of residence*. One case included a husband and wife, natives of England, who were United States permanent residents for 17 years. They were unable to petition for naturalization because of a departure to England for five years due to illness in the family.[956] The principal was employed with the United States Department of the Navy as an architect and scientific advisor, and was one of the first winners of the Gibbs Brothers Medal by the National Academy of Sciences. The Department of the Navy urged support for the private bill, citing his accomplishments and noting that his citizenship could have a "direct bearing on the security of the United States since he deals with the total effectiveness of United States naval ships and submarines including the top priority Polaris."

Other cases of failure to meet residence requirements included that of a 33-year old native of the Philippines, and spouse of a United States citizen with four United States citizen children, who was unable to petition for citizenship due to departure from the United States to reside in the Philippines with his ill oldest child who had a serious stomach ailment. He sought expeditious citizenship in order to meet state requirements to practice medicine.[957]

Another precedent relating to expeditious naturalization in order to fulfill career plans involved a 27-year old native of France who desired citizenship to pursue a law practice.[958]

Other cases included that of a 43-year old native and citizen of India desiring expeditious naturalization to facilitate his nomination for membership in the National Academy of Science. It was said that he "achieved worldwide fame in the field of biochemistry" and his efforts in the field of polynucleotides were instrumental in research development in the field of genetics. He had served on advisory panels of the United States Public Health Service.[959]

Another case involved a 47-year old native and citizen of China employed with the Army Map Service in the translation of Chinese geographic names and who desired expeditious citizenship for access to classified material.[960] Several cases involved doctors who desired expeditious naturalization in order to take medical exams.[961] Another precedent involved a 29-year old native of Yugoslavia employed with the Associated Press who desired expeditious naturalization for travel abroad.[962]

Two beneficiaries were a 22-year old native of Canada and permanent resident of the United States for 10 years and a 62-year old native of Germany, also a permanent resident for 10 years. The former sought expeditious citizenship to accept a post with the Peace Corps, and the latter was unable to comply with the residence requirement in the United States due to employment as administrator of the "Albert Schweitzer" hospital in Peru.[963] Another case involved a 51-year old native of Romania formerly employed by the United States Information Service with the American Legation in Bucharest for four years, and who was arrested by Romanian officials and accused of espionage. She had been imprisoned for 12 years along with her sister who worked with the British Government.[964]

With regard to the *special exemption* category for naturalization, a precedent relating to waiver of prohibitions on naturalization for former members of the Communist Party involved a 32-year old native of the Soviet Union employed by the Department of the Army who had been paroled into the United States in 1959 for the "convenience of the Government" and was the author of the book "Inside a Soviet Embassy."[965]

90th Congress (1967-1968) - The highest number of naturalization private bills in the 100 Congresses were enacted in the 90th Congress. The total naturalization laws was 152, or 70% of the total 216 laws this Congress. This was a sizeable portion of the 695 naturalization bills throughout the 100 Congresses. Three bills concerned those who were unable to confer or derive citizenship; 140 waived the residence period prior to submission of an application for naturalization; seven granted special exemptions (posthumous citizenship bills, and Communist Party membership cases); and two were miscellaneous bills. A Supreme Court decision in 1967 virtually eliminated the need for any private bills relating to voluntary loss of citizenship (*Afroyim v. Rusk*).[966] Additionally, this was one of the few times that the Congress enacted several bills granting posthumous citizenship on behalf of members of the Armed Forces. These types of bills continued through the next few Congresses, primarily on behalf of servicemen who served in Vietnam.

One bill in the category of *conferring or deriving citizenship* involved a 55-year old native and citizen of Canada who entered the United States at the age of 15 with his family, and later discovered that there was no evidence that his father was a citizen and therefore he did not derive citizenship.[967]

In the category of waiver of the *residence* requirements for purposes of naturalization, one case was on behalf of a 45-year old native of Cuba and permanent resident of the United States for five years. He was employed by the W.R. Grace Company in an executive capacity and was married to a United States citizen. The beneficiary was due to return to the United States from an assignment abroad with that company and planned to petition for naturalization, but an airplane crash killing essential company personnel from Peru forced him to return to Peru to assist the company.[968] Another beneficiary, a 33-year old native of Indonesia, sought expeditious citizenship on the basis of employment on a research project with the Department of Defense.[969]

A 24-year old native of Germany and widow of a United States citizen married three years, with a citizen child, sought expeditious citizenship based on marriage to her spouse, who died while serving with the United States Army in Vietnam.[970] Other precedents included relief for a 28-year old native and citizen of Korea who served in the Army for five years. He had applied for suspension of deportation relief, and that application was still pending in Congress. The beneficiary desired expeditious naturalization prior to serving in Vietnam.[971]

Additionally, one precedent involved two beneficiaries, natives and citizens of Canada, who were outstanding hockey players who desired to play for the United States team in international competitions. To make the team they needed to be United States citizens.[972] Another case involved a 46-year old native and citizen of Cuba who desired expeditious naturalization to further his employment as a city engineer in Virginia, and who believed that his lack of citizenship status was a handicap "in supervising United States citizen employees."[973]

Other bills relating to expediting naturalization by retroactively granting permanent residence included that of a 53-year old native and citizen of Cuba employed by the Department of Health, Education and Welfare who wanted to take a dental exam; and a 51-year old native and citizen of Canada and doctor of veterinary medicine with the National Institutes of Health who wished to "advance his professional status" by acquiring United States citizenship.[974]

Three cited precedents in the *special exemption* category involved natives of Italy, Ireland and Germany who were killed in action in Vietnam and were found to be citizens at the time of death.[975]

91st Congress (1969-1970) **-** This Congress granted naturalization benefits on behalf of 33 beneficiaries. This was 29% of the 112 private laws across all categories enacted this Congress. The 33 naturalization bills was a substantial drop from the previous Congress (152,) due to enactment of the Cuban Adjustment Act of 1966 granting permanent status to Cuban nationals, many of whom had previously been required to resort to private bills. Of the 33 bills, one related to those unable to confer or derive citizenship, 16 involved those who failed to meet the residence requirements, and 14 were in the special exemption category (Communist Party membership cases, and posthumous citizenship bills), and two miscellaneous. All of the 11 posthumous citizenship bills were on behalf of Vietnam veterans, the largest number in any Congress.

In the case of bills relating to ability to *confer or derive* citizenship, one case involved a 41-year old native United States citizen who was unable to transmit citizenship to her child born abroad due to a lack of four months residence in the United States.[976]

In the *waivers of residence* category, one case involved that of a 60-year old native of Japan who had resided in the United States for 14 years but who was unable to comply with the requisite residence periods due to his position with a United States company, DuPont Far East.[977] Other precedents included that of a 46-year old native and citizen of India employed as a research physicist for the United States Army at the White Sands Missile Range, who desired access to sensitive research information.[978] Another case involved a 49-year old native and citizen of Italy desiring citizenship in order to apply for a probation officer position.[979]

In the *special exemption* category of various bars to naturalization, one precedent involved a waiver of the prohibition on Communist Party membership on behalf of a 43-year old native of Germany who was employed by the United States Department of Defense and who had "collaborated with the Government in an outstanding manner and continues to make major contributions to the national security."[980] Among those granted posthumous citizenship arising from death due to service in Vietnam were natives of Canada, Germany and Japan, all of whom had close United States citizen relatives.[981]

In the *miscellaneous* category, precedents included the expeditious naturalization of a four-year old native of Japan and adoptive daughter of United States citizens who were employed abroad with the International Christian University, and thus had been unable to fulfill the two year residence requirement for naturalization of an adopted child.[982]

92nd Congress (1971-1972) - In this Congress the number of private laws enacted relating to naturalization sharply decreased, and remained at a low level throughout the decade. Eleven naturalization bills were enacted, of a total of 62 private laws (18%). They included one relating to the inability to confer or derive citizenship; seven relating to those who could not meet the residence requirement prior to submission of an application for naturalization; and three were in the special exemption category (Communist Party membership cases). Amendments in 1972 reducing requirements for retention of citizenship for children born abroad decreased the need for further private bills in this area.

In the category of *conferring or deriving* citizenship, one precedent involved the petitioning rights on behalf of natives of South Africa, ages 13, 10, and 8, who were orphans of a United States citizen mother and a permanent resident father. They did not derive citizenship through the mother because she lacked the requisite residence in the United States to transmit citizenship. After the family entered the

United States in 1962, both parents died in an automobile accident. The sister of the deceased parents, acting as guardian, sought to file a petition for naturalization on behalf of the children.[983]

In the category relating to *waivers of the residence* requirements for naturalization, three precedents are cited which involved natives of Germany, Cuba and Canada who were employed by United States companies abroad. One beneficiary was employed for 20 years as an executive with Goodyear International Corporation, another was employed with Manufacturers Hanover Trust for 10 years, and the last was employed as President of Space Research Corporation and was involved in research in weaponry, space projectiles and other national defense projects with the Department of Defense.[984] Another case involved 19-year old siblings and twins, natives and citizens of Costa Rica, who were incorrectly identified as citizens through faulty birth records. They had been placed in the custody of their foster mother who was married to a United States citizen, when they were two weeks old.[985]

Two precedents for *special exemptions* included waivers of certain prohibitions relating to the bar to naturalization of persons formerly affiliated with the Communist Party. One involved a 35-year old native of Cuba formerly employed with the General Directorate of Intelligence of the Cuban Government prior to defection to the United States.[986] The other related to 48- and 35-year old natives of Romania who defected to the United States. The male beneficiary had spent 14 years as legal adviser for the Romanian Ministry of Foreign Affairs and first secretary of the Romanian Permanent Mission to the United Nations, respectively. It was noted that the male beneficiary made "valuable contributions to the security of the United States."[987]

93rd Congress (1973-1974) - This Congress continued to see a decrease in naturalization bills. There were eight laws enacted, which was 13% of the total of 61 laws passed this Congress. There was one relating to voluntary loss of citizenship, and five concerning those who could not meet the residence requirements. One involved a special exemption due to Communist Party membership, and one was miscellaneous in nature.

Among those laws enacted for failure to meet *residence* requirements was a bill on behalf of a native of Germany and United States permanent resident for eight years who was employed overseas with Kaiser Aluminum.[988] Another case involved a 45-year old native of Iraq previously employed overseas for 25 years, 16 of which were with the

University of Baghdad and nine years with the World Health Organization.[989]

In the *miscellaneous* area one precedent involved a 15-year old native of Mexico and adopted child of a United States citizen. The bill allowed the filing of a petition for naturalization by the parent without the requisite residence, due to the imminent death of the adoptive mother, who was being treated for cancer.[990]

94th Congress (1975-1976) - There were nine private naturalization laws enacted, which represented 9% of the total laws enacted this Congress across all categories (99). There was one relating to loss of citizenship due to a voluntary act; four involving waivers of the residence requirements; two special exemptions (English language), and two miscellaneous bills.

One precedent relating to *voluntary loss of citizenship* involved Hope Namgyl, a 35-year old native of the United States and citizen of India. She lost citizenship through renunciation to marry the then-Crown Prince of Sikkim. Because of conditions in Sikkim, she returned to the United States with her children. Her husband and stepson were subsequently placed under house arrest in Sikkim.[991]

Precedents *waiving residence* requirements involved one of the few times Congress enacted a bill to expedite naturalization to compete in the Winter Olympic Games in 1976. The bill was on behalf of a 34-year old native of Czechoslovakia and lawful permanent resident, who sought to be naturalized for the skiing competition.[992]

Other waivers of residence requirements involved a 51-year old native of the Philippines who was employed with the United States Information Agency for 23 years and while working for that agency in Vietnam was captured and held captive for five years. Favorable action was supported by the Department of State "in view of the special and unusual circumstances of this case."[993] Another precedent related to a 47-year old native of Canada who resided in the United States since the age of three, and needed citizenship status to apply for a civil service appointment.[994]

In the *miscellaneous* category one bill included a 28-year old native and citizen of Mexico brought to the United States at the age of two by her mother, and who did not realize that she lacked United States citizenship until she tried to obtain a teaching certificate in Texas.[995]

95th Congress (1977-1978) - In this Congress five private citizenship bills were enacted into law which represented 4% of all categories of bills enacted this Congress (139). There were three waiving residence periods and two in the special exemption category involving English language waivers. Although, at this time a private bill was amended to provide general relief from the English waiver requirement for aliens 50 years old and who had been in the United States 20 years.

Congress repealed in 1978 most of the expatriating statutes as well as retention of citizenship requirements for a child's return to the United States when born of one United States citizen and an alien parent.

96th Congress (1979-1980) - There were six naturalization laws enacted in this Congress (7% of a total of 82 laws enacted in all categories). There were three relating to residence and three special exemptions (Communist Party membership cases, English language requirement cases, and posthumous citizenship bills).

In the category of *waiver of residence* one case involved a 62-year old native of Poland and United States permanent resident for 12 years who was continuously employed abroad as Acting Director of the United Nations Food and Agriculture Organization.[996]

In the *special exemptions* category one case related to posthumous citizenship on behalf of a 62-year old native of Austria and permanent resident of the United States for 22 years who had filed a petition for naturalization, but was shot to death during a holdup at her family's place of business 15 days after her application had been favorably recommended to the court.[997] This was the first occasion that the Congress granted citizenship posthumously on behalf of a person other than a veteran.

97th Congress (1981-1982) - In this Congress there were only three private naturalization laws (8% of the 40 bills enacted in all categories in this Congress). There was one relating to retention of citizenship, one waiving residence requirements, and one miscellaneous case.

In the category of *failure to retain* one case involved a 39-year old native of Bolivia who derived citizenship through her United States citizen father, but failed to retain citizenship because she did not return to the United States for two years. The citizen father was employed with the United States Embassy in Bolivia for four years and died when she was four months old. She was unaware that she had not retained citizenship.[998]

98th Congress (1983-1984) - In this Congress there was an increase, from only three laws in the previous Congress to ten laws waiving various naturalization provisions. This was 29% of all categories of bills enacted this Congress (35). One case related to the inability to retain citizenship; five involved failure to comply with the residence requirements prior to application for citizenship; three were on behalf of special exemptions (Communist Party membership cases, posthumous bills, and English language cases); and there was also one miscellaneous case.

For the first time in the nation's history relief was granted to a person who could not pass the United States History and Government test, nor comprehend or take the oath of allegiance.

Additionally, three cases waived the residence requirements of the citizenship laws solely in order to allow an individual to participate in Olympic Games for the United States.[999]

Those precedents in the category of *waiving the residence* period for naturalization involved the Olympic cases noted above: a 19-year old native of the Soviet Union who was a rhythmic gymnast, a 30-year old native of Norway and skier, and a native of West Germany who was a soccer player.[1000] All beneficiaries sought naturalization to allow them to participate in the Olympic Games.

In the *special exemption* category, one precedent related to the posthumous conferral of United States citizenship upon a native of Scotland who was killed in action in Vietnam.[1001] The other precedent involved a 63-year old native of Colombia and permanent resident of the United States for 23 years who was unable to comply with the United States History and Government test due to a physical ailment. She also was unable to perform the oath of allegiance. In granting relief Congress stated that although there are "no precedents for waiving the oath of allegiance, and only one precedent for waiver of the test on United States Government, the Committee believes this case is unique."[1002]

99th Congress (1985-1986) - There was only one naturalization bill enacted into law, out of a total of 15 private laws. The one law was a special exemption case.

100th Congress (1987-1988) - This Congress had two bills granting citizenship, of the 21 private laws enacted this Congress. One case related to the inability to confer or derive and one was miscellaneous in nature.

Chapter 5

Controversy

Although the private bill process in both Houses is conducted openly as with any other legislation, its existence has remained a "shadowy" anomaly, with purposes and benefits little understood. This has generated much confusion, misinformation, and controversy. The few occasions where the process has been the subject of abuse have contributed to unwarranted attacks that the system itself has failed.

Private bills have been the subject of three major controversies. First, in 1952 an investigation was undertaken when some Members of Congress admitted introducing bills on behalf of many illegal aliens in the United States. Second, private bills went into disrepute in the 1970s when Members of Congress assisted Chinese shipjumpers and other aliens through private bills. Third, in an FBI "sting" operation in 1980, seven Congressmen were convicted of receiving bribes from men posing as Arab business leaders seeking introduction of private bills to remain in the United States. As a result of the "ABSCAM" scandal, one Member was expelled from the House of Representatives.

There are also controversies within Congress which impact the private bill process and precedents. These include rulings by the Chairmen of the Judiciary Committees and Immigration Subcommittees, rancorous jealousies between the House and the Senate, contempt of the Committee system by certain Members of Congress, and "profiles of privilege" whereby internal and external rules are bypassed for political expediency.

1952 Smuggling Racket

The first private bill controversy involved a "multi-million-dollar racket" of smuggling aliens into the United States in 1952, when it was alleged that many received "the aid of innocent and unwitting members of Congress." The *New York Herald Tribune* noted Members of Congress admitted introducing a large number of bills "without hope of obtaining favorable action because of pressure from groups in their home districts or states." [1]

According to the *New York Herald Tribune* article, one member of Congress, Sen. William D. Langer (D-ND), was known as the "third Senator from New York"--although he represented North Dakota--because many of the bills he introduced involved aliens in New York. Sen. Langer explained that he introduced the bills to stay the deportation of "former Nazis and members of the German-American Bund 'to protect their constitutional rights'." In response to charges of a smuggling racket, he withdrew a "series of bills seeking to stay deportation of more than seventy-five Pakistani seamen who had jumped ship." They had been introduced, Sen. Langer said, because the seamen feared they would be executed if returned home.

Another Congressman, the article noted, had introduced a bill "at the request of attorneys for the Legal Aid Society and other groups," which involved a native of Italy who was smuggled into the United States for $1,000. The Congressman stated that he did not know of any monetary exchanges and that he only introduced bills after ascertaining their special merits. Yet another Member of Congress "used the private bill method" to keep an operator of a food concession in the country long enough to qualify for an administrative remedy, according to the *New York Herald Tribune*.

This controversy resulted in an investigation into private bills and their relationship to stays of deportation in 1953.[2] In addition, the House Judiciary Committee had already been attempting to stem such abuses by conducting frequent hearings on bills and denying many, so that stays of deportation could not be prolonged.

1970 Chinese Shipjumpers

In 1970 Congress again became the subject of intense scrutiny due to allegations of improprieties by Senators introducing private bills on behalf of Chinese shipjumpers. As a result, the Senate conducted its own investigation into private immigration bills introduced on behalf of Chinese crewmen in the 90th and 91st Congress (1967-1970).[3] The Committee found that approximately 80% of the total 657 bills introduced from 1967 to 1969 originated in the offices of four lawyers in New York City and nine lobbyists in Washington, D.C. According to the Senate Committee report on the investigation:

> The magnitude of this influx of bills can be appreciated by noting that in the 88th Congress, for example, bills for only 96 crewmen of all nationalities were introduced. Since our investigation began, no bills for Chinese crewmen have been introduced.[4]

The Special Committee noted that fees as high as $750 for one beneficiary were not uncommon, and that many bills were introduced without the knowledge of a Senator. Although no evidence was found that "any Senator or any employee of the Senate received or accepted a bribe, the promise of a bribe, or anything else of value in consideration of the introduction or attempted introduction of any bill," their impact on the disruption to the Senate's business and its integrity prompted the Special Committee to recommend that

> the Senate Committee on the Judiciary might wish to review the practices disclosed by this investigation and consider some alternative to its present system of handling these bills.[5]

In response, the Senate immediately changed its rules on the procedure for introduction of private bills. Previously, the mere presentation to the Clerk was sufficient to insure the introduction of legislation. Senator Michael J. Mansfield (D-MT) stated that:

> it would appear to us that a stricter interpretation is now in order...bills and resolutions should no longer be received at the desk by the Parliamentarian for reference to the appropriate standing committee unless they are *signed by and delivered at the desk, in person, by the Senator introducing them.*[6]

In another case, a representative was indicted in 1976 for "soliciting and accepting bribes from Chilean and Argentinean aliens in exchange for introducing private immigration bills in Congress." The seven bribery-related charges against Mr. Henry Helstoski (D-NJ) involved receiving at least $8,735 for sponsorship of immigration bills. The United States Supreme Court dismissed the charges, however, under the immunity clause of the Constitution,[7] but his Administrative Assistant was convicted of extortion in 1975.[8]

1980 ABSCAM

The third assault on the private bill system occurred in 1980 after the FBI conducted a "sting" operation (ABSCAM) into the possible improper conduct on behalf of Members of Congress in introducing private bills. Seven Members of Congress were convicted as a result of the investigation: Mr. John W. Jenrette, Jr. (D-SC), Mr. Michael O. Myers (D-PA), Mr. Raymond F. Lederer (D-PA), Mr. Richard Kelly (R-FL), Mr. John M. Murphy (D-NY), Senator Harrison A. Williams, Jr. (D-NJ), and Mr. Frank Thompson, Jr. (D-NJ). One of these Members, Mr. Myers, was expelled, the first Member of Congress since 1861. The Members were charged with accepting bribes in exchange for promising to introduce private immigration bills on behalf of foreign businessmen. In one ABSCAM case $100,000 was paid for the "promise to introduce a private immigration bill."[9]

During debate on the expulsion of Mr. Myers, the House of Representatives discussed the details of his involvement in ABSCAM. The FBI undercover operation began in 1978 with agents and informers posing as representatives of Middle Eastern "sheiks" interested in investing in the United States. On July 26, 1979 an undercover FBI agent (Tony De Vito), posing as a representative of the sheiks, met with Angelo Errichetti, the Mayor of Camden, New Jersey, and several lawyers. Errichetti indicated that he had been previously involved in introducing sheiks to a Congressman in exchange for a fee and asked whether any of the lawyers knew any Congressman who would meet with this group of sheiks. After the meeting, one of the lawyers contacted Mr. Myers and arranged a meeting with Errichetti and DeVito. The following describes the circumstances involved in the Myers case, as set forth in the House debate:

> On August 22, 1979 Myers and Erichetti met with De Vito at the Travel Lodge Hotel at Kennedy Airport, New York. De Vito described to Myers in general terms the sheiks' desire to insure that if they fled their country, they would be able to enter and remain in the U.S., and he asked how Myers could be of assistance in this. Myers replied,
>
> "Where I could be of assistance in this type of a matter, first of all, is private bills that can be introduced." Myers explained that as soon as the sheiks had entered the United States, "I'd have to put a bill in at that

> point". Elaborating on the process, he indicated that once the bill had been introduced, he would be able to use the hearing process to delay any action for a year or 18 months, after which time it would be much easier to arrange for the sheiks to stay in this country...
>
> Myers then suggested that the sheiks invest in Myers' district. He said, "That gives me the out that I need to go full guns".
>
> Throughout the meeting, the Congressman repeatedly promised to assist the unidentified sheiks. "I'll be in the man's corner a hundred percent," he said, and I'll deliver a lot of the people in his corner," he assured De Vito. "Feel free to call me, and, you know, matter of fact, you can come down, we'll meet down in Washington if you want." He also commended DeVito for going about things the right way. "Money talks in this business and bull s--- walks. And it works the same way down in Washington," he explained.
>
> As the meeting drew to a close, Myers again gave his guarantee that he would assist the sheiks. DeVito then handed Myers an envelope containing $50,000 in cash. "Spend it well," DeVito said as Myers accepted the envelope and replied: "Pleasure."[10]

Mr. Myers' defense was that he was play-acting, but the House Members who argued against the resolution to expel him did not use that as support for their opposition to the bill. They noted that the House Rules required a conviction of a criminal offense in order to expel a Member, and that Mr. Myers should be allowed to pursue all legal channels and appeals prior to consideration of any expulsion act by the House.[11] The House of Representatives, however, expelled Mr. Myers by a vote of 376-30 on October 2, 1980.

Internal Controversies

Other internal controversies, such as the volume of bills and sponsors, the role of the Committees, the relationship between the House and the Senate, contempt of the process by certain Members of Congress, and special privileges in some cases reveal the political nature of the beast.

Statistical summary - Often the volume of bills introduced in each Congress gives an inflationary perception, or aura, of abuse, but in fact the majority of Members of Congress never introduce private bills. This is reflected in the 90th Congress (1967-1968) which had the largest number of bills introduced in all Congresses (7,293). Eighty-seven

Members of Congress introduced 68% of those bills. Again in the next Congress (91st Congress: 1969-1970) 82 Members of Congress introduced 70% of the total number of bills (6,266). In the 82nd through the 85th Congress (1951-1958), an earlier period of large numbers of bills, 50 Members of Congress introduced almost 40% of all bills. Most Members represented heavily impacted immigration states, but in not all cases does that appear to be the only reason for introduction. Among those with a high propensity toward a *consistent* introduction of large numbers of bills, with an example of the number of bills introduced in one Congress were: Adam Clayton Powell, D-NY (331 private bills in the 89th Congress, 1965-1966), Mr. Joseph P. Addabbo, D-NY (303 private bills in the 90th Congress, 1967-1968), and Mr. Phillip D. Burton, D-CA (185 in the 90th Congress). In the Senate the following Members also consistently introduced large numbers of bills: Sen. William D. Langer, D-ND (128 in the 82nd Congress, 1951-1952), Sen. Walter F. Mondale, D-MN (86 bills in the 91st Congress, 1969-1970), and Sen. Dennis Chavez, D-NM (103 bills in the 86th Congress, 1959-1960).

Committee Chairmen - Chairmen of the Committees and Subcommittees of the House and Senate wield great power over scheduling and consideration of all legislation, including private bills. In many respects, the precedents and rulings on private bills transcend the changing of the guard of committees and parties. However, in some instances the direct influence of an activist Chairman can lead to changes in rules, or an otherwise passive Member can stymie any action and contribute to possible abuses of the process. In the House, through the steady influence of Judiciary Committee Chairmen Emanuel Celler (D-NY) and Peter W. Rodino, Jr. (D-NJ), private bills have been constantly monitored since 1949.[12] The Chairman of the Immigration Subcommittee through most of that time was Mr. Walter (81st through 87th Congress: 1949-1962), who presided over some of the most important rules changes. When confronted with a rise in bills and continued stays of deportation in 1952, he conducted "operation slaughterhouse" to reduce the 2,500 bills introduced and eliminate nonmeritorious cases.[13] With his departure a rise in bills followed in the 88th Congress (1963-1964), when backlogs developed under Immigration Subcommittee Chairman Michael A. Feighen, who presided over the largest rise in private bills to 7,293 in the 90th Congress (1967-1968).[14]

It was not until the 91st Congress (1969-1970), when Mr. Rodino initiated rules changes and then became Immigration Subcommittee

Chairman in the 92nd Congress, that restrictions to eliminate stays of deportation for *all* nonimmigrants was extended and backlogs became a high priority.[15] The number of bills introduced fell drastically to 2,866 by the end of the 92nd Congress.[16] Since that time, the changing of Subcommittee chairmen under direction of full Committee Chairman Rodino did not alter a closely followed policy on private immigration bills.[17] In fact, under Subcommittee Chairman Romano L. Mazzoli (D-KY) in the 97th Congress through the 100th Congress (1981-1988) the precedents and policy of private bills was expanded and formalized.[18]

In the Senate under the 22 year Chairmanship of James O. Eastland (D-MS), the full Committee held strong control over the process of private bills by also retaining the Subcommittee as his Chairmanship.[19] The early stays of deportation upon introduction of bills continued to be applied in a more liberal fashion than in the House, although the precedents and policies of those enacted into law were similar. Because of the power Sen. Eastland held at both the Subcommittee and full Committee levels, bills moved through the legislative process on many occasions without meetings or debate.

It was the aggressive leadership of Judiciary Committee Chairman Edward M. Kennedy (D-MA) in the 96th Congress (1979-1980), who also had responsibility of the Immigration Subcommittee, that brought about major changes in the Senate mode of operating. The Subcommittee eliminated the automatic stay of deportation upon introduction of a bill; thus requiring the weighing of the hardship before a request for a report would be initiated, as the House Committee rules required. Those changes continued under the leadership of Subcommittee Chairman Alan K. Simpson (R-WY), with the support of full Committee Chairman Strom Thurmond (N-NC), in the 97th through the 99th Congress (1981-1986).

When the Senate returned to Democratic Leadership in the 100th Congress (1987-1988), full Judiciary Committee support of Joseph R. Biden, Jr. (D-DE) provided Immigration Subcommittee Chairman Kennedy the ability to continue the policies that he had initiated in the 96th Congress (1979-1980). Under his tutelage, combined with the House measures, the volume of introduced bills decreased from 347 in the 99th Congress (1985-1986) to 194 in the 100th Congress (1987-1988).

Contempt for the process - Contempt for the process by some Members is reflected in attempts to bypass the Committee system through the inclusion of private bills in other, more general, legislation. While these maneuvers are usually steadfastly refused by the Chairmen of both the House and Senate Judiciary Committees, in a few cases this unusual subterfuge is employed so circuitously as to bypass even the most powerful of Committees.

The principle reason for bypassing the regular order of business is the lack of merit or precedents. In the 98th Congress (1983-1984), for example, a private bill for the relief of the Marfori family was included in a public measure, a "Continuing Appropriations" bill, by Sen. William Proxmire (D-WI).[20] During debate on the measure in the House, the Subcommittee Chairman Mazzoli noted the "highly unusual procedure" and demanded an explanation. In response, Mr. Neal E. Smith (D-IA), a member of the House Appropriations Committee, stated that it was only because of the shortness of time that the Committee would even consider acquiescing to the measure:

> We made it very clear that although in this one instance we were including a private bill in a continuing resolution, it is to be considered an exception and not a precedent...[21]

The bill involved a medical case which was against Committee policy because of the availability of an administrative remedy.[22] In the 100th Congress (1987-1988) another private bill, introduced by Mr. David R. Obey (D-WI), was surreptitiously inserted into an appropriations measure.[23] The bill related to a doctor who entered the United States as an exchange visitor and was obligated to return to his home country. Because the Immigration Subcommittee rules indicated these cases would receive unfavorable action, Mr. Obey flagrantly flaunted the rules. The action also was apparently a spiteful act against an INS officer who ruled that the doctor would have to return home as the law required: "Swan was too damned arrogant..." complained Mr. Obey about the Immigration official.[24]

On occasion the merits of a private bill and its relative significance to a more generic population can sometimes be a vehicle for public legislation. In the 95th Congress (1977-1978), for example, a private bill waiving the English language requirement for citizenship on behalf of an alien was amended to provide for more general relief.[25] The Department of Justice, in its report on the private bill, seemed to endorse more general legislation:

> The present statutory exemption lacks flexibility which would allow older persons with long residence to become eligible for naturalization. H.R. 667 would provide that flexibility and would be a highly desirable legislative change.[26]

The Department estimated that about 15,000 cases would be involved. Additionally, the Committee noted it had "consistently refused to approve private legislation of this type and [is] of the opinion that the general law should be amended to provide uniform benefits."[27]

Also, a bill relating to many individuals may be considered a private bill. In the 91st Congress (1969-1970), a bill to provide admission to the United States for natives of the Bonin Islands was enacted as a private law.[28] Also, in the 98th Congress (1983-1984) a bill to allow employees of the American University of Beirut to re-enter the United States as permanent residents was designated a private bill.[29]

Sometimes, private bills and public legislation may become blurred, as in cases involving honorary or posthumous citizenship. At times, if involving a public figure, the bill is considered a public bill,[30] yet in other cases it is considered a private bill.[31]

House and Senate Jealousies - As with public bills, the House and the Senate jealously guard their turf in private immigration legislation. On occasion the House or the Senate may take private bills "hostage" in return for legislation which an influential Member may seek. In the 83rd Congress (1953-1954), House Chairman Celler noted that legislation sponsored by Sen. Pat McCarran (D-NV) concerning sheepherders was pending in the Committee, and that the House had previously acted favorably upon such legislation. But the Chairman blocked the legislation on this occasion because Sen. McCarran had not allowed the passage of House legislation relating to membership of the United States in the Intergovernmental Committee for European Migration which was "important and meritorious to the Chairman of this Committee." When Sen. McCarran withdrew his objection to the House measure, Mr. Celler urged prompt action of the sheepherder bill.[32]

In the 86th and 87th Congresses (1959-1962), problems developed between the House and Senate relating to adding beneficiaries to House-passed private bills.[33] When a bill passed the House, the Senate then amended that legislation to add the names of other cases which the House Committee had previously denied. This resulted in a conference on the measure, rare in private bill history. In addition, in the 96th Congress (1979-1980) the House was urged to pass some Senate Judiciary Committee private bills which became a pawn for more generic legislation that the House had already passed. The House debate illustrated the dilemma. As Mr. John Seiberling (D-OH), a member of the Judiciary Committee, stated:

> the Senate has insisted that these bills be passed individually in order to stem confusion surrounding their coverage by the public bill, which is H.R. 7273...I have agreed to present these bills so that the Senate, in turn, will pass the general bill, H.R. 7273...even though they would be unnecessary if we first passed H.R. 7273. [34]

One of the Official Objectors for private bills in the House, Mr. Robert E. Bauman (R-MD) did not allow the "trade-off," referring to the Senate demands as "senatorial vanity."[35]

In the next Congress (97th Congress: 1981-1982), the adjournment deadline and the press for finishing private bill business led to a temperamental exchange on bills brought before the House out of the regular procedure. Mr. John Conyers, Jr. (D-MI), a member of the Judiciary Committee, demanded an explanation of the unusual procedure and withheld any action in the House. He said:

> what the gentleman is doing by this procedure is short circuiting the very kinds of questions that I as a member of the full committee would have every right to ask...I think this is an extraordinary procedure, without any particular redeeming merits... [36]

In a bipartisan effort, Mr. F. James Sensenbrenner, Jr. (R-WI), an Official Objector on private bills, supported the process because of the time constraints, and the fact that most of the bills came within Subcommittee precedents and guidelines. He stated:

> Mr. Speaker, as the gentleman from Michigan knows, I have probably got the most restrictive view of private legislation of anyone in the House...During the last Congress, as well as this one, I was one of the three Republican Official Objectors to the private calendar; and on the last or next-to-the-last day of the last Congress there were a number of private bills that were brought up by unanimous consent and were passed because it was deemed to be especially meritorious that the legislation pass.[37]

Other members of the Subcommittee came to the defense of the bills, noting that the bills did not involve special interest measures of the Subcommittee, but merely an attempt to accommodate the sponsors of the bills. Mr. Dan Lungren (R-CA), a member of the Subcommittee on Immigration, noted that the Subcommittee had hard work cut out for them in dealing with private bills, and that there was not a "tremendous propensity for Members to volunteer to serve on that subcommittee to do this work."[38] The Chairman of the Judiciary Committee, Mr. Rodino, stated:

> In my 34 years in the Congress we have during the last waning hours of the Congress considered matters that were urgent matters, where there might have been prejudice to individuals, where serious injury might have occurred, where it might have been not only an act of charity, but an act of justice and equity to take these matters up...I was fully informed of what the subcommittee has done. This is just an act of compassion and justice in these last days. I would hope that we repose confidence in our subcommittee, especially when it is unanimous and that when it takes this kind of action, it is taking action that reflects credit on the committee.[39]

Profiles in Privilege - Although Congress tries very carefully through its rules and procedures to adhere to precedents, the political nature of the beast can override even the best rules, intentions and precedents, and leave a legacy of controversy for future Congresses to face. Some of these "profiles in privilege" reflect the dilemma of politics and private bills.

The most controversial cases are those which are introduced every four years on behalf of Olympic athletes. The privilege extended to these athletes through private bills is hotly debated. In 1960 the Chairman of the Immigration Subcommittee, Mr. Walter, advised his colleagues that five private bills requesting expeditious citizenship had been denied as "highly improper" and that the bootlegging of athletes was not in the spirit of the Olympic Games.[40]

For many years, the Congress withstood pressures to enact special legislation to grant citizenship in such cases, until the 98th Congress (1983-1984), with the enactment of three for elite Olympic athletes. Before that time, a bill had been defeated on the House Floor which would have granted citizenship on behalf of Martina Navratilova to compete in international tennis competition. At that time, the strong leadership of Immigration Subcommittee Chairman Joshua Eilberg (D-PA) stalled efforts for enactment. He took the unprecedented step of filing dissenting views on a private bill because it "would undermine the congressional private bill process and have serious, undesirable, and far-reaching consequences." More importantly, the Chairman believed that citizenship was a privilege not to be lightly bestowed:

> The threshold question to be answered is whether U.S. citizenship should become an 'award for athletic excellence'... H.R. 10210 would have the effect of relegating U.S. citizenship to an award or a reward to superior

athletes--perhaps to be later extended to outstanding artists, scholars, musicians and others.[41]

He noted that conceivably an entire U.S. Olympic team could be made up of beneficiaries of private bills that waived the naturalization requirements. In summary, Chairman Eilberg stated:

> I hope my colleagues will agree that U.S. citizenship is a special privilege indeed and that we should not freely or frivolously waive the citizenship requirements that have been laid down by the Congress in the exercise of its specific constitutional responsibility to 'establish a uniform rule of naturalization' (art. l., sec. 8, cl. 4.).[42]

He also indicated that the prior cases relating to naturalization which had been approved already had the residence requirement, but not in the specific sequence required by law. The Navratilova bill was recommitted from the House Floor to the Judiciary Committee on July 18, 1978, thus ending any further action.

The Navratilova bill set a precedent for refusal of any Olympic or other special cases, that is, until the 98th Congress (1983-1984), when sponsors of legislation for a skier (Mr. Bill Alexander, D-AR), a rhythmic gymnast (Mr. Henry Waxman, D-CA), and a soccer player (Mr. William Lowery, R-CA) sought waivers of the citizenship laws. Proponents argued the importance of the beneficiaries to the United States team and that the athletes would "bring home the Gold." Political expediency undermined the Committee process and precedents. This time the politics of erring on the side of potential medal winners was too much to overcome. The irony of bestowing citizenship and waiving all rules of order was that none of the beneficiaries for whom the gold was pledged came within striking distance of medals. In fact, one did not even make the United States team.[43]

In an effort to stem the controversy in the future, in the 100th Congress (1987-1988) the House Immigration Subcommittee tightened its rules on citizenship bills by requiring a two-thirds majority vote of the Members in order for a bill to be placed on the Subcommittee calendar for scheduling. Also, Chairman Mazzoli addressed a letter to the United States Olympic Committee (USOC) indicating its displeasure at the pressures brought on lawmakers by the sponsoring organizations for special citizenship privileges for athletes. All members of the Subcommittee also signed the letter, which stated:

> The understandable reticence of the Subcommittee to waive the regular five-year naturalization process even for gifted athletes stems from the fact that Congress considers United States citizenship a special privilege, not to be casually or routinely granted...there are many persons who, while not outstanding athletes, wish just as fervently as any athlete to reach the goal of United States citizenship so they can vote and otherwise actively participate in our democratic way of life.

The Subcommittee suggested other alternatives, such as a waiver mechanism by the International Olympic Committee (IOC) for an alien who has indicated an "intention" to become a citizen of his/her adopted land and who desires to represent that country. The Subcommittee also suggested that an advisory board be established to review the credentials of the athletes who requested special exemptions from Congress. A similar letter was addressed from the Senate Subcommittee on Immigration. In response, the USOC met with officers of the IOC, but they advised the Immigration Subcommittee that there was no possibility of changing the international rules. The USOC did, however, establish a board to review the selection process and the bills presented to Congress.[44]

Even with all these safeguards, "Olympic fever" infected the 100th Congress in the Olympic year of 1988, with four bills considered for athletes. The rules were swept aside with the first bill, which was supported by the Speaker of the House, Mr. Jim Wright (D-TX).[45] That bill, on behalf of Tracey McFarlane, was brought onto the floor of the House without Subcommittee or full Committee action and became law. The other pending bills, however, received an extensive hearing before the Subcommittee in April 1988, where Olympic Committee representatives testified on the merits of the bills.[46]

The USOC explained that 38 national governing bodies determine the selection of athletes for each type of competition, such as swimming or skiing, subject to the approval of the USOC. The Rules governing citizenship required that "only citizens of a particular country may compete for that country," and further that athletes who had participated for one country could not represent another country for three years thereafter.[47] The USOC explained a waiver system for some of the rules for dual nationals, those married to nationals of another country, and when the former country agreed to waive the three-year prohibition on behalf of an athlete.

When presenting testimony on the individual bills, the USOC's special committee, which had been assigned the role of reviewing bills in Congress, made an evaluation based on whether there was a strong chance of the athlete making the Olympic Team and earning a medal, and whether the athlete would be eligible to compete even after obtaining citizenship.[48] All three bills which were the subject of the hearing related to former citizens of the Soviet bloc, where Congress would in essence be favoring their competition ahead of other qualified United States citizens.

The first bill related to a Czechoslovak tennis player, Ivan Lendl, sponsored by Mr. Bruce A. Morrison (D-CT). Although the Olympic Committee indicated Lendl was ranked number one in the world and would be a strong contender for a position on the team, it stopped short of endorsing Lendl "because of the eligibility questions which currently exist." Those hurdles included: (1) participation in the Davis Cup, which would require a waiver from the Tennis Federation due to previous representation of another country; (2) selection to the United States Team, which had already been chosen; and (3) waiver of the three-year prohibition under IOC rules because of competition on behalf of another country. The sponsor of the measure noted that age was a hardship factor in that Mr. Lendl would be too old and would be past his tennis-playing prime if not allowed an opportunity in 1988.[49]

The second case involved Gareg Barseghian, an Armenian wrestler, sponsored by Mr. Carlos Moorhead (R-CA). The Olympic Committee concurred with the national governing body that Mr. Barseghian would most likely secure a position on the United States Team and that he had a "high probability" of winning a medal. The USOC also noted his availability for a waiver because he was married to a United States citizen. The sponsor noted that Mr. Barseghian's support had been underwritten by a group of Los Angeles area Armenian businessmen.[50]

The third case involved an East German swimmer, Peter Berndt, sponsored by Mr. Ben Erdreich (D-AL), and the United States Olympic Committee concurred in the national governing body's assessment that he would probably secure a position on the United States Team and had a "high probability" of winning a medal. Like the others, however, he had participated in competition for another country. Mr. Erdreich noted the brief age timeframe for competition of a swimmer.[51]

Notwithstanding the waiver requirements and the prior history of Olympic cases, the Immigration Subcommittee reported on the three bills favorably. But it was at the full Judiciary Committee where there was substantial debate. While the Chairman of the Subcommittee, Mr. Mazzoli, defended the Subcommittee's action by stating that favorable Congressional action would strengthen any efforts by the USOC in obtaining IOC waivers for the athletes,[52] another Member of the

Committee, Mr. F. James Sensenbrenner (R-WI), argued that the Subcommittee violated its own rules and principles by acting in a manner to waive the citizenship laws on behalf of athletes:

> I regret that the Subcommittee on Immigration, Refugees, and International Law has apparently ignored its own rules in approving these three bills. Following the fiasco of special legislation for putative olympic athletes in 1984, the Subcommittee amended its rules to specifically state that they would not approve legislation granting citizenship for an athlete purely on their athletic merits, and there is not anything in any of the records submitted by the Subcommittee to the full Committee today that indicates that there are any circumstances other than the athletic merits in support of each of these three individuals.[53]

As an Official Objector, Mr. Sensenbrenner served notice of his intent to object to such bills on the House Floor, unless the requisite waivers by the IOC were obtained, particularly with respect to past participation on behalf of another government. The full Judiciary Committee reported the three bills favorably, but debate ensued as promised on the House Floor. The bills were passed over without prejudice while allowing the athletes to obtain the appropriate waivers from the IOC. The sponsor of the Lendl bill argued,

> I would like to understand, the gentleman is not trying to impose a condition where the waivers would have to be granted before the House acts because, of course, as the gentleman knows, the application for the waiver cannot be made unless citizenship has already been granted.[54]

In response, Mr. Sensenbrenner stated:

> That is only fair to the House of Representatives which is being asked to take the extraordinary step of accelerating someone's citizenship eligibility date.[55]

The House recommitted the Lendl bill and the Berndt bill to the Judiciary Committee because of the lack of IOC waivers.[56] The bill on behalf of the wrestler, Mr. Barseghian, passed the House after obtaining an IOC waiver but failed in the Senate. The Senate Judiciary Committee held firm in its position of not expediting citizenship based on athletic or other abilities. Mr. Jerry Tinker, an aide to Sen. Edward M. Kennedy (D-MA), said:

> If you start down the slippery slope of granting what most Americans would say is a great right...and start making it available on demand, I think you've eroded a terribly important right and obligation and cherished thing under our law...If you start doing it for (athletes), why not do it for artistic ability or for people who are nuclear physicists... Personal convenience, as opposed to hardship, was not the purpose of private bills.[57]

Internal checks and balances prevented enactment, and again the outcome of the one special act in the 100th Congress on behalf of the swimmer, Tracey McFarlane, who did not win, demonstrated the flaws in the process when its integrity is undermined.

The machinations of granting special privileges to athletes did not escape the attention of the media. The *Philadelphia Enquirer* noted the desperation of Members of Congress for Olympic medals:

> they see nothing wrong with having the country do it with Czechoslovaks and Soviets and East Germans...As bad as our showing was at the Winter Games in Calgary, I can't believe the American public is so hungry for medals in Seoul that it favors 'hiring' mercenaries to win them. Surely, the Olympic movement in this country hasn't come to that.[58]

Additionally, the *Philadelphia Enquirer* produced a letter from the father of a United States citizen who was seeking placement on the United States Team:

> The carefully orchestrated and deliberate process of becoming a United States citizen is surely part of being a citizen. It is not and must not be a maneuver of convenience but part of a meaningful and lasting bond of commitment...for them as individuals, and for America, the journey really is part of the destination.[59]

The *New York Times* added that:

> One would hate to think United States sports agencies were pushing citizenship as a remedy for the lack of gold medals in the recent Winter Games or the second-tier status of the United States Davis Cup Team in recent years.[60]

The controversy over citizenship bills was not confined to only Olympic athlete bills. Even bills conferring citizenship on those who perform heroic deeds for the United States or other countries created controversy, as seen in the 97th Congress (1981-1982), when Congress considered a bill conferring honorary citizenship on Raoul Wallenberg.[61] The controversy again centered on the granting of citizenship, the purpose and its benefits, and the precedents established by such an act. Prior to 1981 the only Act of Congress bestowing honorary citizenship was on behalf of Winston Churchill.

Raoul Wallenberg, who was credited with saving lives of Hungarian Jews facing Nazi extermination during World War II, had disappeared in the Soviet Union. His activities during the war included producing and issuing fake Swedish passports, taking over buildings as official Swedish quarters to protect potential victims, and continuously pressing the Hungarian Government to treat Jews, Catholics, and others humanely.[62] During House Immigration Subcommittee hearings on the legislation, the proponents of the legislation argued that citizenship would enable the United States to obtain information on his whereabouts more effectively.[63] The Department of State testified that it would be a symbolic act which would not obligate the Soviet Union under any legal authority, treaty or international law to respond to United States inquiries, nor would it allow him to become a citizen for purposes of the Immigration and Nationality Act, or confer any citizenship on descendants or relatives.[64]

Because of the controversy surrounding the grant of citizenship and the lack of precedents, the House Judiciary Committee adopted an amendment stating that "honorary citizenship is and should remain an extraordinary honor not lightly conferred nor frequently granted." The Chairman of the Immigration Subcommittee, Mr. Mazzoli, filed additional views on the legislation stating:

> there is a tendancy among the Members of the House to support various resolutions that seek to betsow an honor or award, on someone or another, without always giving sufficient attention to the significance of their action. This is particularly the case where the relief sought is U.S. citizenship. I hope my colleagues will, in the future, weigh the ultimate effect of their actions more carefully.[65]

Other members' dissenting views centered around the precedent and the meaning of citizenship. Mr. George Danielson (D-CA) and Mr. Henry J. Hyde (R-IL) joined in the following views:

> I regret that it is necessary to stand in opposition to legislation which is emotionally and politically charged and which appeals to the humanitarian instincts and principles which we all share. This opposition can easily be misunderstood, or misconstrued, to reflect a lack of

appreciation for the heroic acts of a fine person under the most difficult of circumstances. My opposition is based on other, most fundamental, considerations. I perceive and I cherish American citizenship as the highest honor that our country can confer upon a person who is a citizen of another land. The granting of that citizenship is the admission and welcoming of that person into our national family. It must not be lightly bestowed and the granting of it certainly should never be used as an acknowledgement of appreciation for in doing so we would be diminishing and demeaning the citizenship of those of us who have been born to this land and to the millions before us who have supported the principles we stand for and have fought and died to preserve for our country.[66]

The dissenters cited many heroes, including Marquis de Lafayette, Count Casimir Pulaski, and Congressional Medal of Honor winners as equally, if not more, deserving of United States citizenship:

The history of World War II and its aftermath is filled with the stories of heroic actions by people guided by humanitarian principles. We should commend them, we should revere them, we should remember them and their deeds, and we should try to emulate them. But that does not mean that we must give away American citizenship to those people.[67]

As with other legislation involving public figures, even though the law related to one person, it became a public law. Political expediency again overrode established precedents.

Another case subject to controversy was one seeking to bestow posthumous United States citizenship on a veteran of Vietnam, Corporal Wladyslaw Staniszewski in 1984.[68] Although the Congress had precedents during the Vietnam era of granting citizenship posthumously, there had been few enacted since that time. In fact, because of the unique benefits of the legislation, an amendment was adopted specifying that the surviving relatives could obtain no benefits from the private law. During debate on the measure it appeared that Mr. Brian Donnelly (D-MA), the sponsor, played a heavy hand in enlisting the support of the Speaker of the House, Mr. Thomas "Tip" P. O'Neill (D-MA), in bypassing the Committee process for political gain. The Chairman of the Subcommittee, Mr. Mazzoli, noted:

the decision was made to move this bill extraordinarily from the subcommittee, which had not yet worked on it, right to the floor of the House. It is almost an unprecedented act. At least certainly it is unusual, if not unprecedented, and at a given point, when I yield time to the

> gentleman from Massachusetts, I will ask him perhaps to comment on whether or not there is any precedential value or precedential impact of this activity today...The reason I cannot speak authoritatively is that we never did have our hearings and we never did have the votes in the subcommittee and the full committee which typically would have occurred by this time in the session.[69]

The manner of bypassing the regular rules of order incurred the wrath of the Republicans also. As Mr. Thomas R. Kindness (R-OH) stated during the debate:

> Our committee system has its flaws and its faults and sometimes it is a disappointment or a frustration, but it is a part, an essential part of the effective functioning of the House of Representatives.[70]

The Ranking Member of the Immigration Subcommittee, Mr. Dan Lungren (R-CA), also noted the stampeding manner Mr. Donnelly employed in bypassing Committee procedure and the rights of the minority. "As someone mentioned, it is helpful to have the Speaker of the House from the same State as the author of the bill," said Mr. Lungren.[71]

The bestowal of United States citizenship by Congress on aliens within the United States Embassy in Moscow in 1982 was another controversial legislative endeavor which passed the Senate, but which failed of enactment through the checks and balances of the House and the Executive Branch. In 1978 seven members of a fundamentalist Christian sect from Siberia--Pentacostals--sought visas from the United States Embassy in Moscow, although they had not obtained the proper permission to leave the Soviet Union from Soviet authorities.

Once the "Siberian Seven" entered the United States Embassy compound, they refused to leave and encouraged other family members to join them in the hopes that the Soviet Government would be persuaded to let them emigrate. They remained in the Embassy, conducting hunger strikes and creating a precedent by allowing others around the world to flock to United States Embassies for indeterminate vigils.

Legislation which passed the Senate and was supported by 70 Members of the House, would have granted them United States citizenship while in the Soviet Union. The State Department, as with the Wallenberg case, noted that the legislation was largely a symbolic act which would demonstrate the United States government's commitment to human rights and would serve as a "morale booster" to supporters, but that the legalities and the precedent of such an act prevented the State Department from supporting it. As Mr. Thomas W. Simons, Jr., Office of Soviet Union Affairs, Department of State, testified:

> This provision suggests reliance on the concept of extra-territoriality--the idea that the land occupied by an Embassy is part and parcel of the sovereign territory of the sending state. This is a concept that has no foundation in international law and that has been long rejected by the United States and the international community in general.[72]

While the Department of State noted that the United States Government could protect the seven while in the Embassy compound as inviolable under international law, the seven remained Soviet citizens, subject to Soviet laws: "The United States cannot, whether by legislation or any other means, unilaterally alter this basic legal situation," said the Department. The Executive Branch preferred to deal with their potential emigration within the context of overall refugee policies and diplomatic channels. The Siberian Seven later achieved their immigration without recourse to a special Act of Congress.

One of the largest group of beneficiaries subject to a private bill was on behalf of 653 Mennonites in 1980. As natives of Mexico, they entered the United States believing that if they bought land they could automatically obtain United States citizenship. After the purchase of land, they learned that they did not derive citizenship, nor own water rights to the land. In addition, the Mennonites could not meet payments on the land, which forced foreclosure. The bill was sponsored by Sen. Lloyd Bentsen (D-TX) in the Senate and supported by Mr. Sam Hall (D-TX), another member from Texas, in the House.

During full House Judiciary Committee debate, because of the unusually high number of beneficiaries, controversy developed concerning the manner of entry, the alleged promises of citizenship, and the number of beneficiaries. Chairman of the Committee, Mr. Rodino, and Mr. Hall engaged in an exchange on the merits of the legislation:

> Mr. Hall: I think that this is a bill of equity. These people are of the Mennonite faith. They came up here with the utmost good faith. They spent literally their life savings to acquire land...they are working people, they are welders, they are mechanics, carpenters, and have blended into the society in a very fine way.

Mr. Rodino: Would the gentleman attempt to distinguish for me the status of these people as against Mexicans who cross the border, come in illegally, remain here, are hard working, nonetheless are in an illegal status?

Mr. Hall: I think in this instance you had a group of people who were persecuted literally because they did own property in Mexico, whereas other illegal aliens who come into this country, they are coming strictly from an economic standpoint...

Mr. Rodino: Would the gentleman be suggesting that these people, as distinguished from others who come across the border illegally, that these people did not intend to violate the law? That there was no intention there, or that they acted under some false representation?

Mr. Hall: The real estate agents assured them that the immigration matter would easily be taken care of. And in explaining how this would be done, they referred to the idea of a private bill...[73]

Even with the many unresolved questions, the private law granted permanent residence, bolstered with a great deal of support from the Texas delegation (including the Majority Leader, Jim Wright, D-TX) which provided political expediency to push the bill forward.

Perhaps the most controversial private bill, and one which if enacted would have tested the "bill of attainder" clause of the constitution, involved a bill which required the deportation of Harry Renton Bridges in 1940. Mr. Bridges, a labor organizer accused of Communist agitation, was charged by Members of Congress with attempting to "destroy the American way of life, in the efforts to paralyze the economic, industrial, and political life of San Francisco and the greater part of the Pacific coast."[74]

Deportation hearings were instituted against Mr. Bridges by the Secretary of Labor on the ground that he associated with Communists, but after a study conducted by Harvard University's Dean James M. Landis, which found insufficient evidence of his affiliation, the Secretary of Labor canceled the warrant of arrest. That brought the wrath of Congress both on Mr. Bridges and the Secretary of Labor.

The House Immigration Committee, after a lengthy investigation, passed a resolution ordering Mr. Bridges' deportation. It was presented as a private bill under special rules of the House allowing debate of the measure, which was not the ordinary procedure for private bills. Although its constitutionality was debated on the House Floor, it was politically expedient for Congress to demand his deportation through a private bill. As the Committee stated in its report on the legislation:

> Bridges is regarded by the framers of this bill as a menace to the interests of this country. His close association with known Communists was brought out and admitted by him in the Government's warrant hearing in his deportation case during the summer of 1939...[when] our Nation may at any time become involved in war, it is not a time to equivocate, but it is the primary duty of Congress to act promptly in the interests of the peoples of these United States.[75]

The House Immigration Committee, in acting favorably on the Bridges bill, further noted:

> It is generally conceded that it is an attribute of sovereignty to control and regulate the matter of the alien within our gates. The legislative branch, being a coordinate branch of the Government, is acting within its authority in proposing and acting upon the subject matter covered by H.R. 9766.
>
> The bill has been drawn and voted upon favorably by the Immigration and Naturalization Committee on the theory that if the Congress has the right to authorize and direct by legislation, as has been done in the past, the entry by name of aliens into the United States, it has the right equally to legislate on the question of whether specific aliens may be permitted to remain in this country, notwithstanding such aliens may have been legally admitted under the immigration laws when they came here. No question has been raised of the right of Congress to except from the general provisions of the immigration laws aliens by name who have not in entering complied specifically with such laws, *and the authority to authorize and direct that the alien, Harry Renton Bridges, be deported without assigning any reason is inherent and asserted by this bill.*[76]

As soon as the bill passed the House, the Senate appointed a Committee to look into the legislation. Its investigation, outlined in a legal memorandum by the Senate Committee, found insufficient evidence that Bridges was affiliated with Communist organizations. More importantly, because of the lack of precedent and the possible unconstitutionality of the bill, the Senate amended the bill to require that the Attorney General conduct an investigation, and if the results yielded facts to justify deportation that the Attorney General was authorized "to proceed with the deportation of such alien *in the manner provided by law.*"

Attorney General Robert H. Jackson, commenting on the original bill, stated:

> The Congress has almost unlimited powers over aliens. It has embodied its policies in general laws. If it is convinced, as I am, that recent experiences show the need for additional safeguards, by all means let us have them...But there is no condition, existing or threatened, which needs arbitrary legislation prescribing no rule of conduct, but merely imposing banishment by legislative fiat...Harry Bridges may be all that this bill implies of him. But certainly he does not deserve a place in our history as a martyr. He is insignificant compared to the issues presented by this bill...As an American I would not, for the sake of my own liberty, deny the protection of uniform and indiscriminatory laws, and of fair hearings to even the humblest or meanest of men. As an official of the United States I cannot in good conscience do other than recommend strongly against this bill.[77]

The checks and balances of the Senate, and the Executive Branch, halted the final passage of this measure. The bill was never considered in the full Senate after being reported from the Committee with the amendment language requiring that due process be accorded Mr. Bridges. Most importantly, the problems relating to constitutionality raised by the Executive Branch proved too overwhelming to overcome.

Appendix A

Summary of Rules of Procedure and Policies

1947 House and Senate Committees on the Judiciary enter into Agreements with INS on handling stays of deportation for private immigration bills (80th Congress).

1953 Senate reviews policies on private immigration bills (83rd Congress).

1954 House establishes Rules of Procedure which include: a set date for meeting on private bills, public meetings, a quorum, reports requested from the Executive Branch on bills except Rule 4 (stowaways, seamen, and those entering the U.S. surreptitiously), unless a waiver is obtained required based on separation of families, action is not delayed for nonappearance of the author, tabled bills are not reconsidered unless there is a material change in the facts, and all administrative remedies had to be exhausted. (83rd Congress).

1955 House rules require "extreme hardship" to waive Rule 4, bills are considered in chronological order, and previous Senate adverse bills are not considered unless the Senate alters its position on the legislation (84th Congress).

1959 House rules prohibit consideration where court proceedings are pending (86th Congress).

1967 House rules add aliens in-transit to Rule 4 (90th Congress).

1969 House rules add visitors, exchange visitors, and students to Rule 4 (91st Congress).

1971 House rules require "unusual hardship" for Rule 4 (changed to include all nonimmigrants), and further information is required on naturalization cases (92nd Congress). Staff recommendations are initiated.

1977 House rules require bills that request reconsideration to be scheduled at the earliest possible date (95th Congress).

1979 Senate adopts new policies on private bills similar to the House for aliens in the United States (96th Congress).

1981 Senate adopts Rules of Procedure on private immigration bills, including Rule 3 relating to aliens in the United States. House establishes rules on FMGs requiring passage of certain exams (96th Congress).

1983 House rules require "extreme hardship," FOIA and Privacy Act waiver. Rules incorporate policies on adoptions, investors, medical cases, deferred cases, fraud, FMGs, nurses, drugs, and naturalization (98th Congress).

1985 House adopts a two-thirds rule which requires that two-thirds of the Subcommittee membership is required to schedule consideration of certain controversial private bills. These included medical cases, FMGs, bills previously not scheduled on the agenda, and naturalization cases.

The rules also require a two-year timeframe for obtaining benefits of a private law (99th Congress).

1987 House adds Olympic cases and legalization cases to the two-thirds rule. House and Senate Immigration Subcommittees address letter to the United States Olympic Committee regarding problems with expediting citizenship on behalf of Olympic athletes (100th Congress).

Appendix B

INS and Committee on Judiciary Agreements

[Source: Immigration and Naturalization Service, 1989 FOIA Request. The following letters were re-typed from the original copy for printing purposes]

March 3, 1983

The Honorable Alan C. Nelson
Commissioner
Immigration and Naturalization Service
425 Eye Street, N.W.
Washington, D.C. 20536

Dear Mr. Commissioner:

I wish to restate for your concurrence the policy that was agreed upon by the Immigration and Naturalization Service and the House Committee on the Judiciary relative to the immigration status in the United States of beneficiaries of private bills.

When deportation proceedings are commenced in the case of an alien in the United States who is, or becomes, the beneficiary of a private bill, and a report is requested on the bill by the Committee, the proceedings will be carried to conclusion in the normal course with the entry of a final administrative order in the case, but final action to enforce departure in such cases will be held in abeyance until such time as the Congress has had an opportunity to consider the bill on its merits. If the beneficiary of a pending private bill requests advance permission to reenter the United States after an emergency trip abroad, it shall be within the discretion of the Service to determine if such permission shall be granted and the Committee will be informed of the decision.

In those cases where adverse action is taken, the Service will proceed to enforce the beneficiary's departure.

In the event, during the pendency of a private bill, evidence is developed that the facts are so adverse as to warrant summary enforcement of departure, the Service should seek the agreement of the Committee to enforce immediate departure. We also seek your agreement that beneficiaries of private immigration bills adversely acted upon by either the House or Senate Committee on the Judiciary at any time will not be granted a stay of deportation, notwithstanding the introduction of a bill in the other body unless the acting Committee agrees to vacate its prior action.

As in the past, cases in which the beneficiary of a private bill is subject to Rule 3 or Rule 4 of the Committee Rules of Procedure on private immigration legislation, action to enforce departure will not be held in abeyance unless a formal request by the Committee for such action is made.

Previously there was agreement that the introduction of a private bill to confer permanent resident status upon an alien in the United States as a lawful nonimmigrant would terminate the alien's lawful nonimmigrant status. If such an alien, on being notified of the termination of his lawful nonimmigrant status, claims that the bill was introduced without his knowledge and consent, the Immigration and Naturalization Service will regard such alien as restored to lawful status as nonimmigrant if the bill is formally withdrawn.

Your concurrence in this restatement of policy is appreciated.

With kind regards,

Sincerely,

/s/

PETER W. RODINO, JR.
Chairman

PWR:bms

107-703.785

23 Mar 1983

Honorable Peter W. Rodino, Jr.
Chairman, Committee on the Judiciary
House of Representatives
Washington, D.C. 20515

Dear Mr. Chairman:

Reference is made to your letter of March 3, 1983, in which you restate the policy previously agreed to by this Service at various times relating to the immigration status in the United States of beneficiaries of private bills.

This Service finds your restatement in accord with our understanding of the policy and concurs therein. I would add, however, that in accordance with long-standing policy, the Service will give due consideration to humanitarian and other compelling factors in determining whether the departure of a beneficiary will be enforced following adverse action by your Committee.

Sincerely,

/s/

Alan C. Nelson
Commissioner

Appendix C

Summary of Major Immigration Laws

1790 Requirements for residence and moral character for naturalization established.

1798 President is authorized to order deported any alien dangerous to the United States.

1875-1903 Various bills are enacted prohibiting the admission of prostitutes, criminals, diseased aliens, or persons likely to be public charges, and anarchists.

1882 Chinese exclusion law prohibits immigration of Chinese.

1917 Codification of immigration laws on exclusion. Dillingham Commission is established to study the immigration laws due to a large increase in immigration at the turn of the century. The report was issued in 1911. The literacy provisions set forth language requirements for immigrants. A "barred zone" is designated to exclude Asians from immigration.

1921 First quota law permitted the admission annually of 3% of the number of foreign-born persons of each nationality in the United States.

1922 Cable act allowed women certain rights for naturalization.

1924 Permanent quota law is based on national origins. The law also reenforced the exclusion of aliens from Asian who were "ineligible to citizenship" due to race. It also established priorities for certain family members allowed outside immigration quotas.

1928 Women are provided certain immigration conferral rights.

1929 Provisions for the registry of legal residence for entry before 1921.

1934 Women are allowed the ability to confer citizenship in certain cases.

1939 Registry provisions are updated to entry prior to 1924.

1940 Alien Registration Act extended the classes of deportable aliens and required the registration of all aliens. Suspension of deportation is provided for aliens in the United States. Another new law provided for codification of the naturalization laws and allowances for waivers of residence for spouses of United States citizens.

1942-1964 Bracero program is enacted and extended under various statutes.

1943 Chinese exclusions are repealed.

1945 GI Brides Act allowed spouses of Armed Forces personnel special immigration benefits.

1946 Fiancee Act allowed fiancees of Armed Forces personnel special immigration benefits. A new law allows the entry to the United States of exchange visitors (Fulbright Amendment).

1948 Displaced Persons Act provided for the admission of refugees and orphans from Europe. Another new law expanded suspension of deportation provisions for aliens in the United States.

1950 Internal Security Act expanded the grounds of exclusion, particularly relating to Communist Party Membership. It also required aliens to read and write the English language and take a test of civics for naturalization.

1951 Repeal of expatriation provisions for voting in Italian elections. Another new law allowed a waiver for involuntary membership in the Communist Party.

1952 Revision and codification of the immigration laws which changed the preferences for immigration within the quotas. The highest priority related to skills-based preferences, with other preferences for family. Ineligibility to immigrate based on race is eliminated. Also, the law allowed a waiver of fraud for close relatives.

1953 Refugee Relief Act allowed the admission of refugees from Europe.

1954 Exemption provided for a bar for criminal offenses which were petty in nature. Another new law eliminated expatriation for voting in elections in Japan.

1956 Two year foreign residence requirement for exchange visitors is established with one waiver allowed for public interest.

1957 Provision for the Attorney General to waive tuberculosis, fraud, moral turpitude, and prostitution on behalf of close relatives of United States citizens or permanent residents.

1957-1962 Quota backlog reduction is provided for certain relatives of United States citizens and permanent residents, and skills-based immigrants.

1958 Registry provisions are updated to entry prior to 1940. Another new law expanded adjustment of status provisions.

1959 Expansion of the class of relatives which could immigrate under the quota system to include unmarried sons and daughters of permanent resident aliens and increased the number of visas for brothers and sisters of U.S. citizens. Another new law removed loss of citizenship provisions for certain naturalized citizens.

1960 Refugee Fair Share Act allowed admission of refugees.

1961 Waiver of exchange visitor visa restrictions based on hardship are added, as well as a new visa designated for exchanges. Another new law provided permanent immigration provisions for adopted children and a permanent tuberculosis and fraud waiver for certain relatives of United States citizens or permanent residents.

1964 Supreme Court declared unconstitutional provisions of loss of citizenship based on residence abroad.

1965 National Origins system for immigration is repealed. The new system established two systems of immigration with a maximum number of 170,000 visas per year for the Eastern Hemisphere, and Western Hemisphere immigration was unrestricted. In addition, a preference system was established for the Eastern Hemisphere which included relatives of United States citizens and permanent residents and skilled aliens. It also established a 20,000 per country limitation. The Western Hemisphere system was based on first-come first-served without priority established for relatives and skills persons. In both systems immediate relatives and special immigrants were exempt from numerical limitations. Waivers of health grounds such as epilepsy and mental retardation were provided for relatives of United States citizens or permanent residents.

1966 Cuban Adjustment Act.

1970 New requirements for exchange visitors establish funding requirements in certain cases or skills exchanges. In addition, two waivers of the two-year foreign residence requirement are added based on "no objection" of the home country and based on persecution.

1972 Citizenship retention requirements are liberalized for certain children born abroad.

1975 Immigration of adopted children by single parents is allowed.

1976 A system for Western Hemisphere immigration is established similar to the Eastern Hemisphere with a ceiling 120,000 and a 20,000 per country limitation. Another new law prohibited FMGs from obtaining no objection waivers.

1978 A worldwide system for immigration is established by combining both hemispheric systems with an overall 290,000 visa system, and one preference structure for relatives and skills. A Select Commission on Immigration and Refugee policy is established to review immigration laws. Another new law repealed retention requirements for certain children born abroad. Also, another new law eliminated the two-petition limit on adoption. Yet another law this year provided a waiver for English language for citizenship.

1980 Refugee Relief Act provides structure for the admission of refugees.

1981 Revisions to the immigration law included changes to the adoption definitions, grandfathering provisions for FMGs and investors, exclusion waivers for drug offenses, and naturalization changes.

1985 Naturalization waiver for former members of the Communist Party is provided.

1986 "The Immigration Reform and Control Act" established penalties for employers of illegal aliens and provided legalization of aliens in the United States prior to 1982. Registry provisions are moved to allow permanent residence for those who entered the United States prior to 1972. Another new law reduced transmission requirements for children born abroad of United States citizens.

1990 Provided for increased levels of immigration and certain visas for diversity.

Appendix D1

Precedents Case Summaries

25th Cong., for the relief of John Campbell White. Beneficiary's record was noted incorrectly due to a "misprision" or mistake of the clerk. The law allowed the record to be corrected to read the full name of the beneficiary, John Campbell White for purposes of naturalization. (6 Stat. 750 (1839))-NMSC

44th Cong., S. 32, for the relief of Frederick Hinkel. Beneficiary renounced citizenship and was employed with the government of the North German Empire in the consular service. The law provided that his actions were accepted by the President as evidence of renunciation under the treaty between the United States and the North German Confederation. (Priv. L. No. 9, 19 Stat. 411 (1877))-NVOL

55th Cong., S. 156, for the relief of Nellie Grant Sartoris. Beneficiary lost citizenship due to marriage to a subject of Great Britain and naturalization under a convention between the United States and Great Britain. The law allowed reinstatement of citizenship. (Priv. L. No. 36, 30 Stat. 1496 (1898)) (H.R. Rep. No. 1125)-NVOL

62nd Cong., H.J. Res. 200, for the relief of Eugene Prince. Beneficiary, a 22-year old native of Russia, was employed by International Harvester. His grandfather traveled to Russia to represent exporters of petroleum and died there. His child, John Henry Prince, the father of the beneficiary, was born in Russia and never resided in the United States but retained his American citizenship as an agent of various American firms. He could not transmit citizenship to the beneficiary because he did not reside in the United States. The Committee noted he could have become a Russian subject, but that "it was and is repugnant to his sentiments to abandon his desire to be recognized as a citizen of the United States in view of his descent and in view of his training and sympathies and in view of the fact that until recently he always supposed that his American citizenship was an unquestioned fact." The law admitted him unconditionally to citizenship. (Priv. L. No. 3, 37 Stat. 1346 (1912)) (H.R. Rep. No. 856)-NCOD

63rd Cong., S. 3419, for the relief of George E. Lerrigo. Beneficiary, a 44-year old native of England, sought United States citizenship. His family moved to the United States when he was age 15, and before age 21 made inquiries as to how to obtain United States citizenship. It was alleged his father's naturalization would include all members of the family. The beneficiary was married to a United States citizen and voted in elections. He later went to China with the Young Men's Christian Association and resided four years. When he applied for a passport, it was discovered his father's naturalization was six weeks after he reached the age of 21 therefore he did not derive United States citizenship. The bill sought to waive the residence requirements for United States citizenship. The law admitted the beneficiary to United States citizenship. (Priv. L. No. 184, 38 Stat. 1476 (1915))-NCOD

64th Cong., S. 8075, for the relief of Marguerite Mathilde Slidell D'Erlanger. Beneficiary, a 75-year old native of the United States, lost her United States citizenship by marriage to a German Baron. After her marriage she resided in France with her husband 60 years until his death. She was unaware of provisions in the law whereby a United States citizen widow of a foreign subject could regain United States citizenship, and therefore did not register her intentions within the appropriate timeframe. The beneficiary's relatives in the United States included her only brother, as well as Admirals in the United States Navy. The Senate Committee noted, "It is unnecessary to be reminded of the distinguished place in American public life her father, the Hon. John Slidell, held, being for a time a Member of the House of Representatives of the United States and a Senator of the United States." The law allowed the beneficiary to be readmitted to United States citizenship. (Priv. L. No. 196, 39 Stat. 1588 (1917))-NVOL

64th Cong., S.J. Res. 208, for the relief of Joseph Beech. Beneficiary, a 50-year old native of England, entered the United States with his family at the age of four. At the age of 32 he was appointed a missionary and resided in China 15 years. The beneficiary did not realize his citizenship was in question until application for a United States passport while in China. He sought to be naturalized without the requisite residence periods required for naturalization. The beneficiary wished to return to China as President of the West China Union University. The law held the beneficiary admitted to United States citizenship. (Priv. L. No. 132, 39 Stat. 1495 (1917))-NCOD

66th Cong., S.J. Res. 90, for the relief of Frances Scoville Mumm. Beneficiary, a native-born United States citizen, lost citizenship by marriage to a native of Germany who was the owner of a business in France entitled J.H. Mumm Company, where they resided. The beneficiary and her husband returned to Germany to avoid internment in France. Because of the "neglect and ill treatment" of her husband, the beneficiary sought divorce and a separation agreement was obtained. The Senate Committee noted the beneficiary was in jeopardy because she was not considered a French, German or United States citizen. The need for legislation was also noted in that Congress should protect the interests of an American woman who "even though she married a German" had not expected to reside in Germany or become a German citizen, but who, by her separation from her husband, and her return to and residence in the United States, is, to all intents and purposes--if not under the terms of the law--a citizen of the United States." The law held the beneficiary readmitted to United States citizenship. (Priv. L. No. 1, 41 Stat. 1449 (1919)) (Sen. Rep. No. 343, 1st Sess.) (H.R. Rep. No. 363, 1st Sess.)-NVOL

66th Cong., S.J. Res. 134, for the relief of Augusta Louise De Haven-Alten. Beneficiary, a native-born United States citizen, lost her United States citizenship through marriage to a native of Germany. The beneficiary had resided in the United States with her parents and upon the death of her mother her father took the children to Switzerland. She inherited $100,000 from her mother and had a trust fund established by her grandmother. She later was separated from her husband; but was unable to take advantage of provisions for regaining United States citizenship due to war conditions. According to the Senate Committee "The record of the hearings in this case not only shows a family record of truest Americanism, but shows a record of the highest patriotism displayed by herself from the moment the United States entered the war and even prior thereto. She made constant efforts to return to the United States." Relatives in the United States included many who served in the Armed Forces. Her father had served during the Civil War, and her grandfather was Admiral Abraham Bigelow who distinguished himself with 45 years in the United States Navy. The law held the beneficiary readmitted to United States citizenship. (Priv. L. No. 2, 41 Stat. 1463 (1920)) (H.R. Rep. No. 619, 2nd Sess.)-NVOL

74th Cong., S. 447, for the relief of Rakha Singh Gherwal. Beneficiary, a descendant of a family which ruled India for "thousands of years and still rules the State of Gherwal," was granted United States citizenship by court over the objection of the Naturalization Service because he was not a "free, white person" and was a Hindu, not entitled to citizenship. For two years he exercised his citizenship rights until a complaint was filed by the United States to cancel his citizenship certificate. According to the House Committee, the beneficiary served in the military during the World War and as a result of becoming a citizen forfeited rights to property in India. The Committee found "this bill is a meritorious measure especially since similar cases have been not pressed where a final determination had not been rendered upon them." Upon cancellation of his certificate, the beneficiary sought to file suit but he could not sue the Government without a special act of Congress. The law conferred jurisdiction on the United States District Court to hear and render judgment upon the suit regarding the beneficiary's cancellation of the naturalization certificate and allowed such a suit to be instituted within six months of the Act. (Priv. L. No. 227, 49 Stat. 2145 (1936)) (H.R. Rep. 1225, 1st Sess.)-NMSC

74th Cong., S. 3399, for the relief of Rosalie Piar Sprecher (nee Rosa Piar). Beneficiary, a 28-year old native of Romania, entered the United States with her mother and stepfather at the age of 16 and was excluded because there were no visa numbers available. Subsequently, it was alleged she posed as a United States citizen and daughter of a man she had met. She then entered the United States again three years later and married a United States citizen. She departed the United States and was found excluded based on her false statements. The law waived section 3 of the Act of 1917 relating to crimes involving moral turpitude on behalf of the beneficiary. (Priv. L. No. 425, 49

Stat. 2234 (1936)) (S. Rep. No. 1421, 1st Sess.) (H.R. Rep. No. 2082, 2nd Sess.)-WCRF

75th Cong., H.R. 5597, for the relief of Luigi Mazza. Beneficiary, a 35-year old native of Italy was under deportation based on a rape conviction in Italy when he was 17 years old where he was sentenced to 16 months. The conviction was based on a wager between two friends who bet the woman could not seduce the young man, 11 years her junior. After the seduction she charged him with rape. The beneficiary married a lawful permanent resident alien and had five children. The House Committee noted he never was arrested and that he was not present at the trial. The Committee also noted that "to deport this alien on the charge of rape would inflict a great hardship on the wife and five children and they would be compelled to rely on relief or be taken care of by charitable institutions." The law canceled deportation proceedings on behalf of the beneficiary and granted him lawful permanent resident status. (Priv. L. No. 686, 52 Stat. 1382 (1938)) (H. R. Rep. No. 2080, 3rd Sess.)-WCRF

75th Cong., H.R. 7039, for the relief of Paul Hirschmann. Beneficiary, a 37-year old native of Germany, entered the United States and secured employment as a butler. He was under deportation proceedings due to an arrest at the age of 18 as a result of taking leather from a factory. While employed in the United States, the beneficiary assisted in an arrest at his place of employment. The House Committee noted the beneficiary did not intend to conceal his arrest in Germany and was "very much impressed by the testimony and by the unusual caliber of witnesses who appeared in the alien's behalf." The law canceled deportation proceedings and held the beneficiary to be lawfully admitted to the United States for permanent residence at the time of his entry to the United States. (Priv. L. No. 810, 52 Stat. 1434 (1938)) (H.R. Rep. No. 2055, 2nd Sess.) (Sen. Rep. No. 2213, 2nd Sess.)-WCRF

75th Cong., H.R. 7297, for the relief of Gordon L. Cheasley. Beneficiary, a native of England, entered the United States with documentation indicating he was born in Canada. His spouse and two children also resided in the United States. He was employed 13 years with the same company. He was under deportation orders because of his false statements of country of birth which he explained due to his parents separation and placement in an orphanage. He always believed Canada to be his home since a Canadian family adopted him. The House Committee noted that while the statement that he was born in Canada was false, "it is not of such a nature as to constitute a serious offense, and because of his wife, children, and position, it would be an unjust hardship to deport him." The law canceled deportation proceedings and held the beneficiary to be lawfully admitted for permanent residence on the date of his re-entry to the United States from Canada. (Priv. L. No. 620, 52 Stat. 1355 (1938)) (H.R. Rep. No. 2040, 2nd Sess.) (Sen. Rep. No. 2026, 2nd Sess.)-WCRF

75th Cong., H.R. 9731, for the relief of James J. Coyne. Beneficiary, a 36-year old native of Ireland, entered the United States illegally and enlisted in the United States Army and held the rank of sergeant serving over 12 years. The beneficiary desired to obtain legal status and subsequent United States citizenship. The law held the beneficiary to have been lawfully admitted for permanent residence as of the date of his first entry to the United States. (Priv. L. No. 803, 52 Stat. 1432 (1938)) (H.R. Rep. No. 2224, 2nd Sess.)-QMGN

75th Cong., H.R. 10136, for the relief of John Patrick Toth. Beneficiary, a 31-year old native of Canada married to a United States citizen, first entered the United States illegally with his parents. After departure from the United States as a result of the illegal entry he again entered the United States and married. He was deported to Canada, and his wife remained in the United States. He was refused a visa on the basis of public charge provisions, and a prior offense involving illegal wine possession in Canada when a small boy. Later he entered the United States to rejoin his wife after their child died. The Committee stated, "It appears that since he has resided in the United States he has worked steadily, paid his debts and supported his family, has never been in any trouble....The House Committee is convinced that to deport this man would be a severe hardship." The law canceled deportation proceedings and held the beneficiary to be a lawful permanent resident of the United States. (Priv. L. No. 805, 52 Stat. 1432 (1938)) (H.R. Rep. No. 2355, 2nd Sess.) (Sen. Rep. No. 2201, 2nd Sess.)-WCRF

75th Cong., S. 3064, for the relief of George Henry Levins. Beneficiary, a 55-year old native of Ireland, sought United States citizenship because he believed he had previously derived citizenship from his father's naturalization. It was later learned he was not a minor at the time and therefore did not acquire United States citizenship. The beneficiary was employed as a W.P.A. employee and was the father of eight children. According to the Senate Committee the beneficiary would "lose his employment unless he qualifies for citizenship." The law allowed the beneficiary to file a declaration for citizenship and become naturalized before any court having jurisdiction over naturalization within one year of the enactment. (Priv. L. No. 745, 52 Stat. 1408 (1938)) (Sen. Rep. No. 1451, 2nd Sess.) (H.R. Rep. No. 2697, 2nd Sess.)-NCOD

76th Cong., H.R. 2948, for the relief of Morris Hoppenheim, Lena Hoppenheim, Doris Hoppenheim, and Ruth Hoppenheim. Beneficiaries, a father, spouse and two children, entered the United States through Canada. The male beneficiary was a native of Poland and his spouse a native of Russia, but both were naturalized citizens of Canada. The two children were born in Canada, ages 20 and 16. They entered the United States for a wedding of a relative and resided 15 years. They had one United States citizen child, age 12. The House Committee noted all beneficiaries except the father would be able to obtain an immigrant visa. The Polish quota prolonged the visa wait. The Committee stated: "To require his departure for the purpose of adjustment or regularization of status...would be a distinct hardship." The law canceled deportation and granted lawful permanent resident status upon the beneficiaries. (Priv. L. No. 329, 54 Stat. 1267 (1940)) (H.R. Rep. No. 773, 1st Sess.)-QMGN

76th Cong., H.R. 4066, for the relief of Josefina Alvarado. Beneficiary, a 21-year old native of Cuba entered the United States for medical treatment as an "imbecile." She resided 10 years in the United States with her mother and nine siblings who supported her during this period. The House Committee noted, "It appears to this committee that this alien could not be deported in her present condition and even if she could she has no relatives to take care of her in Cuba and the only place she can be taken care of is with her family. The committee therefore reports this bill favorably." The law canceled deportation proceedings and deemed the beneficiary to have been lawfully admitted for permanent residence. (Priv. L. No. 588, 54 Stat. 1373 (1940)) (H.R. Rep. No. 2351, 2nd Sess.) (Sen. Rep. No. 2154, 80th Cong., 2nd Sess.)-WHEL

76th Cong., H.R. 4954, for the relief of Rosa Paone. Beneficiary, a 53-year old native of Italy and lawful permanent resident of the United States, was under deportation proceedings at the time of her re-entry as likely to become a public charge. She resided in the United States 12 years and returned after a temporary visit abroad. Later she was hospitalized with psychosis and cerebral arteriosclerosis. Her husband and seven children resided legally in the United States, three of whom were native-born United States citizens, and the only relative abroad was a brother. The House Committee noted the condition of her health had grown worse and there was no possibility of her recovering. Although the family was unable to pay for her keep and was on relief from time to time, it was noted it was better to let her remain in the United States. The law allowed her to retain permanent residence status at the time of re-entry. (Priv. L. No. 592, 54 Stat. 1375 (1940)) (H.R. Rep. No. 2413, 2nd Sess.) (Sen. Rep. No. 2008, 2nd Sess.)-WHEL

76th Cong., H.R. 5494, for the relief of John Marinis, Nicolaos Elias, Ihoanis or Jean Demetre Votsitsanos, and Michael Votsitsanos. Beneficiaries, natives of Greece, entered the United States for temporary employment under section 3 of the Act of 1917 for a one year period to engage in deep-sea sponge diving in Tarpon Springs, Florida and stayed approximately seven years. The House Committee noted the importance of that industry in Florida: "It appeared from the evidence presented, from the statement of the chamber of commerce, and the city officials that deep-sea divers are an absolute necessity for the sponge industry. Without the deep-sea divers, only shallow diving can be done, and there are more than necessary boats engaged in the shallow-water diving..." There also appeared before the Committee the Commissioner of Immigration and Naturalization who indicated "American divers would not take the hazard of the deep-sea diving...and that such deep-sea diving causes certain ailments that American divers are subject to." However, the Immigration Service explained their efforts to reduce the importation of any further sponge divers. They indicated it was the first real effort "to shake off the evils of exploitation by the introduction of native labor which is not so gullible or capable of exploitation as the aliens." The quality of the sponges in deep-sea diving, according to testimony, varied from shallow-water sponges in their durability and accessibility. The law canceled deportation proceedings against the beneficiaries and allowed them to remain in the United States so long as they were engaged in deep-sea diving for sponges. (Priv. L. No. 108, 53 Stat. 1485 (1939)) (H.R. Rep. No. 706, 1st Sess.)-QMOC

76th Cong., H.R. 5827, for the relief of John L. Harder and children, Paul William Harder, Irvin W. Harder, Edna Justina Harder, Elsie Anna Harder and Elizabeth Harder. The eldest beneficiary, the father of five children, was formerly a United States citizen who became a Canadian citizen. His spouse was a United States citizen and the minor beneficiaries, ages 19, 18, 17, 16, and 15 years old, were natives of Canada. When the eldest beneficiary became ill, he returned to the United States for a temporary stay but failed to recover enough to return to Canada. He became paralyzed and could neither move nor speak statements, and the physician indicated he would die soon. The House Committee noted it was unlikely Canada would accept him or his family because of his condition, and 14 years absence from that country. The law canceled deportation proceedings and deemed the beneficiaries lawfully admitted for permanent residence. (Priv. L. No. 366, 54 Stat. 1282 (1940)) (H.R. Rep. Rep. No. 790, 2nd Sess.) (Sen. Rep. No. 1479, 2nd Sess.)-WHEL

76th Cong., H.R. 6056, for the relief of Antal or Anthony or Tony Zaicek or Zaiczek. Beneficiary, a native of Romania, entered the United States as a seaman and resided in the United States 15 years. He married a widow with three children, one of whom was an invalid diagnosed with infantile paralysis. Upon institution of deportation proceedings, he proceeded to attempt to obtain travel documents from Romania but was refused. The House Committee was of the opinion that deportation "would be a hardship on his widow and their family" and recommended favorable enactment. The law canceled deportation proceedings and held the beneficiary to be lawfully admitted for permanent residence. (Priv. L. No. 510, 54 Stat. 1341 (1940)) (H.R. Rep. No. 705, 1st Sess.) (Sen. Rep. No. 1915, 2nd Sess.)-QMGN

76th Cong., H.R. 6888, for the relief of Esther Jacobs. Beneficiary, a 32-year old native of Persia, was admitted to the United States for permanent residence. She later entered a hospital for dementia praecox and was ordered deported on the basis that she became a public charge. Her relatives were unable to pay the hospitalization costs in the state institution. Her only relatives, mother (age 75) and two siblings, resided in the United States and there were no relatives abroad. The House Committee was of the opinion that "if there ever was a hardship case this is one" and recommended favorably. The law canceled deportation and recorded admission of the beneficiary for permanent residence. (Priv. L. No. 601, 54 Stat. 1378

(1940)) (H.R. Rep. No. 2168, 2nd Sess.) (Sen. Rep. No. 2176, 2nd Sess.)-WHEL

76th Cong., S. 796, for the relief of Mato, Miljenko, Bozzo, and Augustin Cibilic, or Zibilich. Beneficiaries were natives of Yugoslavia and derivative United States citizens by birth. They had entered the United States as sons of a United States citizen who had his citizenship canceled. It was alleged he did not know his citizenship was canceled because he was in Italy at the time and was ill. He subsequently paid for the services of a lawyer to arrange a visa for his sons' entry to the United States at the ages of 14, 16 and 19. They were engaged in the oyster business their father had established in New Orleans. The Committee noted, "It does not appear that the young men were at any time aware that they were not legally in the United States, nor does it appear they knew that their father had paid a sum of money to secure fraudulent visas." The law canceled deportation proceedings against the beneficiaries and deemed them to have been lawfully admitted for permanent residence. (Priv. L. No. 251, 53 Stat. 1540 (1939)) (Sen. Rep. No. 542, 1st Sess.) (H.R. Rep. No. 111, 1st Sess.)-WCRF

76th Cong., S. 808, for the relief of Calliope Minaca Pilavakis. Beneficiary, a native and citizen of Italy, entered the United States as a temporary visitor but was married a short time after arrival in the United States and had two United States citizen children. Marriage fraud was alleged because of the precipitous entry to the United States. The law canceled deportation proceedings against the beneficiary and allowed her to be admitted for permanent residence. The Act prohibited her from ever becoming eligible for citizenship. (Priv. L. No. 184, 53 Stat. 1514 (1939)) (Sen. Rep. No. 188, 1st Sess.) (H.R. Rep. No. 1105, 1st Sess.)-WCRF

76th Cong., S. 1291, for the relief of William Carl Laude. Beneficiary, a Brother of the religious Order of St. Benedict, entered United States without a visa from Canada. The law canceled deportation proceedings against the beneficiary and held him to be lawfully admitted for permanent residence. (Priv. L. No. 98, 53 Stat. 1481 (1939)) (Sen. Rep. No. 184, 1st Sess.)-QMOC

76th Cong., S. 2427, for the relief of John Ullmann, Jr. Beneficiary, a 55-year old native of the Soviet Union, entered the United States with his parents. He assumed when the father filed his "first papers" that action conferred United States citizenship. Later, the father was naturalized, but the beneficiary had reached his majority and did not derive United States citizenship. He served 30 years in the United States Navy and upon retiring was appointed assistant deputy United States marshal in Shanghai 18 months, and later was employed with United States tobacco firms in China. The law allowed the beneficiary to be naturalized upon taking the oath of allegiance before a court having jurisdiction over naturalization within one year of the date of enactment. (Priv. L. No. 175, 53 Stat. 1510 (1939)) (Sen. Rep. No. 931, 1st Sess)-NCOD

77th Cong., H.R. 6677, for the relief of Ronald Leroy Chen. Beneficiary, an 11-year old native of the Malay States, who was half-Chinese by his father, was inadmissible to immigrate because of racial ineligibility. His mother was widowed and a United States citizen. The law allowed the admission to the United States for permanent residence without regard to racial eligibility. (Priv. L. No. 617, 56 Stat. 1252 (1942))(Sen. Rep. No. 1815, 2nd Sess.)-QIER

77th Cong., H.R. 7828, for the relief of John Sweeney. Beneficiary, a former native-born United States citizen, deserted from the United States Navy after having been to the United States Naval Academy and served three years in the Navy. He was tried and found guilty of desertion. He was pardoned by the President four days after court-martial. He had resided in Canada after desertion and took out naturalization papers. After court-martial he resided in the United States 22 years and subsequently was employed in construction work at a naval operating base. The Secretary of the Navy, in a report to the Committee, found he "rendered outstanding services for the Navy" during his employment connected with the Navy in Trinidad. The law held the beneficiary to be a United States citizen since birth. (Priv. L. No. 633, 56 Stat. 1259 (1942)) (H. R. Rep. No. 2721, 2nd Sess.)-NXDD

78th Cong., H.R. 312, for the relief of Freda Utley. Beneficiary, a 45-year old native of England, was a former member of the Communist Party and was a candidate for that party in a London Council election. She visited the Soviet Union for seven years and subsequently entered the United States with her mother and son for a temporary visit. She was employed as an economic adviser in the United States and denounced affiliation with the Communist Party in a book entitled "The Dream We Lost," and articles including "Must the World Destroy Itself." The law held the provisions of the Act of October 16, 1918, as amended, relating to membership in a proscribed organization, inapplicable. Priv. L. No. 372, 58 Stat. 1021 (1944)) (H.R. Rep. No. 700, 1st Sess.) (Sen. Rep. No. 1078, 2nd Sess.)-WXCP

78th Cong., H.R. 480, for the relief of Francesco P. Mastrilli. Beneficiary, a 35-year old native of Italy who deserted ship and remained in the United States was found deportable based on statements he made registering as an immigrant. He was married to a United States citizen with one United States citizen child. He served five years in the United States Army and was a member of the National Guard. The law canceled deportation and allowed the beneficiary to have been lawfully admitted for permanent residence at the time of his first entry to the United States. (Priv. L. No. 216, 58 Stat. 956 (1944)) (H.R. Rep. No. 230, 1st Sess.) (Sen. Rep. No. 591, 1st Sess.)-WCRF

78th Cong., H.R. 2016, for the relief of William H. Linhart. Beneficiary, a 31-year old native and citizen of Canada, sought to derive United States citizenship through his father. His father was a native-born citizen who became naturalized in Canada and then returned to the United States with his son. The father became a United States citizen again, but his son did not derive citizenship because there was no record of his entry to the United States at the age of two. The beneficiary did not know he was not a United States citizen. He served four years in the Marine Corps and married a United States citizen. The law held the beneficiary to have been lawfully admitted to the United States at the age of two and to have been dwelling in the United States at the time his father was naturalized, thus having derived United States citizenship through his father's naturalization. (Priv. L. No. 516, 58 Stat. 1080 (1944)) (H.R. Rep. No. 247, 1st Sess.) (Sen. Rep. No. 1374, 2nd Sess.)-NCOD

78th Cong., H.R. 2707, for the relief of Henry White. Beneficiary, a 17-year old native of Singapore and subject of Great Britain and orphan, was held racially ineligible for a visa because of birth in China. He had been in the custody of a United States citizen. He was imprisoned for six months during the Japanese capture of Hong Kong and was brought to the United States with 1,500 American prisoners where the United States citizen guardian requested parole for him. The law held the beneficiary to be lawfully admitted for permanent residence. (Priv. L. No. 380, 58 Stat. 1024 (1944)) (H.R. Rep. No. 765, 1st Sess.) (Sen. Rep. No. 1072, 2nd Sess.)-QIER

79th Cong., H.R. 1350, for the relief of Nora R. Neville. Beneficiary, a 37-year old native and citizen of Ireland, entered the United States with her United States citizen mother. She traveled erroneously on her mother's passport as a United States citizen. She did not acquire citizenship automatically upon the naturalization of her parent because she did not reside in the United States at that time. She was unaware of her lack of citizenship until requested to furnish proof at the place of her employment with the N.Y. Telephone Company. The law deemed the beneficiary to have been lawfully admitted for permanent residence. (Priv. L. No. 460, 60 Stat. 1143 (1946)) (H.R. Rep. No. 622, 1st Sess.) (Sen. Rep. No. 1105, 2nd Sess.)-NMSC

79th Cong., H.R. 1402, for the relief of Certain Basque Aliens. Beneficiaries, ages 20 to 55, natives of Spain and of the Basque race, entered the United States at various times as seamen or visitors and then obtained employment in Utah and Nevada as sheepherders. The bill received favorable action because they were "practically indispensable to the war food program in that they make excellent shepherds." (Priv. L. No. 818, 60 Stat. 1292 (1946))(H.R. Rep. No. 165, 1st Sess.) (Sen. Rep. No. 1813, 2nd Sess.)-QMOC

79th Cong., H.R. 3441, for the relief of Master Sgt. Gerhard Neumann. Beneficiary, a 28-year old native of Germany, enlisted in the United States Army in China and served as a mechanic and crew chief training Chinese personnel in American airplane engines. It was desired that the beneficiary obtain a commission, but he was ineligible because he was not a United States citizen and not inducted in the United States. The law held the beneficiary within sections 701 and 702 of the Nationality Act of 1940, and allowed his naturalization notwithstanding enlistment did not occur in the United States, and that he had not previously been admitted for permanent residence. (Priv. L. No. 695, 60 Stat. 1242 (1946)) (H.R. Rep. No. 1111, 1st Sess.) (S. Rep. No. 1446, 2nd Sess.)-NMSC

79th Cong., H.R. 5278, for the relief of Virginia Harris Casardi. Beneficiary, a 38-year old native-born United States citizen who lost her citizenship by taking an oath of allegiance to Italy upon her marriage to an Italian diplomat, sought to regain citizenship. The law held the beneficiary to have been admitted for lawful permanent residence at the time of her return to the United States. (Priv. L. No. 845, 60 Stat. 1303 (1946)) (H.R. Rep. No. 1814, 2nd Sess.) (Sen. Rep. No. 1733, 79th Cong., 2nd Sess.)-NVOL

80th Cong., H.R. 422, for the relief of Francesco and Natalia Picchi. Beneficiaries, 54- and 45-year old natives and citizens of Italy, were parents of five United States children, three of whom served in the United States military. They were found deportable due to their connection with a house of prostitution. The law allowed the beneficiaries to remain permanently in the United States notwithstanding section 19(a) of the Act of February 5, 1917. (Priv. L. No. 168, 62 Stat. 1308 (1948)) (H.R. Rep. No. 112, 1st Sess.) (Sen. Rep. No. 861, 2nd Sess.)-WCRF

80th Cong., H.R. 553, for the relief of Arsenio Acacio Lewis. Beneficiary, a 29-year old native and citizen of the Philippines, was adopted by a United States citizen who met him while in the Philippines where he allegedly assisted in providing assistance to interned prisoners. The law held the beneficiary lawfully admitted for permanent residence. (Priv. L. No. 70, 61 Stat. 993 (1947)) (H.R. Rep. No. 545, 1st Sess.) (Sen. Rep. No. 492, 1st Sess.)-QIRA

80th Cong., H.R. 892, for the relief of Michel Ferapontow. Beneficiary, a 19-year old native of Russia, was taken prisoner by the Germans during the invasion of Russia and later worked in different United States Army camps in Germany. He stowed away on a ship, entered the United States, and visited with an Army official who had befriended him in Germany. The law held the beneficiary to have been lawfully admitted for permanent residence. (Priv. L. No. 330, 62 Stat. 1365 (1948)) (H.R. Rep. No. 1207, 1st Sess.) (Sen. Rep. No. 1328, 2nd Sess.)-QMGN

80th Cong., H.R. 1215, for the relief of Kazue Oda Takahashi. Beneficiary, a 38-year old native and citizen of Japan, entered the United States as a temporary visitor. She later married a lawful permanent resident alien and they had two United States citizen children, ages two and four. She was found deportable and was unable to obtain a visa because of her racial ineligibility. The law held the beneficiary to have been admitted to the United States for lawful permanent residence. (Priv. L. No. 225, 62 Stat. 1328 (1948)) (H.R. Rep. No. 883, 1st Sess.) (Sen. Rep. No. 1006, 2nd Sess.)-QIER

80th Cong., H.R. 1572, for the relief of Basque aliens. Beneficiaries, eight Basque sheepherders of Spain entered the United States as seamen or illegally and were employed as sheepherders in Nevada for five to seven years. The Attorney General noted, "Special consideration has been given in a number of cases in the past to adjust the immigration status of experienced law-abiding Basque shepherds through legislative action... Their continued residence in the United States has proved advantageous to the sheep-raising industry." The law canceled deportation proceedings against the beneficiaries and held them to have been lawfully admitted for permanent residence. (Priv. L. No. 350, 62 Stat. 1373 (1948)) (H. R. Rep. No. 1209, 1st Sess.) (Sen. Rep. No. 1385, 2nd Sess.)-QMOC

80th Cong., H.R. 1652, for the relief of certain United States Army personnel-Yugoslav fliers. Beneficiaries, seven Yugoslav members of the United States Army, sought to be naturalized in the United States under sections 701 and 702 of the Nationality Act of 1940. They were ineligible for expeditious naturalization because they had not been lawfully admitted for permanent residence at the time of their enlistment. The fliers were attached to the United States Army Air Forces in the Mediterranean under an agreement between the United States and the Royal Yugoslav Government for the purpose of flying combat missions for support of the Yugoslav troops. According to a report from the War Department the Yugoslav detachment demonstrated the greatest "bravery, stamina and skill" during the campaigns in Italy, Greece, Bulgaria, Romania, Austria, Germany and France in which they were involved. The beneficiaries were ages 33 through 42. The law allowed the beneficiaries to be naturalized notwithstanding their lack of permanent resident status and inability to meet the expiration date for filing of petitions for naturalization under special provisions for military service. (Priv. L. No. 102, 61 Stat. 1004 (1947)) (H.R. Rep. No. 419, 1st Sess.) (Sen. Rep. No. 661, 1st Sess.)-NMSC

80th Cong., H.R. 1749, for the relief of Johannes or John, Julia, Michael, William, and Anna Kostiuk. Beneficiaries, natives of Canada, entered the United States illegally from Canada. The father became a naturalized United States citizen but his certificate was canceled because of the illegal entry. The law amended previous legislation which canceled deportation and admitted the beneficiaries to lawful permanent residence. (Priv. L. No. 305, 62 Stat. 1357 (1948)) (H. R. Rep. No. 1483, 2nd Sess.) (Sen. Rep. No. 1184, 2nd Sess.)-NMSC

80th Cong., H.R. 1912, for the relief of John A. Dilboy. Beneficiary, a 46-year old native of Turkey and subject of Greece, entered the United States as a deserting seaman and was ordered deported. He was the brother of George Dilboy, a veteran of World War I and possessor of the Congressional Medal of Honor. The law held the beneficiary to be lawfully admitted for permanent residence. (Priv. L. No. 241, 62 Stat. 1334 (1948)) (H.R. Rep. No. 1226, 1st Sess.) (Sen. Rep. No. 1086, 2nd Sess.)-QMGN

80th Cong., H.R. 3243, for the relief of Roman Toporow. Beneficiary, a 27-year old native and citizen of Poland, entered the United States in transit and sought to remain permanently. He had previously been in the Polish Army during World War II serving in the African campaign and Italy. The Attorney General's report was unfavorable indicating "conditions abroad afford an easy explanation of this young man's desire to remain in the United States, but there appear to be no factors involved in his case which would warrant the enactment of special legislation on his behalf." The law canceled deportation proceedings against the beneficiary and held him to have been lawfully admitted for permanent residence. (Priv. L. No. 90, 61 Stat. 1000 (1947)) (H.R. Rep. No. 984, 1st Sess.)-QMGN

80th Cong., H.R. 3742, for the relief of Robert Wilhelm Gerling. Beneficiary, a 34-year old native and citizen of Germany, entered the United States for permanent residence and sought to establish his entry effective the first date of admission. His family was engaged in insurance and he was owner of a large amount of shares in Rheingruppe companies holding a majority ownership. The Swiss Government was anxious to divest the beneficiary of his ownership in view of his German origin. Because of laws in Switzerland and Holland he was unable to administer, transfer or sell his holdings; therefore he sought citizenship as a means of reinstating his business interests abroad. During an investigation of the beneficiary, he said he would be unwilling to fight against Germany although he was not a member of the Nazi Party. The report of the Attorney General noted "Congress has heretofore been reluctant to make exception in the naturalization process through the medium of private legislation except in the most meritorious cases. There appear to be no circumstances in the instant case which would warrant the enactment of special legislation." The law held the beneficiary admitted for lawful permanent residence effective the date of his first entry to the United States. (Priv. L. No. 216, 62 Stat. 1325 (1948)) (H. R. Rep. No. 1216, 1st Sess.) (Sen. Rep. No. 948, 2nd Sess.)-NRES

80th Cong., H.R. 3787, for the relief of Mrs. Maria Smorczewska. Beneficiary, a 54-year old native and citizen of Poland, entered the United States as a visitor. She was employed as a domestic by the United States Ambassador to Poland and he paid her passage to the United States. She was later employed by the President of General Mills. The law held the beneficiary to have been lawfully admitted for permanent residence. (Priv. L. No. 308, 62 Stat. 1357 (1948)) (H.R. Rep. No. 1358, 2nd Sess.) (S. Rep. No. 1189, 80th Cong., 2nd Sess.)-QMOC

80th Cong., H.R. 3880, for the relief of Ludwig Pohoryles. Beneficiary, a 10-year old native and citizen of Poland, entered the United States in transit. He was orphaned at the age of five when his parents were shot before his eyes during the war. He was saved by a Christian servant girl who took care of him when in a labor camp. His uncle and only remaining relative learned of his plight while in a U.N. refugee camp and brought him into the United

States. The law held the beneficiary lawfully admitted for permanent residence. (Priv. L. No. 296, 62 Stat. 1354 (1948)) (H.R. Rep. No. 1431, 2nd Sess.) (Sen. Rep. No. 1191, 2nd Sess.)-QMGN

80th Cong., H.R. 4047, for the relief of Edmund Huppler. Beneficiary, a 55-year old native and citizen of Estonia, entered the United States as a seaman. While serving aboard an Estonian vessel in 1941 a Russian consul boarded and told him to raise the Russian flag. He refused to comply with the orders. He later joined the American merchant marine and served with them three years. He was the recipient of three awards from the War Shipping Administration. The law canceled deportation proceedings against the beneficiary and held him to have been lawfully admitted for permanent residence. (Priv. L. No. 393, 62 Stat. 1392 (1948)) (H.R. Rep. No. 2058, 2nd Sess.) (Sen. Rep. No. 1639, 2nd Sess.)-QMDE

80th Cong., H.R. 4050, for the relief of Moke Tcharoutcheff, Lucie Baptistine Tcharoutcheff, Raymond Tcharoutcheff, and Robert Tcharoutcheff. Beneficiaries, a 38-year old male beneficiary who was a native of Russia, his wife, a native and citizen of France and their daughter and son (ages 10, 8) natives of citizens of France, were unable to adjust status due to the oversubscribed quotas. During 1941 in French Basque the beneficiary facilitated the entry and departure through that area of "persons friendly to the American cause" and "laid the groundwork for such activities by enlisting the aid of the French clergy, school authorities, and farmers." The Military Intelligence Reserve stated that after the beneficiary's departure from Spain he was given United States assistance in obtaining entry to the United States. The Attorney General noted, however, there were "several persons who apparently know Mr. Tcharoutcheff and knew of his activities during World War II...that he was engaged in smuggling and black-market activities in France and Spain, and that he is not trustworthy." The law held the beneficiaries lawfully admitted to the United States for permanent residence. (Priv. L. No. 312, 62 Stat. 1359 (1948)) (H.R. Rep. No. 1359, 2nd Sess.) (Sen. Rep. No. 1192, 2nd Sess.)-QMDE

80th Cong., H.R. 4403, for the relief of Ladislao Vaida, Elena Vaida, and Stefano Vaida. Beneficiaries, ages 52, 50, 15, and natives of Hungary, entered the United States in transit to Brazil. They were former opera singers and, according to documents, rendered service to the Allied intelligence during the war. It was stated the male beneficiary allowed his home to be used as a "haven for Allied fliers and parachutists who were dropped into Hungary...He was unselfish in his devotion to the cause of humanity." When questioned as to how the Allied Intelligence could make reciprocity for his services he stated: "If I can come out of this alive, I will ask but one thing, and that is to find a haven in a peaceful country where I can begin life anew." The law held the beneficiaries lawfully admitted for permanent residence. (Priv. L. No. 254, 62 Stat. 1338 (1948)) (H.R. Rep. No. 1218, 1st Sess.) (Sen. Rep. No. 1097, 2nd Sess.)-QMDE

80th Cong., H.R. 4484, for the relief of Theodore Loetsch. Beneficiary, a 42-year old native and citizen of Luxembourg married to a United States citizen, entered the United States as a seaman. He was found excludable from adjusting status due to theft of a piece of lead weighing 100 pounds in Luxembourg for which he was convicted of petty larceny. The law waived the provisions of the eleventh category of section 3 of the Act of 1917 and allowed issuance of a visa. (Priv. L. No. 338, 62 Stat. 1368 (1948)) (H. R. Rep. No. 1652, 2nd Sess.) (Sen. Rep. No. 1336, 2nd Sess.)-WCRF

80th Cong., S. 53, for the relief of Harold Turcean. Beneficiary was a native of Romania who entered the United States at the age of three without proper documents. He enlisted in the United States Army and was killed in action in Normandy in 1944. The Attorney General noted, "While it might, therefore, seem to be an idle gesture to confer citizenship upon a deceased person, I am not wholly unsympathetic toward the feelings of the boy's mother...I find no objection to the enactment of the bill." It was noted in the same report there were no precedents for such legislation and enactment of the bill would not involve rights of any living person or rights of survivors under Veterans' Administration laws. The law held the beneficiary to be a citizen at the time of his death by conferring United States citizenship posthumously upon him. (Priv. L. No. 51, 61 Stat. 985 (1947)) (Sen. Rep. No. 92, 1st Sess.) (H.R. Rep. No. 660, 1st Sess.)-NXPS

80th Cong., S. 83, for the relief of Elizabeth Pickering Winn. Beneficiary, a native of South Africa and naturalized citizen of the United States, lost her claim to citizenship by prolonged residence abroad. She attained United States citizenship on the basis of her marriage to a United States citizen who later died. Travel to the United States by the beneficiary had been thwarted during the war. Her daughter was a United States citizen. The Attorney General stated there did not appear to be unusual circumstances in this case and expressed his opposition "in principle to the enactment of legislation to restore citizenship." The report also noted there were many other individuals who experienced difficulties in meeting the retention requirements. The law allowed the beneficiary to submit a petition for naturalization within one year after the date of enactment, or become reinstated as a naturalized citizen by taking an oath before a diplomatic office of the United States abroad. (Priv. L. No. 419, 62 Stat. 1403 (1948)) (Sen. Rep. No. 1316, 2nd Sess.) (H.R. Rep. No. 2271, 2nd Sess.)-NRTN

80th Cong., S. 84, for the relief of Mrs. Clinton R. Sharp. Beneficiary, a native of Japan, was married to a United States citizen and veteran of World War I with four United States citizen children. She was ineligible to immigrate because of race. Two daughters were interned by the Japanese with the father, and two boys were permitted to remain with their mother. In order to prevent them being taken into the Japanese Army, the mother and boys trekked into China for five months, but she became bedridden due to the hardships experienced as a result of the journey. The Senate Committee reported, "A mother born Japanese who was so loyal to her husband's country that she risked her own life and the lives of her sons to prevent them from taking up arms against it can hardly be regarded as an undesirable alien." The Committee noted favorable action was consistent with the United States Government policy with respect to alien wives of citizens in the armed forces during the war. The law waived the grounds of excludability relating to persons of races ineligible to citizenship. (Priv. L. No. 144, 62 Stat. 1300 (1948)) (Sen. Rep. No. 485, 1st Sess.) (H.R. Rep. No. 1192, 1st Sess.)-QIER

80th Cong., S. 135, for the relief of Frank Schindler. Beneficiary, a 72-year old former native-born United States citizen and naturalized citizen of Czechoslovakia had resided in the United States until the age of 12 at which time he was taken by his parents to Czechoslovakia. During World War I, he served as sugar commissioner for the food administrator in the Czechoslovakian Government. He entered the United States as a student and subsequently retired as a businessman. The law held the beneficiary to have been lawfully admitted for permanent residence. (Priv. L. No. 12, 61 Stat. 968 (1947)) (Sen. Rep. No. 93, 1st Sess.) (H.R. Rep. No. 448, 1st Sess.)-NMSC

80th Cong., S. 329, for the relief of Gentaro Takahashi. Beneficiary, a 60-year old native and citizen of Japan, entered the United States for permanent residence and remained 19 years until he returned to Japan to marry. He was admitted to the United States as a treaty merchant and remained in the United States 40 years. He had six United States citizen children and sought to remain permanently in the United States. The law canceled deportation proceedings against the beneficiary and held him to have been lawfully admitted for permanent residence. (Priv. L. No. 260, 62 Stat. 1340 (1948)) (Sen. Rep. No. 996, 2nd Sess.) (H.R. Rep. No. 1698, 2nd Sess.)-QMGN

80th Cong., S. 1142, for the relief of Anna Pechnik. Beneficiary, a 27-year old native of Poland, entered the United States as a stowaway. She was excluded from entry as a stowaway and because of the possibility of becoming a public charge due to a leg injury during a bomb explosion in the war. The Department of Justice was unable to recommend enactment of the bill although there were "a number of aspects in this case which arouse normal feelings of pity and sympathy." The Department noted many persons during the war experienced difficulties and her case was most likely not "any more harrowing than thousands of other sufferers throughout war-torn Europe." The Department especially objected to the offense of stowing away on vessels and sought to discourage such practices, particularly in obtaining benefits by means of private legislation. The law canceled deportation proceedings against the beneficiary and held her to have been lawfully admitted for permanent residence. (Priv. L. No. 290, 62 Stat. 1352 (1948)) (Sen. Rep. No. 941, 2nd Sess.) (H.R. Rep. No. 1740, 2nd Sess.)-QMGN

80th Cong., S. 1409, for the relief of Markoto Iwamatsu, Atsushi Jun Iwamatsu, and Tomoe Iwamatsu. Beneficiaries, husband, wife and minor son (ages 39, 39, 13), natives and citizens of Japan, entered the United States as visitors studying art. During the war both elder beneficiaries had been employed by the Office of Strategic Services. An investigation by the Department of Justice revealed that some persons believed the beneficiaries to be inclined toward communism, and others stated they were of good moral character. The male beneficiary wrote a book entitled "The New Sun" and published in several magazines, being a "well-known Japanese artist in this country." The law waived section 303 of the Act of 1940 relating to racial ineligibility to citizenship in order that they immigrate. (Priv. L. No. 400, 62 Stat. 1395 (1948)) (Sen. Rep. No. 1324, 2nd Sess.) (H.R. Rep. No. 2275, 2nd Sess.)-QIER

80th Cong., S. 1451, for the relief of Perfecto M. Biason and Joan Biason. Beneficiaries, a widower and his daughter (ages 47 and 14), and natives and citizens of the Philippines, entered the United States as visitors. The mother was a United States citizen who was killed by the Japanese for refusal to assist them during the war. The law canceled deportation proceedings against the beneficiaries and held them to have been lawfully admitted for permanent residence. (Priv. L. No. 317, 62 Stat. 1360 (1948)) (Sen. Rep. No. 1005, 2nd Sess.) (H. R. Rep. No. 1955, 2nd Sess.)-QIRW

80th Cong., S. 2060, for the relief of Edgar Wikner Percival. Beneficiary, a 51-year old native of Australia, entered the United States as a visitor. He had previously been in the United States during the Second World War on official business for the British Air Commission and was a fighter pilot in the Royal Air Force during World War I. He was the organizer of a commercial flying service in Australia and later founded the Percival Aircraft Company which became the "second largest manufacturer of purely civil aircraft in Great Britain." During World War II his factory assisted the war effort by building motors for the fighter bombers. The law held the beneficiary to have been lawfully admitted for permanent residence and held inapplicable any restrictions on travel which may jeopardize his lawful permanent residence status before or after the date of enactment of the legislation. (Priv. L. No. 342, 62 Stat. 1370 (1948)) (Sen. Rep. No. 1178, 2nd Sess.) (H.R. Rep. No. 2057, 2nd Sess.)-QMDE

81st Cong., H.R. 679, for the relief of Mrs. Julia Balint. Beneficiary, a native and citizen of Czechoslovakia, was married to a United States citizen with three United States citizen children, ages 14, 16, and 18. The father had been making arrangements to move the family to the United States when he was taken by Soviet authorities to Russia in 1944 and was not heard from after that time. According to the Czechoslovak Ministry of Foreign Affairs he had died in a prison camp in Russia. The law held the beneficiary to be entitled to immediate relative status notwithstanding the death or disappearance of her United States citizen husband. (Priv. L. No. 63, 63 Stat. 1098 (1949)) (H.R. Rep. No. 216, 1st Sess.) (Sen. Rep. No. 258, 1st Sess.)-QIRW

81st Cong., H.R. 711, for the relief of Mrs. Margaret Gregg Dilnot. Beneficiary, a 73-year old native-born United States citizen, married a subject of Great Britain in 1924 and accompanied him to England until his death in 1946. While in England she voted in various elections, although she maintained contact with relatives in the United States and filed income tax returns. She had no relatives in England and two citizen siblings resided in the United States. The law allowed the beneficiary to regain the same citizenship status which had existed prior to loss by voting in an election. (Priv. L. No. 43, 63 Stat. 1091 (1949)) (H.R. Rep. No. 135, 1st Sess.) (Sen. Rep. No. 245, 1st Sess.)-NVOL

81st Cong., H.R. 714, for the relief of Pieter Cornelis Ten Wolde and family. Beneficiaries (ages 39, 32, 9, and 6), natives and citizens of the Netherlands, entered the United States as visitors to enable the male beneficiary to inspect a rice mill owned by Rickert Rice Mills, Inc. of New Orleans which had been purchased by the beneficiary's Dutch employer. He had been employed by that company for 17 years. Upon entry to the United States, the rice mill employed the beneficiary due to the ill health of one of the managers. He continued to occupy a position with the company for two years. The Attorney General stated it was unable to recommend enactment to place the beneficiary ahead of other aliens similarly situated who must await a visa. The law held the beneficiaries to have been lawfully admitted for permanent residence. (Priv. L. No. 597, 64 Stat. A94 (1950)) (H.R. Rep. No. 1623, 2nd Sess.) (Sen. Rep. No. 1617, 2nd Sess.)-QMOC

81st Cong., H.R. 750, for the relief of Lee F. Bertuccioli. Beneficiary, a 23-year old native and citizen of Britain and whose mother was a United States citizen, was brought to the United States for residence. He was drafted into the Army and served as a medical technician in China, Burma and India and while abroad received medical treatment for epilepsy. After discharge he left the United States for a short visit with his father in England, but failed to obtain a re-entry permit and was denied a visa due to his affliction. The law waived section 3 of the Act of 1917 relating to mental conditions. (Priv. L. No. 138, 63 Stat. 1128 (1949)) (H.R. Rep. No. 357, 1st Sess.) (Sen. Rep. No. 468, 1st Sess.)-WHEL

81st Cong., H.R. 1010, for the relief of Mrs. May K.Y. Mok, Frederick W.S. Mok, and Vincent W. C. Mok. Beneficiaries (ages 43, 16, 15, and 2), natives and citizens of China and the Philippines, entered the United States as visitors. Their father had been a Chinese consul in Manila who was executed by the Japanese for refusal to cooperate with them. The widow brought her sons to the United States for medical treatment of tuberculosis. The law held the beneficiaries to have been lawfully admitted for permanent residence. (Priv. L. No. 56, 63 Stat. 1096 (1949)) (H.R. Rep. No. 217, 1st Sess.) (Sen. Rep. No. 246, 1st Sess.)-QMGN

81st Cong., H.R. 1079, for the relief of Maria Veltri Magnone. Beneficiary, a 38-year old native and citizen of Italy, was the spouse of a United States citizen and the mother of a United States citizen child. She entered the

United States for permanent residence and resided four years until she was diagnosed as paranoid. The Committee was presented with information which noted her good physical and mental health, until her first-born child died of pneumonia. Her mental condition made her subject to deportation. Her husband, the president of a coal company, desired her return to the United States and provided physician reports of her cure. The law waived section 3 of the Act of 1917 and provisions of the Act of 1929 relating to entry after deportation. (Priv. L. No. 48, (63 Stat. 1093 (1949)) (H.R. Rep. No. 138, 1st Sess.) (Sen. Rep. No. 250, 1st Sess.)-WHEL

81st Cong., H.R. 1170, for the relief of Mrs. John Kaudy (formerly Stella Cappler). Beneficiary, a 24-year old native and citizen of Australia, was the spouse of a United States citizen war veteran. She was found excludable from entry to the United States because of the theft of a pair of ladies' shoes, one handkerchief and other small articles. The law waived the eleventh category of section 3 of the Act of 1917 on behalf of the beneficiary. (Priv. L. No. 535, 64 Stat. A70 (1950)) (H.R. Rep. No. 1624, 2nd Sess.) (Sen. Rep. No. 1620, 2nd Sess.)-WCRF

81st Cong., H.R. 1275, for the relief of Anna Helman. Beneficiary, a 43-year old native of Russia, was the spouse of a permanent resident alien. Upon entering the United States as immigrants, her husband was held and convicted of smuggling diamonds in a suitcase with a value of $8,500. He later received an unconditional pardon from the President but the beneficiary suffered a mental breakdown. Her parents and minor child were citizens of the United States and other sibling relatives resided in the United States. The law waived the second category of section 3 of the Act of 1917 relating to persons who had one or more attacks of insanity. (Priv. L. No. 526, 64 Stat. A70 (1950)) (H.R. Rep. No. 1489, 2nd Sess.) (Sen. Rep. No. 1622, 2nd Sess.)-WHEL

81st Cong., H.R. 1447, for the relief of Ethel Roth. Beneficiary, a 74-year old native of Hungary and former lawful permanent resident of the United States for 50 years, moved to Canada to take care of her married sister who was ill. After her sister died, she sought to return to the United States. It was determined she abandoned her permanent residence due to the 10 year absence. The beneficiary's brother, a United States citizen, also sought her return. The Attorney General did not consider the facts sufficient to "justify considering this alien for preference over the many worthy aliens in other countries...and who would make equally as good citizens." The law held the beneficiary as a returning immigrant upon application at the port of entry. (Priv. L. No. 321, 63 Stat. 1199 (1949)) (H.R. Rep. No. 873, 1st Sess.) (Sen. Rep. No. 992, 1st Sess.)-QPRP

81st Cong., H.R. 1487, for the relief of Lt. (SG) Giacomo Falco. Beneficiary rendered valuable service to American naval forces during 1945 training American crews in submarine warfare and in the operation of Italian submarines. He served in the Italian Navy eight years and during World War II was an officer of the Italian submarine *Dandolo*. Prior to entering the Italian Navy he "risked his life by crossing the German lines in Athens, Greece, to join the British Army after wandering in the Middle East for about 45 days. After joining the British, he gave them valuable information about the German Navy" and positions in Greece. He was awarded a medal by the Ministry of Italian Navy for his activities during this period. The House report included a letter of recommendation of Admiral C.W. Nimitz regarding the beneficiary's naval activities. The law held the beneficiary lawfully admitted for permanent residence. (Priv. L. No. 439, 64 Stat. A37 (1950)) (H.R. Rep. No. 1555, 2nd Sess.) (Sen. Rep. No. 1413, 2nd Sess.)-QMDE

81st Cong., H.R. 1503, for the relief of George Washington. Beneficiary, a citizen of Austria, was the spouse of a United States citizen and the father of a United States citizen child. He claimed relationship to George Washington, the first President, through his half-brother. The Attorney General indicated the beneficiary "presented no documentary evidence to support this claim of relationship." Additionally, he said "the alien has made many conflicting statements concerning his origin and his present and past activities" thus giving rise to doubt as to his identity. He was found deportable on the basis of conviction of a felony for passport alterations and obtaining monies under false pretenses. He was first admitted as an immigrant by petition of his first wife, a United States citizen, who later stated he had deceived her as to his income and that her mother had supported him. The law canceled deportation proceedings against the beneficiary and held him lawfully admitted for permanent residence. (Priv. L. No. 1038, 64 Stat. A255 (1950)) (H.R. Rep. No. 2400, 2nd Sess.) (Sen. Rep. No. 2536, 2nd Sess.)-WCRF

81st Cong., H.R. 1866, for the relief of Honorio Canciller and Nancy Ting Evangelista. Beneficiaries, a 59-year old native and citizen of the Philippines and his spouse, entered the United States as visitors. The Attorney General reported the male beneficiary made "an extremely valuable contribution to the cause of the United States" when he lived in China for more than 26 years using "his influence in behalf of the United States and against the Japanese, particularly with respect to the puppet Filipino organizations." He was imprisoned by the Japanese twice and was decorated by the American consul general in China with the Medal of Freedom for exceptional service. He was later employed by the Bureau of Animal Industry, Department of Agriculture which certified they were unable to "recruit veterinarians to meet its needs". The law held the beneficiaries to be lawfully admitted for permanent residence. (Priv. L. No. 508, 64 Stat. A63 (1950)) (H.R. Rep. No. 1578, 2nd Sess.) (Sen. Rep. No. 1625, 2nd Sess.)-NMSC

81st Cong., H.R. 1991, for the relief of Alexander Stewart. Beneficiary, a 2-year old native of France, became attached to the United States Army as a mascot after American troops invaded Africa and later went to Anzio. He entered the United States with troops as a stowaway. The Committee report noted 300 officers from the Army Division signed a petition on his behalf. The law canceled deportation proceedings on behalf of the beneficiary and held him to have been lawfully admitted for permanent residence. (Priv. L. No. 795, 64 Stat. A163 (1950)) (H.R. Rep. No. 1974, 2nd Sess.) (Sen. Rep. No. 2025, 2nd Sess.)-QMDE

81st Cong., H.R. 2084, for the relief of Teiko Horikawa and Yoshiko Horikawa. Beneficiaries, four-year old twin natives of Japan and stepdaughters of a veteran and United States citizen, were held excludable as racially ineligible for immigration. The mother did not realize her marriage was not registered until after the war and her husband had been killed. The children were later adopted by their grandparents in Japan, but the natural mother and stepfather desired to have them in the United States. The law held section 13(c) of the Act of 1924 relating to racial ineligibility inapplicable on behalf of the beneficiaries and held them to be considered the nature born daughters of their stepfather. (Priv. L. No. 194, 63 Stat. 1150 (1949)) (H.R. Rep. No. 706, 1st Sess.) (Sen. Rep. No. 634, 1st Sess.)-QIER

81st Cong., H.R. 2349, for the relief of Col. Wlodzimierz Onacewicz. Beneficiary, a 55-year old native and citizen of Poland, was commissioned in the Army of Czar Nicholas II of Russia and participated in the First World War. At the outbreak of the Russian Revolution he joined with other Poles in the Polish Army to liberate that country from Germany. He escaped Russia later and joined the Polish Army against the Russian invasion. He was awarded the Legion of Merit by the United States Government for collaborating with the United States and Poland during the war. He was first admitted to the United States as the military attache of the Polish Embassy and later became a permanent resident alien. He was then employed by the Library of Congress and sought early petitioning for citizenship for his permanent employment by the military establishments of the Government. The law held the beneficiary lawfully admitted for permanent residence effective the date of admission as military attache. (Priv. L. No. 170, 63 Stat. 1141 (1949)) (H.R. Rep. No. 550, 1st Sess.) (Sen. Rep. No. 537, 1st Sess.)-QMDE

81st Cong., H.R. 2360, for the relief of Theodore Papachristopoulos. Beneficiary, a five-year old native and citizen of Greece and stepchild of a United States citizen, resided in Greece due to an oversubscription of visas for that country and the fact that the mother was a lawful permanent resident alien. The stepfather served in Greece as Deputy Foreign Trade Administrator in the Ministry of National Economy of Greece as part of the American Mission for Aid to Greece. He had accepted the position after requested by the Department of State, and he dealt with the Greek import and export program. The beneficiary resided with his grandparents, and the stepfather and mother desired his entry to the United States. Although the stepfather indicated he would adopt the beneficiary, the mother believed such action would thwart her divorced husband's entitlement to see the child. The stepfather was employed by Ohio State University. The law held the beneficiary to be the natural-born son of a United States citizen. (Priv. L. No. 64, 63 Stat. 1098 (1949)) (H.R. Rep. No. 358, 1st Sess.) (Sen. Rep. No. 322, 1st Sess.)-QIRM

81st Cong., H.R. 2591, for the relief of Giovanna Parisi, Michelina Valletta, Yolanda Altierei, Generosa Tamburi, Carolina Picciano, and Giovana Turtur. Beneficiaries, ages 61 through 25, natives and citizens of Italy, entered the United States as visitors for the purpose of teaching and performing various charitable types of work of their order as nuns in New York. The law held the beneficiaries to have been lawfully admitted for permanent residence. (Priv. L. No. 441, 64 Stat. A38 (1950)) (H.R. Rep. No. 1777, 81st Cong., 2nd Sess.) (Sen. Rep. No. 1416, 81st Cong., 2nd Sess.)-QMOC

81st Cong., H.R. 2602, for the relief of John B. Boyle. Beneficiary, a 33-year old native and citizen of Canada, was the spouse of a lawful permanent resident with one United States citizen child. He was held excludable from entering the United States due to a conviction for mail fraud in Canada. The law waived the eleventh category of section 3 of the Act of 1917 relating to crimes involving moral turpitude on behalf of the beneficiary. (Priv. L. No. 226, 63 Stat. 1162 (1949)) (H.R. Rep. No. 876, 81st Cong., 1st Sess.) (Sen. Rep. No. 823, 1st Sess.)-WCRF

81st Cong., H.R. 2921, for the relief of Nicholas C.. Kalcoutsakis. Beneficiary, a 41-year old native and citizen of Greece, entered the United States as a visitor and subsequently became a partner in a large textile organization, Pee Dee Mills, North Carolina. The Committee noted the beneficiary and other managers worked out many serious labor and modernizing problems of the mills which were necessary to the local communities. The law held the beneficiary lawfully admitted for permanent residence. (Priv. L. No. 305, 63 Stat. 1193 (1949)) (H.R. Rep. No. 1079, 81st Cong., 1st Sess.) (Sen. Rep. No. 1007, 81st Cong., 1st Sess.)-QMOC

81st Cong., H. R. 3018, for the relief of Camilla Fabris. Beneficiary, a 35-year old native and citizen of Italy, entered the United States as a student. She had previously worked as a secretary for the Allied and Military Government in Rome and as a translator. Her mother was a United States citizen who married an Italian native and moved to Italy. Her grandparents resided in the United States. The law held the beneficiary lawfully admitted for permanent residence. (Priv. L. No. 577, 64 Stat. A87 (1950)) (H.R. Rep. No. 1580, 2nd Sess.) (Sen. Rep. No. 1702, 2nd Sess.)-QMGN

81st Cong., H.R. 3127, for the relief of Jacob Gross. Beneficiary, a two-year old native and citizen of Romania, was orphaned in an airplane crash in Czechoslovakia in which his parents died. The beneficiary was the only survivor. He was pinned to a pillow and thrown clear of the wreckage. The beneficiary's grandfather became the legal guardian and at the time of his immigration to the United States was unable to confer immigration benefits. The law held the beneficiary to be the child of his grandfather for purposes of immigration. (Priv. L. No. 175, 63 Stat. 1143 1949)) (H.R. Rep. No. 566, 1st Sess.) (Sen. Rep. No. 539, 1st Sess.)-QIRA

81st Cong., H.R. 3169, for the relief of Certain Spanish Physicians Residing in Puerto Rico. Beneficiaries, seven physicians and their families, natives and citizens of Spain, entered the United States on various types of documents, and were employed in Puerto Rico as doctors in the areas of surgery, psychiatry, tubercular work and other types of medical specialties. The Attorney General noted he was unable to recommend favorably because of the oversubscribed condition of visas from Spain and stated: "The enactment of special legislation to adjust individual cases, however, encourages other aliens to circumvent our immigration laws by entering the United States, allegedly as visitors, then remaining here and taking steps to adjust their status to permanent residence." The law held the beneficiaries to have been lawfully admitted for permanent residence. (Priv. L. No. 767, 64 Stat. A153 (1950)) (H.R. Rep. No. 1910, 2nd Sess.) (Sen. Rep. No. 1976, 2nd Sess.)-QMOC

81st Cong., H.R. 3330, for the relief of Therese Hohman. Beneficiary, a 28-year old native and citizen of Germany, entered the United States as a fiancee of a United States citizen. However, the engaged couple found differences in religion would impair the relationship. She later found employment as a maid for the vice president of Bethlehem Steel Corporation. The Attorney General noted no basis for exempting the beneficiary from general provisions of the law and was unable to recommend favorably on the legislation. The law held the beneficiary to have been lawfully admitted for permanent residence. (Priv. L. No. 776, 64 Stat. A157 (1950)) (H.R. Rep. No. 1626, 1st Sess.) (Sen. Rep. No. 2054, 2nd Sess.)-QMGN

81st Cong., H.R. 3771, for the relief of Mrs. Marie Gulbenkian. Beneficiary, a 72-year old native of Turkey, entered the United States as a visitor. She was formerly admitted for lawful permanent residence, however, she abandoned her status to live in France for 27 years. She worked at various charitable purposes among Armenians with a trust fund established by her husband. The law held the beneficiary lawfully admitted for permanent residence. (Priv. L. No. 442, 64 Stat. A38 (1950)) (H.R. Rep. No. 1819, 2nd Sess.) (Sen. Rep. 1392, 2nd Sess.)-QMGN

81st Cong., H.R. 3921, for the relief of Nicholas C.. Hadjipateras, Pipitsa N. Hadjipateras, and Costas N. Hadjipateras. Beneficiaries, 65-, 54-, 30-year old natives and citizens of Greece, entered the United States as visitors. The elder beneficiary indicated he entered the United States to study American shipping methods and to buy vessels. He and his brothers owned three ships worth $1.15 million. Some of his ships became involved in litigation in the United States during the war. The ships were engaged in delivering cargo under the Marshall Plan. The Attorney General indicated enactment of such legislation would encourage the entry of others whose ultimate goal was to remain in the United States. The law held the beneficiaries to have been lawfully admitted for permanent residence. (Priv. L. No. 894, 64 Stat. A203 (1950)) (H.R. Rep. No. 2402, 2nd Sess.) (Sen. Rep. No. 2294, 2nd Sess.)-QMGN

81st Cong., H.R. 4042, for the relief of Konstantinos Yannopoulos. Beneficiary, a 29-year old native and citizen of Greece, entered the United States as a visitor and sought to remain with his United States citizen parents. He had applied for a visa to enter the United States before the war but was unable to enter during wartime. He was employed in the United States as a stage director with the Metropolitan Opera in New York. The law held the beneficiary to have been lawfully admitted for permanent residence. (Priv. L. No. 346, 63 Stat. 1209 (1949)) (H.R. Rep. No. 1098, 1st Sess.) (Sen. Rep. No. 1183, 1st Sess.)-QMOC

81st Cong., H.R. 4306, for the relief of Zora B. Vulich. Beneficiary, a native and citizen of Yugoslavia, was the widow of a Yugoslav flyer serving in the United States Armed Forces killed during World War II. She sought nonquota status by virtue of her husband's military record. The beneficiary's uncle, a permanent resident alien, also supplied information stating her three brothers were killed during the war, and her 70-year old father had been placed in a concentration camp by the Yugoslav regime. The law held the beneficiary entitled to immediate relative status. (Priv. L. No. 310, 63 Stat. 1194 (1949)) (H.R. Rep. No. 954, 1st Sess.) (Sen. Rep. No. 869, 1st Sess.)-QIRW

81st Cong., H.R. 4365, for the relief of Fe'R. Dumaguing. Beneficiary, a 28-year old native and citizen of the Philippines, who had "rendered highly meritorious service during World War II" as a nurse sought permanent residence in the United States. She entered the United States as a visitor and later was employed as a nurse. The law held the beneficiary to have been lawfully admitted to the United States for permanent residence. (Priv. L. No. 976, 64 Stat. A231 (1950)) (H.R. Rep. No. 2971, 2nd Sess.) (Sen. Rep. No. 2518, 2nd Sess.)-QMOC

81st Cong., H.R. 4604, for the relief of certain aliens possessing special skills, namely, Teodor Egle, Karlis Fogelis, Vasily Kils, and Aleksanders Zelmenis. Beneficiaries, natives and citizens of Latvia, were "highly skilled specialists." Most resided in Canada and were needed for the operation of a textile mill in Rhode Island. The prospective employer had previously employed the individuals in Europe. As an émigré from Latvia he smuggled his dismantled mills to Norway and later desired to set up his plant in Rhode Island. The Attorney General indicated that "unique technical skill will be required to set up Mr. Hirss' foreign-made machinery properly and to train local employees in its use and that individuals having such skill may not be readily available in this country." The law provided for the temporary admission to the United States of the beneficiaries and held that if any of the beneficiaries failed to maintain a satisfactory employment status within a year after admission they would be subject to deportation. (Priv. L. No.

821, 64 Stat. A173 (1950)) (H.R. Rep. No. 1627, 2nd Sess.) (Sen. Rep. No. 1636, 2nd Sess.)-QMOC

81st Cong., H.R. 4747, for the relief of Louise Ahting. Beneficiary, a native of Germany, acquired United States citizenship through her mother. She lost her claim to citizenship by protracted residence abroad. She had departed the United States to Germany in order to take care of some inheritance money and was unable to return due to her mother's illness. The Attorney General's report on the case noted many persons had become expatriated and could await an immigrant visa along with others in similar circumstances. The law allowed the beneficiary to be reinstated as a citizen upon filing for naturalization or upon taking an oath of allegiance before a consular officer abroad. (Priv. L. No. 570, 64 Stat. A85 (1950)) (H.R. Rep. No. 1556, 2nd Sess.) (Sen. Rep. No. 1638, 2nd Sess.)-NRTN

81st Cong., H.R. 5354, for the relief of Itzchak Shafer. Beneficiary was a six-year old orphan adopted by United States citizens. He had been brought to Germany in a convoy at the age of two from Poland. In Poland he was saved from an extermination camp by the Catholic Church and later he was sent to an orphanage in Paris. The law held the beneficiary to have been born in France for the purposes of section 12(a) of the Act of 1924. (Priv. L. No. 350, 63 Stat. 1211 (1949)) (H.R. Rep. No. 1285, 1st Sess.) (Sen. Rep. No. 1185, 1st Sess.)-QIRA

81st Cong., H.R. 5375, for the relief of Mrs. Hilda De Silva. Beneficiary, 49 years old, entered the United States in 1917. She had four United States citizen children. Twelve years later she and her family traveled to Bermuda during the depression where her husband found employment. Two of her sons served in the United States military, and they petitioned for the remaining family to return to the United States. The beneficiary was ineligible for a visa because of illiteracy. The law waived exclusion under section 3 of the Act of 1917. (Priv. L. No. 329, 63 Stat. 1202 (1949)) (H.R. Rep. No. 1222, 1st Sess.) (Sen. Rep. No. 1030, 81st Cong., 1st Sess.)-WXIL

81st Cong., H.R. 5947, for the relief of Alfio Batelli. Beneficiary, a 46-year old native and citizen of Italy, entered the United States temporarily and was a highly skilled violin repairman. He was employed by Kagan & Gaines Company in the United States which manufactured and distributed band and orchestra instruments. The law held the beneficiary to have been lawfully admitted for permanent residence. (Priv. L. No. 779, 64 Stat. A158 (1950)) (H.R. Rep. No. 1995, 2nd Sess.) (Sen. Rep. No. 1984, 2nd Sess.)-QMOC

81st Cong., H.R. 6006, for the relief of Anthony Charles Bartley. Beneficiary, a native of India and subject of Great Britain, was a surviving RAF fighter pilot who participated in the Battle of Britain and was decorated twice with the Distinguished Flying Cross. He was shot down three times in flames during the Battle of Britain and participated in the Battle of Dunkerque and in the Northern Africa and South Pacific campaigns with the United States Marines on Palau. He was married to Deborah Kerr, an MGM actress and they had a United States citizen child.

The law held the beneficiary lawfully admitted for permanent residence. (Priv. L. No. 282, 63 Stat. 1183 (1949)) (H.R. Rep. No. 1286, 1st Sess.) (Sen. Rep. No. 1089, 1st Sess.)-QMDE

81st Cong., H.R. 6106, for the relief of Daniel Kokal. Beneficiary, a 27-year old native and citizen of Yugoslavia, entered the United States as a student and was under the sponsorship of a Member of Congress for whom he did various farm chores. The Congressman met him during a tour of one of the refugee camps in Italy. The Attorney General did not recommend enactment because the "considerations presented do not appear sufficient to justify the enactment of special legislation" when so many other aliens from oversubscribed countries must wait their turn to immigrate. The law held the beneficiary lawfully admitted for permanent residence. (Priv. L. No. 977, 64 Stat. A232 (1950)) (H.R. Rep. No. 2973, 2nd Sess.) (Sen. Rep. No. 2466, 2nd Sess.)-QMGN

81st Cong., H.R. 6283, for the relief of Johny Nielsen. Beneficiary, a four-year old native of Denmark, was adopted by United States citizens. The adoptive parents had been visiting Denmark with their five-year old child who was attacked by a mad dog. The boy was rushed to a hospital where Pasteur treatment was implemented but the hypodermic needle broke which necessitated an operation. Because the child had eaten beforehand and this was not known to the doctors, the ether caused the child to choke to death. The parents then sought to adopt a child to bring to the United States and to overcome the waiting period for visa issuance. The law held the beneficiary to be the natural son of the adoptive parents thereby entitling him to immediate relative status. (Priv. L. No. 434, 64 Stat. A35 (1950)) (H.R. Rep. No. 1485, 2nd Sess.) (Sen. Rep. No. 1428, 2nd Sess.)-QIRA

81st Cong., H.R. 6386, for the relief of Amos Chen. Beneficiary, a 37-year old native of Jamaica, British West Indies and of the Chinese race, was ineligible to immigrate due to racial ineligibility and illiteracy. He was married to a United States citizen who had four minor children from a previous marriage and two children by the beneficiary. The beneficiary's former employer stated he would employ him again should he enter the United States. His spouse indicated that unless her husband returned to the United States she would have to work and board her children. The law waived section 3 of the Act of 1917 and section 2 of the Act of 1943 as well as provisions of sections 6(a) and 9 of the Act of 1924 relating to illiteracy, racial ineligibility, and preference status on behalf of the beneficiary. (Priv. L. No. 898, 64 Stat. A204 (1950)) (H.R. Rep. No. 2507, 2nd Sess.) (Sen. Rep. No. 2305, 2nd Sess.)-QIER

81st Cong., H.R. 6442, for the relief of Mrs. Martha Reid. Beneficiary, an 86-year old native and citizen of Canada, believed herself to be a United States citizen by virtue of her marriage. However, her husband later learned he did not derive citizenship and therefore neither had such status. The daughter of the beneficiary was admitted as a United States citizen. Mrs. Reid entered the United States as a visitor and sought to remain without leaving the country to obtain a visa. It was indicated the beneficiary's health would be better by living in Honolulu rather than in Canada. The law held the beneficiary lawfully admitted for permanent residence. (Priv. L. No. 887, 64 Stat. A201 (1950)) (H.R. Rep. No. 2471, 2nd Sess.) (Sen. Rep. No. 2307, 2nd Sess.)-NMSC

81st Cong., H.R. 6747, for the relief of Helga Holleb. Beneficiary, a 13-month old native of Germany, was adopted by United States citizens. The adoptive parents had two children, both of whom died as the result of a degeneration of the liver at the ages of 14 months and 10 weeks. The adoptive father was an officer in the United States Army. The adoptive parents sought to provide a home for the newborn child and overcome the lengthy delay of oversubscribed visas for that country. The law held the beneficiary to be the natural daughter of the adoptive parents thereby entitling her to immediate relative status. (Priv. L. No. 585, 64 Stat. A90 (1950)) (H.R. Rep. No. 1713, 2nd Sess.) (Sen. Rep. No. 1717, 2nd Sess.)-QIRA

81st Cong., H.R. 6758, for the relief of Ruby Thaw and Hla Sein. Beneficiaries, natives and citizens of Burma, were nurses who had performed "distinguished service with the United States Armed Forces in the Far East." They had been awarded a Bronze Star Medal and a citation from President Roosevelt. In 1942 they volunteered to serve in a medical unit and were assigned to the Stillwell mission "where they provided the only medical care available for the Chinese-American armies in Burma," and accompanied the Stillwell group on their trek out of Burma in retreat. They set up a hospital for the medical care of American and Chinese forces in India and during the reinvasion of Burma accompanied forces during raids and scouting expeditions. The beneficiaries entered the United States as students. The law held the beneficiaries lawfully admitted for permanent residence. (Priv. L. No. 789, 64 Stat. A161 (1950)) (H.R. Rep. No. 2170, 2nd Sess.) (Sen. Rep. No. 2135, 2nd Sess.)-QMDE

81st Cong., H.R. 6804, for the relief of Certain Italian Aliens. Beneficiaries, 14 Catholic nuns, natives and citizens of Italy, entered the United States for the purpose of teaching in orphanages for mixed races in Louisiana. The law held the beneficiaries lawfully admitted for permanent residence. (Priv. L. No. 943, 64 Stat. A218 (1950)) (H.R. Rep. No. 2474, 2nd Sess.) (Sen. Rep. No. 2357, 2nd Sess.)-QMOC

81st Cong., H.R. 7071, for the relief of Mrs. Masa Iyoki. Beneficiary, a 71-year old native and citizen of Japan, was formerly a lawful permanent resident of the United States for 37 years prior to return to Japan for five years because of the illness of her husband. She had three United States citizen children in Hawaii but lost her permanent residence because of her extended residence in Japan. The law waived section 13(c) of the Act of 1924 relating to ineligibility for an immigrant visa due to race and found the beneficiary entitled to status under section 4(b) of the Act of 1924 as a returning permanent resident alien. (Priv. L. No. 790, 64 Stat. A161 (1950)) (H.R. Rep. No. 2241, 2nd Sess.) (Sen. Rep. No. 2086, 2nd Sess.)-QPRP

81st Cong., H.R. 7282, for the relief of Cornelius Ver Sluis. Beneficiary, a 21-year old native and citizen of the Netherlands, entered the United States as a student attending school to become an ordained minister in the Salvation Army. The Salvation Army was reluctant to assign the beneficiary unless his immigration status was permanent. The Attorney General stated the case did not appear to have sufficient "impelling" reasons to justify a preference by enactment of special legislation. The law held the beneficiary lawfully admitted for permanent residence. (Priv. L. No. 902, 64 Stat. A206 (1950)) (H.R. Rep. No. 2476, 2nd Sess.) (Sen. Rep. No. 2314, 2nd Sess.)-QMGN

81st Cong., H.R. 7428, for the relief of Mrs. Erna Tvedt. Beneficiary, a 23-year old native and citizen of Germany, and spouse of a United States citizen and veteran of World War II as well as mother of two United States citizen children, was excluded from entry to the United States because of a conviction for breaking into a chicken coop and stealing two chickens at the age of 21. The law waived the eleventh category of section 3 of the Act of 1917 relating to crimes involving moral turpitude on behalf of the beneficiary. (Priv. L. No. 706, 64 Stat. A133 (1950)) (H.R. Rep. No. 2094, 2nd Sess.) (Sen. Rep. No. 1992, 2nd Sess.)-WCRF

81st Cong., H.R. 7563, for the relief of Dr. Nicola Di Palma. Beneficiary, a 26-year old native and citizen of Italy who entered the United States as a visitor, formerly derived United States citizenship through his father and later expatriated himself by voting in an Italian election. He was employed in New York as a doctor. The Attorney General noted there were many former United States citizens who lost citizenship by voting in political elections and that "the problem of granting relief to such individuals is a general one and should be resolved, if at all, by general legislation. The facts in Dr. Di Palma's case fail to present considerations sufficient to justify the enactment of special legislation granting him a preference over other former United States citizens similarly situated." The law held the beneficiary lawfully admitted for permanent residence. (Priv. L. No. 1018, 64 Stat. A246 (1950)) (H.R. Rep. No. 2558, 2nd Sess.) (Sen. Rep. No. 2491, 2nd Sess.)-NVOL

81st Cong., H.R. 7733, for the relief of Sisters Rita Pinto de Carvalho, Maria Leite Da Silva, Carmelinda Lopes de Aguiar, Maria Adozinda da Fonseca Melo, Joaquine de Jesus, and Maria Luisa Pinto Carvalho. Beneficiaries, six natives and citizens of Portugal, were Catholic nuns employed in educational work by the Order of the Sisters of the Sacred Heart in New York. They entered the United States on temporary visas for religious training. Among the subjects taught were sewing, cooking and Portuguese at Marymount College. The law held the beneficiaries lawfully admitted for permanent residence. (Priv. L. No. 981, 64 Stat. A233 (1950)) (H.R. Rep. No. 2633, 2nd Sess.) (Sen. Rep. No. 2407, 2nd Sess.)-QMOC

81st Cong., H.R. 7815, for the relief of John Yee Horn. Beneficiary, a one-year old native and citizen of China, failed to derive United States citizenship through his father because his father had not acquired the requisite period of residence to transmit citizenship to a child born abroad. Although the father could petition for his spouse as an immediate relative, the statute did not allow petitioning for the child of Chinese descent. The Secretary of State indicated such relief would not establish a "bothersome precedent." The law held section 4(a) and section 9 of the Act of 1924 relating to unmarried minor children applicable to the beneficiary. (Priv. L. No. 708, 64 Stat. A133 (1950)) (H.R. Rep. No. 2243, 2nd Sess.) (Sen. Rep. No. 2065, 2nd Sess.)-QIRM

81st Cong., H.R. 8219, for the relief of Tadeusz Herka. Beneficiary, a 24-year old native and citizen of Poland enlisted in the United States Army and served 3 years. He was ineligible to apply for naturalization under special provisions because he had not enlisted while in the United States, nor had he been lawfully admitted for permanent residence. The law held the beneficiary lawfully admitted for permanent residence. (Priv. L. No. 944, 64 Stat. A219 (1950)) (H.R. Rep. No. 2482, 2nd Sess.) (Sen. Rep. No. 2351, 2nd Sess.)-NMSC

81st Cong., H.R. 8289, for the relief of Yee Balche Yee. Beneficiary, a six-month old native and citizen of China (Hong Kong), did not derive United States citizenship through her father because he had not acquired sufficient residence for transmission of citizenship. Although he could submit a petition for his spouse, he could not petition for his child of the Chinese race except under the 25% quota for Chinese persons not born in China. The law held section 4(a) of the Act of 1924 applicable to the beneficiary as the unmarried minor child of a United States citizen. (Priv. L. No. 757, 64 Stat. A150 (1950)) (H.R. Rep. 2244, 2nd Sess.) (Sen. Rep. 2072, 2nd Sess.)-QIRM

81st Cong., H.R. 8759, for the relief of Rev. Andrew Chai Kyung Whang. Beneficiary, a 44-year old native and citizen of Korea, was found ineligible for entry to the United States because of race. He entered the United States as a visitor and was employed as a translator-announcer by the Voice of America and was an ordained minister of the Presbyterian religion. The law waived section 13(c) of the Act of 1924 relating to ineligibility to citizenship and held the beneficiary lawfully admitted to permanent residence. (Priv. L. No. 1094, 64 Stat. A276 (1951)) (H.R. Rep. No. 2417, 2nd Sess.) (Sen. Rep. No. 2609, 2nd Sess.)-QIER

81st Cong., H.R. 9082, for the relief of Mrs. Chang-Sei Kim, David Kim, and Arthur Kim. Beneficiaries, 47-, 32- and 20-year old natives of Korea and China, had five sibling relatives who were United States citizens. One relative was a captain in the Army Reserves and another had been naturalized in recognition of World War II achievements in Shanghai, China. Another son, a United States citizen, had been naturalized after enlistment in the United States Army in China. The law waived section

13(c) relating to racial ineligibility on behalf of the mother and one son and admitted the other beneficiary who was already in the United States for lawful permanent residence. (Priv. L. No. 1028, 64 Stat. A251 (1950)) (H.R. Rep. No. 2805, 2nd Sess.) (Sen. Rep. No. 2423, 2nd Sess.)-QIER

81st Cong., H.R. 9144, for the relief of Mrs. Olga Kowalik and Czeslawa Kowalik. Beneficiaries, Polish refugees, mother and daughter, had been in Poland at the time of the partition and were sent to Siberia. They were later released by the Russians and sent by direction of the Polish Government to Iran and then to India. The elder beneficiary's parents, husband, and brothers and sisters had been killed in Poland. In 1945 she was sent from India to Africa where she applied for entry to the United States as a displaced person but was unable to qualify due to residence requirements. The law waived paragraph (l) of subsection 2(c) of the Displaced Persons Act of 1948 and deemed them to be eligible as displaced persons. (Priv. L. No. 1042, 64 Stat. A256 (1950)) (H.R. Rep. No. 2977, 2nd Sess.) (Sen. Rep. No. 2542, 2nd Sess.)-QMDP

81st Cong., S. 27, for the relief of Certain Basque Aliens. Beneficiaries, 48-year old natives and citizens of Spain who entered the United States temporarily, were sheepherders in the State of Nevada. The Senate Committee noted that the aliens' services were "urgently needed in the sheep-raising industry." The Committee amended the bill to require that they remain in the same employment. The Attorney General had previously noted: "it would be an unsound policy to condition the stay of these aliens in the United States on their continued employment in a designated industry." The law held the beneficiaries lawfully admitted for permanent residence and provided that one of the beneficiaries be admitted to permanent residence irrespective of his ineligibility under section 3 of the Act of 1917 relating to illiteracy. (Priv. L. No. 13, 63 Stat. 1079 (1949)) (Sen. Rep. No. 9, 1st Sess.) (H.R. Rep. No. 193, 1st Sess.)-QMOC

81st Cong., S. 118, for the relief of Clemente Sabin Dopico. Beneficiary, a 78-year old native and citizen of Spain, was admitted for lawful permanent residence at the age of 30 and resided in the United States and Spain intermittently. He last entered the United States as a visitor and had been convicted one year after entry in 1902 for selling liquor without a State license. The law canceled deportation proceedings against the beneficiary and held him lawfully admitted for permanent residence. (Priv. L. No. 630, 64 Stat. Al05 (1950)) (Sen. Rep. No. 1379, 2nd Sess.) (H.R. Rep. No. 2193, 2nd Sess.)-WCRF

81st Cong., S. 315, for the relief of Dr. Chung Kwai Lui. Beneficiary, a 40-year old native and citizen of China, entered the United States as a student and thereafter was employed by Westinghouse Electric Corporation. The Attorney General stated the beneficiary was engaged in "confidential and secret work in connection with contracts for the Army and Navy. During the war she performed valuable service on the highly secret Manhattan project." The law canceled deportation proceedings against the beneficiary and held her lawfully admitted for permanent residence. (Priv. L. No. 3, 63 Stat. 1073 (1949)) (Sen. Rep. No. 16, 1st Sess.) (H.R. Rep. No. 195, 1st Sess.)-QMDE

81st Cong., S. 356, for the relief of Hugo Geiger. Beneficiary, a 24-year old native and citizen of Germany and son of United States citizen parents, was excluded from entry to the United States due to a conviction of theft of food at the age of 20. When his parents immigrated to the United States they intended to return to Germany and bring the beneficiary to the United States but because of the outbreak of World War II, they could not do so. Later they learned he had lost a leg in Russia while in the German Army and petitioned for his entry to the United States. The law waived section 3 of the Act of 1917 relating to crimes involving moral turpitude on behalf of the beneficiary. (Priv. L. No. 494, 64 Stat. A59 (1950)) (Sen. Rep. No. 1376, 2nd Sess.) (H.R. Rep. No. 2106, 2nd Sess.)-WCRF

81st Cong., S. 609, for the relief of Mrs. Bertie Grace Chan Leong. Beneficiary, a 62-year old native of Hong Kong of the Chinese race and widow of a United States citizen, was the mother of three United States citizen children. She returned to China with her husband after 19 years in the United States. He planned to practice dentistry but then died. She sought to return to the United States. Because of her Chinese ancestry she did not acquire United States citizenship upon marriage to her citizen husband. The law held the beneficiary lawfully admitted for permanent residence. (Priv. L. No. 403, 64 Stat. A23 (1950)) (Sen. Rep. No. 721, 1st Sess.) (H.R. Rep. No. 1761, 2nd Sess.)-QIRW

81st Cong., S. 753, for the relief of Sisters Antoinette Cometti, Mary Gibin, Angela Pelosin, Emma Ghisleni, Elisabetta De Caterin, and Onorina Franzina. Beneficiaries, six nuns of the Order of the Daughters of St. Mary of Providence, and natives and citizens of Italy, entered the United States as temporary visitors destined to Chicago where they instructed mentally retarded and physically handicapped children. The law held the beneficiaries lawfully admitted for permanent residence. (Priv. L. No. 363, 64 Stat. A7 (1950)) (Sen. Rep. No. 1043 1st Sess.) (H.R. Rep. No. 1553, 2nd Sess.)-QMOC

81st Cong., S. 905, for the relief of John Sewen. Beneficiary, a 62-year old native and citizen of Luxembourg, had previously been a naturalized United States citizen who lost his citizenship when he returned to his home country after 18 years in the United States. He desired to be with his mother who had a stroke. After her death he was unable to return to the United States because of the war. He later entered the United States as a visitor to be with his brother and tend to his 200 acres of farmland which he had acquired by homestead. The law held the beneficiary lawfully admitted for permanent residence. (Priv. L. No. 199, 63 Stat. 1152 (1949)) (Sen. Rep. No. 522, 1st Sess.) (H.R. Rep. No. 1078, 1st Sess.)-NRTN

81st Cong., S. 918, for the relief of Clara Sogor. Beneficiary, a 38-year old native of Hungary and citizen of France, entered the United States as a temporary visitor. She served as a lieutenant in the French Army Feminine Auxiliary Ground Forces during World War II and was said to have contributed exceptional services to the Allied cause. She was employed in the Kresge Department Store in the United States. The Attorney General noted there were many aliens performing patriotic duty to their own country, and who "rendered valuable service to the Allied cause," but that did not justify granting the beneficiary a preference, and that to do so would encourage others to seek an exemption to the immigration laws on the same basis. The law held the beneficiary to have been lawfully admitted for permanent residence. (Priv. L. No. 847, 64 Stat. A184 (1950)) (Sen. Rep. No. 1955, 2nd Sess.) (H.R. Rep. No. 2785, 2nd Sess.)-QMGN

81st Cong., S. 1026, for the relief of Roman Szymanski and Anastosia Szymanski. Beneficiaries, natives of Poland, ages 51 and 43 respectively and naturalized citizens of Canada, entered the United States on a temporary visa to visit with a sister. The beneficiaries' in-laws were Mr. and Mrs. Switlik who was the president of the Switlik Parachute Company, "the leading supplier of parachutes to our armed forces." The Attorney General noted the oversubscription of visas for the country of Poland but indicated the record failed to disclose sufficient reason for special privileges for the beneficiaries. The law held the beneficiaries lawfully admitted for permanent residence. (Priv. L. No. 245, 63 Stat. 1169 (1949)) (Sen. Rep. No. 628, 1st Sess.) (H.R. Rep. No. 1219, 1st Sess.)-QMGN

81st Cong., S. 1192, for the relief of Certain Basque Aliens. Beneficiaries, 152 Spanish Basques, entered the United States between 1943 and 1949 as temporary visitors for the purpose of herding sheep and were employed in Western states including Nevada and Idaho. The beneficiaries were brought to the United States "to relieve the acute shortage of sheepherders in certain Western States." The Senate Committee noted attempts to find sheepherders were not successful and that if the beneficiaries were required to leave the United States "the sheep growing industry would suffer substantial losses." The law held the beneficiaries lawfully admitted for permanent residence. (Priv. L. No. 1031, 64 Stat. A251 (1950)) (Sen. Rep. No. 2352, 2nd Sess.) (H.R. Rep. No. 3066, 2nd Sess.)-QMOC

81st Cong., S. 1405, for the relief of Poon Lim. Beneficiary, a 31-year old native and citizen of China, was the sole survivor of the British freighter *Ben Lomand* when it was torpedoed in 1942. He spent 133 days adrift and then was picked up by a Brazilian fishing boat and subsequently entered the United States temporarily as a distressed seaman. He later received the British Empire Medal and returned to the United States on a temporary visit employed as a seaman in the United States merchant marine. The report of the Attorney General noted the beneficiary exhibited great "fortitude and ingenuity in overcoming the perils of the sea." The report noted his efforts raised the "morale of all seaman...the recruiting of seaman for vessels destined for dangerous waters increased." Also, because of his experience in devising equipment for the use of survivors of torpedoed vessels, the

Attorney General posed no objection to the enactment of the legislation. The law held the beneficiary lawfully admitted for permanent residence. (Priv. L. No. 178, 63 Stat. 1144 (1949)) (Sen. Rep. No. 490, 1st Sess.) (H.R. Rep. No. 1032, 1st Sess.)-QMDE

81st Cong., S. 1506, for the relief of Andre Lan. Beneficiary, a 38-year old native of France, born in French Indochina, was admitted to the United States for permanent residence. He was an importer and exporter and President of United States South Asia Corporation. He was awarded the Medal of Freedom for meritorious service during the period 1942 to 1945 for organizing and operating an "extensive intelligence net throughout French Indochina." He had abandoned successful business enterprises at the time to perform such activities. The beneficiary desired to petition for naturalization but was short one year of the requisite five year residence period for naturalization. The law held the beneficiary to have resided in the United States for five years as a lawful permanent resident. (Priv. L. No. 870, 64 Stat. A194 (1950)) (Sen. Rep. No. 1396, 2nd Sess.) (H.R. Rep. No. 2836, 2nd Sess.)-NMSC

81st Cong., S. 1551, for the relief of Jose Augusto Pereira. Beneficiary, a 44-year old native of Portugal who entered the United States by means of a fraudulent visa, was ineligible for permanent residence having committed acts constituting perjury in connection with his visa which were found to be crimes involving moral turpitude. He resided in the United States 25 years, and was married to a lawful permanent resident alien. According to the report of the Committee, he "reared seven stepchildren...has the reputation of being a good workman, a good family man, hard working, and a good provider, devoted to his wife and stepchildren." The law canceled deportation proceedings against the beneficiary and held him lawfully admitted for permanent residence. (Priv. L. No. 730, 64 Stat. A142 (1950)) (Sen. Rep. No. 1397, 2nd Sess.) (H.R. Rep. No. 2614, 2nd Sess.)-WCRF

81st Cong., S. 1552, for the relief of Ernest E. Heintz. Beneficiary, a 36-year old native of Canada whose brother was a United States citizen, was ineligible for a visa because he was convicted of entering property illegally when he and some other boys at the age of 16 or 17 were looking for empty bottles. Favorable action was taken because "the offense for which the beneficiary received the suspended sentence was little more than a youthful indiscretion...the beneficiary of the bill has led an exemplary life since the offense, and that he and his family, if admitted, would be prospective good citizens." The law waived section 3 of the Act of 1917 relating to crimes involving moral turpitude. (Priv. L. No. 398, 64 Stat. A21 (1950)) (Sen. Rep. No. 1056, 1st Sess.) (H.R. Rep. No. 1724, 2nd Sess.)-WCRF

81st Cong., S. 1637, for the relief of Marie Henriette de Bruyn. Beneficiary, a 26-year old native and citizen of the Netherlands, was caretaker for numerous graves of American soldiers, among them being the grave of Mr. and Mrs. Ridenhour's son. She entered the United States as a visitor. The Attorney General noted there were no compelling reasons to grant the beneficiary preference over other immigrants awaiting a visa. The law held the beneficiary lawfully admitted for permanent residence. (Priv. L. No. 619, 64 Stat. A102 (1950)) (Sen. Rep. No. 1476, 2nd Sess.) (H.R. Rep. No. 2197, 2nd Sess.)-QMGN

81st Cong., S. 1856, for the relief of Sisters Maria Rita Rossi, Maria Domenica Paone, Rachele Orlando, Assunta Roselli, Rosa Innocenti, and Maria Mancinelli. Beneficiaries, six nuns of the Carmelite Order in Massachusetts who were engaged in religious activities educating young boys for priesthood, were natives and citizens of Italy. The law held the beneficiaries lawfully admitted for permanent residence. (Priv. L. No. 489, 64 Stat. A57 (1950)) (Sen. Rep. No. 1404, 2nd Sess.) (H.R. Rep. No. 2107, 2nd Sess.)-QMOC

81st Cong., S. 1866, for the relief of Mrs. Clayre Louise Forsyth. Beneficiary, a 49-year old native-born United States citizen, lost her citizenship by voting in an election in Newfoundland. She was employed as a nurse for 20 years. The Attorney General opposed relief indicating the issue of loss of citizenship should be addressed in general legislation, and specifically stated "the facts in this case fail to present considerations sufficient to justify the enactment of special legislation." The law deemed section 401(e) would not apply to the beneficiary. (Priv. L. No. 864, 64 Stat. A191 (1950)) (Sen. Rep. No. 1879, 2nd Sess.) (H.R. Rep. No. 2788, 2nd Sess.)-NVOL

81st Cong., S. 1869, for the relief of Marcantonio Doria D'Angri and his wife, Sonia Stampa Doria D'Angri. Beneficiaries, natives and citizens of Italy, assisted the Allies in World War II. The male beneficiary held the position of Italian Vice-Consul in Freiburg, Germany and established contact with the British consul through the underground to communicate with his brother-in-law, who had crossed the lines to join the government which had overthrown Mussolini in Salerno. His communications were intercepted and he was then arrested by the German Gestapo and imprisoned for treason. The Senate Committee noted he would have been executed "except for the intervention of the papal annuncio." He "rendered unusually meritorious services to our allies as a member of the underground in Italy." The law held the beneficiaries lawfully admitted for permanent residence. (Priv. L. No. 650, 64 Stat. A112 (1950)) (Sen. Rep. No. 1405, 2nd Sess.) (H.R. Rep. No. 2441, 2nd Sess.)-QMDE

81st Cong., S. 1915, for the relief of Viktor A. Kravchenko. Beneficiary, a 41-year old native of the Soviet Union, entered the United States as a representative of the Soviet Purchasing Commission. He was the author of a publication entitled "I Chose Freedom" which was highly critical of the Communist system and he was afraid of return to the Soviet Union because of his writings. The law held the beneficiary lawfully admitted for permanent residence and held inapplicable provisions of the Act of October 16, 1918 and sections 3 and 19(a) of the Act of 1917 relating to aliens who were members of certain political parties or who advocated the overthrow of the United States government. The bill also waived section 305 of the Act of 1940 relating to naturalization. (Priv. L. No. 365, 64 Stat. A8 (1950)) (Sen. Rep. No. 525, 1st Sess.) (H.R. Rep. No. 1480, 2nd Sess.)-NXCP

81st Cong., S. 2047, for the relief of Marie C. Araujo, also known as Marie Conceipaco de Brito. Beneficiary, a 20-year old native of Portugal who was born out of wedlock was adopted by the natural parent, a United States citizen who contributed to her support since birth. The law held the beneficiary as the natural child of a United States citizen. (Priv. L. No. 947, 64 Stat. A220 (1950)) (Sen. Rep. No. 1588, 2nd Sess.) (H.R. Rep. No. 2940, 2nd Sess.)-QIRA

81st Cong., S. 2077, for the relief of Francisco Gonzalez Perez. Beneficiary, a 28-year old native and citizen of Mexico and spouse of a United States citizen with two United States citizen children, was unable to obtain a visa due to the commission of perjury in attempting to immigrate. His spouse was on relief and had been in "serious need of support from her husband for herself and children." The law waived the eleventh category of section 3 of the Act of 1917 and provisions of the Act of March 4, 1929 relating to entry after deportation. (Priv. L. No. 672, 64 Stat. A119 (1950)) (Sen. Rep. No. 1797, 2nd Sess.) (H.R. Rep. No. 2502, 2nd Sess.)-WCRF

81st Cong., S. 2100, for the relief of Penelope Carolyn Cox. Beneficiary, a 27-year old native of India with a British father and American mother, did not derive United States citizenship at birth because her mother had lost citizenship upon marriage. Although the mother regained citizenship through naturalization the child did not derive because she lacked permanent resident status. The father's employment required extensive travel, and while employed in India the beneficiary was born. Her parents later resided in the United States but she could not readily obtain a visa because of the oversubscribed visas for India. The law deemed the beneficiary to have been born in Great Britain. (Priv. L. No. 366, 64 Stat. A8 (1950)) (Sen. Rep. No. 1060, 1st Sess.) (H.R. Rep. No. 1482, 2nd Sess.)-NMSC

81st Cong., S. 2107, for the relief of Georges Gregory Alpiar. Beneficiary, a 52-year old native of Turkey, entered the United States temporarily to establish a perfume business. He was later employed as a research technician in the manufacture of candies and fruit juice. His technical knowledge was "necessary to the development of an infant American industry." The law held the beneficiary lawfully admitted for permanent residence. (Priv. L. No. 633, 64 Stat. A106 (1950)) (Sen. Rep. No. 1475, 2nd Sess.) (H.R. Rep. No. 2165, 2nd Sess.)-QMOC

81st Cong., S. 2108, for the relief of Italo Vespa de Chellis. Beneficiary, a 22-year old native and citizen of China, desired to join his sister and mother who were permanent residents. They both were employed as librarians at the Library of Congress and the sister worked part time for Rev. Msgr. Fulton J. Sheen. The beneficiary was unable to immigrate with the family because he had attained the age of 21. The law held the beneficiary as the minor child of a lawful permanent resident alien. (Priv. L. No. 490, 64 Stat. A57 (1950)) (Sen. Rep. No. 1406, 2nd Sess.) (H.R. Rep. No. 2108, 2nd Sess.)-QPRF

81st Cong., S. 2420, for the relief of Shaoul Minashi Shami, Emily Shami, Joseph Clement Shami, and Charles Henry Shami. Beneficiaries (ages 50, 49, 16, 14), citizens of Iraq and Great Britain, entered the United States as visitors. Subsequently, Mr. Shami established a textile mill in Massachusetts in which his imports and exports totaled a quarter of a million dollars for one year. The Senate Committee noted the beneficiary appeared to have made a "definite contribution...to the American textile industry" and employed a number of United States citizens. The law held the beneficiaries lawfully admitted for permanent residence. (Priv. L. No. 1060, 64 Stat. A262 (1950)) (Sen. Rep. No. 2384, 2nd Sess.) (H.R. Rep. No. 3160, 2nd Sess.)-QMOC

81st Cong., S. 2429, for the relief of Henrique Santos. Beneficiary, a lawful permanent resident of the United States, was ineligible for citizenship due to his application for exemption from United States military service. The Senate Committee noted that after initially applying for citizenship "he became engaged in a confidential capacity by the Government of the United States and in order to preserve his usefulness to the United States Government, 'pursuant to direction of his superiors' deferred his naturalization" and then claimed exemption from the military service. The law waived section 3(a) of the Act of September 16, 1940 relating to ineligibility for citizenship. (Priv. L. No. 402, 64 Stat. A23 (1950)) (Sen. Rep. No. 1062, 1st Sess.) (H.R. Rep. No. 1727, 2nd Sess.)-NXDD

81st Cong., S. 2556, for the relief of Mrs. Billy J. Knight and Dorothea Knight. Beneficiaries, widow and daughter, natives and citizens of Germany, desired to enter the United States to be with the deceased husband's relatives. The deceased spouse, a United States citizen in the Armed Forces, had requested permission to marry from his parents who first refused. He then became married but did not want the military authorities to know because of prohibitions against such marriages. The husband drowned when on furlough to the United States. The law held the child to be a United States citizen at birth and held the widow entitled to immediate relative status. (Priv. L. No. 635, 64 Stat. A107 (1950)) (Sen. Rep. No. 1452, 2nd Sess.) (H.R. Rep. No. 2201, 2nd Sess.)-QIRW

81st Cong., S. 2611, for the relief of Roland Roger Alfred Boccia, also known as Roland Barbera. Beneficiary, an eight-year old native and citizen of France born in Algeria, entered the United States on a temporary visa for medical treatment for tuberculosis and was thereafter hospitalized at public expense. It was stated his case would require a long period of hospitalization. His mother, a United States citizen and his stepfather, a United States citizen and veteran of World War II, accompanied the child to the United States. The stepfather had adopted him from the mother's previous marriage. The law held the beneficiary lawfully admitted for permanent residence. (Priv. L. No. 502, 64 Stat. A61 (1950)) (Sen. Rep. No. 1303, 2nd Sess.) (H.R. Rep. No. 2109, 2nd Sess.)-WHEL

81st Cong., S. 2682, for the relief of Naum Ionescu and his wife. Beneficiaries, 52- and 38-year old natives and citizens of Bulgaria and Romania, served in various posts with the Romanian Government. They left Romania with King Mihai when he abdicated his crown and remained in France until their entry to the United States as visitors. The law held the beneficiaries lawfully admitted for permanent residence. (Priv. L. No. 653, 64 Stat. A113 (1950)) (Sen. Rep. No. 1606, 2nd Sess.) (H.R. Rep. No. 2448, 2nd Sess.)-QMGN

81st Cong., S. 2795, for the relief of Fortunato Giulio Torre. Beneficiary, a 57-year old native and citizen of Italy, entered the United States as a visitor and later was employed by the Concord Cheese Corporation as a cheese bacteriologist and technician for which he had experience when employed by the City of Milan. The law held the beneficiary lawfully admitted for permanent residence. (Priv. L. No. 660, 64 Stat. A115 (1950)) (Sen. Rep. No. 1692, 2nd Sess.) (H.R. Rep. No. 2451, 2nd Sess.)-QMOC

81st Cong., S. 2897, for the relief of Hyman D. Langer and Alta Jourard Langer. Beneficiaries, 48- and 40-year old natives of Poland and citizens of Canada, entered the United States as visitors. The male beneficiary was employed as an organizer and business agent for the International Ladies Garment Workers' Union. (Priv. L. No. 856, 64 Stat. A188 (1950)) (Sen. Rep. No. 1884, 2nd Sess.) (H.R. Rep. No. 2994, 2nd Sess.)-QMOC

81st Cong., S. 2981, for the relief of Giuseppe Merlinet Forgnone. Beneficiary, a 38-year old native and citizen of Italy, entered the United States as a visitor and was engaged in supervising construction work relating to a State-sponsored agricultural project including breeding cattle and other livestock husbandry and poultry farming. His father had resided in the United States for 20 years and had extensive holdings in Nevada, one-fourth share of which went to the beneficiary upon his death. The law held the beneficiary lawfully admitted for permanent residence. (Priv. L. No. 1097, 64 Stat. A277 (1951)) (Sen. Rep. No. 2191, 2nd Sess.) (H.R. Rep. No. 3214, 2nd Sess.)-QMOC

81st Cong., S. 3125, for the relief of Dr. Lutfu Lahut Uzman. Beneficiary, a 27-year old native and citizen of Turkey, entered the United States as a student and graduated from Harvard Medical School, subsequently working in the field of biochemistry. He was then employed at Children's Hospital in Boston and was regarded as "one of the most promising investigators in medical research in this country." The law held the beneficiary lawfully admitted for permanent residence. (Priv. L. No. 1098, 64 Stat. A277 (1951)) (Sen. Rep. No. 2591, 2nd Sess.) (H.R. Rep. No. 3216, 2nd Sess.)-QMOC

81st Cong., S. 3238, for the relief of Dr. Frederick Daniel McDade. Beneficiary, a 40-year old native and citizen of Canada, was admitted for permanent residence and was employed as a surgeon in Montana. The state licensing laws for physicians required United States citizenship, and he needed the requisite time period to file for naturalization. The Attorney General was unable to recommend favorably in the case because it would "establish an undesirable precedent by permitting the naturalization of an alien who had resided in the United States for less than the required period of time . . . it appears that the relief sought in this case could be obtained more directly by appropriate action by the State government rather than by the Federal Government." The law waived the residence requirement for purposes of naturalization of the beneficiary. (Priv. L. No. 873, 64 Stat. A195 (1950)) (Sen. Rep. No. 1969, 2nd Sess.) (H.R. Rep. No. 2797, 2nd Sess.)-NRES

81st Cong., S. 3378, for the relief of Armando Santini. Beneficiary, a 46-year old native and citizen of Italy, entered the United States as a visitor and was later employed by Da Prato Statuary Company of Illinois as a silversmith. He was sought by that company to "bring new ideas into the manufacture of religious articles." The report of the Attorney General noted no significant merit in the case, and that the deliberate entry into the United States as nonimmigrants for the ultimate purpose of remaining in the United States was not fair to those aliens who had to wait their turn for a visa abroad. The law held the beneficiary lawfully admitted for permanent residence. (Priv. L. No. 1099, 64 Stat. A277 (1951)) (Sen. Rep. No. 2595, 2nd Sess.) (H.R. Rep. No. 3221, 2nd Sess.)-QMOC

81st Cong., S.J. Res. 105, for the relief of Sister Elizabeth Kenny. Beneficiary, a native and citizen of Australia, evolved a treatment for infantile paralysis. She entered the United States as a visitor on many occasions and in 1942 the Sister Kenny Foundation, Inc. was founded in Minneapolis. During World War II, United States medical officers were instructed by her at Mayo Clinic. Because of her extended stays in the United States the beneficiary would have normally been classified as an immigrant, however, she did not choose to "sever her ties with her native country." The law granted the beneficiary the privilege of entering the United States "as frequently as she may desire" notwithstanding section 3 of the Act of 1924 which held such persons to be classified as immigrants. In addition, the act exempted Sister Kenny from the Alien Registration Act of 1940, section 2 of the Act of 1917 relating to tax levies, and section 15 of the Act of 1924 relating to duration of stay for visitors. The Act did not, however, waive any ground of exclusion for admission to the United States. (Priv. L. No. 357, 64 Stat. A4 (1950)) (Sen. Rep. No. 1063, 1st Sess.)-QMGN

82nd Cong., H.R. 616, for the relief of Tomas J. Zafiriadis. Beneficiary, a 41-year old native of Turkey, was taken to Uruguay as a child and became a citizen of that country. He served in the American Embassy in Uruguay for 20 years and was elevated to the position of special assistant to the commercial attaché, John P. Hoover. He was unable to obtain a visa due to the oversubscription of visas for Turkey, the country to which his visa would be chargeable. The law deemed the beneficiary to be a native of Uruguay. (Priv. L. No. 99, 65 Stat. A39 (1951)) (H.R. Rep. No. 402, 1st Sess.) (Sen. Rep. No. 393, 1st Sess.)-QPRF

82nd Cong., H.R. 617, for the relief of Franz Furtner, Valentina Furtner, Nina Tuerck, and Victoria Tuerck. Beneficiaries, 44-, 35-, 19-, and 8-year old natives of Austria, Russia, and Germany, entered the United States as visitors employed by Ringling Brothers, and Barnum and Bailey Circus. One of the beneficiaries was represented as being the only man in the world who could balance himself on one finger. The Attorney General stated there were not compelling reasons to justify enactment of special legislation on their behalf. The law held the beneficiaries lawfully admitted for permanent residence. (Priv. L. No. 215, 65 Stat. A82 (1951)) (H.R. Rep. No. 403, 1st Sess.) (Sen. Rep. No. 617, 1st Sess.)-QMOC

82nd Cong., H.R. 622, for the relief of Mrs. Oksana Stepanovna Kasenkina. Beneficiary, a 55-year old native and citizen of Russia, entered the United States for employment in the Russian consulate and taught students of Russian diplomats in New York City. She had been scheduled to return to Russia but sought asylum. She received much publicity as a result of her stay at the Reed Farm, sponsored by Tolstoy Foundation, where the Soviet consular officials allegedly arranged her "kidnapping or rescue." She escaped by her leap from the third floor window of the Soviet consulate August 12, 1948. She subsequently published her memoirs in a book entitled "Leap to Freedom." The law held the beneficiary lawfully admitted for permanent residence. (Priv. L. No. 30, 65 Stat. A14 (1951)) (H.R. Rep. No. 68, 1st Sess.) (Sen. Rep. No. 255, 1st Sess.)-QMDE

82nd Cong., H.R. 627, for the relief of Mrs. Tjitske Bandstra Van Der Velde. Beneficiary, a native and citizen of the Netherlands, and spouse of a United States citizen, was ineligible for a visa due to previous attacks of insanity for which she was institutionalized eight years. She was in good health until her two children died tragically, one death occurred when she was washing clothes and the child fell into a tub of boiling water. The second death occurred when another child swallowed a piece of copper money causing poisoning and death. It was stated after eight years of treatment she did not show any mental disturbances. She had two surviving children. The law waived the second category of section 3 of the Act of 1917 relating to mental conditions for attacks on insanity. (Priv. L. No. 241, 65 Stat. A92 (1951)) (H.R. Rep. No. 598, 1st Sess.) (Sen. Rep. No. 664, 1st Sess.)-WHEL

82nd Cong., H.R. 648, for the relief of Max Mayer Hirsch Winzelberg and Mrs. Jenty Fuss De Winzelberg. Beneficiaries, 55- and 54-year old natives of Poland entered the United States on the basis of the male beneficiary being an ordained minister of religion. It was later discovered he had not practiced his religion for two years prior to admission to the United States. They had two sons in the United States, one of whom was to become a citizen and who served in the United States Army. The law held the beneficiaries lawfully admitted for permanent residence and deducted visas from section 4 of the Displaced Persons Act. (Priv. L. No. 528, 66 Stat. A40 (1952)) (H.R. Rep. No. 943, 1st Sess.) (Sen. Rep. No. 1238, 2nd Sess.)-QMDP

82nd Cong., H.R. 664, for the relief of Mrs. Coral E. Alldritt. Beneficiary, a 41-year old native and citizen of Australia, entered the United States as a student and was associated with the Medical Arts School of Johns Hopkins University and later employed in a Veterans Administration hospital as a medical illustrator. She served in the Women's Auxiliary Air Force of the Royal Australian Air Force four years assisting in "constructing bombing target maps." She was a highly skilled technician who had rendered meritorious service to the United States. The law held the beneficiary lawfully admitted for permanent residence. (Priv. L. No. 32, 65 Stat. A15 (1951)) (H.R. Rep. No. 108, 1st Sess.) (Sen. Rep. No. 257, 1st Sess.)-QMOC

82nd Cong., H.R. 702, for the relief of Karl Chimani and Ada Chimani. Beneficiaries, 62- and 53-year old natives and citizens of Austria, entered the United States as visitors and were subsequently employed as a trainer of Lippizaner horses in Kansas. The employer owned six mares and one stallion which had grown to 20 head. The horses had been rescued and brought to the United States by the Third Army. The beneficiary was a graduate of the Spanish Riding Academy. The Attorney General did not recommend enactment because it appeared the beneficiaries entered the United States "allegedly as visitors when they were in fact coming here to accept employment and remain permanently." The law held the beneficiaries lawfully admitted for permanent residence. (Priv. L. No. 164, 65 Stat. A63 (1951)) (H.R. Rep. No. 525, 1st Sess.) (Sen. Rep. No. 507, 1st Sess.)-QMOC

82nd Cong., H.R. 711, for the relief of George Lukes. Beneficiary, a native of Japan, was an orphan who was to be adopted by United States citizens. He was racially ineligible to enter the United States. The child was born out of wedlock to a Japanese mother who had been institutionalized, and an American soldier. He was then placed in an orphanage. The law held section 13(c) of the Act of 1924 relating to racial ineligibility inapplicable to the beneficiary and held him to be the natural-born child of United States citizens under section 4(a) and 9 of the Act. (Priv. L. No. 289, 65 Stat. A109 (1951)) (H.R. Rep. No. 848, 1st Sess.) (Sen. Rep. No. 809, 1st Sess.)-QIER

82nd Cong., H.R. 714, for the relief of James A. G. Martindale. Beneficiary, a 33-year old native and citizen of Great Britain who had resided in Canada, was the spouse of a United States citizen with one United States citizen child. He was excluded from admission to the United States based on several convictions in Canada for crimes of theft, forgery, and fraud. He served in the Canadian Army 1941 to 1945. The report of the Attorney General noted there did not appear to be sufficient grounds to justify enactment of special legislation. The law waived the eleventh category of section 3 of the Act of 1917 relating to crimes involving moral turpitude. (Priv. L. No. 46, 65 Stat. A19 (1951)) (H.R. Rep. No. 72, 1st Sess.) (Sen. Rep. No. 259, 1st Sess.)-WCRF

82nd Cong., H.R. 715, for the relief of Aenny Blank. Beneficiary, a 55-year old native of Turkey and citizen of Germany lost her mother and three sisters during an accidental bombing of their home in World War II. Three brothers resided in the United States upon whom she was dependent for support. Her niece who also survived the bombing was eligible for a visa under the German quota, but the beneficiary was chargeable to the Turkey quota which was oversubscribed. The law held the beneficiary to have been born in Germany. (Priv. L. No. 100, 65 Stat. A39 (1951)) (H.R. Rep. No. 73, 1st Sess.) (Sen. Rep. No. 339, 1st Sess.)-QPRF

82nd Cong., H.R. 853, for the relief of Maximilian Otto Ricker-Huetter and Mrs. Eugenia Ricker-Huetter. Beneficiaries, husband and wife, ages 46 and 41, natives of Czechoslovakia and citizens of Austria, entered the United States as visitors. The male beneficiary was a successful journalist, publisher, and manufacturer prior to the war and opposed the Nazi regime and Communism. An aunt, a United States citizen and opera singer, was known as Madam Maria Jeritza. They applied for relief under the Displaced Persons Act but were denied, because they were unable to prove they could not return to Austria due to possible persecution. The male beneficiary was employed in the United States organizing an umbrella company. The law held the beneficiaries lawfully admitted for permanent residence under section 4 of the Displaced Persons Act. (Priv. L. No. 399, 65 Stat. A146 (1951)) (H.R. Rep. No. 946, 1st Sess.) (Sen. Rep. No. 986, 1st Sess.)-QMDP

82nd Cong., H.R. 880, for the relief of Giuseppe Biolzi. Beneficiary, a 19-year old native and citizen of Italy, was adopted by his United States citizen uncle with whom he had resided since entering the United States as a visitor. His parents and four siblings resided in Italy. The law held the beneficiary lawfully admitted for permanent residence. (Priv. L. No. 996, 66 Stat. A202 (1952)) (H.R. Rep. No. 1904, 2nd Sess.) (Sen. Rep. No. 2060, 2nd Sess.)-QIRA

82nd Cong., H.R. 884, for the relief of Johanna A. Stoots. Beneficiary, a 36-year old native and citizen of the Netherlands, entered the United States at the invitation of the Gold Star Mothers whose sons had been billeted in her home in the Netherlands during the war. The law held the beneficiary lawfully admitted for permanent residence. (Priv. L. No. 386, 65 Stat. A142 (1951)) (H.R. Rep. No. 967, 1st Sess.) (Sen. Rep. No. 987, 1st Sess.)-QMGN

82nd Cong., H.R. 885, for the relief of Heinrich von Biel, Margarethe von Biel, and Doris Schumann. Beneficiaries, 53-, 44- and 19-year old natives and citizens of Germany, entered the United States accompanying the male beneficiary who was chief of the shipping section of the German Mission. He later resigned that position and was employed by the United States Lines

Company. He had been drafted into the German Army in 1944 and participated in an uprising against Hitler for which he was imprisoned and reduced to the rank of private. He had one son, a United States citizen, who was attending school in the United States. The law held the beneficiaries lawfully admitted for permanent residence. (Priv. L. No. 777, 66 Stat. A123 (1952)) (H.R. Rep. No. 1476, 2nd Sess.) (Sen. Rep. No. 1643, 2nd Sess.)-QMGN

82nd Cong., H.R. 890, for the relief of Athina Mary Onassis. Beneficiary, a 22-year old native of England and citizen of Greece, entered the United States as a student and thereafter for lawful permanent residence. She then married Aristotle Socrates Onassis and had a two-year old United States citizen child. She was unable to petition for citizenship due to absences abroad. The law deemed the beneficiary to have been lawfully admitted for permanent residence on the date she first entered the United States as a student, thus making her eligible to petition for naturalization eight months earlier than had been anticipated. (Priv. L. No. 35, 65 Stat. A16 (1951)) (H.R. Rep. No. 78, 1st Sess.) (Sen. Rep. No. 265, 1st Sess.)-NRES

82nd Cong., H.R. 896, for the relief of Mrs. Clara Raffloer Droesse. Beneficiary, a 71-year old native-born United States citizen, was taken to Germany by her father at the age of eight. She lost her citizenship through marriage to a German citizen and subsequently regained citizenship through reinstatement laws. In 1946 she voted in an election in Germany, thus losing her citizenship. Challenges were pending in the courts at the time of consideration: "it would appear that there will be a considerable lapse of time before the matter is finally adjudicated...Mrs. Droesse is 70 years of age and has limited means. In view of this situation the committee feels that the facts in this case warrant a favorable recommendation." The law allowed retention of citizenship. (Priv. L. No. 144, without the President's approval, 65 Stat. A55 (1951)) (H.R. Rep. No. 330, 1st Sess.) (Sen. Rep. No. 451, 1st Sess.) -NVOL

82nd Cong., H.R. 898, for the relief of Gunter Arno Thelemann. Beneficiary, a 20-year old native of Germany born out of wedlock and acknowledged by his putative father, was unable to immigrate on that basis because of difficulties locating the legitimization decree because of the war. The putative father and his spouse sought adoption of the child, but due to the oversubscribed visas for Germany he was unable to immigrate. The law held the beneficiary to be within sections 4(a) and (9) of the Act of 1924 as the natural son of the adoptive parents. (Priv. L. No. 37, 65 Stat. A16 (1951)) (H.R. Rep. No. 80, 1st Sess.) (Sen. Rep. No. 267, 1st Sess.)-QIRA

82nd Cong., H.R. 901, for the relief of Janet and Daisy Wong. Beneficiaries were 20- and 18-year old natives and citizens of China. Their United States citizen mother had planned to bring them to the United States but died, and their father was also deceased. They resided in Hong Kong and were cared for by a teacher. There were several aunts and uncles in the United States who were willing to guarantee care of the children. The beneficiaries were heir to their mother's interest in a Chinese restaurant in San Francisco. The Attorney General did not recommend enactment in view of the many other alien Chinese children of United States citizens awaiting visas and the facts did not present justification for special preference. The law held the beneficiaries to be within section 4(a) of the Act of 1924 as the natural-born children of a deceased United States citizen. (Priv. L. No. 302, 65 Stat. A123 (1951)) (H.R. Rep. No. 162, 1st Sess.) (Sen. Rep. No. 811, 1st Sess.)-QIER

82nd Cong., H.R. 961, for the relief of Zbigniew Jan Dunikowski, Karolina Dunikowski, Wanda Octavia Dunikowski, and Janina Grospera Dunikowski. Beneficiaries were husband, wife and two children, ages 62, 52, 23, and 17. The parents were natives of Poland and the children were born in Monaco and Italy, respectively. They entered the United States as visitors and applied for relief under the Displaced Persons Act but were denied because they could not show they were unable to return to the Philippines, the place of their last residence. It was stated the beneficiaries "were active in giving aid and comfort to American prisoners held by the Japanese in the Philippines, doing so with great danger to their lives." They suffered the destruction of $100,000 property during the war. The law held the beneficiaries lawfully admitted for permanent residence under section 4 of the Displaced Persons Act of 1948. (Priv. L. No. 420, 66 Stat. A6 (1952)) (H.R. Rep. No. 331, 1st Sess.) (Sen. Rep. No. 1079, 2nd Sess.)-QMDP

82nd Cong., H.R. 970, for the relief of Antonios Charalambou. Beneficiary, a 49-year old native and citizen of Greece was a seaman who had been employed on United States vessels 10 years. He was ineligible to file for naturalization on the basis of five years service under the Internal Security Act of 1950 because its provisions had expired. The law held the beneficiary lawfully admitted for permanent residence. (Priv. L. No. 256, 65 Stat. A97 (1951)) (H.R. Rep. No. 601, 1st Sess.) (Sen. Rep. No. 666, 1st Sess.)-NMSC

82nd Cong., H.R. 978, for the relief of Mrs. Michi Masaoka. Beneficiary, a 57-year old native and citizen of Japan and the mother of eight United States citizen children, was inadmissible for immigration due to racial ineligibility. Four sons served in the United States Armed Forces during World War II, one of whom was killed in France. She was widowed and her son desired her admission to the United States. The law held section 13(c) of the Act of 1924 inapplicable to the beneficiary. (Priv. L. No. 562, 66 Stat. A52 (1952)) (H.R. Rep. No. 1350, 2nd Sess.) (Sen. Rep. No. 1368, 2nd Sess.)-QIER

82nd Cong., H.R. 1092, for the relief of Mrs. Mercedes Hernandez Saguar. Beneficiary, a 60-year old native of Spain and widow who had four United States citizen siblings in the United States and two United States citizen children, was excluded from entry due to previous attacks of insanity. She had previously resided in the United States seven years and was deported on the basis of mental health. The Attorney General did not recommend enactment: "While the case admittedly has appealing elements, the excluding provisions of the immigration laws nevertheless were enacted for the protection of the citizenry of this country as a whole. The question of granting relief to incompetent relatives of United States citizens is a general one which should be resolved, if at all, by general legislation and not by a series of private bills." The law held the second category of section 3 of the Act of 1917 relating to attacks of insanity inapplicable in the case of the beneficiary. (Priv. L. No. 869, 66 Stat. A162 (1952)) (H.R. Rep. No. 1970, 82nd Sess.) (Sen. Rep. No. 2006, 2nd Sess.)-WHEL

82nd Cong., H.R. 1100, for the relief of Eugenio Bellini. Beneficiary, a 64-year old native of Italy and citizen of Germany entered the United States as a visitor and was employed by Vanity Fair Mills, Inc. as a consulting engineer. It was stated he was regarded as an "expert designer and builder of tricot machines" (knitting machines). He had formerly been the designer of a Saupe model of tricot machines built in the 1930's and in use in Saxony. He had been affiliated with the Nazi Party but did not seek membership in that party and only paid dues in order to conduct business. The law held the beneficiary lawfully admitted for permanent residence. (Priv. L. No. 341, 65 Stat. A127 (1951)) (H.R. Rep. No. 819, 1st Sess.) (Sen. Rep. No. 907, 1st Sess.)-QMOC

82nd Cong., H.R. 1103, for the relief of Sidney Young Hughes. Beneficiary, a 53-year old native of Wales and citizen of England, was deported on the basis of a conviction of assault arising out of a fight with three other persons. He later entered the United States as a seaman and married a United States citizen. The law held the beneficiary lawfully admitted for permanent residence. (Priv. L. No. 238, 65 Stat. A91 (1951)) (H.R. Rep. No. 333, 1st Sess.) (Sen. Rep. No. 410, 1st Sess.) (Conf. Rep. No. 805, 82nd Cong., 1st Sess.)-WCRF

82nd Cong., H.R. 1150, for the relief of Mario Pucci, Giacomo Favetti, Giuseppe Omati, Vincenzo Andreani, Lambruno Sarzanini, and Alessandro Costa. Beneficiaries, natives and citizens of Italy (ages 39, 59, 50, 53, 39, 55), entered the United States as visitors to work in the granite and marble industry in Vermont. The Senate Committee noted they were all "expert granite and marble workers whose services are said to be vitally needed in such industries in New England." The House Committee noted similar legislation had been passed by the Congress. As temporary visitors under section 3(2) of the Act of 1924, they were admitted as an exemption from the alien contract labor laws. The beneficiaries were employed as sculptors and instructors in various granite and marble quarries. The law held the beneficiaries lawfully admitted for permanent residence. (Priv. L. No. 63, 65 Stat. A25 (1951)) (H.R. Rep. No. 84, 1st Sess.) (Sen. Rep. No. 271, 1st Sess.)-QMOC

82nd Cong., H.R. 1157, for the relief of Lum Ying. Beneficiary, a 56-year old native of China, entered the United States claiming to be a United States citizen but was unable to establish his claim because of conflicting statements concerning his parents' place of birth and periods of residence in the United States. He claimed his records were destroyed in a 1906 earthquake. He had allegedly been in the United States 30 years and was the owner of a Chinese restaurant. The law held the beneficiary lawfully admitted for permanent residence. (Priv. L. No. 169, 65 Stat. A65 (1951)) (H.R. Rep. No. 85, 1st Sess.) (Sen. Rep. No. 512, 1st Sess.)-NMSC

82nd Cong., H.R. 1158, for the relief of Isao Ishimoto. Beneficiary, a native of Japan, was adopted by United States citizens who desired to bring the child to the United States. The law held the beneficiary within section 4(a) and 9 of the Act of 1924 as the natural-born child of United States citizens and waived the grounds of exclusion relating to races ineligible to citizenship. (Priv. L. No. 563, 66 Stat. A52 (1952)) (H.R. Rep. No. 1326, 2nd Sess.) (Sen. Rep. No. 1369, 2nd Sess.)-QIER

82nd Cong., H.R. 1162, for the relief of Kaiko Sugimote (Kay Fair) and her minor children. Beneficiaries, natives of Japan, were the widow and children of a United States citizen member of the Armed Forces who was killed in action in Korea. The beneficiaries would have been entitled to status under a previous private law as nonquota immigrants under section 4(a) of the Act of 1924, but because of his death and ineligibility due to race they were unable to immigrate. The law held section 13(c) of the Act of 1924 relating to races ineligible to citizenship inapplicable to the beneficiaries. (Priv. L. No. 676, 66 Stat. A88, (1952)) (H.R. Rep. No. 1574, 2nd Sess.) (Sen. Rep. No. 1531, 2nd Sess.)-QIER

82nd Cong., H.R. 1165, for the relief of Richard Gregory Rundle and Valiquette Adele Rundle. Beneficiaries, adopted children of United States citizens ages 13 and 5, were natives of Germany and Austria. One of the parents was employed by United Press for 21 years, during which he spent a significant period of time abroad. This made it difficult for the adopted children to comply with the two-year residence requirement for naturalization. The law deemed the provisions of sections 316(b) and (c) inapplicable to the beneficiaries and stated they could be naturalized after five months continuous residence in the United States. (Priv. L. No. 5, 65 Stat. A4 (1951)) (H.R. Rep. No. 112, 1st Sess.) (Sen. Rep. No. 110, 1st Sess.)-NRES

82nd Cong., H.R. 1234, for the relief of Mrs. Selma Cecelia Gahl. Beneficiary, a 63-year old native of Australia, acquired United States citizenship on the basis of her marriage to a United States citizen. She resided in the United States 30 years and then went to Peru with her husband where he later died. She was unable to retain citizenship due to residence abroad because of a lawsuit in the Peruvian courts. The report of the Attorney General noted there were insufficient facts to justify special legislation. The law held the beneficiary lawfully admitted for permanent residence. (Priv. L. No. 522, 66 Stat. A38 (1952)) (H.R. Rep. No. 406, 1st Sess.) (Sen. Rep. No. 1240, 2nd Sess.)-NRTN

82nd Cong., H.R. 1236, for the relief of Rhoda Akiko Nishiyama. Beneficiary, a four-year old native of Japan, whose mother was a permanent resident and whose father entered the United States under section 4(e) of the Act of 1924, was unable to join her mother in the United States because she was excluded on the basis of racial ineligibility. The law held section 13(c) of the Act of 1924 inapplicable to the beneficiary. (Priv. L. No. 360, 65 Stat. A133 (1951)) (H.R. Rep. No. 873, lst Sess.) (Sen. Rep. No. 878, 1st Sess.)-QIER

82nd Cong., H.R. 1252, for the relief of Mr. and Mrs. Miroslav Kudrat. Beneficiaries, 64- and 53-year old natives and citizens of Czechoslovakia, entered the United States as visitors, three days after the provisions of the Displaced Persons Act would have provided relief. The male beneficiary was formerly the Czechoslovakian Minister in Iraq and Iran and was later employed in Washington, D.C. by the National Committee for Free Europe. The law held the beneficiaries lawfully admitted for permanent residence under section 4 of the Displaced Persons Act. (Priv. L. No. 342, 65 Stat. A127 (1951)) (H.R. Rep. No. 735, 1st Sess.) (Sen. Rep. No. 861, 1st Sess.)-QMDP

82nd Cong., H.R. 1464, for the relief of Arokiaswami Arumai Singh. Beneficiary, a 25-year old native of India, entered the United States as a visitor on consignment as an animal trainer for elephants for the Daily Brothers circus. At the time of his entry he brought eleven elephants to the circus and intended to remain until the elephants were accustomed to English language and another trainer. He was later employed as a lion trainer with another circus. The law held the beneficiary lawfully admitted for permanent residence. (Priv. L. No. 922, 66 Stat. A179 (1952)) (H.R. Rep. No. 1478, 2nd Sess.) (Sen. Rep. No. 1903, 2nd Sess.)-QMOC

82nd Cong., H.R. 1477, for the relief of Linda Azar Karam Batrouny. Beneficiary, a 39-year old native and citizen of Lebanon, entered the United States as a visitor and subsequently was engaged in teaching Arabic at Berlitz Schools. She was also employed on contract with the Office of International Information, Department of State and gave special instructions in Arabic to military units in New York. The Attorney General noted it would be unjust to grant preference to the beneficiary over others awaiting visas abroad. The law held the beneficiary lawfully admitted for permanent residence. (Priv. L. No. 923, 66 Stat. A180 (1952)) (H.R. Rep. No. 1736, 2nd Sess.) (Sen. Rep. No. 1904, 2nd Sess.)-QMOC

82nd Cong., H.R. 1479, for the relief of Joseph Bernstein. Beneficiary, a 36-year old native of Romania, and citizen of Palestine, entered the United States as a visitor and as a violinist and soloist with the Palestinian Orchestra. He gave various concerts in the United States on behalf of the United Jewish Appeal. The law held the beneficiary lawfully admitted for permanent residence. (Priv. L. No. 14, 65 Stat. A7 (1951)) (H.R. Rep. No. 250, 1st Sess.) (Sen. Rep. No. 181, 1st Sess.)-QMOC

82nd Cong., H.R. 1598, for the relief of Hanoh Sarapanovschi (also known as Hanoh Charat), Gizela (Gisele) Sarapanovschi (nee Levy), and Philippe Sarapanovschi. Beneficiaries, natives of Russia and France were husband, wife, and child. They had escaped Germany to enter France and were seized by the Germans during its occupation. Upon release they went to Spain, later to Cuba and proceeded to Mexico where they established a business in drapery materials. They returned to France where the male beneficiary acquired United States patent rights to a "catalytic agent for water treatment." Later they entered the United States where he set up business in this area and owned 49 of the 100 shares of stock in Texas Sola Catalytic Company. The law held the parents lawfully admitted for permanent residence under section 4 of the Displaced Persons Act and held the children lawfully admitted for permanent residence. (Priv. L. No. 321, 65 Stat. A120 (1951)) (H.R. Rep. No. 677, 1st Sess.) (Sen. Rep. No. 816, 1st Sess.)-QMDP

82nd Cong., H.R. 1791, for the relief of Joe Tortolini. Beneficiary, a 39-year old native and citizen of Italy entered the United States for permanent residence and resided 20 years. After entry he and his mother were ordered deported due to management of a house of prostitution. His mother was deported, but the beneficiary remained in the country due to war conditions. He had also been admitted to United States citizenship, which was later canceled because of these facts. His spouse was a citizen and veteran of World War II. The Attorney General noted enactment of such a measure was a matter of legislative policy and no recommendation was forthcoming. The law canceled deportation proceedings against the beneficiary and held him lawfully admitted for permanent residence. (Priv. L. No. 107, 65 Stat. A42 (1951)) (H.R. Rep. No. 342, 1st Sess.) (Sen. Rep. No. 396, 1st Sess.)-WCRF

82nd Cong., H.R. 1818, for the relief of Hego Fuchino. Beneficiary, a 63-year old native and citizen of Japan entered the United States as a seaman. His spouse and seven children were United States citizens and resided in the United States with him 45 years. He desired to return to Japan to visit an ill brother but was not able to secure a visa due to racial ineligibility. The Attorney General noted enactment of such legislation was a matter of legislative policy and no recommendation on the bill was made. The law held the beneficiary lawfully admitted for permanent residence. (Priv. L. No. 307, 65 Stat. A114 (1951)) (H.R. Rep. No. 822, 1st Sess.) (Sen. Rep. No. 818, 1st Sess.)-QIER

82nd Cong., H.R. 1836, for the relief of Mrs. Carla Mulligan. Beneficiary, a 28-year old native of Germany and spouse of a United States citizen veteran who had one United States citizen child, was ineligible for a visa due to a conviction for black-marketing of flour and the theft of sugar. The law waived the eleventh category of section 3 of the Act of 1917 relating to crimes involving moral turpitude. (Priv. L. No. 567, 66 Stat. A54 (1952)) (H.R. Rep. No. 1342, 2nd Sess.) (Sen. Rep. No. 1373, 2nd Sess.)-WCRF

82nd Cong., H.R. 1968, for the relief of Senta Ziegler. Beneficiary, a 35-year old native and citizen of Germany, entered the United States for medical treatment. She had previously suffered a nervous breakdown when separated from her family who had immigrated to the United States. They later became United States citizens. She spent eight years in a hospital in England and had two operations which were quite successful. A petition under the ninth proviso for a temporary visa was denied because it appeared she was cured and further treatment could be obtained in England. The Attorney General noted the exclusion from the United States of persons who had one or more attacks of insanity and stated the record failed to present facts to justify enactment of special legislation. The Attorney General also noted the conditions of her temporary stay were for medical treatment and that two years had passed in which post-operative rehabilitation took place. The law held the beneficiary lawfully admitted for permanent residence, provided a bond was posted to secure that the beneficiary would not become a public charge. (Priv. L. No. 592, 66 Stat. A60 (1952)) (H.R. Rep. No. 1479, 2nd Sess.) (Sen. Rep. No. 1413, 2nd Sess.)-WHEL

82nd Cong., H.R. 2180, for the relief of Mrs. Florence E. Homann and John A. Villas. Beneficiaries, mother and child of a United States citizen, natives of Britain and China (ages 28, 5), were excluded from entering the United States on the basis that the mother had tuberculosis. The spouse indicated he planned to adopt his stepson and provided support for the beneficiaries when they were paroled into the United States. The law held the beneficiaries lawfully admitted for permanent residence. (Priv. L. No. 181, 65 Stat. A69, (1951)) (H.R. Rep. No. 472, 1st Sess.) (Sen. Rep. No. 518, 1st Sess.)-WHEL

82nd Cong., H.R. 2299, for the relief of Biagio Poidimani. Beneficiary, a 41-year old native and citizen of Italy, entered the United States as a visitor. He was a sculptor and former assistant in the Department of Sculpture of the Royal Academy of Fine Arts in Rome, Italy. His works had been exhibited in Europe and the United States. The Attorney General noted there were not sufficient reasons to grant special relief to the beneficiary ahead of others who desire to enter the United States and "enjoy the cultural and economic advantages available in this country." The law held the beneficiary lawfully admitted for permanent residence. (Priv. L. No. 176, 65 Stat. A67 (1951)) (H.R. Rep. No. 473, 1st Sess.) (Sen. Rep. No. 520, 1st Sess.)-QMOC

82nd Cong., H.R. 2307, for the relief of Jean (John) Plewniak and Anna Piotrowska Plewniak. Beneficiaries, 56- and 45-year old natives of Poland, entered the United States as visitors. The male beneficiary served in World War I in both the German and Polish Armies. During World War II he joined the Polish Armed Forces under British command. While in the United States they were employed as a butler and cook for the Embassy of Saudi-Arabia in Washington, D.C. The Attorney General noted enactment of this legislation "would encourage others to circumvent our immigration laws by entering the United States in the guise of visitors and then attempting to adjust their status to permanent residence, thereby obtaining an unjust preference over the alien who complies with the law." The law held the beneficiaries lawfully admitted for permanent residence under section 4 of the Displaced Persons Act. (Priv. L. No. 25, 66 Stat. A95 (1951)) (H.R. Rep. No. 743, 1st Sess.) (Sen. Rep. No. 1535, 2nd Sess.)-QMDP

82nd Cong., H.R. 2310, for the relief of Jindrich (Henri) Nosek and Mrs. Zdenka Nosek. Beneficiaries, 55- and 48-year old natives and citizens of Czechoslovakia, entered the United States as visitors. The male beneficiary had formerly been the Czechoslovakian Ambassador to France, but resigned in protest against the Communist takeover of that country. He was employed in the United States by the National Committee for Free Europe at the Library of Congress. The Attorney General noted that there were no compelling facts to justify preference for immigration in the case of the beneficiaries. The law held the beneficiaries lawfully admitted for permanent residence under section 4 of the Displaced Persons Act. (Priv. L. No. 124, 65 Stat. A47 (1951)) (H.R. Rep. No. 409, 1st Sess.) (Sen. Rep. No. 455, 1st Sess.)-QMDP

82nd Cong., H.R. 2346, for the relief of Odette Louise Tirman. Beneficiary, a 26-year old native and citizen of France and spouse of a United States citizen serving in the Armed Forces, was ineligible for a visa because she had previously been married under bigamous circumstances. She and her husband had three United States citizen children. The law waived the eleventh category of section 3 of the Act of 1917 and deportation provisions of the Act of March 4, 1929 relating to crimes involving moral turpitude on behalf of the beneficiary. (Priv. L. No. 659, 66 Stat. A82 (1952)) (H.R. Rep. No. 1580, 2nd Sess.) (Sen. Rep. No. 1536, 2nd Sess.)-WCRF

82nd Cong., H.R. 2455, for the relief of Mrs. Maryanna Boppel. Beneficiary, a 43-year old native and citizen of Poland was admitted to the United States for permanent residence, and later found deportable due to engaging in prostitution. She was married to a United States citizen and also took care of two of her sister's children. The House Committee noted "she has effected a complete reformation and rehabilitation and...her deportation would seriously affect her foster children and her husband." The law held the beneficiary lawfully admitted for permanent residence. (Priv. L. No. 183, 65 Stat. A70 (1951)) (H.R. Rep. No. 474, 1st Sess.) (Sen. Rep. No. 523, 1st Sess.)-WCRF

82nd Cong., H.R. 2498, for the relief of Marianne and Michel Speelman. Beneficiaries, a 74-year old native and citizen of the Netherlands and his wife, a 34-year old native of China and citizen of the Netherlands, entered the United States as visitors. The male beneficiary was associated with financial companies and went to China to assist as financial adviser for the New Chinese Republic at the request of Sun Yat Sen where he remained 50 years engaged in various businesses. The law held the beneficiaries lawfully admitted for permanent residence under section 4 of the Displaced Persons

Act. (Priv. L. No. 310, 65 Stat. A116 (1951)) (H.R. Rep. No. 679, 1st Sess.) (Sen. Rep. No. 709, 1st Sess.)-QMDP

82nd Cong., H.R. 2505, for the relief of Carl Weitlanner. Beneficiary, a 49-year old native of Austria, was lawfully admitted for permanent residence and filed a declaration of intention to become a citizen. He traveled with a United States company for a short period of time and returned to Austria for personal reasons in 1940, where he became involved in the war effort, later teaching in a Displaced Persons Camp. The Attorney General stated he was unable to recommend enactment of the bill because the record presented "no compelling reasons for granting him a preference in naturalization over other resident aliens, many of whom rendered valuable assistance to the United States during World War II..." The law deemed inapplicable to the beneficiary section 307(a) (l) of the Nationality Act of 1940, relating to the requisite residence period for naturalization. (Priv. L. No. 423, 66 Stat. A7 (1952)) (H.R. Rep. No. 745, 1st Sess.) (Sen. Rep. No. 1083, 2nd Sess.)-NRES

82nd Cong., H.R. 2714, for the relief of Marcelle Lecomte. Beneficiary, a native and citizen of France, was lawfully admitted to permanent residence in the United States and was employed with the United States Department of State in France and other posts for 20 years. She was found ineligible to file for naturalization because she had not been continuously present in the United States for a portion of the five-year residence requirement. A letter from the Deputy Under Secretary of State was submitted in support of the beneficiary. The law deemed the beneficiary to have fulfilled a one-year physical presence requirement in the United States for purposes of filing for naturalization. (Priv. L. No. 16, 65 Stat. A8 (1951)) (H.R. Rep. No. 166, 1st Sess.) (Sen. Rep. No. 235, 1st Sess.)-NRES

82nd Cong., H.R. 2718, for the relief of Enrique M. Orpilla. Beneficiary, a 34-year old native and citizen of the Philippines, entered the United States while in the Armed Forces and was discharged. He was part of the Philippine Scouts and served in the United States Air Force for four years. He was unable to petition for naturalization because he had enlisted in the Philippines. The law held the beneficiary lawfully admitted for permanent residence. (Priv. L. No. 744, 66 Stat. A111 (1952)) (H.R. Rep. No. 1757, 2nd Sess.) (Sen. Rep. No. 1769, 2nd Sess.)-NMSC

82nd Cong., H.R. 2719, for the relief of Philip Fugh, Sarah Liu Fugh, and John Fugh. Beneficiaries, 54-, 52-, and 18-year old natives of China, entered the United States as visitors. The male beneficiary was employed by Chiang Kai-shek and later became political adviser to the United States Ambassador in China five years. Two daughters were married to United States citizens. The Attorney General did not make any recommendation and determined enactment would be a matter of legislative policy. The law held the beneficiaries lawfully admitted for permanent residence. (Priv. L. No. 745, 66 Stat. A112 (1952)) (H.R. Rep. No. 1758, 2nd Sess.) (Sen. Rep. No. 1770, 2nd Sess.)-QMDE

82nd Cong., H.R. 2906, for the relief of Kenji Kusumoto. Beneficiary, a native and citizen of Japan, was the spouse of a United States citizen. His wife had gone to China and started an orphanage asylum for Chinese children and was later employed in the United States Armed Forces. They had two citizen children. The law waived section 13(c) relating to exclusion of races ineligible to naturalization. (Priv. L. No. 934, 66 Stat. A183 (1952)) (H.R. Rep. No. 1760, 2nd Sess.) (Sen. Rep. No. 1919, 2nd Sess.)-QIER

82nd Cong., H.R. 2920, for the relief of Priscilla Ogden Dickerson Gillson de 1a Fregonniere. Beneficiary, a 47-year old native-born United States citizen, renounced her citizenship under section 3 of the Act of May 24, 1934 and voted in British elections. She returned to the United States in 1947 to purchase an estate in Middleburg, Virginia. The beneficiary's grandfather was the Secretary of the Navy under President Andrew Jackson, and her uncle was a Governor of the State of New Jersey. The Secretary of State reported "it is inexpedient to enact special legislation providing for the restoration of American citizenship to a person who, as an adult, voluntarily divested herself of such citizenship." The law allowed the beneficiary to regain citizenship upon taking the oaths required within one year after date of enactment. (Priv. L. No. 713, 66 Stat. A100 (1952)) (H.R. Rep. No. 1354, 2nd Sess.) (Sen. Rep. No. 1543, 2nd Sess.)-NVOL

82nd Cong., H.R. 3124, for the relief of Mehmet Salih Topcuoglu. Beneficiary, a 28-year old native and citizen of Turkey, entered the United States as a visitor in order to obtain an artificial leg which he had lost serving in the Turkish Navy. He later became employed in the Artificial Limb Company, and the Senate Committee stated that "his knowledge and skill in this particular field are needed because of the shortage of such labor and the increasing large number of amputees." The law held the beneficiary lawfully admitted for permanent residence. (Priv. L. No. 684, 66 Stat. A91 (1952)) (H.R. Rep. No. 1356, 2nd Sess.) (Sen. Rep. No. 1545, 2nd Sess.)-QMOC

82nd Cong., H.R. 3152, for the relief of Mrs. Setsuyo Sumida. Beneficiary, a 63-year old native and citizen of Japan, resided in the United States 28 years and then went to Japan with her husband and two children. She became widowed and sought reentry to the United States, but World War II began and she was unable to obtain the appropriate documents. She had eight United States citizen children, four of whom served in the United States Army and one of whom was killed in action. The Attorney General considered such legislation a matter of legislative policy and did not make any recommendation. The law held the beneficiary a returning resident alien under section 4(b) of the Act of 1924. (Priv. L. No. 686, 66 Stat. A92 (1952)) (H.R. Rep. No. 1583, 2nd Sess.) (Sen. Rep. No. 1547, 2nd Sess.)-QPRP

82nd Cong., H.R. 3155, for the relief of Sebastiano Bello, Dino Bianchi, Pierino Ciccarese, Vincenzo Dall'alda, Vittorio de Gasperi, Salvatore

Puggioni, Giovanni Battista Volpato, and Leone Montini. Beneficiaries (ages 51 through 27), natives and citizens of Italy and priests of the Society of the Sons of the Sacred Heart, entered the United States to assist in establishing a seminary doing missionary work in Ohio. The law held the beneficiaries lawfully admitted for permanent residence. (Priv. L. No. 747, 66 Stat. A112 (1952)) (H.R. Rep. No. 1484, 2nd Sess.) (Sen. Rep. No. 1649, 2nd Sess.)-QMOC

82nd Cong., H.R. 3271, for the relief of Toshiaki Shimada. Beneficiary, a seven-year old native of Japan and son of a United States citizen, was racially excluded from entering the United States. Additionally, he did not derive United States citizenship from his mother because he lacked the requisite period of residence in the United States. The law waived section 13(c) of the Act of 1924 relating to races ineligible for citizenship. (Priv. L. No. 588, 66 Stat. A59 (1952)) (H.R. Rep. No. 1358, 2nd Sess.) (Sen. Rep. No. 1418, 2nd Sess.)-NCOD

82nd Cong., H.R. 3280, for the relief of Mrs. Emi Yasuda and her minor son, Keichiro Yasuda. Beneficiaries, a former United States citizen and her child, a native of Japan, were excluded from admission to the United States on the basis of race. The mother had left the United States to study in Japan and visit her grandparents. She left that country to return to the United States, but the ship was attacked near Pearl Harbor and returned to Japan. She was married in that country and later widowed. Her five brothers and sisters were United States citizens. She lost her citizenship by voting in a Japanese election in 1946, and the son did not derive citizenship because she lacked sufficient residence in the United States to transmit citizenship. The law waived section 13(c) of the Act of 1924 relating to races ineligible citizenship. (Priv. L. No. 937, 66 Stat. A184 (1952)) (H.R. Rep. No. 1982, 2nd Sess.) (Sen. Rep. No. 1923, 2nd Sess.)-NCOD

82nd Cong., H.R. 3524, for the relief of Jan Yee Young. Beneficiary, a 10-year old native of China and son of a United States citizen, did not derive United States citizenship through his father because he had not accumulated sufficient residence to confer citizenship at that time. Three children did derive United States citizenship. The beneficiary was chargeable to the Chinese quota which was oversubscribed. The family, except for the beneficiary, resided in the United States. The law held the beneficiary within sections 4(a) and 9 of the Act of 1924. (Priv. L. No. 599, 66 Stat. A62 (1952)) (H.R. Rep. No. 1359, 2nd Sess.) (Sen. Rep. No. 1419, 2nd Sess.)-QIER

82nd Cong., H.R. 3600, for the relief of Dr. Alexander Symeonidis. Beneficiary, a 41-year old native of Greece and a doctor, was admitted to the United States as a visitor to do research under a Rockefeller fellowship at the National Cancer Institute in Washington, D.C. He resided in the United States five years, three years of which were as a permanent resident. His research involved epidemic hepatitis and gynecomastia produced by malnutrition. He desired expeditious naturalization. The Attorney General noted, "Congress has been most reluctant to interfere in naturalization proceedings in individual cases. The granting of United States citizenship is a high privilege, and should not be indiscriminately bestowed to suit the individual needs of recently arrived aliens who do not want to comply with the residence requirements in order to become citizens." Although the Attorney General waived making any recommendation, it was noted "The alien in this case is one whose services would appear to be invaluable to the United States and to all humanity." The law held the beneficiary lawfully admitted for permanent residence effective the date of his first entry to the United States. (Priv. L. No. 792, 66 Stat. A131 (1952)) (H.R. Rep. No. 1167, 1st Sess.) (Sen. Rep. No. 1666, 2nd Sess.)-NRES

82nd Cong., H.R. 3965, for the relief of Five Sisters of the Franciscan Missionaries of Mary. Beneficiaries, natives of Spain and nuns (ages 51 through 29), were engaged in duties in Massachusetts attending to crippled and mentally handicapped children at the Joseph P. Kennedy Memorial Hospital. The law held the beneficiaries lawfully admitted for permanent residence. (Priv. L. No. 296, 65 Stat. A111 (1951)) (H.R. Rep. No. 737, 1st Sess.) (Sen. Rep. No. 824, 1st Sess.)-QMOC

82nd Cong., H.R. 4250, for the relief of Ruben George Varga and Mrs. Ilona Varga. Beneficiaries, ages 23 and 54, were natives of Israel and Hungary and citizens of Israel. The son was blind and a well-known concert violinist. The law held the beneficiaries lawfully admitted for permanent residence. (Priv. L. No. 948, 66 Stat. A187 (1952)) (H.R. Rep. No. 1986, 2nd Sess.) (Sen. Rep. No. 1937, 2nd Sess.)-QMOC

82nd Cong., H.R. 4396, for the relief of Elias Papadopoulos. Beneficiary, a 40-year old native and citizen of Greece and spouse of a United States citizen, entered the United States as a seaman. He was ineligible to adjust his status because of a conviction for theft of a letter containing funds. The Attorney General waived making any recommendation in the case but noted the offense occurred over 20 years ago and the amount of money involved at the time in United States terms was $3.00. There was one United States citizen child born of the marriage. The law held the beneficiary lawfully admitted for permanent residence. (Priv. L. No. 950, 66 Stat. A188 (1952)) (H.R. Rep. No. 1987, 2nd Sess.) (Sen. Rep. No. 2016, 2nd Sess.)-WCRF

82nd Cong., H.R. 4535, for the relief of Nigel C. S. Salter-Mathieson. Beneficiary, a 20-year old native of Great Britain, was the stepson of a United States citizen, Brig. Gen. Sory Smith of the United States Air Force. He desired an appointment to the United States Military Academy; however, he had not completed the requisite residence period for purposes of filing for naturalization. The Attorney General stated "the circumstances in this case do not appear to warrant enactment of special legislation." The law exempted the beneficiary from section 307(a)(1) and 331 of the Nationality Act of 1940 in order to file a petition for naturalization. (Priv. L. No. 603, 66 Stat. A63 (1952)) (H.R. Rep. No. 1268, 2nd Sess.) (Sen. Rep. No. 1423, 2nd Sess.)-NRES

82nd Cong., H.R. 4588, for the relief of Mark Yen Hui. Beneficiary, a 17-year old native of China and former United States citizen who derived citizenship through his father, lost entitlement to his citizenship because he did not return to the United States before his sixteenth birthday. It was stated he could not return because he was unable to obtain permission to exit China. The law held the beneficiary within sections 4(a) and 9 of the Act of 1924 as the natural child of a United States citizen. (Priv. L. No. 953, 66 Stat. A189 (1952)) (H.R. Rep. No. 1910, 2nd Sess.) (Sen. Rep. No. 1941, 2nd Sess.)-NRTN

82nd Cong., H.R. 4709, for the relief of Baron Fred Alexander D'Osten-Sacken. Beneficiary, a 66-year old native of Russia, entered the United States as a visitor and was engaged in training thoroughbred horses in Kentucky. He was internationally known having won the Warsaw Derby in 1921 with Barbara Belle and managed the stables of Marcel Boussac. Toward the end of the war, he rescued the stallion Pharis and later won other Derbies. It was stated he was instrumental in introducing to the United States the French stallion Ardan as a new breed of stock from France. The law held the beneficiary lawfully admitted for permanent residence. (Priv. L. No. 955, 66 Stat. A189 (1952)) (H.R. Rep. No. 1782, 2nd Sess.) (Sen. Rep. No. 1943, 2nd Sess.)-QMOC

82nd Cong., H.R. 4788, for the relief of Yoko Takeuchi. Beneficiary, a nine-year old native of Japan and stepchild of a United States citizen employed with the United States Army in a civilian capacity, was unable to obtain a visa due to racial ineligibility. Her mother was able to obtain a visa under a new law. The law held the beneficiary within sections 4(a) and 9 of the Act of 1924 relating to natural children of United States citizens and waived section 13(c) relating to persons ineligible to citizenship. (Priv. L. No. 605, 66 Stat. A64 (1952)) (H.R. Rep. No. 1409, 2nd Sess.) (Sen. Rep. No. 1425, 2nd Sess.)-QIER

82nd Cong., H.R. 5208, for the relief of Sor Eufrasia Gomez Gallego, Sor Francisca Gil Martinez, and Sor Rasalia de La Maza. Beneficiaries, natives and citizens of Spain and nuns of the Carmelite Order, entered the United States as visitors and were engaged in the treatment of mental diseases in a hospital in Puerto Rico where most of the patients were Army veterans referred from the Veterans' Administration. The law held the beneficiaries lawfully admitted for permanent residence. (Priv. L. No. 752, 66 Stat. A114 (1952)) (H.R. Rep. No. 1588, 2nd Sess.) (Sen. Rep. No. 1654, 2nd Sess.)-QMOC

82nd Cong., H.R. 5238, for the relief of Albert O. Holland and Bergtor Haaland. Beneficiaries, natives of Norway, who were naturalized in the United States, were skilled craftsmen in the plumbing and heating trade and had been sent to Venezuela by the United States firm of Meritt-Chapman, Scott, Fuller. The beneficiaries were engaged in the construction of buildings in that country, thereby losing their citizenship through residence abroad. The Secretary of State noted that the services of the beneficiaries were a worthwhile contribution to that country and were "beneficial to the United States in that they further amicable relations between the two countries and also promote American trade and commerce through the introduction of American material, methods, and techniques," but that no matter what the "natural justice in individual cases...it is the duty of the Department to construe and apply it [the law] as appears necessary from its language." Although no objections were posed, the State Department recommended that the remedy to prevent such hardships and "undeserved loss of citizenship" was to change the law. The law deemed the beneficiaries not to have lost their citizenship through residence in a foreign state. (Priv. L. No. 867, 66 Stat. A162 (1952)) (H.R. Rep. No. 1487, 2nd Sess.) (Sen. Rep. No. 1974, 2nd Sess.)-NRTN

82nd Cong., H.R. 5347, for the relief of Fusako Terao Scogin. Beneficiary, a native and citizen of Japan, was married in a family ceremony to a United States citizen member of the Armed Forces. They had one child. The United States citizen subsequently was killed in action. The child was declared to be legitimate by a Texas court and derived citizenship through the father, however, the mother was unable to obtain a visa. The law waived section 13 (c) of the Act of 1924 relating to races ineligible for a visa, and held the beneficiary entitled to a nonquota visa. (Priv. L. No. 516, 66 Stat. A36 (1952)) (H.R. Rep. No. 1266, 2nd Sess.) (Sen. Rep. No. 1329, 82nd Cong., 2nd Sess.)-QIER

82nd Cong., H.R. 6117, for the relief of Deliana Meulenkamp. Beneficiary, an 18-year old native of the Netherlands who entered the United States in 1947 and acquired permanent residence in 1951, sought waiver of the residence period for naturalization in order to compete at the swimming competition in the Olympic Games in Helsinki. The law exempted the beneficiary from sections 307 and 331 of the Nationality Act of 1940 relating to residence requirements. (Priv. L. No. 761, 66 Stat. A117 (1952)) (H.R. Rep. No. 1444, 2nd Sess.) (Sen. Rep. No. 1707, 2nd Sess.)-NRES

82nd Cong., H.R. 7095, for the relief of Ruth Ann Holecek. Beneficiary, a three-year old native and citizen of Japan, was born out of wedlock and released to United States citizen missionaries who adopted her. She was unable to obtain a visa due to racial ineligibility. The law held the beneficiary within sections 4(a) and 9 of the Act of 1924 relating to natural-born children of United States citizens and waived section 13(c) of that Act relating to exclusion of persons on the basis of race. (Priv. L. No. 986, 66 Stat. A198 (1952)) (H.R. Rep. No. 2095, 2nd Sess.) (Sen. Rep. No. 1962, 2nd Sess.)-QIER

82nd Cong., H.R. 7833, for the relief of Prof. Werner Richter and Prof. Max Horkheimer. Beneficiary Richter, a 65-year old native of Germany and naturalized United States citizen, experienced difficulties with potential loss of citizenship because of protracted residence abroad in fulfillment of a contract with the University of Bonn. The other beneficiary also experienced similar problems at the Frankfort University, both as rectors.

Although the Department of State did not oppose enactment of the bill, it reported "as a general rule, it is inexpedient to extend relief... where the beneficiary has spent so little time in the United States during his lifetime." The law exempted the beneficiaries from section 404(b) of the Nationality Act of 1940 provided they return to the United States within two years following the date of enactment of the legislation. (Priv. L. No. 1023, 66 Stat. A213 (1952)) (H.R. Rep. No. 2304, 2nd Sess.) (Sen. Rep. No. 2065, 2nd Sess.)-NRTN

82nd Cong., S. 44, for the relief of John E. Turri and Edward H. Turri. Beneficiaries, 38- and 36-year old natives of Italy and citizens of the United States, were brothers who served in the United States Army and returned to Italy to settle the family estate after the war. Because of their protracted residence in Italy, they divested themselves of citizenship. Beneficiaries' occupations were architect and lawyer. The Attorney General stated there were no special circumstances to warrant the special relief, and that "the problem of preserving the nationality of such naturalized citizens is a general one and should be resolved by general legislation." The law exempted the beneficiaries from section 404(b) and (c) of the Nationality Act of 1940 in order to retain their citizenship provided they returned to the United States for permanent residence within one year after the Act. (Priv. L. No. 2, 65 Stat. A3 (1951)) (Sen. Rep. No. 6, 1st Sess.) (H.R. Rep. No. 153, 1st Sess.)-NRTN

82nd Cong., S. 118, for the relief of Nouhad Ann Khoury. Beneficiary, an 18-year old native and citizen of Lebanon, entered the United States as a visitor in order to obtain medical treatment. Her United States citizen aunt filed a petition for adoption. The Attorney General indicated a reluctance to recommend favorably on the bill due to the oversubscription of visas for that country, and that it failed to justify granting a preference over other relatives desiring to enter the United States. The report noted that at the time the beneficiary entered the United States she claimed eye treatment was needed; however, no medical attention was sought after arrival in the United States. The law held the beneficiary lawfully admitted for permanent residence. (Priv. L. No. 376, 65 Stat. A139 (1951)) (Sen. Rep. No. 60, 1st Sess.) (H.R. Rep. No. 1133, 1st Sess.)-QIRA

82nd Cong., S. 178, for the relief of Zdenek Marek. Beneficiary, a 25-year old native of Czechoslovakia, entered the United States as a student. He had been a member of the Czechoslovak Olympic hockey team who defected in Sweden. He was befriended by United States hockey team members, who invited him to play local hockey in the United States and attend school. The law held the beneficiary within section 4 of the Displaced Persons Act. (Priv. L. No. 95, 65 Stat. A37 (1951)) (Sen. Rep. No. 64, 1st Sess.) (H.R. Rep. No. 510, 1st Sess.)-QMDP

82nd Cong., S. 291, for the relief of Claudio Pier Connelly. Beneficiary, a seven-year old native and citizen of Italy, and stepchild of a United States citizen, entered the United States with his parents. He had erroneously been included in the passport of the family for a visa. The law held the beneficiary lawfully admitted for permanent residence. (Priv. L. No. 81, 65 Stat. A32 (1951)) (Sen. Rep. No. 245, 1st Sess.) (H.R. Rep. No. 513, 1st Sess.)-QMGN

82nd Cong., S. 364, for the relief of Mrs. Suzanne Wiernik and her daughter, Genevieve. Beneficiaries, ages 36 and 13, were natives of Poland and France respectively and entered the United States as visitors being supported by a United States citizen uncle. They were the "sole survivors of a family of approximately 60 people in Europe," lost either in the war or in camps in Poland. The law held the beneficiaries lawful permanent residents under section 4 of the Displaced Persons Act. (Priv. L. No. 93, 65 Stat. A37 (1951)) (Sen. Rep. No. 146, 1st Sess.) (H.R. Rep. No. 519, 1st Sess.)-QMDP

82nd Cong., S. 420, for the relief of Gloria Wilson. Beneficiary, a 27-year old native-born United States citizen, lost her citizenship by voting in a foreign election. The beneficiary was a member of the United States Women's Army Corps in 1943 until her marriage to an Australian Air Force pilot when she moved to Australia. The Attorney General indicated there were no special facts in the case to warrant relief. The law allowed the beneficiary to be reinstated to United States citizenship upon an oath of allegiance, and undertake the same status which had existed before loss under section 401(e) of the Nationality Act of 1940. (Priv. L. No. 639, 66 Stat. A75 (1952)) (Sen. Rep. No. 1311, 2nd Sess.) (H.R. Rep. No. 1876, 2nd Sess.)-NVOL

82nd Cong., S. 440, for the relief of Evangelos and Michael Dumas. Beneficiaries, 21- and 19-year old natives of Greece, entered the United States as students and were adopted by United States citizens. The law held the beneficiaries lawfully admitted for permanent residence. (Priv. L. No. 457, 66 Stat. A17 (1952)) (Sen. Rep. No. 896, 1st Sess.) (H.R. Rep. No. 1302, 2nd Sess.)-QIRA

82nd Cong., S. 471, for the relief of Ai Mei Yu and Ai Mei Chen. Beneficiaries, sisters ages five and three and natives of China, were adopted by a United States citizen, who was employed with the World Health Organization as a public health nurse specializing in tuberculosis. She had performed service in China. The adoptive parent sought entry of the children to the United States without regard to the numerical limitations of China. The Attorney General stated, "There are no doubt many alien children, some of them war orphans, who wish to obtain the benefits of residence in this country, but who are unable to obtain immigration visas...The record in the instant case fails to present considerations which would justify the enactment of special legislation to grant these two children a preference over the natural-born Chinese children of American citizens, and over other alien children, who desire to come to this country for permanent residence but are precluded from doing so at the present time because of the oversubscription of the quotas." The law held the beneficiaries to be the natural-born children of the adoptive parents for the purposes of sections 4(a) and 9 of the Act of 1924. (Priv. L. No. 427, 66 Stat. A9 (1952)) (Sen. Rep. No. 897, 1st Sess.) (H.R. Rep. No. 1232, 2nd Sess.)-QIRA

82nd Cong., S. 674, for the relief of Arthur Koestler. Beneficiary, a 46-year old native of Hungary and citizen of Great Britain, entered the United States as a visitor. He was an author and former member of the Communist Party of Germany and then enlisted in the British Army. According to the Senate Committee report, the beneficiary, after breaking with the Party, "used his experiences as a Communist for the exposure of Communist methods and had continued a relentless fight against the Communist menace." The law held the beneficiary lawfully admitted for permanent residence. (Priv. L. No. 221, without Presidential approval, 65 Stat. A84 (1951)) (Sen. Rep. No. 407, 1st Sess.)-WXCP

82nd Cong., S. 1420, for the relief of Pinfang Hsia. Beneficiary, a 49-year old native of China and former manager of the Bank of China in London, entered the United States as a visitor. His position with the Bank was terminated upon recognition by the British Government of the Peoples Government of China. The law held the beneficiary lawfully admitted for permanent residence. (Priv. L. No. 647, 66 Stat. A77 (1952)) (Sen. Rep. No. 1266, 2nd Sess.) (H.R. Rep. No. 1887, 2nd Sess.)-QMGN

82nd Cong., S. 1462, for the relief of Joseph Boris Tchertkoff. Beneficiary, a 36-year old native of Switzerland and son of United States citizens, entered the United States for medical treatment. At the age of six weeks he was given improper medication resulting in brain damage. The law held the beneficiary lawfully admitted for permanent residence. (Priv. L. No. 467, 66 Stat. A20 (1952)) (Sen. Rep. No. 901, 1st Sess.) (H.R. Rep. No. 1315, 2nd Sess.)-WHEL

82nd Cong., S. 1469, for the relief of Julie Bettelheim and Evelyn Lang Hirsch. Beneficiaries, 63-and 17-year old natives of Austria, entered the United States as visitors to see their paternal grandmother. The spouse of the elder beneficiary was formerly the manager of the House of Rothschild. Applications as Displaced Persons were denied. Their remaining family died in Europe. The law held the beneficiaries lawfully admitted for permanent residence under section 4 of the Displaced Persons Act. (Priv. L. No. 550, 66 Stat. A47 (1952)) (Sen. Rep. No. 1267, 2nd Sess.)-QMDP

82nd Cong., S. 1470, for the relief of Panagiotes Roumeliotis. Beneficiary, a 20-year old native and citizen of Greece, entered the United States as a seaman and proceeded to reside with his United States citizen uncle who intended to make the beneficiary his heir. The Committee noted there was "confidential information that the presence in the United States of the beneficiary of the bill would be beneficial to the security interests of this country." The law held the beneficiary lawfully admitted for permanent residence. (Priv. L. No. 859, 66 Stat. A159 (1952)) (Sen. Rep. No. 1147, 2nd Sess.) (H.R. Rep. No. 2232, 2nd Sess.)-QMDE

82nd Cong., S. 1541, for the relief of Dr. Francis S. N. Kwok. Beneficiary, a 35-year old native of the Fiji Islands and citizen of Great Britain of the Chinese race, entered the United States as a student and became a doctor engaged in otolaryngology in New York. The law held the beneficiary lawfully admitted for permanent residence. (Priv. L. No. 500, 66 Stat. A31 (1952)) (Sen. Rep. No. 763, 1st Sess.) (H.R. Rep. No. 1472, 2nd Sess.)-QMOC

82nd Cong., S. 1724, for the relief of Elina Branlund. Beneficiary, a 45-year old native and citizen of Finland, entered the United States as an employee of the Minister of Finland as a cook and later was employed as a maid for Mr. Lamont du Pont, Jr. The law held the beneficiary lawfully admitted for permanent residence. (Priv. L. No. 836, 66 Stat. Al5O (1952)) (Sen. Rep. No. 1522, 2nd Sess.) (H.R. Rep. No. 2236, 2nd Sess.)-QMOC

82nd Cong., S. 2145, for the relief of Certain Displaced Persons. Beneficiaries, 386 natives of Estonia, Latvia, Finland, Sweden, Poland and Russia, sought refuge in Sweden after fleeing from Communism. They purchased sloops and schooners and arrived on the United States eastern seaboard between 1945 and 1950, and were paroled into the United States. Because they did not enter the United States as nonimmigrants or in another status they were ineligible for relief under the Displaced Persons Act. The Attorney General noted "While their plight naturally evokes sympathy, it must be borne in mind that they deliberately came to this country in violation of the immigration laws of the United States. It appears that many of the aliens were aware that the quotas to which they are chargeable were oversubscribed, and that they were excludable from the United States...To enact this bill would undoubtedly serve to encourage others, in whose cases immigration visas are not readily obtainable, to deliberately violate the immigration laws of this country." A report from the Attorney General three months later, noted that the case was "sufficiently remote to justify a modification of the Department's prior conclusion" that it would have been an undesirable precedent. The report stated enactment was a matter of legislative policy and no recommendation would be forthcoming. The law held the beneficiaries within section 4 of the Displaced Persons Act of 1948 and allowed them to file applications thereunder. (Priv. L. No. 655, 66 Stat. A80 (1952)) (Sen. Rep. No. 1362, 1st Sess.) (H.R. Rep. No. 1897, 1st Sess.)-QMDP

82nd Cong., S. 2231, for the relief of Tina Bentsen. Beneficiary, a one-week old child and native of Norway, was adopted by Congressman and Mrs. Bentsen who desired to bring the child to the United States without regard to the waiting period for natives of that country. The law held the beneficiary to be the natural-born child of the adoptive parents for the purposes of sections 4(a) and 9 of the Act of 1924. (Priv. L. No. 330, 65 Stat. A123 (1951)) (Sen. Rep. No. 1898, 2nd Sess.) (H.R. Rep. No. 1898, 2nd Sess.)-QIRA

82nd Cong., S. 2566, for the relief of Niccolo Luvisotti. Beneficiary, a native of Italy, was admitted for permanent residence based on a petition filed by his spouse, a United States citizen. When they attempted to obtain a visa for their child it was discovered she had not derived United States citizenship through her father because he had lost citizenship through naturalization in Italy. The beneficiary's status was therefore under question, and he sought to legitimate his stay in the United States and bring the child. The law held the beneficiary lawfully admitted for permanent residence. (Priv. L. No. 737, 66 Stat. A109 (1952)) (Sen. Rep. No. 1152, 2nd Sess.) (H.R. Rep. No. 2057, 2nd Sess.)-QMGN

82nd Cong., S. 2588, for the relief of Dulcie Ann Steinhardt Sherlock. Beneficiary, a 27-year old native-born United States citizen, resided abroad with her father, the late Ambassador Lawrence A. Steinhardt, and because of that did not have the requisite 10 year period of residence in the United States to transmit citizenship to her child when born abroad. The Department of State recommended favorably on the legislation noting she was obliged to reside with her family abroad, and she should not be "deprived of the privilege of transmitting citizenship to her child born abroad." The law deemed the time she resided abroad with her parents, when her father was in the Foreign Service, to meet the requirements of section 201(g) of the Nationality Act of 1940, thereby allowing her child to derive United States citizenship at birth. (Priv. L. No. 657, 66 Stat. A82 (1952)) (Sen. Rep. No. 1364, 2nd Sess.) (H.R. Rep. No. 1899, 2nd Sess.)-NCOD

82nd Cong., S. 2770, for the relief of Matheos Alafouzos. Beneficiary, a native and citizen of Greece and spouse of a United States citizen, was unable to obtain a visa due to oversubscription of visas. The lag in approving the petition and forwarding it to the appropriate office was sufficient to change the circumstance of visa availability. The law deemed the marriage of the beneficiaries to have occurred prior to the occurrence of overdemand for visas for natives of Greece under section 4(a) of the Act of 1924. (Priv. L. No. 658, 66 Stat. A82 (1952)) (Sen. Rep. No. 1275, 2nd Sess.) (H.R. Rep. No. 1900, 2nd Sess.)-QIRM

83rd Cong., H.R. 675, for the relief of Mrs. Romola Nijinsky and Paul Bohus-Vilagosi. Beneficiaries, 63- and 57-year old natives of Hungary, entered the United States as visitors. The female beneficiary was an author and lecturer and the widow of the famous dancer, Nijinsky. The male beneficiary assisted in motion picture contracts for productions on the dancer. The daughter of Mrs. Nijinsky was a lawful permanent resident. Mrs. Nijinsky's two books were entitled "Last Days of Nijinsky" and the "Life Stories of the Great Dancers of Past Centuries." The law held the beneficiaries lawfully admitted for permanent residence. (Priv. L. No. 404, 68 Stat. A68 (1954)) (H.R. Rep. No. 1390, 2nd Sess.) (Sen. Rep. No. 1440, 2nd Sess.)-QMOC

83rd Cong., H.R. 711, for the relief of Mrs. Ruth R. Ekholm. Beneficiary, a 44-year old native and citizen of Finland, entered the United States as a visitor. She was a widow, after her husband died serving in the United States Merchant Marine when his vessel was torpedoed. The law held the beneficiary lawfully admitted for permanent residence. (Priv. L. No. 272, 68 Stat. Al7 (1954)) (H.R. Rep. No. 574, 1st Sess.) (Sen. Rep. No. 951, 2nd Sess.)-QIRW

83rd Cong., H.R. 765, for the relief of Tien Koo Chen. Beneficiary, a 65-year old native and citizen of China, entered the United States as a visitor and had resided seven years. He was formerly the Chinese Ambassador to Mexico and Brazil. Two of his sons resided in the United States and were United States citizens. The law held the beneficiary lawfully admitted for permanent residence. (Priv. L. No. 110, 67 Stat. A40 (1953)) (H.R. Rep. No. 402, 1st Sess.) (Sen. Rep. No. 546, 1st Sess.)-QMGN

83rd Cong., H.R. 804, for the relief of Enrichetta F. C. Meda-Novara. Beneficiary, a 63-year old native and citizen of Italy, entered the United States as a visitor. She had previously resided in the United States 17 years, and made trips to Italy upon the death of her mother and father. Her sister resided in the United States. The law held the beneficiary lawfully admitted for permanent residence. (Priv. L. No. 728, 68 Stat. A183 (1954)) (H.R. Rep. No. 1932, 2nd Sess.) (Sen. Rep. No. 2100, 2nd Sess.)-QMGN

83rd Cong., H.R. 871, for the relief of Orsola Jacopelli Leggio. Beneficiary, a 37-year old native and citizen of Italy and spouse of a United States citizen, was ineligible for a visa due to a conviction of attempted homicide. The offense involved shots she fired at a young man who refused to marry her, after a suit brought against him by her parents for rape was dismissed. The law waived section 212(a) (9) concerning offenses for moral turpitude. (Priv. L. No. 177, 67 Stat. A63 (1953)) (H.R. Rep. No. 577, 1st Sess.) (Sen. Rep. No. 761, 1st Sess.)-WCRF

83rd Cong., H.R. 944, for the relief of Mr. and Mrs. Zygmunt Sowinski. Beneficiaries, 46- and 35-year old natives and citizens of Poland, entered the United States as visitors. They claimed to have been active in the underground movement during World War II in Poland, by counterfeiting passports. Their applications for relief under the Displaced Persons Act of 1948 were denied, because they had established a residence in Brazil. The male beneficiary was involved in the painting of miniatures for which he was renown. The law held the beneficiaries lawfully admitted for permanent residence. (Priv. L. No. 537, 68 Stat. A121 (1954)) (H.R. Rep. No. 1494, 2nd Sess.) (Sen. Rep. No. 1725, 2nd Sess.)-QMGN

83rd Cong., H.R. 954, for the relief of Edith Smith. Beneficiary, a 27-year old native and citizen of Germany and spouse of a United States citizen was ineligible for a visa due to a conviction for theft. The offense occurred when her sister climbed a walnut tree and tried to shake some nuts from the tree. She fell and fractured her arms. The beneficiary accompanied her sister to the police for questioning and both were charged for theft. The law waived section 212(a) (9) relating to crimes involving moral turpitude. (Priv. L. No. 180, 67 Stat. A64 (1953)) (H.R. Rep. No. 578 1st Sess.) (Sen. Rep. No. 765, 1st Sess.)-WCRF

83rd Cong., H.R. 962, for the relief of Gabrielle Marie Smith (nee Staub). Beneficiary, a 25-year old native of Germany, was admitted for permanent residence accompanied by her stepmother and charged to the quota of France. She was found deportable because her stepmother erroneously declared her birthplace in France. She was employed by Life Magazine and resided in the United States 13 years. The law held the beneficiary lawfully admitted for permanent residence on the date of her entry to the United States. (Priv. L. No. 330, 68 Stat. A38 (1954)) (H.R. Rep. No. 1179, 2nd Sess.) (Sen. Rep. No. 1115, 2nd Sess.)-QMGN

83rd Cong., H.R. 974, for the relief of Dr. Morad Malek-Aslani. Beneficiary, a 29-year old native of Iran, entered the United States to study at the Colorado School of Mines and later accepted employment at the Texas Gulf Sulphur Company as a sulfur geologist. Although the visas for Iran were oversubscribed, the report of the Attorney General noted the beneficiary could be eligible for a preference under section 203(a) (1) (A). The law held the beneficiary lawfully admitted for permanent residence. (Priv. L. No. 50, 67 Stat. A19 (1953)) (H.R. Rep. No. 295, 1st Sess.) (Sen. Rep. No. 252, 1st Sess.)-QMOC

83rd Cong., H.R. 1103, for the relief of Maria Buffoni and Emma Botta. Beneficiaries, 36- and 29-year old natives and citizens of Italy and nuns of the Missionary Sisters of Verona, entered the United States as visitors and were teachers on behalf of Black children in Alabama. The law held the beneficiaries lawfully admitted for permanent residence. (Priv. L. No. 62, 67 Stat. A24 (1953)) (H.R. Rep. No. 241, 1st Sess.) (Sen. Rep. No. 331, 1st Sess.)-QMOC

83rd Cong., H.R. 1148, for the relief of Antonino Cangialosi (or Anthony Consola). Beneficiary, a 43-year old native and citizen of Italy and former permanent resident of the United States, entered the United States at the age of three and remained for 20 years. He then visited Canada and was convicted for armed robbery and sentenced 15 years. He was released after eight years and deported to the United States. In the United States he was ordered deported to Italy on the basis of his conviction. He remained in the United States 15 years with his father, a United States citizen. The law held the beneficiary lawfully admitted for permanent residence. (Priv. L. No. 324, 68 Stat. A37 (1954)) (H.R. Rep. No. 731, 1st Sess.) (Sen. Rep. No. 1072, 2nd Sess.)-WCRF

83rd Cong., H.R. 1358, for the relief of Dr. Marcelino J. Avecilla and Dr. Teodora A. Fidelino-Avecilla. Beneficiaries, 41- and 46-year old natives and citizens of the Philippines, entered the United States as visitors and later studied medicine. They were employed as physicians at Harlem Hospital in New York where "their services are extremely necessary because of the shortage of doctors." The law held the beneficiaries lawfully admitted for permanent residence. (Priv. L. No. 296, 68 Stat. A26 (1954)) (H.R. Rep. No. 799, 1st Sess.) (Sen. Rep. No. 961, 2nd Sess.)-QMOC

83rd Cong., H.R. 1657, for the relief of Antonio Messina. Beneficiary, a 77-year old native and citizen of Italy and former United States citizen who lost citizenship due to protracted residence abroad, was ineligible for a visa due to a conviction for theft of wheat at the age of 23. He had resided in the United States 29 years and left to look after some property but was unable to return because of the war. His spouse was a lawful permanent resident, and they had one United States citizen son. His family and siblings resided in the United States. The law waived section 212(a) (9) relating to crimes involving moral turpitude. (Priv. L. No. 410, 68 Stat. A70 (1954)) (H.R. Rep. No. 1405, 2nd Sess.) (Sen. Rep. No. 1443, 2nd Sess.)-WCRF

83rd Cong., H.R. 1673, for the relief of James I. Smith. Beneficiary, a 28-year old native and citizen of Canada and the spouse of a United States citizen with a son, entered the United States as a visitor. He was excluded from entry due to four different convictions for minor thefts and possession of stolen goods. His spouse was a licensed pilot and instructor with the Civilian Air Patrol until she was injured in a crash necessitating the amputation of her left leg. The law waived section 212(a) (9) relating to crimes involving moral turpitude. (Priv. L. No. 558, 68 Stat. A128 (1954)) (H.R. Rep. No. 1496, 2nd Sess.) (Sen. Rep. No. 1744, 2nd Sess.)-WCRF

83rd Cong., H.R. 1688, for the relief of Henry Ty. Beneficiary, a native of the Philippines of the Chinese race, entered the United States as a student. He had been employed in an American officers' club in Manila, and was befriended by a group of American officers who arranged for him to study in the United States. He dropped out of school because of financial difficulties and found employment as a tool designer. The law held the beneficiary lawfully admitted for permanent residence. (Priv. L. No. 297, 68 Stat. A26 (1954)) (H.R. Rep. No. 581, 1st Sess.) (Sen. Rep. No. 964, 2nd Sess.)-QMGN

83rd Cong., H.R. 1695, for the relief of Irtene Proios (nee Vagianos). Beneficiary, a 27-year old native and citizen of Greece, entered the United States as a visitor fiancee' destined to marry a United States citizen, but the marriage did not occur. The Department of Justice opposed the relief. She later married another United States citizen in a civil ceremony, but both parties indicated that the purpose was to allow her to remain in the United States. She was found deportable because the marriage which was the basis for her entering the United States did not occur. The law held the beneficiary lawfully admitted for permanent residence. (Priv. L. No. 166, 67 Stat. A59 (1953)) (H.R. Rep. No. 246, 1st Sess.) (Sen. Rep. No. 663, 1st Sess.)-QMGN

83rd Cong., H.R. 1756, for the relief of Eugene de Thassy. Beneficiary, a native of Hungary, entered the United States as a visitor. He was a member of the Hungarian armed forces and engaged in underground activities. He was an aide-de-camp to General Nagy and was cited by the Hungarian

Government for his anti-Nazi role. The French Government decorated him with the Silver Medal of the Gratitude of France. He was employed in the United States by the National Committee for a Free Europe. The law held the beneficiary lawfully admitted for permanent residence. (Priv. L. No. 185, 67 Stat. A65 (1953)) (H.R. Rep. No. 405, 1st Sess.) (Sen. Rep. No. 770, 1st Sess.)-QMDE

83rd Cong., H.R. 1768, for the relief of Claire Louise Carey and Vincent F. Carey. Beneficiaries, nine and eight-year old natives and citizens of Australia, were admitted to the United States as visitors. The adoptive father deserted the family as soon as they left for the United States. The adoptive mother was a United States citizen who had an excessive drinking problem. The children were taken away from her for that reason and because of the ill treatment of them. They were in the custody of the United States courts but spent weekends with families who expressed an interest in adopting them. (Priv. L. No. 677, 68 Stat. A166 (1954)) (H.R. Rep. No. 1498, 2nd Sess.) (Sen. Rep. No. 1851, 2nd Sess.)-QIRA

83rd Cong., H.R. 1886, for the relief of Paul Myung Ha Chung. Beneficiary, a 23-year old native and citizen of Korea, entered the United States as a student. His parents and three siblings were permanent residents who immigrated on the basis of the father's status as a minister. The beneficiary was ineligible for a visa because he had reached his 18th birthday. The law held the beneficiary lawfully admitted for permanent residence. (Priv. L. No. 116, 67 Stat. A42 (1953)) (H.R. Rep. No. 406, 1st Sess.) (Sen. Rep. No. 558, 1st Sess.)-QMGN

83rd Cong., H.R. 2061, for the relief of Regine du Planty. Beneficiary, a 57-year old native and citizen of France and former permanent resident of the United States, was found deportable based on fraudulent statements in connection with her visa applications. She stated her false statements were made because of a conviction in absentia by a political court in France, for collaboration with the enemy, and she feared extradition to France. She had been a member of the town council at Versailles and adhered to the Vichy Government. Because of her association with the Free French Forces she was taken into custody, but later escaped. She was a French teacher in the United States, and resided in the United States seven years. The law held the beneficiary lawfully admitted for permanent residence. (Priv. L. No. 889, 68 Stat. A239 (1954)) (H.R. Rep. No. 1954, 2nd Sess.) (Sen. Rep. No. 2454, 2nd Sess.)-WCRF

83rd Cong., H.R. 2499, for the relief of Adolfo L. Kalb and Mrs. Eugenia G. Kalb. Beneficiaries, 67- and 65-year old natives of Poland and citizens of Mexico had resided in the United States six years and became United States citizens. They returned to Mexico to attend to the husband's business and lost their citizenship as a result of protracted residence abroad. The law held the beneficiaries within section 101(a) (27) (B) as returning permanent resident aliens. (Priv. L. No. 693, 68 Stat. A171 (1954)) (H.R. Rep. No. 1788, 2nd Sess.) (Sen. Rep. No. 1858, 2nd Sess.)-QPRP

83rd Cong., H.R. 2604, for the relief of Lauri Allan Torni. Beneficiary, a 34-year old native and citizen of Finland, entered the United States as a seaman under false pretenses. He stated that he used an alias because he was a former captain in the Finnish Army imprisoned in Finland and was a part of the resistance movement against Russia. He was "one of the few living holders of the highest Finnish war decoration, Knight of the Mannerheim Cross." The law held the beneficiary lawfully admitted for permanent residence. (Priv. L. No. 168, 67 Stat. A60 (1953)) (H.R. Rep. No. 483, 1st Sess.) (Sen. Rep. No. 668, 1st Sess.)-QMDE

83rd Cong., H.R. 2879, for the relief of Juan Onativia. Beneficiary, a 43-year old native and citizen of Spain, entered the United States as a visitor. He was a musician participating in choirs and a known authority on Basque music traditions. The law held the beneficiary lawfully admitted for permanent residence. (Priv. L. No. 744, 68 Stat A188 (1954)) (H.R. Rep. No. 1957, 2nd Sess.) (Sen. Rep. No. 2116, 2nd Sess.)-QMOC

83rd Cong., H.R. 3566, for the relief of Pimen Maximovitch Sofronov. Beneficiary, a 55-year old native and citizen of Estonia, entered the United States as a visitor. He was reputed to be an outstanding icon painter and came to the United States at the request of various officials of the Eastern Orthodox Catholic Church in connection with work to be done for the churches and monasteries. The law held the beneficiary lawfully admitted for permanent residence. (Priv. L. No. 807, 68 Stat. A208 (1954)) (H.R. Rep. No. 2134, 2nd Sess.) (Sen. Rep. No. 2457, 2nd Sess.)-QMOC

83rd Cong., H.R. 3678, for the relief of George Prokofieff de Seversky and Isabelle Prokofieff de Seversky. Beneficiaries, 57- and 53-year old natives of Russia and Poland, respectively, entered the United States as visitors. Male beneficiary was a pilot and aeronautical engineer consulting with his brother Maj. Alexander P. de Seversky. The law held the beneficiaries lawfully admitted for permanent residence. (Priv. L. No. 70, 67 Stat. A26 (1953)) (H.R. Rep. No. 253, 1st Sess.) (Sen. Rep. No. 342, 1st Sess.)-QMOC

83rd Cong., H.R. 3831, for the relief of Panagiotes G. Karras. Beneficiary, a 27-year old native of Greece, was unable to qualify as a Displaced Person at the same time as his parents and four siblings because he was in the Greek Army prior to the Act's expiration, and there was insufficient time to process his case. The law held the beneficiary within sections 203(a) (3) and 205 relating to aliens under 21 years of age. (Priv. L. No. 169, 67 Stat. A60 (1953)) (H.R. Rep. No. 484, 1st Sess.) (Sen. Rep. No. 669, 1st Sess.)-QPRF

83rd Cong., H.R. 3855, for the relief of Sister Agrippina (Agrippina Palermo), Sister Battistina (Franceschina Serpa), Sister Romana (Angela Iolanda Morelli), Sister Franceschina (Maria Caruso), and Sister Bruna (Giuseppina de Caro). Beneficiaries, five nuns of the Sisters of Charity of the Most Precious Blood, were natives of Italy (ages 43 through 27). They entered the United States as visitors destined to

Massachusetts to perform duties of the mission, consisting of caring for chapels and altars. The law held the beneficiaries lawfully admitted for permanent residence. (Priv. L. No. 752, 68 Stat. A190 (1954)) (H.R. Rep. No. 1964, 2nd Sess.) (Sen. Rep. No. 2124, 2nd Sess.)-QMOC

83rd Cong., H.R. 3874, for the relief of Roberto Johnson. Beneficiary, a seven-year old native and citizen of Italy, entered the United States as a United States citizen accompanying his mother, the spouse of a United States citizen veteran. It was later learned the father was already married, and therefore the child did not derive United States citizenship. The mother remarried and the child was placed in the care of the grandparents of the natural father who proposed to adopt him. The law held the beneficiary lawfully admitted for permanent residence. (Priv. L. No. 810, 68 Stat. A209 (1954)) (H.R. Rep. No. 2136, 2nd Sess.) (Sen. Rep. No. 2405, 2nd Sess.)-QMGN

83rd Cong., H.R. 4522, for the relief of Petrus Van Keer. Beneficiary, a 23-year old native and citizen of Belgium, was excluded from entry to the United States with his parents and siblings due to a mental defect from a childhood injury when he fell to the floor from a table at the age of three months. He was capable of simple duties but was unable to read or write adequately. The law waived section 212 (a)(4) relating to mental illness and provided the posting of a bond. (Priv. L. No. 816, 68 Stat. A211 (1954)) (H.R. Rep. No. 2571, 2nd Sess.) (Sen. Rep. No. 2408, 2nd Sess.)-WHEL

83rd Cong., H.R. 4701, for the relief of Josip Stanic. Beneficiary, a 59-year old native of Yugoslavia with six siblings, two of whom were United States citizens, entered the United States as a visitor and was a highly qualified cabinetmaker. The law held the beneficiary lawfully admitted for permanent residence. (Priv. L. No. 487, 68 Stat. A101 (1954)) (H.R. Rep. No. 1412, 2nd Sess.) (Sen. Rep. No. 1518, 2nd Sess.)-QMOC

83rd Cong., H.R. 5085, for the relief of Mrs. Marie Tcherepnin. Beneficiary, a 76-year old native of Russia and resident of France 30 years, was a widow and blind. She entered the United States as a visitor. Her son, a lawful permanent resident, expressed a desire to support her. The law held the beneficiary lawfully admitted for permanent residence. (Priv. L. No. 329, 68 Stat. A38 (1954)) (H.R. Rep. No. 1183, 2nd Sess.) (Sen. Rep. No. 1122, 2nd Sess.)-QMGN

83rd Cong., H.R. 5238, for the relief of Franciszek Jarecki. Beneficiary, a 21-year old native and citizen of Poland, escaped from that country in a Soviet Mig 15 fighterplane and landed it on the Danish island of Bornholm, thus "giving the technicians of the free world their first opportunity to examine an undamaged aircraft of that type." He was granted asylum in Denmark, and later entered the United States as a visitor to engage in large-scale rallies sponsored by the Polish National Alliance and supported by United States Government agencies. The law waived section 212(a) (28) relating to Communist Party membership, and held him lawfully admitted for permanent residence. (Priv. L. No. 109, 67 Stat. A40 (1953)) (H.R. Rep. No. 468, 1st Sess.) (Sen. Rep. No. 434, 1st Sess.)-WXCP

83rd Cong., H.R. 5354, for the relief of Liborio Guido Rutilio. Beneficiary, a 48-year old native and citizen of Italy and spouse of a United States citizen, was ineligible for a visa due to aiding and abetting theft of a chain used to hook up horses to plows. Five children were admitted to the United States for permanent residence and one child was a United States citizen. The law waived section 212(a) (9) relating to grounds involving moral turpitude. (Priv. L. No. 766, 68 Stat. A194 (1954)) (H.R. Rep. No. 1531, 2nd Sess.) (Sen. Rep. No. 1869, 2nd Sess.)-WCRF

83rd Cong., H.R. 5816, for the relief of Mrs. Caridad Rosa Avila Leyva de Ernest. Beneficiary, a 22-year old native and citizen of Cuba and spouse of a United States citizen, was denied a visa based on reports she engaged in prostitution. The law waived section 212(a) (12) relating to prostitution. (Priv. L. No. 761, 68 Stat. A193 (1954)) (H.R. Rep. No. 1533, 2nd Sess.) (Sen. Rep. No. 1870, 2nd Sess.)-WCRF

83rd Cong., H.R. 6650, for the relief of Joseph Cerny. Beneficiary, a 69-year old native and citizen of Czechoslovakia, entered the United States as a visitor. He was a prominent political force in Czechoslovakia, having been a member of the Czechoslovak Parliament and Minister of the Interior from 1934 to 1938. He was jailed by the Communists for two years and fled that country in 1948. In the United States he was employed by the National Committee for a Free Europe. An application for relief under the Displaced Persons Act was favorable but failed of passage in the Congress. The law held the beneficiary lawfully admitted for permanent residence. (Priv. L. No. 543, 68 Stat. A123 (1954)) (Sen. Rep. No. 1731, 2nd Sess.)-QMDE

83rd Cong., H.R. 6955, for the relief of Margers Nulle-Siecenieks. Beneficiary, a 33-year old native of Latvia and spouse of a lawful permanent resident, was refused a visa due to concealing his membership in the Baltic Legion when applying for admission as a Displaced Person. His actions were explained in that he feared deportation to Latvia. The law waived section 212(a) (19) relating to fraudulent attempts to procure a visa. (Priv. L. No. 829, 68 Stat. A215 (1954)) (H.R. Rep. No. 1832, 2nd Sess.) (Sen. Rep. No. 2137, 2nd Sess.)-WCRF

83rd Cong., H.R. 6998, for the relief of Erna White. Beneficiary, a 33-year old native of Germany and spouse of a United States citizen in the Armed Forces, was ineligible for a visa due to conviction of abortion. The law waived section 212(a) (9) relating to crimes involving moral turpitude. (Priv. L. No. 544, 68 Stat. A123 (1954)) (H.R. Rep. No. 1440, 2nd Sess.) (Sen. Rep. No. 1732, 2nd Sess.)-WCRF

83rd Cong., H.R. 7151, for the relief of Mazal Kolman. Beneficiary was a 30-year old native of Arabia and national of Israel, and spouse of a United States citizen. Although an administrative remedy was available on the basis of her marriage to a United States citizen, the House Committee noted, "in view of the fact that Mrs. Kolman's United States citizen husband is totally blind," and he had received a law degree, the Committee recommended favorably on the bill. The law held the beneficiary lawfully admitted to the United States for permanent residence. (Priv. L. No. 835, 68 Stat. A217 (1954)) (H.R. Rep. No. 2156, 2nd Sess.) (Sen. Rep. No. 2423, 2nd Sess.)-QMGN

83rd Cong., H.R. 7559, for the relief of Mrs. Madeleine Alice Aquarone. Beneficiary, a 35-year old native of France and naturalized United States citizen, was in jeopardy of losing her citizenship due to her residence abroad, while her husband was employed as an interpreter to the Court of International Justice at the Hague. The Department of State supported enactment of the legislation. The law deemed section 352(a) (2) inapplicable to the beneficiary, provided that she return to the United States for permanent residence prior to one year after the termination of her husband's employment. (Priv. L. No. 369, 68 Stat. A53 (1954)) (H.R. Rep. No. 1226, 2nd Sess.) (Sen. Rep. No. 1236, 2nd Sess.)-NRTN

83rd Cong., H.R. 7761, for the relief of John Lewis Pyles, Jr. Beneficiary, a native of England and three-year old son of a United States citizen who was a member of the Armed Forces, was ineligible for a visa due to mental retardation and was unable to walk or speak. The law waived sections 212(a) (1) and (4) relating to mental illness and provided for the posting of a bond to overcome possible public charge aspects. (Priv. L. No. 711, 68 Stat. A177 (1954)) (H.R. Rep. No. 1537, 2nd Sess.) (Sen. Rep. No. 1880, 2nd Sess.)-WHEL

83rd Cong., H.R. 8334, for the relief of Helmut Cermak and Hana Cermak. Beneficiaries, 30- and 31-year old natives of Austria and Czechoslovakia, entered the United States under the auspices of the United States Government at Andrews Air Force Base. They had escaped Czechoslovakia by overpowering the Communist crew of a Czechoslovak airplane. They flew that plane to Frankfurt, Germany where they were granted asylum. The law held the beneficiaries lawfully admitted for permanent residence. (Priv. L. No. 716, 68 Stat. A179 (1954)) (H.R. Rep. No. 2022, 2nd Sess.) (Sen. Rep. No. 2155, 2nd Sess.)-QMDE

83rd Cong., H.R. 8557, for the relief of Ezio Bertoni. Beneficiary, a 49-year old native and citizen of Italy and spouse of a United States citizen with two United States citizen children, was ineligible for a visa due to paranoia, a person afflicted with insanity. It was stated he had no disturbances for 20 years. The law waived section 212(a) (3) relating to persons with attacks of insanity and provided for a posting of bond to overcome possible public charge aspects. (Priv. L. No. 848, 68 Stat. A221 (1954)) (H.R. Rep. No. 2401, 2nd Sess.) (Sen. Rep. No. 2436, 2nd Sess.)-WHEL

83rd Cong., S. 69, for the relief of Dr. Peter C. T. Kao. Beneficiary, a 34-year old native and citizen of China, entered the United States as a visitor-trainee continuing dental work in New York at the Guggenheim Dental Clinic. The law held the beneficiary lawfully admitted for permanent residence. (Priv. L. No. 121, 67 Stat. A44 (1953)) (Sen. Rep. No. 105, 1st Sess.) (H.R. Rep. No. 719, 1st Sess.)-QMOC

83rd Cong., S. 196, for the relief of Alejandro de La Cruz Hernandez. Beneficiary, a 30-year old native of Spain, entered the United States as a visitor for medical treatment. He had been undergoing plastic surgery for his chin which was struck by a bomb fragment. He was employed as a skilled cabinet maker. The law held the beneficiary lawfully admitted for permanent residence. (Priv. L. No. 125, 67 Stat. A45 (1953)) (Sen. Rep. No. 345, 1st Sess.) (H.R. Rep. No. 721, 1st Sess.)-QMGN

83rd Cong., S. 205, for the relief of Evdoxia J. Kitsos. Beneficiary, a 58-year old native and citizen of Albania, entered the United States for permanent residence as the spouse of a United States citizen. It was later disclosed that her husband had died two months prior to her entry and she was not entitled to an immigrant visa. She resided in the United States with her United States citizen brother. Her daughter also resided in the United States. The law held the beneficiary lawfully admitted for permanent residence. (Priv. L. No. 250, 68 Stat. A10 (1954)) (Sen. Rep. No. 567, 1st Sess.) (H.R. Rep. No. 1151, 2nd Sess.)-QIRW

83rd Cong., S. 233, for the relief of Jeno Cseplo. Beneficiary, a 33-year old native of Hungary, entered the United States as a visitor to attend the Congress of the International Peasants Alliance. He stated he fled from the Communists because of his connection as head of the Peasants Alliance in Hungary. In the United States he operated a dairy farm owned by Ferenc Nagy, former Hungarian Premier. The law held the beneficiary lawfully admitted for permanent residence. (Priv. L. No. 608, 68 Stat. A144 (1954)) (Sen. Rep. No. 992, 2nd Sess.) (H.R. Rep. No. 2216, 2nd Sess.)-QMGN

83rd Cong., S. 278, for the relief of Szyga (Saul) Morgenstern. The beneficiary was a 22-year old native of Poland, who entered the United States as a student studying at the Mesifta Yeshiva Rabbi Chaim Berlin Rabbinical Academy in New York. Relatives abroad included three sisters residing in Israel. The law held the beneficiary lawfully admitted for permanent residence. (Priv. L. No. 566, 68 Stat. A130 (1954)) (Sen. Rep. No. 1152, 2nd Sess.) (H.R. Rep. No. 2049, 2nd Sess.)-QMOC

83rd Cong., S. 315, for the relief of Owen Lowery. Beneficiary, a 14-year old native of China, had been taken by his mother to Macao after the Japanese invasion at Canton in 1938. His father had been with the Chinese Army. When the mother died, shortly after arriving in Macao, a United States citizen missionary, with the Congregational Church in China, cared for him. He was six months old at that time. The missionary later adopted the beneficiary in the United States, and sought to confer immigration benefits without regard to the waiting period for visa issuance. The law held the beneficiary to be the natural-born child of the adoptive mother for purposes of section 101(a) (27) (A). (Priv. L. No. 83, 67 Stat. A31 (1953)) (Sen. Rep. No. 256, 1st Sess.) (H.R. Rep. No. 610, 1st Sess.)-QIRA

83rd Cong., S. 506, for the relief of Horst F.W. Dittmar and Heinz-Erik Dittmar. Beneficiaries, brothers (ages 30, 28), natives of the Netherlands East Indies, entered the United States as visitors. Their parents were permanent residents. The father was an ordained minister of the Seventh Day Adventist Church. The law held the beneficiaries lawfully admitted for permanent residence. (Priv. L. No. 257, 68 Stat. A12 (1954)) (Sen. Rep. No. 658, 1st Sess.) (H.R. Rep. No. 1159, 2nd Sess.)-QMGN

83rd Cong., S. 569, for the relief of Lina Anna Adelheid (Adam) Hoyer. Beneficiary, a 27-year old native and citizen of Germany, entered the United States as an exchange visitor to study banking, and subsequently married a United States citizen and veteran who had a 100% disability. The law held the beneficiary lawfully admitted for permanent residence. (Priv. L. No. 258, 68 Stat. A13 (1954)) (Sen. Rep. No. 537, 1st Sess.) (H.R. Rep. No. 1161, 2nd Sess.)-QMGN

83rd Cong., S. 579, for the relief of Wong You Henn. Beneficiary, a native of China, entered the United States based on a claim to United States citizenship. However, it was determined by the courts that he was not a United States citizen. The father died declaring him his heir and next of kin. The law held the beneficiary lawfully admitted for permanent residence. (Priv. L. No. 529, 68 Stat. A118 (1954)) (Sen. Rep. No. 1154, 2nd Sess.) (H.R. Rep. No. 1983, 2nd Sess.)-QMGN

83rd Cong., S. 629, for the relief of Igor Michael Bogolepov (alias Ivar Nyman) and Margaret Johanna Bogolepov (alias Margaret Johanna Nyman). Beneficiaries, a 50-year old native of Russia and a 44-year old native of Estonia, entered the United States as visitors. It was stated they "cooperated with various congressional committees in their investigations of communism." The law held the beneficiaries lawfully admitted for permanent residence (Priv. L. No. 456, 68 Stat. A91 (1954)) (Sen. Rep. No. 1174, 2nd Sess.) (H.R. Rep. No. 1717, 2nd Sess.)-QMDE

83rd Cong., S. 676, for the relief of Eftychios Mourginakis. Beneficiary, a 36-year old native and citizen of Greece, entered the United States as a crewman. During the war he was chief mate on a destroyer. When Germany invaded Greece, he took the destroyer to sea to join the British Fleet. He received the Distinguished Service Cross for his action, and later was employed as port captain for a steamship company in New York. He owned interest in two shipping companies, including part ownership of four vessels. The law held the beneficiary lawfully admitted for permanent residence. (Priv. L. No. 530, 68 Stat. A119 (1954)) (Sen. Rep. No. 1205, 2nd Sess.) (H.R. Rep. No. 1984, 2nd Sess.)-QMDE

83rd Cong., S. 740, for the relief of Santa Muciaccia (Sister Maria Fridiana), Teresa Saragaglia (Sister Maria Eutropia), and Caterina Isonni (Sister Maria Giovita). Beneficiaries, three Italian nuns (ages 30, 37, 30), entered the United States as visitors engaged in nursing work at the Joseph P. Kennedy Memorial Hospital in Massachusetts caring for young children mentally ill or who had cerebral palsy. The law held the beneficiaries lawfully admitted for permanent residence. (Priv. L. No. 457, 68 Stat. A92 (1954)) (Sen. Rep. No. 1000, 2nd Sess.) (H.R. Rep. No. 1720, 2nd Sess.)-QMOC

83rd Cong., S. 795, for the relief of Josef Radziwill. Beneficiary, a 35-year old native of Poland, entered the United States as a seaman. He served in the Polish Army and was with the Anders Army in England. His mother and brother were admitted to the United States as displaced persons, but his documents were not processed in a timely fashion because he was at sea. The law held the beneficiary lawfully admitted for permanent residence. (Priv. L. No. 588, 68 Stat. A137 (1954))(Sen. Rep. No. 1002, 2nd Sess.) (H.R. Rep. No. 2056, 2nd Sess.)-QMGN

83rd Cong., S. 855, for the relief of Kirill Mihailovich Alexeev, Antonina Ivanovna Alexeev, and minor children, Victoria and Vladimir Alexeev. Beneficiaries, 45-, 40-, 17-, and 16-year old natives of Russia, entered the United States in transit to the Soviet Union. The male beneficiary had been assigned to Mexico City with the Russian Embassy. It was stated he "disavowed his loyalty to the Soviet Government and has written several anti-Soviet articles in magazines." The law held the beneficiaries lawfully admitted for permanent residence. (Priv. L. No. 591, 68 Stat. A138 (1954)) (Sen. Rep. No. 1133, 2nd Sess.) (H.R. Rep. No. 2060, 2nd Sess.)-QMDE

83rd Cong., S. 1212, for the relief of Alice Masaryk. Beneficiary, a 75-year old native of Austria, entered the United States as a visitor and was granted the privilege of pre-examination under section 3(c) of the Displaced Persons Act of 1948 as an "especially meritorious case." However, a visa was not available. She was the daughter of Thomas Masaryk, the first President of the Republic of Czechoslovakia and the sister of Jan Masaryk, the Prime Minister of the Czechoslovakian Government in exile during World War II. She was engaged in the preparation of her memoirs and was a lecturer and speaker on the Voice of America and Radio Free Europe. The law held the beneficiary lawfully admitted for permanent residence. (Priv. L. No. 621, 68 Stat. A148 (1954)) (Sen. Rep. No. 1715, 2nd Sess.) (H.R. Rep. No. 2510, 2nd Sess.)-QMDE

83rd Cong., S. 1262, for the relief of Stefanos A. Spilios (also known as Stephen A. Harrison). Beneficiary, a 23-year old native and citizen of Greece, entered the United States as a visitor and resided with his uncle, Peter S. Harrison, the publisher of Harrison's Reports. The report of the Attorney General opposed its enactment as it would encourage others to obtain visas to overcome backlogged visa subscription in other countries. The law held the beneficiary lawfully admitted for permanent residence. (Priv. L. No. 89, 67 Stat. A33 (1953)) (Sen. Rep. No. 259, 1st Sess.) (H.R. Rep. No. 617, 1st Sess.)-QMOC

83rd Cong., S. 1382, for the relief of Elie Joseph Hakim and Family. Beneficiaries, 41-, 39-, 8-, and 5-year old natives and citizens of Egypt, entered the United States as a visitors. The male beneficiary was an expert in the cotton exchange field and was granted a preference for immigration but it expired. He was employed by James Lawrence & Company as a cotton classifier. His expertise in Egyptian cotton was invaluable in advising of materials for parachutes, uniforms, and army shoelaces. He had one brother in the United States as a citizen. The law held the beneficiaries lawfully admitted for permanent residence. (Priv. L. No. 509, 68 Stat Al12 (1954)) (Sen. Rep. No. 1345, 2nd Sess.) (H.R. Rep. No. 1988, 2nd Sess.)-QMOC

83rd Cong., S. 1682, for the relief of Branimir V. Popovitch and Mila B. Popovitch. Beneficiaries, 54- and 45-year old natives of Yugoslavia, entered the United States as visitors. The male beneficiary was formerly a Yugoslav diplomat serving as first attaché and second secretary with the Foreign Office. He became first secretary of the Embassy in Romania, Italy and London. He was private secretary to ex-King Peter in 1948 and refused to return to Yugoslavia. In the United States he was employed in the Library of Congress. The law held the beneficiary lawfully admitted for permanent residence. (Priv. L. No. 473, 68 Stat. A96 (1954)) (Sen. Rep. No. 1249, 2nd Sess.) (H.R. Rep. No. 1744, 2nd Sess.)-QMGN

83rd Cong., S. 1955, for the relief of Giorgio Salvini Thompson. Beneficiary, a nine-year old native and citizen of Italy and stepson of a United States citizen, was unable to immigrate because he was born out of wedlock. His mother married a United States citizen. The law held the beneficiary within section 101(a) (27) (A) and 205 relating to natural-born children of United States citizens. (Priv. L. No. 475, 68 Stat. A97 (1954)) (Sen. Rep. No. 543, 1st Sess.) (H.R. Rep. No. 1748, 2nd Sess.)-QIRM

83rd Cong., S. 2065, for the relief of Mr. and Mrs. Hendrik Van der Tuin. Beneficiaries, 68- and 69-year old natives and citizens of the Netherlands, entered the United States as visitors and were subsequently offered employment in the raising and sorting of tulip bulbs for which the male beneficiary was skilled. Their daughter resided in the United States as a lawful permanent resident and was in need of assistance during an illness. The law held the beneficiaries lawfully admitted for permanent residence. (Priv. L. No. 603, 68 Stat. A142 (1954)) (Sen. Rep. No. 1165, 2nd Sess.) (H.R. Rep. No. 2081, 2nd Sess.)-QMOC

83rd Cong., S. 2135, for the relief of Fernando A. Rubio, Jr. Beneficiary, a 28-year old native of Spain, entered the United States for permanent residence and requested relief from military service in 1944 on the basis of being a neutral alien. He stated he signed the form because of his father's threats of removing him from the United States. He was married to a United States citizen and had one minor child. Beneficiary actually served in the United States Army October 1950 to June 1953. The Committee noted in acting on such legislation that although it did not condone signing the exemption form, "his subsequent honorable service of 32 months…warrants the granting of the waiver." The law waived section 315 relating to ineligibility to citizenship. (Priv. L. No. 665, 68 Stat. A163 (1954)) (Sen. Rep. No. 1543, 2nd Sess.) (H.R. Rep. No. 2414, 2nd Sess.)-NXDD

83rd Cong., S. 2156, for the relief of John Enepekides, his wife, Anna, and his son, George. Beneficiaries, husband, wife, and son, natives and citizens of Greece and ages 52, 44 and 14, were found eligible for nonquota status. The basis for immigration was due to the husband's position as Chief of the Commercial Unit of the Economic Section at the American Embassy in Greece, where he had been employed over 27 years. The law provided the beneficiary be allowed to fulfill the one-year physical presence requirement for citizenship in a similar fashion as provided in section 316(c). (Priv. L. No. 967, 68 Stat. A278 (1954)) (Sen. Rep. No. 1422, 2nd Sess.) (H.R. Rep. No. 2594, 2nd Sess.)-NRES

83rd Cong., S. 2210, for the relief of Frank (Franz) Homolka, Olga Homolka (nee Mandel), Adolf Homolka, Helga Maria Homolka, and Frieda Homolka. Beneficiaries entered the United States for permanent residence as Displaced Persons. They were natives of Romania, Czechoslovakia, and Germany (ages 47, 40, 13, 9, 7). It was learned the husband had previously been in the United States, and had been deported. Because of this misrepresentation he was found deportable. The law held the beneficiaries lawfully admitted for permanent residence. (Priv. L. No. 640, 68 Stat. A155 (1954)) (Sen. Rep. No. 1522, 2nd Sess.) (H.R. Rep. No. 2568, 2nd Sess.)-WCRF

83rd Cong., S. 2259, for the relief of Rev. Charles V. Rossini. Beneficiary, a 64-year old native of Italy and naturalized United States citizen, divested himself of United States citizenship by continuous residence abroad, when he went to Rome for service in the Vatican from 1949 to 1952. The law allowed the beneficiary to regain his citizenship status by taking an oath of allegiance. (Priv. L. No. 902, 68 Stat. A244 (1954)) (Sen. Rep. No. 1829, 2nd Sess.)-NRTN

83rd Cong., S. 2345, for the relief of Yun Tai Miao and his wife, Chao Pei Tsang Miao. Beneficiaries, natives and citizens of China, entered the United States as visitors. The male beneficiary was later employed as President of an export and import company. He had been involved in several trading companies in China, and was the chairman of the Yunnan Economic Council for two years and later adviser to Gen. R.B. McClure with the American ground forces in China in 1945. The law held the beneficiaries lawfully admitted to permanent residence. (Priv. L. No. 969, 68 Stat. A279 (1954)) (Sen. Rep. No. 1831, 2nd Sess.)-QMOC

83rd Cong., S. 2360, for the relief of Jacob Vandenbergh. Beneficiary, a 46-year old native and citizen of Holland, who entered the United States as a visitor, had been formerly lawfully admitted for permanent residence. It was later discovered he had returned to Holland and entered the United States without documents. He was president of a textile mill in Massachusetts and had one United States citizen child. The law held the beneficiary lawfully admitted for permanent residence. (Priv. L. No. 476, 68 Stat. A97 (1954)) (Sen. Rep. No. 1130, 2nd Sess.) (H.R. Rep. No. 1750, 2nd Sess.)-WCRF

83rd Cong., S. 2369, for the relief of Karl Ullstein. Beneficiary, a 61-year old native of Germany and naturalized United States citizen, was in jeopardy of losing his United States citizenship by protracted residence abroad. He was a member of the famous family of Germany known as the House of Ullstein, a large publishing firm. The properties of the publishing house had been seized during the war and restored to the owners by the German courts. The beneficiary was concerned with his printing business. The Department of State reported it would be against the interests of the United States if the beneficiary was forced to discontinue his activities in Germany where he employed 4,000 persons, and was involved in the publishing of newspapers advocating democratic principles. The law permitted the beneficiary to reside abroad without losing citizenship under section 352 (a). (Priv. L. No. 533, 68 Stat. A119 (1954)) (Sen. Rep. No. 1407, 2nd Sess.) (H.R. Rep. No. 1994, 2nd Sess.)-NRTN

83rd Cong., S. 2504, for the relief of Elisa Albertina Cioccio Rigazzi or Elisa Cioccio. Beneficiary, a 24-year old native and citizen of Italy, entered the United States as a visitor intending to marry a United States citizen. The marriage failed to materialize. She had previously been adopted six months prior to her entry to the United States by her aunt and uncle. They later refused to have anything to do with her when she refused to marry their selected husband. The law held the beneficiary lawfully admitted for permanent residence). (Priv. L. No. 650, 68 Stat. A158 (1954)) (Sen. Rep. No. 1739, 2nd Sess.) (H.R. Rep. No. 2519, 2nd Sess.)-QIRA

83rd Cong., S. 2512, for the relief of Jeannette Kalker and Abraham Benjamin Kalker. Beneficiaries, 13- and 12-year old natives and citizens of Holland whose parents died in a concentration camp, were supported by their aunt and uncle. Her relatives were held eligible to enter the United States as permanent residents, and desired to have their niece and nephew join them. The law held the beneficiaries within section 203(a) (3) and 205 as the natural-born children of a lawful permanent resident. (Priv. L. No. 651, 68 Stat. A158 (1954)) (Sen. Rep. No. 1740, 2nd Sess.) (H.R. Rep. No. 2569, 2nd Sess.)-QPRF

83rd Cong., S. 2534, for the relief of Dora Vida Lyew Seixas. Beneficiary, a 36-year old native and citizen of Panama, was chargeable to the quota for China because her father was Chinese. Those visas were oversubscribed, however. Her spouse was a lawful permanent resident and their three children were entitled to nonquota status. Her spouse had been employed by the United States Air Corps in the Canal Zone. The Committee noted that the "continued separation of this family with young children is unwise" and recommended favorable action. The law waived section 202(b) and classified the beneficiaries as children under section 101(a) (27) (C). (Priv. L. No. 344, 68 Stat. A44 (1954)) (Sen. Rep. No. 950, 2nd Sess.) (H.R. Rep. No. 1366, 2nd Sess.)-QPRF

83rd Cong., S. 2618, for the relief of Ertogroul Osman. Beneficiary, a 41-year old native of Turkey, was admitted for permanent residence by previous private legislation. He was unable to travel because he did not have the requisite seven year consecutive residence to qualify for a waiver of excludability for draft exemption as a returning permanent resident. The law waived section 212(a) (22) relating to exclusion of persons who claim exemption from the draft and allowed the beneficiary to be readmitted to permanent residence. (Priv. L. No. 999, 68 Stat. A289 (1954)) (Sen. Rep. No. 1463, 2nd Sess.) (H.R. Rep. No. 2596, 2nd Sess.)-QPRP

83rd Cong., S. 3145, for the relief of Bonita Lee Simpson. Beneficiary, a four-year old native of New Zealand, was adopted by a former United States citizen who served eight years with the United States Marine Corps. His spouse was a native of New Zealand. The United States citizen father had become a citizen of New Zealand after moving to that country with his spouse. Upon seeking return to the United States as an immigrant, he sought to bring his wife and adopted child to the United States. The law held the beneficiary to be the natural-born child of the adoptive parents. (Priv. L. No. 986, 68 Stat. A285 (1954)) (Sen. Rep. No. 1668, 2nd Sess.)-QIRA

83rd Cong., S. 3433, for the relief of Andreja Glusic. Beneficiary, a 21-year old native of Yugoslavia, was unable to immigrate with her parents because she had already attained the age of 21. The delay in obtaining the visa was caused by difficulties attaining exit permits from the Yugoslav Government. The law held the beneficiary within the purview of section 203(a) (3) and 205 as the natural child of her parents. (Priv. L. No. 659, 68 Stat A161 (1954)) (Sen. Rep. No. 1669, 2nd Sess.) (H.R. Rep. No. 2233, 2nd Sess.)-QPRF

84th Cong., H. R. 877, for the relief of Mrs. Rose Amoresano and her children. Beneficiaries, natives and citizens of Italy, planned to immigrate to the United States on the basis of the husband's approved petition under the Refugee Relief Act of 1953 filed by his mother. On the day they were leaving to obtain visas, the father was killed by a relative of the fiance of his oldest daughter, who believed she would not return to Italy to marry his son. The beneficiaries therefore lost their eligibility for a visa. The law held the beneficiaries eligible for nonquota visas under section 4(a)(6) of the Refugee Relief Act of 1953. (Priv. L. No. 744, 70 Stat. A111 (1956)) (H.R. Rep. No. 2072, 2nd Sess.) (Sen. Rep. No. 2336, 2nd Sess.)-QPRF

84th Cong., H.R. 962, for the relief of Maria Louise Andreis. Beneficiary, a 24-year old native and citizen of Italy, sought to join her mother, a lawful permanent resident, and her stepfather, a United States citizen, in the United States. Her parents were self-employed as voice teachers and opera singers, "highly regarded in their profession." It was stated the beneficiary could become one of the greatest coloratura sopranos of the opera stage. She was unable to immigrate immediately because she was over the age of 21. The law held the beneficiary within 203(a)(3) and 205 as the natural-born child of a lawful permanent resident of the United States. (Priv. L. No. 249, 69 Stat. A88 (1955)) (H.R. Rep. No. 497, 1st Sess.) (Sen. Rep. No. 753, 1st Sess.)-QPRF

84th Cong., H.R. 968, for the relief of Max Kozlowski. Beneficiary, a 56-year old native of Poland, and the father and grandfather of citizens of the United States, was found ineligible for a visa for membership in a proscribed organization. In addition, he fraudulently attempted to impersonate his brother-in-law in obtaining an immigrant visa. He had been imprisoned by the Nazi Government in Poland six years, and was later released with the stipulation he repatriate to countries under Soviet domination and join organizations championing their cause. The Committee noted that "liberated victims of Nazi camps cannot be made--as a rule--responsible for their short-lived membership in those organizations." The law waived section 212(a)(9), (19) and (28) relating to crimes involving moral turpitude, fraudulently attempting to obtain a visa, and membership in certain proscribed organizations on behalf of the beneficiary. (Priv. L. No. 149, 69 Stat. A52 (1955)) (H.R. Rep. No. 411, 1st Sess.) (Sen. Rep. No. 594, 1st Sess.)-WXCP

84th Cong., H.R. 973, for the relief of Mrs. Elizabeth Dowds. Beneficiary, a 56-year old native of Northern Ireland and citizen of Great Britain, and former United States citizen, had her naturalization revoked and was found deportable based on misrepresenting herself as her sister-in-law in being admitted to the United States, and committing perjury and forgery. She had two adult children in the United States and worked as a nursemaid. The law held the beneficiary lawfully admitted for permanent residence. (Priv. L. No. 150, 69 Stat. A52 (1955)) (H.R. Rep. No. 307, 1st Sess.) (Sen. Rep. No. 595, 1st Sess.)-WCRF

84th Cong., H.R. 995, for the relief of Frieda Quirling and Tina Quirling. Beneficiaries, 15- and 12-year old natives of Russia, whose parents became separated in Russia during World War II and subsequently were placed in a refugee camp with their mother, were befriended by the Mennonite Church. The Church friends arranged to move the family to Paraguay where they resided with a distant relative, until their mother died. The prospective United States citizen adoptive parents supported the beneficiary, and desired to have them enter the United States. The adoptive parents had three other adoptive children, citizens of the United States, and owned a ranch and farming operation. They sought exemption from placing the children on the nonpreference visa waiting list. The law held the beneficiaries within section 101(a)(27)(A). (Priv. L. No. 153, 69 Stat. A53 (1955)) (H.R. Rep. No. 353, 1st Sess.) (Sen. Rep. No. 598, 1st Sess.)-QIRA

84th Cong., H.R. 1022, for the relief of Antonio Andrea Chitato. Beneficiary, a national of Portugal, entered the United States accompanied by his employers, United States citizens in the Foreign Service. He was employed by them as a houseboy and they were "very much attached to the beneficiary and hoped to retain him in their household indefinitely." The law held the beneficiary lawfully admitted for permanent residence. (Priv. L. No. 491, 70 Stat. A3 (1956)) (H.R. Rep. No. 382, 1st Sess.) (Sen. Rep. No. 2187, 2nd Sess.)-QMOC

84th Cong., H.R. 1081, for the relief of Anna Tokatlian Gulezian. Beneficiary, a 60-year old native of Turkey, entered the United States as a visitor. She subsequently married a United States citizen who died one year later and she lost her eligibility for nonquota status. She resided in the United States with her daughter, a lawful permanent resident. The law held the beneficiary lawfully admitted for permanent residence. (Priv. L. No. 107, 69 Stat. A37 (1955)) (H.R. Rep. No. 184, 1st Sess.) (Sen. Rep. No. 526, 1st Sess.)-QIRW

84th Cong., H.R. 1160, for the relief of Vittorio Capano. Beneficiary, an 18-year old native and citizen of Italy, whose father was a United States citizen, desired to enter the United States to reside with his United States citizen aunt and uncle. His father, a totally disabled veteran, had returned to Italy due to illness and lost his citizenship through protracted residence abroad. The law held the beneficiary within sections 101(a)(27)(A) and 205 relating to natural-born children of United States citizens. (Priv. L. No. 330, 69 Stat. A113 (1955)) (H.R. Rep. No. 382, 1st Sess.) (Sen. Rep. No. 2187, 2nd Sess.)-QIRM

84th Cong., H.R. 1166, for the relief of Florence Meister. Beneficiary, a 26-year old native-born United States citizen, lost citizenship by service in the Israeli Army two years. The law allowed the beneficiary to regain United States citizenship after its loss under section 401(c) by an oath of allegiance to the United States. (Priv. L. No. 12, 69 Stat. A6 (1955)) (H.R. Rep. No. 187, 1st Sess.) (Sen. Rep. No. 306, 1st Sess.)-NVOL

84th Cong., H.R. 1185, for the relief of Jose Domingo Quintanar. Beneficiary, a 42-year old native and citizen of Mexico, entered the United States fraudulently claiming to be a United States citizen. His spouse was a lawful permanent resident and they had seven children, five of whom were United States citizens. The law waived 212(a)(19) relating to fraud. (Priv. L. No. 287, 69 Stat. A99 (1955)) (H.R. Rep. No. 957, 1st Sess.) (Sen. Rep. No. 928, 1st Sess.)-WCRF

84th Cong., H.R. 1193, for the relief of Dr. and Mrs. Ivan Pernar. Beneficiaries, 56- and 55-year old natives of Yugoslavia, entered the United States as visitors. The male beneficiary served as Senator and Under Secretary of the Interior for the Kingdom of Yugoslavia and fled that country when the Communists took over. Their applications as displaced persons were denied because they had resettled in Canada. The law held the beneficiaries lawfully admitted for permanent residence. (Priv. L. No. 512, 70 Stat. A10 (1956)) (H.R. Rep. No. 1316, 1st Sess.) (Sen. Rep. No. 1417, 2nd Sess.)-QMDE

84th Cong., H.R. 1203, for the relief of Ivan Bruno Lomm, also known as Ivan B. Johnson. Beneficiary, a 61-year old native and citizen of Sweden, entered the United States first as a seaman and later illegally after a temporary absence from the United States He was married to a United States citizen and resided in the United States 29 years, and was employed as a watchmaker. He had been convicted of embezzlement prior to entering the United States. The law held the beneficiary lawfully admitted for permanent residence. (Priv. L. No. 15, 69 Stat. A7 (1955)) (H.R. Rep. No. 251, 1st Sess.) (Sen. Rep. No. 310, 1st Sess.)-WCRF

84th Cong., H.R. 1275, for the relief of Gennaro Savarese. Beneficiary, a 37-year old native and citizen of Italy, entered the United States as a stowaway. His parents were United States citizens who returned to Italy to bring their children to the United States; but the beneficiary was refused a visa because of an eye disease. After he was discharged from medical treatment, the war broke out and he was over 21 and unable to immigrate as a child. The House Committee report noted it had consistently refused to pass legislation on behalf of persons who entered the United States surreptitiously. "However, the long history of Mr. Savarese's endeavors to secure entry to the United States in order to reside with his parents and brothers and sisters…points up to a rather unusual and truly touching set of adverse circumstances beyond the control of the beneficiary of this bill." The law held the beneficiary lawfully admitted for permanent residence. (Priv. L. No. 253, 69 Stat. A89 (1955)) (H.R. Rep. No. 692, 1st Sess.) (Sen. Rep. No. 786, 1st Sess.)-WHEL

84th Cong., H.R. 1301, for the relief of Karlis Abele. Beneficiary, a 65-year old native of Latvia, entered the United States as a Displaced Person. He was excluded due to a mental defect and admitted as a temporary visitor under bond for psychiatric treatment. He was employed performing odd jobs for the Latvian Evangelical Lutheran Church of New York, and was considered free from his mental illness after treatment. The law held the beneficiary lawfully admitted for permanent residence and required the posting of a bond in order to overcome the possibility of the beneficiary becoming a public charge. (Priv. L. No. 415, 69 Stat. A142 (1955)) (H.R. Rep. No. 773, 1st Sess.) (Sen. Rep. No. 1002, 1st Sess.)-WHEL

84th Cong., H.R. 1410, for the relief of Giovanna Scano. Beneficiary, a 37-year old former United States citizen by birth, lost her citizenship by acquiring Italian citizenship. She resided in the United States 20 years, when she left for Italy and resided in that country seven years. The beneficiary and her husband entered the United States as visitors with two children and had another child born in the United States Her parents and four siblings were United States citizens. The beneficiary's father was a sculptor by profession and constructed the architectural models for many historical buildings including the Metropolitan Museum of Art in New York and the State seals in the House Chamber of the Congress of the United States in Washington, D.C. The law held the beneficiary lawfully admitted for permanent residence. (Priv. L. No. 720, 70 Stat. A98 (1956)) (H.R. Rep. No. 1370, 1st Sess.) (Sen. Rep. No. 2224, 2nd Sess.)-NVOL

84th Cong., H.R. 1487, for the relief of Rosa Marie Phillips. Beneficiary, a 24-year old native and citizen of Germany and spouse of a United States citizen, was ineligible for a visa because of a conviction for prostitution. Her spouse was in the Armed Forces and they had one child of the marriage.

The law waived sections 212(a)(9) and (12) relating to crimes involving moral turpitude, and prostitution. (Priv. L. No. 89, 69 Stat. A31 (1955)) (H.R. Rep. No. 370, 1st Sess.) (Sen. Rep. No. 455, 1st Sess.)-WCRF

84th Cong., H.R. 1501, for the relief of Andrea Hernandes Montes Rocha. Beneficiary, a 29-year old native and citizen of Mexico and spouse of a United States citizen with two United States citizen children, was ineligible for a visa based on fraudulently representing herself as a United States citizen and committing perjury. She was also refused readmission to the United States after having been excluded and deported. The law waived sections 212(a)(9), (16), and (19) relating to crimes involving moral turpitude and visa fraud. (Priv. L. No. 46, 69 Stat. A16 (1955)) (H.R. Rep. No. 277, 1st Sess.) (Sen. Rep. No. 315, 1st Sess.)-WCRF

84th Cong., H.R. 1525, for the relief of Ardes Albacete Yanez. Beneficiary, a 44-year old native and citizen of Spain, entered the United States as a stowaway. He resided in the United States 28 years, and was married to a lawful permanent resident with two children. He applied for an exemption from service in the Armed Forces, and later requested that it be withdrawn. The House Committee noted in its report it was not departing from its policy of unfavorably recommending bills "designed to grant permanent residence to aliens who have entered the United States as stowaways, or for aliens who have claimed exemption from military service...However, considering the fact that the beneficiary has resided in the United States for over 27 years...and that he supports his lawfully resident alien wife and his two citizen children," this particular case was meritorious. The Committee noted that it would not allow him to obtain permanent residence nor would it allow him to be eligible "to the privilege and benefits of United States citizenship." The law canceled deportation proceedings against the beneficiary. (Priv. L. No. 197, 69 Stat. A68 (1955)) (H.R. Rep. No. 415, 1st Sess.) (Sen. Rep. No. 660, 1st Sess.)-WXDD

84th Cong., H.R. 1552, for the relief of Dalisay Lourdes Cruz. Beneficiary, a 22-year old native and citizen of the Philippines, was unable to immigrate with her family including six siblings because she had attained the age of 21 and no longer entitled to a nonquota visa. Her father, a United States citizen and 30-year veteran of the United States Army, desired the family join him in the United States. The law held the beneficiary within sections 101(a)(27)(A) and 205 as immediate relatives and the natural-born child of a United States citizen. (Priv. L. No. 418, 69 Stat. A143 (1955)) (H.R. Rep. No. 709, 1st Sess.) (Sen. Rep. No. 1003, 1st Sess.)-QIRM

84th Cong., H.R. 1667, for the relief of Lieselotte Boehme. Beneficiary, a 32-year old native of Germany and daughter of a United States citizen, was admitted to the United States for medical treatment. She had previously been denied a visa as mentally retarded. When the family immigrated to the United States she resided with an aunt, but when her aunt died the family sought her admission to the United States. It was stated she received medical treatment in the United States which showed improvement, and that the family was willing to assume full responsibility for her support. The law held the beneficiary lawfully admitted for permanent residence upon the posting of a bond to overcome possible public charge. (Priv. L. No. 597, 70 A41 (1956)) (H.R. Rep. No. 973, 1st Sess.) (Sen. Rep. No. 1344, 2nd Sess.)-WHEL

84th Cong., H.R. 1887, for the relief of Dr. Tsi Au Li (Tsi Gziou Li). Beneficiary, a 46-year old native of Belgium and citizen of China, entered the United States in transit. He was employed as a doctor of pathology and conducted cancer research in New York. His spouse and two children were granted relief under section 6 of the Refugee Relief Act but his application was denied because he was born in Belgium. While in China he had been a major general in the Chinese Nationalist Army and served as liaison for Chiang Kai-Shek. The law held the beneficiary lawfully admitted for permanent residence under section 4(a)(13) of the Refugee Relief Act of 1953. (Priv. L. No. 533, 70 Stat. A17 (1956)) (H.R. Rep. No. 1148, 1st Sess.) (Sen. Rep. No. 1438, 2nd Sess.)-QMGN

84th Cong., H.R. 1897, for the relief of Giuseppe Tumbarello. Beneficiary, a 79-year old native and citizen of Italy, and father of three United States citizen children and one who was a permanent resident, was ineligible for a visa due to a conviction at the age of 22 for assault with a dangerous weapon. The law waived section 212(a)(9) relating to crimes involving moral turpitude. (Priv. L. No. 228, 69 Stat. A79 (1955)) (H.R. Rep. No. 513, 1st Sess.) (Sen. Rep. No. 738, 1st Sess.)-WCRF

84th Cong., H.R. 1935, for the relief of Giuseppa Curro Tati. Beneficiary, a 44-year old native and citizen of Italy and spouse of a United States citizen, was excluded from entry to the United States due to a conviction for attempted murder. The victim seduced the beneficiary with the promise of marriage, and when this did not occur she fired five revolver shots at him. She was sentenced to three years imprisonment. Her United States citizen spouse was employed by the New York, New Haven and Hartford Railroad over 40 years and was injured on the job and disabled. He was under continuous medical treatment. The law waived section 212(a)(9) relating to crimes involving moral turpitude. (Priv. L. No. 229, 69 Stat. A79 (1955)) (H.R. Rep. No. 514, 1st Sess.) (Sen. Rep. No. 739, 1st Sess.)-WCRF

84th Cong., H.R. 2054, for the relief of Induk Pahk. Beneficiary, a 58-year old native and citizen of Korea, entered the United States as a visitor. She had worked for the American military in the Department of Public Information as a radio lecturer on democracy, and the "enlightenment of Korean women" during the American occupation of South Korea. When the Korean war broke out, she delivered speeches encouraging the Korean people. In the United States she traveled lecturing at churches and schools and was the author of the book "September Monkey." The law held the beneficiary lawfully admitted for permanent residence. (Priv. L. No. 554, 70 Stat. A24 (1956)) (H.R. Rep. No. 1324, 1st Sess.) (Sen. Rep. No. 1531, 2nd Sess.)QMOC

84th Cong., H.R. 2059, for the relief of Edward Patrick Cloonan. Beneficiary, a 20-year old native and citizen of Ireland, attempted to enter the United States for permanent residence. He was excluded as mentally deficient and subsequently entered as a visitor for medical treatment. He derived United States citizenship at birth, but was unable to meet the retention requirements for maintaining citizenship requiring him to enter the United States prior to his sixteenth birthday. He resided in the United States with his mother, a lawful permanent resident, and he had ten United States citizen siblings also residing in the United States. He was employed as a landscape laborer at a cemetery. The law held the beneficiary lawfully admitted for permanent residence upon the posting of a bond to overcome possibility of the beneficiary becoming a public charge. (Priv. L. No. 303, 69 Stat. A104 (1955)) (H.R. Rep. No. 776, 1st Sess.) (Sen. Rep. No. 944, 1st Sess.)-WHEL

84th Cong., H.R. 2072, for the relief of Julian Nowakowski or William Nowak (Novak). Beneficiary, a 45-year old subject of Poland and former United States citizen, entered the United States as a citizen employed in the Foreign Service of the Department of State. He had been born in the United States and was taken to Poland at the age of 11 where he remained 15 years, and returned to the United States. One year thereafter he returned to Poland and accepted employment with a British concern and was advised he should obtain Polish citizenship, which he did, thus losing his United States citizenship. It was stated he had posed as a United States citizen while employed by the Embassy because of threats of harm to his wife and their child. He reported his contacts to the American Embassy and later was advised by the Embassy that he should leave Poland. The law held the beneficiary lawfully admitted for permanent residence. (Priv. L. No. 555, 70 Stat. A24 (1956)) (H.R. Rep. No. 1325, 1st Sess.) (Sen. Rep. No. 1532, 2nd Sess.)-NVOL

84th Cong., H.R. 2087, for the relief of Erika Rambauske. Beneficiary, a 48-year old native of Germany and sister of a lawful permanent resident of the United States, was excluded from entry to the United States for a previous attack of insanity for which she was institutionalized two years. Her brother, a United States citizen, was employed as a scientist by the United States Air Force and was the sole support for the beneficiary. The law waived section 212(a)(3) relating to persons with attacks of insanity and provided for the posting of a bond to overcome possible public charge aspects. (Priv. L. No. 52, 69 Stat. A18 (1955)) (H.R. Rep. No. 255, 1st Sess.) (Sen. Rep. No. 325, 1st Sess.)-WHEL

84th Cong., H.R. 2242, for the relief of Kim Joong Yoon. Beneficiary, a 20-year old native and citizen of Korea, entered the United States as a student. The sponsor, a United States citizen, desired to educate him in memory of their son who was killed in action. The beneficiary had been an ammunition carrier for his son, and they planned to adopt him. The law held the beneficiary lawfully admitted for permanent residence. (Priv. L. No. 307,

69 Stat. A106 (1955)) (H.R. Rep. No. 797, 1st Sess.) (Sen. Rep. No. 948, 1st Sess.)-QMGN

84th Cong., H.R. 2261, for the relief of Giuseppe Carollo. Beneficiary, a 49-year old native and citizen of Italy and spouse of a United States citizen, was ineligible for a visa due to convictions at the age of 19 for theft of grass and theft from an orchard. There were five children of the marriage, three of whom were United States citizens. The law waived section 212(a)(9) relating to crimes involving moral turpitude. (Priv. L. No. 22, 69 Stat. A9 (1955)) (H.R. Rep. No. 192, 1st Sess.) (Sen. Rep. No. 326, 1st Sess.)-WCRF

84th Cong., H.R. 2339, for the relief of Monika Schefbanker. Beneficiary, a 10-year old native and citizen of Austria, was the stepchild of a United States citizen. The child was the illegitimate child of the spouse and was to be adopted by the United States citizen. The law held the beneficiary within sections 101(a)(27)(A) and 205 relating to natural-born children of a United States citizen. (Priv. L. No. 449, 69 Stat. A153 (1955)) (H.R. Rep. No. 1216, 1st Sess.) (Sen. Rep. No. 1293, 1st Sess.)-QIRA

84th Cong., H.R. 2345, for the relief of Jean Henri Buchet. Beneficiary, a 32-year old native and citizen of France, entered the United States as a returning permanent resident. It was discovered he had procured an entry document fraudulently. He was the son of a French Army officer and resided in France until 1944. In 1945 he was denounced as a German collaborator and was imprisoned. He was later released and fled France with the passport of a friend. He was condemned to death in absentia. The beneficiary later returned to France to stand trial and was exonerated. His spouse was a United States citizen with three United States citizen children. The law held the beneficiary lawfully admitted for permanent residence. (Priv. L. No. 558, 70 Stat. A25 (1956)) (H.R. Rep. No. 1375, 1st Sess.) (Sen. Rep. No. 1535, 2nd Sess.)-WCRF

84th Cong., H.R. 2354, for the relief of Basil Theodossiou. Beneficiary, a 25-year old native of Egypt, served in the British Army during World War II as a wireless operator. After discharge, he served on other ships and played a role in the rescue of the steamship *Greenville* by the *Ile de France* in 1953. It was learned the rescue took place only because the beneficiary, while aboard the *Greenville*, substituted a make-shift antenna for a broken one thus making contact with the other vessel. The House Committee Report noted the beneficiary's rescue was the subject of a story in the March 1954 Reader's Digest which reflected his decisive role during the affair. The law held the beneficiary within Public Law 203, 83rd Congress, Chapter 336 relating to eligibility to apply for a visa as a refugee under section 4(a)(7) of that Act notwithstanding the residence requirement for section 7(d)(2). (Priv. L. No. 27, 69 Stat. A10 (1955)) (H.R. Rep. No. 45, 1st Sess.) (Sen. Rep. No. 332, 1st Sess.)-QMGN

84th Cong., H.R. 2495, for the relief of Antoni Rajkowski. Beneficiary, a 29-year old native and citizen of Poland, entered the United States as a visitor to see his brother who had been involved in an auto accident and subsequently died. The mother, 10-year old brother and 14-year old sister, were admitted for permanent residence and were dependent on the beneficiary for support. The law held the beneficiary lawfully admitted for permanent residence. (Priv. L. No. 272, 69 Stat. A95 (1955)) (H.R. Rep. No. 699, 1st Sess.) (Sen. Rep. No. 803, 1st Sess.)-QMGN

84th Cong., H.R. 2788, for the relief of Miguel Sandoval-Michel (also known as Arturo Rodriguez-Gomez). Beneficiary, a 27-year old native and citizen of Mexico entered the United States as an agricultural laborer. He re-entered the United States illegally and was deported three times to Mexico and later found guilty of illegal entry after deportation. He was placed on probation and deported on the condition he not seek re-entry to the United States without permission. He subsequently entered the United States without the necessary application for entry. He was married to a United States citizen and they had two United States citizen children. The law waived sections 212(a)(17) and (19) relating to offenses for fraud and misrepresentation and re-entry of persons deported from the United States. (Priv. L. No. 425, 69 Stat. A145 (1955)) (H.R. Rep. No. 1149, 1st Sess.) (Sen. Rep. No. 1120, 1st Sess.)-WCRF

84th Cong., H.R. 2916, for the relief of Mrs. Elfrieda Schoeppe. Beneficiary, a 30-year old native of Austria and widow of a United States citizen serviceman, wished to accompany their two United States citizen children to the United States and reside with her in-laws. The law held the beneficiary eligible to immigrate as the immediate relative of a United States citizen. (Priv. L. No. 483, 69 Stat. A164 (1955)) (H.R. Rep. No. 1217, 1st Sess.) (Sen. Rep. No. 1296, 1st Sess.)-QIRW

84th Cong., H.R. 2949, for the relief of Jose Armando Quaresma. Beneficiary, a 25-year old native and citizen of Portugal, entered the United States as a seaman. He was inducted into the United States Army and served in Korea where he received the Purple Heart. He had tuberculosis while in the service and was treated in the United States. He was ineligible for special provisions relating to granting permanent residence on behalf of servicemen, because he did not reside in the United States one year prior to induction. The law held the beneficiary lawfully admitted for permanent residence provided a proper bond was posted to overcome possible public charge aspects. (Priv. L. No. 335, 69 Stat. A114 (1955)) (H.R. Rep. No. 1009, 1st Sess.) (Sen. Rep. No. 1064, 1st Sess.)-WHEL

84th Cong., H.R. 3075, for the relief of Virgil Won (also known as Virgilio Jackson). Beneficiary, a 34-year old native and citizen of Nicaragua of Chinese ancestry, was orphaned at an early age and brought to the United States in transit to China when he became ill and was placed in a boys' home, where he remained while in the United States eight years. He later proceeded to China where he became an interpreter for the United States Army in China and served two years as a parachutist and guerrilla warfare expert with the OSS in that country. He then was employed with General

Chennault's Air Transport Association in Formosa. He moved from Formosa and resided in Korea where he was employed with the United States Army in a civilian capacity. His application to the United States as a refugee was denied in Korea. The law held section 202(b) relating to visa chargeability inapplicable on behalf of the beneficiary. (Priv. L. No. 200, 69 Stat. A69 (1955)) (H.R. Rep. No. 406, 1st Sess.) (Sen. Rep. No. 664, 1st Sess.)-QMDE

84th Cong., H.R. 3857, for the relief of Constantin David, Paula Marie David, Claire Edmonde David, and Ariane Constance David. Beneficiaries, a 67-year old native of Turkey and citizen of France and 46-, 13-, and 10-year old natives and citizens of France, entered the United States as visitors. The male beneficiary was engaged in producing motion pictures in Europe and in the United States. He and his spouse later operated a private language school. An application for relief under section 244 relating to suspension of deportation was denied. The law held the beneficiaries lawfully admitted for permanent residence. (Priv. L. No. 583, 70 Stat. A34 (1956)) (H.R. Rep. No. 1114, 1st Sess.) (Sen. Rep. No. 1543, 2nd Sess.)-QMGN

84th Cong., H.R. 4039, for the relief of Julian, Dolores, Jaime, Dennis, Roldan, and Julian, Jr., Lizardo. Beneficiaries, natives and citizens of the Philippines, entered the United States as visitors. The adult male beneficiary was employed with the United States Department of Agriculture, Bureau of Animal Industry, as a veterinary meat inspector. The Department of Agriculture noted nine Filipino veterinarians were employed by their Meat Inspection Branch, and that they were "confronted with the perplexing problem of an insufficient number of veterinarians," and had been only able to employ 1400 qualified veterinarians. The law held the beneficiaries lawfully admitted for permanent residence. (Priv. L. No. 598, 70 Stat. A41 (1956)) (H.R. Rep. No. 1433, 1st Sess.) (Sen. Rep. No. 1566, 2nd Sess.)-QMOC

84th Cong., H.R. 4147, for the relief of Angelo DeVito. Beneficiary, a 59-year old native and citizen of Italy, was ineligible for a visa due to a conviction for theft and a conviction for assault with a deadly weapon. The latter offense was a result of the beneficiary threatening his wife's lover, and chasing him through the streets of town with a knife. His United States citizen brother owned a dairy bar, motel and restaurant in New York. The law waived section 212(a)(9) relating to crimes involving moral turpitude. (Priv. L. No. 348, 69 Stat. A119 (1955)) (H.R. Rep. No. 977, 1st Sess.) (Sen. Rep. No. 970, 1st Sess.)-WCRF

84th Cong., H.R. 4152, for the relief of Maria Pintos and her daughter, Eugenia Pintos. Beneficiaries, 45- and 10-year old natives and citizens of Greece, entered the United States as visitors, destined to the husband, an employee of the United Nations. Upon arrival, the beneficiary was told by her husband that he divorced her and remarried. The House Committee noted a detailed investigation of the beneficiary's husband was undertaken in light of the fact that he had not been divorced, and his second wife was entitled to diplomatic status, while the beneficiary did not have that status. The Chairman of the House Committee noted in a letter to the United States Ambassador to the United Nations, "It appears that this is a clear case of bigamy and perjury where prosecution seems to be impossible due to immunities with which Mr. Pintos is clothed. Simultaneously, two perfectly innocent persons...are made to suffer hardship." A later report from the Royal Greek Embassy stated the beneficiary was the lawful wife of Jerome Pintos. The law held the beneficiaries lawfully admitted for permanent residence. (Priv. L. No. 827, 70 Stat. A156 (1956)) (H.R. Rep. No. 2442, 2nd Sess.) (Sen. Rep. No. 2604, 2nd Sess.)-QMGN

84th Cong., H.R. 4544, for the relief of Andrew Carrigan. Beneficiary, a three-year old native of Germany, was adopted by United States citizens. The adoptive father was assigned with the United States Information Service in Saigon, Indochina and the family resided with him. The adoptive parents sought to allow the child to retain his eligibility to re-enter the United States as a permanent resident and thus be eligible to acquire sufficient time to qualify for the naturalization requirements. The law held the beneficiary eligible to retain a re-entry permit until he attained the age of 10 years or until the adoptive father was able to resume permanent residence in the United States. (Priv. L. No. 456, 69 Stat. A155 (1955)) (H.R. Rep. No. 1385, 1st Sess.) (Sen. Rep. No. 1298, 1st Sess.)-QPRP

84th Cong., H.R. 4548, for the relief of Michele Pica. Beneficiary, a 47-year old native and citizen of Italy, and spouse of a United States citizen, was ineligible for a visa due to a conviction for assault with a weapon at the age of 18. The incident involved an argument concerning the affections of a girl where the parties involved exchanged gunshots. He and his spouse had seven children, two of whom were United States citizens. The law waived section 212(a)(9) relating to crimes involving moral turpitude. (Priv. L. No. 524, 70 Stat. A14 (1956)) (H.R. Rep. No. 1386, 1st Sess.) (Sen. Rep. No. 1430, 2nd Sess.)-WCRF

84th Cong., H.R. 5041, for the relief of Mrs. Margaret Dows Thyberg. Beneficiary, a 50-year old native-born United States citizen, lost her citizenship by voting in a Swedish election. Her husband was a career diplomat holding the post of Swedish Minister to Portugal. The report noted Mrs. Thyberg's family established itself in the 17th century among the early settlers of Dutchess County, N.Y. where she owned a large estate. The law allowed the beneficiary to regain citizenship upon oath of allegiance to the United States (Priv. L. No. 763, 70 Stat. A119 (1956)) (H.R. Rep. No. 2206, 2nd Sess.) (Sen. Rep. No. 2341, 2nd Sess.)-NVOL

84th Cong., H.R. 5546, for the relief of Francisca Alemany. Beneficiary, a 32-year old native and citizen of Spain, was the daughter of permanent residents of the United States. The father of the beneficiary was an expert on the structure of the eye for special surgery, and was employed as a medical artist. The Committee on the Judiciary noted the enactment of the legislation would "serve as a recognition of the contribution to this country of the services of her father, who has recently been spoken of as the greatest expert on the physical structure of the eye for special surgery." The law held the beneficiary to be the minor child of lawful permanent residents of the United States. (Priv. L. No. 486, 69 Stat. A164 (1955)) (H.R. Rep. No. 1124, 1st Sess.) (Sen. Rep. No. 1137, 1st Sess.)-QPRF

84th Cong., H.R. 5870, for the relief of Jesajahu Braun. Beneficiary, a 27-year old native of Hungary and citizen of Israel, entered the United States as a visitor. His parents and five siblings died in the Auschwitz concentration camp. His surviving brothers, two of whom were United States citizens, resided in the United States. The law held the beneficiary lawfully admitted for permanent residence. (Priv. L. No. 528, 70 Stat. A15 (1956)) (H.R. Rep. No. 1392, 1st Sess.) (Sen. Rep. No. 1434, 2nd Sess.)-QMGN

84th Cong., H.R. 6363, for the relief of Edward Barnett. Beneficiary, a 69-year old native and citizen of England, and father of a United States citizen, was ineligible for a visa due to a conviction of embezzlement for which he served three months. He had been an officer of the British Red Cross seven years. The law waived section 212(a)(9) relating to crimes involving moral turpitude. (Priv. L. No. 570, 70 Stat. A29 (1956)) (H.R. Rep. No. 1411, 1st Sess.) (Sen. Rep. No. 1550, 2nd Sess.)-WCRF

84th Cong., H.R. 6613, for the relief of Yuji Doi and Mrs. Matsuyo Yamaoka Doi. Beneficiaries, 68- and 66-year old natives and citizens of Japan, were the parents of five children, four of whom were United States citizens and three of whom were sons serving during World War II. The female beneficiary had been lawfully admitted for permanent residence; but her husband was discovered not to have been entitled to a permanent resident visa. They had resided in Japan after 15 years residence in the United States. The law waived section 212(a)(17) relating to persons previously deported and allowed them to return to the United States under section 101(a)(27)(B) as returning permanent resident aliens. (Priv. L. No. 360, 69 Stat. A122 (1955)) (H.R. Rep. No. 1028, 1st Sess.) (Sen. Rep. No. 976, 1st Sess.)-QPRP

84th Cong., H.R. 6617, for the relief of Boris Kowerda. Beneficiary, a 47-year old native of Poland and spouse of a permanent resident alien, was ineligible for a visa due to a conviction at the age of 19 for premeditated manslaughter. At the age of 19 the beneficiary had "fired 6 fatal shots at the Soviet diplomatic representative in Poland, formerly one of the chief administrators of the Ural region of Russia, where most of the massacres of anti-Bolsheviks were perpetrated [and who was] allegedly a direct participant in the execution of the Czar and his family." His sentence of life imprisonment was commuted by the President of Poland after 10 years of labor. He had a seven-year old daughter who had also been admitted for permanent residence with her mother as Displaced Persons. The beneficiary had qualified as a Displaced Person but was found excludable for his manslaughter offense. The law waived section 212(a)(9) relating to crimes involving moral turpitude. (Priv. L. No. 572, 70 Stat. A29 (1956)) (H.R. Rep. No. 965, 1st Sess.) (Sen. Rep. No. 1588, 2nd Sess.)-WCRF

84th Cong., H.R. 6955, for the relief of Inna Hekker Grade. Beneficiary, a 31-year old native of the Soviet Union, entered the United States as a visitor. Private legislation on her behalf had previously conferred lawful permanent residence status. She was awarded a scholastic grant by the John Hay Whitney Foundation, but all recipients were required to be United States citizens. She had appeared before the Select Committee on Communist Aggression of the House of Representatives and submitted "valuable testimony." The law granted permanent residence retroactively to the date of the beneficiary's first entry to the United States. (Priv. L. No. 712, 70 Stat. A95 (1956)) (H.R. Rep. No. 1851, 2nd Sess.) (Sen. Rep. No. 2182, 2nd Sess.)-NXCP

84th Cong., H.R. 10088, for the relief of Rupert Waltl. Beneficiary, a 20-year old native of Germany, was admitted to the United States for permanent residence in 1951. Since 1956 he had been on active duty with the United States Navy and was considered to be a top-ranking bicyclist for competition in the Olympic games in Australia. He was one month short of being eligible for filing a petition for naturalization. The law exempted the beneficiary from the residence requirements for purposes of naturalization. (Priv. L. No. 824, 70 Stat. A155 (1956)) (H.R. Rep. No. 2443, 2nd Sess.) (Sen. Rep. No. 2606, 2nd Sess.)-NRES

84th Cong., H.R. 10984, for the relief of Nikolai E. Khokhlov. Beneficiary, a 34-year old native and citizen of the Soviet Union, entered the United States after defecting from the Soviet Union. He had served in the Soviet Army and later held the rank of captain in the Soviet Intelligence Service. He defected upon refusing a Soviet assignment to kill a Russian resistance leader in Frankfurt, Germany. The House Report noted he "rendered valuable service to United States agencies and congressional committees. He also contributed to the knowledge of the Western World of the methods of operation of the internal Communist conspiracy by publishing on two occasions extensive articles in the United States News World Report." The law held the beneficiary lawfully admitted for permanent residence and waived section 212(a)(28) relating to membership in Communist organizations. (Priv. L. No. 851, 70 Stat. A174 (1956)) (H.R. Rep. No. 2444, 2nd Sess.) (Sen. Rep. No. 2607, 2nd Sess.)-WXCP

84th Cong., S. 97, an omnibus bill for the relief of Barbara D. Colthurst, Pedro P. Dagamac and Edith Kahler. Beneficiary Colthurst, a 23-year old native of Canada and lawful permanent resident of the United States, had accumulated more than five years residence in the United States but because of a two year absence due to her father's employment abroad with the United States General Accounting Office, was unable to meet the physical presence requirement. Beneficiary Dagamac, a 51-year old native of the Philippines and lawful permanent resident of the United States, departed the United States for a civilian position with the United States Army in Japan. He did not obtain the approval of the Attorney General to allow absence over one year to count towards the continuous residence requirements of the law, although he appeared eligible for such a waiver. Beneficiary Kahler, a 42-year old native of Czechoslovakia and lawful permanent resident of the United States, was unable to meet the residence requirements for naturalization due to temporary absences from the United States while employed with United States Government. (Priv. L. No. 534, 70 Stat. A17 (1956)) (Sen. Rep. No. 813, 1st Sess.) (H.R. Rep. No. 1734, 2nd Sess.)-NRES

84th Cong., S. 129, for the relief of Miroslav Slovak. Beneficiary, a 25-year old native of Czechoslovakia, entered the United States on board a United States Air Force flight. He was one of a group of Czechoslovaks who commandeered a Czechoslovakian passenger airplane as its chief pilot, and used it to escape to the West Zone of Germany where he was granted asylum. The law held the beneficiary lawfully admitted for permanent residence and waived section 212(a)(28) relating to membership in the Communist Party. (Priv. L. No. 74, 69 Stat. A26 (1955)) (Sen. Rep. No. 65, 1st Sess.) (H.R. Rep. No. 673, 1st Sess.)-WXCP

84th Cong., S. 245, for the relief of Ahmet Haldun Koca Taskin Ursula and Jadwiga Milarski Goodman. Mr. Taskin, one of the beneficiaries and a native of Turkey, entered the United States as a student and later married a United States citizen and had one child. He claimed exemption from military service as a neutral alien, thus rendering him ineligible for a visa. The law waived section 212(a)(22) relating to persons who sought to evade military obligations. (Priv. L. No. 739, 70 Stat. A109 (1956)) (Sen. Rep. No. 101, 1st Sess.) (H.R. Rep. No. 2335, 2nd Sess.)-WXDD

84th Cong., S. 432, for the relief of Aniceto Sparagna. Beneficiary, a 41-year old native and citizen of Italy, entered the United States as a nonquota immigrant and as a minister of religion. He was found deportable as having obtained a visa by fraudulently claiming his destination to a church where he was no longer a member. His spouse was a United States citizen. The law held the beneficiary lawfully admitted for permanent residence. (Priv. L. No. 146, without the President's approval, 69 Stat. A51 (1955)) (Sen. Rep. No. 86, 1st Sess.) (H.R. Rep. No. 760, 1st Sess.)-WCRF

84th Cong., S. 884, for the relief of Gabor Lanyi. Beneficiary, an eight-year old native of Hungary, was ineligible for a visa due to a glandular disturbance which resulted in a Mongoloid condition. His father divorced the mother because she would not leave the child to come to the United States. Later they were remarried and both had permanent residence. The mother returned to Austria when the beneficiary's nurse became ill. The law waived sections 212(a)(1) and (4) relating to mental conditions and provided for a posting of a bond to overcome possible public charge aspects. (Priv. L. No. 396, 69 Stat. A136 (1955)) (Sen. Rep. No. 985, 1st Sess.) (H.R. Rep. No. 1517, 1st Sess.)-WHEL

84th Cong., S. 1044, for the relief of Edward Naarits. Beneficiary, a 53-year old native and citizen of Estonia, was employed on a United States vessel for five years. His service on shore for two years made him ineligible to take advantage of provisions for special naturalization benefits based on service aboard United States vessels. The law waived the timeperiod limitations under section 330(a)(2) and allowed the beneficiary to file a petition for naturalization within one year of the Act. (Priv. L. No. 469, 69 Stat. A159 (1955)) (Sen. Rep. No. 191, 1st Sess.) (H.R. Rep. No. 1246, 1st Sess.)-NMSC

84th Cong., S. 1627, for the relief of Alexander Orlov and his wife, Maria Orlov. Beneficiaries, 60- and 52-year old natives of Russia, were admitted to the United States as Soviet diplomats. The male beneficiary held several positions with the Soviet Government and was a counterintelligence officer who broke from the Communist Party in 1938 when in Spain as an adviser of the Politburo to the Spanish Republican Government. His other occupations included Chief of the Information Service of the Supreme Finance Council of the Soviet Union 1917-1918, service in the Red Army two years, and Deputy Chief of the Economic administration of the NKVD. He broke with the Stalin regime and the Communist Party during his service in Spain in 1938 and then entered the United States The female beneficiary had also been employed with various departments of the Soviet Government. An article published by the beneficiary included in Life Magazine in 1953 was titled "The Ghastly Secrets of Stalin's Power," and his book was entitled, "The Secret History of Stalin's Crimes." The Department of State noted in its report "the arrest or deportation of Alexander Orlov, who is a well-known Soviet defector, would have a seriously detrimental impact on the United States defector program. Such action could be used by propagandists of the Soviet-bloc governments to demonstrate that the United States is indifferent and even hostile to persons from the Soviet orbit seeking asylum." It was also stated the beneficiaries cooperated with various United States Government agencies in anti-Communist activities. The law held the beneficiaries lawfully admitted for permanent residence. (Priv. L. No. 810, 70 Stat. A149 (1956)) (Sen. Rep. No. 2075, 2nd Sess.) (H.R. Rep. No. 2654, 2nd Sess.)-WXCP

84th Cong., S. 2088, for the relief of Ladislav Mencl. Beneficiary, a 21-year old native of Czechoslovakia who escaped to West Germany Christmas Day 1951, entered the United States Army. He bailed out of a plane on a routine jump and sustained a broken back and injuries to his left leg. The law held the beneficiary lawfully admitted for permanent residence. (Priv. L. No. 446, 69 Stat. A152 (1955)) (Sen. Rep. No. 1207, 1st Sess.)-QMDE

85th Cong., H.R. 1451, for the relief of Cecelia Vaccaro. Beneficiary, a 53-year old native-born United States citizen, expatriated by voting in an election in Italy. She claimed that she lived in an isolated area and was unaware of citizenship requirements. The law allowed the beneficiary to regain citizenship through an oath of allegiance within one year of enactment. (Priv. L. No. 43, 71 Stat. A19 (1957)) (H.R. Rep. No. 232, 1st Sess.) (Sen. Rep. No. 378, 1st Sess.)-NVOL

85th Cong., H.R. 1677, for the relief of Gilbert B. Mar. Beneficiary, a 27-year old native and citizen of China, was admitted for permanent residence. He sought employment with General Dynamics Corporation engaged in the production planning of submarine construction work. The Senate Committee Report noted it was not their policy to retroactively grant permanent residence for naturalization purposes but "in view of his potential employment in an industry vital to the United States Government...this is warranted." The law held the beneficiary lawfully admitted for permanent residence retroactively. (Priv. L. No. 304, 71 Stat. A120 (1957)) (H.R. Rep. No. 628, 1st Sess.) (Sen. Rep. No. 1135, 1st Sess.)-NRES

85th Cong., H.R. 1757, for the relief of Nicola Marcello. Beneficiary, a 52-year old native and citizen of Italy, resided in the United States 22 years. He was found deportable for convictions involving larceny and burglary, assault to rob and other offenses. He was later pardoned by the Governor of Pennsylvania. His four United States citizen siblings resided in the United States. The law held the beneficiary a returning permanent resident under section 101(a)(27)(B). (Priv. L. No. 15, 71 Stat. A7 (1957)) (H.R. Rep. No. 166, 1st Sess.) (Sen. Rep. No. 177, 1st Sess.)-QPRP

85th Cong., H.R. 3184, for the relief of Gordon Broderick. Beneficiary, a 24-year old native and citizen of Canada, entered the United States as a United States citizen, having been adopted by United States citizen parents. During college training it was discovered he was not a citizen. He served four years with the United States Air Force. The Senate Report noted its reluctance to grant retroactive permanent residence but in view of his erroneous admission as a United States citizen, relief would be granted. The law held the beneficiary lawfully admitted for permanent residence retroactively. (Priv. L. No. 212, 71 Stat. A82 (1957)) (H.R. Rep. No. 856, 1st Sess.) (Sen. Rep. No. 936, 1st Sess.)-NMSC

85th Cong., H.R. 4854, for the relief of Victoria Galea. Beneficiary, a 54-year old native of Malta and citizen of Great Britain, sought to enter the United States with her sister as a nonquota immigrant. She was handicapped by a hearing deficiency and entirely dependent upon her sister and brother who was a United States citizen. The law held section 202(c)(1) relating to visa chargeability inapplicable on behalf of the beneficiary. (Priv. L. No. 169, 71 Stat. A105 (1957)) (H.R. Rep. No. 857, 1st Sess.) (Sen. Rep. No. 950, 1st Sess.)-QPRF

85th Cong., H.R. 7729, for the relief of August Widmer. Beneficiary, a 54-year old native and citizen of Switzerland, was sponsored for admission to the United States by a priest in Colorado. The beneficiary, also a priest, was to assist the pastor in view of the "critical shortage of Catholic clergymen in the United States." The law waived section 212(a)(6) relating to those afflicted with tuberculosis and provided a suitable posting of bond to overcome possible public charge aspects. (Priv. L. No. 507, 72 Stat. A72

(1958)) (H.R. Rep. No. 1649, 2nd Sess.) (Sen. Rep. No. 1775, 2nd Sess.)-WHEL

85th Cong., H.R. 7826, for the relief of Israel Baird Poskanzer. Beneficiary, a 37-year old native-born United States citizen, expatriated on the basis of service in the Israeli Air Force Reserves. He had also served in the United States Army Air Corps from 1942 until 1945 when he moved to Israel to attend school. The law allowed the beneficiary to regain his United States citizenship by taking an oath of allegiance to the United States. (Priv. L. No. 623, 72 Stat. A128 (1958)) (H.R. Rep. No. 1853, 2nd Sess.) (Sen. Rep. No. 2140, 2nd Sess.)-NVOL

85th Cong., H.R. 8014, for the relief of Edith Dorn. Beneficiary, a 52-year old native and citizen of Germany, was ineligible for a visa due to a conviction for embezzlement of property. Her admission to the United States was sponsored by a writer-producer for Warner Brothers who was to employ her as an office worker. The law waived section 212(a)(9) relating to crimes involving moral turpitude. (Priv. L. No. 740, 72 Stat. A200 (1958)) (H.R. Rep. No. 2409, 2nd Sess.) (Sen. Rep. No. 2433, 2nd Sess.)-WCRF

85th Cong., H.R. 8348, for the relief of Michael Romanoff. Beneficiary, a 65-year old adult male and spouse of a United States citizen, entered the United States after the age of nine, and was placed in a Juvenile Asylum for lack of guardianship. The beneficiary traveled abroad, and thereafter sought entry as a United States citizen but he was excluded and found deportable. He escaped custody and sought re-entry on several occasions as a stowaway. He was unable to be deported because there was no documentation as to his country of birth. He and his spouse were principal owners of Romanoff's Restaurant in California. The Senate Report noted its reluctance to retroactively grant permanent residence; but it stated that because the beneficiary consistently maintained birth in the United States and attempted to establish United States citizenship, favorable action was taken. The law held the beneficiary lawfully admitted for permanent residence retroactively. (Priv. L. No. 401, 72 Stat. A30 (1958)) (H.R. Rep. No. 1385, 2nd Sess.) (Sen. Rep. No. 1450, 2nd Sess.)-QMGN

85th Cong., H.R. 8374, for the relief of Virginia Ray Potts. Beneficiary, a 44-year old native-born United States citizen, married a Canadian citizen and permanent resident of the United States in 1936. After their marriage, she went to India with her husband who was employed in that country. In 1942 she returned to the United States after being evacuated because of war. Her husband was transferred to South Africa and she sought to travel there on a United States passport. The passport was not issued, because it was determined that her travel was nonessential. She then proceeded to renounce her citizenship in Canada for the purposes of obtaining a Canadian passport to be with her husband. Her parents resided in the United States, her father being a Member of Congress. The law allowed the beneficiary to regain United States citizenship upon an oath of allegiance to the United

States. (Priv. L. No. 310, 71 Stat. A123 (1957)) (H.R. Rep. No. 1069, 1st Sess.) (Sen. Rep. No. 1138, 1st Sess.)-NVOL

85th C., H.R. 12903, for the relief of Wolfgang Stresemann. Beneficiary, a 54-year old native of Germany and naturalized United States citizen resided in Germany where he was in jeopardy of losing his citizenship because of prolonged absence abroad. He was employed as the chief official of the Radio Symphony Orchestra in Berlin in which his work was of "direct and substantial benefit to the interests of the United States," according to the Department of State. His wife and son as well as one of his parents were United States citizens. He had been was on assignment in Germany as a historical advisor for a motion picture based on the life of his father, Gustav Stresemann, the former Chancellor of Germany. The law held section 352(a)(1) relating to residence abroad inapplicable to the beneficiary provided he return to the United States within three years of enactment of the legislation. (Priv. L. No. 616, 72 Stat. A126 (1958)) (H.R. Rep. No. 2252, 2nd Sess.) (Sen. Rep. No. 2182, 2nd Sess.)-NRTN

85th Cong., S. 530, for the relief of Shun Wen Lung (also known as Van Long and Van S. Lung). Beneficiary, a 31-year old native and citizen of China, entered the United States as a representative of the Chinese Nationalist Government. He studied in the United States and owned the Peking Palace Restaurant in Washington, D.C. His father was Governor of Yunnan Province 1924-1945, and later served as a puppet figure in Communist China. One of his sons was executed by the Communists for leading an insurrection against them. The beneficiary's father and Chiang Kai-shek became disassociated with each other shortly after the war, and he was removed from his post as Governor and moved to Hong Kong. He later returned to China. The beneficiary was a lieutenant colonel in the Chinese Nationalist Army 1944-1945 and acted as liaison between that Army and the United States until his entry to the United States His application for relief under the Displaced Persons Act of 1948 was denied. The Senate Committee report stated there was information that he was "completely cooperative with the United States Armed Forces." The law held the beneficiary lawfully admitted for permanent residence. (Priv. L. No. 84, 71 Stat. A36 (1957)) (Sen. Rep. No. 148, 1st Sess.) (H.R. Rep. No. 723, 1st Sess.)-QMDE

85th Cong., S. 660, for the relief of Ursula Rosa Pazdro. Beneficiary, a 22-year old native and citizen of Germany and spouse of a United States citizen serving in the Armed Forces, was ineligible for a visa due to convictions for petty larceny. She gave birth to twins, one month old, and had two other children (ages two and one) who were temporarily residing with their paternal grandparents in the United States. The court waived section 212(a)(9) relating to crimes involving moral turpitude. (Priv. L. No. 253, 71 Stat. A97 (1957)) (Sen. Rep. No. 422, 1st Sess.) (H.R. Rep. No. 1081, 1st Sess.)-WCRF

85th Cong., S. 701, for the relief of Karl Eigil Engedal Hansen and his wife, Else Viola Agnethe Hansen, and their minor child, Jessie Engedal Hansen. Beneficiaries, a 34-year old couple and 11-year old child, natives and citizens of Denmark, entered the United States as visitors. They had one United States citizen child, age three. Their occupation was as acrobats on tour in the United States. They were denied immigrant visas because the male beneficiary had previously forged a birth date. The incident occurred in order to change the age of a member of the troupe in order to work in the United States. The law waived section 212(a)(9) relating to crimes involving moral turpitude. (Priv. L. No. 133, 71 Stat. A52 (1957)) (Sen. Rep. No. 152, 1st Sess.) (H.R. Rep. No. 731, 1st Sess.)-WCRF

85th Cong., S. 803, for the relief of Claudio Guillen. Beneficiary, a 33-year old native and citizen of France, was admitted to the United States as a permanent resident and requested relief from military service in 1943 as a neutral alien on the basis of his dual citizenship from Spain. He later enlisted in the Free French Forces in which he served from 1943 until 1945. His father was a lawful permanent resident and his sister a United States citizen. The beneficiary was employed at Princeton University. In approving the legislation the Committee noted, "while it is the general policy of the committee not to look with favor upon bills which remove the bar to naturalization...in the instant case the alien actually enlisted in the Allied Forces...and thereafter served for over two years during which time he saw combat action." The law waived the ground of exclusion relating to persons who claim exemption from military service and waived the bar to naturalization. (Priv. L. No. 464, 72 Stat. A56 (1958)) (Sen. Rep. No. 1307, 2nd Sess.) (H.R. Rep. No. 1819, 2nd Sess.)-NXDD

85th Cong., S. 1175, for the relief of Helene Cordery Hall. Beneficiary, a 37-year old native of Poland and spouse of a United States citizen, entered the United States as a visitor. She was unable to adjust status to permanent resident because her citizen husband disappeared, and she did not have documents to demonstrate their marriage. The law held the beneficiary lawfully admitted for permanent residence. (Priv. L. No. 317, 71 Stat. A125 (1957)) (Sen. Rep. No. 627, 1st Sess.) (H.R. Rep. No. 1090, 1st Sess.)-QIRW

85th Cong., S. 1290, for the relief of Lee-Ana Roberts. Beneficiary, a three-year old native and citizen of Canada, was paroled into the United States with her United States citizen adoptive parents and their five other adopted children who were admitted for permanent residence. She was not eligible for a visa because she was 50 percent Japanese and visas for that country were oversubscribed. The law held the beneficiary lawfully admitted for permanent residence. (Priv. L. No. 271, 71 Stat. A106 (1957)) (Sen. Rep. No. 629, 1st Sess.) (H.R. Rep. No. 1093, 1st Sess.)-QIER

85th Cong., S. 1456, for the relief of Refugio Guerrero-Monje. Beneficiary, a 32-year old native and citizen of Mexico and father of six United States citizen children, entered the United States on parole. He had previously made 20 illegal entries. The beneficiary was convicted of statutory rape, and he later married a woman who became a United States citizen. According to the Senate Committee the beneficiary was the "sole support of his family and were he required to depart from the United States, it is stated that they would suffer severe economic hardship." The law held the beneficiary lawfully admitted for permanent residence. (Priv. L. No. 321, 71 Stat. A126 (1957)) (Sen. Rep. No. 794, 1st Sess.) (H.R. Rep. No. 1250, 1st Sess.)-WCRF

85th Cong., S. 1519, for the relief of Isaac Lidji, Henry Isaac Lidji, and Sylvio Isaac Gattegno. Beneficiaries, 64-, 27-, and 68-year old natives of Turkey, Egypt, and Greece, respectively, entered the United States as visitors. The beneficiaries owned a department store in Cairo, Egypt and could not safely return to that country because of their Jewish faith. It was further noted that the Egyptian Government confiscated certain of their holdings. The law held the beneficiaries lawfully admitted for permanent residence as refugee-escapees under section 15 of the Act of September 11, 1957. (Priv. L. No. 378, 72 Stat. A20 (1958)) (Sen. Rep. No. 492, 1st Sess.) (H.R. Rep. No. 1362, 2nd Sess.)-QMGN

85th Cong., S. 1578, for the relief of Hovhannes H. Haidostian. Beneficiary, a 37-year old native of Turkey, entered the United States as a visitor. He was subsequently employed with the library of the University of Southern California. A United States citizen brother also resided in the United States. According to the Senate Committee, the beneficiary rendered "valuable services" to a United States Government Agency. The law held the beneficiary lawfully admitted for permanent residence. (Priv. L. No. 394, 72 Stat. A27 (1958)) (Sen. Rep. No. 1215, 2nd Sess.) (H.R. Rep. No. 1652, 2nd Sess.)-QMDE

85th Cong., S. 1782, for the relief of Carolina M. Gomes. Beneficiary, a 55-year old native and citizen of Portugal, was unable to derive citizenship from her father's naturalization because she did not enter the United States during her minority. She was married to a United States citizen 17 years but was divorced. She remained in Portugal during her adult years to care for her ill mother. Her four United States citizen brothers contributed to her support. The House Committee noted reluctance to grant full restoration of citizenship to the beneficiary as was provided in the Senate measure, but that there was "sufficient equity to warrant placing her in a position to enter the United States for permanent residence, thereby giving her an opportunity to regain her United States citizenship through the naturalization process." The law held the beneficiary entitled to the status of a nonquota immigrant.. (Priv. L. No. 594, 72 Stat. A116 (1958)) (Sen. Rep. No. 1444, 2nd Sess.) (H.R. Rep. No. 2209, 2nd Sess.)-NCOD

85th Cong., S. 1833, for the relief of Janos Schreiner. Beneficiary, an 81-year old native of Austria-Hungary and citizen of Hungary, desired to immigrate to the United States with his spouse. His stepdaughter conferred immigration benefits upon her mother; however, the beneficiary, as the stepfather, was not entitled to benefits. It was stated the beneficiary was "old, ill, and destitute" and his wife would not immigrate without him. The law held the beneficiary within section 101(b)(2) as the natural father of a United States citizen. (Priv. L. No. 105, 71 Stat. A42 (1957)) (Sen. Rep. No. 356, 1st Sess.) (H.R. Rep. No. 753, 1st Sess.)-QIRM

85th Cong., S. 2095, for the relief of Vaclav Uhlik, Marta Uhlik, Vaclav Uhlik, Jr., and Eva Uhlik. Beneficiaries, a family, ages 35, 30, 9 and 7, were natives and citizens of Czechoslovakia and entered the United States as visitors. They escaped from Czechoslovakia in a homemade tank the male beneficiary constructed from an old British command car which took three years to build. They entered the United States to publicize their escape and raise funds for Radio Free Europe. The law held the beneficiaries lawfully admitted for permanent residence. (Priv. L. No. 282, 71 Stat. A109 (1957)) (Sen. Rep. No. 751, 1st Sess.) (H.R. Rep. No. 1118, 1st Sess.)-QMDE

85th Cong., S. 2168, for the relief of Armas Edvin Jansson-Viik. Beneficiary, a 54-year old native and citizen of Finland, entered the United States for permanent residence but was found ineligible to immigrate because he claimed exemption from military service. He was married to a United States citizen and had four brothers residing in the United States, two of whom served in the Armed Forces. The law held the beneficiary lawfully admitted for permanent residence. The bill specifically did not waive section 315 prohibiting petitioning for United States citizenship. (Priv. L. No. 465, 72 Stat. A56 (1958)) (Sen. Rep. No. 1268, 2nd Sess.) (H.R. Rep. No. 1783, 2nd Sess.)-WXDD

85th Cong., S. 2301, for the relief of Genevieve M. Scott Bell. Beneficiary, a 34-year old native of England and United States citizen, resided abroad with her father, a career Foreign Service Officer. She attended the University of Virginia and in 1947 married a British subject. They had one child who did not derive citizenship because the beneficiary lacked the requisite residence in the United States to transmit citizenship. Her husband died in 1957, and she returned to the United States. The law deemed the beneficiary to have met the residence requirements under section 301(a)(7) for the purposes of transmitting United States citizenship to her child. (Priv. L. No. 439, 72 Stat. A47 (1958)) (Sen. Rep. No. 1196, 2nd Sess.) (H.R. Rep. No. 1789, 2nd Sess.)-NCOD

85th Cong., S. 2469, for the relief of Dr. Brant Bonner. Beneficiary, a 48-year old native of Canada and United States citizen, lost citizenship by prolonged residence abroad. He was in the United States Marine Corps during World War II and in 1947 returned to Canada as a professor at the University of Western Ontario. During residence in Canada, he continued to be active with the United States Marine Corps Reserve, and made frequent entries to the United States The law allowed the beneficiary to be reinstated to United States citizenship by taking an oath of allegiance to the United States. (Priv. L. No. 771, 72 Stat. A214 (1958)) (Sen. Rep. No. 2394, 2nd Sess.)-NRTN

85th Cong., S. 2935, for the relief of Mary Louise Shields Wilkinson. Beneficiary, a 37-year old native-born United States citizen, resided abroad for substantial periods of time, and was unable to transmit United States citizenship to her two children born abroad. In 1936 she went to China where her father served as District Attorney to the United States Court. She returned to the United States with her parents in 1942, and then went to Cuba and married a Cuban citizen. Her husband was involved in the advertising business and was also a correspondent for Columbia Broadcasting System. The law deemed the residence abroad with her father as an employee of the United States Government to be physical presence in the United States for purposes of section 201(g), thereby allowing her to transmit United States citizenship to her children. (Priv. L. No. 631, 72 Stat. A131 (1958)) (Sen. Rep. No. 1773, 2nd Sess.) (H.R. Rep. No. 2369, 2nd Sess.)-NCOD

85th Cong., S. 2936, for the relief of Feofania Bankevitz. Beneficiary, a 59-year old native and citizen of Russia, desired to immigrate with her parents who were ages 83 and 78. The beneficiary was ineligible for a visa due to a tubercular condition. Her father was blind and the mother was also afflicted with tuberculosis, but was able to obtain a waiver under the law as the parent of a United States citizen. It was stated that because of the advanced ages of the parents, the beneficiary's assistance would be helpful to them. The law waived section 212(a)(6) relating to persons afflicted with tuberculosis and provided for the posting of a bond to overcome possible public charge aspects. (Priv. L. No. 674, 72 Stat. A146 (1958)) (Sen. Rep. No. 1634, 2nd Sess.) (H.R. Rep. No. 2370, 2nd Sess.)-WHEL

85th Cong., S. 2989, for the relief of Salvador Miranda. Beneficiary, a 35-year old native-born United States citizen, lost his citizenship by serving in the Mexican Army and accepting employment with the Mexican Police Force. He was taken to Mexico at the age of eight by his Mexican citizen parents, and resided in that country thereafter until attempting surreptitiously to enter the United States. His next entry was attempted as a United States citizen but he was held excludable. He later married a United States citizen, and had one child of that marriage. The beneficiary was also fined for having transported an alien who was in the United States illegally. The law held the beneficiary lawfully admitted for permanent residence. (Priv. L. No. 634, 72 Stat. A132 (1958)) (Sen. Rep. No. 1900, 2nd Sess.) (H.R. Rep. No. 2373, 2nd Sess.)-NVOL

85th Cong., S. 3060, for the relief of Romulo A. Manriquez. Beneficiary, a 46-year old native and citizen of the Philippines, entered the United States as a visitor. He was inducted into the United States Army and served five years, attaining the rank of Colonel. He was awarded the Legion of Merit and the Presidential Unit Citation with two clusters. He was notified by the Department of the Army that he was erroneously granted status in the Army. It was learned that the officer who inducted him did not have the authority to induct or grant such commissions. While in the United States, the beneficiary attended school and was employed as a waiter at the Metropolitan Club in Washington, D.C. The Senate Committee noted it did not usually recommend permanent residence as of the date of entry, but the beneficiary had filed an application for naturalization prior to the naturalization commissioner being returned to the United States from the Philippines. The report also stated that "Because of the unusual circumstances in this case, and the beneficiary's long and honorable service with the Army of the United States, the committee feels that the beneficiary should be granted the status of a lawful permanent resident..." The law held the beneficiary lawfully admitted for permanent residence. (Priv. L. No. 513, 72 Stat. A74 (1958)) (Sen. Rep. No. 1566, 2nd Sess.) (H.R. Rep. No. 1992, 2nd Sess.)-QMGN

85th Cong., S. 3219, for the relief of Mrs. Margaret Graham Bonnalie. Beneficiary, a 46-year old native of England and naturalized United States citizen, was in jeopardy of losing her citizenship by prolonged absences abroad. She was first married to a United States citizen, Hubert Scott-Paine, the pioneer of PT boats. Upon his death in 1954, she returned to England to settle the estate and later married a native of England. They planned to return to the United States when her husband retired. The Department of State advised there was no objection to the bill: "There have been compelling reasons for her residence in England since 1953. She has kept her money and property in this country. She has maintained ties with this country...She appears to be a true and loyal citizen of the United States." The law deemed section 352(a)(1) inapplicable to the beneficiary, thereby allowing her to prolong her stay in England. (Priv. L. No. 729, 72 Stat. A196 (1958)) (Sen. Rep. No. 1992, 2nd Sess.) (H.R. Rep. No. 2603, 2nd Sess.)-NRTN

85th Cong., S. 3221, for the relief of Erika Margaretha Zintl Pearce. Beneficiary, a 27-year old native of Czechoslovakia and citizen of the United States, was in jeopardy of losing her citizenship by prolonged residence abroad. She had derived United States citizenship through her mother upon entry to the United States in 1932, and resided in the United States until 1954 when she departed for England to attend school. The beneficiary was two years short of being eligible to take advantage of certain retention of citizenship requirements. The law deemed the beneficiary within the purview of section 354(5) of the Act allowing her to have resided in the United States the requisite period of years. (Priv. L. No. 730, 72 Stat. A196 (1958)) (Sen. Rep. No. 2111, 2nd Sess.) (H.R. Rep. No. 2604, 2nd Sess.)-NRTN

86th Cong., H.R. 1422, for the relief of Alessandro Maraessa. Beneficiary, a 55-year old native and citizen of Italy, had been entitled to a nonquota visa. The beneficiary was ineligible for a visa due to a conviction for assault with a dangerous weapon, a pitchfork. A United States brother resided in the United States. The law waived Section 212(a)(9) of the act relating to crimes involving moral turpitude. (Priv. L. No. 424, 74 Stat. A76 (1960)) (H.R. Rep. No. 1700, 2nd Sess.) (Sen. Rep. No. 1786, 2nd Sess.)-WCRF

86th Cong., H.R. 1705, for the relief of Louis J. DeWinter and Simone H. DeWinter. Beneficiaries, a 38-year old native of the Netherlands and a 34-year old native of French Morocco, both naturalized United States citizens, were in jeopardy of losing United States citizenship through residence abroad. The male beneficiary accepted a position with N.V. Leo DeWinter & Company in the Netherlands, which was involved in the manufacture and sales of processed milk. The firm was wholly owned by United States citizens, and the male beneficiary was to preserve and look after the interests of the stockholders. They had three United States citizen children. The law allowed the beneficiaries to reside abroad by deeming section 352 inapplicable so long as they established residence in the United States within seven years or within one year of the termination of the beneficiary's employment. (Priv. L. No. 125, 73 Stat. A56 (1959)) (H.R. Rep. No. 349, 1st Sess.) (Sen. Rep. No. 642, 1st Sess.)-NRTN

86th Cong., H.R. 2645, for the relief of Jesus Cruz-Figueroa. Beneficiary, a 35-year old native and citizen of Mexico, was formerly a permanent resident of the United States residing in the country 14 years and then returned to Mexico. He was married to a United States citizen and had four United States citizen children. The beneficiary had been excluded as a person who departed the United States during time of war to evade service in the Armed Forces. The beneficiary's family received public assistance, and although the House Committee noted its reluctance to approve such legislation, it acted favorably based on the hardship which would be caused to the beneficiary's citizen family. The law canceled deportation proceedings against the beneficiary. (Priv. L. No. 349, 74 Stat. A48 (1960)) (H.R. Rep. No. 1349, 2nd Sess.) (Sen. Rep. No. 1476, 2nd Sess.)-WXDD

86th Cong., H.R. 2944, for the relief of Luciano Di Franco. Beneficiary, a 33-year old native and citizen of Italy, received a preference petition as an ironwork specialist. He was ineligible for a visa due to a conviction for rape in Italy which was later pardoned. His parents and sister were admitted for permanent residence, and another sister was a United States citizen. The law waived section 212(a) (9) relating to crimes involving moral turpitude. (Priv. L. No. 432, 74 Stat. A78 (1960)) (H.R. Rep. No. 1806, 2nd Sess.) (Sen. Rep. No. 1794, 2nd Sess.)-WCRF

86th Cong., H.R. 2946, for the relief of Cecil E. Finley. Beneficiary, a 47-year old native-born United States citizen, expatriated himself by service in the Canadian military for four years. He later entered the United States claiming to be a United States citizen and was found deportable. He sought reinstatement of citizenship under preserving clauses of the Nationality Act of 1940, but the court found him ineligible to file a petition due to his deportability. He was also ineligible for a visa due to convictions for setting fire to a truck and theft of an automobile battery. He had two siblings residing in the United States as citizens. The law held the beneficiary lawfully admitted for permanent residence. (Priv. L. No. 200, 73 Stat. A88 (1959)) (H.R. Rep. No. 751, 1st Sess.) (Sen. Rep. No. 847, 1st Sess.)-WCRF

86th Cong., H.R. 3534, for the relief of Epifanio Trupiano. Beneficiary, a 30-year old native and citizen of Italy, resided in the United States illegally four years and was deported to Italy. His spouse and child were United States citizens. He was found ineligible for a visa due to institutionalization in a mental hospital which was later vacated by the courts. The law waived section 212(a) (3) relating to mental health conditions and provided for the posting of a bond to overcome possible public charge aspects. (Priv. L. No. 399, 74 Stat. A65 (1960)) (H.R. Rep. No. 1807, 2nd Sess.) (Sen. Rep. No. 1704, 2nd Sess.)-WHEL

86th Cong., H.R. 4242, for the relief of certain aliens. Beneficiaries, 18 individuals comprising two households, were members of the family of the Patriarch of the Church of the East, a United States citizen. The bill provided the beneficiaries to be considered nonquota immigrants as members of the family of a minister of a religious denomination. The beneficiaries were natives of Turkey, Iran, Israel, Cyprus, and Lebanon. The following information was provided by the House Committee: "The Church of the East is one of the oldest Christian churches in the world. Its ancient home was Turkey and when driven from that country in 1915, the church moved to Iran, where it remained until 1933. At that time its headquarters was moved to Cyprus. The patriarch desires to move the church's permanent headquarters to the United States. While the members of a patriarchal family are not in church orders, they are looked upon by the members of the church to set an example in their life and their faith, the patriarch delegates churchwork to the family members...Because of the uniqueness of the patriarchal family system in the Church of the East, it is stated that it is imperative for the work of the patriarch himself to have his family in the United States." The patriarch was a naturalized citizen and held his position with the church 39 years. The law held the beneficiaries eligible for nonquota visas under sections 101(a) (27) (F) and 204. (Priv. L. No. 122, 73 Stat. A55 (1959)) (H.R. Rep. No. 307, 1st Sess.) (Sen. Rep. No. 603, 1st Sess.)-QMGN

86th Cong., H.R. 4834, for the relief of Giuseppe Antonio Turchi. Beneficiary, a 25-year old native and citizen of Italy, was found eligible for admission to the United States under the Refugee Relief Act of 1953. However, his visa number was allocated to another person by the same name erroneously, and the Act expired before another visa could be issued. The law held the beneficiary eligible for a nonquota immigrant and admission to the United States for permanent residence. (Priv. L. No. 337, 74 Stat. A42 (1960)) (H.R. Rep. No. 1371, 2nd Sess.) (Sen. Rep. No. 1458, 2nd Sess.)-QIRM

86th Cong., H.R. 5645, for the relief of Christopher J. Mulligan. Beneficiary, a 27-year old native and citizen of Ireland, was admitted to the

United States for permanent residence, and in 1953 claimed exemption from military service under a treaty between the United States and Ireland. In 1956 he was inducted into the United States Army and served through 1959. His only relatives, parents, a brother and sister were residents and citizens of the United States. The law deemed section 315 inapplicable to the beneficiary. (Priv. L. No. 209, 73 Stat. A91 (1959)) (H.R. Rep. No. 754, 1st Sess.) (Sen. Rep. No. 948, 1st Sess.)-NXDD

86th Cong., H.R. 5910, for the relief of Zelda Glick. Beneficiary, a 31-year old native of Latvia and permanent resident of the United States, was unable to automatically derive United States citizenship by her father's naturalization because she had reached her 18th birthday four months prior to the naturalization. The beneficiary was employed with the United States Army twelve years and was unable to go through the regular petition process by return to the United States, because it would jeopardize her civil service status benefits. Additionally, she would have to wait four years before submission of an application, and meet the six month residence requirements within a State for naturalization. The law held section 314 inapplicable to the beneficiary and deemed her to have acquired derivative citizenship from the naturalization of her father. (Priv. L. No. 210, 73 Stat. A91 (1959)) (H.R. Rep. No. 866, 1st Sess.) (Sen. Rep. No. 949, 1st Sess.)-NCOD

86th Cong., H.R. 6804, for the relief of Mary Elizabeth Tighe Crespo. Beneficiary, a 23-year old native and citizen of Ireland and spouse of a United States citizen, was found ineligible for a visa due to affliction with epilepsy from childhood. She and her husband had two United States citizen children and the illness was "well controlled by drugs." The law waived section 212 (a) (4) relating to mental health conditions and provided for the posting of a bond to overcome possible public charge aspects. (Priv. L. No. 438, 74 Stat. A80 (1960)) (H.R. Rep. No. 1813, 2nd Sess.) (Sen. Rep. No. 1799, 2nd Sess.)-WHEL

86th Cong., H.R. 6886, for the relief of Liliana Caprara. Beneficiary, a 36-year old native and citizen of Italy, was lawfully admitted for permanent residence. She was married to a United States citizen four years, but the marriage was terminated by divorce before an application for naturalization could be pursued based on the three years residence for persons married to United States citizens. The law held the beneficiary retroactively admitted for permanent residence effective the date of first entry to the United States. (Priv. L. No. 217, 73 Stat. A94 (1959)) (H.R. Rep. No. 755, 1st Sess.) (Sen. Rep. No. 952, 1st Sess.)-NRES

86th Cong., H.R. 6954, for the relief of Frol Martin Simonov. Beneficiary, a 38-year old native of the Soviet Union and permanent resident of the United States was a Lt. Col. of the Soviet Army who defected through West Berlin in 1953. He was unable to obtain citizenship because he had been formerly associated with the Communist Party. His wife and two children were United States citizens. The report indicated that information supplied was "to the effect that he has unalterably changed his loyalty from the Soviet Union to the United States." The law held the beneficiary to be exempt from sections 313(a) and (c) relating to residence requirements for former Communist Party Members. (Priv. L. No. 218, 73 Stat. A95 (1959)) (H.R. Rep. No. 756, 1st Sess.) (Sen. Rep. No. 953, 1st Sess.)-NXCP

86th Cong., H.R. 7551, for the relief of Hubert O. Beckles. Beneficiary, a 27-year old native of the British West Indies, entered the United States as a visitor. He was inducted into the United States Army, and while performing guard duty in Korea was accidentally shot by another member of the Armed Forces which left him totally paralyzed. The law held the beneficiary lawfully admitted for permanent residence. (Priv. L. No. 442, 74 Stat. A82 (1960)) (H.R. Rep. No. 1702, 2nd Sess.) (Sen. Rep. No. 1802, 2nd Sess.)-QMGN

86th Cong., H.R. 8156, for the relief of Jack Kent Cooke. The beneficiary was a 47-year old native and citizen of Canada. He entered the United States on various occasions for temporary visits, spending approximately six months of each year in the United States. The beneficiary had interests in various enterprises including the Toronto Broadcasting Company, Toronto Mapleleaf Baseball and Hockey Clubs and joint owner of a radio station, Donald Cooke Inc., with his brother, a United States citizen. The law held the beneficiary to have been lawfully admitted for permanent residence retroactively and held him to have complied with the residence requirements relating to naturalization under section 316. (Priv. L. No. 486, 74 Stat. A100 (1960)) (H.R. Rep. No. 1506, 2nd Sess.) (Sen. Rep. No. 1933, 2nd Sess.)-NRES

86th Cong., H.R. 9444, for the relief of Hsiao-li Lindsay (nee Li-Hsiao-li). Beneficiary, a 41-year old native of China and citizen of Australia, was the spouse of a lawful permanent resident who was an expert in developments in Communist China and was on the staff of American University. It was stated he was "universally recognized as probably the outstanding critic of Red China." The spouse and his family resided in Britain and Australia, where he was engaged in research and academic works, and was bestowed with the title in Australia of Lord Lindsay of Birker. While the beneficiary's children would be eligible for visas as joining him, the beneficiary was unable to obtain a visa immediately because of the oversubscription of visas for the Chinese quota. The law held the beneficiary to have been born in Great Britain and sections 201(a), 202(a) (5), and 202(b) (2) relating to visa chargeability were held inapplicable. (Priv. L. No. 259, 74 Stat. A13 (1960)) (H.R. Rep. No. 1227, 2nd Sess.) (Sen. Rep. No. 1150, 2nd Sess.)-QPRF

86th Cong., S. 32, for the relief of Uwe-Thorsten Scobel. Beneficiary was a 22-year old native of Germany and lawful permanent resident of the United States He was found ineligible for derivative United States citizenship, and was unable to fulfill the five year residence requirement for naturalization prior to being offered a commission in the Air Force Reserve, and training at the United States Air Force Academy. He was one year short of meeting the five year residence period. The law waived the residence requirement for purposes of naturalization. (Priv. L. No. 34, 73 Stat. A17 (1959)) (Sen. Rep. No. 254, 1st Sess.) (H.R. Rep. No. 468, 1st Sess.)-NCOD

86th Cong., S. 46, for the relief of Ben Chassin. The beneficiary, a 50-year old native of England and citizen of the United States, was in jeopardy of losing citizenship by protracted residence abroad, when he was employed with the United States Government in the Panama Canal Zone for 14 years. He operated a large poultry ranch in Panama supplying military dependents in that Zone. His two sons were United States citizens. The law held the beneficiary to meet the requirements of section 354(5) relating to residence abroad. (Priv. L. No. 36, 73 Stat. A18 (1959)) (Sen. Rep. No. 70, 1st Sess.) (H.R. Rep. No. 470, 1st Sess.)-NRTN

86th Cong., S. 110, for the relief of Yaeko Inouye. Beneficiary, a 74-year old native and citizen of Japan, was admitted for permanent residence to the United States and resided in the country 30 years. She left for Japan to obtain a divorce and during World War II was unable to return to the United States. By the time she made plans to return, the second preference visas for that country was oversubscribed. She was entirely dependent on the support of her United States citizen adopted daughter who resided in the United States. The law held the beneficiary with section 101(a) (27) (B) relating to returning permanent resident aliens. (Priv. L. No. 37, 73 Stat. A18 (1959)) (Sen. Rep. No. 71, 1st Sess.) (H.R. Rep. No. 471, 1st Sess.)-QPRP

86th Cong., S. 762, for the relief of Manuel Alves de Carvalho. Beneficiary, a 45-year old native and citizen of Portugal, was admitted for permanent residence on the basis of his marriage to a United States citizen. He had been honorary consul for Portugal in Rhode Island and sought to obtain expeditious naturalization so that he could be admitted to practice law. The law held the beneficiary retroactively admitted for permanent residence effective the date of his first entry to the United States. (Priv. L. No. 358, 74 Stat. A51 (1960)) (Sen. Rep. No. 1479, 2nd Sess.) (H.R. Rep. No. 1832, 2nd Sess.)-NRES

86th Cong., S. 855, for the relief of Saeko Higa and Masako Higa. Beneficiaries, 21- and 19-year old natives of Okinawa and citizens of Japan, as well as sisters, sought to enter the United States to join their mother, a lawful permanent resident. The parents had been divorced, and the mother immigrated to the United States believing she could file third preference petitions for her minor children. Since entering the United States, that portion of the visas for Japan became oversubscribed. The law held the beneficiaries within section 202(b) (3) relating to admission of minor children of lawful permanent residents. (Priv. L. No. 57, 73 Stat. A25 (1959)) (Sen. Rep. No. 261, 1st Sess.) (H.R. Rep. No. 500, 1st Sess.)-QPRF

86th Cong., S. 977, for the relief of Nasubit Mildred Milkie. Beneficiary was a 40-year old native-born United States citizen and later citizen of Lebanon. She lost her United States citizenship through the naturalization of her father in Lebanon, and did not return to the United States within the required timeframe in order to retain citizenship. She entered the United States as a nonimmigrant servant of a diplomat. Two brothers were United States citizens residing in the United States. The beneficiary was later employed as a practical nurse. The law held the beneficiary lawfully admitted for permanent residence. (Priv. L. No. 172, 73 Stat. A75 (1959)) (Sen. Rep. No. 322, 1st Sess.) (H.R. Rep. No. 1001, 1st Sess.)-RTN

86th Cong., S. 1557, for the relief of Allen Howard Pilgrim, Cheryl Ann Pilgrim, Robb Alexander Pilgrim, and Jocelyn Mari Pilgrim. Beneficiaries were ages 7, 6, 4, and 2. They were adopted by United States citizens. The adoptive parents were visiting a cousin in Canada, and found the beneficiaries in an abandoned truck with their parents without heat, electricity or water. They suffered from malnutrition from which one of the children was lame. The Senate Committee in acting favorably noted the beneficiaries were entitled to nonquota status, but because of the "humanitarian factors involved" granting of permanent residence was warranted. The law held the beneficiaries lawfully admitted for permanent residence. (Priv. L. No. 142, 73 Stat. A62 (1959)) (Sen. Rep. No. 496, 1st Sess.) (H.R. Rep. No. 786, 1st Sess.)-QIRA

86th Cong., S. 1684, for the relief of Mr. and Mrs. Carl Skogen Woods. The beneficiaries, 66- and 65-year old natives and former citizens of the United States, lost citizenship by prolonged absence from the United States. The male beneficiary had been transferred in his employment, after nine years with a United States railroad, to the Canadian National Railways and worked as a lineman until his retirement. The law reinstated United States citizenship to the beneficiaries, provided an oath of allegiance was taken within one year. (Priv. L. No. 102, 73 Stat. A48 (1959)) (Sen. Rep. No. 496, 1st Sess.) (H.R. Rep. No. 786, 1st Sess.)-NRTN

86th Cong., S. 1915, for the relief of Chung Ching Wei. Beneficiary, a 45-year old native and citizen of China, entered the United States as an official of a foreign government and had his status adjusted to permanent residence under a recently enacted law. The beneficiary had previously been denied adjustment of status as a Displaced Person by Congress and had an application for suspension of deportation denied. For ten years, he was an officer or employee of subsidiary companies of the China International Foundation. The beneficiary and other officers, in 1953, were indicted for having a vessel chartered to a person who was not a United States citizen; and the Government was paid two million dollars. The Ingalls-Taiwan Shipbuilding Dry Dock Company was anxious that the beneficiary become a United States citizen in order to more effectively conduct the company's work. The company had various contracts with Government agencies. The Department of Navy indicated "in the event of increased activity in the Taiwan Straits, the Ingalls-Taiwan yards would be required for the repair and dry docking of United States vessels." The Senate Committee noted that, "Because of the potential benefit to the United States Government, the committee feels that granting the beneficiary permanent residence as of the date of a prior entry is warranted." The law held the beneficiary retroactively admitted for permanent residence. (Priv. L. No. 145, 73 Stat. A63 (1959)) (Sen. Rep. No. 767, 1st Sess.) (H.R. Rep. No. 1065, 1st Sess.)-NRES

86th Cong., S. 2142, for the relief of George C. McKinney. Beneficiary, a 34-year old native of Latvia and United States citizen was born abroad while his father was on assignment with the United States Foreign Service. He continued to reside with his father during assignments in Latvia and London, and took various jobs abroad including assignment with the Virginia State Ports Authority in Belgium. The beneficiary married a Swedish national and had a child who did not derive United States citizenship, because the father lacked the necessary residence for transmission of citizenship. The law held the beneficiary to have been physically present in the United States during the time he was residing abroad with his parents. (Priv. L. No. 320, 74 Stat. A36 (1960)) (Sen. Rep. No. 1113, 2nd Sess.) (H.R. Rep. No. 1679, 2nd Sess.)-NCOD

86th Cong., S. 2177, for the relief of Peter J. Waterton. Beneficiary, a 36-year old native and citizen of Great Britain, was ineligible for a visa due to two previous attacks of epilepsy. He was offered employment associated with the Bendix Corporation on development work on patents relating to guided missiles. It was stated the beneficiary had no medical problems for ten years. The law waived section 212(a)(4) relating to mental health and provided for the posting of a bond to overcome possible public charge aspects. (Priv. L. No. 321, 74 Stat. A36 (1960)) (Sen. Rep. No. 1102, 2nd Sess.) (H.R. Rep. No. 1680, 2nd Sess.)-WHEL

86th Cong., S. 2319, for the relief of Sergiusz Rudczenko. Beneficiary, a 29-year old native and citizen of Poland, was ineligible for a visa due to a tubercular condition. His father, a United States citizen and mother, a lawful permanent resident, resided in the United States. The beneficiary had an approved first preference petition filed by a firm of architects. The law waived sections 212(a)(6) and 212(a)(15) relating to mental health conditions and public charge. It also provided an appropriate bond be posted to overcome possible public charge aspects. The act also precluded the denying of a preference classification on behalf of the beneficiary. (Priv. L. No. 226, 73 Stat. A98 (1959)) (Sen. Rep. No. 842, 1st Sess.)-WHEL

86th Cong., S. 2528, for the relief of John Lipset. Beneficiary, a 25-year old native and citizen of Japan, was born out of wedlock to a United States citizen and Japanese mother. He was the beneficiary of previous private law which granted him eligibility for a nonquota visa. His United States citizen father died prior to filing a petition on his behalf. He was also heir to a substantial trust fund in the United States. The law held the beneficiary to have retained the status conferred by prior legislation, and waived provisions of section 205 relating to the filing of a petition on his behalf.

(Priv. L. No. 361, 74 Stat. A52 (1960)) (Sen. Rep. No. 1251, 2nd Sess.) (H.R. Rep. No. 1835, 2nd Sess.)-QPRF

86th Cong., S. 2554, for the relief of Leila Finlay Bohin. Beneficiary, a native-born United States citizen, resided in the United States 15 years until she accompanied her parents abroad where her father was assigned as Deputy for Defense Efforts to the United States special representative in Europe. She married a French national employed with a United States corporation, Singer Sewing Machine, and continued to reside abroad thus disallowing her to transmit United States citizenship to her son. The law deemed the beneficiary to have been physically present in the United States for the purposes of section 301(a) (7), thus allowing her to transmit United States citizenship to her son. (Priv. L. No. 328, 74 Stat. A39 (1960)) (Sen. Rep. No. 1171, 2nd Sess.) (H.R. Rep. No. 1689, 2nd Sess.)-NCOD

86th Cong., S. 2566, for the relief of Peter Leo Bahr. Beneficiary, a 39-year old native of China and citizen of Germany, sought admission to the United States to join his spouse, a lawful permanent resident. Her mother was handicapped with one leg amputated. The beneficiary stated that he would assume responsibility for support of his wife's mother. His visa under the third preference classification was oversubscribed for the Chinese quota. The law held sections 201(a), 202(a) (5) and 202(b) inapplicable on behalf of the beneficiary. (Priv. L. No. 394, 74 Stat. A64 (1960)) (Sen. Rep. No. 1172, 2nd Sess.) (H.R. Rep. No. 1690, 2nd Sess.)-QPRF

86th Cong., S. 2646, for the relief of Lloyd C. Kimm. Beneficiary, a 54-year old native and citizen of Korea, entered the United States for permanent residence. He was employed as an instructor in the Korean language by the National Security Agency, Department of Defense. He was also employed with the United States Army 12 years in Japan. The beneficiary sought expeditious naturalization in order to obtain civil service status. The law retroactively granted permanent residence to the beneficiary effective his first date of entry to the United States. (Priv. L. No. 363, 74 Stat. A53 (1960)) (Sen. Rep. No. 1438, 2nd Sess.) (H.R. Rep. No. 1837, 2nd Sess.)-NRES

86th Cong., S. 2768, for the relief of Frederick T.C. Yu and his wife, Alice Siao-Fen Chen Yu. Beneficiaries, 39- and 35-year old natives of China and lawful permanent residents of the United States, were scheduled to travel in conjunction with the male beneficiary's employment and desired citizenship. The male beneficiary had been granted a Ford Foundation fellowship in social relations and government at Harvard, and a fellowship in international communications at MIT. He also received a grant to travel to examine Far East attitudes of Asians toward other Asians, with particular reference toward Communist China. Their two children were United States citizens. Although they had resided in the United States for four years they were short one year of meeting the residence requirements for naturalization. The law waived the residence requirements for naturalization and the court jurisdiction for making the application to petition for naturalization. (Priv.

L. No. 365, 74 Stat. A53 (1960)) (Sen. Rep. No. 1440, 2nd Sess.) (H.R. Rep. No. 1839, 2nd Sess.)-NRES

86th Cong., S. 2886, for the relief of Nikolija Lazic. Beneficiary was a 38-year old widow, native and citizen of Yugoslavia. The beneficiary's husband was accorded fourth preference status on the basis of a visa petition filed by his mother. Prior to visa issuance, he died of cancer. The law held the beneficiary within section 4 of the Act of September 22, 1959, and eligible for a quota visa under section 203(a)(4), and held the approved petition valid. (Priv. L. No. 367, 74 Stat. A54 (1960)) (Sen. Rep. No. 1321, 2nd Sess.) (H.R. Rep. No. 1840, 2nd Sess.)-QPRF

86th Cong., S. 2991, for the relief of Ah See Lee Chin. Beneficiary, a 63-year old native of Hong Kong and lawful permanent resident of the United States, was unable to acquire enough knowledge of the English language to take the test for naturalization because of her advanced age. She resided in the United States 12 years, was married to a United States citizen, and had three United States citizen children. Her husband was employed as a manager of the New China Daily Press in Hawaii. The law held the beneficiary to have complied with the English language requirements under section 312(1). (Priv. L. No. 371, 74 Stat. A55 (1960)) (Sen. Rep. No. 1474, 2nd Cong.) (H.R. Rep. No. 1844, 2nd Sess.)-NXEN

86th Cong., S. 3016, for the relief of Walter F. Beecroft. Beneficiary, a 37-year old native of Britain and lawful permanent, was unable to meet the residence requirement because of his employment with the World Health in Switzerland. Prior to his employment with the World Health, he was employed with the United Nations and Refugee Organizations. The law waived the residence for purposes of naturalization, and the court jurisdiction for making such application. (Priv. L. No. 372, 74 Stat. A55 (1960)) (Sen. Rep. No. 1448, 2nd Sess.) (H.R. Rep. No. 1847, 2nd Sess.)-NRES

86th Cong., S. 3130, for the relief of Anne-Marie Stehlin. Beneficiary, a 33-year old native of France and citizen of the United States, was in jeopardy of losing United States citizenship by prolonged absence from the United States. She had resided in the United States 10 years and returned to France with her mother where she then was employed with the Economic Cooperation Administration. She married a French national and accompanied him to the United States on a NATO assignment, but he was later assigned to France as General, Vice Chief of Staff of the French Army. The law permitted the beneficiary to reside abroad four years without losing United States citizenship under section 352(a). (Priv. L. No. 352, 74 Stat. A49 (1960)) (Sen. Rep. No. 1363, 2nd Sess.) (H.R. Rep. No. 1851, 2nd Sess.)-NRTN

87th Cong., H.R. 1394, for the relief of Laszlo Hamori. Beneficiary, a 46-year old native and citizen of Hungary, was employed with the United Nations Narcotics Bureau and served in other capacities with the U.N. 12 years. He was married to a citizen with two citizen but was unable to attain permanent residence through administrative channels due to his status as a representative of an international organization. He was eligible for a visa but could not comply with residence requirements for naturalization. The law held the beneficiary to have complied with the residence requirements for naturalization upon admission for permanent residence. (Priv. L. No. 221, 75 Stat. 932 (1961)) (H.R. Rep. No. 304, 1st Sess.) (Sen. Rep. No. 918, 1st Sess.)-NRES

87th Cong., H.R. 1395, for the relief of Sydney Gruson. Beneficiary, a 46-year old native of Ireland and lawful permanent resident of the United States, was unable to meet the residence requirements for naturalization due to prolonged employment abroad as chief correspondent in Germany to the New York Times. He had returned to the United States on temporary visits and had failed to obtain a re-entry permit. The law held the beneficiary to have complied with the residence requirements for naturalization upon admission for permanent residence. (Priv. L. No. 408, 76 Stat 1309 (1962)) (H.R. Rep. No. 589, 1st Sess.) (Sen. Rep. No. 1500, 2nd Sess.)-NRES

87th Cong., H.R. 1404, for the relief of Mrs. Frances Mangiaracina. Beneficiary, a 52-year old native and citizen of Italy and former United States citizen, lost her citizenship by returning to Italy. She resided in the United States 17 years. Her mother and five siblings were United States citizens. Her spouse was convicted of murder in Italy and was serving an extended prison sentence. She had three children and desired to enter the United States with her children and reside with her family. The law held the beneficiary within section 101(a) (27) (B) relating to returning permanent resident aliens. (Priv. L. No. 409, 76 Stat. 1309 (1962)) (H.R. Rep. No. 1537, 2nd Sess.) (Sen. Rep. No. 1501, 2nd Sess.)-QPRP

87th Cong., H.R. 1458, for the relief of Lee Dock On. Beneficiary, a 39-year old native of China, entered the United States misrepresenting himself as a United States citizen, having derived citizenship through his father. It was later discovered his relative was in fact an uncle and not his father. His passport was revoked while he was abroad. The beneficiary had resided in the United States 16 years. The House Committee noted the legislation was acted upon unfavorably in the first instance because of visa fraud; but an investigation resulted in favorable action in view of his "prolonged residence in the United States and his moral record shown during that period of time [which] represent an equity warranting the enactment of legislation." The law held the beneficiary within section 101(a) (27) (B) relating to returning permanent resident aliens, and the bill also waived section 212(a) (19) relating to visa fraud. (Priv. L. No. 530, 76 Stat. 1350 (1962)) (H.R. Rep. No. 303, 1st Sess.) (Sen. Rep. No. 1448, 2nd Sess.)-QPRP

87th Cong., H.R. 1469, for the relief of Mrs. Leslie M. Paterson, Janet Paterson, and Mary Paterson. Beneficiary, a 53-year old widow of a United States citizen and her daughters, ages 22 and 19, were natives of Jamaica and subjects of Great Britain. One of the younger beneficiaries entered the United States as a student. The father of the beneficiaries obtained United States citizenship through naturalization, but was in ill health and planned to bring his family to the United States when he recovered. He died before accomplishing that objective. The interested party, the sister of Mrs. Paterson and a United States citizen, desired that the family join them in the United States. Her husband had been cited by the British and French Governments for intelligence work during World War II. The law held section 202(c) (1) inapplicable on behalf of the beneficiaries. (Priv. L. No. 473, 76 Stat. 1330 (1962)) (H.R. Rep. No. 1743, 2nd Sess.) (Sen. Rep. No. 1662, 2nd Sess.)-QPRF

87th Cong., H.R. 1653, for the relief of William Falby. Beneficiary, a 28-year old native of the United States and citizen of Great Britain, lost his United States citizenship by accepting employment as a customs officer in the British West Indies. His parents were natives of the British West Indies and had taken the beneficiary with them at the age of five where he had resided since that time. His sister, a United States citizen, sponsored him. The law allowed the beneficiary to regain his citizenship by taking the oath of allegiance to the United States within two years after the Act. (Priv. L. No. 420, 76 Stat. 1312 (1962)) (H.R. Rep. No. 1600, 2nd Sess.) (Sen. Rep. No. 1516, 2nd Sess.)-NVOL

87th Cong., H.R. 2156, for the relief of Mrs. Tui Hing Tow Woo. Beneficiary, a 65-year old native of China and lawful permanent resident of the United States, was unable to meet the requirements of the naturalization law regarding understanding of the English language. She had resided in the United States 22 years as a permanent resident alien and her husband and four children were United States citizens. The law held the beneficiary to have complied with section 312(1) relating to English language requirements. (Priv. L. No. 107, 75 Stat. 886 (1961)) (H.R. Rep. No. 339, 1st Sess.) (Sen. Rep. No. 464, 1st Sess.)-NXEN

87th Cong., H.R. 2187, for the relief of Augustin Ramirez-Trejo. Beneficiary, a 47-year old native and citizen of Mexico, was admitted for permanent residence and later claimed exemption from military service. He had also been convicted of a crime of burglary and was excluded. His spouse and eight children were lawful permanent residents. The House Committee noted in its recommendation for action that it was prompted to do so "solely on the ground that hardship would be caused to the beneficiary's wife and eight minor children if he were to be deported and they were deprived of his support." The Senate noted that the beneficiary would never be eligible for naturalization. The law canceled deportation proceedings against the beneficiary and provided that nothing should be construed to waive the provisions of section 315 relating to the bar to naturalization of persons who claimed exemption from military service. (Priv. L. No. 485, 76 Stat. 1334 (1962)) (H.R. Rep. No. 1596, 1st Sess.) (Sen. Rep. No. 1504, 1st Sess.)-WXDD

87th Cong., H.R. 2666, for the relief of Adelina Benedict (nee Rosasco). Beneficiary, a 55-year old native and citizen of Italy, resided in the United

States seven years and returned to Italy. She was married to a United States citizen, and he divorced her on grounds of desertion. Three United States citizen siblings resided in the United States. The law held the beneficiary within section 101(a) (27) (B) as a returning permanent resident alien. (Priv. L. No. 243, 75 Stat. 939 (1961)) (H.R. Rep. No. 929, 1st Sess.) (Sen. Rep. No. 1011, 1st Sess.)-QPRP

87th Cong., H.R. 3401, for the relief of Salvatore Cairo. Beneficiary, a 53-year old native and citizen of Italy, was admitted for permanent residence at the age of two with his parents. Twenty-nine years later in the United States, he was convicted of the sale of narcotics and was deported. He had a wife and three children who were permanent residents. The law waived 212(a)(23) relating to drug violations. (Priv. L. No. 279, 75 Stat. 952 (1961)) (H.R. Rep. No. 1074, 1st Sess.) (Sen. Rep. No. 1014, 1st Sess.)-WCRF

87th Cong., H.R. 3718, for the relief of Matthias Nock, Jr. Beneficiary, a 32-year old native of Yugoslavia and citizen of Germany, was found ineligible for a visa due to convictions involving demolishing a barracks for wood, and theft of green tobacco and onions from a farm. His father was a United States citizen and his mother and sister were lawfully admitted for permanent residence. The law waived section 212(a) (9) relating to crimes involving moral turpitude. (Priv. L. No. 249, 75 Stat. 940 (1961)) (H.R. Rep. No. 763, 1st Sess.) (Sen. Rep. No. 942, 1st Sess.)-WCRF

87th Cong., H.R. 4028, for the relief of Lennon May. Beneficiary, a 16-year old native of Jamaica and illegitimate child of a United States citizen, resided in Jamaica with his paternal grandmother. His putative father supported him while in Jamaica, but his grandmother with whom he resided was in failing health. The law held the beneficiary within section 101(a) (27) (A) and 205 as the natural-born alien child of a United States citizen. (Priv. L. No. 251, 75 Stat. 941 (1961)) (H.R. Rep. No. 930, 1st Sess.) (Sen. Rep. No. 1015, 1st Sess.)-QIRM

87th Cong., H.R. 4384, for the relief of Richard Fordham. Beneficiary, a 23-year old native of Brazil, acquired United States citizenship at birth but was unable to meet the retention requirements for citizenship prior to his 23rd birthday. His entry to the United States was six months after he turned 23. He desired to enter Air Force Officers' Candidate School for which he needed United States citizenship. The law held the beneficiary to have met the retention requirements for citizenship by entering the United States prior to his 23rd birthday. (Priv. L. No. 253, 75 Stat. 942 (1961)) (H.R. Rep. No. 704, 1st Sess.) (Sen. Rep. No. 944, 1st Sess.)-NRTN

87th Cong., H.R. 6226, for the relief of Arlin David English. Beneficiary, a 22-year old native of the United States, was taken to Canada at the age of 13 by his parents and re-entered the United States as a United States citizen eight years later, erroneously. It was discovered he expatriated himself by serving in the Canadian military reserve. His entire family resided in the United States, and his mother and 10 siblings were United States citizens.

The law allowed the beneficiary to regain citizenship upon taking an oath of allegiance to the United States within one year of the date of the Act. (Priv. L. No. 299, 76 Stat. 1268 (1962)) (H.R. Rep. No. 1124, 1st Sess.) (Sen. Rep. No. 1186, 2nd Sess.)-NVOL

87th Cong., H.R. 6343, for the relief of Mrs. Izabel A. Miguel. Beneficiary, a 63-year old native and citizen of Portugal, was formerly a permanent resident alien who resided in the United States 10 years. She was found deportable due to a hospitalization for dementia praecox, catatonic type and returned to her home in the Azores with her husband who deserted her 19 days later and returned to the United States to obtain a divorce. She had two sons born in the United States who served in the Armed Forces, and one of whom filed a second preference petition on her behalf. She was found inadmissible due to previous attacks of insanity. She had not been hospitalized for over 30 years. The law waived section 212(a) (3) relating to mental health conditions and provided an appropriate bond be posted to overcome possible public charge aspects. (Priv. L. No. 339, 76 Stat. 1283 (1962)) (H.R. Rep. No. 1335, 2nd Sess.) (Sen. Rep. No. 1299, 2nd Sess.)-WHEL

87th Cong., H.R. 6833, for the relief of Frantisek Tisler. Beneficiary, a 37-year old native and lawful permanent resident of the United States, first entered the United States as a government official attached to the Embassy of Czechoslovakia as a military and air attaché, and defected to the United States four years later. The Senate Committee indicated he "cooperated with our Government." The law held the beneficiary to be exempt from sections 313(a) and (c) relating to residence requirements for former Communist Party Members. (Priv. L. No. 492, 76 Stat. 1336 (1962)) (H.R. Rep. No. 1744, 2nd Sess.) (Sen. Rep. No. 1766, 2nd Sess.)-NXCP

87th Cong., H.R. 7582, for the relief of Dario Tacquechel. Beneficiary, a 24-year old native of Brazil and citizen of Cuba, entered the United States for permanent residence and desired United States citizenship to qualify as a naval aviation cadet in the United States Navy. The law held the beneficiary retroactively admitted for permanent residence effective the date of his first entry to the United States. (Priv. L. No. 549, 76 Stat. 1358 (1962)) (H.R. Rep. No. 2081, 2nd Sess.) (Sen. Rep. No. 1976, 2nd Sess.)-NRES

87th Cong., H.R. 9588, for the relief of Claude Homann-Herimberg (nee Wagner). Beneficiary, a 32-year old native of Egypt and naturalized United States citizen, was in jeopardy of losing citizenship through prolonged absence abroad where her husband was employed as special assistant to the High Commissioner for Refugees. The law deemed section 352(a) (2) relating to residence abroad inapplicable to the beneficiary provided she return to the United States within three years of the date of the Act. (Priv. L. No. 471, 76 Stat. 1329 (1962)) (H.R. Rep. No. 1695, 2nd Sess.) (Sen. Rep. No. 1655, 2nd Sess.)-NRTN

87th Cong., H.R. 9669, for the relief of Molly Kwauk. Beneficiary, a 25-year old native and citizen of China, resided in Hong Kong. Her United

States citizen mother filed a petition on her behalf, but she was denied as feebleminded. Her mother was formerly chief of anesthesia at the Peiping Union Medical College Hospital in China, and was chief of anesthesiology for the Veteran's Administration in Louisville, Kentucky. The House Committee noted taking favorable action "the committee wishes to stress it in no way intends to deviate from its general policy of not approving private bills in behalf of aliens who are afflicted with feeblemindedness or who are mentally defective and who may become public charges [but]...Its disapproval would mean her return to Communist China where her only relative is an 80 year old grandmother." The law waived section 212(a) (1) relating to mental health conditions and provided an appropriate bond be posted to overcome possible public charge aspects. (Priv. L. No. 676, 76 Stat. 1408 (1962)) (H.R. Rep. No. 1603, 2nd Sess.) (Sen. Rep. No. 2099, 2nd Sess.)-WHEL

87th Cong., H.R. 9915, for the relief of Umberto Brezza. Beneficiary, a 23-year old native of Yugoslavia and citizen of Italy, desired to enter the United States to join his mother and twin sister, lawful permanent residents. He was denied a visa due to a conviction for aggravated assault with a knife involving an attempt to protect his mother who was being attacked by two women. The law waived section 212 (a) (9) relating to crimes involving moral turpitude. (Priv. L. No. 528, 76 Stat. 1350 (1962)) (H.R. Rep. No. 1874, 2nd Sess.) (Sen. Rep. No. 1900, 2nd Sess.)-WCRF

87th Cong., H.R. 10160, for the relief of Mrs. A. R. Lendian. Beneficiary, a 30-year old native-born United States citizen, married a native of Cuba and moved to that country where she resided and had four children. Three children derived United States citizenship at birth, but the fourth child came under newly enacted transmission requirements which did not provide relief for him. The beneficiary and her husband returned to the United States, where her husband claimed asylum and she sought the citizenship status of her fourth child. The law held the beneficiary to have complied with section 201(g) relating to residence in the United States for transmission of United States citizenship. (Priv. L. No. 562, 76 Stat. 1363 (1962)) (H.R. Rep. No. 2110, 2nd Sess.) (Sen. Rep. No. 2007, 2nd Sess.)-NCOD

87th Cong., S. 217, for the relief of Alessandro Gellhorn. Beneficiary, a 12-year old native of Italy and lawful permanent resident of the United States, was adopted by United States citizens and was unable to acquire citizenship through administrative channels because of prolonged residence abroad. His father, Thomas Stanley Matthews, was formerly editor of Time magazine and was a journalist and listed in Who's Who in America. Mrs. Matthews was formerly married to Ernest Hemingway five years, and she too was listed in Who's Who in America as a foreign correspondent for Collier's Weekly. (Priv. L. No. 7, 75 Stat. 853 (1961)) (Sen. Rep. No. 93, 1st Sess.) (H.R. Rep. No. 286, 1st Sess.)-NMSC

87th Cong., S. 231, for the relief of Helga G. F. Koehler. Beneficiary, a 26-year old native of Czechoslovakia and citizen of Germany, was ineligible for a visa due to her affiliation with a proscribed organization in East Germany. She was a member of the Socialist Unity party for three years, but she severed her ties with the organization when leaving East Germany. The beneficiary did not have the cumulative five year period necessary, since her termination of those activities, to qualify for an administrative waiver. Her husband, a United States citizen, served in the Armed Forces and was later employed as a civilian with the United States Army. They were expecting a child. The law waived section 212(a) (28) relating to membership in proscribed organizations. (Priv. L. No. 155, 75 Stat. 901 (1961)) (Sen. Rep. No. 396, 1st Sess.) (H.R. Rep. No. 769, 1st Sess.)-WXCP

87th Cong., S. 235, for the relief of Evagelos Mablekos. Beneficiary, a 31-year old native and citizen of Greece, entered the United States as a nonquota immigrant based on his marriage to a United States citizen. It was later discovered the marriage was annulled and he was not entitled to a visa. The beneficiary served in the Royal Hellenic Air Force five years, and since entry was employed by the University of Wisconsin which filed a first preference visa petition on his behalf. The law waived section 212(a) (19) relating to visa fraud. (Priv. L. No. 308, 76 Stat. 1272 (1962)) (Sen. Rep. No. 810, 1st Sess.) (H.R. Rep. No. 1337, 2nd Sess.)-WCRF

87th Cong., S. 333, for the relief of Godofredo M. Herzog. Beneficiary, a native of Germany and citizen of Bolivia, was lawfully admitted for permanent residence. He was a doctor of Medicine and received a temporary commission in the United States Air Force for two years. His spouse was a lawful permanent resident, and they had two United States citizen children. The beneficiary desired a regular commission in the Air Force; however, United States citizenship was a prerequisite. The law held the beneficiary retroactively admitted for permanent residence effective the date of his first entry to the United States. (Priv. L. No. 158, 75 Stat. 903 (1961)) (Sen. Rep. No. 512, 1st Sess.) (H.R. Rep. No. 933, 1st Sess.)-NRES

87th Cong., S. 400, for the relief of Mrs. Keum Ja Asato (Mrs. Thomas R. Asato). Beneficiary, a 26-year old native and citizen of Korea and widow of a United States citizen, had two United States citizen children, ages 3 and 1. Her husband served in the Armed Forces 15 years and died from leukemia. The law held the beneficiary within section 101(a) (27) (A) and 205 relating to nonquota visas. (Priv. L. No. 73, 75 Stat. 874 (1961)) (Sen. Rep. No. 188, 1st Sess.) (H.R. Rep. No. 479, 1st Sess.)-QIRW

87th Cong., S. 438, for the relief of Mrs. Maria Giovanna Hopkins. Beneficiary, a 35-year old native and citizen of Italy, was married to a United States citizen member of the Army for eight years. Her husband died and left her with five United States citizen children. The law deemed the beneficiary to have been admitted for permanent residence as of the date of her marriage, and to have met the residence requirements for naturalization. (Priv. L. No. 126, 75 Stat. 892 (1961)) (Sen. Rep. No. 102, 1st Sess.) (H.R. Rep. No. 696, 1st Sess.)-NRES

87th Cong., S. 546, for the relief of In Fil Chung, In Ae Chung, In Sook Chung, and In Ja Chung. Beneficiaries, one-year old quadruplets and natives and citizens of Korea, were released for adoption by their father. Their mother died at birth. The United States citizen prospective adoptive parents had two other Korean orphans admitted to the United States. The adoptive parents sought a waiver of the two-petition limitation on the immigration of adopted children. The law held the children to be the natural-born children of the adoptive parents for purposes of sections 101(a) (27) (A) and 205, and waived the two petition limit thus allowing them to enter as immediate relatives. (Priv. L. No. 35, 75 Stat. 862 (1961)) (Sen. Rep. No. 123, 1st Sess.) (H.R. Rep. No. 396, 1st Sess.)-QIRA

87th Cong., S. 570, for the relief of Giuseppa Alonzi. Beneficiary, a 54-year old native and citizen of Italy, desired to join her eight siblings, United States citizens, in the United States. Her brother filed a fourth preference petition on her behalf, but the visas for that category were oversubscribed. The Senate Committee reported in acting favorably that there were unusual circumstances warranting relief. The law held the beneficiary registered on a visa waiting list under section 4 of the Act of September 22, 1959 and section 203(c) with an early priority date in order for visa issuance to be valid. (Priv. L. No. 178, 75 Stat. 910 (1961)) (Sen. Rep. No. 229, 1st Sess.) (H.R. Rep. No. 774, 1st Sess.)-QPRF

87th Cong., S. 689, for the relief of Karl Heinz Agar. Beneficiary, a 20-year old native of Germany and lawful permanent resident of the United States, was unable to fulfill the residence requirements for naturalization while under the age of 18 because his adoptive mother was assigned overseas in the Armed Forces. The adoptive mother was a United States Army nurse, widowed upon the death of her husband in a Japanese prison camp, and her only natural son was killed in Korea. Unless the beneficiary obtained citizenship, he would not be eligible for advanced ROTC training while attending the New Mexico Military Institute. The law deemed the beneficiary to have complied with the residence requirements of section 323. (Priv. L. No. 599, 76 Stat. 1377 (1962)) (Sen. Rep. No. 1831, 2nd Sess.) (H.R. Rep. No. 2388, 2nd Sess.)-NMSC

87th Cong., S. 722, for the relief of Aideh Kobler. Beneficiary, a 39-year old native and citizen of China and doctor, was married to a lawful permanent resident alien who immigrated to the United States as a first preference beneficiary employed by the Kentucky State Department of Mental Health in Louisville. His spouse was unable to join him because the quota for natives of China was oversubscribed. The law held inapplicable sections 201(a), 202(a)(5) and 202(b)(2), and considered the beneficiary to be the accompanying spouse within section 202(a) (2) provided an application for a visa was made within six months. (Priv. L. No. 180, 75 Stat. 910 (1961)) (Sen. Rep. No. 305, 1st Sess.) (H.R. Rep. No. 775, 1st Sess.)-QPRF

87th Cong., S. 899, for the relief of Liu Shui Chen. Beneficiary, a 40-year old native and citizen of China, entered the United States as a crewman. He sailed on British merchant marine vessels carrying munitions in World War II, and immediately prior to entering the United States was employed on a Chinese Nationalist vessel. The beneficiary was granted status by the Attorney General under the Refugee Relief Act of 1953, but the Congress did not approve his case. The law held the beneficiary lawfully admitted for permanent residence. (Priv. L. No. 328, 76 Stat. 1279 (1962)) (Sen. Rep. No. 912, 1st Sess.) (H.R. Rep. No. 1519, 2nd Sess.)-QMGN

87th Cong., S. 1074, for the relief of Chao Yao Koh. Beneficiary, a 35-year old native and citizen of China, entered the United States as an exchange visitor and obtained a waiver of the two-year foreign residence requirement at the request of the Defense Department, while engaged in research at the Institute of Technology of the University of Minnesota. He was later employed at Boeing Airplane Company which had filed a first preference petition on his behalf. It was claimed he could contribute to the defense program if his citizenship could be expedited for security clearance purposes. The first preference visas for China were oversubscribed. Among those projects which he worked on were thermodynamics and heat transfer fluid sponsored by the Atomic Energy Commission; aerodynamics and heat transfer of parachutes at supersonic speed on behalf of the Air Force; and the analytic study of techniques of film cooling gas turbine blades and rocket nozzles. The law held the beneficiary lawfully admitted for permanent residence in lieu of granting citizenship. (Priv. L. No. 481, 76 Stat. 1333 (1962)) (Sen. Rep. No. 1413, 2nd Sess.) (H.R. Rep. No. 1865, 2nd Sess.)-NRES

87th Cong., S. 1234, for the relief of Max Haleck. Beneficiary, a 69-year old native of Germany who immigrated to American Samoa at the age of 22, was married three times to natives of American Samoa, United States nationals. He had 5 children who were also natives of American Samoa and two served in the United States Armed Forces. It was stated he was an "outstanding and highly respected resident" of American Samoa, but because he was not born in American Samoa was not a national. He was the owner of five merchandise stores, and according to the Department of Interior report, a person of "considerable influence in support of our Government." The law held the beneficiary to have been born in American Samoa and regarded as residing therein on February 16, 1900, as well as held the beneficiary within the purview of section 325 relating to special naturalization benefits available to nationals of American Samoa. (Priv. L. No. 268, 75 Stat. 948 (1961)) (Sen. Rep. No. 719, 1st Sess.)-NRES

87th Cong., S. 1786, for the relief of Heripsime Hovnanian. Beneficiary, a 67-year old native and citizen of Turkey, was found eligible for nonquota status but could not obtain a visa due to illiteracy. Since the death of her husband, she was cared for by her brother and family and became totally dependent upon them. They were admitted to the United States for permanent residence and the beneficiary was left in the care of a religious order. The law waived section 212(a) (25) relating to illiteracy. (Priv. L. No. 271, 75 Stat. 949 (1961)) (Sen. Rep. No. 669, 1st Sess.)-WXIL

87th Cong., S. 1791, for the relief of Dr. Tzy-Cheng Peng. Beneficiary, a 32-year old native and citizen of China, entered the United States as a student. He was employed as a research analyst by Boeing Airplane Company, which filed a first preference visa petition on his behalf. Because of the oversubscription of visas for China, he was unable to obtain a visa. His work was important to defense and missile programs, and United States citizenship was necessary to obtain proper security clearances for government contracts. The law held the beneficiary retroactively admitted for lawful permanent residence effective the first date of entry to the United States. (Priv. L. No. 317, 76 Stat. 1275 (1962)) (Sen. Rep. No. 1026, 1st Sess.) (H.R. Rep. No. 1344, 2nd Sess.)-NRES

87th Cong., S. 2011, for the relief of Antonia Longfield-Smith. Beneficiary, a 15-year old native and citizen of Greece, was adopted by United States citizens who had previously adopted her 13-year old twin sisters. The twin sisters entered the United States under the Act of September 11, 1957. The adoptive male parent was a career officer in the United States Air Force. The adoptive parents sought a waiver of the two-petition limitation on the immigration of adopted children. The law held the child to be the natural-born child of the adoptive parents for purposes of sections 101(a) (27) (A) and 205, thus waiving the two-petition limit and allowing them to enter the United States as immediate relatives. (Priv. L. No. 417, 76 Stat. 1311 (1962)) (Sen. Rep. No. 1255, 2nd Sess.) (H.R. Rep. No. 1731, 2nd Sess.)-QIRA

87th Cong., S. 2385, for the relief of Dr. Hau Cheong Kwaan, his wife, Tech Phaik Loui Kwaan, and their Daughter, Laura Wai Man Kwaan. Beneficiaries were 29-, 28- and 1-year old natives of Hong Kong, and the spouse, a native of Malaysia. They entered the United States as exchange visitors and returned to Hong Kong after research studies of the male beneficiary. He was a physician employed as a lecturer at the University of Hong Kong. His services were "urgently needed" by the James F. Mitchell Foundation for Medical Education and Research in Washington, D.C., and a first preference petition was filed on his behalf. His medical specialty was diseases of the heart and circulatory system, and he was the author or co-author of 15 related publications. The Foundation required his services in connection with a five-year grant from the United States Public Health Service, National Heart Institute for a study of arteriosclerosis. His spouse was also a medical doctor serving in tuberculosis work in Hong Kong. The law deemed sections 201(a), 202(a)(5) and 202(b) inapplicable in the case of the beneficiaries. (Priv. L. No. 323, 76 Stat. 1277 (1962)) (Sen. Rep. No. 1006, 1st Sess.) (H.R. Rep. No. 1351, 2nd Sess.)-QPRF

87th Cong., S. 2555, for the relief of Fong Yee Hin. Beneficiary, a 31-year old native and citizen of China, entered the United States claiming to be a United States citizen. It was later discovered, after his father's confession, that he was not a United States citizen. He was one month short of eligibility for relief under section 249 which allowed the creation of a record of lawful admission based on residence in the United States. He was married and had two United States citizen children. The beneficiary was employed by the New York City Transit Authority, and he needed United States citizenship to continue his employment. The law held the beneficiary retroactively admitted for lawful permanent residence effective the date of first entry to the United States. (Priv. L. No. 670, 76 Stat. 1406 (1962) (Sen. Rep. No. 1419, 2nd Sess.)-NRES

87th Cong., S. 2679, for the relief of John Axel Arvidson. Beneficiary, a 66-year old native of Sweden, entered the United States as an immigrant. In 1918, he served several months in the United States Army, and two days before the armistice in 1918 he applied for relief from military service on the grounds of alienage. The beneficiary was naturalized, but later denaturalized because his citizenship had been erroneously granted. He did not know of the cancellation until 19 years later when applying for a passport. The beneficiary was placed in deportation proceedings on the basis of an invalid immigrant visa. His status was then adjusted by a prior private law, but that bill did not waive his ineligibility to citizenship. In enacting the legislation, the Committee noted it "has been the consistent policy of the committee not to look with favor upon bills which would remove ineligibility to citizenship, however...it is felt that the unique facts and extenuating circumstances of this case justify the relief granted." The Committee noted his Army unit had been disbanded before his application for a waiver was acted upon. The beneficiary was married to a United States citizen. The law waived the bar to naturalization and the decree which denaturalized the beneficiary. (Priv. L. No. 460, 76 Stat. 1326 (1962)) (Sen. Rep. No. 1422, 2nd Sess.) (H.R. Rep. No. 1932, 2nd Sess.)-NXDD

87th Cong., S. 2865, for the relief of Ferdinand A. Hermens. Beneficiary, a 55-year old native of Germany and United States citizen, was in danger of losing citizenship by protracted residence abroad. He was employed as a teacher in political science at the Political Science Research Institute at the University of Cologne, and was author of 13 books on government and political science. He was on leave of absence from Notre Dame, and served three years as a consultant to the United States High Commissioner for Germany, as well as assisting the United States Information Agency program. The Committee stated continuation of his work appeared to be "in the interests of the United States." The law held section 352(a) relating to residence abroad not applicable to the beneficiary provided he return to the United States within three years. (Priv. L. No. 430, 76 Stat. 1316 (1962)) (Sen. Rep. No. 1515, 2nd Sess.)-NRTN

87th Cong., S. 3026, for the relief of Jeno Nagy. Beneficiary, a 24-year old native and citizen of Hungary, was paroled into the United States as a Hungarian refugee. He was ineligible for adjustment of status under special legislation because it was discovered he was afflicted with tuberculosis. The law waived section 212(a) (6) relating to persons afflicted with tuberculosis and allowed his adjustment of status under the Act of July 25, 1958. The bill also provided for the posting of a bond to overcome possible public charge aspects. (Priv. L. No. 565, 76 Stat. 1364 (1962)) (Sen. Rep. No. 1659, 2nd Sess.) (H.R. Rep. No. 2284, 2nd Sess.)-WHEL

87th Cong., S. 3267, for the relief of Gunter Heinz Hillebrand. Beneficiary, a 37-year old native of Germany and lawful permanent resident of the United States, was unable to meet the residence requirements for purposes of naturalization because of frequent business trips abroad. He was employed with the Von Kohorn International Corporation, an industry involved in erecting plants and machinery for the production of manmade fibers. (Priv. L. No. 641, 76 Stat. 1393 (1962)) (Sen. Rep. No. 1666, 2nd Sess.) (H.R. Rep. No. 2424, 2nd Sess.)-NRES

87th Cong., S. 3336, for the relief of Lazaro Loyola Arinque, Jr. Beneficiary, a 30-year old native and citizen of the Philippines, entered the United States on military orders, having served with the United States Coast Guard. He was injured on active duty during a fall from a gymnastic bar and was confined to a wheelchair as a quadriplegic, and retired from service. The law held the beneficiary lawfully admitted for permanent residence. (Priv. L. No. 608, 76 Stat. 1381 (1962)) (Sen. Rep. No. 1938, 2nd Sess.) (H.R. Rep. No. 2428, 2nd Sess.)-QMGN

88th Cong., H.R. 1174, for the relief of Elfriede Unterholzer Sharble. Beneficiary, a 31-year old native and citizen of Austria and spouse of a United States citizen veteran with two United States citizen children, was ineligible for a visa due to various arrests and convictions for fraud, theft, larceny, embezzlement, and prostitution. An application for waiver was denied because "the beneficiary had not demonstrated any substantial reformation." The beneficiary was previously granted relief under a private law, but it was learned that there were offenses which the Immigration and Naturalization Service and the Department of State did not have knowledge. The law waived section 212(a) (9) and (12) relating to crimes involving moral turpitude and prostitution. (Priv. L. No. 294, 78 Stat. 1173 (1964)) (H.R. Rep. No. 815, 1st Sess.) (Sen. Rep. No. 892, 2nd Sess.)-WCRF

88th Cong., H.R. 1182, for the relief of Willy Sapuschnin. Beneficiary, a 42-year old native of Poland and citizen of Germany, served in the German Navy and was held prisoner of war by the Russians eight years, until he escaped to Italy. He entered the United States as a visitor and was previously married to a United States citizen. The law held the beneficiary paroled into the United States under the Act of July 14, 1960. (Priv. L. No. 177, 78 Stat. 1125 (1964)) (H.R. Rep. No. 943, 1st Sess.)(Sen. Rep. No. 893, 2nd Sess.)-QMGN

88th Cong., H.R. 1398, for the relief of Margaret Barker. Beneficiary, a 22-year old native and citizen of the Philippines, entered the United States as a student. She did not derive United States citizenship at birth due to an invalid marriage of her father which was deemed bigamous. There was no evidence the beneficiary knew she was not a United States citizen, until she went to register at the Embassy for a United States passport. The law held the beneficiary lawfully admitted for permanent residence. (Priv. L. No. 50, 77 Stat. 890 (1963)) (H.R. Rep. No. 462, 1st Sess.) (Sen. Rep. No. 423, 1st Sess.)-QMGN

88th Cong., H.R. 1521, for the relief of Lororko Lucic. Beneficiary, a 25-year old native and citizen of Yugoslavia, was ineligible for a visa due to a conviction of assault with a dangerous weapon, for which he was sentenced to two months. The offense involved the beneficiary and two other men who were intoxicated, and who caused a brawl in the street by attempting involvement with a young lady. The beneficiary's mother and stepfather were United States citizens. The law waived section 212(a) (9) relating to crimes involving moral turpitude. (Priv. L. No. 183, 78 Stat. 1127 (1964)) (H.R. Rep. No. 968, 1st Sess.) (Sen. Rep. No. 899, 2nd Sess.)-WCRF

88th Cong., H.R. 1560, for the relief of Constantinos A. Grigoras (Gregoras). Beneficiary, a 38-year old native and citizen of Greece, was found ineligible for a visa as a fourth preference applicant due to violation of his nonimmigrant status following entries into the United States as a seaman. The violation of status canceled his priority date for visa issuance and reinstated a new date, the date of his deportation from the United States. The law held section 4 of the Act of September 22, 1959 and section 42.66(a) (7) of title 22 of the Code of Federal Regulations inapplicable on behalf of the beneficiary and deemed him registered as an immigrant on his original date of eligibility. (Priv. L. No. 158, 77 Stat. 932 (1963)) (H.R. Rep. No. 266, 1st Sess.) (Sen. Rep. No. 803, 1st Sess.)-QPRF

88th Cong., H.R. 2287, for the relief of Shin Sook (Renee) Whang. Beneficiary, a six-year old native and citizen of Korea who was an orphan, was adopted by a United States citizen who was employed by the United States Government. Because the United States citizen was a single person, she sought a waiver of the law requiring two parents for the petition of immigration for adopted children. The law allowed a petition to be filed for the beneficiary by the United States citizen adoptive parent. (Priv. L. No. 56, 77 Stat. 892 (1963)) (H.R. Rep. No. 338, 1st Sess.) (Sen. Rep. No. 429, 1st Sess.)-QIRA

88th Cong., H.R. 2305, for the relief of Zoltan Friedmann. Beneficiary, a 55-year old native and citizen of Hungary, was found ineligible for a nonquota visa as a minister of religion, due to a fraudulent certificate of his qualifications as a rabbi. It was discovered that although the beneficiary was educated as a rabbi, he lost his certificate and had a duplicate prepared by unauthorized authorities. His United States citizen brother resided in the United States. The law waived section 212(a) (19) relating to visa fraud. (Priv. L. No. 134, 77 Stat. 921 (1963)) (H.R. Rep. No. 818, 1st Sess.) (Sen. Rep. No. 713, 1st Sess.)-WCRF

88th Cong., H.R. 2309, for the relief of Luigi Giuseppe Luraschi. Beneficiary, a 57-year old native of England and United States citizen, was in jeopardy of losing citizenship by prolonged absence abroad in Italy, the country of which he was formerly a national. He was a permanent resident 11 years and United States citizen 23 years, but his employment as a producer with the movie industry required him to remain abroad. The beneficiary worked with Dino De Laurentus as a specialist and his work, according to the House Committee was of "valuable service to the United States . . . in presenting the best possible image of our country to others abroad." The law held section 352(a)(l) relating to residence abroad inapplicable to the beneficiary provided he return to the United States within two years. (Priv. L. No. 38, 77 Stat. 887 (1963)) (H.R. Rep. No. 316, 1st Sess.) (Sen. Rep. No. 430, 1st Sess.)-NRTN

88th Cong., H.R. 2444, for the relief of Mrs. Mabel Constance Kennedy. Beneficiary, an 80-year old widow and native of the British West Indies, entered the United States as a visitor and resided with her United States citizen daughter. She was ineligible to adjust status in the United States, and because of her ill health was unable to travel abroad to obtain a visa. The law held section 245(c) inapplicable in the case of the beneficiary. (Priv. L. No. 57, 77 Stat. 892 (1963)) (H.R. Rep. No. 340, 1st Sess.) (Sen. Rep. No. 431, 1st Sess.)-QMGN

88th Cong., H.R. 2737, for the relief of Pedro Aguinaldo. Beneficiary, a 70-year old native and citizen of the Philippines, entered the United States as a visitor. He served in the Philippine Scouts and in the United States Navy. He was a prisoner of war three years. The law held the beneficiary lawfully admitted for permanent residence. (Priv. L. No. 256, 78 Stat. 1157 (1964)) (H.R. Rep. No. 1334, 2nd Sess.) (Sen. Rep. No. 1141, 2nd Sess.)-NRES

88th Cong., H.R. 2757, for the relief of Woo You Lyn (also known as Hom You Fong and Lyn Fong Y. Hom). Beneficiary, a 34-year old native and citizen of China, entered the United States falsely claiming United States citizenship. His father, who entered on the same basis, later became a United States citizen and his mother and brother were admitted for lawful permanent residence. The beneficiary was ineligible to apply for relief under section 244 for suspension of deportation due to an absence from the United States during the requisite seven year period presence in the United States. The law held the beneficiary physically present in the United States for purposes of section 244. (Priv. L. No. 102, 77 Stat. 909 (1963)) (H.R. Rep. No. 684, 1st Sess.) (Sen. Rep. No. 611, 1st Sess.)-QMGN

88th Cong., H.R. 5507, for the relief of Michal Goleniewski. Beneficiary, a 40-year old native of Poland and permanent resident of the United States, was a defector from Poland in 1958 and he was employed by the United States Government. His services to the United States Government, according to the House Committee, "are rated as truly significant." Because of his former association with the Communist Party, he was unable to be naturalized for 10 years. The law held the beneficiary exempt from sections 313(a) and 313(c), and to have met the residence requirements of section

316(a). (Priv. L. No. 59, 77 Stat. 893 (1963)) (H.R. Rep. No. 468, 1st Sess.) (Sen. Rep. No. 437, 1st Sess.)-NXCP

88th Cong., H.R. 7347, for the relief of Teresa Elliopoulos and Anastasia Elliopoulos. Beneficiaries, one-year old twin sisters and natives and citizens of Greece, were coming to the United States for adoption by United States citizens who had no natural children. The beneficiaries' parents were living but were unable financially to care for them. The law held the beneficiaries to be classified as eligible orphans within section 101(b)(l)(F). (Priv. L. No. 195, 78 Stat. 1132 (1964)) (H.R. Rep. No. 1070, 1st Sess.) (Sen. Rep. No. 917, 2nd Sess.)-QIRA

88th Cong., H.R. 9090, for the relief of Mrs. Audrey Rossmann. Beneficiary, a 35-year old native of England, was the spouse of a lawful permanent resident. She was found ineligible for a visa due to prior attacks of insanity which stemmed from pregnancies resulting in depression. After her third child she was sterilized, and was free from any symptoms of puerperium 15 years. Her husband was engaged in research at Purdue University in the area of determining the structure of biologically significant large molecules. This involved grants from the National Science Foundation and the National Institutes of Health. The law waived section 212(a) (3) relating to previous attacks of insanity and provided posting of a bond to overcome possible public charge aspects. (Priv. L. No. 250, 78 Stat. 1155 (1964)) (H.R. Rep. No. 1263, 2nd Sess.) (Sen. Rep. No. 1064, 2nd Sess.)-WHEL

88th Cong., S. 584, for the relief of Yih-Ho Pao and his wife, Joanne T. Pao. Beneficiaries, 29- and 31-year old natives and citizens of China, entered the United States as students. The male beneficiary was employed by Boeing Company. His services with Boeing Company were needed in connection with research involving defense contracts which required permanent resident status. Visas were unavailable due to the oversubscribed categories for China. A first preference petition was filed on his behalf by his employer. The law held the beneficiary eligible for an immigrant visa under section 203(a) (1) of section 2 of the Act of October 24, 1962. (Priv. L. No. 329, 78 Stat. 1188 (1964)) (Sen. Rep. No. 106, 2nd Sess.) (H.R. Rep. No. 1849, 2nd Sess.)-QPRF

88th Cong., S. 1014, for the relief of Mrs. Joyce Mark Bouvier. Beneficiary, a 35-year old native of the United States and citizen of Switzerland, lost her United States citizenship by voting in foreign elections. Her four children derived United States citizenship at birth, but the youngest child did not because of her mother's loss of citizenship. The law restored citizenship to the beneficiary upon taking an oath of allegiance to the United States, and allowed derivative naturalization benefits for her fifth child by deeming the child be considered a citizen at birth under section 301(a) (7), relating to acquisition of birth abroad. (Priv. L. No. 153, 77 Stat. 930 (1963)) (Sen. Rep. No. 221, 1st Sess.) (H.R. Rep. No. 965, 1st Sess.)-NCOD

88th Cong., S. 1096, for the relief of Mrs. Susanna Grun (Susanne Roth). Beneficiary, a 71-year old native of Yugoslavia and citizen of West Germany, entered the United States for permanent residence and resided eleven years; thereafter she departed the United States and returned to Yugoslavia and remained abroad 25 years. Her husband and son were deceased and her remaining relative was her daughter-in-law and granddaughter, United States citizens, who wished her to remain with them in the United States. The law held the beneficiary within section 101(a) (27) (B) as a returning permanent resident alien. (Priv. L. No. 154, 77 Stat. 930 (1963)) (Sen. Rep. No. 520, 1st Sess.) (H.R. Rep. No. 955, 1st Sess.)-QPRP

88th Cong., S. 1999, for the relief of Francisco Navarro-Paz. Beneficiary, a 32-year old native and citizen of Mexico, entered the United States falsely claiming United States citizenship. He was married to a United States citizen with three United States citizen children dependent upon him for support. One child was mentally retarded, crippled, and required constant attention. He served one year in the United States Army. The beneficiary was unable to proceed to Mexico for a visa due to financial difficulties and, according to the Senate Committee Report, "his absence to obtain a visa would increase the hardship." The law held the beneficiary lawfully admitted for permanent residence. (Priv. L. No. 333, 78 Stat. 1189 (1964)) (Sen. Rep. No. 946, 2nd Sess.) (H.R. Rep. No. 1853, 2nd Sess.)-WCRF

89th Cong., H.R. 1236, for the relief of Salvador Munoz-Tostado. Beneficiary, a 66-year old native and citizen of Mexico, entered the United States as a visitor. He was later arrested for possession of 50 grains of cocaine and deported to Mexico. The beneficiary was married to a United States citizen with six United States citizen children. His spouse had been convicted of alien smuggling and served five months in jail. The law waived section 212(a) (23) relating to possession of narcotics. (Priv. L. No. 11, 79 Stat. 1336 (1965)) (H.R. Rep. No. 297, 1st Sess.) (Sen. Rep. No. 397, 1st Sess.)-WCRF

89th Cong., H.R. 1393, for the relief of Mrs. Maria Eduvigis Aran Heffernan. Beneficiary, a 44-year old native and citizen of the Philippines and widow of a United States citizen who was killed in action at Bataan, entered the United States as a visitor to testify on behalf of the United States Government in litigation pending before the Court of Claims. She returned to the Philippines to care for her father after studying in the United States. The law held the beneficiary within section 101(a) (27) (A) as an immediate relative of a United States citizen. (Priv. L. No. 178, 79 Stat. 1403 (1965)) (H.R. Rep. No. 825, 1st Sess.) (Sen. Rep. No. 889, 1st Sess.)-QIRW

89th Cong., H.R. 1414, for the relief of Jacobo Temel. Beneficiary, a 63-year old native of Poland and citizen of Colombia, was ineligible for admission to the United States due to a conviction in the United States of illegally dealing in drugs for which he was deported. His spouse and four children were lawful permanent residents, and one child was a United States citizen. The beneficiary also had three United States citizen siblings residing in the United States. In Colombia, he was the owner of a restaurant with assets in excess of $500,000. The law waived section 212(a) (23) relating to conviction on drug possession. (Priv. L. No. 269, 80 Stat. 1638 (1966)) (H.R. Rep. No. 1377, 2nd Sess.) (Sen. Rep. No. 1387, 2nd Sess.)-WCRF

89th Cong., H.R. 1627, for the relief of Esterina Ricupero. Beneficiary, a 20-year old native and citizen of Italy, was ineligible for a visa due to feeblemindedness. Her father was a United States citizen, and her mother and seven siblings were admitted for permanent residence. The beneficiary resided in Italy with her aunt and a 77-year old grandmother and was supported by her parents. She was unable to immigrate at the time of her family's immigration due to her health condition. The law waived section 212(a)(1) relating to feeblemindedness, and required the posting of a bond to overcome possible public charge aspects. (Priv. L. No. 66, 79 Stat. 1358 (1965)) (H.R. Rep. No. 462, 1st Sess.) (Sen. Rep. No. 660, 1st Sess.)-WHEL

89th Cong., H.R. 2005, for the relief of Miss Gloria Seborg. Beneficiary, a 22-year old native of Canada and lawful permanent resident of the United States for 10 years, was unable to meet the residence requirements for naturalization due to prolonged studies abroad. She was accepted for an overseas post with the Peace Corps but needed United States citizenship to serve. The law held the beneficiary to have met the residence requirements under section 316 for purposes of naturalization. (Priv. L. No. 152, 79 Stat. 1392 (1965)) (H.R. Rep. No. 761, 1st Sess.) (Sen. Rep. No. 825, 1st Sess.)-NRES

89th Cong., H.R. 2290, for the relief of Charlotte Schulz. Beneficiary, a 62-year old native of Germany and lawful permanent resident of the United States 10 years, was unable to meet the residence requirements for naturalization because of prolonged absence from the United States in her employment as administrator of the "Albert Schweitzer" hospital in Peru working with Peruvian Indians. The law deemed the period the beneficiary resided in the United States to have met the residence requirements under section 316. (Priv. L. No. 247, 80 Stat. 1627 (1966)) (H.R. Rep. No. 1371, 2nd Sess.) (Sen. Rep. No. 1256, 2nd Sess.)-NRES

89th Cong., H.R. 2752, for the relief of Kock Kong Fong. Beneficiary, a 31-year old native and citizen of China, entered the United States as the son of a United States citizen. It was later discovered his claim to citizenship was based on a misinterpretation of law for residents of Hawaii at the time of his father's birth in 1882. His parents, a United States citizen and a lawful permanent resident, resided in the United States. The law held the beneficiary lawfully admitted for permanent residence. (Priv. L. No. 234, 80 Stat. 1623 (1966)) (H.R. Rep. No. 864, 1st Sess.) (Sen. Rep. No. 1037, 2nd Sess.)-WCRF

89th Cong., H.R. 3233, for the relief of Emanuel G. Topakas. Beneficiary, a 31-year old native and citizen of Greece, was ineligible for a visa due to his previous fraudulent marriage for the purpose of obtaining permanent residence. His new spouse and daughter were United States citizens. The law held section 204(c), relating to prohibition on filing of petitions on behalf of persons who entered into marriage for the sole purpose of obtaining permanent residence, inapplicable on behalf of the beneficiary. (Priv. L. No. 283, 80 Stat. 1642 (1966)) (H.R. Rep. No. 1517, 2nd Sess.) (Sen. Rep. No. 1497, 2nd Sess.)-WCRF

89th Cong., H.R. 3292, for the relief of Consuelo Alvarado de Corpus. Beneficiary, a 36-year old native and citizen of Mexico, entered the United States for permanent residence. She and her United States citizen husband were convicted of importing aliens for prostitution and for assisting contract laborers to enter the United States two years after her entry. She was imprisoned six months. They had five United States citizen children. Her spouse served 20 years in the United States Navy. The law waived section 212(a) (31) relating to smuggling. (Priv. L. No. 70, 79 Stat. 1359 (1965)) (H.R. Rep. No. 486, 1st Sess.) (Sen. Rep. No. 664, 1st Sess.)-WCRF

89th Cong., H.R. 5231, for the relief of Jack Ralph Walker. Beneficiary, a 35-year old native of Canada, was brought to the United States at the age of six months by his United States adoptive parents. He learned he was not a United States citizen when he and his spouse filed for the adoption of a child. He later applied for permanent residence based on his entry but no record could be verified, and permanent residence was granted effective a later date. He served one year in the United States Navy. The law held the beneficiary retroactively lawfully admitted for permanent residence effective the date of his first entry to the United States. (Priv. L. No. 226, 80 Stat. 1619 (1966)) (H.R. Rep. No. 1057, 1st Sess.) (Sen. Rep. No. 1034, 2nd Sess.)-QMGN

89th Cong., H.R. 6235, for the relief of Chun Soo Kim. Beneficiary, a 10-year old native and citizen of Korea and an orphan, was adopted by United States citizens. He had paralysis, atrophy and shortening of both legs due to polio. They already had adopted two Korean children. The law held the beneficiary to be an orphan under section 101(b) (1) (F) and waived section 205(c) relating to the number of petitions which could be filed on behalf of adopted children. (Priv. L. No. 144, 79 Stat. 1389 (1965)) (H.R. Rep. No. 870, 1st Sess.) (Sen. Rep. No. 845, 1st Sess.)-QIRA

89th Cong., H.R. 7453, for the relief of Margaret Elizabeth and Frederick Henry Todd. Beneficiaries, husband and wife and natives of England and lawful permanent resident aliens of the United States for 12 years, were unable to petition for naturalization because of a departure to England due to illness in the family, where they remained for five years. The male beneficiary was employed with the United States Department of the Navy as an architect and scientific advisor in the David Taylor Model Basin. He was the first winner of the Gibbs Brothers Medal for outstanding contributions to naval architecture by the National Academy of Sciences, and the Department of the Navy urged support for providing expeditious naturalization. The Navy stated that his accomplishments could have a "direct bearing on the security of the United States since he deals with the total effectiveness of United States naval ships and submarines, including the top priority Polaris." The law held the beneficiaries to have met the residence requirements for purposes of naturalization under section 316. (Priv. L. No. 194, 79 Stat. 1408 (1965)) (H.R. Rep. No. 874, 1st Sess.) (Sen. Rep. No. 882, 1st Sess.)-NRES

89th Cong., H.R. 10288, for the relief of Dr. Antonio B. Santillano. Beneficiary, a 33-year old native of the Philippines and lawful permanent resident of the United States for one and a half years, was unable to petition for naturalization because he did not have the requisite residence period. He was admitted to the United States as a visitor seven years prior to attaining permanent residence, and he had a United States citizen wife with four United States citizen children. He left the United States to reside in the Philippines in 1959, but returned four years later because his oldest child was diagnosed as having a serious stomach ailment. He desired to practice medicine but needed United States citizenship to meet the state requirements. The law held the period of time he resided in the United States to meet the residence requirements of section 316. (Priv. L. No. 398, 80 Stat. 1685 (1966)) (H.R. Rep. No. 2033, 2nd Sess.) (Sen. Rep. No. 1914, 2nd Sess.)-NRES

89th Cong., H.R. 11718, for the relief of Jack L. Philippot. Beneficiary, a 47-year old native-born United States citizen, was unable to transmit United States citizenship to his three children due to prolonged absence from the United States. The beneficiary was born in the United States to parents who were citizens of Belgium. They took him abroad on their return to Belgium. He resided abroad with his family during his childhood. He served in the United States Armed forces and later returned to Europe serving for three years as a clerk in the American Embassy in Paris. Later he worked for the Economic Cooperation Administration for seven years. The law held the period of time the beneficiary was employed by the United States to have met the requirements of section 301(a) (7) thus enabling him to transmit United States citizenship to his children. (Priv. L. No. 277, 80 Stat. 1640 (1966)) (H.R. Rep. No. 1459, 2nd Sess.) (Sen. Rep. No. 1381, 2nd Sess)-NCOD

89th Cong., S. 374, for the relief of Dr. Guillermo Castrillo (Fernandez). Beneficiary, a 27-year old native of France and lawful permanent resident of the United States, was unable to meet the residence requirements for naturalization and desired to do so in order to meet state requirements to practice law. The law deemed the period of time the beneficiary resided in the United States since his entry as a visitor to have met the residence requirements, for purposes of naturalization under section III. (Priv. L. No. 169, 79 Stat. 1399 (1965)) (Sen. Rep. No. 282, 1st Sess.) (H.R. Rep. No. 1142, 1st Sess.)-NRES

89th Cong., S. 442, for the relief of Carleen Coen. Beneficiary, a 20-year old native and citizen of Canada, was unaware she did not derive United States citizenship through her father, a United States citizen. He served in the Royal Air Force two years and was transferred to the United States Air Force where he served two years until his death in action in the Normandy invasion in 1944. He had married a citizen of Canada and because of his act of expatriation by taking an oath of allegiance to the British Crown he was unable to transmit citizenship to the beneficiary. Her erroneous admission to the United States as a citizen was held to be an admission for permanent residence. She would have been eligible to petition for naturalization administratively, but the beneficiary sought full United States citizenship at birth. The law deemed the beneficiary to have been the daughter of a United States citizen under section 301(a) relating to acquisition of United States citizenship at birth. (Priv. L. 40, 79 Stat. 1347 (1965)) (Sen. Rep. No. 210, 1st Sess.) (H.R. Rep. No. 751, 1st Sess.)-NCOD

89th Cong., S. 582, for the relief of Aleksandr Kaznacheev. Beneficiary, a 32-year old native of the U.S.S.R., and permanent resident of the United States was employed by the Department of the Army as a translator-analyst. He was paroled into the United States in 1959 for the "convenience of the Government," and was the author of the book "Inside a Soviet Embassy." He had served in the Soviet Embassy in Burma for two years. The law held the beneficiary to be exempt from section 313(a) and 313(c) relating to a 10 year residence requirement for former members of the Communist Party in order to be naturalized. (Priv. L. No. 42, 79 Stat. 1347 (1965)) (Sen. Rep. No. 214, 1st Sess.) (H.R. Rep. No. 753, 1st Sess.)-NXCP

89th Cong., S. 619, for the relief of Nora Isabella Samuelli. Beneficiary, a 51-year old native of Romania, entered the United States as a visitor. She was formerly employed by the United States Information Service with the American Legation in Bucharest four years, when she was arrested by Romanian officials and accused of espionage. She was imprisoned 12 years on that offense along with her sister who worked with the British Government. Upon their release, they were stripped of their possessions and allowed to travel to France. The law held the beneficiary lawfully retroactively lawfully admitted for permanent residence effective the date of her first entry to the United States. (Priv. L. No. 203, 79 Stat. 1413 (1965)) (Sen. Rep. No. 94, 1st Sess.) (H.R. Rep. No. 1149, 1st Sess.)-NRES

89th Cong., S. 826, for the relief of Har Gobind Khorana. Beneficiary, a 43-year old native and citizen of India, entered the United States for permanent residence and desired expeditious naturalization to facilitate his nomination for membership in the National Academy of Science. He "achieved worldwide fame in the field of biochemistry" and was considered to be a "man of great genius" by the scientific community. Attestations concerning his abilities included Nobel winner Arthur Kornberg, the National Science Foundation, Rockefeller Institute and Harvard University. His efforts in the field of polynucleotides were instrumental in revolutionary developments in the field of genetics. He was employed by the University of Wisconsin as a professor and chairman of the Institute for Enzyme Research. He also served on advisory panels of the United States Public Health Service. The law held the beneficiary retroactively lawfully admitted for permanent residence effective the date of his first entry to the United States. (Priv. L. No. 44, 79 Stat. 1348 (1965)) (Sen. Rep. No. 238, 1st Sess. (H.R. Rep. No. 756, 1st Sess.)-NRES

89th Cong., S. 1084, for the relief of Shu Hsien Chang. Beneficiary, a 57-year old native and citizen of China, entered the United States for permanent residence on the basis of a first preference petition filed by the Army Map Service. He was previously employed by the Nationalist Government in China, and in Taiwan with the American military attaché. His duties with the United States Army Map Service involved translation of geographic names as a specialist in Chinese matters. Citizenship would allow him access to material which would more effectively utilize his expertise. The law held the beneficiary retroactively lawfully admitted for permanent residence effective the date of his first entry to the United States. (Priv. L. No. 82, 79 Stat. 1363 (1965)) (Sen. Rep. No. 220, 1st Sess.) (H.R. Rep. No. 919, 1st Sess.)-NRES

89th Cong., S. 1111, for the relief of Pola Bodenstein. Beneficiary, a 48-year old native of Poland and citizen of France, was ineligible for a visa due to a prior attack of insanity. She was the only survivor of her immediate family who were persecuted during World War II, and she suffered severe depression because of that loss. The beneficiary was under treatment and prognosis for continued stability was good. Her husband was the beneficiary of a fourth preference visa petition and their two children were also eligible for immigration. The law waived section 212(a) (3) relating to persons who had one or more attacks of insanity. (Priv. L. No. 109, 79 Stat. 1374 (1965)) (Sen. Rep. No. 395, 1st Sess.) (H.R. Rep. No. 859, 1st Sess.)-WHEL

89th Cong., S. 1919, for the relief of Laura MacArthur Goditiabois-Deacon. Beneficiary, a 28-year old native-born United States citizen, spent most of her life abroad as a family member of Ambassador Douglas MacArthur II. She married a citizen of Belgium and had one child, who was unable to derive United States citizenship at birth because the beneficiary did not have the required 10 year residence in the United States for transmission of United States citizenship. She was two months short of meeting the requirement. The law held the time the beneficiary resided abroad with her parents to have met the residence requirements under section 301(a) (7) for transmitting United States citizenship to her child. (Priv. L. No. 93, 79 Stat. 1366 (1965)) (Sen. Rep. No. 560, 1st Sess.) (H.R. Rep. No. 920, 1st Sess.)-NCOD

89th Cong., S. 2010, for the relief of Fun Wat Hoy. Beneficiary, a 32-year old native and citizen of China, entered the United States as a visitor. He was employed in a restaurant and made an application for relief under provisions for suspension of deportation, but was unable to meet the requirements of presence in the United States due to brief excursions to Canada. The law held the beneficiary lawfully admitted for permanent residence. (Priv. L. No. 451, 80 Stat. 1706 (1966)) (Sen. Rep. No. 1389, 89th Cong., 2nd Sess.)-QMGN

89th Cong., S. 2451, for the relief of Che Yim Loh. Beneficiary, a one-year old child, was adopted by a United States citizen who desired to bring the child to the United States. The single adoptive parent was a reporter and foreign correspondent with the Buffalo Evening News, Associated Press and the New York Times. She was also a researcher-reporter for "David Brinkley's Journal," and producer for National Educational Television. The law held the beneficiary to be classified as a child under section 101(b)(1)(F) and allowed a single parent to file a petition on behalf of the child. (Priv. L. No. 455, 80 Stat. 1708 (1966)) (Sen. Rep. No. 1122, 2nd Sess.) (H.R. Rep. No. 1942, 2nd Sess.)-QIRA

89th Cong., S. 2555, for the relief of Kim Kin Soon. Beneficiary, a five-year old native and citizen of Korea who was an orphan, had been adopted by United States citizens who previously adopted eight Korean orphans. Five of the previously adopted orphans had been destined to other families when they entered the United States, but were placed with the adoptive parents because they were neglected or mistreated. They also had petitions approved for three other orphans including a set of twins. The law held inapplicable section 204(c) relating to a restriction of two petitions for the immigration of adopted children. (Priv. L. No. 337, 80 Stat. 1662 (1966)) (Sen. Rep. No. 1130, 2nd Sess.) (H.R. Rep. No. 1943, 2nd Sess.)-QIRA

89th Cong., S. 3189, for the relief of Dr. Alonso Portuondo. Beneficiary, a 48-year old native and citizen of Cuba, entered the United States for permanent residence and had served as a visiting professor of medicine at the University of Miami Medical School. He desired expeditious naturalization in order to take the requisite medical exam to practice medicine in Florida. The law held the beneficiary retroactively lawfully admitted for permanent residence effective the date of his first entry to the United States. (Priv. L. No. 327, 80 Stat. 1659 (1966)) (Sen. Rep. No. 1315, 2nd Sess.) (H.R. Rep. No. 1981, 2nd Sess.)-NRES

89th Cong., S. 3222, for the relief of Dusko Doder. Beneficiary, a 29-year old native of Yugoslavia, entered the United States for permanent residence on the basis of his wife's petition, and desired expeditious naturalization in order to accept overseas positions as a newspaperman with his employer, the Associated Press. The law held the beneficiary retroactively lawfully admitted for permanent residence effective the date of his first entry to the United States. (Priv. L. No. 465, 80 Stat. 1711 (1966)) (Sen. Rep. No. 1337, 2nd Sess.)-NRES

89th Cong., S. 3272, for the relief of Dr. Jacobo Albo Maya. Beneficiary, a 41-year old native and citizen of Cuba, entered the United States for permanent residence. He was a doctor employed in Florida as a staff physician. He wished expeditious naturalization in order to take the medical examination in the State of Florida for licensing. The law held the beneficiary retroactively lawfully admitted for permanent residence effective the date of his first entry to the United States. (Priv. L. No. 328, 80 Stat. 1659 (1966)) (Sen. Rep. No. 1392, 2nd Sess.) (H.R. Rep. No. 1982, 2nd Sess.)-NRES

90th Cong., H.R. 2048, for the relief of William John Masterton and Louis Vincent Nanne. Beneficiaries, 28- and 26-year old natives and citizens of Canada, were admitted to the United States for permanent residence. They were outstanding hockey players and desired expeditious naturalization in order to play for the United States team in international competitions. One beneficiary was a freshman hockey coach for the University of Minnesota, and the other a professional hockey player with the Omaha Knights of Nebraska. A letter from the United States National Hockey Team stated, "both Masterton and Nanne played with us up to the world championships and in doing so, made many financial sacrifices while giving the program the much-needed experience and stability." The letter also responded to various concerns of the Committee concerning the expeditious naturalization of athletes. The law held the beneficiaries retroactively lawfully admitted for permanent residence effective the date of their first entry to the United States. (Priv. L. No. 18, 81 Stat. 992 (1967)) (H.R. Rep. No. 47, 1st Sess.) (Sen. Rep. No. 330, 1st Sess.)-NRES

90th Cong., H.R. 3221, for the relief of Dr. Alexander D. Cross. Beneficiary, a 35-year old native and citizen of Great Britain, was ineligible for a visa due to evasion of duty on a watch. He was employed by Syntex Research in the field of pharmaceutical manufacturing and was an "internationally known and widely respected scientist." The beneficiary was formerly married to a United States citizen two years. The law waived section 212(a) (9) relating to exclusion for crimes involving moral turpitude. (Priv. L. No. 64, 81 Stat. 1005 (1967)) (H.R. Rep. No. 309, 1st Sess.) (Sen. Rep. No. 434, 1st Sess.)-WCRF

90th Cong., H.R. 5216, for the relief of Roberto Martin Del Campo. Beneficiary, a 42-year old native and citizen of Mexico, was ineligible for a visa due to a conviction for smuggling aliens into the United States. He and his spouse resided in Mexico with four children. Their fifth child was a permanent resident alien. The law waived section 212(a) (31) relating to exclusion of persons involved in smuggling aliens into the United States. (Priv. L. No. 138, 81 Stat. 1030 (1967)) (H.R. Rep. No. 467, 1st Sess.) (Sen. Rep. No. 658, 1st Sess.)-WCRF

90th Cong., H.R. 5862, for the relief of Dr. Juan F. Chaves. Beneficiary, a 46-year old native and citizen of Cuba, entered the United States for permanent residence and desired expeditious naturalization in order to assist in his employment. He was employed as a city engineer in Virginia and believed his status was a handicap "in supervising United States citizen employees." The law held the beneficiary retroactively lawfully admitted for permanent residence the date of his first entry to the United States. (Priv. L. No. 57, 81 Stat. 1004 (1967)) (H.R. Rep. No. 310, 1st Sess.) (Sen. Rep. No. 437, 1st Sess.)-NRES

90th Cong., H.R. 13301, for the relief of PFC John R. Aneli. Beneficiary was a native of Italy admitted to the United States as a permanent resident alien. He enlisted in the United States Army in 1966 and was killed in Vietnam in 1967. The law held the beneficiary to be a United States citizen at the time of his death by conferring United States citizenship posthumously. (Priv. L. No. 299, 82 Stat. 1021 (1968)) (H.R. Rep. No. 1027, 1st Sess.) (Sen. Rep. No. 1217, 2nd Sess.)-NXPS

90th Cong., H.R. 15591, for the relief of PFC John Patrick Collopy. Beneficiary was a native of Ireland admitted to the United States for permanent residence with his parents, a brother, and twin sisters. He served in the United States Army from 1966 to 1967 and was killed in action in Vietnam. The law held the beneficiary to be a United States citizen at the time of his death by conferring United States citizenship posthumously. (Priv. L. No. 263, 82 Stat. 1393 (1968)) (H.R. Rep. No. 1216, 2nd Sess.) (Sen. Rep. No. 1205, 2nd Sess.)-NXPS

90th Cong., S. 164, for the relief of Dr. Cesar A. Mena. Beneficiary, a 53-year old native and citizen of Cuba, entered the United States for permanent residence and desired expeditious naturalization in order to take an exam for dental license in Florida. He was employed by the Department of Health, Education and Welfare at the Cuban Refugee Emergency Center and was intent in pursuing a career in public health. The law held the beneficiary retroactively lawfully admitted for permanent residence the date of his first entry to the United States. (Priv. L. No. 33, 81 Stat. 996 (1967)) (Sen. Rep. No. 100, 1st Sess.) (H.R. Rep. No. 443, 1st Sess.)-NRES

90th Cong., S. 168, for the relief of Maria Jordan Ferrando. Beneficiary, a 65-year old native of Spain and citizen of Venezuela, entered the United States as a visitor. She resided with her adoptive daughter, a United States citizen, for whom she had custody since the age of two. The daughter was not formally adopted until the age of 17. The law held the beneficiary the parents of a United States citizen for the purposes of section 201(b). (Priv. L. No. 42, 81 Stat. 999 (1967)) (Sen. Rep. No. 103, 1st Sess.) (H.R. Rep. No. 444, 1st Sess.)-QIRM

90th Cong., S. 445, for the relief of Rosemarie Gauch Neth. Beneficiary, a 24-year old native of Germany and lawful permanent resident of the United States, was married to a United States citizen three years prior to his death while serving in the United States Army in Vietnam. He received a Silver Star posthumously for his deeds. She had a three-year old United States citizen child. The beneficiary was desirous of filing a petition for naturalization under the three-year residence period for persons married to United States citizens. The law held the beneficiary within the purview of section 319(a) relating to naturalization benefits for spouses of United States citizens. (Priv. L. No. 139, 81 Stat. 1030 (1967)) (Sen. Rep. No. 314, 1st Sess.) (H.R. Rep. No. 670, 1st Sess.)-NRES

90th Cong., S. 534, for the relief of Setsuko Wilson (nee Hiranaka). Beneficiary, a 34-year old native and citizen of Japan and spouse of a United States citizen serving in the Armed Forces, was ineligible for a visa due to conviction for larceny and a narcotics law violation involving a small quantity of heroin. The law waived section 212(a) (23) relating to exclusion for drug possession. (Priv. L. No. 93, 81 Stat. 1016 (1967)) (Sen. Rep. No. 174, 1st Sess.) (H.R. Rep. No. 456, 1st Sess.)-WCRF

90th Cong., S. 747, for the relief of Earl C. Chamberlain. Beneficiary, a 51-year old native and citizen of Canada, entered the United States for permanent residence. He was a doctor of veterinary medicine and was employed at the National Institute of Health. The beneficiary desired expeditious naturalization in order to "advance his professional status." The law held the beneficiary retroactively lawfully admitted for permanent residence as of the date of his first entry to the United States. (Priv. L. No. 328, 82 Stat. 1425 (1968)) (Sen. Rep. No. 332, 1st Sess.) (H.R. Rep. No. 1650, 2nd Sess.)-NRES

90th Cong., S. 866, for the relief of Giuseppe Pacino Biancarosso. Beneficiary was a 10-year old native and citizen of Italy who was placed in the care of his aunt since the age of eight months. The aunt's husband died prior to the issuance of the adoption decree, however. The natural mother was deceased and the whereabouts of the natural father was unknown. The aunt desired to bring the child to the United States notwithstanding the requirement of two parents filing a petition for the child. The law held the beneficiary to be a child within section 101(b) (l) (F) and allowed the adoptive parent to file a petition on his behalf. (Priv. L. No. 204, 81 Stat. 1050 (1968)) (Sen. Rep. No. 659, 1st Sess.) (H.R. Rep. No. 1000, 1st Sess.)-QIRA

90th Cong., S. 1021, for the relief of Antonio Luis Navarro. Beneficiary, a 45-year old native of Cuba and lawful permanent resident of the United States six years, was employed by W.R. Grace Company in various executive capacities including Lima, Peru. He was also married to a United States citizen. The beneficiary first entered the United States for permanent residence in 1943, after which he returned to Cuba 10 years later. He re-entered and obtained refugee status in 1961, and from that time he was in the employ of W.R. Grace. He was due to return to the United States from his assignment abroad with that company and planned to petition for naturalization. An airplane crash killing essential personnel from Peru forced him to return to Peru to assist the company. The law held the beneficiary to have fulfilled the residence requirements of section 316. (Priv. L. No. 114, 81 Stat. 1024 (1967)) (Sen. Rep. No. 270, 1st Sess.) (H.R. Rep. No. 684, 1st Sess.)-NRES

90th Cong., S. 1458, for the relief of Lee Duk Hee. Beneficiary, a two-year old native and citizen of Korea and orphan was to be adopted by United

States citizens who had previously adopted three Korean orphans. One of the previously adopted orphans had died. The adoptive parents then found two orphan twins. They also journeyed to the orphanage where their deceased child was found and learned of the beneficiary who they also wanted to adopt. The law held inapplicable section 204(c) relating to the two-petition limitation for immigration of adopted children. (Priv. L. No. 121, 81 Stat. 1026 (1967)) (Sen. Rep. No. 441, 1st Sess.) (H.R. Rep. No. 694, 1st Sess.)-QIRA

90th Cong., S. 1652, for the relief of Anastasia D. Mpatziani. Beneficiary, a 67-year old native and citizen of Greece and widow, was ineligible for a visa due to illiteracy. Her only close relative, a United States citizen, contributed to her support 30 years and filed a petition on her behalf. The law waived section 212(a) (25) relating to exclusion of persons due to illiteracy. (Priv. L. No. 346, 82 Stat. 1430 (1968)) (Sen. Rep. No. 784, 1st Sess.) (H.R. Rep. No. 1671, 2nd Sess.)-WXIL

90th Cong., S. 1781, for the relief of Kyong Hwan Chang. Beneficiary, a 28-year old native and citizen of Korea, entered the United States as a student. He was inducted into the Army and served five years. He was granted relief under suspension of deportation, and his case was referred to Congress. Because he was under orders for service in Vietnam, he was anxious to have his status adjusted and take advantage of special naturalization provisions for members of the Armed Forces. The law held the beneficiary lawfully admitted for permanent residence. (Priv. L. No. 160, 81 Stat. 1037)) (1967) (Sen. Rep. No. 328, 1st Sess.) (H.R. Rep. No. 945, 2nd Sess.)-NRES

90th Cong., S. 2706, for the relief of Yung Ran Kim. Beneficiary, a four-month old native and citizen of Korea and orphan, was to be adopted by United States citizens. They had previously adopted two Korean orphans, one of whom died within 13 hours of arrival in the United States. The law held section 204(c) inapplicable as it related to the limitation of two petitions for the immigration of adopted children. (Priv. L. No. 339, 82 Stat. 1428 (1968)) (Sen. Rep. No. 1209, 2nd Sess.) (H.R. Rep. No. 1731, 2nd Sess.)-QIRA

90th Cong., S. 2720, for the relief of Heng Liong Thung. Beneficiary, a 33-year old native of Indonesia and lawful permanent resident of the United States, desired expeditious citizenship due to his employment on a research project under contract with the Department of Defense. He had resided in the United States six years, four of which were as a permanent resident. His employment was with Cornell Aeronautical Laboratory as a systems engineer, and his travel plans involved a project in Thailand. The law held the periods of time the beneficiary resided in the United States to have met the statutory requirements of section 316. (Priv. L. No. 340, 82 Stat. 1428 (1968)) (Sen. Rep. No. 1062, 2nd Sess.) (H.R. Rep. No. 1675, 2nd Sess.)-NRES

90th Cong., S. 2759, for the relief of S. Sgt. Ivan Claus King. Beneficiary was a native of Germany and citizen of China, who was admitted to the

United States for permanent residence and filed a declaration for citizenship February 2, 1965. He enlisted in the United States Army in 1965 and was killed in Vietnam 1967. His mother was a United States citizen, and one brother was a permanent resident. The law held the beneficiary to be a United States citizen at the time of his death by conferring United States citizenship posthumously. (Priv. L. No. 343, 82 Stat. 1429 (1968)) (Sen. Rep. No. 1212, 2nd Sess.) (H.R. Rep. No. 1732, 2nd Sess.)-NXPS

90th Cong., S. 2897, for the relief of James T. O'Brien. Beneficiary, a 55-year old native and citizen of Canada, entered the United States at the age of 15 with his family as a United States citizen. It was later discovered there was no evidence his father was a United States citizen at the time of his birth, thus he did not derive United States citizenship. The law held the beneficiary retroactively lawfully admitted for permanent residence effective the date of his first entry to the United States. (Priv. L. No. 347, 82 Stat. 1430 (1968)) (Sen. Rep. No. 1197, 2nd Sess.) (H.R. Rep. No. 1733, 2nd Sess.)-NCOD

91st Cong., H.R. 1828, for the relief of James F. Wegener. Beneficiary was a native of Canada who was admitted to the United States as an immigrant. He served in the United States Army two years, including a year in Vietnam. He had been scheduled for naturalization but was killed while at work in the United States 17 days prior to the citizenship ceremony. His wife was a United States citizen and they had one child. The law deemed the beneficiary to be a citizen at the time of his death by conferring United States citizenship posthumously. (Priv. L. No. 22, 83 Stat. 874 (1969)) (H.R. Rep. No. 251, 1st Sess.) (Sen. Rep. No. 303, 1st Sess.)-NXPS

91st Cong., H.R. 1939, for the relief of Mrs. Marjorie J. Hottenroth. Beneficiary, a 22-year old native and citizen of China, was the widow of a United States citizen killed while serving with the United States Air Force in Vietnam. She entered the United States as a visitor and desired to remain with her husband's relatives and attend school. The law deemed the beneficiary an immediate relative for purposes of the Immigration Act and section 204 inapplicable in her case. (Priv. L. No. 17, 83 Stat. 872 (1969)) (H.R. Rep. No. 86, 1st Sess.) (Sen. Rep. No. 253, 1st Sess.)-QIRW

91st Cong., H.R. 3165, for the relief of Martin H. Loeffler. Beneficiary, a 43-year old native of Germany and lawful permanent resident of the United States was employed by the Department of Defense as a research specialist. Because of his former association with the Communist Party in East Berlin, he was subject to a 10-year residence requirement for naturalization. According to the House Committee, the beneficiary "collaborated with the Government in an outstanding manner and continues to make major contributions to the national security." The law exempted the beneficiary from section 313 relating to residence requirements of former Communist Party members. (Priv. L. No. 51, 83 Stat. 885 (1969)) (H.R. Rep. No. 224, 1st Sess.) (Sen. Rep. No. 441, 1st Sess.)-NXCP

91st Cong., H.R. 3376, for the relief of Maria da Conceicao Evaristo. Beneficiary, a 54-year old native and citizen of Portugal, was ineligible for a visa as an illiterate. She was afflicted with spinal meningitis at the age of three which resulted in her being deaf. She was supported by four siblings, three of whom were United States citizens. The law waived section 212(a)(25) relating to persons who were illiterate. The bill also provided for the posting of a bond to overcome possible public charge aspects. (Priv. L. No. 30, 83 Stat. 876 (1969)) (H.R. Rep. No. 229, 1st Sess.) (Sen. Rep. No. 316, 1st Sess.)-WHEL

91st Cong., H.R. 5136, for the relief of George Tilson Weed. Beneficiary, a 60-year old native of Japan and lawful permanent resident of the United States, desired expeditious naturalization due to his travel in connection with employment with DuPont Far East, Inc. He had resided in the United States as a nonimmigrant 14 years, and after attaining permanent residence worked with the United States occupation forces in Japan six years. Because of his position with DuPont in Japan, he was unable to fulfill the residence requirements for naturalization. The law held the beneficiary to have complied with section 316 relating to residence for naturalization. (Priv. L. No. 20, 83 Stat. 873 (1969)) (H.R. Rep. No. 124, 1st Sess.) (Sen. Rep. No. 256, 1st Sess.)-NRES

91st Cong., H.R. 6600, for the relief of Panagiotis, Georgia, and Constantina Malliaras. Beneficiaries, 17-, 22-, and 13-year old siblings, two as natives and citizens of Greece, and the youngest as a native and citizen of Australia, entered the United States as visitors several months after their father killed their mother and then committed suicide. The two youngest resided in the United States with their aunt and uncle, United States citizens. The eldest worked as a clerk and lived alone. The law held the beneficiaries lawfully admitted for permanent residence. (Priv. L. No. 69, 83 Stat. 891 (1969)) (H.R. Rep. No. 519, 1st Sess.) (Sen. Rep. No. 591, 1st Sess.)-QMGN

91st Cong., H.R. 6607, for the relief of SP4C. Klaus Josef Strauss. Beneficiary was a native of Germany admitted to the United States as an immigrant. He was drafted into the United States Army in 1966 and was killed in Vietnam 1968. His mother was a United States citizen, and two brothers were permanent resident aliens. The law held the beneficiary to be a United States citizen at the time of his death by conferring United States citizenship posthumously. (Priv. L. No. 15, 83 Stat. 871 (1969)) (H.R. Rep. No. 125, 1st Sess.) (Sen. Rep. No. 257, 1st Sess.)-NXPS

91st Cong., H.R. 13997, for the relief of S. Sgt. Ryuzo Somma. Beneficiary was a native of Japan admitted for permanent residence. He was inducted in the Army in 1966 and served until he was killed in Vietnam 1969. He had been awarded two Bronze Star medals and a Purple Heart. His mother was a United States citizen. The law deemed the beneficiary to be a citizen at the time of his death by conferring United States citizenship posthumously.

(Priv. L. No. 151, 84 Stat. 2128 (1970)) (H.R. Rep. No. 1259, 2nd Sess.) (Sen. Rep. No. 1110, 2nd Sess.)-NXPS

91st Cong., S. 85, for the relief of Dr. Jagir Singh Randhawa. Beneficiary, a 46-year old native and citizen of India, entered the United States for permanent residence. He was employed as a research physicist for the United States Army at the White Sands Missile Range. He desired expeditious naturalization in order to have access to a "much broader scope of sensitive research problems." The law held the beneficiary retroactively lawfully admitted for permanent residence effective the date of his first entry to the United States. (Priv. L. No. 48, 83 Stat. 884 (1969)) (H.R. Rep. No. 25, 1st Sess.) (Sen. Rep. No. 401, 1st Sess.)-NRES

91st Cong., S. 265, for the relief of John (Giovanni) Denaro. Beneficiary, a 49-year old native and citizen of Italy, entered the United States for permanent residence and desired expeditious naturalization in order to apply for the position of a probation officer. The law held the beneficiary retroactively lawfully admitted for permanent residence effective the date of his first entry to the United States. (Priv. L. No. 53, 83 Stat. 885 (1969)) (Sen. Rep. No. 126, 1st Sess.) (H.R. Rep. No. 503, 1st Sess.)-NRES

91st Cong., S. 537, for the relief of Noriko Susan Duke (Nakano). Beneficiary, a four-year old native of Japan and lawful permanent resident of the United States, was the adoptive daughter of a United States citizen couple, one of whom was employed abroad as a teacher for the International Christian University. In order for the child to be naturalized, a two-year residence requirement after lawful admission to the United States was required. The beneficiary's parents were anxious that the beneficiary remain with them during their employment in Japan. The law held the beneficiary within the purview of section 323(c) relating to the ability to be expeditiously naturalized without regard to residence requirements for adopted children. (Priv. L. No. 11, 83 Stat. 870 (1969)) (Sen. Rep. No. 110, 1st Sess.) (H.R. Rep. No. 235, 1st Sess.)-NMSC

91st Cong., S. 737, for the relief of Konrad Ludwig Staudinger. Beneficiary, a 42-year old native and citizen of Austria, entered the United States as a nonimmigrant ski instructor and resided for 12 years during the skiing season. He was ineligible for a visa due to a conviction of theft involving a drill and other tools in Austria. The law waived section 212(a)(9) relating to crimes involving moral turpitude. (Priv. L. No. 187, 84 Stat. 2150 (1970)) (Sen. Rep. No. 942, 2nd Sess.) (H.R. Rep. No. 1483, 2nd Sess.)-WCRF

91st Cong., S. 1704, for the relief of Lillian Biazzo. Beneficiary, a 32-year old native and citizen of Italy, entered the United States for permanent residence, and then returned to Italy due to the illness of her father. She then re-entered six years later as a visitor and obtained a sixth preference visa petition as a stenographer. The law held the beneficiary within section 101(a) (27) (B) as a returning permanent resident alien. (Priv. L. No. 146,

84 Stat. 2127 (1970)) (Sen. Rep. No. 248, 1st Sess.) (H.R. Rep. No. 1325, 2nd Sess.)-QPRP

91st Cong., S. 2863, for the relief of Mrs. Cumorah Kennington Romney. Beneficiary, a 41-year old native-born United States citizen, was unable to transmit United States citizenship to her child because she was four months short of the 10 year residence requirement for transmission purposes. The law held the beneficiary to have complied with transmission requirement under section 201(g), thus allowing her 20-year old daughter to automatically derive United States citizenship from birth. (Priv. L. No. 148, 84 Stat. 2128 (1970)) (Sen. Rep. No. 830, 2nd Sess.) (H.R. Rep. No. 1326, 2nd Sess.)-NCOD

91st Cong., S. 2976, for the relief of Margarita Anne Marie Baden (Nguyen Tan Nga). Beneficiary, a one-year old native and citizen of South Vietnam, was an orphan. She was adopted by a United States citizen nurse employed by the United States Agency for International Development in that country. The law held the beneficiary to be a child under section 101(b) (1) (F) upon the filing of a petition. (Priv. L. No. 162, 84 Stat. 2132 (1970)) (Sen. Rep. No. 815, 2nd Sess.) (H.R. Rep. No. 1327, 2nd Sess.)-QIRA

91st Cong., S. 3136, for the relief of Guy Andre Blanchette. Beneficiary was a native of Canada admitted to the United States as a permanent resident. He enlisted in the Army in 1965 and served in Vietnam from 1968 until his death in 1969. He had been awarded the National Defense Service Medal, Vietnam Service Medal with one Bronze Service Star, and the Vietnam Campaign Ribbon, and posthumously the Bronze Star Medal, Purple Heart, and Good Conduct Medal. His wife was a United States citizen as well as his father and brother. The law held the beneficiary to be a United States citizen posthumously. (Priv. L. No. 149, 84 Stat. 2128 (1970)) (Sen. Rep. No. 816, 2nd Sess.) (H.R. Rep. No. 1328, 2nd Sess.)-NXPS

91st Cong., S. 3620, for the relief of Mrs. Anastasia Pertsovitch. Beneficiary, a 63-year old native and citizen of Russia and widow of a United States citizen, was separated from her spouse when he was forcibly taken from Russia to Germany as a laborer. He later became a United States citizen. The beneficiary was not granted permission to leave Russia until six years later, but her husband died shortly after her arrival. The law held the beneficiary within section 201(b) and 204 relating to immediate relatives of United States citizens. (Priv. L. No. 190, 84 Stat. 2151 (1970)) (Sen. Rep. No. 1175, 2nd Sess.) (H.R. Rep. No. 1491, 2nd Sess.)-QIRW

92nd Cong., H.R. 1899, for the relief of Mrs. Maria G. Orsini (nee Mari). Beneficiary, a 41-year old native and citizen of Italy, entered the United States for permanent residence as the spouse of a United States citizen. It was later discovered her husband's previous marriage had not been terminated, and that her husband had been discharged from the Army due to service-connected mental illness and declared mentally incompetent. He had failed to disclose a prior marriage due to the illness. A divorce was sought, but he died prior to his remarriage to the beneficiary. The law held the beneficiary lawfully admitted for permanent residence. (Priv. L. No. 42, 85 Stat. 850 (1971)) (H.R. Rep. No. 138, 1st Sess.) (Sen. Rep. No. 462, 1st Sess.)-QMGN

92nd Cong., H.R. 1974, for the relief of Mrs. Gloria Vazquez Herrera. Beneficiary, a 22-year old native and citizen of Mexico, entered the United States as a visitor. She was the widow of a United States citizen who was murdered six years after her entry to the United States. There were three minor United States citizen children of the marriage. The law held the beneficiary lawfully admitted for permanent residence. (Priv. L. No. 90, 86 Stat. 1538 (1972)) (H.R. Rep. No. 856, 2nd Sess.) (Sen. Rep. No. 878, 2nd Sess.)-QIRW

92nd Cong., H.R. 2076, for the relief of Vladimir Rodriguez LaHera. Beneficiary, a 35-year old native of Cuba and lawful permanent resident of the United States, was formerly employed with the General Directorate of Intelligence of the Cuban Government, and was in the Cuban Rebel Army before he defected to the United States. He was desirous of becoming a naturalized citizen without having to comply with the total 10-year residence period required of former members of the Communist Party, although he had already fulfilled eight years of that requirement. The law held the beneficiary to be exempt from section 313 relating to residence requirements for persons formerly associated with the Communist Party. (Priv. L. No. 92, 86 Stat. 1539 (1972)) (H.R. Rep. No. 818, 2nd Sess.) (Sen. Rep. No. 880, 2nd Sess.)-NXCP

92nd Cong., H.R. 2394, for the relief of Antonio Benavides. Beneficiary, a 61-year old native and citizen of Mexico, was ineligible for a visa due to a conviction for aiding in the smuggling of aliens into the United States. His United States citizen spouse and five children resided in the United States. The law waived section 212(a) (31) relating to smuggling aliens into the United States. (Priv. L. No. 117, 86 Stat. 1549 (1972)) (H.R. Rep. No. 619, 1st Sess.) (Sen. Rep. No. 1053, 2nd Sess.)-WCRF

92nd Cong., H.R. 3929, for the relief of Gheorghe Jucu and Aurelia Jucu. Beneficiaries, 48- and 35-natives of Romania and lawful permanent residents of the United States, defected to the United States after having served 14 years as legal adviser for the Romanian Ministry of Foreign Affairs. He also served as first secretary of the Romanian Permanent Mission to the United Nations in New York two years. They had two children, one who was handicapped, but attended school and walked with prosthetic aids. According to the House Report, the male beneficiary made "valuable contributions to the security of the United States." The law held the beneficiaries exempt from section 313 relating to the prohibition of naturalization for former members of the Communist Party. (Priv. L. No. 9, 85 Stat. 836 (1971)) (H.R. Rep. No. 106, 1st Sess.) (Sen. Rep. No. 218, 1st Sess.)-NXCP

92nd Cong., H.R. 6907, for the relief of Matyas Hunyadi. Beneficiary, a 49-year old native and citizen of Hungary, was paroled into the United States and was employed as a physician in Washington, D.C. He was found ineligible for a visa due to a conviction 12 years previously for forging a false prescription for narcotics (morphine). The law waived section 212(a) (23) relating to possession of drugs. (Priv. L. No. 99, 86 Stat. 1541 (1972)) (H.R. Rep. 821, 2nd Sess.) (Sen. Rep. No. 883, 2nd Sess.)-WCRF

92nd Cong., H.R. 7641, for the relief of Chung Chi Lee. Beneficiary, a 30-year old native and citizen of China, was ineligible for a visa due to a conviction of two counts of armed robbery at the age of 16. His father was a United States citizen and his mother a lawful permanent resident. He had four siblings, three of whom were lawful permanent residents and one of whom was a United States citizen. The law waived section 212(a) (9) and 212(a) (10) relating to crimes involving moral turpitude and exclusion for two or more convictions. (Priv. L. No. 100, 86 Stat. 1541 (1972)) (H.R. Rep. No. 827, 2nd Sess.) (Sen. Rep. No. 884, 2nd Sess.)-WCRF

92nd Cong., H.R. 14173, for the relief of Walter Eduard Koenig. Beneficiary, a 42-year old native of Germany and lawful permanent resident of the United States, was employed as an executive with Goodyear International Corporation 20 years and because of his extensive travel was unable to meet the residence requirements of the Immigration Act. The law held the beneficiary to have complied with section 316 relating to residence requirements for naturalization. (Priv. L. No. 132, 86 Stat. 1555 (1972)) (H.R. Rep. No. 1248, 2nd Sess.) (Sen. Rep. No. 1172, 2nd Sess.)-NRES

92nd Cong., S. 306, for the relief of Eddie Troy Jaynes, Jr. and Rosa Elena Jaynes. Beneficiaries, 19-year old siblings and twins who were natives and citizens of Costa Rica, entered the United States for permanent residence. It was later discovered they were incorrectly identified as United States citizens because of faulty birth records. The beneficiaries had been placed in the custody of their foster mother at two weeks old who was married to a United States citizen. She was later divorced and immigrated to the United States with the beneficiaries. The beneficiaries were not aware of their lack of citizenship until 20-years old. The law held the beneficiaries lawfully admitted for permanent residence. (Priv. L. No. 36, 85 Stat. 849 (1971)) (Sen. Rep. No. 121, 1st Sess.) (H.R. Rep. 492, 1st Sess.)-NRES

92nd Cong., S. 389, for the relief of Stephen Lance Pender, Patricia Jenifer Pender, and Denese Gene Pender. Beneficiaries, 13-, 10-, and 8-year old natives of South Africa and lawful permanent residents of the United States, were orphans of a United States citizen mother and lawful permanent resident alien father. They were unable to derive United States citizenship through the mother, because she did not have the requisite residence period in the United States in order to transmit United States citizenship to children born abroad. The entire family entered the United States in 1962 and the parents died in an automobile accident in 1970. The sister of the deceased parents, serving as guardian, sought their naturalization prior to their 18th birthdays, at which time they were eligible to petition on their own behalf. The law allowed the legal guardian of the beneficiaries to petition for their naturalization under section 322(a) relating to naturalization of children upon the petition of their parent. (Priv. L. No. 35, 85 Stat. 848 (1971)) (Sen. Rep. No. 274, 1st Sess.) (H.R. Rep. No. 646, 1st Sess.)-NCOD

92nd Cong., S. 513, for the relief of Maria Badalamenti. Beneficiary, a 54-year old native and citizen of Italy, entered the United States as a visitor. She was found ineligible for a visa due to mental retardation and illiteracy resulting from spinal meningitis. Her United States citizen sister and brother residing in the United States supported her and filed a visa petition on her behalf. The law waived section 212(a) (1) and (25) relating to mental retardation and illiteracy, and provided for the posting of a bond to overcome possible public charge aspects. (Priv. L. No. 88, 86 Stat. 1537 (1972)) (Sen. Rep. No. 69, 1st Sess.) (H.R. Rep. No. 999, 2nd Sess.)-WHEL

92nd Cong., S. 559, for the relief of Albina Lucio Z. Manlucu. Beneficiary, a 70-year old native and citizen of the Philippines, entered the United States as a visitor. She was the widow of a veteran of guerrilla forces who served with Philippine-American troops in World War II. She was the beneficiary of a third preference visa petition as a teacher but two years after approval, the Department of Labor would not revalidate the labor certification. The law held the beneficiary lawfully admitted for permanent residence. (Priv. L. No. 115, 86 Stat. 1548 (1972)) (Sen. Rep. No. 113, 1st Sess.) (H.R. Rep. No. 647, 1st Sess.)-QMGN

92nd Cong., S. 672, for the relief of Nicholas Demitrios Apostolakis. Beneficiary, a 19-year old native and citizen of Greece, was coming to the United States for adoption by his United States citizen uncle and aunt. The prospective adoptive parents were also the sponsors of previous private legislation for two other nephews. The beneficiaries' natural parents resided in Greece, and they supported the proposed adoption. The law held the beneficiary to be a child under section 101(b) (1) (F) in order to immigrate as an immediate relative. (Priv. L. No. 14, 85 Stat. 838 (1971)) (Sen. Rep. No. 65, 1st Sess.) (H.R. Rep. No. 286, 1st Sess.)-QIRA

92nd Cong., S. 2270, for the relief of Magnus David Forrester. The beneficiary, a 23-year old native and citizen of Canada, was married to a United States citizen with two children. He was deported from the United States, after entering as a visitor, due to a conviction for possession of marijuana for which he was later pardoned. The law waived section 212(a) (23) relating to drug possession. (Priv. L. No. 154, 86 Stat. 1565 (1972)) (Sen. Rep. No. 870, 2nd Sess.) (H.R. Rep. No. 1561, 2nd Sess.)-WCRF

92nd Cong., S. 2575, for the relief of William John West. Beneficiary, a two-year old native and citizen of Italy, was born out of wedlock and his natural father, a United States citizen serving in the Air Force, was unable to legitimate him. His mother was killed in an accident. The law held the beneficiary within section 101(b) (1) as the natural-born alien child of a United States citizen. (Priv. L. No. 129, 86 Stat. 1554 (1972)) (Sen. Rep. No. 872, 2nd Sess.) (H.R. Rep. No. 1238, 2nd Sess.)-QIRM

92nd Cong., S. 2822, for the relief of Alberto Rodriguez. Beneficiary, a 66-year old native of Cuba and lawful permanent resident of the United States for 10 years, was unable to meet the residence requirement for naturalization because of his duties abroad as bank representative for Spain and Portugal with Manufacturers Hanover Trust Company. He had been employed with that company for 10 years. The law held the beneficiary to have satisfied the residence requirements under section 316 and to be able to file a petition for naturalization with any court. (Priv. L. No. 150, 86 Stat. 1563 (1972)) (Sen. Rep. No. 876, 2nd Sess.) (H.R. Rep. No. 1564,, 2nd Sess.)-NRES

92nd Cong., S. 3583, for the relief of Gerald Vincent Bull. Beneficiary, a 44-year old native of Canada and lawful permanent resident of the United States was unable to meet the residence requirements for naturalization because of his position as President of Space Research Corporation which necessitated temporary visits to Canada. His research with that corporation in weaponry and space projectiles, and other national defense projects for the Department of Defense proved valuable to the United States. The law held the beneficiary to have met the requirements of section 316 relating to residence for naturalization. (Priv. L. No. 152, 86 Stat. 1564 (1972)) (Sen. Rep. No. 1059, 2nd Sess.) (H.R. Rep. No. 1565, 2nd Sess.)-NRES

93rd Cong., H.R. 1356, for the relief of Ann E. Shepherd. Beneficiary, a 39-year old native and citizen of Great Britain, entered the United States for permanent residence based on marriage to a United States citizen. She resided in the United States 18 years and did not obtain a re-entry permit when she left the United States due to marital difficulties. She later entered the United States as a visitor. The beneficiary and her husband were later divorced. They had two United States citizen children, one of whom resided with the beneficiary while undergoing therapy from a rare speech defect resulting in an inability to talk since birth. The law held the beneficiary within section 101(a) (27) (B) as a returning permanent resident alien. (Priv. L. No. 21, 87 Stat. 1104 (1973)) (H.R. Rep. No. 503, 1st Sess.) (Sen. Rep. No. 531, 1st Sess.)-QPRP

93rd Cong., H.R. 1366, for the relief of Juan Marcos Cordova-Campos. Beneficiary, a 23-year old native and citizen of Mexico, was adopted by United States citizens who were missionaries in Mexico. He resided with them 16 years, and entered the United States as a student two years after being in their care. They later adopted him. He did not know the whereabouts of his parents and seven siblings. The adoptive parents indicated that the beneficiary left their home and had "become independent." They also indicated that they were "no longer interested in pursuing the purpose of the bill." However, the author of the bill reaffirmed the intent of the bill of family reunification. The law held the beneficiary to be a child under section 101(b) (1) (F) and held section 245(c) inapplicable relating to unauthorized employment in the United States. (Priv. Law No. 12, 87 Stat. 1101 (1973)) (H.R. Rep. No. 197, 1st Sess.) (Sen. Rep. No. 436, 1st Sess.)-QIRA

93rd Cong., H.R. 1367, for the relief of Bertha Alicia Sierra. Beneficiary, a 20-year old native and citizen of Mexico, entered the United States as a visitor. Her mother was a permanent resident alien prior to death, and the whereabouts of her father were unknown. The beneficiary resided with her sister, a lawful permanent resident. The law held the beneficiary lawfully admitted for permanent residence. (Priv. L. No. 22, 87 Stat. 1104 (1973)) (H.R. Rep. No. 504, 1st Sess.) (Sen. Rep. No. 532, 1st Sess.)-QMGN

93rd Cong., H.R. 1377, for the relief of Michael Joseph Wendt. Beneficiary, a 19-year old native of British Guiana and citizen of Guyana was adopted by United States citizen parents at the age of seven, and entered the United States as a visitor. He had been raised since infancy by the adoptive parents. The adoptive father, deceased, was a founder of British Guiana Airways and died while preparing for his return to the United States. He had been awarded the Order of the British Empire and the King's Medal for Service in the Cause of Freedom for his service during World War II. They had previously adopted two children. The law held the beneficiary to be a child for the purposes of section 101(b) (1) (F) and held section 245(c) inapplicable relating to unauthorized employment in the United States. (Priv. L. No. 13, 87 Stat. 1101 (1973)) (H.R. Rep. No. 198, 1st Sess.) (Sen. Rep. No. 437, 1st Sess.)-QIRA

93rd Cong., H.R. 3754, for the relief of Mrs. Bruna Turni and Miss Graziella Turni. Beneficiaries, a 27-year old widow and 7- and 3-year old children, two of whom were natives and citizens of Italy, and the youngest a native of the United States born in diplomatic status, entered the United States as members of a diplomatic mission. The spouse was the beneficiary of a fifth preference visa petition filed by his sister. While the family was in the process of adjusting status in the United States, the spouse died and they were no longer entitled to immigrant visas. The law held the beneficiaries to retain the priority date assigned under the fifth preference. (Priv. L. No. 29, 87 Stat. 1107 (1973)) (H.R. Rep. No. 507, 1st Sess.) (Sen. Rep. No. 544, 1st Sess.)-QPRF

93rd Cong., H.R. 3758, for the relief of Isabel Eugenia Serrane Macias Ferrier. Beneficiary, a 28-year old native and citizen of Colombia, entered the United States as a visitor, and resided with her United States citizen aunt and uncle who were attempting to adopt her. The beneficiary had previously remained in her native country to care for her ill mother and younger brothers. Her mother was later placed in a mental institution and her father was deceased. The law held the beneficiary within section 21(e) of the Act of October 3, 1965 as a lawful permanent resident and provided for the deduction of a visa number under section 101(a) (27) (A). (Priv. L. No. 49, 87 Stat. 1114 (1973)) (H.R. Rep. No. 525, 1st Sess.) (Sen. Rep. No. 544, 1st Sess.)-QPRF

93rd Cong., H.R. 6477, for the relief of Lucille de Saint Andre. Beneficiary, a 53-year old native of Germany and citizen of Canada, entered the United States as a visitor. She was formerly a permanent resident alien and was deported for engaging in prostitution. She resided in the United States with her United States citizen mother who suffered from hypertension and arthritis. Her United States citizen brother filed a visa petition on her behalf. The law waived section 212(a) (12) relating to persons who engaged in prostitution. (Priv. L. No. 97, 88 Stat. 2382 (1974)) (H.R. Rep. No. 584, 1st Sess.) (Sen. Rep. No. 1197, 2nd Sess.)-WCRF

93rd Cong., S. 89, for the relief of Kuay Ten Chang (Kuay Hong Chang). Beneficiary, a 56-year old native and citizen of China, entered the United States as a visitor. His spouse and child entered the United States previously on the basis of a fifth preference visa petition filed by her United States citizen sister, but they died in a traffic accident. The beneficiary was ineligible for a visa under the fifth preference because his name was not included on the petition. The law held the beneficiary within section 203(a) (2) relating to spouses and unmarried sons and daughters of lawful permanent residents. (Priv. L. No. 7, 87 Stat. 1099 (1973)) (Sen. Rep. No. 73, 1st Sess.) (H.R. Rep. No. 474, 1st Sess.)-QPRF

93rd Cong., S. 428, for the relief of Ernest Edward Scofield (Ernesto Espino). Beneficiary, a 22-year old native and citizen of the Philippines, entered the United States as a visitor. He was adopted at the age of 21 by a retired United States citizen Air Force sergeant. The beneficiary served as a houseboy for one and a half years to the adoptive father prior to entry to the United States. His parents and eight siblings resided in the Philippines. The law held the beneficiary within section 203(a) (1) and 204 as the natural-born alien son of a United States citizen. (Priv. L. No. 70, 88 Stat. 2371 (1974)) (Sen. Rep. No. 288, 1st Sess.) (H.R. Rep. No. 819, 2nd Sess.)-QPRF

93rd Cong., S. 507, for the relief of Wilhelm J. R. Maly. Beneficiary, a 52-year old native of Germany and lawful permanent resident of the United States for eight years, was unable to meet the residence requirements for naturalization because of his overseas employment with Kaiser Aluminum. The law held the residence the beneficiary acquired in the United States to meet section 316 for purposes of naturalization. (Priv. L. No. 62, 88 Stat. 2368 (1974)) (Sen. Rep. No. 286, 1st Sess.) (H.R. Rep. No. 820, 2nd Sess.)-NRES

93rd Cong., S. 816, for the relief of Mrs. Jozefa Sokolowska Domanski. Beneficiary, a 25-year old native and citizen of Poland, entered the United States as a visitor. She was married to a lawful permanent resident who filed a visa petition on her behalf, but he died of a gunshot wound prior to visa issuance. The law held the beneficiary within sections 203(a) (2) and 204 relating to spouses and unmarried sons and daughters of lawful permanent residents. (Priv. L. No. 63, 88 Stat. 2369 (1974)) (Sen. Rep. No. 290, 1st Sess.) (H.R. Rep. No. 821, 2nd Sess.)-QPRF

93rd Cong., S. 912, for the relief of Mahmood Shareef Suleiman. Beneficiary, a 45-year old native of Iraq and lawful permanent resident of the United States for 16 years, was unable to meet the residence requirements for naturalization because of his employment overseas with the University of Baghdad, and then with the World Health Organization with which he was employed nine years. The law held the residence the beneficiary acquired in the United States to meet section 316 for purposes of naturalization. (Priv. L. No. 64, 88 Stat. 2369 (1974)) (Sen. Rep. No. 432, 1st Sess.) (H.R. Rep. No. 822, 2nd Sess.)-NRES

93rd Cong., S. 1852, for the relief of Georgina Henrietta Harris. Beneficiary, a 15-year old native of Mexico and lawful permanent resident of the United States, was the adoptive child of a United States citizen. The adoptive mother was being treated for cancer, and she desired the beneficiary to have citizenship prior to her death. The beneficiary had resided with the adoptive mother six years, but had only one year of residence as a lawful permanent resident alien. The law held the beneficiary within the purview of section 323 relating to special benefits for adopted children of United States citizens. (Priv. L. No. 54, 88 Stat. 2366 (1974)) (Sen. Rep. No. 441, 1st Sess.) (H.R. Rep. No. 824, 2nd Sess.)-NMSC

94th Cong., H.R. 1388, for the relief of Guadalupe Villegas-Cantu. Beneficiary, a 28-year old native and citizen of Mexico, was brought to the United States at the age of two by her mother illegally, and did not know she was not a United States citizen until graduation from college. She was unable to obtain a teaching certificate in the State of Texas because she was not a citizen. The law held the beneficiary retroactively lawfully admitted for permanent residence effective the date of first entry under section 21(e) of the Act of October 3, 1965. (Priv. L. No. 2, 89 Stat. 1164 (1975)) (H.R. Rep. No. 127, 1st Sess.) (Sen. Rep. No. 232, 1st Sess.)-NMSC

94th Cong., H.R. 1394, for the relief of Suk Chin and Hae Suk Chin. Beneficiaries, six- and four-year old natives of Korea whose parents were afflicted with Hansen's disease, were coming to the United States for adoption by a single United States citizen parent. The natural father was blind and the mother had one leg amputated. They resided in Saint Lazarus Village, a leper colony. The prospective adoptive parent was employed by the United States Government and had previously adopted one child. The law held the beneficiaries to be children within section 101 (b) (1) (F) and allowed the filing of more than two petitions for the immigration of adopted children. (Priv. L. No. 60, 90 Stat. 2980 (1976)) (H.R. Rep. No. 583, 1st Sess.) (Sen. Rep. No. 1083, 2nd Sess.)-QIRA

94th Cong., H.R. 1395, for the relief of Mee Kyung Cho and Hee Kyung Cho. Beneficiaries, five- and two-year old natives and citizens of Korea who were afflicted with Hansen's disease resided in a leper colony in Korea with their father. They were coming to the United States for adoption by United States citizens. The law held the beneficiaries to be children under section 101(b) (1) (F) for purposes of immigration. (Priv. L. No. 61, 90 Stat. 2980 (1976)) (H.R. Rep. No. 584, 1st Sess.) (Sen. Rep. No. 1084, 2nd Sess.)-QIRA

94th Cong., H.R. 1396, for the relief of Sang Kook Chung and Hwa Soon Chung. Beneficiaries were 13- and 11-year old natives of Korea afflicted with Hansen's disease and resided in a leper colony in Korea with their parents. They were coming to the United States for adoption by United States citizens. The law classified the beneficiaries as children under section 101(b) (1) (F) for purposes of deriving immediate relative status. (Priv. L. No. 62, 90 Stat. 2980 (1976)) (H.R. Rep. No. 621, 1st Sess.) (Sen. Rep. No. 1085, 2nd Sess.)-QIRA

94th Cong., H.R. 1425, for the relief of Juliet Elizabeth Tozzi. Beneficiary, a 24-year old native and citizen of Great Britain, was admitted for permanent residence and returned to England. She reentered the United States several times. She was found ineligible for a visa due to drug possession. It was stated she suffered injuries in a car accident in the United States, which precipitated her drug involvement (cannabis) and led to stealing. She was married to a United States citizen and had a minor United States citizen child. Her father was a United States citizen residing in the United States, and her mother was divorced residing in England. A report from the United States Public Health Service indicated her "prognosis is good in view of her excellent adjustment." The law waived section 212(a) (23) relating to drug possession. (Priv. L. No. 64, 90 Stat. 2981 (1976)) (H.R. Rep. No. 406, 1st Sess.) (Sen. Rep. No. 1087, 2nd Sess.)-WCRF

94th Cong., H.R. 1553, for the relief of Victor Henrique Carlos Gibson. Beneficiary, a 55-year old native of the United States and citizen of Peru was born while his family was in diplomatic status in the United States. His father was the Secretary of the Peruvian Embassy. He was admitted for permanent residence three years and employed by the Rubber Development Corporation, an agency of the United States Government. He subsequently applied for relief from military service due to his father's position. He remained in the United States 30 years in diplomatic service, having relinquished his permanent residence status, until termination of his position due to a conflict of policies between the United States and Peru. He then requested political asylum. He was married to a United States citizen 25 years, and they had four United States citizen children. The beneficiary was ineligible for a visa due to his application for relief from military service. The law waived section 212(a) (22) relating to exclusion of persons who sought to evade military service, and waived section 245(c) prohibiting adjustment of status in the United States of those who work without authorization. The act provided that nothing in the law should be construed to waive the provisions of section 315 relating to prohibition of naturalization for those who claimed exemption from military service. (Priv. L. No. 17, 89 Stat. 1179 (1975)) (H.R. Rep. No. 131, 1st Sess.) (Sen. Rep. No. 346, 1st Sess.)-WXDD

94th Cong., H.R. 1556, for the relief of Hendrika Koenders Lyne. Beneficiary, a 44-year old native and citizen of the Netherlands, entered the United States as a visitor. She was married to a United States citizen with two United States citizen children (ages 11, 7), and was deserted by her spouse seven years after marriage. She was able to obtain support for her children as military dependents. The law held the beneficiary lawfully admitted for permanent residence. (Priv. L. No. 3, 89 Stat. 1165 (1975)) (H.R. Rep. No. 132, 1st Sess.) (Sen. Rep. No. 238, 1st Sess.)-QMGN

94th Cong., H.R. 1645, for the relief of Kevin Patrick Saunders. Beneficiary, a 47-year old native and citizen of England, and spouse of a United States citizen, was ineligible for a visa due to conviction at the age of 23 for possession of 3 grains of cocaine, 161 4/5 grains of heroin and morphine. The law waived section 212(a) (23) relating to drug possession. (Priv. L. No. 66, 90 Stat. 2982 (1976)) (H.R. Rep. No. 396, 1st Sess.) (Sen. Rep. No. 1090, 2nd Sess.)-WCRF

94th Cong., H.R. 2399, for the relief of Leonard Alfred Brownrigg. Beneficiary, a 46-year old native and citizen of Great Britain, entered the United States for permanent residence and was found deportable 11 years thereafter for possession of marijuana. The record was later expunged. He was married to a United States citizen and employed as a land surveyor. The law waived section 212(a) (23) relating to drug possession. (Priv. L. No. 69, 90 Stat. 2983 (1976)) (H.R. Rep. No. 398, 1st Sess.) (Sen. Rep. No. 1092, 2nd Sess.)-WCRF

94th Cong., H.R. 2565, for the relief of Luisa Marillac Hughes, Marco Antonio Hughes, Maria del Cisne Hughes, Maria Augusta Hughes, Miguel Vicente Hughes, Veronica del Rocio Hughes, and Ivan Hughes. Beneficiaries, (ages 13 through 5), natives and citizens of Ecuador, entered the United States as visitors. They were adopted by United States citizen parents who already had two other adopted children. The older beneficiary was blind and two others suffered from cerebral palsy. They had no known living natural parents and resided with the adoptive parents four years after the adoption. The law held the beneficiaries to be children for purposes of section 101(b) (1) (F) as well as waived sections 204(c) relating to the two-petition limitation on the immigration of adopted children and section 245(c) relating to prohibition on working in the United States. (Priv. L. No. 73, 90 Stat. 2984 (1976)) (H.R. Rep. No. 790, 2nd Sess.) (Sen. Rep. No. 1096, 2nd Sess.)-QIRA

94th Cong., H.R. 2776, for the relief of Candido Badua. Beneficiary, a 51-year old native of the Philippines and lawful permanent resident of the United States for three years, had been employed with the United States Information Agency 23 years and while in Vietnam with that Agency in 1968 was taken captive and held prisoner five years. The Department of State supported the beneficiary's efforts to become naturalized in light of the "special and unusual circumstances of this case." The law held the beneficiary to have satisfied the residence requirements of section 316 relating to naturalization. (Priv. L. No. 44, 90 Stat. 2973 (1976)) (H.R. Rep. No. 400, 1st Sess.) (Sen. Rep. No. 784, 2nd Sess.)-NRES

94th Cong., H.R. 4583, for the relief of Rosina C. Beltran. Beneficiary, a 47-year old native and citizen of the Philippines, entered the United States as a visitor to care for the three children of her sister who suffered from terminal cancer and died. She was appointed guardian of the United States citizen children, and the beneficiary's family was paroled into the United States to join her. The law held the beneficiary lawfully admitted for permanent residence. (Priv. L. No. 111, 90 Stat. 2999 (1976)) (H.R. Rep. No. 1619, 2nd Sess.)-QMGN

94th Cong., H.R. 6093, for the relief of Maria D'Arpino. Beneficiary, a 53-year old native and citizen of Italy, entered the United States as a visitor. She resided with her United States citizen sister and was ineligible for a visa due to illiteracy and mental retardation. Her father was a United States citizen, and he died 10 days after the beneficiary's arrival in the United States. The law waived section 212(a) (1) and (25) relating to mental retardation and illiteracy. (Priv. L. No. 81, 90 Stat. 2988 (1976)) (H.R. Rep. No. 779, 2nd Sess.) (Sen. Rep. No. 1104, 2nd Sess.)-WHEL

94th Cong., H.R. 7404, for the relief of Christine Donnelly. Beneficiary, a 47-year old native of Canada and lawful permanent resident of the United States, had resided in the United States since the age of three. She was unaware of her lack of citizenship until she applied for a Civil Service appointment. The law held the beneficiary to have satisfied the requirements of section 316 relating to residence for purposes of naturalization. (Priv. L. No. 4, 90 Stat. 2989 (1976)) (H.R. Rep. No. 1277, 2nd Sess.) (Sen. Rep. No. 1107, 2nd Sess.)-NRES

94th Cong., H.R. 8119, for the relief of Fernando Alves Macos. The beneficiary, a 27-year old native and citizen of Portugal and spouse of a United States citizen, was ineligible for a visa due to a previous attempt to immigrate based on a fraudulent marriage. They had one United States citizen child. The House Committee noted, "The Committee does not wish to condone such reprehensible behavior but believes that the bill should be approved solely on the basis of hardship which is being caused to the beneficiary's second wife and child." The Committee also noted in acting favorably that convincing evidence was presented establishing that the beneficiary's wife was unaware of the circumstances surrounding his previous marriage. The law waived sections 204(c) and 212(a) (19) relating to fraud. (Priv. L. No. 121, 90 Stat. 3004 (1976)) (H.R. Rep. No. 907, 2nd Sess.) (Sen. Rep. No. 1291, 2nd Sess.)-WCRF

94th Cong., H.R. 9543, for the relief of Eupert Anthony Grant. The beneficiary, a 20-year old native and citizen of Jamaica, was adopted by a United States citizen at the age of 17. He had resided with his adoptive mother from infancy, until her admission to the United States. The law held the beneficiary to be the natural-born child of a lawful permanent resident with a priority date effective the date of the adoption. (Priv. L. No. 128, 90 Stat. 3007 (1976)) (H.R. Rep. No. 1529, 2nd Sess.) (Sen. Rep. No. 1380, 2nd Sess.)-QPRF

94th Cong., H.R. 10792, for the relief of Jana Hlavaty. Beneficiary, a 34-year old native of Czechoslovakia, entered the United States for permanent residence, and desired expeditious naturalization in order to participate as a member of the United States Ski Team, in the Winter Olympic Games, in 1976. The law held the beneficiary retroactively lawfully admitted for permanent residence effective the date of first entry to the United States. (Priv. L. No. 27, 89 Stat. 1189 (1975)) (Sen. Rep. No. 579, 1st Sess.)-NRES

94th Cong., H.R. 10793, for the relief of Afaf Yassine and her children, Najla Yassine, Walid Yassine, Mona Yassine, and Maher Yassine. Beneficiaries were a widow and sons and daughters (ages 41 through 12), natives and citizens of Lebanon. They were beneficiaries of a fifth preference visa petition filed on behalf of the husband. Prior to visa issuance, he was killed by sniper fire in Lebanon; and his United States citizen brother assumed full financial responsibility for the beneficiaries. The law held the beneficiaries eligible for fifth preference classification with the same priority date under section 203(a) (9) of the Act of June 6, 1974. (Priv. L. No. 115, 90 Stat. 3001 (1976)) (H.R. Rep. No. 921, 2nd Sess.) (Sen. Rep. No. 1118, 2nd Sess.)-QPRF

94th Cong., H.R. 11890, for the relief of Bernard Julian Phillips. Beneficiary, a 32-year old native and citizen of England and spouse of a United States citizen, was ineligible for a visa due to conviction for possession of 19.8 grams of marijuana. The beneficiary's spouse desired to return to the United States because of the illness of both parents, one of whom was undergoing treatment for cancer, and the other suffered from Parkinson's disease. The law waived section 212(a) (23) relating to drug possession and provided that the beneficiary would be subject to deportation under section 241(a) (11) if convicted of drug possession subsequent to the date of enactment of the legislation. (Priv. L. No. 116, 90 Stat. 3001 (1976)) (H.R. Rep. No. 1301, 2nd Sess.) (Sen. Rep. No. 1290, 2nd Sess.)-WCRF

94th Cong., S. 52, for the relief of Miss Rosario Y. Quijano, Walter York Quijano, Ramon York Quijano, Tarcisus York Quijano, Denis York Quijano, and Paul York Quijano. Beneficiaries, six siblings, natives and citizens of the Philippines (ages 27 through 10), were children of a United States citizen who was killed by her husband who then committed suicide. One beneficiary entered the United States as a student and the others resided in the Philippines with their aunt who had ten children of her own. The United States citizen mother had filed petitions on their behalf but died before their immigration. Their United States citizen brother filed immigration petitions on their behalf, but visas were oversubscribed in that category. The law held the beneficiaries within section 203(a) (1) and 201(b) relating to unmarried sons and daughters of United States citizens, and immediate relatives of United States citizens, as well as waiving section 204 relating to filing of petitions. (Priv. L. No. 51, 90 Stat. 2975 (1976)) (Sen. Rep. No. 245, 1st Sess.) (H.R. Rep. No. 908, 2nd Sess.)-QPRF

94th Cong., S. 447, for the relief of Jesus Cortez Pineda. Beneficiary, an 18-year old native and citizen of Mexico, entered the United States as a student. He was adopted by his sister, a permanent resident alien and her United States citizen spouse, at the age of 16. The natural mother was ill and unable to care for him, and the natural father deceased. His younger brother had already been adopted. The law classified the beneficiary as a child under section 101(b) (1) (F). (Priv. L. No. 24, 89 Stat. 1186 (1975)) (Sen. Rep. No. 226, 1st Sess.) (H.R. Rep. No. 588, 2nd Sess.)-QIRA

94th Cong., S. 1699, for the relief of Mrs. Hope Namgyal. Beneficiary, a 35-year old native of the United States and citizen of India, renounced her United States citizenship to marry the Crown Prince of Sikkim. Because of conditions in Sikkim, the beneficiary returned to the United States as a student with her two children, ages 12 and 8. Her husband and stepson were placed under house arrest in Sikkim. The law held the beneficiary lawfully admitted for permanent residence. (Priv. L. No. 52, 90 Stat. 2976 (1976)) (Sen. Rep. No. 437, 1st Sess.) (H.R. Rep. No. 912, 2nd Sess.)-NVOL

95th Cong., H.R. 1396, for the relief of Mrs. Sun Pok Winer. Beneficiary, a 29-year old native and citizen of Korea and spouse of a United States citizen serving in the Army, was excluded from entry to the United States due to a conviction for possession of 120 grams of marijuana six years prior to an application for a visa. The law waived section 212(a)(23) relating to drug possession. (Priv. L. No. 63, 92 Stat. 3818 (1978)) (H.R. Rep. No. 935, 2nd Sess.) (Sen. Rep. No. 1336, 2nd Sess.)-WCRF

95th Cong., H.R. 1420, for the relief of Umberto Ruffolo. Beneficiary, a 31-year old native and citizen of Italy, was inadmissible due to mental retardation. His parents, a United States citizen and lawful permanent resident, were deceased; and his United States citizen sister contributed $100 per month to his support. The law waived section 212(a)(1) relating to mental retardation and provided for the posting of a bond to overcome possible public charge aspects. (Priv. L. No. 48, 92 Stat. 3811 (1978)) (H.R. Rep. No. 250, 1st Sess.) (Sen. Rep. No. 1017, 2nd Sess.)-WHEL

95th Cong., H.R. 1422, for the relief of Julio Ortiz-Medina. Beneficiary, a 28-year old native and citizen of Mexico and spouse of a United States citizen, was excluded from entry to the United States due to smuggling aliens into the United States for which he was deported. There was one United States citizen child of the marriage. The law waived sections 212(a)(17) and (31) relating to smuggling aliens into the United States, and the readmission of aliens who had previously been deported from the United States. (Priv. L. No. 158, 92 Stat. 3857 (1978)) (H.R. Rep. No. 680, 1st Sess.) (Sen. Rep. No. 1335, 2nd Sess.)-WCRF

95th Cong., H.R. 1432, for the relief of Mrs. Desolina Sciulli. Beneficiary, a 46-year old native and citizen of Italy, had a fifth preference petition filed on her behalf by her United States citizen sister. She was found excludable due to two convictions for theft of firewood for which she was fined $8.00. The law waived section 212(a)(9) relating to conviction of crimes involving moral turpitude. (Priv. L. No. 31, 92 Stat. 3804 (1978)) (H.R. Rep. No. 251, 1st Sess.) (Sen. Rep. No. 681, 2nd Sess.)-WCRF

95th Cong., H.R. 1446, for the relief of Lester Bruce Priday. Beneficiary, a 27-year old native and citizen of Australia and spouse of a United States citizen, was excluded from entry to the United States due to two convictions for possession of cannabis and Indian hemp seeds, five years prior to visa application. There was one United States citizen child of the marriage. The law waived section 212(a)(23) relating to drug possession. (Priv. L. No. 64, 92 Stat. 3819 (1978)) (H.R. Rep. No. 1440, 2nd Sess.) (Sen. Rep. No. 1340, 2nd Sess.)-WCRF

95th Cong., H.R. 1552, for the relief of Oh Soon Yi. Beneficiary, a seven-year old native and citizen of Korea, was adopted by Andre Previn and Mia Farrow, United States citizens, who had five children, two of whom were adopted. Mr. Previn was employed by the London Symphony Orchestra and Mia Farrow was an actress. The bill waived section 101(b)(1)(F) relating to the two adoption petition limitation. (Priv. L. No. 95-37, 92 Stat. 3806 (1978)) (H.R. Rep. No. 328, 1st Sess.) (Sen. Rep. No. 95-692, 2nd Sess.)-QIRA

95th Cong., H.R. 1748, for the relief of Carmela Scudieri. Beneficiary, a 33-year old native and citizen of Italy, sought to immigrate as the sister of a United States citizen. She was raised in the household of her natural father and was not aware she and the petitioner were not sisters until a petition on her behalf was denied. The law held the beneficiary within section 203(a)(5) and 204 relating to eligibility to immigrate as the sibling of a United States citizen. (Priv. L. No. 159, 92 Stat. 3858 (1978)) (H.R. Rep. No. 169, 1st Sess.) (Sen. Rep. No. 1342, 2nd Sess.)-QPRF

95th Cong., H.R. 1750, for the relief of Anthony Rogers. Beneficiary, a 24-year old native and citizen of Morocco, entered the United States as a visitor. He was adopted by a United States citizen, the president of American Express Corporation., who befriended him while visiting Morocco. The beneficiary was a deaf-mute and received medical treatment in the United States. His adoptive father established a trust fund on his behalf. The law held the beneficiary within section 203(a)(1) and 204 relating to immigration as the son of a United States citizen. (Priv. L. No. 86, 92 Stat. 3829 (1978)) (H.R. Rep. No. 256, 1st Sess.) (Sen. Rep. No. 1343, 2nd Sess.)-QPRF

95th Cong., H.R. 1939, for the relief of Meda Abilay Florin. Beneficiary, a three-year old native and citizen of the Philippines, was paroled into the United States. He was adopted by lawful permanent residents of the United States with whom he resided until immigrating to the United States. The adoptive parents, the mother being the aunt of the beneficiary, had no children of their own. The natural parents and five siblings remained in the Philippines. The law held the beneficiary to be within section 101(b)(1)(E) relating to fulfillment of a two-year residence and legal custody requirement for adoption. (Priv. L. No. 32, 92 Stat. 3804 (1978)) (H.R. Rep. No. 508, 1st Sess.) (Sen. Rep. No. 682, 2nd Sess.)-QIRA

95th Cong., H.R. 2256, for the relief of Edmundo Alfredo Oreiro Espinueva. Beneficiary, a 34-year old native and citizen of the Philippines, entered the United States with the United States Navy where he served 15 years, until it was learned he suffered from a hearing loss and he retired on disability. His United States citizen brother resided in the United States. The law held the beneficiary lawfully admitted for permanent residence. Priv. L. No. 131, 92 Stat. 3846 (1978)) (H.R. Rep. No. 682, 1st Sess.) (Sen. Rep. No. 1355, 2nd Sess.)-QMGN

95th Cong., H.R. 2291, for the relief of Carmen Cecilia Blanquicett. Beneficiary, a 21-year old native and citizen of Colombia, sought to enter the United States and reside with her United States citizen godmothers. Her natural mother died when the beneficiary was at the age of three months, and she resided with her godmothers until their immigration to the United States Her natural father refused to execute the necessary documents to allow the beneficiary to immigrate, and she resided with him four years until she was forced to reside with her aunt and uncle. The law held the beneficiary within section 101(b)(1) as the natural daughter of a United States citizen. (Priv. L. No. 162, 92 Stat. 3859 (1978)) (H.R. Rep. No. 938, 2nd Sess.) (Sen. Rep. No. 1357, 2nd Sess.)-QIRM

95th Cong., H.R. 2756, for the relief of Marlene Holder. Beneficiary, a 19-year old native and citizen of Guyana who was admitted to the United States as a visitor, was adopted by United States citizens at the age of 17. At the age of three her natural mother gave her to her grandmother for caring. Because the grandmother had difficulty supporting her and three sisters, she went to live with the grandmother's cousin at the age of 10. That cousin died three years later. The adoptive parents, age 81 and 70, were related to the child by virtue of being the grandmother's cousin's brother. The law deemed the beneficiary to be a child for purposes of section 101(b)(1)(F). (Priv. L. No. 94, 92 Stat. 3832 (1978)) (H.R. Rep. No. 178, 1st Sess.) (Sen. Rep. No. 1332, 2nd Sess.)-QIRA

95th Cong., H.R. 2940, for the relief of Daniel Crowley. Beneficiary, a 43-year old native and citizen of Ireland, entered the United States as a visitor. He was found inadmissible for an immigrant visa due to mental retardation and illiteracy. Relatives in the United States included his three United States citizen sisters and a lawful permanent resident brother. He had previously been employed for 21 years as a bookbinder and had no relatives in Ireland. The law waived section 212(a)(1) and (25) relating to mental retardation and illiteracy and provided for the posting of a bond to overcome possible public charge aspects. (Priv. L. No. 67, 92 Stat. 3820 (1978)) (H.R. Rep. No. 179, 1st Sess.) (Sen. Rep. No. 1367, 2nd Sess.)-WHEL

95th Cong., H.R. 3461, for the relief of Chin-Ho An. Beneficiary, a 67-year old native and citizen of Korea, was the natural father of a United States citizen who filed a petition on his behalf. Because there was no marriage between her parents, the daughter's petition was denied. Petitions for the mother and sister were approved and the beneficiary desired to accompany them to the United States. The law held the beneficiary within section 201(b) relating to immediate relatives of United States citizens. (Priv. L. No. 17, 91 Stat. 1655 (1977)) (H.R. Rep. No. 185, 1st Sess.) (Sen. Rep. No. 534, 1st Sess.)-QIRM

95th Cong., H.R. 3996, for the relief of Mrs. Young Hee Kim Kang, Hee Jae Kang, Hee Jin Kang and Hee Soo Kang. Beneficiaries (ages 39 through 9), natives and citizens of Korea, one of whom was a widow, were in the process of obtaining immigrant visas when the father died of cancer. The petition by his United States citizen brother became invalid. The law held the beneficiaries entitled to fifth preference status under section 203(a)(9) of the Act as of the date of the visa petition, notwithstanding the death of the principal beneficiary. (Priv. L. No. 40, 92 Stat. 3807 (1978)) (H.R. Rep. No. 981, 2nd Sess.) (Sen. Rep. No. 902, 2nd Sess.)-QPRF

95th Cong., H.R. 4246, for the relief of Hee Kyung Yoo. Beneficiary, a three-year old native and citizen of Korea, was coming to the United States for adoption by United States citizens who had one natural child and one adopted child. The prospective adoptive parents had also petitioned, and provided for the immigration of another adopted child who had died at the age of three in a drowning accident. The law held the beneficiaries to be classified as children within section 101(b)(1)(F) and waived section 204(c) relating to the limitation of two petitions for adopted children. (Priv. L. No. 5, 91 Stat. 1648 (1977)) (H.R. Rep. No. 262, 1st Sess.) (Sen. Rep. No. 294, 1st Sess.)-QIRA

95th Cong., H.R. 4401, for the relief of Kwi Sok Buckingham (nee Kim). Beneficiary, a 22-year old native and citizen of Korea and spouse of a United States citizen serving in the Army, was excluded from entry to the United States because of a conviction for giving two individuals 69 tablets of valium. The law waived section 212(a)(23) relating to drug possession. (Priv. L. No. 35, 92 Stat. 3805 (1978)) (H.R. Rep. No. 525, 1st Sess.) (Sen. Rep. No. 685, 2nd Sess.)-WCRF

95th Cong., H.R. 4875, for the relief of Elizabeth D. Yee Kraus. Beneficiary, a 27-year old native and citizen of the Philippines, entered the United States as a visitor and was subsequently adopted by a United States citizen who was a Roman Catholic priest. It was stated he intended to retire in eight years and wished the beneficiary to "care for him during his retirement years." The law held the beneficiary within section 203(a)(1) as the natural daughter of a United States citizen. (Priv. L. No. 103, 92 Stat. 3835 (1978)) (H.R. Rep. No. 677, 1st Sess.) (Sen. Rep. No. 1377, 2nd Sess.)-QPRF

95th Cong., H.R. 8192, for the relief of Andree Marie Helene McGiffin. Beneficiary, a 37-year old native and citizen of France, was formerly a permanent resident on the basis of a seven year marriage to a United States citizen, but was divorced. She was granted custody of their two United

States citizen children, and accompanied her second husband to France and was subsequently divorced from him. The law held the beneficiary within section 101(a)(27)(A) as a returning resident alien. (Priv. L. No. 165, 92 Stat. 3860 (1978)) (H.R. Rep. No. 957, 2nd Sess.) (Sen. Rep. No. 1389, 2nd Sess.)-QPRP

95th Cong., H.R. 8927, for the relief of Monika Grantz. Beneficiary, a 32-year old native and citizen of Germany and spouse of a United States citizen serving in the United States Air Force, was ineligible for a visa due to a conviction at the age of 24 for trafficking in narcotics (hashish), fraud, forgery and tax evasion. She received six months probation because of "extenuating circumstances" and her assistance in investigating the principals of the case. The law waived section 212(a)(23) relating to drug possession. (Priv. L. No. 74, 92 Stat. 3822 (1978)) (H.R. Rep. No. 1442, 2nd Sess.) (Sen. Rep. No. 1393, 2nd Sess.)-WCRF

95th Cong., S. 455, for the relief of Ermelinda Rossi. Beneficiary, an 80-year old native and citizen of Italy, was ineligible for a visa due to illiteracy. The beneficiary cared for the interested party, a United States citizen, since the death of her mother, although she never adopted her. The beneficiary was registered within the nonpreference classification for purposes of immigration. The law waived section 212(a)(25) relating to illiteracy, and provided for the posting of a bond to overcome possible public charge aspects. (Priv. L. No. 11, 91 Stat. 1653 (1977)) (Sen. Rep. No. 269, 1st Sess.) (H.R. Rep. No. 687, 1st Sess.)-WXIL

95th Cong., S. 1142, for the relief of Kam Lin Cheung. Beneficiary, a 79-year old native and citizen of China, entered the United States as a visitor and resided with her United States citizen godson. He had previously resided with her sixteen years after the death of his mother. She was ineligible for a visa due to illiteracy. The law waived section 212(a)(25) relating to illiteracy and provided for the posting of a bond to overcome possible public charge aspects. (Priv. L. No. 19, 91 Stat. 1656 (1977)) (Sen. Rep. No. 270, 1st Sess.) (H.R. Rep. No. 685, 1st Sess.)-WXIL

95th Cong., S. 3109, for the relief of Ricardo Rosas Salazar. Beneficiary, a 22-year old native and citizen of Mexico, entered the United States as a student and was adopted by United States citizen missionaries at the age of 14. He was found guilty of petty larceny and given one year probation at the age of 20. The law held the beneficiary within sections 203(a)(1) and 204 as the natural-born son of United States citizens. (Priv. L. No. 125, 92 Stat. 3844 (1978)) (Sen. Rep. No. 1252, 2nd Sess.)-QPRF

96th Cong., H.R. 1619, for the relief of Rolando R. Gaza, Teresita C. Gaza, and Rolynne Therese Gaza. Beneficiaries, ages 25, 22, and 2, natives and citizens of the Philippines, entered the United States as visitors. The male beneficiary served in the United States Navy one year, and was discharged after an accident aboard a United States vessel on combat duty in the Tonkin Gulf, which resulted in amputation of his leg. He received medical treatment from the Veteran's Administration in the United States. The law held the beneficiaries lawfully admitted for permanent residence. (Priv. L. No. 42, 93 Stat. 1406 (1979)) (H.R. Rep. No. 639, 1st Sess.) (Sen. Rep. No. 520, 1st Sess.)-QMDE

96th Cong., H.R. 1829, for the relief of Loraine Smart and Robert Clarke. Beneficiaries, ages 21 and 18, natives and citizens of Jamaica, entered the United States as a student and visitor. The natural mother died when they were three years old and two days, respectively. The United States citizen grandmother became their legal guardian until her death. The daughter of the grandmother, a permanent resident alien, sought to have them remain with her and her spouse in the United States. The law held the beneficiaries lawfully admitted for permanent residence. (Priv. L. No. 50, 94 Stat. 3593 (1980)) (H.R. Rep. No. 671, 2nd Sess.) (Sen. Rep. No. 585, 1st Sess.)-QMGN

96th Cong., H.R. 2145, for the relief of Florette Ivoree Gayle and Keisha Dajaran Karr. Beneficiaries, mother and child, ages 21 and 3, natives and citizens of Jamaica, were coming to the United States to reside with the mother's adoptive mother, a United States citizen who adopted her at the age of 17. The elder beneficiary, although adopted, resided in Jamaica with her natural mother and the three year old child. The House Committee noted a "warm relationship exists between the adoptive mother and the beneficiary." The grandmother had not known of the adoptive daughter's child, but said that the child "would be welcome in her home." The law held the adoptive daughter to be an immediate relative under section 101(b)(1)(F) and held the child to be a lawful permanent resident of the United States. (Priv. L. No. 103, 94 Stat. 3629 (1980)) (H.R. Rep. No. 1507, 2nd Sess.)-QIRA

96th Cong., H.R. 2433, for the relief of Zora Singh Sunga. Beneficiary, a 21-year old native and citizen of India, was adopted at the age of 16 by United States citizens, ages 76 and 78, who had no natural children. The child was to be readopted in the United States because there were questions regarding traditional adoption customs in India. The House Committee reported that it had requested the Department of State and the Library of Congress to establish the correctness of the deed of adoption. The beneficiary's natural parents and four siblings resided in India. The law held the beneficiary to be a child within section 101(b)(1)(F) relating to immigration as an immediate relative. (Priv. L. No. 92, 94 Stat. 3625 (1980)) (H.R. Rep. No. 1509, 2nd Sess.)-QIRA

96th Cong., H.R. 3138, for the relief of Surip Karmowiredjo. Beneficiary, a 22-year old native and citizen of Indonesia adopted at the age of 19 by United States citizens, had previously been employed by them for six months as a domestic. The House Committee noted it was "convinced that a true parent-child relationship exists between the adoptive parents and the beneficiary and the intentions of providing a home are valid." Her natural parents and seven siblings resided in Indonesia. The law held the beneficiary to be a child for purposes of section 101(b)(1)(F) relating to immigration of adopted children as immediate relatives. (Priv. L. No. 95, 94 Stat. 3626 (1980)) (H.R. Rep. No. 1510, 2nd Sess.)-QIRA

96th Cong., H.R. 4013, for the relief of Jozef Swiderski. Beneficiary, a 62-year old native of Poland and lawful permanent resident of the United States for 12 years, was unable to fulfill the residence requirements for naturalization because of his employment as the Acting Director of the United Nations Food and Agriculture Organization in Italy 14 years. The law held the beneficiary to have complied with the residence requirements under section 316. (Priv. L. No. 52, 94 Stat. 3594 (1980)) (H.R. Rep. No. 647, 1st Sess.) (Sen. Rep. No. 624, 2nd Sess.)-NRES

96th Cong., H.R. 6739, for the relief of Leopoldine Marie Schmid. Beneficiary, a 62-year old native of Austria and lawful permanent resident of the United States for 22 years, had filed a petition for naturalization but was shot to death during a holdup at her business 15 days after her application had been favorably recommended to the court. The law conferred posthumously citizenship on the beneficiary. (Priv. L. No. 101, 94 Stat. 3628 (1980)) (H.R. Rep. No. 1306, 2nd Sess.)-NXPS

96th Cong., S. 215, for the relief of Renuka Pavla. Beneficiary, a 15-year old native and citizen of India, orphaned at an early age, and the victim of polio which had paralyzed both her legs from the knees down, entered the United States as a visitor to be adopted by United States citizens. The adoptive parents had two natural children and eleven adopted children. The law held the beneficiary to be within section 101(b)(1)(F) relating to the immigration of adopted children. (Priv. L. No. 60, 94 Stat. 3598 (1980)) (Sen. Rep. No. 82, 1st Sess.) (H.R. Rep. No. 1298, 2nd Sess.)-QIRA

96th Cong., S. 707, for the relief of Certain Aliens. Beneficiaries, 653 members of the Mennonite Church, entered the United States from Mexico and Canada, allegedly under the belief that they could continue to live in the United States and purchase land as farmers "in communities somewhat by themselves." The majority of the Mennonites left Mexico when land reforms were introduced, and some were dispossessed of land. Under special agreements made with other governments such as Bolivia and Paraguay, they had been able to immigrate and practice their religion. They believed that they could do the same in the United States. The Mennonites bought land in the United States, and were allegedly assured "necessary immigration papers" would follow after purchase. They settled in Seminole, Texas and bought 7,500 acres of farm land inexpensively, where there was little water in the area. It was alleged the beneficiaries were "lured" into the land scheme by unscrupulous real estate agents in the United States. According to the author of the Senate bill, the legislation was "not intended to have value as precedent for anyone besides the 653 persons involved." The law held the beneficiaries lawfully admitted for permanent residence. (Priv. L. No. 63, 94 Stat. 3599 (1980)) (Sen. Rep. No. 287, 1st Sess.) (H.R. Rep. No. 1324, 2nd Sess.)-QMGN

96th Cong., S. 1772, for the relief of Min-Zen Lin. Beneficiary, a one-year old native and citizen of China, was adopted by United States citizens who were unable to have children. The natural parents relinquished the child for economic reasons. After the adoption, the adoptive mother resided with the child for six months. The law held the child within section 101(b)(1)(F) relating to immigration of adopted children as immediate relatives. (Priv. L. No. 99, 94 Stat. 3628 (1980)) (Sen. Rep. No. 806, 1st Sess.)-QIRA

96th Cong., S. 2961, for the relief of Viktor Ivanovich Belenko. Beneficiary, a 33-year old native of the Soviet Union and lawful permanent resident of the United States, had defected from the Soviet Union in 1976 by flying a Soviet Mig-25 Foxbat interceptor from the Soviet Union to northern Japan. According to a letter from the Central Intelligence Agency, the beneficiary presented the United States with the most "advanced operational aircraft in the Soviet inventory along with his knowledge of related Soviet armament, technology, and tactical doctrine... Because of his unique contribution to our country and the benefits we expect from him in years to come, Viktor Belenko merits special consideration in his quest for American citizenship." The law held the beneficiary to have met the residence requirements for purposes of naturalization and exempted him from the prohibition relating to naturalization of former members of the Communist Party. (Priv. L. No. 62, 94 Stat. 3599 (1980)) (Sen. Rep. No. 963, 2nd Sess.)-NXCP

97th Cong., H.R. 684, for the relief of Ok-Boon Kang. Beneficiary, a 21-year old native and citizen of Korea and orphan, entered the United States as a visitor with the prospective United States citizen adoptive parents. They had already adopted five other Korean children. The beneficiary was allegedly the offspring of an American soldier and Korean woman, an "Amerasian." The law held the beneficiary within section 101(b)(1)(E) on behalf of adopted children. (Priv. L. No. 34, 96 Stat. 2627 (1982)) (H.R. Rep. No. 716, 1st Sess.) (Sen. Rep. No. 623, 2nd Sess.)-QIRA

97th Cong., H.R. 783, for the relief of Roland Karl Heinz Vogel. Beneficiary, a 35-year old native and citizen of Germany, was excludable due to two counts of assault with a deadly weapon during a jealous rage with a previous close friend at the age of 25. He was supported by his United States citizen mother until he joined the German Navy, at the age of 17; and she desired to have him join her in the United States The law waived section 212(a)(9) relating to crimes involving moral turpitude. (Priv. L. No. 3, 95 Stat. 1733 (1981)) (H.R. Rep. No. 113, 1st Sess.) (Sen. Rep. No. 232, 1st Sess.)-WCRF

97th Cong., H.R. 828, for the relief of George G. Barrios, Doctor of Medicine, his wife Olga T. Cruz, and their children Kurt F. Barrios and Karl S. Barrios, Katrina Adelaida Theresa. Beneficiaries (ages 38 through 2), were natives and citizens of the Philippines. The male beneficiary entered the United States as an exchange visitor and completed the requisite visa and medical exams for admission to the United States, and obtained a waiver of the two-year foreign residence requirement applicable to certain exchange visitors. His specialty was in colon rectal surgery, and he served the New York area three years. According to a report from the Department of Health and Human Services, portions of the county in which the beneficiary served were health manpower shortage areas for primary care. His spouse and four children resided in the Philippines, one child as a United States citizen. The House Committee noted the bill sought to provide temporary relief for a period of two years, and thereafter permanent residence due to "concerns revealed by past precedents" that indicated beneficiaries of private relief laws in the medical profession "did not serve the community on whose behalf the legislation was sought, or shortly after the granting of permanent residence, they left the community in need of their services for more lucrative employment." In order to assure the beneficiary served the needs of the community for whose benefit relief was sought, the Committee required assurances that the beneficiary remain in the area as a physician for a period of two years prior to the granting of full relief. The law suspended the deportation of the male beneficiary for two years and required assurances to the Attorney General that he would practice medicine in the area. Deportation proceedings would be reinstituted in the event he failed to comply with the law. The bill also allowed that the principal beneficiary's family would be eligible to enter the United States under section 101(a)(15)(B) as nonimmigrant visitors. Further, the Attorney General was directed to admit the beneficiaries for lawful permanent residence at the expiration of the two-year period if the above requirements were met regarding practice of medicine in a specific area. (Priv. L. No. 44, 96 Stat. 2631 (1982)) (H.R. Rep. No. 467, 2nd Sess.) (Sen. Rep. No. 625, 2nd Sess.)-QMOC

97th Cong., H.R. 1469, for the relief of Madeleine Mesnager. Beneficiary, an 81-year old native and citizen of France, sought to enter the United States to reside with her adoptive United States citizen daughter. The beneficiary raised the adoptive child, also her niece, since the age of two. At that time the natural mother became paralyzed. The putative adoptive mother supported her 29 years and adopted her at the age of 31. The House Committee noted adoption was delayed due to various problems including war conditions. The adoptive daughter wished to care for her mother "during her final years as she was cared for by the beneficiary during her formative years." The law held the beneficiary within section 201(b) as the immediate relative of a United States citizen. The bill also provided there would be no compensation by any agent or attorney for services rendered relating to the introduction of the legislation and provided for a misdemeanor upon conviction thereof and fine not exceeding $1,000. (Priv. L. No. 4, 95 Stat. 1734 (1981)) (H.R. Rep. No. 114, 1st Sess.) (Sen. Rep. No. 233, 1st Sess.)-QIRM

97th Cong., H.R. 1482, for the relief of Christina Boltz Sidders. Beneficiary, a 39-year old native of Bolivia, entered the United States as a visitor. She derived United States citizenship through her United States citizen father. The beneficiary forfeited citizenship because she did not return to the United States between the ages of 14 and 28. The House Committee noted it granted permanent residence in lieu of restoration of citizenship: "The Committee holds United States citizenship in the highest regard and precedents for restoring or conferring this honor are few...there was sufficient merit, however, in the case based on her father's service to the United States." The beneficiary's United States citizen father was an employee of the United States Embassy for four years, and he died when she was four months old. She resided with her mother thereafter, and later married a native of Argentina. The beneficiary claimed she was unaware of retention requirements. She maintained contact with her father's relatives in the United States since the age of 14. The law held the beneficiary lawfully admitted for permanent residence effective the date of entry to the United States (Priv. L. No. 24, 96 Stat. 2622 (1982)) (H.R. Rep. No. 581, 2nd Sess.) (Sen. Rep. No. 626, 2nd Sess.)-NRTN

97th Cong., H.R. 1681, for the relief of Andre Bartholo Eubanks. Beneficiary, a six-year old native and citizen of Brazil who entered the United States as a visitor, was relinquished by her parents for adoption by a United States citizen parent and lawful permanent resident, an aunt, at the age of five. The adoptive mother attempted to comply with the two-year residence period required by law for immigration of adopted children. The adoptive parents were married 15 years with no children. The law held the beneficiary to be within section 101(b)(1)(E) relating to the immigration of adopted children. (Priv. L. No. 17, 96 Stat. 2619 (1982)) (H.R. Rep. No. 129, 1st Sess.) (Sen. Rep. No. 358, 2nd Sess.)-QIRA

97th Cong., H.R. 1785, for the relief of Gladys Belleville Schultz. Beneficiary, a 17-year old native and citizen of Haiti was adopted at the age of 15 by United States citizens. She resided in an orphanage since the age of nine and met her adoptive parents on a visit to the United States with a church group, one year prior to adoption. The law classified the beneficiary as an adopted child under section 101(b)(1)(F) for purposes of immigrating. (Priv. L No. 7, 95 Stat. 1735 (1981)) (H.R. Rep. No. 130, 1st Sess.) (Sen. Rep. No. 236, 1st Sess.)-QIRA

97th Cong., H.R. 1826, for the relief of Shinji Oniki. Beneficiary, a 19-year old native and citizen of Japan, entered the United States as a visitor. He resided with his natural mother in the United States. The beneficiary was born illegitimately and was given to the maternal grandmother thirty days after birth for adoption. The natural mother left the child at the age of six in Japan, and departed to the United States with her United States citizen husband and later sought immigration. In granting relief, the House Committee noted, "While the Committee cannot condone the abandonment by the natural mother of her child, it appears she has been kept apprised of his developments in Japan by the maternal grandmother and has exhibited some concern of his well being during that time." The law held the beneficiary lawfully admitted for permanent residence. (Priv. L. No. 36, 96

Stat. 2627 (1982)) (H.R. Rep. No. 471, 2nd Sess.) (Sen. Rep. No. 628, 2nd Sess.)-QIRA

97th Cong., H.R. 2185, for the relief of Hanife Frantz. Beneficiary, a 31-year old native and citizen of Turkey and widow of a United States citizen, entered the United States as a visitor. She had been married four years and her spouse was employed by Boeing Services International under contract to the United States Air Force. He was killed in an ambush with three other Americans in Turkey on Christmas Day 1979. There was one United States citizen child, age three. The law held the beneficiary within section 201(b)and 204 relating to immediate relatives of United States citizens. (Priv. L. No. 9, 95 Stat. 1736 (1981)) (H.R. Rep. No. 118, 1st Sess.) (Sen. Rep. No. 238, 1st Sess.)-QIRW

97th Cong., S. 167, for the relief of Juan Esteban Ramirez. Beneficiary, a 23-year old native and citizen of Ecuador, entered the United States as a visitor through the efforts of a United States citizen doctor, who met him during a visit to a missionary hospital where the beneficiary was treated for malnutrition and had surgery on his legs to correct the effects of polio. He was one of seven illegitimate children and was sold to restaurant owners, until his contact with the American doctor. He was later given to the care of foster parents in the United States and attended school for the physically handicapped. The law held the beneficiary lawfully admitted for permanent residence. (Priv. L. No. 26, 96 Stat. 2623 (1982)) (Sen. Rep. No. 220, 1st Sess.) (H.R. Rep. No. 715, 2nd Sess.)-QMGN

98th Cong., H.R. 960, conferring citizenship posthumously on Corporal Wladyslaw Staniszewski. Beneficiary, a 20-year old native of Scotland who was admitted for permanent residence, served in the Marine Corps and was killed in action in Vietnam. His parents and two siblings were United States citizens. The law held the beneficiary to be a United States citizen at the time of his death, and provided that no benefits would derive to survivors. (Priv. L. No. 33, 98 Stat. 3429 (1984))-NXPS

98th Cong., H.R. 1150, for the relief of Teodoro N. Salanga, Jr. Beneficiary, a 48-year old native and citizen of the Philippines, entered the United States as a visitor. His family had sympathized with American prisoners of war during World War II, and the beneficiary smuggled food and supplies at the age of six. His sister, a United States citizen, filed a petition on his behalf. Various letters attesting to his deeds were included in the report. The law held the beneficiary lawfully admitted for permanent residence. (Priv. L. No. 27, 98 Stat. 3426 (1984)) (H.R. Rep. No. 973, 1st Sess.)-QMDE

98th Cong., H.R. 1236, for the relief of Andrew and Julia Lui. Beneficiaries, natives of Hong Kong, ages 30 and 26, entered the United States as students and resided here ten and eight years, respectively. The male beneficiary graduated from MIT, and was employed by a company involved in marketing a system for evaluating the economics of various chemicals industries. He received labor certification by that company. The beneficiaries had one United States citizen child. The law held the beneficiaries lawfully admitted for permanent residence. (Priv. L. No. 28, 98 Stat. 3426 (1984)) (H.R. Rep. No. 940, 1st Sess.)-QMOC

98th C., H.R. 1865, for the relief of Nery De Maio. Beneficiary, a 63-year old native of Colombia and permanent resident of the United States for 23 years, was denied United States citizenship because she was unable to respond to questions concerning United States History and Government due to a stroke. The House noted "Congress has no precedents for waiving the oath of allegiance...but the Committee believes this case is unique." The law held the beneficiary satisfied the requirements of section 312(2) relating to knowledge and understanding of United States Government, and section 337(a) of the Act relating to taking an oath of allegiance. (Priv. L. No. 41, 98 Stat. 3432 (1984)) (H.R. Rep. No. 521, 1st Sess.)-NXEN

98th C., H.R. 3131, for the relief of Marina Kunyavsky. Beneficiary, a 19-year old native and citizen of the U.S.S.R., entered the United States as a refugee for permanent residence. She was a rhythmic gymnast and a member of the United States national team. She placed fourth during 1983 USA National Championships. She desired to participate in the 1984 Olympics. The Senate Committee noted, "documents from the United States Olympic Committee support the bill and this may well be her one chance to participate in Olympic competition." The law held the beneficiary within section 316 to residence in the United States. (Priv. L. No. 13, 98 Stat. 3420 (1984)) (Sen. Rep. No. 520, 2nd Sess.)-NRES

98th Cong., S. 1060, for the relief of Samuel Joseph Edgar. Beneficiary, a 19-year old native of Scotland and citizen of England, entered the United States as a visitor. He had been a ward of the Government of Scotland since birth because his father was in prison, and his mother could not adequately provide for him. He had been placed in a full time foster home at the age of 12, and when they moved to the United States he later accompanied them. After several years, there was a "breakdown in the relationship," and the beneficiary was placed with a different set of foster parents who then adopted him. The law held the beneficiary lawfully admitted for permanent residence. (Priv. L. No. 25, 98 Stat. 3425 (1984)) (Sen. Rep. No. 327, 1st Sess.) (H.R. Rep. No. 949, 2nd Sess.)-QMGN

98th C., S. 1863, for the relief of Audun Endestad. Beneficiary, a 30-year old native of Norway and permanent resident of the United States, desired to compete in the 1984 Winter Olympics as a member of the United States Ski Team. The Senate Committee noted the beneficiary "contributed a great deal to the development of the strongest cross country team the United States has ever had...Audun's warm personality and natural love of people have made him a central focus of the 'team group,' which we feel has contributed to the amazing success of the men's cross country ski team the last few years." The beneficiary was eight months short of the period required to meet the naturalization residence requirement. The law held the beneficiary within section 319(a) relating to the three-year residence requirement for persons married to United States citizens. (Priv. L. No. 7, 98 Stat. 3417 (1984)) (Sen. Rep. No. 330, 1st Sess.)-NRES

98th Cong. S. 2729, for the relief of Jean Willhelm Willrich. Beneficiary, a 31-year old native of West Germany who entered the United States in 1981 as a permanent resident, was a soccer player. He was married to a United States citizen. The law held the beneficiary to have satisfied section 319(a) relating to residence for purposes of naturalization for persons married to United States citizens. (Priv. L. No. 15, 98 Stat. 3420 (1984)) (Sen. Rep. No. 519, 1st Sess.)-NRES

99th C., H.R. 483, for the relief of Edwin Marcos Rios and Geovanna Rios. Beneficiaries, 21- and 18-year old natives and citizens of Bolivia, who entered the United States as visitors, were the nephew and niece of United States citizens, who adopted them in the United States. The natural mother died in March 1981 of cancer, and the father died in September of that same year. The law held the beneficiaries within section 101(b)(1)(F) as the adopted children of United States citizens. (Priv. L. No. 5, 100 Stat. 4314 (1986)) (H.R. Rep. No. 514, 2nd Sess.)-QIRA

99th Cong., H.R. 737, for the relief of Ms. Chang Ai Bae. Beneficiary, a 45-year old native and citizen of Korea, was the victim of spousal abuse from her Korean husband. She entered the United States as an exchange visitor and had custody of two citizen children. The law held the beneficiary lawfully admitted for permanent residence and provided that application for relief must be made within two years of enactment. (Priv. L. No. 2, 100 Stat. 4313 (1986)) (H.R. Rep. No. 515, 2nd Sess.)-QMGN

99th C., H.R. 3154, for the relief of John Patrick Brady, Ann M. Brady, and Mark P. Brady. Beneficiaries, 39-, 39- and 13-year old natives and citizens of Ireland, entered the United States as treaty traders employed with Aer Lingus. The principal beneficiary sought to change employment. The Immigration and Naturalization Service erroneously approved a petition allowing the beneficiary to be employed with another airline sharing operations with Aer Lingus. They were denied visas abroad because they were no longer eligible for treaty trader status, since they were not associated with an employer of their native country. They had two citizen children, ages 12 and 6. The House Committee noted that although "there are few precedents for granting nonimmigrant status by means of private legislation, the unique circumstances of this case merit relief. The Committee is convinced that the 17 year employer relationship was severed solely on the basis of erroneous advice from the Immigration and Naturalization Service and in order to correct this inequity, the beneficiary should be eligible to retain the status for which he originally qualified." The law held the beneficiaries within section 101(a)(15)(E)(i) as treaty traders while employed by the new company. (Priv. L. No. 9, 100 Stat. 4316 (1986)) (H.R. Rep. No. 520, 1st Sess.)-QMGN

99th Cong., H.R. 5016, for the relief of Sueng Ho Jang and Sueng Il Jang. Beneficiaries, 24- and 20-year old natives and citizens of Korea, entered the

United States with their parents as dependents of treaty traders. The parents and two brothers died aboard the Korean Airline (KAL) 007 flight which was sabotaged in 1983. The father had been employed with KAL seven years. The law held the beneficiaries lawfully admitted for permanent residence. (Priv. L. No. 19, 100 Stat. 4321 (1986)) (H.R. Rep. No. 749, 2nd Sess.) (Sen. Rep. No. 527, 2nd Sess.)-QMGN

99th Cong., S. 381, for the relief of Mishleen Earle. Beneficiary was an 18-year old native and citizen of Lebanon and widow of a United States citizen. Her spouse served in the Armed Forces, and was killed in the 1983 bombing of the Marine Headquarters in Beirut, Lebanon. They had been married seven days and the citizen had filled out the necessary forms for her immigration. The completed papers rested in his pockets at the time of the massacre. The law held the beneficiary admitted for permanent residence. (Priv. L. No. 1, 100 Stat. 4313 (1986)) (Sen. Rep. No. 252, 2nd Sess.) (H.R. Rep. No. 524, 2nd Sess.)-QIRW

100th Cong., H.R. 1191, for the relief of Jose Maria Vas. Beneficiary, a 23-year old native and citizen of Hong Kong, was over the age of 21 when the family adjusted to permanent residence, and therefore could not be included in the process. A second preference petition was approved. The bill provided that the beneficiary be considered a child for purposes of 202(b)(1). (Priv. L. No. 4, 101 Stat. 1975 (1987)) (H. R. Rep. No. 348, 1st Sess.)-QPRF

100th Cong., H.R. 2109, for the relief of Rosa Pratts. Beneficiary, a 27-year old native and citizen of Honduras, entered the United States on a diplomatic visa in 1982. She married a United States citizen who filed a petition on her behalf, but he committed suicide prior to her obtaining status. They had a four-year old citizen child. The law provided that the beneficiary be considered an immediate relative of a United States citizen. (Priv. L. No. 38, 102 Stat. 4861 (1988)) (H.R. Rpt. No. 841, 2nd Sess.)-QIRW

100th Cong., S. 391, for the relief of Hyong Cha Kim Kay. Beneficiary was a 37-year old native and citizen of Korea who resided in Korea with her 11 year old citizen daughter, and 7 year old citizen son. She was married to a United States serviceman who filed a petition on her behalf but was killed. She was then engaged to another United States citizen. She was excludable due to a conviction in 1975 of possession of fifty grams of marijuana. The law waived section 212(a)(23) of the Act, but first provided for suspension of deportation for two years during which the beneficiary had to satisfy the Attorney General that she exhibited good moral character, no other convictions, and rehabilitation. (Priv. L. No. 23, 102 Stat. 4851 (1988)) (H.R. Rep. No. 848, , 2nd Sess.) (Sen. Rep. No. 278, 2nd Sess.)-WCRF

100th Cong., S. 1842, for the relief of Wilhelm Jahn Schlechter, Monica Pino Schlechter, Ingrid Daniela Schlechter, and Arturo David Schlechter. Beneficiaries were 32-, 35-, 5-, and 8-year old natives of Chile. One child, Daniela, was undergoing medical treatment for a rare birth defect called bladder exstrophy, a condition where the bladder is formed outside the body. They first entered the United States for medical treatment in 1980 and last entered 1984. The law granted permanent residence on behalf of the beneficiary. (Priv. L. No. 48, 102 Stat. 4867 (1988)) (Sen. Rep. No. 349, 1st Sess.) (H.R. Rep. No. 1046, 2nd Sess.)-QMGN

100th Cong., S. 1919, for the relief of Michael Wilding. Beneficiary, a native-born United States citizen who renounced citizenship in 1971, was excludable due to a conviction for cultivating 10 milligrams of cannibis. He was the son of actress Elizabeth Taylor. The beneficiary was married to a United States citizen. The bill waived exclusion due to drugs and suspended deportation for three years with a requirement for community service. (Priv. L. No. 36, 102 Stat. 4859 (1988)) (*Congressional Record*, 134, 32446)-WCRF

100th Cong., S. 2637, for the relief of Gillian Lesley Sackler. Beneficiary was a 48-year old native and citizen of England who was married to philanthropist Arthur M. Sackler, a United States citizen, who endowed the Sackler Museum in Washington, D.C. A petition was filed on her behalf 14 days prior to his death. The bill granted permanent residence. (Priv. L. No. 35, 102 Stat. 4859 (1988)-QIRW

VETOES

76th Cong., H.R. 5156, for the relief of Adolph Ernest Helms. Beneficiary first entered the United States as a seaman in 1927 and subsequently married a United States citizen with two children. His wife died after eleven years of marriage. In approving the bill, the Committee noted the alien testified before the Committee, and his entries to the United States were not the result of fraud. (H.R. Rep. No. 789, 1st Sess.) (Sen. Rep. No. 1921, 3rd Sess.)

Message of President Franklin D. Roosevelt dated July 3, 1940, (H.R. Doc. 868, 3rd Sess.) returned the bill without approval stating, "It seems highly questionable whether a person who is to be considered ineligible to become a citizen of the United States should, nevertheless, be admitted to permanent residence in this country. If a person is to be so admitted, he should be permitted to apply for naturalization if he so desires. If he is not regarded as a fit subject for naturalization, no reason is discernible why he should be admitted to permanent residence."

76th Cong., H.R. 5640, for the relief of Richard Paul Rehn. Beneficiary, a native of Germany, was a deserting crewman who resided in the United States 14 years, and married a lawful permanent resident alien with one United States citizen child. (H.R. Rep. No. 1793, 3rd Sess.) (Sen. Rep. No. 1922, 3rd Sess.)

Message of President Franklin D. Roosevelt dated August 26, 1940 (H.R. Doc. 935, 3rd Sess.) returned the bill without approval because administrative relief under the Alien Registration Act of 1940 existed, wherein the Attorney General could suspend deportation of those who resided in the United States five years and whose deportation would result in serious economic detriment to United States citizen relatives.

76th Cong., H.R. 5641, for the relief of Johann Rudolf Hueneberg. Beneficiary, a 40-year old native of Germany and deserting crewman, was married to a United States citizen and resided in the United States 14 years. (H.R. Rep. No. 1805, 3rd Sess.) (Sen. Rep. No. 1914, 3rd Sess.)

Message of President Franklin D. Roosevelt dated August 26, 1940 (H.R. Doc. 936, 3rd Sess.) returned the bill without approval because administrative relief existed under the Alien Registration Act of 1940, whereby the Attorney General could suspend deportation if economic hardship was shown to United States citizens. The President noted the case appeared within the provisions of the new law and "It is therefore in the interest of orderly procedure that the matter be handled administratively."

76th Cong., H.R. 6409, for the relief of Motiejus Buzas and Bernice Buzas, his wife. Beneficiaries, natives of Lithuania, entered the United States as visitors where they resided 14 years. They had previously resided in Canada, but when they sought travel documents to that country the

Government of Canada declared their status to be invalid. Additionally, they were not able to obtain travel documents from the Soviet Union for return to Lithuania. (H.R. Rep. No. 726, 1st Sess.) (Sen. Rep. No. 1679, 3rd Sess.)

Message of President Franklin D. Roosevelt dated October 10, 1940 (H.R. Doc. 968, 3rd Sess.) returned without approval the legislation because it did not allow the beneficiaries a permanent lawful status which would then allow them to become United States citizens. The President declared it "highly questionable whether it is in the best interests of the United States to place persons living in this country in such a peculiar status."

76th Cong., H.R. 7179, for the relief of Louis D. Friedman. Beneficiary, a native-born United States citizen moved to Canada and expatriated himself on the basis that he wanted to engage in business for which Canadian citizenship was required. He was married to a United States citizen. Upon finding out that he lost his claim to United States citizenship because of his actions, he liquidated his holdings in Canada and returned to the United States. (H.R. Rep. No. 1797, 3rd Sess.) (Sen. Rep. No. 1685, 3rd Sess.)

Message of President Franklin D. Roosevelt dated October 10, 1940 (H.R. Doc. 975, 3rd Sess.) returned the legislation without approval noting: "No reason is discernible why a special dispensation should be accorded to him from compliance with all of the requirements of the naturalization laws. Resort to naturalization by private act should be permitted, if at all, only in unusual and unique situations".

76th Cong., H.R. 7563, for the relief of Salomon Georg Kaufmann, Doris Kaufmann, and John Michael Peter Kaufmann. Beneficiaries were born in Germany and the Netherlands and the principal was the owner of 20% of an exporting and importing business in Holland and Canada. In acting favorably, the Committee noted the assets of the company and the fact that they would not become a public charge. Also noted was support from various banks, including Guaranty Trust Company of New York and the Commodity Exchange. (H.R. Rep. No. 1692, 3rd Sess.) (Sen. Rep. No. 1916, 3rd Sess.)

Message of President Franklin D. Roosevelt dated July 3,1940 (H.R. Doc. 865, 3rd Sess.) returned the bill without approval because it was an exception of "such a broad scope" and administrative authorities did not have any discretion to review other provisions of law which might be applicable.

76th Cong., H.R. 9651, for the relief of Meier Langermann, his wife, Friederik, and son, Joseph. Beneficiaries, 53-, 29-, and 18-month old natives of Poland who later resided in Germany were admitted to the United States as visitors. The principal beneficiary was engaged in manufacturing shoes and was in "well-to-do" circumstances with $18,000 in the bank. It was stated that "it would be impossible for Mr. Langermann, his wife and child to return to the country to which they owe allegiance." (H.R. Rep. No. 2271, 3rd Sess.) (Sen. Rep. No. 1918, 3rd Sess.)

Message of President Franklin D. Roosevelt dated July 2, 1940 (H. Doc. 862 3rd Sess.) returned the bill because of its broad scope. In the instant case, the bill did not only waive the requirements of the Quota Act, but set aside all other limitations to immigration statutes. The President stated, "It does not seem to me to be advisable to grant an exception of such a broad scope" preventing review of other provisions of law.

76th Cong., S. 1384, for the relief of Egon Karl Freiherr Von Mauchenheim and Margarete Von Mauchenheim. Beneficiaries, 26- and 22-year old natives of Germany, entered the United States as visitors, and the male beneficiary was employed by Ford Motor Company. Both were fugitives from Germany. The male beneficiary was tried in Germany in absentia and sentenced to death for avoiding the draft under Hitler's regime. The wife received a prison sentence as an accessory. While visiting Monaco, they were ordered extradited. The Prince Sovereign of Monaco refused extradition, however, and the beneficiaries traveled to the United States. (H.R. Rep. No. 787, 1st Sess.) (Sen. Rep. No. 553, 1st Sess.)

Message of President Franklin D. Roosevelt dated May 29, 1940 (S. Doc. 201, 3rd Sess.) returned the bill without approval due to the fact that beneficiaries made false statements concerning their acts in Germany, and that they were actually involved in criminal proceedings for "fraud and civil claims for the recovery of property." The President noted that the investigation by the Department of State revealed these misrepresentations had not been known to the Congress at the time the legislation was considered.

76th Cong., S. 3673, for the relief of Kurt Frings. Beneficiary, a 31-year old native of Germany and spouse of a United States citizen, was ineligible for a visa due to fraud. He was a writer and had been a European lightweight champion boxer, and also instructed in skiing. His spouse was a writer in Hollywood for Warner Brothers. (Sen. Rep. No. 1464, 3rd Sess.) (H.R. Rep. No. 2087, 3rd Sess.)

Message of President Franklin D. Roosevelt dated June 19, 1940 (S. Doc. 248, 3rd Sess.) returned without approval the legislation because the beneficiary had been refused a visa due to perjury which constituted moral turpitude when applying for a visa.

76th Cong., S. 4085, for the relief of Max Von Der Porten and wife, Charlotte Von Der Porten. Beneficiaries, 61- and 30-year old natives and citizens of Germany, entered the United States as visitors. Shortly before Hitler became Chancellor of Germany, the male beneficiary was a director in various industrial corporations controlled by the German Government in ores and metals. According to the Senate report, the Department of Justice was "instrumental in helping Dr. von der Porten obtain a visa...because it appeared that he had obtained valuable information in connection with his industrial activities in Germany." (Sen. Rep. No. 2157, 3rd Sess.) (H.R. Rep. No. 3106, 3rd Sess.)

Pocket veto. Presented to President Franklin D. Roosevelt January 2, 1941, *Congressional Record* 86:14012.

77th Cong., S. 381, for the relief of Marcel M. Roman, Clara M. Roman, and Rodica E. Roman. Beneficiaries, 46, 40 and 32 years of age, entered the United States as visitors. The male beneficiary claimed to have a patent for improving refining gasoline. (Sen. Rep. No. 797, 1st Sess.) (H.R. Rep. No. 1701, 2nd Sess.)

Message from President Franklin D. Roosevelt dated February 17, 1942 (S. Doc. 180, 2nd Sess.) returned the bill without approval because an administrative remedy appeared to be available.

80th C., H.R. 1502, for the relief of Herman Trahn. Beneficiary, a 43-year old native of Sweden, entered the United States as a visitor and claimed exemption from military service. He stated he applied for exemption in order to leave the United States to visit Mexico. He was deaf in his right ear, and indicated he made several attempts to enlist in the armed forces but was rejected. The Department of Justice saw "no unusual circumstances" in the case and recommended adversely. (H.R. Rep. No. 652, 1st Sess.) (Sen. Rep. No. 500, 1st Sess.)

Pocket veto. Presented to President Harry S. Truman July 18, 1947, *Congressional Record* 93:9343.

80th C., H.R. 2347, for the relief of Mrs. Akiko Tsukado Miller. Beneficiary, a 40-year old native of Japan and spouse of a United States citizen serving in the Armed Forces, and mother of two citizen children entered the United States as a visitor. She was not eligible for permanent residence under the Soldier Brides Act because she was a native of a race ineligible to citizenship. (H.R. Rep. No. 907, 1st Sess.) (Sen. Rep. No. 1007, 2nd Sess.)

Message from President Truman dated April 12, 1948 (H.R. Doc. 609, 2nd Sess.) returned without approval the bill due to a remedy under a law enacted in the 80th Congress allowing all races eligible to the Soldier Brides Act.

80th C., H.R. 3061, for the relief of Victor C. Kaminski. Beneficiary, a 34-year old native of Poland, was a deserting crewman who resided in the United States one year. He spent two years in the Polish underground fighting Germans, and after one-month imprisonment he joined the merchant marines. (H.R. Rep. No. 1125, 1st Sess.) (Sen. Rep. No. 1008, 2nd Sess.)

Message from President Harry S. Truman dated April 12, 1948 (H.R. Doc. 607, 2nd Sess.) returned without approval the above legislation noting that although the beneficiary's plight was a sympathetic one, his situation was "not unlike thousands of others throughout the world who are seeking a haven in the United States, but who are obliged to await their turn under established immigration quotas." To grant special privileges to the beneficiary "would postpone the entry of some other hopeful Polish person rightfully awaiting the opportunity to enjoy the blessings of a new life in this country."

80th Cong., H.R. 4199, for the relief of George Haniotis. Beneficiary, a 53-year old native of Turkey and citizen of Greece, entered the United States as an attaché of the Greek Embassy. His two children were married to United States citizens. In acting favorably, the Committee took into consideration his record in both World Wars, command of the English language and intellectual qualifications. (H.R. Rep. No. 1651, 2nd Sess.) (Sen. Rep. No. 1723, 2nd Sess.)

Pocket veto. Presented to President Harry S. Truman June 21, 1948, *Congressional Record* 94:9371.

81st Cong., H.R. 3464, for the relief of John Michael Ancker Rasmussen. Beneficiary, a 32-year old native and citizen of Denmark, entered the United States as a visitor followed by his mother and sister who entered for permanent residence. The beneficiary had previously resided in China where his parents were missionaries, and he was later employed. His wife and children resided in Sweden at the time of his visit to the United States. (H.R. Rep. No. 1818, 2nd Sess.) (Sen. Rep. No. 2015, 2nd Sess.). The case subsequently became law. (Priv. L. No. 1012, 82nd Cong., 65 Stat. A63 (1951))

Message from President Harry S. Truman dated August 14, 1950 (H.R. Doc. 683, 2nd Sess.) returned the legislation without approval because there were insufficient equities "justifying the enactment of special legislation granting him a preference over such others" who are awaiting permanent residence. The President noted enactment of such a bill would "undoubtedly encourage other aliens to attempt to enter the United States as visitors for a temporary period and, thereafter, seek exemption from the requirements of the immigration laws."

81st Cong., H.R. 5016, for the relief of Mrs. Virginia Dalla Rosa Prati and her Minor son, Rolando Dalla Rosa Prati. Beneficiaries, 43- and 11-years old, sought permanent resident status in the United States. Mrs. Prati was a native born United States citizen and her son was born in Romania. Mrs. Prati lost her citizenship by becoming a naturalized citizen of Italy for the purpose of marrying her husband, an employee of the Italian consular service. (H.R. Rep. No. 2127, 2nd Sess.) (Sen. Rep. No. 2133, 2nd Sess.)

Message from President Harry S. Truman dated August 14, 1950 (H.R. Doc. 685, 2nd Sess.) returned without approval the above legislation because Mrs. Prati voluntarily relinquished her United States citizenship with full knowledge of her act. The case, said the President, "does not present considerations justifying the enactment of special legislation granting them a preference over the many other aliens" awaiting permanent residence.

81st Cong., S. 305, for the relief of Julio Laffitte. Beneficiary, a 53-year old native and citizen of Spain, was admitted to the United States as a visitor and possessed exceptional skills as a designer of furs and dresses which would contribute to economic interests in that industry. He worked with Saks Fifth Avenue and was chosen as one of the 10 best designers in the United States. (Sen. Rep. No. 2006, 2nd Sess.) (H.R. Rep. No. 2835, 2nd Sess.)

Message from President Harry S. Truman dated August 29, 1950 (S. Doc. 210, 2nd Sess.) returned without approval the bill citing the fact that while the beneficiary may possess unique talents in the fashion industry, that in itself was not an area which was of such scope as to impact the "economic welfare of the United States as a whole," warranting an exemption from the normal requirements of the law. "The enactment of this measure would undoubtedly encourage other aliens, also chargeable to oversubscribed quotas, to attempt to enter the United States as visitors for a temporary period and, thereafter, seek exemption from the requirements of the immigration laws," the President said.

82nd Cong., S. 46, for the relief of Ruth Obre Dubonnet. Beneficiary, a 51-year old native-born United States citizen, lost her citizenship by acquiring French citizenship while residing in France during the war. She later returned to the United States as a lawful permanent resident. The beneficiary had worked with the Red Cross during the war, but had also made disparaging statements of the United States. (Sen. Rep. No. 7, 1st Sess.) (H.R. Rep. No. 155, 1st Sess.). The case subsequently became law. (Priv. L. No.. 634, 82nd Cong., 66 Stat. 73 (1952))

Message from President Harry S. Truman dated March 16, 1951 (S. Doc. 15, 1st Sess.) returned the legislation without approval as "unnecessary and unwise." The President stated the beneficiary could proceed toward United States citizenship through the normal administrative channels, and there were no "compelling reasons" to accelerate the procedure. Additionally, the President did not believe it was proper to set aside the judgment of a District Court denying her reinstatement to citizenship.

82nd Cong., S. 1436, for the relief of Mrs. Marie Y. Mueller. Beneficiary, a 43-year old native and citizen of Canada who entered the United States as a visitor, was subject to deportation having maintained a bawdy-house in Canada in 1929 and 1932 and had previously been married four times and her husband three times. Her spouse was arrested for Federal violations and claimed the alien was dependent upon him. She was married to a United States citizen and had effected a "complete rehabilitation". (Sen. Rep. No. 464, 1st Sess.) (H.R. Rep. No. 1143, 1st Sess.). This bill later became law without the President's approval. (Priv. L. No. No. 1, 66 Stat. A120 (1952)).

Pocket veto. Presented to President Harry S. Truman Oct. 19, 1951, *Congressional Record* 97:13534.

83rd Cong., H.R. 692, for the relief of Nina Makeef, also known as Nina Berberova. Beneficiary, a 52-year old native of Russia, entered the United States as a visitor and was employed first as a journalist with Tolstoy Foundation, and later under contract with the Voice of America. The bill would have granted the beneficiary lawful permanent resident status. (H.R. Rep. No. 1392, 2nd Sess.) (Sen. Rep. No. 1847, 2nd Sess.)

Pocket veto. Presented to President Dwight D. Eisenhower August 24, 1954, *Congressional Record* 100:14683.

83rd Cong., S. 153, for the relief of Wilhelm Engelbert. Beneficiary, a 45-year old native and citizen of Germany, was a deserting crewman who entered the United States. He was a former member of the Nazi Party in Germany and was interned as an alien enemy during World War II. He was married to a United States citizen. (Sen. Rep. No. 67, 1st Sess.) (H.R. Rep. No. 1149, 2nd Sess.)

Message from President Dwight D. Eisenhower dated March 17, 1954 (S. Doc. 106, 2nd Sess.) returned the bill without approval on the basis that during the beneficiary's stay in the United States for 13 years, including during the outbreak of World War II, he did nothing to regularize his status; and in fact, "his actions indicate clearly that he thought of himself as a German and showed his allegiance time and again as that of a German national." Further, the President noted the beneficiary did not show any real "willingness to accept the responsibilities of a permanent resident of the United States. On the contrary, he sought repatriation to Germany during the war, and it was not until after victory had been assured in Europe in 1945 that he withdrew his application and requested adjustment of his immigration status."

83rd Cong., S. 154, for the relief of George Pantelas. Beneficiary, a 47-year old native and citizen of Greece, first entered the United States in 1921, and nine years later was convicted and imprisoned for issuing bad checks and was deported. He later reentered the United States with false documents, and subsequently married a United States citizen and had a seven-year old child. The Department of Justice noted the visas for Greece were oversubscribed, and the beneficiary's past criminal record and "disregard for the laws and principles of the United States" presented no justification for granting him special relief. In support of its contention of merit in the bill, the Senate noted "cancellation of the outstanding deportation proceedings is warranted solely on the ground that his support is necessary for his citizen wife and child." (Sen. Rep. No. 322, 1st Sess.) (H.R. Rep. 2640, 2nd Sess.). This case subsequently became law. (Priv. L. No. No. 768, 84th Cong., 70 Stat. A122 (1956))

Pocket veto. Presented to President Dwight D. Eisenhower August 17, 1954, *Congressional Record* 100:14707.

84th Cong., H.R. 3963, for the relief of Ashot Mnatzakanian and Ophelia Mnatzakanian. Beneficiaries were 35- and 24-year old natives of Iran and Russia. The principal beneficiary had entered the United States as an exchange student with funds from the World Health Organization to return to Iran with the Ministry of Health in sanitary engineering. He attended Johns Hopkins University, and the spouse had entered as a visitor. He subsequently sought employment in violation of his student status. They had twins, United States citizens. (H.R. Rep. No. 1382, 1st Sess.) (Sen. Rep. No. 1546, 2nd Sess.)

Pocket veto. Presented to President Dwight D. Eisenhower March 22, 1956, *Congressional Record* 102:5696.

84th Cong., S. 143, for the relief of Kurt Glaser. Beneficiary, a 28-year old native of Czechoslovakia and citizen of Austria, entered the United States as an exchange visitor and was employed by Reynolds Metals Company as a metallurgical engineer. (Sen. Rep. No. 67, 1st Sess.) (H.R. Rep. No. 557, 1st Sess.)

Message from President Dwight D. Eisenhower dated June 3, 1955 (S. Doc. 557, 1st Sess.) returned without approval the legislation based on the concept of the exchange program as "effective instruments for promoting international understanding and good will." The President noted both the beneficiary and his sponsor understood their obligations under the exchange program, and there were no exceptional circumstances which served the beneficiary's case to override the requirements and purpose of the exchange program. The President further recommended Congress take steps to restrict waivers available under the exchange program stating, "Such provisions of law will protect the purposes of the exchange program, will prevent unjustifiable evasion of immigration procedures, and will establish legislative policy to guide the committees of Congress in taking action on future private bills which would set aside the general law."

85th Cong., S. 2110, for the relief of Shirley Leeke Kilpatrick. Beneficiary, a 21-year old native and citizen of Australia, entered the United States as a visitor, and was the spouse of a United States citizen serving in the Armed Forces. She was expecting a child and could not afford to travel to Canada under pre-examination procedures to obtain a visa. (Sen. Rep. No. 1028, 1st Sess.) (H.R. Rep. No. 1472, 2nd Sess.)

Message of President Dwight D. Eisenhower dated March 31, 1958 (S. Doc. 84, 2nd Sess.) returned the bill without approval due to enactment of a new law making the bill unnecessary.

87th Cong., S. 1934, for the relief of Mrs. Chow Chui Ha. Beneficiary, a 27-year old native and citizen of China residing in Hong Kong, was registered on the quota list for immigration by virtue of a petition filed by United States citizen adoptive parents. She had resided with her adoptive parents 12 years prior to marriage. She was married with six children. The adoptive father suffered paralysis, and they were anxious to have their daughter and grandchildren with them. (Sen. Rep. No. 623, 1st Sess.) (H.R. Rep. No. 1123, 1st Sess.)

Message of President John F. Kennedy dated April 16, 1962 (S. Doc. 87, 2nd Sess.) returned the above bill without approval due to the fact that the law cited in the legislation was repealed March 25, 1962 therefore "the intended relief is no longer available and approval of the bill would serve no useful purpose."

98th Cong., H.R. 2859, for the relief of John Brima Charles. Beneficiary, a 24-year old native and citizen of Sierra Leone, entered the United States at the age of 11 as a visitor. His mother had deserted him at birth and the father, a lawful permanent resident, abandoned his residence in the United States when the beneficiary was 17. The beneficiary had been under investigation due to fraudulently obtaining student loans. (H.R. Rep. No. 970, 1st Sess.)

Pocket veto. Presented to President Ronald Reagan October 17, 1984, *Congressional Record*, 130:31086.

Appendix D2

Alphabetical Index

Abele, Karlis, 84th Cong., H.R. 1301, Priv. L. No. 415, 69 Stat. A142 (1955)-WHEL

Agar, Karl Heinz, 87th Cong., S. 689, Priv. L. No. 599, 76 Stat. 1377 (1962)-NMSC

Agrippina, Sister (Agrippina Palermo), Sister Battistina (Franceschina Serpa), Sister Romana (Angela Iolanda Morelli), Sister Franceschina (Maria Caruso), and Sister Bruna (Giuseppina de Caro) 83rd Cong., H.R. 3855, Priv. L. No. 752, 68 Stat. A190 (1954)-QMOC

Aguinaldo, Pedro, 88th Cong., H.R. 2737, Priv. L. No. 256, 78 Stat. 1157 (1964)-NRES

Ahting, Louise, 81st Cong., H.R. 4747, Priv. L. No. 570, 64 Stat. A85 (1950)-NRTN

Alafouzos, Matheos, 82nd Cong., S. 2770, Priv. L. No. 658, 66 Stat. A82 (1952)-QIRM

Alemany, Francisca, 84th Cong., H.R. 5546, Priv. L. No. 486, 69 Stat. A164 (1955)-QPRF

Alexeev, Kirill Mihailovich, Antonina Ivanovna Alexeev, and minor children, Victoria and Vladimir Alexeev, 83rd Cong., S. 855, Priv. L. No. 591, 68 Stat. A138 (1954)-QMDE

Alldritt, Mrs. Coral E., 82nd Cong., H.R. 664, Priv. L. No. 32, 65 Stat. A15 (1951)-QMOC

Alonzi, Giuseppa, 87th Cong., S. 570, Priv. L. No. 178, 75 Stat. 910 (1961)-QPRF

Alpiar, Georges Gregory, 81st Cong., S. 2107, Priv. L. No. 633, 64 Stat. A106 (1950)-QMOC

Alvarado, Josefina, 76th Cong., H.R. 4066, Priv. L. No. 588, 54 Stat. 1373 (1940)-WHEL

Amoresano, Mrs. Rose and her children, 84th Cong., H.,R. 877, Priv. L. No. 744, 70 Stat. A111 (1956)-QPRF

An, Chin-Ho, 95th Cong., H.R. 3461, Priv. L. No. 17, 91 Stat. 1655 (1977)-QIRM

Andreis, Maria Louise, 84th Cong., H.R. 962, Priv. L. No. 249, 69 Stat. A88 (1955)-QPRF

Aneli, PFC John R., 90th Cong., H.R. 13301, Priv. L. No. 299, 82 Stat. 1021 (1968)-NXPS

Apostolakis, Nicholas Demitrios, 92nd Cong., S. 672, Priv. L. No. 14, 85 Stat. 838 (1971)-QIRA

Aquarone, Mrs. Madeleine Alice, 83rd Cong., H.R. 7559, Priv. L. No. 369, 68 Stat. A53 (1954)-NRTN

Araujo, Marie C., also known as Marie Conceipaco de Brito, 81st Cong., S. 2047, Priv. L. No. 947, 64 Stat. A220 (1950)-QIRA

Arinque, Lazaro Loyola Jr., 87th Cong., S. 3336, Priv. L. No. 608, 76 Stat. 1381 (1962)-QMGN

Arvidson, John Axel, 87th Cong., S. 2679, Priv. L. No. 460, 76 Stat. 1326 (1962)-NXDD

Asato, Mrs. Keum Ja (Mrs. Thomas R. Asato), 87th Cong., S. 400, Priv. L. No. 73, 75 Stat. 874 (1961)-QIRW

Avecilla, Dr. Marcelino J. and Dr. Teodora A. Fidelino-Avecilla, 83rd Cong., H.R. 1358, Priv. L. No. 296, 68 Stat. A26 (1954)-QMOC

Badalamenti, Maria, 92nd Cong., S. 513, Priv. L. No. 88, 86 Stat. 1537 (1972)-WHEL

Baden, Margarita Anne Marie (Nguyen Tan Nga), 91st Cong., S. 2976, Priv. L. No. 162, 84 Stat. 2132 (1970)-QIRA

Badua, Candido, 94th Cong., H.R. 2776, Priv. L. No. 44, 90 Stat. 2973 (1976)-NRES

Bae, Chang, 99th Cong., H.R. 737, Priv. L. No. 2, 100 Stat. 4313 (1986)-QMGN

Bahr, Peter Leo, 86th Cong., S. 2566, Priv. L. No. 394, 74 Stat. A64 (1960)-QPRF

Balint, Mrs. Julia, 81st Cong., H.R. 679, Priv. L. No. 63, 63 Stat. 1098 (1949)-QIRW

Bankevitz, Feofania, 85th Cong., S. 2936, Priv. L. No. 674, 72 Stat. A146 (1958)-WHEL

Barker, Margaret, 88th Cong., H.R. 1398, Priv. L. No. 50, 77 Stat. 890 (1963)-QMGN

Barnett, Edward, 84th Cong., H.R. 6363, Priv. L. No. 570, 70 A29 (1956)-WCRF

Barrios, George G., Doctor of Medicine, his wife Olga T. Cruz, and their children Kurt F. Barrios and Karl S. Barrios, Katrina Adelaida Theresa, 97th Cong., H.R. 828, Priv. L. No. 44, 96 Stat. 2631 (1982)-QMOC

Bartley, Anthony Charles, 81st Cong., H.R. 6006, Priv. L. No. 282, 63 Stat. 1183 (1949)-QMDE

Batelli, Alfio, 81st Cong., H.R. 5947, Priv. L. No. 779, 64 Stat. A158 (1950)-QMOC

Batrouny, Linda Azar Karam, 82nd Cong., H.R. 1477, Priv. L. No. 923, 66 Stat. A180 (1952)-QMOC

Beckles, Hubert O., 86th Cong., H.R. 7551, Priv. L. No. 442, 74 Stat. A82 (1960)-QMGN

Beech, Joseph, 64th Cong., S.J. Res. 208, Priv. L. No. 132, 39 Stat. 1495 (1917)-NCOD

Beecroft, Walter F., 86th Cong., S. 3016, Priv. L. No. 372, 74 Stat. A55 (1960)-NRES

Belenko, Viktor Ivanovich, 96th Cong., S. 2961, Priv. L. No. 62, 94 Stat. 3599 (1980)-NXCP

Bell, Genevieve M. Scott, 85th Cong., S. 2301, Priv. L. No. 439, 72 Stat. A47 (1958)-NCOD

Bellini, Eugenio, 82d Cong., H.R. 1100, Priv. L. No. 341, 65 Stat. A127 (1951)-QMOC

Bello, Sebastiano, Dino Bianchi, Pierino Ciccarese, Vincenzo Dall'alda, Vittorio de Gasperi, Salvatore Puggioni, Giovanni Battista Volpato, and Leone Montini, 82nd Cong., H.R. 3155, Priv. L. 747, 66 Stat. A112 (1952)-QMOC

Beltran, Rosina C., 94th Cong., H.R. 4583, Priv. L. No. 111, 90 Stat. 2999 (1976)-QMGN

Benavides, Antonio, 92nd Cong., H.R. 2394, Priv. L. No. 117, 86 Stat. 1549 (1972)-WCRF

Benedict, Adelina (nee Rosasco), 87th Cong., H.R. 2666, Priv. L. No. 243, 75 Stat. 939 (1961)-QPRP

Bentsen, Tina, 82nd Cong., S. 2231, Priv. L. N. 330, 65 Stat. A123 (1951)-QIRA

Bernstein, Joseph, 82d Cong., H.R. 1479, Priv. L. No. 14, 65 Stat. A7 (1951)-QMOC

Bertoni, Ezio, 83rd Cong., H.R. 8557, Priv. L. No. 848, 68 Stat. A221 (1954)-WHEL

Bertuccioli, Lee F., 81st Cong., H.R. 750, Priv. L.. No. 138, 63 Stat. 1128 (1949)-WHEL

Bettelheim, Julie and Evelyn Lang Hirsch, 82nd Cong., S. 1469, Priv. L. No. 550, 66 Stat. 47 (1952)-QMDP

Biancarosso, Giuseppe Pacino, 90th Cong., S. 866, Priv. L. No. 204, 81 Stat. 1050 (1968)-QIRA

Biason, Perfecto M. and Joan, 80th Cong., S. 1451, Priv. L. No. 317, 62 Stat. 1360 (1948)-QIRW

Biazzo, Lillian, 91st Cong., S. 1704, Priv. L. No. 146, 84 Stat. 2127 (1970)-QPRP

Biolzi, Giuseppe, 82nd Cong., H.R. 880, Priv. L. No. 996, 66 Stat. A202 (1952)-QIRA

Blanchette, Guy Andre, 91st Cong., S. 3136, Priv. L. No. 149, 84 Stat. 2128 (1970)-NXPS

Blank, Aenny, 82nd Cong., H.R. 715, Priv. L. No. 100, 65 Stat. A39 (1951)-QPRF

Blanquicett, Carmen Cecilia, 95th Cong., H.R. 2291, Priv. L. No. 162, 92 Stat. 3859 (1978)-QIRM

Boccia, Roland Roger Alfred, also known as Roland Barbera, 81st Cong., S. 2611, Priv. L. No. 502, 64 Stat. A61 (1950)-WHEL

Bodenstein, Pola, 89th Cong., S. 1111, Priv. L. No. 109, 79 Stat. 1374 (1965)-WHEL

Boehme, Lieselotte, 84th Cong., H.R. 1667, Priv. L. No. 597, 70 Stat. A41 (1956)-WHEL

Bogolepov, Igor Michael (alias Ivar Nyman) and Margaret Johanna Bogolepov (alias Margaret Johanna Nyman), 83rd Cong., S. 629, Priv. L. No. 456, 68 Stat. A91 (1954)-QMDE

Bohin, Leila Finlay, 86th Cong., S. 2554, Priv. L. No. 328, 74 Stat. A39 (1960)-NCOD

Bonnalie, Mrs. Margaret Graham, 85th Cong., S. 3219, Priv. L. No. 729, 72 Stat. A196 (1958)-NRTN

Bonner, Dr. Brant, 85th Cong., S. 2469, Priv. L. No. 771, 72 Stat. A214 (1958) NRTN

Boppel, Mrs. Maryanna, 82nd Cong., H.R. 2455, Priv. L. No. 183, 65 Stat. A70 (1951)-WCRF

Bouvier, Mrs. Joyce Mark, 88th Cong., S. 1014, Priv. L. No. 153, 77 Stat. 930 (1963)-NCOD

Boyle, John B., 81st Cong., H.R. 2602, Priv. L. No. 226, 63 Stat. 1162 (1949)-WCRF

Brady, John Patrick, 99th Cong., H.R. 3154, Priv. L. No. 9, 100 Stat. 4316 (1986)-QMGN

Branlund, Elina, 82nd Cong., S. 1724, Priv. L. 836, 66 Stat. A150 (1952)-QMOC

Braun, Jesajahu, 84th Cong., H.R. 5870, Priv. L. No. 528, 70 Stat. A15 (1956)-QMGN

Brezza, Umberto, 87th Cong., H.R. 9915, Priv. L. No. 528, 76 Stat. 1350 (1962)-WCRF

Broderick, Gordon, 85th Cong., H.R. 3184, Priv. L. No. 212, 71 Stat. A82 (1957)-NMSC

Brownrigg, Leonard Alfred, 94th Cong., H.R. 2399, Priv. L. No. 69, 90 Stat. 2983 (1976)-WCRF

Buchet, Jean Henri, 84th Cong., H.R. 2345, Priv. L. No. 558, 70 Stat. A25 (1956)-WCRF

Buckingham, Kwi Sok (nee Kim), 95th Cong., H.R. 4401, Priv. L. No. 35, 92 Stat. 3805 (1978)-WCRF

Buffoni, Maria and Emma Botta, 83rd Cong., H.R. 1103, Priv. L. No. 62, 67 Stat. A24 (1953)-QMOC

Bull, Gerald Vincent, 92nd Cong., S. 3583, Priv. L. No. 152, 86 Stat. 1564 (1972)-NRES

Buzas, Motiejus and Bernice, and his wife, 76th Cong., H.R. 6409, Veto Message October 10, 1940 (H.R. Doc. 968, 3d Sess.)-VETO

Cairo, Salvatore, 87th Cong., H.R. 3401,Priv. L. No. 279, 75 Stat. 952 (1961)-WCRF

Canciller, Honorio and Nancy Ting Evangelista, 81st Cong., H.R. 1866, Priv. L. No. 508, 64 Stat. A63 (1950)-NMSC

Cangialosi, Antonino (or Anthony Consola), 83rd Cong., H.R. 1148, Priv. L. No. 324, 68 Stat. A37 (1954)-WCRF

Capano, Vittorio, 84th Cong., H.R. 1160, Priv. L. No. 330, 69 Stat. A113 (1955)-QIRM

Caprara, Liliana, 86th Cong., H.R. 6886, Priv. L. No. 217,73 Stat. A94 (1959)-NRES

Carey, Claire Louise and Vincent F. Carey, 83rd Cong., H.R. 1768, Priv. L. No. 677, 68 Stat. A166 (1954)-QIRA

Carollo, Giuseppe, 84th Cong., H.R. 2261, Priv. L. No. 22, 69 Stat A9 (1955)-WCRF

Carrigan, Andrew, 84th Cong., H.R. 4544, Priv. L. No. 456, 69 Stat. A155 (1955)-QPRP

Casardi, Virginia Harris, 79th Cong., H.R. 5278, Priv. L. No. 845, 60 Stat. 1303 (1946)-NVOL

Castrillo, Dr. Guillermo (Fernandez), 89th Cong., S. 374, Priv. L. No. 169, 79 Stat. 1399 (1965)-NRES

Cermak, Helmut and Hana Cermak, 83rd Cong., H.R. 8334, Priv. L. No. 716,68 Stat. A179 (1954)-QMDE

Cerny, Joseph, 83rd Cong., H.R. 6650, Priv. L. No. 543, 68 Stat. A123 (1954)-QMDE

Certain aliens, 86th Cong., H.R. 4242, Priv. L. No. 122, 73 Stat. A55 (1959)-QMGN

Certain Aliens, 96th Cong., S. 707, Priv. L. No. 63, 94 Stat. 3599 (1980)-QMGN

Certain aliens possessing special skills, namely, Teodor Egle, Karlis Fogelis, Vasily Kils, and Aleksanders Zelmenis, 81st Cong., H.R. 4604, Priv. L. No. 821, 64 Stat. A173 (1950)-QMOC

Certain Basque Aliens, 79th Cong., H.R. 1402, Priv. L. No. 818, 60 Stat. 1292 (1946)-QMOC

[Certain] Basque Aliens, 80th Cong., H.R. 1572, Priv. L. No. 350, 62 Stat. 1373 (1948)-QMOC

Certain Basque Aliens, 81st Cong., S. 27, Priv. L. No. 13, 63 Stat. 1079 1949)-QMOC

Certain Basque Aliens, 81st Cong., S. 1192, Priv. L. No. 1031, 64 Stat. A251 (1950)-QMOC

Certain Displaced Persons, 82nd Cong., S. 2145, Priv. L. No. 655, 66 Stat. A80 (1952)-QMDP

Certain Italian Aliens, 81st Cong., H.R. 6804, Priv. L. No. 943, 64 Stat. A218 (1950)-QMOC

Certain Spanish Physicians Residing in Puerto Rico, 81st Cong., H.R. 3169, Priv. L. No. 767, 64 Stat. A153 (1950)-QMOC

Certain U.S. Army personnel-Yugoslav fliers, 80th Cong., H.R. 1652, Priv. L. No. 102, 61 Stat. 1004 (1947)-NMSC

Chamberlain, Earl C., S. 747, 90th Cong., Priv. L. No. 328, 82 Stat. 1425 (1968)-NRES

Chang, Kuay Ten (Kuay Hong Chang), 93rd Cong., S. 89, Priv. L. No. 7, 87 Stat. 1099 (1973)-QPRF

Chang, Kyong Hwan, 90th Cong., S. 1781, Priv. L. No. 160, 81 Stat. 1037 (1967)-NRES

Chang, Shu Hsien, 89th Cong., S. 1084, Priv. L. No. 82, 79 Stat. 1363 (1965)-NRES

Charalambou, Antonios, 82nd Cong., H.R. 970, Priv. L. No. 256, 65 Stat. A97 (1951)-NMSC

Chassin, Ben, 86th Cong., S. 46, Priv. L. No. 36, 73 Stat. A18 (1959)-NRTN

Charles, John Brima, 98th Cong., H.R. 2895, Pocket Veto, October 17, 1984, *Congressional Record* 130:31086-VETO

Chaves, Dr. Juan F., 90th Cong., H.R. 5862, Priv. L. No. 57, 81 Stat. 1004 (1967)-NRES

Cheasley, Gordon L., 75th Cong., H.R. 7297, Priv. L. No. 620, 52 Stat. 1355 (1938)-WCRF

Chen, Amos, 81st Cong., H.R. 6386, Priv. L. No. 898, 64 Stat. A204 (1950)-QIER

Chen, Liu Shui, 87th Cong., S. 899, Priv. L. No. 328, 76 Stat. 1279 (1962)-QMGN

Chen, Ronald Leroy, 77th Cong., H.R. 6677, Priv. L. No. 617, 56 Stat. 1252 (1942)-QIER

Chen, Tien Koo, 83rd Cong., H.R. 765, Priv. L. No. 110, 67 Stat. A40 (1953)-QMGN

Cheung, Kam Lin, 95th Cong., S. 1142, Priv. L. No. 19, 91 Stat. 1656, (1977)-WXIL

Chimani, Karl and Ada Chimani, 82nd Cong., H.R. 702, Priv. L. No. 164, 65 Stat. A63 (1951)-QMOC

Chin, Ah See Lee, 86th Cong., S. 2991, Priv. L. No. 371, 74 Stat. A55 (1960)-NXEN

Chin, Suk and Hae Suk Chin, 94th Cong., H.R. 1394, Priv. L. No. 60, 90 Stat. 2980 (1976)-QIRA

Chitato, Antonio Andrea, 84th Cong., H.R. 1022, Priv. L. No. 491, 70 Stat. A3 (1956)-QMOC

Cho, Mee Kyung and Hee Kyung Cho, 94th Cong., H.R. 1395, Priv. L. No. 61, 90 Stat. 2980 (1976)-QIRA

Chung, In Fil, In Ae Chung, In Sook Chung, and In Ja Chung, 87th Cong., S. 546, Priv. L. No. 35, 75 Stat. 862 (1961)-QIRA

Chung, Paul Myung Ha, 83rd Cong., H.R. 1886, Priv. L. No. 116, 67 Stat. A42 (1953)-QMGN

Chung, Sang Kook and Hwa Soon Chung, 94th Cong., H.R. 1396, Priv. L. No. 62, 90 Stat. 2980 (1976)-QIRA

Cibilic or Zibilich, Mato, Miljenko, Bozzo, and Augustin, 76th Cong., S. 796, Priv. L. No. 251, 53 Stat. 1540 (1939)-WCRF

Cloonan, Edward Patrick, 84th Cong., H.R. 2059, Priv. L. No. 303, 69 Stat. A104 (1955)-WHEL

Coen, Carleen, 89th Cong., S. 442, Priv. L. No. 40, 79 Stat. 1347 (1965)-NCOD

Collopy, PFC John Patrick, 90th Cong., H.R. 15591, Priv. L. No. 263, 82 Stat. 1393 (1968)-NXPS

Colthurst, Barbara D., Dagamac, Pedro P. and Kahler, Edith, 84th Cong., S. 97, Priv. L. No. 534, 70 Stat. A17 (1956)-NRES

Cometti, Sisters Antoinette, Mary Gibin, Angela Pelosin, Emma Ghisleni, Elisabetta De Caterin, and Onorina Franzina, 81st Cong., S. 753, Priv. L. No. 363, 64 Stat. A7 (1950)-QMOC

Connelly, Claudio Pier, 82nd Cong., S. 291, Priv. L. No. 81, 65 Stat. A32 1951)-QMGN

Cooke, Jack Kent, 86th Cong., H.R. 8156, Priv. L. No. 486, 74 Stat. A100 (1960)-NRES

Cordova-Campos, Juan Marcos, 93rd Cong., H.R. 1366, Priv. L. No. 12, 87 Stat. 1101 (1973)-QIRA

Cox, Penelope Carolyn, 81st Cong., S. 2100, Priv. L. No. 366, 64 Stat. A8, (1950)-NMSC

Coyne, James J., 75th Cong., H.R. 9731, Priv. L. No. 803, 52 Stat. 1432 (1938)-QMGN

Crespo, Mary Elizabeth Tighe, 86th Cong., H.R. 6804, Priv. L. No. 438, 74 Stat. A80 (1960)-WHEL

Cross, Dr. Alexander D., 90th Cong., H.R. 3221, Priv. L. No. 64, 81 Stat. 1005 (1967)-WCRF

Crowley, Daniel, 95th Cong., H.R. 2940, Priv. L. No. 67, 92 Stat. 3820 (1978)-WHEL

Cruz, Dalisay Lourdes, 84th Cong., H.R. 1552, Priv. L. No. 418, 69 Stat. A143 (1955)-QIRM

Cruz-Figueroa, Jesus, 86th Cong., H.R. 2645, Priv. L. No. 349, 74 Stat. A48 (1960)-WXDD

Cseplo, Jeno, 83rd Cong., S. 233, Priv. L. No. 608, 68 Stat. A144 (1954)-QMGN

D'Angri, Marcantonio Doria and his wife, Sonia Stampa Doria D'Angri, 81st Cong., S. 1869, Priv. L. No. 650, 64 Stat. A112 (1950)-QMDE

D'Arpino, Maria, 94th Cong., H.R. 6093, Priv. L. No. 81, 90 Stat. 2988 (1976)-WHEL

D'Erlanger, Marguerite Mathilde Slidell, 64th Cong., S. 8075, Priv. L. No. 196, 39 Stat. 1588 (1917)-NVOL

D'Osten-Sacken, Baron Fred Alexander, 82nd Cong., H.R. 4709, Priv. L. No. 955, 66 Stat. A189 (1952)-QMOC

David, Constantin, Paula Marie David, Claire Edmonde David, and Ariane Constance David, 84th Cong., H.R. 3857, Priv. L. No. 583, 70 Stat. A34 (1956)-QMGN

de Bruyn, Marie Henriette, 81st Cong., S. 1637, Priv. L. No. 619, 64 Stat. A102 (1950)-QMGN

de Carvalho, Manuel Alves, 86th Cong., S. 762, Priv. L. No. 358, 74 Stat. A51 (1960)-NRES

de Carvalho, Sisters Rita Pinto de, Maria Leite Da Silva, Carmelinda Lopes de Aguiar, Maria Adozinda da Fonseca Melo, Joaquine de Jesus, and Maria

Luisa Pinto Carvalho, 81st Cong., H.R. 7733, Priv. L. No. 981, 64 Stat. A233 (1950)-QMOC

de Chellis, Italo Vespa, 81st Cong., S. 2108, Priv. L. No. 490, 64 Stat. A57 (1950)-QPRF

de Corpus, Consuelo Alvarado, 89th Cong., H.R. 3292, Priv. L. No. 70, 79 Stat. 1359 (1965)-WCRF

de Ernest, Mrs. Caridad Rosa Avila Leyva, 83rd Cong., H.R. 5816, Priv. L. No. 761, 68 Stat. A193 (1954)-WCRF

De Haven-Alten, Augusta Louise, 66th Cong., S.J. Res. 134, Priv. L. No. 2, 41 Stat. 1463 (1920)-NVOL

de La Cruz Hernandez, Alejandro, 83rd Cong., S. 196, Priv. L. No. 125, 67 Stat. A45 (1953)-QMGN

de la Fregonniere, Priscilla Ogden Dickerson Gillson, 82nd Cong., H.R. 2920, Priv. L. No. 713, 66 Stat. A100 (1952)-NVOL

De Maio, Nery, 98th Cong., H.R. 1865, Priv. L. No. 41, 98 Stat. 3432 (1984)-NXEN

de Saint Andre, Lucille, 93rd Cong., H.R. 6477, Priv. L. No. 97, 88 Stat. 2382 (1974)-WCRF

de Seversky, George Prokofieff and Isabelle Prokofieff de Seversky, 83rd Cong., H.R. 3678, Priv. L. No. 70, 67 Stat. A26 (1953)-QMOC

De Silva, Mrs. Hilda, 81st Cong., H.R. 5375, Priv. L. No. 329, 63 Stat. 1202 (1949)-WXIL

de Thassy, Eugene, 83rd Cong., H.R. 1756, Priv. L. No. 185, 67 Stat. A65 (1953)-QMDE

De Vito, Angelo, 84th Cong., H.R. 4147, Priv. L. No. 348, 69 Stat. A119 (1955)-WCRF

Del Campo, Roberto Martin, 90th Cong., H.R. 5216, Priv. L. No. 138, 81 Stat. 1030 (1967)-WCRF

Denaro, John (Giovanni), 91st Cong., S. 265, Priv. L. No. 53, 83 Stat. 885 (1969)-NRES

DeWinter, Louis J. and Simone H., 86th Cong., H.R. 1705, Priv. L. No. 125, 73 Stat. A56 (1959)-NRTN

Di Franco, Luciano, 86th Cong., H.R. 2944, Priv. L. No. 432, 74 Stat. A78 (1960)-WCRF

Di Palma, Dr. Nicola, 81st Cong., H.R. 7563, Priv. L. No. 1018, 64 Stat. A246 (1950)-NVOL

Dilboy, John A., 80th Cong., H.R. 1912, Priv. L. No. 241, 62 Stat. 1334 (1948)-QMGN

Dilnot, Mrs. Margaret Gregg, 81st Cong., H.R. 711, Priv. L. No. 43, 63 Stat. 1091 (1949)-NVOL

Dittmar, Horst F. W. and Heinz-Erik, S. 506, 83rd Cong., Priv. L. 257, 68 Stat. A12 (1954)-QMGN

Doder, Dusko, 89th Cong., S. 3222, Priv. L. No. 465, 80 Stat. 1711, (1966)-NRES

Doi, Yuji and Mrs. Matsuyo Yamaoka Doi, 84th Cong., H.R. 6613, Priv. L. No. 360, 69 Stat. A122 (1955)-QPRP

Domanski, Mrs. Jozefa Sokolowska, 93rd Cong., S. 816, Priv. L. No. 63, 88 Stat. 2369 (1974)-QPRF

Donnelly, Christine, 94th Cong., H.R. 7404, Priv. L. No. 4, 90 Stat. 2989 (1976)-NRES

Dopico, Clemente Sabin, 81st Cong., S. 118, Priv. L. No. 630, 64 Stat. A105 (1950)-WCRF

Dorn, Edith, 85th Cong., H.R. 8014, Priv. L. No. 740, 72 Stat. A200 (1958)-WCRF

Dowds, Mrs. Elizabeth, 84th Cong., H.R. 973, Priv. L. No. 150, 69 Stat. A52 (1955)-WCRF

Droesse, Mrs. Clara Raffloer, 82nd Cong., H.R. 896, Priv. L. No. 144 (65 Stat. A55-NVLOS

du Planty, Regine, 83rd Cong., H.R. 2061, Priv. L. No. 889, 68 Stat. A239 (1954)-WCRF

Dubonnet, Ruth Obre, 82nd Cong., S. 46, Veto Message March 16, 1951 (S. Doc. 15, 1st Sess.)-VETO

Duke, Noriko Susan (Nakano), 91st Cong., S. 537, Priv. L. No. 11, 84 Stat. 870 (1969)-NMSC

Dumaguing, Fe'R., 81st Cong., H.R. 4365, Priv. L. No. 976, 64 Stat. A231 (1950)-QMOC

Dumas, Evangelos and Michael, 82nd Cong., S. 440, Priv. L. No. 457, 66 Stat A17 (1952)-QIRA

Dunikowski, Zbigniew Jan, Karolina Dunikowski, Wanda Octavia Dunikowski, and Janina Grospera Dunikowski, 82nd Cong., H.R. 961, Priv. L. No. 420, 66 Stat. A6 (1952)-QMDP

Earle, Mishleen, 99th Cong., S. 381, Priv. L. No. 1, 100 Stat. 4313, (1986)-QIRW

Edgar, Samuel Joseph, 98th Cong., S. 1060, Priv. L. No. 25, 98 Stat. 3425 (1984)-QMGN

Ekholm, Mrs. Ruth R., 83rd Cong., H.R. 711, Priv. L. No. 272, 68 Stat. A17 (1954)-QIRW

Elliopoulos, Teresa and Anastasia Elliopoulos, 88th Cong., H.R. 7347, Priv. L. No. 195, 78 Stat. 1132 (1964)-QIRA

Endestad, Audun, 98th Cong., S. 1863, Priv. L. No. 7, 98 Stat. 3417 (1984)-NRES

Enepekides, John, his wife, Anna, and his son, George, 83rd Cong., S. 2156, Priv. L. No. 967, 68 Stat. A278 (1954)-NRES

Engelbert, Wilhelm, 83rd Cong., S. 153,Veto Message March 17, 1954 (S. Doc. 106, 2nd Sess.)-VETO

English, Arlin David, 87th Cong., H.R. 6226, Priv. L. No. 299, 76 Stat. 1268 (1962)-NVOL

Espinueva, Edmundo Alfredo Oreiro, 95th Cong., H.R. 2256, Priv. L. No. 131, 92 Stat. 3846 (1978)-QMGN

Eubanks, Andre Bartholo, 97th Cong., H.R. 1681, Priv. L. No. 17, 96 Stat. 2619 (1982)-QIRA

Evaristo, Maria da Conceicao, 91st Cong., H.R. 3376, Priv. L. No. 30, 83 Stat. 876 (1969)-WHEL

Fabris, Camilla, 81st Cong., H.R. 3018, Priv. L. No. 577, 64 Stat. A87 (1950)-QMGN

Falby, William, 87th Cong., H.R. 1653, Priv. L. No. 420, 76 Stat. 1312 (1962)-NVOL

Falco, Lt. (SG) Giacomo, 81st Cong., H.R. 1487, Priv. L. No. 439, 64 Stat. A37 (1950)-QMDE

Ferapontow, Michel, 80th Cong., H.R. 892, Priv. L. No. 330, 62 Stat. 1365 (1948)-QMGN

Ferrando, Maria Jordan, 90th Cong., S. 168, Priv. L. No. 42, 81 Stat. 999, (1967)-QIRM

Ferrier, Isabel Eugenia Serrane Macias, 93rd Cong., H. R. 3758, Priv. L. 49, 87 Stat. 1114 (1973)-PRF

Finley, Cecil E., 86th Cong., H.R. 2946, Priv. L. No. 200, 73 Stat. A88 (1959)-WCRF

Five Sisters of the Franciscan Missionaries of Mary, 82nd Cong., H.R. 3965, Priv. L. No. 296, 65 Stat. A111 (1951)-QMOC

Florin, Meda Abilay, 95th Cong., H.R. 1939, Priv. L. No. 32, 92 Stat. 3804 (1978)-QIRA

Fong, Kock Kong, 89th Cong., H.R. 2752, Priv. L. No. 234, 80 Stat. 1623 (1966)-WCRF

Fordham, Richard, 87th Cong., H.R. 4384, Priv. L. No. 253, 75 Stat. 942 (1961)-NRTN

Forgnone, Giuseppe Merlinet, 81st Cong., S. 2981, Priv. L. No. 1097, 64 Stat. A277 (1951)-QMOC

Forrester, Magnus David, 92nd Cong., S. 2270, Priv. L. No. 154, 86 Stat. 1565 (1972)-WCRF

Forsyth, Mrs. Clayre Louise, 81st Cong., S. 1866, Priv. L. No. 864, 64 Stat. A191 (1950)-NVOL

Frantz, Hanife, 97th Cong., H.R. 2185, Priv. L. No. 9, 95 Stat. 1736 (1981)-QIRW

Friedman, Louis D., 76th Cong., H.R. 7179, Veto Message October 10, 1940 (H.R. Doc. 975, 3rd Sess.)-VETO

Friedmann, Zoltan, 88th Cong., H.R. 2305, Priv. L. No. 134, 77 Stat. 921 (1963)-WCRF

Frings, Kurt, 76th Cong., S. 3673, Veto Message June 19, 1940 (S. Doc. 248, 3rd Sess.)-VETO

Fuchino, Hego, 82nd Cong., H.R. 1818, Priv. L. No. 307, 65 Stat. A114 (1951)-QIER

Fugh, Philip, Sarah Liu Fugh, and John Fugh, 82nd Cong., H.R. 2719, Priv. L. No. 745, 66 Stat. A112 (1952)-QMDE

Furtner, Franz, Valentina Furtner, Nina Tuerck, and Victoria Tuerck, 82nd Cong., H.R. 617, Priv. L. No. 215, 65 Stat. A82 (1951)-QMOC

Gahl, Mrs. Selma Cecelia, 82nd Cong., H.R. 1234, Priv. L. No. 522, 66 Stat. A38 (1952)-NRTN

Galea, Victoria, 85th Cong., H.R. 4854, Priv. L. No. 169, 71 Stat. A105 (1957)-QPRF

Gallego, Sor Eufrasia Gomez, Sor Francisca Gil Martinez, and Sor Rasalia de La Maza, 82nd Cong., H.R. 5208, Priv. L. No. 752, 66 Stat. A114 (1952)-QMOC

Gattegno, Sylvio Isaac, Isaac Lidji, Henry Isaac Lidji, 85th Cong., S. 1519, Priv. L. No. 378, 72 Stat. A20 (1958)-QMGN

Gayle, Florette Ivoree and Keisha Dajaran Karr, 96th Cong., H.R. 2145, Priv. L. No. 103, 94 Stat. 3629 (1980)-QIRA

Gaza, Rolando R., Teresita C., and Rolynne Therese Gaza, 96th Cong., H.R. 1619, Priv. L. No. 42, 93 Stat. 1406 (1979)-QMDE

Geiger, Hugo, 81st Cong., S. 356, Priv. L. No. 494, 64 Stat. A59 (1950)-WCRF

Gellhorn, Alessandro, 87th Cong., S. 217, Priv. L. No. 7, 75 Stat. 853 (1961)-NMSC

Gerling, Robert Wilhelm, 80th Cong., H.R. 3742, Priv. L. No. 216, 62 Stat. 1325 (1948)-NRES

Gherwal, Rakha Singh, 74th Cong., S. 447, Priv. L. No. 227, 49 Stat. 2145 (1935)-NMSC

Gibson, Victor Henrique Carlos, 94th Cong., H.R. 1553, Priv. L. No. 17, 89 Stat. 1179 (1975)-WXDD

Glaser, Kurt, 84th Cong., S. 143, Veto Message June 3, 1955 (S. Doc. 557, 1st Sess.)-VETO

Glick, Zelda, 86th Cong., H.R. 5910, Priv. L. No. 210, 73 Stat. A91 (1959)-NCOD

Glusic, Andreja, 83rd Cong., S. 3433, Priv. L. No. 659, 68 Stat. A161 (1954)-QPRF

Goditiabois-Deacon, Laura MacArthur, 89th Cong., S. 1919, Priv. L. No. 93, 79 Stat. 1366 (1965)-NCOD

Goleniewski, Michal, 88th Cong. H.R. 5507, Priv. L. No. 59, 77 Stat. 893 (1963)-NXCP

Gomes, Carolina M., 85th Cong., S. 1782, Priv. L. No. 594, 72 Stat. A116 (1958)-NCOD

Grade, Inna Hekker, 84th Cong., H.R. 6955, Priv. L. No. 712, 70 Stat. A95 (1956)-NXCP

Grant, Eupert Anthony, 94th Cong., H.R. 9543, Priv. L. No. 128, 90 Stat. 3007 (1976)-QPRF

Grantz, Monika, 95th Cong., H.R. 8927, Priv. L. No. 74, 92 Stat. 3822 (1978)-WCRF

Grigoras, Constantinos A. (Gregoras), 88th Cong., H.R. 1560, Priv. L. No. 158, 77 Stat. 932 (1963)-QPRF

Gross, Jacob, 81st Cong., H.R. 3127, Priv. L. No. 175, 63 Stat. 1143 (1949)-QIRA

Grun, Mrs. Susanna (Susanne Roth), 88th Cong., S. 1096, Priv. L. No. 154, 77 Stat. 930 (1963)-QPRP

Gruson, Sydney, 87th Cong., H.R. 1395, Priv. L. No. 408, 76 Stat. 1309 (1962)-NRES

Guerrero-Monje, Refugio, 84th Cong., S. 1456, Priv. L. No. 321, 71 Stat. A126 (1957)-WCRF

Guillen, Claudio, 85th Cong., S. 803, Priv. L. No. 464, 72 Stat. A56 (1958)-NXDD

Gulbenkian, Mrs. Marie, 81st Cong., H.R. 3771, Priv. L. No. 442, 64 Stat. A38 (1950)-QMGN

Gulezian, Anna Tokatlian, 84th Cong., H.R. 1081, Priv. L. No. 107, 69 Stat. A37 (1955)-QIRW

Ha, Mrs. Chow Chui, 87th Cong., S. 1934, Veto Message April 16, 1962 (S. Doc. 87, 2nd Sess.)-VETO

Hadjipateras, Nicholas C., Pipitsa N. Hadjipateras, and Costas N. Hadjipateras, 81st Cong., H.R. 3921, Priv. L. No. 894, 64 Stat. A203 (1950)-QMGN

Haidostian, Hovhannes H., 85th Cong., S. 1578, Priv. L. No. 394, 72 Stat. A27 (1958)-QMDE

Hakim, Elie Joseph and Family, 83rd Cong., S. 1382, Priv. L. No. 509, 68 Stat. A112 (1954)-QMOC

Haleck, Max, 87th Cong., S. 1234, Priv. L. No. 268, 75 Stat. 948 (1961)-NRES

Hall, Helene Cordery, 85th Cong., S. 1175, Priv. L. No. 317, 71 Stat. A125 (1957)-QIRW

Hamori, Laszlo, 87th Cong., H.R. 1394, Priv. L. 221, 75 Stat. 932 (1961)-NRES

Haniotis, George, 80th Cong., H.R. 4199, Pocket veto June 21, 1948, 94 *Congressional Record*, 94:9371-VETO

Hansen, Karl Eigil Engedal and his wife, Else Viola Agnethe Hansen, and their minor child, Jessie Engedal Hansen, 85th Cong., S. 701, Priv. L. No. 133, 71 Stat. A52 (1957)-WCRF

Harder, John L., and children, Paul William Harder, Irvin W. Harder, Edna Justina Harder, Elsie Anna Harder and Elizabeth Harder, 76th Cong., H.R. 5827, Priv. L. No. 366, 54 Stat. 1282 (1940)-WHEL

Harris, Georgina Henrietta, 93rd Cong., S. 1852, Priv. L. No. 54, 88 Stat. 2366 (1974)-NMSC

Hee, Lee Duk, 90th Cong., S. 1458, Priv. L. No. 121, 81 Stat. 1026 (1967)-QIRA

Heffernan, Mrs. Maria Eduvigis Aran, 89th Cong., H.R. 1393, Priv. L. No. 178, 79 Stat. 1403 (1965)-QIRW

Heintz, Ernest E., 81st Cong., S. 1552, Priv. L. No. 398, 64 Stat. A21 (1950)-WCRF

Helman, Anna, 81st Cong., H.R. 1275, Priv. L. No. 526, 64 Stat. A70 (1950)-WHEL

Helms, Adolph Ernest, 76th Cong., H.R. 5156, Veto Message July 3, 1940 (H.R. Doc. 868, 3rd Sess.)-VETO

Henn, Wong You, 83rd Cong., S. 579, Priv. L. No. 529, 68 Stat. A118 (1954)-QMGN

Herka, Tadeusz, 81st Cong., H.R. 8219, Priv. L. No. 944, 64 Stat. A219 (1950)-NMSC

Hermens, Ferdinand A., 87th Cong., S. 2865, Priv. L. No. 430, 76 Stat. 1316 (1962)-NRTN

Herrera, Mrs. Gloria Vazquez, 92nd Cong., H.R. 1974, Priv. L. No. 90,86 Stat. 1538 (1972)-QIRW

Herzog, Godofredo M., 87th Cong., S. 333, Priv. L. No. 158, 75 Stat. 903 (1961)-NRES

Higa, Saeko and Masako Higa, 86th Cong., S. 855, Priv. L. No. 57, 73 Stat. A25 (1959)-QPRF

Hillebrand, Gunter Heinz, 87th Cong., S. 3267, Priv. L. No. 641, 76 Stat. 1393 (1962)-NRES

Hin, Fong Yee, 87th Cong., S. 2555, Priv. L. No. 670, 76 Stat. 1406 (1962)-NRES

Hinkel, Frederick, 44th Cong., S. 32, Priv. L. No. 9, 19 Stat. 411 (1877)-NVOL

Hirschmann, Paul, 75th Cong., H.R. 7039, Priv. L. No. 810, 52 Stat. 1434 (1938)-WCRF

Hlavaty, Jana, 94th Cong., H.R. 10792, Priv. L. No. 27, 89 Stat. 1189 (1975)-NRES

Hohman, Therese, 81st Cong., H.R. 3330, Priv. L. No. 776, 64 Stat. A157 (1950)-QMGN

Holder, Marlene, 95th Cong., H.R. 2756, Priv. L. No. 94, 92 Stat. 3832 (1978)-QIRA

Holecek, Ruth Ann, 82nd Cong., H.R. 7095, Priv. L. No. 986, 66 Stat. A198 (1952)-QIER

Holland, Albert O. and Bergtor Haaland, 82nd Cong., H.R. 5238, Priv. L. No. 867, 66 Stat. A162 (1952)-NRTN

Holleb, Helga, 81st Cong., H.R. 6747, Priv. L. No. 585, 64 Stat. A90 (1950)-QIRA

Homann, Mrs. Florence E. and John A. Villas, 82nd Cong., H.R. 2180, Priv. L. No. 181, 65 Stat. A69 (1951)-WHEL

Homann-Herimberg, Claude (nee Wagner), 87th Cong., H.R. 9588, Priv. L. No. 471, 76 Stat. 1329 (1962)-NRTN

Homolka, Frank (Franz), Olga Homolka (nee Mandel), Adolf Homolka, Helga Maria Homolka, and Frieda Homolka, 83rd Cong., S. 2210, Priv. L. No. 640, 68 Stat. A155 (1954)-WCRF

Hopkins, Mrs. Maria Giovanna, 87th Cong., S. 438, Priv. L. No. 126, 75 Stat. 892 (1961)-NRES

Hoppenheim, Morris, Lena Hoppenheim, Doris Hoppenheim, and Ruth Hoppenheim, 76th Cong., H.R. 2948, Priv. L. No. 329, 54 Stat. 1267 (1940)-QMGN

Horikawa, Teiko and Yoshiko Horikawa, 81st Cong., H.R. 2084, Priv. L. No. 194, 63 Stat. 1150 (1949)-QIER

Horn, John Yee, 81st Cong., H.R. 7815, Priv. L. No. 708, 64 Stat. A133 (1950)-QIRM

Hottenroth, Mrs. Marjorie J., 91st Cong., H.R. 1939, Priv. L. No. 17, 83 Stat. 872 (1969)-QIRW

Hovnanian, Heripsime, 87th Cong., S. 1786, Priv. L. No. 271, 75 Stat. 949 (1961)-WXIL

Hoy, Fun Wat, 89th Cong., S. 2010, Priv. L. No. 451, 80 Stat. 1706 (1966)-QMGN

Hoyer Lina Anna Adelheid (Adam) Hoyer, 83rd Cong., S. 569, Priv. L. No. 258, 68 Stat. A13 (1954)-QMGN

Hsia, Pinfang, 82nd Cong., S. 1420, Priv. L. No. 647, 66 Stat. A77 (1952)-QMGN

Hueneberg, Johann Rudolf, 76th Cong., H.R. 5641, Veto Message August 26, 1940 (H.R. Doc. 936, 3rd Sess.)-VETO

Hughes, Luisa Marillac, Marco Antonio Hughes, Maria del Cisne Hughes, Maria Augusta Hughes, Miguel Vicente Hughes, Vernoica del Rocio Hughes, and Ivan Hughes, 94th Cong., H.R. 2565, Priv. L. No. 73, 90 Stat. 2984 (1976)-QIRA

Hughes, Sidney Young, 82nd Cong., H.R. 1103, Priv. L. No. 238, 65 Stat. A91 (1951)-WCRF

Hui, Mark Yen, 82nd Cong., H.R. 4588, Priv. L. No. 953, 66 Stat. A189 (1952)-NRTN

Hunyadi, Matyas, 92nd Cong., H.R. 6907, Priv. L. No. 99, 86 Stat. 1541 (1972)-WCRF

Huppler, Edmund, 80th Cong., H.R. 4047, Priv. L. No. 393, 62 Stat. 1392 (1948)-QMDE

Inouye, Yaeko, 86th Cong., S. 110, Priv. L. No. 37, 73 Stat. A18 (1959)-QPRP

Ionescu, Naum and his wife, 81st Cong., S. 2682, Priv. L. No. 653, 64 Stat. A113 (1950)-QMGN

Ishimoto, Isao, 82nd Cong., H.R. 1158, Priv. L. No. 563, 66 Stat. A52 (1952)-QIER

Iwamatsu, Markoto, Atsushi Jun Iwamatsu, and Tomoe Iwamatsu, 80th Cong., S. 1409, Priv. L. No. 400, 62 Stat. 1395 (1948)-QIER

Iyoki, Mrs. Masa, 81st Cong., H.R. 7071, Priv. L. No. 790, 64 Stat. A161 (1950)-QPRP

Jacobs, Esther, 76th Cong., H.R. 6888, Priv. L. No. 601, 54 Stat. 1378 (1940)-WHEL

Jang, Sueng Ho and Sueng Il Jang, 99th Cong., H.R. 5016, Priv. L. No. 19, 100 Stat. 4321 (1986)-QMGN

Jansson-Viik, Armas Edvin, 85th Cong., S. 2168, Priv. L. No. 465, 72 Stat. A56 (1958)-WXDD

Jarecki, Franciszek, 83rd Cong., H.R. 5238, Priv. L. No. 109, 67 Stat. A40 (1953)-WXCP

Jaynes, Eddie Troy, Jr. and Rosa Elena Jaynes, 92nd Cong., S. 306, Priv. L. No. 36, 85 Stat. 849 (1971)-NRES

Johnson, Roberto, 83rd Cong., H.R. 3874, Priv. L. No. 810, 68 Stat. A209 (1954)-QMGN

Jucu, Gheorghe and Aurelia Jucu, 92nd Cong., H.R. 3929, Priv. L. No. 9, 85 Stat. 836 (1971)-NXCP

Kalb, Adolfo L. and Mrs. Eugenia G. Kalb, 83rd Cong., H.R. 2499, Priv. L. No. 693, 68 Stat. A171 (1954)-QPRP

Kalcoutsakis, Nicholas C., 81st Cong., H.R. 2921, Priv. L. No. 305, 63 Stat. 1193 (1949)-QMOC

Kalker, Jeannette and Abraham Benjamin Kalker, 83rd Cong., S. 2512, Priv. L. No. 651, 68 Stat. A158 (1954)-QPRF

Kaminski, Victor C., 80th Cong., H.R. 3061, Veto Message April 12, 1948 (H.R. Doc. 607, 2nd Sess.)-VETO

Kang, Ok-Boon, 97th Cong., H.R. 684, Priv. L. No. 34, 96 Stat. 2627 (1982)-QIRA

Kang, Mrs. Young Hee Kim, Hee Jae Kang, Hee Jin Kang and Hee Soo Kang, 95th Cong., H.R. 3996, Priv. L. No. 40, 92 Stat. 3807 (1978)-QPRF

Kao, Dr. Peter C. T., 83rd Cong., S. 69, Priv. L. No. 121, 67 Stat. A44 (1953)-QMOC

Karmowiredjo, Surip, 96th Cong., H.R. 3138, Priv. L. No. 95, 94 Stat. 3626 (1980)-QIRA

Karras, Panagiotes G., 83rd Cong., H.R. 3831, Priv. L. No. 169, 67 Stat. A60 (1953)-QPRF

Kasenkina, Mrs. Oksana Stepanovna, 82nd Cong., H.R. 622, Priv. L. No. 30, 65 Stat. A14 (1951)-QMDE

Kaudy, Mrs. John (formerly Stella Cappler), 81st Cong., Priv. L. No. 535, H.R. 1170, 64 Stat. A70 (1950)-WCRF

Kaufman, Salomon Georg, Doris Kaufmann, and John Michael Peter Kaufmann, 76th Cong., H.R. 7563, Veto Message July 3, 1940 (H.R. Doc. 865, 3rd Sess.)-VETO

Kay, Hyong Cha Kim, 100th Cong., S. 391, Priv. L. No. 23, 102 Stat. 4851 (1988)-WCRF

Kaznacheev, Aleksandr, 89th Cong., S. 582, Priv. L. No. 42, 79 Stat. 1347 (1965)-NXCP

Kennedy, Mrs. Mabel Constance, 88th Cong., H.R. 2444, Priv. L. No. 57, 77 Stat. 892 (1963)-QMGN

Kenny, Sister Elizabeth, 81st Cong., S.J. Res. 105, Priv. L. No. 357, 64 Stat. A4 (1950)-QMGN

Khokhlov, Nikolai E., 84th Cong., H.R. 10984, Priv. L. No. 851, 70 Stat. A174 (1956)-WXCP

Khorana, Har Gobind, 89th Cong., S. 826, Priv. L. No. 44, 79 Stat. 1348 (1965)-NRES

Khoury, Nouhad Ann, 82nd Cong., S. 118, Priv. L. No. 376, 65 Stat. A139 (1951)-QIRA

Kilpatrick, Shirley Leeke, 85th Cong., S. 2110, Veto Message March 31, 1958 (S. Doc. 84, 2nd Sess.)-VETO

Kim, Mrs. Chang-Sei, David Kim, and Arthur Kim, 81st Cong., H.R. 9082, Priv. L. No. 1028, 64 Stat. A251 (1950)-QIER

Kim, Chun Soo, 89th Cong., H.R. 6235, Priv. L. No. 144, 79 Stat. 1389 (1965)-QIRA

Kim, Yung Ran, 90th Cong., S. 2706, Priv. L. No. 339, 82 Stat. 1428 (1968)-QIRA

Kimm, Lloyd C., 86th Cong., S. 2646, Priv. L. No. 363, 74 Stat. A53 (1960)-NRES

King, S. Sgt. Ivan Claus, 90th Cong., S. 2759, Priv. L. No. 343, 82 Stat. 1429 (1968)-NXPS

Kitsos, Evdoxia J., 83rd, S. 205, Priv. L. No. 250, 68 Stat. A10 (1954)-QIRW

Knight, Mrs. Billy J. Knight and Dorothea Knight, 81st Cong., S. 2556, Priv. L. No. 635, 64 Stat. A107 (1950)-QIRW

Kobler, Aideh, 87th Cong., S. 722, Priv. L. No. 180, 75 Stat. 910 (1961)-QPRF

Koehler, Helga G. F., 87th Cong., S. 231, Priv. L. No. 155, 75 Stat. 901 (1961)-WXCP

Koenig, Walter Eduard, 92nd Cong., H.R. 14173, Priv. L. No. 132, 86 Stat. 1555 (1972)-NRES

Koestler, Arthur, 82nd Cong., S. 674, Priv. L. No. 221, 65 Stat. A84 (1951)-WXCP

Koh, Chao Yao, 87th Cong., S. 1074, Priv. L. No. 481, 76 Stat. 1333 (1962)-NRES

Kokal, Daniel, 81st Cong., H.R. 6106, Priv. L. No. 977, 64 Stat. 232 (1950)-QMGN

Kolman, Mazal, 83rd Cong., H.R. 7151, Priv. L. No. 835, 68 Stat. A217 (1954)-QMGN

Kostiuk, Johannes or John, Julia, Michael, William, and Anna, 80th Cong., H.R. 1749, Priv. L. No. 305, 62 Stat. 1357 (1948)-NMSC

Kowalik, Mrs. Olga, and Czeslawa Kowalik, 81st Cong., H.R. 9144, Priv. L. No. 1042, 64 Stat. A256 (1950)-QMDP

Kowerda, Boris, 84th Cong., H.R. 6617, Priv. L. No. 572, 70 Stat. A29 (1956)-WCRF

Kozlowski, Max, 84th Cong., H.R. 968, Priv. L. No. 149, 69 Stat. A52 (1955)-WXCP

Kraus, Elizabeth D. Yee, 95th Cong., H.R. 4875, Priv. L. No. 103, 92 Stat. 3835 (1978)-QPRF

Kravchenko, Viktor A., 81st Cong., S. 1915, Priv. L. No. 365, 64 Stat. A8 (1950)-NXCP

Kudrat, Mr. and Mrs. Miroslav, 82nd Cong., H.R. 1252, Priv. L. No. 342, 65 Stat. A127 (1951)-QMDP

Kunyavsky, Marina, 98th Cong., H.R. 3131, Priv. L. No. 13, 98 Stat. 3420 (1984)-NRES

Kusumoto, Kenji, 82nd Cong., H.R. 2906, Priv. L. No. 934, 66 Stat. A183 (1952)-QIER

Kwaan, Dr. Hau Cheong, his wife, Tech Phaik Loui Kwaan, and their daughter, Laura Wai Man Kwaan, 87th Cong., S. 2385, Priv. L. No. 323, 76 Stat. 1277 (1962)-QPRF

Kwauk, Molly, 87th Cong., H.R. 9669, Priv. L. No. 676, 76 Stat. 1408 (1962)-WHEL

Kwok, Dr. Francis S.N., 82nd Cong., S. 1541, Priv. L. No. 500, 66 Stat. A31 (1952)-QMOC

Laffitte, Julio, 81st Cong., S. 305, Veto Message August 29, 1950 (S. Doc. 210, 2nd Sess.)-VETO

LaHera, Vladimir Rodriguez, 92nd Cong., H.R. 2076, Priv. L. No. 92, 86 Stat. 1539 (1972)-NXCP

Lan, Andre, 81st Cong., S. 1506, Priv. L. No. 870, 64 Stat. A194 (1950)-NMSC

Langer, Hyman D., and Alta Jourard Langer, 81st Cong., S. 2897, Priv. L. No. 856, 64 Stat. A188 (1950)-QMOC

Langermann, Meier and his wife, Friederik, and son, Joseph, 76th Cong., H.R. 9651, Veto Message July 2, 1940, H.R. Doc. 862, 3rd Sess.)-VETO

Lanyi, Gabor, 84th Cong., S. 884, Priv. L. No. 396, 69 Stat. A136 (1955)-WHEL

Laude, William Carl, 76th Cong., S. 1291, Priv. L. No. 98, 53 Stat. 1481 (1939)-QMOC

Lazic, Nikolija, 86th Cong., S. 2886, Priv. L. No. 367, 74 Stat. A54 (1960)-QPRF

Lecomte, Marcelle, 82nd Cong., H.R. 2714, Priv. L. No. 16, 65 Stat. A8 (1951)-NRES

Lee, Chung Chi, 92nd Cong., H.R. 7641, Priv. L. No. 100, 86 Stat. 1541 1972)-WCRF

Leggio, Orsola Jacopelli, 83rd Cong., H.R. 871, Priv. L. No. 177, 67 Stat. A63 (1953)-WCRF

Lendian, Mrs. A.R., 87th Cong., H.R. 10160, Priv. L. No. 562, 76 Stat. 1363 (1962)-NCOD

Leong, Mrs. Bertie Grace Chan, 81st Cong., S. 609, Priv. L. No. 403, 64 Stat. A23 (1950)-QIRW

Lerrigo, George E., 63rd Cong., S. 3419, Priv. L. No. 184, 38 Stat. 1476 (1915)-NCOD

Levins, George Henry, 75th Cong., S. 3064, Priv. L. No. 745, 52 Stat. 1408 (1938)-NCOD

Lewis, Arsenio Acacio, 80th Cong., H.R. 553, Priv. L. No. 70, 61 Stat. 993 (1947)-QIRA

Li, Dr. Tsi Au (Tsi Gziou Li), 84th Cong., H.R. 1887, Priv. L. 533, 70 Stat. A17 (1956)-QMGN

Lim, Poon, 81st Cong., S. 1405, Priv. L. No. 178, 63 Stat. 1144 (1949)-QMDE

Lin, Min-Zen, 96th Cong., S. 1772, Priv. L. No. 99, 94 Stat. 3628 1980)-QIRA

Lindsay, Hsiao-li (nee Li-Hsiao-li), 86th Cong., H.R. 9444, Priv. L. No. 259, 74 Stat. A13 (1960)-QPRF

Linhart, William H., 78th Cong., H.R. 2016, Priv. L. No. 516, 58 Stat. 1080 (1944)-NCOD

Lipset, John, 86th Cong., S. 2528, Priv. L. No. 361, 74 Stat. A52 (1960)-QPRF

Lizardo, Julian, Dolores, Jaime, Dennis, Roldan, and Julian Jr., 84th Cong., H.R. 4039, Priv. L. No. 598, 70 Stat. A41 (1956)-QMOC

Loeffler, Martin H., 91st Cong., H.R. 3165, Priv. L. No. 51, 83 Stat. 885 (1969)-NXCP

Loetsch, Theordore, 80th Cong., H.R. 4484, Priv. L. No. 338, 62 Stat. 1368 (1948)-WCRF

Loh, Che Yim, 89th Cong., S. 2451, Priv. L. No. 455, 80 Stat. 1708 (1966)-QIRA

Lomm, Ivan Bruno, also known as Ivan B. Johnson, 84th Cong., H.R. 1203, Priv. L. No. 15, 69 Stat. A7 (1955)-WCRF

Longfield-Smith, Antonia, 87th Cong., S. 2011, Priv. L. No. 417, 76 Stat. 1311 (1962)-QIRA

Lowery, Owen, 83rd Cong., S. 315, Priv. L. No. 83, 67 Stat. A31 (1953)-QIRA

Lucic, Lororko, H.R. 1521, 88th Cong., Priv. L. No. 183, 78 Stat. 1127 (1964)-WCRF

Lui, Andrew and Julia, 98th Cong., H.R. 1236, Priv. L. No. 28, 98 Stat. 3426 (1984)-QMOC

Lui, Dr. Chung Kwai, 81st Cong., S. 315, Priv. L. No. 3, 63 Stat. 1073 (1949)-QMDE

Lukes, George, 82nd Cong., H.R. 711, Priv. L. No. 289, 65 Stat. A109 (1951)-QIER

Lung, Shun Wen (also known as Van Long and Van S. Lung), 85th Cong., S. 530, Priv. L. No. 84, 71 Stat. A36 (1957)-QMDE

Luraschi, Luigi Giuseppe, 88th Cong., H.R. 2309, Priv. L. No. 38, 77 Stat. 887 (1963)-NRTN

Luvisotti, Niccolo, 82nd Cong., S. 2566, Priv. L. No. 737, 66 Stat. A109 (1952)-QMGN

Lyn, Woo You (also known as Hom You Fong and Lyn Fong Y. Hom), 88th Cong., H.R.2757, Priv. L. No. 102, 77 Stat. 909 (1963)-QMGN

Lyne, Hendrika Koenders, 94th Cong., H.R. 1556, Priv. L. No. 3, 89 Stat. 1165 (1975)-QMGN

McDade, Dr. Frederick Daniel, 81st Cong., S. 3238, Priv. L. No. 873, 64 Stat. A195 (1950)-NRES

McGiffin, Andree Marie Helene, 95th Cong., H.R. 8192, Priv. L. No. 165, 92 Stat. 3860 (1978)-QPRP

McKinney, George C., 86th Cong., S. 2142, Priv. L. No. 320, 74 Stat. A36 (1960)-NCOD

Mablekos, Evagelos, 87th Cong., S. 235, Priv. L. No. 308, 76 Stat. 1272 (1962)-WCRF

Macos, Fernando Alves, 94th Cong., H.R. 8119, Priv. L. No. 121, 90 Stat. 3004 (1976)-WCRF

Magnone, Maria Veltri, 81st Cong., H.R. 1079, Priv. L. No. 48, 63 Stat. 1093 (1949)-WHEL

Makeef, Nina, also known as Nina Berberova, 83rd Cong., H.R. 692, Pocket Veto, *Congressional Record* 100:14683-VETO

Malek-Aslani, Dr. Morad, 83rd Cong., H.R. 974, Priv. L. No. 50, 67 Stat. A19 (1953)-QMOC

Malliaras, Panagiotis, Georgia, and Constantina, 91st Cong., H.R. 6600, Priv. L. No. 69, 83 Stat. 891 (1969)-QMGN

Maly, Wilhelm, J.R., 93rd Cong., S. 507, Priv. L. No. 62, 88 Stat. 2368 (1974)-NRES

Mangiaracina, Mrs. Frances, 87th Cong., H.R. 1404, Priv. L. No. 409, 76 Stat. 1309 (1962)-QPRP

Manlucu, Albina Lucio Z., 92nd Cong., S. 559, Priv. L. 115, 86 Stat. 1548 (1972)-QMGN

Manriquez, Romulo A. 85th Cong., S. 3060, Priv. L. No. 513, 72 Stat. A74 (1958)-QMGN

Mar, Gilbert B., 85th Cong., H.R. 1677, Priv. L. No. 304, 71 Stat. A120 (1957)-NRES

Maraessa, Alessandro, 86th Cong., H.R. 1422, Priv. L. No. 424, 74 Stat. A76 (1960)-WCRF

Marcello, Nicola, 85th Cong., H.R. 1757, Priv. L. No. 15, 71 Stat. A7 (1957)-QPRP

Marek, Zdenek, 82nd Cong., S. 178, Priv. L. No. 95, 65 Stat. A37 (1951)-QMDP

Martindale, James A.G., 82nd Cong., H.R. 714, Priv. L. No. 46, 65 Stat. A19 (1951)-WCRF

Masaoka, Michi Mrs., 82nd Cong., H.R. 978, Priv. L. No. 562, 66 Stat. A52 (1952)-QIER

Masaryk, Alice, 83rd Cong., S. 1212, Priv. L. No. 621, 68 Stat. A148 (1954)-QMDE

Masterton, William John and Louis Vincent Nanne, 90th Cong., H.R. 2048, Priv. L. No. 18, 81 Stat. 992 (1967)-NRES

Mastrilli, Francesco P. 78th Cong., H.R. 480, Priv. L. No. 216, 58 Stat. 956 (1944)-WCRF

May, Lennon, 87th Cong., H.R. 4028, Priv. L. No. 251, 75 Stat. 941 (1961)-QIRM

Maya, Dr. Jacobo Albo, 89th Cong., S. 3272, Priv. L. No. 328, 80 Stat. 1659 (1966)-NRES

Mazza, Luigi, 75th Cong., H.R. 5597, Priv. L. No. 686, 52 Stat. 1382 (1938)-WCRF

Meda-Novara, Enrichetta F.C., 83rd Cong., H.R. 804, Priv. L. No. 728, 68 Stat. A183 (1954)-QMGN

Meister, Florence, 84th Cong., H.R. 1166, Priv. L. No. 12, 69 Stat. A6 (1955)-NVOL

Mena, Dr. Cesar A., 90th Cong., S. 164, Priv. L. No. 33, 81 Stat. 996 (1967)-NRES

Mencl, Ladislav, 84th Cong., S. 2088, Priv. L. No. 446, 69 Stat. A152 (1955)-QMDE

Mesnager, Madeleine, 97th Cong., H.R. 1469, Priv. L. No. 4, 95 Stat. 1734 (1981)-QIRM

Messina, Antonio, 83rd Cong., H.R. 1657, Priv. L. No. 410, 68 Stat. A70 (1954)-WCRF

Meulenkamp, Deliana, 82nd Cong. H.R. 6117, Priv. L. No. 761, 66 Stat. A117 (1952)-NRES

Miao, Yun Tai and his wife, Chao Pei Tsang Miao, 83rd Cong., S. 2345, Priv. L. No. 969, 68 Stat. A279 (1954)-QMOC

Miguel, Mrs. Izabel A., 87th Cong., H.R. 6343, Priv. L. No. 339, 76 Stat. 1283 (1962)-WHEL

Milkie, Nasubit Mildred, 86th Cong., S. 977, Priv. L. No. 172, 73 Stat. A75 (1959)-NRTN

Miller, Mrs. Akiko Tsukado, 80th Cong., H.R. 2347, Veto Message April 12, 1948 (H.R. Doc. 609, 2nd Sess.)-VETO

Miranda, Salvador, 85th Cong., S. 2989, Priv. L. No. 634, 72 Stat. A132 (1958)-NVOL

Mnatzakanian, Ashot and Ophelia Mnatzakanian, 84th Cong., H.R. 3963, Pocket Veto March 22, 1956, *Congressional Record* 102:5696-VETO

Mok, Mrs. May K.Y., Frederick W.S. Mok, and Vincent W. C. Mok, 81st Cong., H.R. 1010, Priv. L. No. 56, 63 Stat. 1096 (1949)-QMGN

Morgenstern, Szyga (Saul), 83rd Cong., S. 278, Priv. L. No. 566, 68 Stat. A130 (1954)-QMOC

Mourginakis, Eftychios, 83rd Cong., S. 676, Priv. L. No. 530, 68 Stat. A119 (1954)-QMDE

Mpatziani, Anastasia D., 90th Cong., S. 1652, Priv. L. No. 346, 82 Stat. 1430 (1968)-WXIL

Muciaccia, Santa (Sister Maria Fridiana), and Teresa Saragaglia (Sister Maria Eutropia), and Caterina Isonni (Sister Maria Giovita), 83rd Cong., S. 740, Priv. L. No. 457, 68 Stat. A92 (1954)-QMOC

Mueller, Mrs. Marie Y., 82nd Cong., S. 1436, Pocket veto Oct. 19, 1951, *Congressional Record* 97:13534-VETO

Mulligan, Mrs. Carla, 82nd Cong., H.R. 1836, Priv. L. No. 567, 66 Stat. A54 (1952)-WCRF

Mulligan, Christopher J., 86th Cong., H.R. 5645, Priv. L. No. 209, 73 Stat. A91 (1959)-NXDD

Mumm, Frances Scoville, 66th Cong., S.J. Res. 90, Priv. L. No. 1, 41 Stat. 1449 (1919)-NVOL

Munoz-Tostado, Salvador, 89th Cong., H.R. 1236, Priv. L. No. 11, 79 Stat. 1336 (1965)-WCRF

Naarits, Edward, 84th Cong., S. 1044, Priv. L. No. 469, 69 Stat. A159 (1955)-NMSC

Nagy, Jeno, 87th Cong., S. 3026, Priv. L. No. 565, 76 Stat. 1364 (1962)-WHEL

Namgyal, Mrs. Hope, 94th Cong., S. 1699, Priv. L. No. 52, 90 Stat. 2976 (1976)-NVOL

Navarro, Antonio Luis, 90th Cong., S. 1021, Priv. L. No. 114, 81 Stat. 1024 (1967)-NRES

Navarro-Paz, Francisco, 88th Cong., S. 1999, Priv. L. No. 333, 78 Stat. 1189 (1964)-WCRF

Neth, Rosemarie Gauch, 90th Cong., S. 445, Priv. L. No. 139, 81 Stat. 1030 (1967)-NRES

Neumann, Master Sgt. Gerhard, 79th Cong., H.R. 3441, Priv. L. No. 695, 60 Stat. 1242 (1946)-NMSC

Neville, Nora R. 79th Cong., H.R. 1350, Priv. L. No. 460, 60 Stat. 1143 (1946)-NMSC

Nielsen, Johny, 81st Cong., H.R. 6283, Priv. L. No. 434, 64 Stat. A35 (1950)-QIRA

Nijinsky, Mrs. Romola and Paul Bohus-Vilagosi, 83rd Cong., H.R. 675, Priv. L. No. 404, 68 Stat. A68 (1954)-QMOC

Nishiyama, Rhoda Akiko, 82nd Cong., H.R. 1236, Priv. L. No. 360, 65 Stat. A133 (1951)-QIER

Nock, Matthias, Jr., 87th Cong., H.R. 3718, Priv. L. No. 249, 75 Stat. 940 (1961)-WCRF

Nosek, Jindrich (Henri) and Mrs. Zdenka Nosek, 82nd Cong., H.R. 2310, Priv. L. No. 124, 65 Stat. A47 (1951)-QMDP

Nowakowski, Julian or William Nowak (Novak), 84th Cong., H.R. 2072, Priv. L. No. 555,70 Stat. A24 (1956)-NVOL

Nulle-Siecenieks, Margers, 83rd Cong., H.R. 6955, Priv. L. 829, 68 Stat. A215 (1954)-WCRF

O'Brien, James T., 90th Cong., S. 2897, Priv. L. No. 347, 82 Stat. 1430 (1968)-NCOD

On, Lee Dock, 87th Cong., H.R. 1458, Priv. L. No. 530, 76 Stat. 1350 (1962)-QPRP

Onacewicz, Col. Wlodzimierz, 81st Cong., H.R. 2349, Priv. L. No. 170, 63 Stat. 1141 (1949)-QMDE

Onassis, Athina Mary, 82nd Cong., H.R. 890, Priv. L. No. 35, 65 Stat. A16 (1951)-NRES

Onativia, Juan, 83rd Cong., H.R. 2879, Priv. L. No. 744, 68 Stat. A188 (1954)-QMOC

Oniki, Shinji, 97th Cong., H.R. 1826, Priv. L. No. 36, 96 Stat. 2627 (1982)-QIRA

Orlov, Alexander and his wife, Maria Orlov, 84th Cong., S. 1627, Priv. L. No. 810, 70 Stat. A149 (1956)-WXCP

Orpilla, Enrique M., 82nd Cong., H.R. 2718, Priv. L. No. 744, 66 Stat. A111 (1952)-NMSC

Orsini, Mrs. Maria G. (nee Mari), 92nd Cong., H.R. 1899, Priv. L. No. 42, 85 Stat. 850 (1971)-QMGN

Ortiz-Medina, Julio, 95th Cong., H.R. 1422, Priv. L. No. 158, 92 Stat. 3857 (1978)-WCRF

Osman, Ertogroul, 83rd Cong., S. 2618, Priv. L. No. 999, 68 Stat. A289 (1954)-QPRP

Pahk, Induk, 84th Cong., H.R. 2054, Priv. L. No. 554, 70 Stat. A24 (1956)-QMOC

Pantelas, George, 83rd Cong., S. 154, Pocket veto August 17, 1954, *Congressional Record*, 100:14707-VETO

Pao, Yih-Ho and his wife, Joanne T. Pao, 88th Cong., S. 584, Priv. L. No. 329, 78 Stat. 1188 (1964)-QPRF

Paone, Rosa, 76th Cong., H.R. 4954, Priv. L. No. 592, 54 Stat. 1375 (1940)-WHEL

Papachristopoulos, Theodore, 81st Cong., H.R. 2360, Priv. L. No. 64, 63 Stat. 1098 (1949)-QIRM

Papadopoulos Elias, 82nd Cong., H.R. 4396, Priv. L. No. 950, 66 Stat. A188 (1952)-W

Parisi, Giovanna, Michelina Valletta, Yolanda Altieri, Generosa Tamburi, Carolina Picciano, and Giovana Turtur, 81st Cong., H.R. 2591, Priv. L. No. 441, 64 Stat. A38 (1950)-QMOC

Paterson, Mrs. Leslie M., Janet Paterson and Mary Paterson, 87th Cong., H.R. 1469, Priv. L. No. 473, 76 Stat. 1330 (1962)-QPRF

Pavla, Renuka, 96th Cong., S. 215, Priv. L. 60, 94 Stat. 3598 (1980)-QIRA

Pazdro, Ursula Rosa, 85th Cong., S. 660, Priv. L. No. 253, 71 Stat. A97 (1957)-WCRF

Pearce, Erika Margaretha Zintl, 85th Cong., S. 3221, Priv. L. No. 730, 72 Stat. A196 (1958)-NRTN

Pechnik, Anna, 80th Cong., S. 1142, Priv. L. No. 290, 62 Stat. 1352 (1948)-QMGN

Pender, Stephen Lance, Patricia Jenifer Pender, and Denese Gene Pender, 92nd Cong., S. 389, Priv. L. No. 35, 85 Stat. 848 (1971)-NCOD

Peng, Dr. Tzy-Cheng, 87th Cong., S. 1791, Priv. L. No. 317, 76 Stat. 1275 (1962)-NRES

Percival, Edgar Wikner, 80th Cong., S. 2060, Priv. L. No. 342, 62 Stat. 1370 (1948)-QMDE

Pereira, Jose Augusto, 81st Cong., S. 1551, Priv. L. No. 730, 64 Stat. A142 (1950)-WCRF

Perez, Francisco Gonzalez, 81st Cong., S. 2077, Priv. L. No. 672, 64 Stat. A119 (1950)-WCRF

Pernar, Dr. and Mrs. Ivan, 84th Cong., H.R. 1193, Priv. L. No. 512, 70 Stat. A10 (1956)-QMDE

Pertsovitch, Mrs. Anastasia, 91st Cong., S. 3620, Priv. L. No. 190, 84 Stat. 2151 (1970)-QIRW

Philippot, Jack L., 89th Cong., H.R. 11718, Priv. L. No. 277, 80 Stat. 1640 (1966)-NCOD

Philips, Bernard Julian, 94th Cong., H.R. 11890, Priv. L. No. 116, 90 Stat. 3001 (1976)-WCRF

Phillips, Rosa Marie, 84th Cong., H.R. 1487, Priv. L. No. 89, 69 Stat. A31 (1955)-WCRF

Pica, Michele, 84th Cong., H.R. 4548, Priv. L. No. 524, 70 Stat. A14 (1956)-WCRF

Picchi, Francesco and Natalia, 80th Cong., H.R. 422, Priv. L. No. 168, 62 Stat. 1308 (1948)-WCRF

Pilavakis, Calliope Minaca, 76th Cong., S. 808, Priv. L. No. 184, 53 Stat. 1514 (1939)-WCRF

Pilgrim, Allen Howard, Cheryl Ann Pilgrim, Robb Alexander Pilgrim, and Jocelyn Marie Pilgrim, 86th Cong., S. 1557, Priv. L. No. 142, 73 Stat. A62 (1959)-QIRA

Pineda, Jesus Cortez, 94th Cong., S. 447, Priv. L. No. 24, 89 Stat. 1186 (1975)-QIRA

Pintos, Maria and her daughter, Eugenia Pintos, 84th Cong., H.R. 4152, Priv. L. No. 827, 70 Stat. A156 (1956)-QMGN

Plewniak, Jean (John) and Anna Piotrowska Plewniak, 82nd Cong., H.R. 2307, Priv. L. No. 25, 66 Stat. A95 (1951)-QMDP

Pohoryles, Ludwig, 80th Cong., H.R. 3880, Priv. L. No. 296, 62 Stat. 1354 (1948)-QMGN

Poidimani, Biagio, 82nd Cong., H.R. 2299, Priv. L. No. 176, 65 Stat. A67 (1951)-QMOC

Popovitch, Branimir V. and Mila B. Popovitch, 83rd Cong., S. 1682, Priv. L. No. 473, 68 Stat. A96 (1954)-QMGN

Portuondo, Dr. Alonso, 89th Cong., S. 3189, Priv. L. No. 327, 80 Stat. 1659 (1966)-NRES

Poskanzer, Israel Baird, 85th Cong., H.R. 7826, Priv. L. No. 623, 72 Stat. A128 (1958)-NVOL

Potts, Virginia Ray, 85th Cong., H.R. 8374, Priv. L. No. 310, 71 Stat. A123 (1957)-NVOL

Prati, Mrs. Virginia Dalla Rosa and her Minor son, Rolando Dalla Rosa Prati, 81st Cong., H.R. 5016, Veto Message August 14, 1950 (H.R. Doc. 685, 2nd Sess.)-VETO

Pratts, Rosa, 100th Cong., H.R. 2109, Priv. L. No. 38, 102 Stat. 4861 (1988)-QIRW

Priday, Lester Bruce, 95th Cong., H.R. 1446, Priv. L. No. 64, 92 Stat. 3819 (1978)-WCRF

Prince, Eugene, 62nd Cong., H.J. Res. 200,, 37 Stat. 1346 (1912)-NCOD

Proios, Irtene (nee Vagianos), 83rd Cong., H.R. 1695, Priv. L. No. 166, 67 Stat. A59 (1953)-QMGN

Pucci, Mario Giacomo Favetti, Giuseppe Omati, Vincenzo Andreani, Lambruno Sarzanini, Alessandro Costa, 82nd Cong., H.R. 1150, Priv. L. No. 63, 65 Stat. A25 (1951)-QMOC

Pyles, John Lewis, Jr., 83rd Cong., H.R. 7761, Priv. L. No. 711, 68 Stat. A177 (1954)-WHEL

Quaresma, Jose Armando, 84th Cong., H.R. 2949, Priv. L. No. 335, 69 Stat. A114 (1955)-WHEL

Quijano, Miss Rosario Y., Walter York Quijano, Ramon York Quijano, Tarcisus York Quijano, Denis York Quijano, and Paul York Quijano, 94th Cong., S. 52, Priv. L. No. 51, 90 Stat. 2975 (1976)-QPRF

Quintanar, Jose Domingo, 84th Cong., H.R. 1185, Priv. L. No. 287, 69 Stat. A99 (1955)-WCRF

Quirling, Frieda and Tina Quirling, 84th Cong., H.R. 995, Priv. L. No. 153, 69 Stat. A53 (1955)-QIRA

Radziwill, Josef, 83rd Cong., S. 795, Priv. L. No. 588, 68 Stat. A137 (1954)-QMGN

Rajkowski, Antoni, 84th Cong., H.R. 2495, Priv. L. No. 272, 69 Stat. A95 (1955)-QMGN

Rambauske, Erika, 84th Cong., H.R. 2087, Priv. L. No. 52, 69 Stat. A18 (1955)-WHEL

Ramirez, Juan Esteban, 97th Cong., S. 167, Priv. L. No. 26, 96 Stat. 2623 (1982)-QMGN

Ramirez-Trejo, Augustin, 87th Cong., H.R. 2187, Priv. L. No. 485, 76 Stat. 1334 (1962)-WXDD

Randhawa, Dr. Jagir Singh, 91st Cong., S. 85, Priv. L. No. 48, 83 Stat. 884 (1969)-NRES

Rasmussen, John Michael Ancker, 81st Cong., H.R. 3464, Veto Message August 14, 1950 (H.R. Doc. 683, 2nd Sess.)-VETO

Rehn, Richard Paul, 76th Cong., H.R. 5640, Veto Message August 26, 1940 (H.R. Doc. 935, 3rd Sess.)-VETO

Reid, Mrs. Martha, 81st Cong., H.R. 6442, Priv. L. No. 887, 64 Stat. A201 (1950)-NMSC

Richter, Prof. Werner and Horkheimer, Prof. Max , 82nd Cong., H.R. 7833, Priv. L. No. 1023, 66 Stat. A213 (1952)-NRTN

Ricker-Huetter, Maximilian Otto, and Mrs. Eugenia Ricker-Huetter, 82nd Cong., H.R. 853, Priv. L. No. 399, 65 Stat. A146 (1951)-QMDP

Ricupero, Esterina, 89th Cong., H.R. 1627, Priv. L. No. 66, 79 Stat. 1358 (1965)-WHEL

Rigazzi, Elisa Albertina Cioccio or Elisa Ciocci, 83rd Cong., S. 2504, Priv. L. No. 650, 68 Stat. A158 (1954)-QIRA

Rios, Edwin Marcos and Geovanna Rios, 99th Cong., H.R. 483, Priv. L. No. 5, 100 Stat. 4314 (1986)-QIRA

Roberts, Lee-Ana, 85th Cong., S. 1290, Priv. L. No. 271, 71 Stat. A106 (1957)-QIER

Rocha, Andrea Hernandes Montes, 84th Cong., H.R. 1501, Priv. L. No. 46, 69 Stat. A16 (1955)-WCRF

Rodriguez, Alberto, 92nd Cong., S. 2822, Priv. L. No. 150, 86 Stat. 1563 (1972)-NRES

Rogers, Anthony, 95th Cong., H.R. 1750, Priv. L. No. 86, 92 Stat. 3829 (1978)-QPRF

Roman, Marcel M., Clara M. Roman, and Rodica E. Roman, 77th Cong., S. 381, Veto Message February 17, 1942 (S. Doc. 180, 2nd Sess.)-VETO

Romanoff, Michael, 85th Cong., H.R. 8348, Priv. L. No. 401, 72 Stat. A30 (1958)-QMGN

Romney, Mrs. Cumorah Kennington, 91st Cong., S. 2863, Priv. L. No. 148, 84 Stat. 2128 (1970)-NCOD

Rossi, Ermelinda, 95th Cong., S. 455, 91 Stat. 1653, Priv. L. No. 11 (1977)-WXIL

Rossi, Sisters Maria Rita, Maria Domenica Paone, Rachele Orlando, Assunta Roselli, Rosa Innocenti, and Maria Mancinelli, 81st Cong., S. 1856, Priv. L. No. 489, 64 Stat. A57 (1950)-QMOC

Rossini, Rev. Charles V., 83rd Cong., S. 2259, Priv. L. No. 902, 68 Stat. A244 (1954)-NRTN

Rossmann, Mrs. Audrey, 88th Cong., H.R. 9090, Priv. L. No. 250, 78 Stat. 1155 (1964)-WHEL

Roth, Ethel, 81st Cong., H.R. 1447, Priv. L. No. 321, 63 Stat. 1199 (1949)-QPRP

Roumeliotis, Panagiotes, 82nd Cong., S. 1470, Priv. L. No. 859, 66 Stat. A159 (1952)-QMDE

Rubio, Fernando A., Jr., 83rd Cong., S. 2135, Priv. L. No. 665, 68 Stat. A163 (1954)-NXDD

Rudczenko, Sergiusz, S. 2319, 86th Cong., Priv. L. 226, 73 Stat. A98 (1959)-WHEL

Ruffolo,Umberto, 95th Cong., H.R. 1420, Priv. L. No. 48, 92 Stat. 3811 (1978)-WHEL

Rundle, Richard Gregory and Valiquette Adele, 82nd Cong., H.R. 1165, Priv. L. No. 5, 65 Stat. A4 (1951)-NRES

Rutilio, Liborio Guido, 83rd Cong., H.R. 5354, Priv. L. No. 766, 68 Stat. A194 (1954)-WCRF

Sackler, Gillian Lesley, 100th Cong., S. 2637, Priv. L. No. 35, 102 Stat. 4859 (1988)-QIRW

Saguar, Mrs. Mercedes Hernandez, 82nd Cong., H.R. 1092, Priv. L. No. 869, 66 Stat. A162 (1952)-WHEL

Salanga, Teodoro N., Jr., 98th Cong., H.R. 1150, Priv. L. No. 27, 98 Stat. 3426 (1984)-QMDE

Salazar, Ricardo Rosas, 95th Cong., S. 3109, Priv. L. No. 125, 92 Stat. 3844 (1978)-QPRF

Salter-Mathieson, Nigel C.S., 82nd Cong., H.R. 4535, Priv. L. No. 603, 66 Stat. A63 (1952)-NRES

Samuelli, Nora Isabella, 89th Cong., S. 619, Priv. L. No. 203, 79 Stat. 1413 (1965)-NRES

Sandoval-Michel, Miguel (also known as Arturo Rodriguez-Gomez), 84th Cong., H.R. 2788, Priv. L. No. 425, 69 Stat. A145 (1955)-WCRF

Santillano, Dr. Antonio B., 89th Cong., H.R. 10288, Priv. L. No. 398, 80 Stat. 1685 (1966)-NRES

Santini, Armando, 81st Cong., S. 3378, Priv. L. No. 1099, 64 Stat. A277 (1951)-QMOC

Santos, Henrique, 81st Cong., S. 2429, Priv. L. No. 402, 64 Stat. A23 (1950)-NXDD

Sapuschnin, Willy, 88th Cong., H.R. 1182, Priv. L. No. 177, 78 Stat. 1125 (1964)-QMGN

Sarapanovschi, Hanoh (also known as Hanoh Charat), Gizela Gisele) Sarapanovschi (nee Levy), and Philippe Sarapanovschi, 82nd Cong., H.R. 1598, Priv. L. No. 321, 65 Stat. A120 (1951)-QMDP

Sartoris, Nellie Grant, 55th Cong., S. 156, Priv. L. No. 36, 30 Stat. 1496 (1898)-NVOL

Saunders, Kevin Patrick, 94th Cong., H.R. 1645, Priv. L. No. 66, 90 Stat. 2982 (1976)-WCRF

Savarese, Gennaro, 84th Cong., H.R. 1275, Priv. L. No. 253, 69 Stat. A89 (1955)-WHEL

Scano, Giovanna, 84th Cong., H.R. 1410, Priv. L. No. 720, 70 Stat. A98 (1956)-NVOL

Schefbanker, Monika, 84th Cong., H.R. 2339, Priv. L. No. 449, 69 Stat. A153 (1955)-QIRA

Schindler, Frank, 80th Cong., S. 135, Priv. L. No. 12, 61 Stat. 968 (1947)-NMSC

Schlechter, Wilhelm Jahn, Monica Pino Schlechter, Ingrid Daniela Schlechter, and Arturo David Schlechter, 100th Cong., S. 1842, Priv. L. No. 48, 102 Stat. 4867 (1988)-QMGN

Schmid, Leopoldine Marie, 96th Cong., H.R. 6739, Priv. L. No. 101, 94 Stat. 3628 (1980)-NXPS

Schoeppe, Mrs. Elfrieda, 84th Cong., H.R. 2916, Priv. L. No. 483, 69 Stat. A164 (1955)-QIRW

Schreiner, Janos, 85th Cong., S. 1833, Priv. L. No. 105, 71 Stat. A42 (1957)-QIRM

Schultz, Gladys Belleville, 97th Cong., H.R. 1785, Priv. L. No. 7, 95 Stat. 1735 (1981)-QIRA

Schulz, Charlotte, 88th Cong., H.R. 2290, Priv. L. No. 247, 80 Stat. 1627 (1966)-NRES

Sciulli, Mrs. Desolina, 95th Cong., H.R. 1432, Priv. L. No. 31, 92 Stat. 3804 (1978)-WCRF

Scobel, Uwe-Thorsten, 86th Cong., S. 32, Priv. L. No. 34, 73 Stat. A17 (1959)-NCOD

Scofield, Ernest Edward (Ernesto Espino), 93rd Cong., S. 428, Priv. L. No. 70, 88 Stat. 2371 (1974)-QPRF

Scogin, Fusako Terao, 82nd Cong., H.R. 5347, Priv. L. No. 516, 66 Stat. A36 (1952)-QIER

Scudieri, Carmela, 95th Cong., H.R. 1748, Priv. L. No. 159, 92 Stat. 3858 (1978)-QPRF

Seborg, Miss Gloria, 88th Cong., H.R. 2005, Priv. L. No. 152, 79 Stat. 1392 (1965)-NRES

Seixas, Dora Vida Lyew, 83rd Cong., S. 2534, Priv. L. No. 344, 68 Stat. A44 (1954)-QPRF

Sewen, John, 81st Cong., S. 905, Priv. L. No. 199, 63 Stat. 1152 (1949)-NRTN

Shafer, Itzchak, 81st Cong., H.R. 5354, Priv. L. No. 350, 63 Stat. 1211 (1949)-QIRA

Shami, Shaoul Minashi, Emily Shami, Joseph Clement Shami, and Charles Henry Shami, 81st Cong., S. 2420, Priv. L. No. 1060, 64 Stat. A262 (1950)-QMOC

Sharble, Elfriede Unterholzer, 88th Cong., H.R. 1174, Priv. L. No. 294, 78 Stat. 1173 (1964)-WCRF

Sharp, Mrs. Clinton R., 80th Cong., S. 84, Priv. L. No. 144, 62 Stat. 1300 (1948)-QIER

Shepherd, Ann E., 93rd Cong., H.R. 1356, Priv. L. No. 21, 87 Stat. 1104 (1973)-QPRP

Sherlock, Dulcie Ann Steinhardt, S. 3588, 82nd Cong., Priv. L. No. 657, 66 Stat. A82 (1952)-NCOD

Shimada, Toshiaki, 82nd Cong., H.R. 3271, Priv. L. No. 588, 66 Stat. A59 (1952)-NCOD

Sidders, Christina Boltz, 97th Cong., H.R. 1482, Priv. L. No. 24, 96 Stat. 2622 (1982)-NRTN

Sierra, Bertha Alicia, 93rd Cong., H.R. 1367, Priv. L. No. 22, 87 Stat. 1104 (1973)-QMGN

Simonov, Frol Martin, 86th Cong., H.R. 6954, Priv. L. 218, 73 Stat. A95, (1959)-NXCP

Simpson, Bonita Lee, 83rd Cong., S. 3145, Priv. L. No. 986, 68 Stat. A285 (1954)-QIRA

Singh, Arokiaswami Arumai, 82nd Cong., H.R. 1464, Priv. L. No. 922, 66 Stat. A179 (1952)-QMOC

Slovak, Miroslav, 84th Cong., S. 129, Priv. L. No. 74, 69 Stat. A26 (1955)-WXCP

Smart, Loraine, and Robert Clarke, 96th Cong., H.R. 1829, Priv. L. No. 50, 94 Stat. 3593 (1980)-QMGN

Smith, Edith, 83rd Cong., H.R. 954, Priv. L. No. 180, 67 Stat. A64 (1953)-WCRF

Smith, Gabrielle Marie (nee Staub), 83rd Cong., H.R. 962, Priv. L. No. 330, 68 Stat. A38 (1954)-QMGN

Smith, James I., 83rd Cong., H.R. 1673, Priv. L. No. 558, 68 Stat. A128 (1954)-WCRF

Smorczewska, Mrs. Maria, 80th Cong., H.R. 3787, Priv. L. No. 308, 62 Stat. 1357 (1948)-QMOC

Sofronov, Pimen Maximovitch, 83rd Cong., H.R. 3566, Priv. L. No. 807, 68 Stat. A208 (1954)-QMOC

Sogor, Clara, 81st Cong., S. 918, Priv. L. No. 847, 64 Stat. A184 (1950)-QMGN

Somma, S. Sgt. Ryuzo, 91st Cong., H.R. 13997, Priv. L. No. 151, 84 Stat. 2128 (1970)-NXPS

Soon, Kim Kin, 89th Cong., S. 2555, Priv. L. No. 337, 80 Stat. 1662 (1966)-QIRA

Sowinski, Mr. and Mrs. Zygmunt, 83rd Cong., H.R. 944, Priv. L. No. 537, 68 Stat. A121 (1954)-QMGN

Sparagna, Aniceto, 84th Cong., S. 432, Priv. L. No. 146, 69 Stat. A51 (1955)-WCRF

Speelman, Marianne and Michel, 82nd Cong., H.R. 2498, Priv. L. No. 310, 65 Stat. A116 (1951)-QMDP

Spilios, Stefanos A. (also known as Stephen A. Harrison), 83rd Cong., S. 1262, Priv. L. No. 89, 67 Stat. A33 (1953)-QMOC

Sprecher, Rosalie Piar (nee Rosa Piar), 74th Cong., S. 3399, Priv. L. No. 425, 49 Stat. 2234 (1936)-WCRF

Stanic, Josip, 83rd Cong., H.R. 4701, Priv. L. No. 487, 68 Stat. A101 (1954)-QMOC

Staniszewski, Corporal Wladyslaw, 98th Cong., H.R. 960, Priv. L. No. 33, 98 Stat. 3429 (1984)-NXPS

Staudinger, Konrad Ludwig, 91st Cong., S. 737, Priv. L. No. 187, 84 Stat. 2150 (1970)-WCRF

Stehlin, Anne-Marie, 86th Cong., S. 3130, Priv. L. No. 352, 74 Stat. A49 (1960)-NRTN

Stewart, Alexander, 81st Cong., H.R. 1991, Priv. L. No. 795, 64 Stat. A163 (1950)-QMDE

Stoots, Johanna A., 82nd Cong., H.R. 884, Priv. L. No. 386, 65 Stat. A142 (1951)-QMGN

Strauss, SP4C Klaus Josef, 91st Cong., HR. 6607, Priv. L. No. 15, 83 Stat. 871 (1969)-NXPS

Stresemann, Wolfgang, 85th Cong., H.R. 12903, Priv. L. No. 616, 72 Stat. A126 (1958)-NRTN

Sugimote, Kaiko (Kay Fair) and her minor children, 82nd Cong., H.R. 1162, Priv. L. No. 676, 66 Stat. A88 (1952)-QIER

Suleiman, Mahmood Shareef, 93rd Cong., S. 912, Priv. L. No. 64, 88 Stat. 2369 (1974)-NRES

Sumida, Mrs. Setsuyo, 82nd Cong., H.R. 3152, Priv. L. No. 686, 66 Stat. A92 (1952)-QPRP

Sunga, Zora Singh, 96th Cong., H.R. 2433, Priv. L. No. 92, 94 Stat. 3625 (1980)-QIRA

Sweeney, John, 77th Cong., H.R. 7828, Priv. L. No. 633, 56 Stat. 1259 (1942)-NXDD

Swiderski, Jozef, 96th Cong., H.R. 4013, Priv. L. No. 52, 94 Stat. 3594 (1980)-NRES

Symeonidis, Dr. Alexander, 82nd Cong., H.R. 3600, Priv. L. No. 792, 66 Stat. A131 (1952)-NRES

Szymanski, Roman and Anastosia Szymanski, 81st Cong., S. 1026, Priv. L. No. 245, 63 Stat. 1169 (1949)-QMGN

Tacquechel, Dario, 87th Cong., H.R. 7582, Priv. L. No. 549, 76 Stat. 1358 (1962)-NRES

Takahashi, Gentaro, 80th Cong., S. 329, Priv. L. No. 260, 62 Stat. 1340 (1948)-QMGN

Takahashi, Kazue Oda, 80th Cong., H.R. 1215, Priv. L. No. 225, 62 Stat. 1328 (1948)-QIER

Takeuchi, Yoko, 82nd Cong., H.R. 4788, Priv. L. No. 605, 66 Stat. A64 (1952)-QIER

Taskin, Ahmet Haldun Koca Taskin and Jadwiga Milarski Goodman, 84th Cong., S. 245, Priv. L. No. 739, 70 Stat. A109 (1956)-WXDD

Tati, Giuseppa Curro, 84th Cong., H.R. 1935, Priv. L. No. 229, 69 Stat. A79 (1955)-WCRF

Tcharoutcheff, Moke, Lucie Baptistine Tcharoutcheff, Raymond Tcharoutcheff, and Robert Tcharoutcheff, 80th Cong., H.R. 4050, Priv. L. No. 312, 62 Stat. 1359 (1948)-QMDE

Tcherepnin, Mrs. Marie, 83rd Cong., H.R. 5085, Priv. L. No. 329, 68 Stat. A38 (1954)-QMGN

Tchertkoff, Joseph Boris, 82nd Cong., S. 1462, Priv. L. No. 467, 66 Stat. A20 (1952)-WHEL

Temel, Jacobo, 89th Cong., H.R. 1414, Priv. L. No. 269, 80 Stat. 1638 (1966)-WCRF

Thaw, Ruby and Hla Sein, 81st Cong., H.R. 6758, Priv. L. No. 789, 64 Stat. A161 (1950)-QMDE

Thelemann, Gunter Arno, 82nd Cong., H.R. 898, Priv. L. No. 37, 65 Stat. A16 (1951)-QIRA

Theodossiou, Basil, 84th Cong., H.R. 2354, Priv. L. No. 27, 69 Stat. A10 (1955)-QMGN

Thompson, Giorgio Salvini, 83rd Cong., S. 1955, Priv. L. No. 475, 68 Stat. A97 (1954)-QIRM

Thung, Heng Liong, 90th Cong., S. 2720, Priv. L. No. 340, 82 Stat. 1428 (1968)-NRES

Thyberg, Mrs. Margaret Dows, 84th Cong., H.R. 5041, Priv. L. No. 763, 70 Stat. A119 (1956)-NVOL

Tirman, Odette Louise, 82nd Cong., H.R. 2346, Priv. L. No. 659, 66 Stat. A82 (1952)-WCRF

Tisler, Frantisek, 87th Cong., H.R. 6833, Priv. L. No. 492, 76 Stat. 1336 (1962)-NXCP

Todd, Margaret Elizabeth and Frederick Henry, 89th Cong., H.R. 7453, Priv. L. 194, 79 Stat. 1408 (1965)-NRES

Topakas, Emanuel G., 89th Cong., H.R. 3233, Priv. L. No. 283, 61 Stat. 1642 (1966)-WCRF

Topcuoglu, Mehmet Salih, 82nd Cong., H.R. 3124, Priv. L. No. 684, 66 Stat. A91 (1952)-QMOC

Toporow, Roman, 80th Cong., H.R. 3243, Priv. L. No. 90, 61 Stat. 100 (1947)-QMGN

Torni, Lauri Allan, 83rd Cong., H.R. 2604, Priv. L. 168, 67 Stat. A60 (1953)-QMDE

Torre, Fortunato Giulio, 81st Cong., S. 2795, Priv. L. No. 660, 64 Stat. A115 (1950)-QMOC

Tortolini, Joe, 82nd Cong., H.R. 1791, Priv. L. No. 107, 65 Stat. A42 (1951)-WCRF

Toth, John Patrick, 75th Cong., H.R. 10136, Priv. L. No. 805, 52 Stat. 1432 (1938)-WCRF

Tozzi, Juliet Elizabeth, 94th Cong., H.R. 1425, Priv. L. No. 64, 90 Stat. 2981 (1976)-WCRF

Trahn, Herman, 80th Cong., H.R. 1502, Pocket veto July 18, 1947, 93 *Congressional Record*, 93:9343)-VETO

Trupiano, Epifanio,86th Cong., H.R. 3534, Priv. L. No. 399, 74 Stat. A65 (1960)-WHEL

Tumbarello, Giuseppe, 84th Cong., H.R. 1897, Priv. L. No. 228, 69 Stat. A79 (1955)-WCRF

Turcean, Harold, 80th Cong., S. 53, Priv. L. No. 51, 61 Stat. 985 (1947)-NXPS

Turchi, Giuseppe Antonio, 86th Cong., H.R. 4834, Priv. L. No. 337, 74 Stat. A42 (1960)-QIRM

Turni, Mrs. Bruna and Miss Graziella Turni, 93rd Cong., H.R. 3754, Priv. L. No. 29, 87 Stat. 1107 (1973)-QPRF

Turri, John E. and Edward H., 82nd Cong., S. 44, Priv. L. No. 2, 65 Stat. A3 (1951)-NRTN

Tvedt, Mrs. Erna, 81st Cong., H.R. 7428, Priv. L. No. 706, 64 Stat. A133 (1950)-WCRF

Ty, Henry, 83rd Cong., H.R. 1688, Priv. L. No. 297, 68 Stat. A26 (1954)-QMGN

Uhlik, Vaclav, Marta Uhlik, Vaclav Uhlik, Jr. and Eva Uhlik, 85th Cong., S. 2095, Priv. L. No. 282, 71 Stat. A109 (1957)-QMDE

Ullmann, John Jr., 76th Cong., S. 2427, Priv. L. No. 175, 53 Stat. 1510 (1939)-NCOD

Ullstein, Karl, 83rd Cong., S. 2369, Priv. L. No. 533, 68 Stat. A119 (1954)-NRTN

Utley, Freda, 78th Cong., H.R. 312, Priv. L. No. 372, 58 Stat. 1021 (1944)-WXCP

Uzman, Dr. Lutfu Lahut, 81st Cong., S. 3125, Priv. L. No. 1098, 64 Stat. A277 (1951)-QMOC

Vaccaro, Cecelia, 85th Cong., H.R. 1451, Priv. L. No. 43, 70 Stat. A19 (1957)-NVOL

Vaida, Ladislao, Elena Vaida, and Stefano Vaida, 80th Cong., H.R. 4403, Priv. L. No. 254, 62 Stat. 1338 (1948)-QMDE

Van der Tuin, Mr. and Mrs. Hendrik, 83rd Cong., S. 2065, Priv. L. No. 603, 68 Stat. A142 (1954)-QMOC

Van Der Velde, Mrs. Tjitske Bandstra, 82nd Cong., H.R. 627, Priv. L. No. 241, 65 Stat. A92 (1951)-WHEL

Van Keer, Petrus, 83rd Cong., H.R. 4522, Priv. L. No. 816, 68 Stat. A211 (1954)-WHEL

Vandenbergh, Jacob, 83rd Cong., S. 2360, Priv. L. No. 476, 68 Stat. A97 (1954)-WCRF

Varga, Ruben George and Mrs. Ilona Varga, 82nd Cong., H.R. 4250, Priv. L. No. 948, 68 Stat. A187 (1952)-QMOC

Vas, Jose Maria, 100th Cong., H.R. 1191, Priv. L. No. 4, 101 Stat. 1975 (1987)-QPRF

Ver Sluis, Cornelius, 81st Cong., H.R. 7282, Priv. L. No. 902, 64 Stat. A206 (1950)-QMGN

Villegas-Cantu, Guadalupe, 94th Cong., H.R. 1388, Priv. L. No. 2, 89 Stat. 1164 (1975)-NMSC

Vogel, Roland Karl Heinz, 97th Cong., H.R. 783, Priv. L. No. 3, 95 Stat. 1733 (1981)-WCRF

Von Biel, Heinrich, Margarethe Von Biel, and Doris Schumann, 82nd Cong., H.R. 885, Priv. L. No. 777, 66 Stat. A123 (1952)-QMGN

Von Der Porten, Max and wife, Charlotte Von Der Porten, 76th Cong., S. 4085, Pocket veto January 2, 1941, *Congressional Record* 86:14012-VETO

Von Mauchenheim, Egon Karl Freiherr and Margarete Von Mauchenheim, 76th Cong., S. 1384, Veto Message May 29, 1940 (S. Doc. 201, 3rd Sess.)-VETO

Votsitsanos, John Marinis, Nicolaos Elias, Ihoanis or Jean Demetre, and Michael Votsitsanos, 76th Cong., H.R. 5494, Priv. L. No. 108, 53 Stat. 1485 (1939)-QMOC

Vulich, Zora B., 81st Cong., H.R. 4306, Priv. L. No. 310, 63 Stat. 1194 (1949)-QIRW

Walker, Jack Ralph, 89th Cong., H.R. 5231, Priv. L. No. 226, 80 Stat. 1619 (1966)-QMGN

Waltl, Rupert, 84th Cong., H.R. 10088, Priv. L. No. 824, 70 Stat. A155 (1956)-NRES

Washington, George, 81st Cong., H.R. 1503, Priv. L. No. 1038, 64 Stat. A255 (1950)-WCRF

Waterton, Peter J., 86th Cong., S. 2177, Priv. L. No. 321, 74 Stat. A36 (1960)-WHEL

Weed, George Tilson, 91st Cong., H.R. 5136, Priv. L. No. 20, 83 Stat. 873 (1969)-NRES

Wegener, James F., 91st Cong., H.R. 1828, Priv. L. No. 22, 83 Stat. 874 (1969)-NXPS

Wei, Chung Ching, 86th Cong., S. 1915, Priv. L. No. 145, 73 Stat. A63 (1959)-NRES

Weitlanner, Carl, 82nd Cong., H.R. 2505, Priv. L. No. 423, 66 Stat. A7 (1952)-NRES

Wendt, Michael Joseph, 93rd Cong., H.R. 1377, Priv. L. No. 13, 87 Stat. 1101 (1973)-QIRA

West, William John, 92nd Cong., S. 2575, Priv. L. No. 129, 86 Stat. 1554 (1972)-QIRM

Whang, Rev. Andrew Chai Kyung, 81st Cong., H.R. 8759, Priv. L. No. 1094, 64 Stat. A276 (1951)-QIER

Whang, Shin Sook (Renee), 88th Cong., H.R. 2287, Priv. L. No. 56, 77 Stat. 892 (1963)-QIRA

White, Erna, 83rd Cong., H.R. 6998, Priv. L. No. 544, 68 Stat. A123 (1954)-WCRF

White, Henry, 78th Cong., H.R. 2707, Priv. L. No. 380, 58 Stat. 1024 (1944)-QIER

White, Dr. John Campbell, 25th Cong., 6 Stat. 750 (1839)-NMSC

Widmer, August, 85th Cong., H.R. 7729, Priv. L. No. 507, 72 Stat. A72 (1958)-WHEL

Wiernik, Mrs. Suzanne and her daughter, Genevieve, 82nd Cong., S. 364, Priv. L. No. 93, 65 Stat. A37 (1951)-QMDP

Wilding, Michael, 100th Cong., S. 1919, Priv. L. 36, 102 Stat. 4859 (1988)-WCRF

Wilkinson, Mary Louise Shields, 85th Cong., S. 2935, Priv. L. No. 631, 72 Stat. A131 (1958)-NCOD

Willrich, Jean Willhelm, 98th Cong., S. 2729, Priv. L. No. 15, 98 Stat. 3420 (1984)-NRES

Wilson, Gloria, 82nd Cong., S. 420, Priv. L. No. 639, 66 Stat. A75 (1952)-NVOL

Wilson, Setsuko (nee Hiranaka), 90th Cong., S. 534, Priv. L. No. 93, 81 Stat. 1016 (1967)-WCRF

Winer, Mrs. Sun Pok, 95th Cong., H.R. 1396, Priv. L. No. 63, 92 Stat. 3818 (1978)-WCRF

Winn, Elizabeth Pickering, 80th Cong., S. 83, Priv. L. No. 419, 62 Stat. 1403 (1948)-NRTN

Winzelberg, Max Mayer Hirsch, and Mrs. Jenty Fuss De Winzelberg, 82nd Cong., H.R.648, Priv. L. No. 528, 66 Stat. A40 (1952)-QMDP

Wolde, Pieter Cornelis Ten and family, 81st Cong., H.R. 714, Priv. L. No. 597, 64 Stat. A94 (1950)-QMOC

Won, Virgil (also known as Virgilio Jackson), 84th Cong., H.R. 3075, Priv. L. No. 200, 69 Stat. A69 (1955)-QMDE

Wong, Janet and Daisy, 82nd Cong., H.R. 901, Priv. L. No. 302, 65 Stat. A123 (1951)-QIER

Woo, Mrs. Tui Hing Tow, 87th Cong., H.R. 2156, Priv. L. No. 107, 75 Stat. 886 (1961)-NXEN

Woods, Mr. and Mrs. Carl Skogen, 86th Cong., S. 1684, Priv. L. No. 102, 73 Stat. A48 (1959)-NRTN

Yanez, Ardes Albacete, 84th Cong., H.R. 1525, Priv. L. No. 197, 69 Stat. A68 (1955)-WXDD

Yannopoulos, Konstantinos, 81st Cong., H.R. 4042, Priv. L. No. 346, 63 Stat. 1209 (1949)-QMOC

Yassine, Afaf Yassine and her children, Najla Yassine, Walid Yassine, Mona Yassine, and Maher Yassine, 94th Cong., H.R. 10793, Priv. L. No. 115, 90 Stat. 3001 (1976)-QPRF

Yasuda, Mrs. Emi and her minor son, Keichiro Yasuda, 82nd Cong., H.R. 3280, Priv. L. No. 937, 66 Stat. A184 (1952)-NCOD

Yee, Yee Balche, 81st Cong., H.R. 8289, Priv. L. No. 757, 64 Stat. A150 (1950)-QIRM

Yi, Oh Soon, 95th Cong., H.R. 1552, Priv. L. No. 95-37, 92 Stat. 3806 (1978)-QIRA

Ying, Lum, 82nd Cong., H.R. 1157, Priv. L. No. 169, 65 Stat. A65 (1951)-NMSC

Yoo, Hee Kyung, 95th Cong., H.R. 4246, Priv. L. No. 5, 91 Stat. 1648 (1977)-QIRA

Yoon, Kim Joong, 84th Cong., H.R. 2242, Priv. L. No. 307, 69 Stat. A106 (1955)-QMGN

Young, Jan Yee, 82nd Cong., H.R. 3254, Priv. L. No. 599, 66 Stat. A62 (1952)-QIER

Yu, Ai Mei and Ai Mei Chen, 82nd Cong., S. 471, Priv. L. No. 427, 66 Stat. A9 (1952)-QIRA

Yu, Frederick T.C. and his wife, Alice Siao-Fen Chen Yu, 86th Cong., S. 2768, Priv. L. No. 365, 74 Stat. A53 (1960)-NRES

Zafiriadis, Tomas J., 82nd Cong., H.R. 616, Priv. L. No. 99, 65 Stat. A39 (1951)-QPRF

Zaicek, Antal or Anthony or Tony Zaicek or Zaiczek, 76th Cong., H.R. 6056, Priv. L. No. 510, 54 Stat. 1341 (1940)-QMGN

Ziegler, Senta, 82nd Cong., H.R. 1968, Priv. L. No. 592, 66 Stat. A60 (1952)-WHEL

Appendix D3

Categorical Index

QUOTA

Immediate relative - Adoption (QIRA)

80th Cong., H.R. 553, Priv. L. No. 70, 61 Stat. 993 (1947), for the relief of Arsenio Acacio Lewis

81st Cong., H.R. 3127, Priv. L. No. 175, 63 Stat. 1143 (1949), for the relief of Jacob Gross

81st Cong., H.R. 5354, Priv. L. No. 350, 63 Stat. 1211 (1949), for the relief of Itzchak Shafer

81st Cong., H.R. 6283, Priv. L. No. 434, 64 Stat. A35 (1950), for the relief of Johny Nielsen

81st Cong., H.R. 6747, Priv. L. No. 585, 64 Stat. A90 (1950), for the relief of Helga Holleb

81st Cong., S. 2047, Priv. L. No. 947, 64 Stat. A220 (1950), for the relief of Marie C. Araujo, also known as Marie Conceipaco de Brito

82nd Cong., H.R. 880, Priv. L. No. 996, 66 Stat. A202 (1952), for the relief of Giuseppe Biolzi

82nd Cong., H.R. 898, Priv. L. No. 37, 65 Stat. A16 (1951), for the relief of Gunter Arno Thelemann

82nd Cong., S. 118, Priv. L. No. 376, 65 Stat. A139 (1951), for the relief of Nouhad Ann Khoury

82nd Cong., S. 440, Priv. L. No. 457, 66 Stat. A17 (1952), for the relief of Evangelos and Michael Dumas

82nd Cong., S. 471, Priv. L. No. 427, 66 Stat. A9 (1952), for the relief of Ai Mei Yu and Ai Mei Chen

82nd Cong., S. 2231, Priv. L. No. 330, 65 Stat. A123 (1951), for the relief of Tina Bentsen

83rd Cong., H.R. 1768, Priv. L. No. 677, 68 Stat. A166 (1954), for the relief of Claire Louise Carey and Vincent F. Carey

83rd Cong., S. 315, Priv. L. No. 83, 67 Stat. A31 (1953), for the relief of Owen Lowery

83rd Cong., S. 2504, Priv. L. No. 650, 68 Stat. A158 (1954), for the relief of Elisa Albertina Cioccio Rigazzi or Elisa Cioccio

83rd Cong., S. 3145, Priv. L. No. 986, 68 Stat. A285 (1954), for the relief of Bonita Lee Simpson

84th Cong., H.R. 995, Priv. L. No. 153, 69 Stat. A53 (1955), for the relief of Frieda Quirling and Tina Quirling

84th Cong., H.R. 2339, Priv. L. No. 449, 69 Stat. A153 (1955), for the relief of Monika Schefbanker

86th Cong., S. 1557, Priv. L. No. 142, 73 Stat. A62 (1959), for the relief of Allen Howard Pilgrim, Cheryl Ann Pilgrim, Robb Alexander Pilgrim, and Jocelyn Mari Pilgrim

87th Cong., S. 546, Priv. L. No. 35, 75 Stat. 862 (1961), for the relief of In Fil Chung, In Ae Chung, In Sook Chung, and In Ja Chung

87th Cong., S. 2011, Priv. L. No. 417, 76 Stat. 1311 (1962), for the relief of Antonia Longfield-Smith

88th Cong., H.R. 2287, Priv. L. No. 56, 77 Stat. 892 (1963), for the relief of Shin Sook (Renee) Whang

88th Cong., H.R. 7347, Priv. L. No. 195, 78 Stat. 1132 (1964), for the relief of Teresa Ellipoulos and Anastasia Ellipoulos

89th Cong., H.R. 6235, Priv. L. No. 144, 79 Stat. 1389 (1965), for the relief of Chun Soo Kim

89th Cong., S. 2451, Priv. L. No. 455, 80 Stat. 1708 (1966), for the relief of Che Yim Loh

89th Cong., S. 2555, Priv. L. No. 337, 80 Stat. 1662 (1966), for the relief of Kim Kin Soon

90th Cong., S. 866, Priv. L. No. 204, 81 Stat. 1050 (1968), for the relief of Giuseppe Pacino Biancarosso

90th Cong., S. 1458, Priv. L. No. 121, 81 Stat. 1026 (1967), for the relief of Lee Duk Hee

90th Cong., S. 2706, Priv. L. No. 339, 82 Stat. 1428 (1968), for the relief of Yung Ran Kim

91st Cong., S. 2976, Priv. L. No. 162, 84 Stat. 2132 (1970), for the relief of Margarita Anne Marie Baden (Nguyen Tan Nga)

92nd Cong., S. 672, Priv. L. No. 14, 85 Stat. 838 (1971), for the relief of Nicholas Demitrios Apostolakis

93rd Cong., H.R. 1366, Priv. L. No. 12, 87 Stat. 1101 (1973), for the relief of Juan Marcos Cordova-Campos

93rd Cong., H.R. 1377, Priv. L. No. 13, 87 Stat. 1101 (1973), for the relief of Michael Joseph Wendt

94th Cong., H.R. 1394, Priv. L. No. 60, 90 Stat. 2980 (1976), for the relief of Suk Chin and Hae Suk Chin

94th Cong., H.R. 1395, Priv. L. No. 61, 90 Stat. 2980 (1976), for the relief of Mee Kyung Cho and Hee Kyung Cho

94th Cong., H.R. 1396, Priv. L. No. 62, 90 Stat. 2980 (1976), for the relief of Sang Kook Chung and Hwa Soon Chung

94th Cong., H.R. 2565, Priv. L. No. 73, 90 Stat. 2984 (1976), for the relief of Luisa Marillac Hughes, Marco Antonio Hughes, Maria del Cisne Hughes, Maria Augusta Hughes, Miguel Vicente Hughes, Veronica del Rocio Hughes, and Ivan Hughes

94th Cong., S. 447, Priv. L. No. 24, 89 Stat. 1186 (1975), for the relief of Jesus Cortez Pineda

95th Cong., H.R. 1552, Priv. L. No. 95-37, 92 Stat. 3806 (1978), for the relief of Oh Soon Yi

95th Cong., H.R. 1939, Priv. L. No. 32, 92 Stat. 3804 (1978), for the relief of Meda Abilay Florin
95th Cong., H.R. 2756, Priv. L. No. 94, 92 Stat. 3832 (1978), for the relief of Marlene Holder
95th Cong., H.R. 4246, Priv. L. No. 5, 91 Stat. 1648 (1977), for the relief of Hee Kyung Yoo
96th Cong., H.R. 2145, Priv. L. No. 103, 94 Stat. 3629 (1980), for the relief of Florette Ivoree Gayle and Keisha Dajaran Karr
96th Cong., H.R. 2433, Priv. L. No. 92, 94 Stat. 3625 (1980), for the relief of Zora Singh Sunga
96th Cong., H.R. 3138, Priv. L. No. 95, 94 Stat. 3626 (1980), for the relief of Surip Karmowiredjo
96th Cong., S. 215, Priv. L. No. 60, 94 Stat. 3598 (1980), for the relief of Renuka Pavla
96th Cong., S. 1772, Priv. L. No. 99, 94 Stat. 3628 (1980), for the relief of Min-Zen Lin
97th Cong., H.R. 684, Priv. L. No. 34, 96 Stat. 2627 (1982), for the relief of Ok-Boon Kang
97th Cong., H.R. 1681, Priv. L. No. 17, 96 Stat. 2619 (1982), for the relief of Andre Bartholo Eubanks
97th Cong., H.R. 1785, Priv. L. No. 7, 95 Stat. 1735 (1981), for the relief of Gladys Belleville Schultz
97th Cong., H.R. 1826, Priv. L. No. 36, 96 Stat. 2627 (1982), for the relief of Shinji Oniki
99th Cong., H.R. 483, Priv. L. No. 5, 100 Stat. 4314, (1986), for the relief of Edwin Marcos Rios and Geovanna Rios

Immediate Relative - Miscellaneous (QIRM)

81st Cong., H.R. 7815, Priv. L. No. 708,64 Stat. A133 (1950), for the relief of John Yee Horn
81st Cong., H.R. 8289, Priv. L. No. 757, 64 Stat. A150 (1950), for the relief of Yee Balche Yee
82nd Cong., S. 2770, Priv. L. No. 658, 66 Stat. A82 (1952), for the relief of Matheos Alafouzos
83rd Cong., S. 1955, Priv. L. No. 475, 68 Stat. A97 (1954), for the relief of Giorgio Salvini Thompson
84th Cong., H.R. 1160, Priv. L. No. 330, 69 Stat. A113 (1955), for the relief of Vittorio Capano
84th Cong., H.R. 1552, Priv. L. No. 418, 69 Stat. A143 (1955), for the relief of Dalisay Lourdes Cruz
85th Cong., S. 1833, Priv. L. No. 105, 71 Stat. A42 (1957), for the erelief of Janos Schreiner
86th Cong., H.R. 4834, Priv. L. No. 337, 74 Stat. A42 (1960), for the relief of Giuseppe Antonio Turchi
87th Cong., H.R. 4028, Priv. L. No. 251, 75 Stat. 941 (1961), for the relief of Lennon May

90th Cong., S. 168, Priv. L. No. 42, 81 Stat. 999 (1967), for the relief of Maria Jordan Ferrando

92nd Cong., S. 2575, Priv. L. No. 129, 86 Stat. 1554 (1972), for the relief of William John West

95th Cong., H.R. 2291, Priv. L. No. 162, 92 Stat. 3859 (1978), for the relief of Carmen Cecilia Blanquicett

95th Cong., H.R. 3461, Priv. L. No. 17, 91 Stat. 1655 (1977), for the relief of Chin-Ho An

97th Cong., H.R. 1469, Priv. L. No. 4, 95 Stat. 1734 (1981), for the relief of Madeleine Mesnager

Immediate Relative - Widows of U.S. Citizens (QIRW)

80th Cong., S. 1451, Priv. L. No. 317, 62 Stat. 1360 (1948), for the relief of Perfecto M. Biason and Joan Biason

81st Cong., H.R. 679, Priv. L. No. 63, 63 Stat. 1098 (1949), for the relief of Mrs. Julia Balint

81st Cong., H.R. 4306, Priv. L. No. 310, 63 Stat. 1194 (1949), for the relief of Zora B. Vulich

81st Cong., S. 609, Priv. L. No. 403, 64 Stat. A23 (1950), for the relief of Mrs. Bertie Grace Chan Leong

81st Cong., S. 2556, Priv. L. No. 635, 64 Stat. A107 (1950), for the relief of Mrs. Billy J. Knight and Dorothea Knight

83rd Cong., H.R. 711, Priv. L. No. 272, 68 Stat. A17 (1954), for the relief of Mrs. Ruth R. Ekholm

83rd Cong., S. 205, Priv. L. No. 250, 68 Stat. A10 (1954), for the relief of Evdoxia J. Kitsos

84th Cong., H.R. 1081, Priv. L. No. 107, 69 Stat. A37 (1955), for the relief of Anna Tokatlian Gulezian

84th Cong., H.R. 2916, Priv. L. No. 483, 69 Stat. A164 (1955), for the relief of Mrs. Elfrieda Schoeppe

85th Cong., S. 1175, Priv. L. No. 317, 71 Stat. A125 (1957), for the relief of Helene Cordery Hall

87th Cong., S. 400, Priv. L. No. 73, 75 Stat. 874 (1961), for the relief of Mrs. Keum Ja Asato (Mrs. Thomas R. Asato)

89th Cong., H.R. 1393, Priv. L. No. 178, 79 Stat. 1403 (1965), for the relief of Mrs. Maria Eduvigis Aran Heffernan

91st Cong., H.R. 1939, Priv. L. No. 17, 83 Stat. 872 (1969), for the relief of Mrs. Marjorie J. Hottenroth

91st Cong., S. 3620, Priv. L. No. 190, 84 Stat. 2151 (1970), for the relief of Mrs. Anastasia Pertsovitch

92nd Cong., H.R. 1974, Priv. L. No. 90, 86 Stat. 1538 (1972), for the relief of Mrs. Gloria Vazquez Herrara

97th Cong., H.R. 2185, Priv. L. No. 9, 95 Stat. 1736 (1981), for the relief of Hanife Frantz

99th Cong., S. 381, Priv. L. No. 1, 100 Stat. 4313 (1986), for the relief of Mishleen Earle

100th Cong., H.R. 2109, Priv. L. No. 38, 102 Stat. 4861 (1988), for the relief of Rosa Pratts

100th Cong., S. 2637, Priv. L. No. 35, 102 Stat. 4859 (1988), for the relief of Gillian Lesley Sackler

Ineligible Due to Race (QIER)

77th Cong., H.R. 6677, Priv. L. No. 617, 56 Stat. 1252 (1942), for the relief of Ronald Leroy Chen

78th Cong., H.R. 2707, Priv. L. No. 380, 58 Stat. 1024 (1944), for the relief of Henry White

80th Cong., H.R. 1215, Priv. L. No. 225, 62 Stat. 1328 (1948), for the relief of Kazue Oda Takahashi

80th Cong., S. 84, Priv. L. No. 144, 62 Stat. 1300 (1948), for the relief of Mrs. Clinton R. Sharp

80th Cong., S. 1409, Priv. L. No. 400, 62 Stat. 1395 (1948), for the relief of Markoto Iwamatsu, Atsushi Jun Iwamatsu, and Tomoe Iwamatsu

81st Cong., H.R. 2084, Priv. L. No. 194, 63 Stat. 1150 (1949), for the relief of Teiko Horikawa and Yoshiko Horikawa

81st Cong., H.R. 6386, Priv. L. No. 898, 64 Stat. A204 (1950), for the relief of Amos Chen

81st Cong., H.R. 8759, Priv. L. No. 1094, 64 Stat. A276 (1951), for the relief of Rev. Andrew Chai Kyung Whang

81st Cong., H.R. 9082, Priv. L. No. 1028, 64 Stat. A251 (1950), for the relief of Mrs. Chang-Sei Kim, David Kim, and Arthur Kim

82nd Cong., H.R. 711, Priv. L. No. 289, 65 Stat. A109 (1951), for the relief of George Lukes

82nd Cong., H.R. 978, Priv. L. No. 562, 66 Stat. A52 (1952), for the relief of Mrs. Michi Masaoka

82nd Cong., H.R. 901, Priv. L. No. 302, 65 Stat. A123 (1951), for the relief of Janet and Daisy Wong

82nd Cong., H.R. 1158, Priv. L. No. 563, 66 Stat. A52 (1952), for the relief of Isao Ishimoto

82nd Cong., H.R. 1162, Priv. L. No. 676, 66 Stat. A88 (1952), for the relief of Kaiko Sugimote (Kay Fair) and her minor children

82nd Cong., H.R. 1236, Priv. L. No. 360, 65 Stat. A133 (1951), for the relief of Rhoda Akiko Nishiyama

82nd Cong., H.R. 1818, Priv. L. No. 307, 65 Stat. A114 (1951), for the relief of Hego Fuchino

82nd Cong., H.R. 2906, Priv. L. No. 934, 66 Stat. A183 (1952), for the relief of Kenji Kusumoto

82nd Cong., H.R. 3271, Priv. L. No. 588, 66 Stat. A59 (1952), for the relief of Toshiaki Shimada

82nd Cong., H.R. 3280, Priv. L. No. 937, 66 Stat. A184 (1952), for the relief of Mrs. Emi Yasuda and her minor son, Keichiro Yasuda

82nd Cong., H.R. 3524, Priv. L. No. 599, 66 Stat. A62 (1952), for the relief of Jan Yee Young

82nd Cong., H.R. 4788, Priv. L. No. 605, 66 Stat. A64 (1952), for the relief of Yoko Takeuchi

82nd Cong., H.R. 5347, Priv. L. No. 516, 66 Stat. A36 (1952), for the relief of Fusako Terao Scogin

82nd Cong., H.R. 7095, Priv. L. No. 986, 66 Stat. A198 (1952), for the relief of Ruth Ann Holecek

85th Cong., S. 1290, Priv. L. No. 271, 71 Stat. A106 (1957, for the relief of Lee-Ana Roberts

Miscellaneous - Displaced Persons Act of 1948 (QMDP)

81st Cong., H.R. 9144, Priv. L. No. 1042, 64 Stat. A256 (1950), for the relief of Mrs. Olga Kowalik and Czeslawa Kowalik

82nd Cong., H.R. 648, Priv. L. No. 528, 66 Stat. A40 (1952), for the relief of Max Mayer Hirsch De Winzelberg and Mrs. Jenty Fuss De Winzelberg

82nd Cong., H.R. 853, Priv. L. No. 399, 65 Stat. A146 (1951), for the relief of Maximilian Otto Ricker-Huetter and Mrs. Eugenia Ricker-Huetter

82nd Cong., H.R. 961, Priv. L. No. 420, 66 Stat. A6 (1952), for the relief of Zbigniew Jan Dunikowski, Karolina Dunikowski, Wanda Octavia Dunikowski, and Janina Grospera Dunikowski

82nd Cong., H.R. 1252, Priv. L. No. 342, 65 Stat. A127 (1951), for the relief of Mr. and Mrs. Miroslav Kudrat

82nd Cong., H.R. 1598, Priv. L. No. 321, 65 Stat. A120 (1951), for the relief of Hanoh Sarapanovschi (also known as Hanoh Charat), Gizela (Gisele) Sarapanovschi (nee Levy), and Philippe Sarapanovschi

82nd Cong., H.R. 2307, Priv. L. No. 25, 66 Stat. A95 (1951), for the relief of Jean (John) Plewniak and Anna Piotrowska Plewniak

82nd Cong., H.R. 2310, Priv. L. No. 124, 65 Stat. A47 (1951), for the relief of Jindrich (Henri) Nosek and Mrs. Zdenka Nosek

82nd Cong., H.R. 2498, Priv. L. No. 310, 65 Stat. A116 (1951), for the relief of Marianne and Michel Speelman

82nd Cong., S. 178, Priv. L. No. 95, 65 Stat. A37 (1951), for the relief of Zdenek Marek

82nd Cong., S. 364, Priv. L. No. 93, 65 Stat. A37 (1951), for the relief of Mrs. Suzanne Wiernik and her daughter, Genevieve

82nd Cong., S. 1469, Priv. L. No. 550, 66 Stat. A47 (1952), for the relief of Julie Bettelheim and Evelyn Lang Hirsch

Miscellaneous - Due to Deeds (QMDE)

80th Cong., H.R. 4047, Priv. L. No. 393, 62 Stat. 1392 (1948), for the relief of Edmund Huppler

80th Cong., H.R. 4050, Priv. L. No. 312, 62 Stat. 1359 (1948), for the relief of Moke Tcharoutcheff, Lucie Baptistine Tcharoutcheff, Raymond Tcharoutcheff, and Robert Tcharoutcheff

80th Cong., H.R. 4403, Priv. L. No. 254, 62 Stat. 1338 (1948), for the relief of Ladislao Vaida, Elena Vaida, and Stefano Vaida

80th Cong., S. 2060, Priv. L. No. 342, 62 Stat. 1370 (1948), for the relief of Edgar Wikner Percival

81st Cong., H.R. 1487, Priv. L. No. 439, 64 Stat. A37 (1950), for the relief of Lt. (SG) Giacomo Falco

81st Cong., H.R. 1991, Priv. L. No. 795, 64 Stat. A163 (1950), for the relief of Alexander Stewart

81st Cong., H.R. 2349, Priv. L. No. 170, 63 Stat. 1141 (1949), for the relief of Col. Wlodzimierz Onacewicz

81st Cong., H.R. 6006, Priv. L. No. 282, 63 Stat. 1183 (1949), for the relief of Anthony Charles Bartley

81st Cong., H.R. 6758, Priv. L. No. 789, 64 Stat. A161 (1950), for the relief of Ruby Thaw and Hla Sein

81st Cong., S. 315, Priv. L. No. 3, 63 Stat. 1073 (1949), for the relief of Dr. Chung Kwai Lui

81st Cong., S. 1405, Priv. L. No. 178, 63 Stat. 1144 (1949), for the relief of Poon Lim

81st Cong., S. 1869, Priv. L. No. 650, 64 Stat. A112 (1950), for the relief of Marcantonio Doria D'Angri and his wife, Sonia Stampa Doria D'Angri

82nd Cong., H.R. 622, Priv. L. No. 30, 65 Stat. A14 (1951), for the relief of Mrs. Oksana Stepanovna Kasenkina

82nd Cong., H.R. 2719, Priv. L. No. 745, 66 Stat. A112 (1952), for the relief of Philip Fugh, Sarah Liu Fugh, John Fugh

82nd Cong., S. 1470, Priv. L. No. 859, 66 Stat. A159 (1952), for the relief of Panagiotes Roumeliotis

82nd Cong., S. 2145, Priv. L. No. 655, 66 Stat. A80 (1952), for the relief of Certain Displaced Persons

83rd Cong., H.R. 1756, Priv. L. No. 185, 67 Stat. A65 (1953), for the relief of Eugene de Thassy

83rd Cong., H.R. 2604, Priv. L. No. 168, 67 Stat. A60 (1953), for the relief of Lauri Allan Torni

83rd Cong., H.R. 6650, Priv. L. No. 543, 68 Stat. A123 (1954), for the relief of Joseph Cerny

83rd Cong., H.R. 8334, Priv. L. No. 716, 68 Stat. A179 (1954), for the relief of Helmut Cermak and Hana Cermak

83rd Cong., S. 629, Priv. L. No. 456, 68 Stat. A91 (1954), for the relief of Igor Michael Bogolepov (alias Ivar Nyman) and Margaret Johanna Bogolepov (alias Margaret Johanna Nyman)

83rd Cong., S. 676, Priv. L. No. 530, 68 Stat. A119 (1954), for the relief of Eftychios Mourginakis

83rd Cong., S. 855, Priv. L. No. 591, 68 Stat. A138 (1954), for the relief of Kirill Mihailovich Alexeev, Antonina Ivanovna Alexeev, and minor children, Victoria and Vladimir Alexeev

83rd Cong., S. 1212, Priv. L. No. 621, 68 Stat. A148 (1954), for the relief of Alice Masaryk

84th Cong., H.R. 1193, Priv. L. No. 512, 70 Stat. A10 (1956), for the relief of Dr. and Mrs. Ivan Pernar

84th Cong., H.R. 3075, Priv. L. No. 200, 69 Stat. A69 (1955), for the relief of Virgil Won (also known as Virgilio Jackson)

84th Cong., S. 2088, Priv. L. No. 446, 69 Stat. A152 (1955), for the relief of Ladislav Mencl

85th Cong., S. 530, Priv. L. No. 84, 71 Stat. A36 (1957), for the relief of Shun Wen Lung (also known as Van Long and Van S. Lung)

85th Cong., S. 1578, Priv. L. No. 394, 72 Stat. A27 (1958), for the relief of Hovhannes H. Haidostian

85th Cong., S. 2095, Priv. L. No. 282, 71 Stat. A109 (1957), for the relief of Vaclav Uhlik, Marta Uhlik, Vaclav Uhlik, Jr. and Eva Uhlik

96th Cong., H.R. 1619, Priv. L. No. 42, 93 Stat. 1406 (1979), for the relief of Rolando R. Gaza, Teresita C. Gaza, and Rolynne Therese Gaza

98th Cong., H.R. 1150, Priv. L. No. 27, 98 Stat. 3426 (1984), for the relief of Teodoro N. Salanga, Jr.

Miscellaneous - General (QMGN)

75th Cong., H.R. 9731, Priv. L. No. 803, 52 Stat. 1432 (1938), for the relief of James J. Coyne

76th Cong., H.R. 2948, Priv. L. No. 329, 54 Stat. 1267 (1940), for the relief of Morris Hoppenheim, Lena Hoppenheim, Doris Hoppenheim, and Ruth Hoppenheim

76th Cong., H.R. 6056, Priv. L. No. 510, 54 Stat. 1341 (1940), for the relief of Antal or Anthony or Tony Zaicek or Zaiczek

80th Cong., H.R. 892, Priv. L. No. 330, 62 Stat. 1365 (1948), for the relief of Michel Ferapontow

80th Cong., H.R. 1912, Priv. L. No. 241, 62 Stat. 1334 (1948), for the relief of John A. Dilboy

80th Cong., H.R. 3243, Priv. L. No. 90, 61 Stat. 1000 (1947), for the relief of Roman Toporow

80th Cong., H.R. 3880, Priv. L. No. 296, 62 Stat. 1354 (1948), for the relief of Ludwig Pohoryles

80th Cong., S. 329, Priv. L. No. 260, 62 Stat. 1340 (1948), for the relief of Gentaro Takahashi

80th Cong., S. 1142, Priv. L. No. 290, 62 Stat. 1352 (1948), for the relief of Anna Pechnik

81st Cong., H.R. 1010, Priv. L. No. 56, 63 Stat. 1096 (1949), for the relief of Mrs. May K. Y. Mok, Frederick W. S. Mok, and Vincent W. C. Mok

81st Cong., H.R. 2360, Priv. L. No. 64, 63 Stat. 1098 (1949), for the relief of Theodore Papachristopoulos

81st Cong., H.R. 3018, Priv. L. No. 577, 64 Stat. A87 (1950), for the relief of Camilla Fabris

81st Cong., H.R. 3330, Priv. L. No. 776, 64 Stat. A157 (1950), for the relief of Therese Hohman

81st Cong., H.R. 3771, Priv. L. No. 442, 64 Stat. A38 (1950), for the relief of Mrs. Marie Gulbenkian

81st Cong., H.R. 3921, Priv. L. No. 894, 64 Stat. A203 (1950), for the relief of Nicholas C. Hadjipateras, Pipitsa N. Hadjipateras, and Costas N. Hadjipateras

81st Cong., H.R. 6106, Priv. L. No. 977, 64 Stat. A232 (1950), for the relief of Daniel Kokal

81st Cong., H.R. 7282, Priv. L. No. 902, 64 Stat. A206 (1950), for the relief of Cornelius Ver Sluis

81st Cong., S. 918, Priv. L. No. 847, 64 Stat. A184 (1950), for the relief of Clara Sogor

81st Cong., S. 1026, Priv. L. No. 245, 63 Stat. 1169 (1949), for the relief of Roman Szymanski and Anastosia Szymanski

81st Cong., S. 1637, Priv. L. No. 619, 64 Stat. A102 (1950), for the relief of Marie Henriette de Bruyn

81st Cong., S. 2682, Priv. L. No. 653, 64 Stat. A113 (1950), for the relief of Naum Ionescu and his wife

81st Cong., S.J. Res. 105, Priv. L. No. 357, 64 Stat. A4 (1950), for the relief of Sister Elizabeth Kenny

82nd Cong., H.R. 884, Priv. L. No. 386, 65 Stat. A142 (1951), for the relief of Johanna A. Stoots

82nd Cong., H.R. 885, Priv. L. No. 777, 66 Stat. A123 (1952), for the relief of Heinrich Von Biel, Margarethe Von Biel, and Doris Schumann

82nd Cong., S. 291, Priv. L. No. 81, 65 Stat. A32 (1951), for the relief of Claudio Pier Connelly

82nd Cong., S. 1420, Priv. L. No. 647, 66 Stat. A77 (1952), for the relief of Pinfang Hsia

82nd Cong., S. 2566, Priv. L. No. 737, 66 Stat. A109 (1952), for the relief of Niccolo Luvisotti

83rd Cong., H.R. 765, Priv. L. No. 110, 67 Stat. A40 (1953), for the relief of Tien Koo Chen

83rd Cong., H.R. 804, Priv. L. No. 728, 68 Stat. A183 (1954), for the relief of Enrichetta F. C. Meda-Novara

83rd Cong., H.R. 944, Priv. L. No. 537, 68 Stat. A121 (1954), for the relief of Mr. and Mrs. Zygmunt Sowinski

83rd Cong., H.R. 962, Priv. L. No. 330, 68 Stat. A38 (1954), for the relief of Gabrielle Marie Smith (nee Staub)

83rd Cong., H.R. 1688, Priv. L. No. 297, 68 Stat. A26 (1954), for the relief of Henry Ty

83rd Cong., H.R. 1695, Priv. L. No. 166, 67 Stat. A59 (1953), for the relief of Irtene Proios (nee Vagianos)

83rd Cong., H.R. 1886, Priv. L. No. 116, 67 Stat. A42 (1953), for the relief of Paul Myung Ha Chung

83rd Cong., H.R. 3874, Priv. L. No. 810, 68 Stat. A209 (1954), for the relief of Roberto Johnson

83rd Cong., H.R. 5085, Priv. L. No. 329, 68 Stat. A38 (1954), for the relief of Mrs. Marie Tcherepnin

83rd Cong., H.R. 7151, Priv. L. No. 835, 68 Stat. A217 (1954), for the relief of Mazal Kolman

83rd Cong., S. 196, Priv. L. No. 125, 67 Stat. A45 (1953), for the relief of Alejandro de La Cruz Hernandez

83rd Cong., S. 233, Priv. L. No. 608, 68 Stat. A144 (1954), for the relief of Jeno Cseplo

83rd Cong., S. 506, Priv. L. No. 257, 68 Stat. A12 (1954), for the relief of Horst F.W. Dittmar and Heinz-Erik Dittmar

83rd Cong., S. 569, Priv. L. No. 258, 68 Stat. A13 (1954), for the relief of Lina Anna Adelheid (Adam) Hoyer

83rd Cong., S. 579, Priv. L. No. 529, 68 Stat. A118 (1954), for the relief of Wong You Henn

83rd Cong., S. 795, Priv. L. No. 588, 68 Stat. A137 (1954), for the relief of Josef Radziwill

83rd Cong., S. 1682, Priv. L. No. 473, 68 Stat. A96 (1954), for the relief of Branimir V. Popovitch and Mila B. Popovitch

84th Cong., H.R. 1887, Priv. L. No. 533, 70 Stat. A17 (1956), for the relief of Dr. Tsi Au Li (Tsi Gziou Li)

84th Cong., H.R. 2242, Priv. L. No. 307, 69 Stat. A106 (1955), for the relief of Kim Joong Yoon

84th Cong., H.R. 2354, Priv. L. No. 27,69 Stat. A10 (1955), for the relief of Basil Theodossiou

84th Cong., H.R. 2495, Priv. L. No. 272, 69 Stat. A95 (1955), for the relief of Antoni Rajkowski

84th Cong., H.R. 3857, Priv. L. No. 583, 70 Stat. A34 (1956), for the relief of Constantin David, Paula Marie David, Claire Edmonde David, and Ariane Constance David

84th Cong., H.R. 4152, Priv. L. No. 827, 70 Stat. A156 (1956), for the relief of Maria Pintos and her daughter, Eugenia Pintos

84th Cong., H.R. 5870, Priv. L. No. 528, 70 Stat. A15 (1956), for the relief of Jesajahu Braun

85th Cong., H.R. 8348, Priv. L. No. 401, 72 Stat. A30 (1958), for the relief of Michael Romanoff

85th Cong., S. 1519, Priv. L. No. 378, 72 Stat. A20 (1958), for the relief of Isaac Lidji, Henry Isaac Lidji, and Sylvio Isaac Gattegno

85th Cong., S. 3060, Priv. L. No. 513, 72 Stat. A74 (1958), for the relief of Romulo A. Manriquez

86th Cong., H.R. 4242, Priv. L. No. 122, 73 Stat. A55, (1959), for the relief of certain aliens

86th Cong., H.R. 7551, Priv. L. No. 442, 74 Stat. A82 (1960), for the relief of Hubert O. Beckles

87th Cong., S. 899, Priv. L. No. 328, 76 Stat. 1279 (1962), for the relief of Liu Shui Chen

87th Cong., S. 3336, Priv. L. No. 608, 76 Stat. 1381 (1962), for the relief of Lazaro Loyola Arinque, Jr.

88th Cong., H.R. 1182, Priv. L. No. 177, 78 Stat. 1125 (1964), for the relief of Willy Sapuschnin

88th Cong., H.R. 1398, Priv. L. No. 50, 77 Stat. 890 (1963), for the relief of Margaret Barker

88th Cong., H.R. 2444, Priv. L. No. 57, 77 Stat. 892 (1963), for the relief of Mrs. Mabel Constance Kennedy

88th Cong., H.R. 2757, Priv. L. No. 102, 77 Stat. 909 (1963), for the relief of Woo You Lyn (also known as Hom You Fong and Lyn Fong Y. Hom)

89th Cong., H.R. 5231, Priv. L. No. 226, 80 Stat. 1619 (1966), for the relief of Jack Ralph Walker

89th Cong., S. 2010, Priv. L. No. 451, 80 Stat. 1706 (1966), for the relief of Fun Wat Hoy

91st Cong., H.R. 6600, Priv L. No. 69, 83 Stat. 891 (1969), for the relief of Panagiotis, Georgia, and Constantina Malliaras

92nd Cong., H.R. 1899, Priv. L. No. 42, 85 Stat. 850 (1971), for the relief of Mrs. Maria G. Orsini (nee Mari)

92nd Cong., S. 559, Priv. L. No. 115, 86 Stat. 1548 (1972), for the relief of Albina Lucio Z. Manlucu

93rd Cong., H.R. 1367, Priv. L. No. 22, 87 Stat. 1104 (1973), for the relief of Bertha Alicia Sierra

94th Cong., H.R. 1556, Priv. L. No. 3, 89 Stat. 1165 (1975), for the relief of Hendrika Koenders Lyne

94th Cong., H.R. 4583, Priv. L. No. 111, 90 Stat. 2999 (1976), for the relief of Rosina C. Beltran

95th Cong., H.R. 2256, Priv. L. No. 131, 92 Stat. 3846 (1978), for the relief of Edmundo Alfredo Oreiro Espinueva

96th Cong., H.R. 1829, Priv. L. No. 50, 94 Stat. 3593 (1980), for the relief of Loraine Smart and Robert Clarke

96th Cong., S. 707, Priv. L. No. 63, 94 Stat. 3599 (1980), for the relief of Certain Aliens

97th Cong., S. 167, Priv. L. No. 26, 96 Stat. 2623 (1982), for the relief of Juan Esteban Ramirez

98th Cong., S. 1060, Priv. L. No. 25, 98 Stat. 3425 (1984), for the relief of Samuel Joseph Edgar

99th Cong., H.R. 737, Priv. L. No. 2, 100 Stat. 4313, for the relief of Ms. Chang Ai Bae

99th Cong., H.R. 3154, Priv. L. No. 9, 100 Stat. 4316 (1986), for the relief of John Patrick Brady, Ann M. Brady, and Mark P. Brady

99th Cong., H.R. 5016, Priv. L. No. 19, 100 Stat. 4321 (1986), for the relief of Sueng Ho Jang and Sueng Il Jang

100th Cong., S. 1842, Priv. L. No. 48, 102 Stat. 4867 (1988), for the relief of Wilhelm Jahn Schlechter, Monica Pino Schlechter, Ingrid Daniela Schlechter, and Arturo David Schlechter

Miscellaneous - Occupations (QMOC)

76th Cong., H.R. 5494, for the relief of John Marinis, Nicolaos Elias, Ihoanis or Jean Demetre Votsitsanos, and Michael Votsitsanos

76th Cong., S. 1291, Priv. L. No. 98, 53 Stat. 1481 (1939), for the relief of William Carl Laude

79th Cong., H.R. 1402, Priv. L. No. 818, 60 Stat. 1292 (1946), for the relief of Certain Basque Aliens

80th Cong., H.R. 1572, Priv. L. No. 350, 62 Stat. 1373 (1948), for the relief of [Certain] Basque aliens

80th Cong., H.R. 3787, Priv. L. No. 308, 62 Stat. 1357 (1948), for the relief of Mrs. Maria Smorczewska

81st Cong., H.R. 714, Priv. L. No. 597, 64 Stat. A94 (1950), for the relief of Pieter Cornelis Ten Wolde and family

81st Cong., H.R. 2591, Priv. L. No. 441, 64 Stat. A38 (1950), for the relief of Giovanna Parisi, Michelina Valleta, Yolanda Altierei, Generosa Tamburi, Carolina Picciano, and Giovana Turtur

81st Cong., H.R. 2921, Priv. L. No. 305, 63 Stat. 1193 (1949), for the relief of Nicholas C. Kalcoutsakis

81st Cong., H.R. 3169, Priv. L. No. 767, 64 Stat. A153 (1950), for the relief of Certain Spanish Physicians residing in Puerto Rico

81st Cong., H.R. 4042, Priv. L. No. 346, 63 Stat. 1209 (1949), for the relief of Konstantinos Yannopoulos

81st Cong., H.R. 4365, Priv. L. No. 976, 64 Stat. A231 (1950), for the relief of Fe'R. Dumaguing

81st Cong., H.R. 4604, Priv. L. No. 821, 64 Stat. A173 (1950), for the relief of certain aliens possessing special skills, namely, Teodor Egle, Karlis Fogelis, Vasily Kils, and Aleksanders Zelmenis

81st Cong., H.R. 5947, Priv. L. No. 779, 64 Stat. A158 (1950), for the relief of Alfio Batelli

81st Cong., H.R. 6804, Priv. L. No. 943, 64 Stat. A218 (1950), for the relief of Certain Italian Aliens

81st Cong., H.R. 7733, Priv. L. No. 981, 64 Stat. A233 (1950), for the relief of Sisters Rita Pinto de Carvalho, Maria Leite Da Silva, Carmelinda Lopes de Aguiar, Maria Adozinda da Fonseca Melo, Joaquine de Jesus, and Maria Luisa Pinto Carvalho

81st Cong., S. 27, Priv. L. No. 13, 63 Stat. 1079 (1949), for the relief of certain Basque aliens

81st Cong., S. 753, Priv. L. No. 363, 64 Stat. A7 (1950), for the relief of Sisters Antoinette Cometti, Mary Gibin, Angela Pelosin, Emma Ghisleni, Elisabetta De Caterin, and Onorina Franzina

81st Cong., S. 1192, Priv. L. No. 1031, 64 Stat. A251 (1950), for the relief of Certain Basque Aliens

81st Cong., S. 1856, Priv. L. No. 489, 64 Stat. A57 (1950), for the relief of Sisters Maria Rita Rossi, Maria Domenica Paone, Rachele Orlando, Assunta Roselli, Rosa Innocenti, and Maria Mancinelli

81st Cong., S. 2107, Priv. L. No. 633, 64 Stat. A106 (1950), for the relief of Georges Gregory Alpiar

81st Cong., S. 2420, Priv. L. No. 1060, 64 Stat. A262 (1950), for the relief of Shaoul Minashi Shami, Emily Shami, Joseph Clement Shami, and Charles Henry Shami

81st Cong., S. 2795, Priv. L. No. 660, 64 Stat. A115 (1950), for the relief of Fortunato Giulio Torre

81st Cong., S. 2897, Priv. L. No. 856, 64 Stat. A188 (1950), for the relief of Hyman D. Langer and Alta Jourard Langer

81st Cong., S. 2981, Priv. L. No. 1097, 64 Stat. A277 (1951), for the relief of Giuseppe Merlinet Forgnone

81st Cong., S. 3125, Priv. L. No. 1098, 64 Stat. A277 (1951), for the relief of Dr. Lutfu Lahut Uzman

81st Cong., S. 3378, Priv. L. No. 1099, 64 Stat. A277 (1951), for the relief of Armando Santini

82nd Cong., H.R. 617, Priv. L. No. 215, 65 Stat. A82 (1951), for the relief of Franz Furtner, Valentina Furtner, Nina Tuerck, and Victoria Tuerck

82nd Cong., H.R. 664, Priv. L. No. 32, 65 Stat. A15 (1951), for the relief of Mrs. Coral E. Alldritt

82nd Cong., H.R. 702, Priv. L. No. 164, 65 Stat. A63 (1951), for the relief of Karl Chimani and Ada Chimani

82nd Cong., H.R. 1100, Priv. L. No. 341, 65 Stat. A127 (1951), for the relief of Eugenio Bellini

82nd Cong., H.R. 1150, Priv. L. No. 63, 65 Stat. A25 (1951), for the relief of Mario Pucci, Giacomo Favetti, Giuseppe Omati, Vincenzo Andreani, Lambruno Sarzanini, and Alessandro Costa

82nd Cong., H.R. 1464, Priv. L. No. 922, 66 Stat. A179 (1952), for the relief of Arokiaswami Arumai Singh

82nd Cong., H.R. 1477, Priv. L. No. 923, 66 Stat. A180 (1952), for the relief of Linda Azar Karam Batrouny

82nd Cong., H.R. 1479, Priv. L. No. 14, 65 Stat. A7 (1951), for the relief of Joseph Bernstein

82nd Cong., H.R. 2299, Priv. L. No. 176, 65 Stat. A67 (1951), for the relief of Biagio Poidimani

82nd Cong., H.R. 3124, Priv. L. No. 684, 66 Stat. A91 (1952), for the relief of Mehmet Salih Topcuoglu

82nd Cong., H.R. 3155, Priv. L. No. 747, 66 Stat. A112 (1952), for the relief of Sebastiano Bello, Dino Bianchi, Pierino Ciccarese, Vincenzo Dall'alda, Vittorio de Gasperi, Salvatore Puggioni, Giovanni Battista Volpato, and Leone Montini

82nd Cong., H.R. 3965, Priv. L. No. 296, 65 Stat. A111 (1951), for the relief of Five Sisters of the Franciscan Missionaries of Mary

82nd Cong., H.R. 4250, Priv. L. No. 948, 66 Stat. A187 (1952), for the relief of Ruben George Varga and Mrs. Ilona Varga

82nd Cong., H.R. 4709, Priv. L. No. 955, 66 Stat. A189 (1952), for the relief of Baron Fred Alexander D'Osten-Sacken

82nd Cong., H.R. 5208, Priv. L. No. 752, 66 Stat. A114 (1952), for the relief of Sor Eufrasia Gomez Gallego, Sor Francisca Gil Martinez, and Sor Rosalia de La Maza

82nd Cong., S. 1541, Priv. L. No. 500, 66 Stat. A31 (1952), for the relief of Dr. Francis S. N. Kwok

82nd Cong., S. 1724, Priv. L. 836, 66 Stat. A150 (1952), for the relief of Elina Branlund

83rd Cong., H.R. 675, Priv. L. No. 404, 68 Stat. A68 (1954), for the relief of Mrs. Romola Nijinsky and Paul Bohus-Vilagosi

83rd Cong., H.R. 974, Priv. L. No. 50, 67 Stat. A19 (1953), for the relief of Dr. Morad Malek-Aslani

83rd Cong., H.R. 1103, Priv. L. No. 62, 67 Stat. A24 (1953), for the relief of Maria Buffoni and Emma Botta

83rd Cong., H.R. 1358, Priv. L. No. 296, 68 Stat. A26 (1954), for the relief of Dr. Marcelino J. Avecilla and Dr. Feodora A. Fidelino-Avecilla

83rd Cong., H.R. 2879, Priv. L. No. 744, 68 Stat. A188 (1954), for the relief of Juan Onativia

83rd Cong., H.R. 3566, Priv. L. No. 807, 68 Stat. A208 (1954), for the relief of Pimen Maximovitch Sofronov

83rd Cong., H.R. 3678, Priv. L. No. 70, 67 Stat. A26 (1953), for the relief of George Prokofieff de Seversky and Isabelle Prokofieff de Seversky

83rd Cong., H.R. 3855, Priv. L. No. 752, 68 Stat. A190 (1954), for the relief of Sister Agrippina (Agrippina Palermo), Sister Battistina (Franceschina Serpa, Sister Romana (Angela Iolanda Morelli), Sister Franceschina (Maria Caruso), and Sister Bruna (Giuseppina de Caro)

83rd Cong., H.R. 4701, Priv. L. No. 487, 68 Stat. A101 (1954), for the relief of Josip Stanic

83rd Cong., S. 69, Priv. L. No. 121, 67 Stat. A44 (1953), for the relief of Dr. Peter C. T. Kao

83rd Cong., S. 278, Priv. L. No. 566, 68 Stat. A130 (1954), for the relief of Szyga (Saul) Morgenstern

83rd Cong., S. 740, Priv. L. No. 457, 68 Stat. A92 (1954), for the relief of Santa Muciaccia (Sister Maria Fridiana), and Teresa Saragaglia (Sister Maria Eutropia), and Caterina Isonni (Sister Maria Giovita)

83rd Cong., S. 1262, Priv. L. No. 89, 67 Stat. A33 (1953), for the relief of Stefanos A. Spilios (also known as Stephen A. Harrison)

83rd Cong., S. 1382, Priv. L. No. 509, 68 Stat. A112 (1954), for the relief of Elie Joseph Hakim and Family

83rd Cong., S. 2065, Priv. L. No. 603, 68 Stat. A142 (1954), for the relief of Mr. and Mrs. Henrik Van der Tuin

83rd Cong., S. 2345, Priv. L. No. 969, 68 Stat. A279 (1954), for the relief of Yun Tai Miao and his wife, Chao Pei Tsang Miao

84th Cong., H.R. 1022, Priv. L. No. 491, 70 Stat. A3 (1956), for the relief of Antonio Andrea Chitato

84th Cong., H.R. 2054, Priv. L. No. 554, 70 Stat. A24 (1956), for the relief of Induk Pahk

84th Cong., H.R. 4039, Priv. L. No. 598, 70 Stat. A41 (1956), for the relief of Julian, Dolores, Jaime, Dennis, Roldan, and Julian Jr. Lizardo

97th Cong., H.R. 828, Priv. L. No. 44, 96 Stat. 2631 (1982), for the relief of George G. Barrios, Doctor of Medicine, his wife Olga T. Cruz, and their children Kurt F. Barrios and Karl S. Barrios, Katrina Adelaida Theresa

98th Cong., H.R. 1236, Priv. L. No. 28, 98 Stat. 3426 (1984), for the relief of Andrew and Julia Lui

Preference

81st Cong., S. 2108, Priv. L. No. 490, 64 Stat. A57 (1950), for the relief of Italo Vespa de Chellis

82nd Cong., H.R. 616, Priv. L. No. 99, 65 Stat. A39 (1951), for the relief of Tomas J. Zafiriadis

82nd Cong., H.R. 715, Priv. L. No. 100, 65 Stat. A39 (1951), for the relief of Aenny Blank

83rd Cong., H.R. 3831, Priv. L. No. 169, 67 Stat. A60 (1953), for the relief of Panagiotes G. Karras

83rd Cong., S. 2512, Priv. L. No. 651, 68 Stat. A158 (1954), for the relief of Jeannette Kalker and Abraham Benjamin Kalker

83rd Cong., S. 2534, Priv. L. No. 344, 68 Stat. A44 (1954), for the relief of Dora Vida Lyew Seixas

83rd Cong., S. 3433, Priv. L. No. 659, 68 Stat. A161 (1954), for the relief of Andreja Glusic

84th Cong., H.R. 877, Priv. L. No. 744, 70 Stat. A111 (1956), for the relief of Mrs. Rose Amoresano and her children

84th Cong., H.R. 962, Priv. L. No. 249, 69 Stat. A88 (1955), for the relief of Maria Louise Andreis

84th Cong., H.R. 5546, Priv. L. No. 486, 69 Stat. A164 (1955), for the relief of Francisca Alemany

85th Cong., H.R. 4854, Priv. L. No. 169, 71 Stat. A105 (1957), for the relief of Victoria Galea

86th Cong., H.R. 9444, Priv. L. No. 259, 74 Stat. Al3 (1960), for the relief of Hsiao-li Lindsay (nee Li- Hsiao-li)

86th Cong., S. 855, Priv. L. No. 57, 73 Stat. A25 (1959), for the relief of Saeko Higa and Masako Higa

86th Cong., S. 2528, Priv. L. No. 361, 74 Stat. A52 (1960), for the relief of John Lipset

86th Cong., S. 2566, Priv. L. No. 394, 74 Stat. A64 (1960), for the relief of Peter Leo Bahr

86th Cong., S. 2886, Priv. L. No. 367, 74 Stat. A54 (1960), for the relief of Nikolija Lazic

87th Cong., H.R. 1469, Priv. L. No. 473, 76 Stat. 1330 (1962), for the relief of Mrs. Leslie M. Paterson, Janet Paterson and Mary Paterson

87th Cong., S. 570, Priv. L. No. 178, 75 Stat. 910 (1961), for the relief of Giuseppa Alonzi

87th Cong., S. 722, Priv. L. No. 180, 75 Stat. 910 (1961), for the relief of Aideh Kobler

87th Cong., S. 2385, Priv. L. No. 323, 76 Stat. 1277 (1962), for the relief of Dr. Hau Cheong Kwaan, his wife, Tech Phaik Loui Kwaan, and their daughter, Laura Wai Man Kwaan

88th Cong., H.R. 1560, Priv. L. No. 158, 77 Stat. 932 (1963), for the relief of Constantinos A. Grigoras (Gregoras)

88th Cong., S. 584, Priv. L. No. 329, 78 Stat. 1188 (1964), for the relief of Yih-Ho Po and his wife, Joanne T. Pao

93rd Cong., H.R. 3754, Priv. L. No. 29, 87 Stat. 1107 (1973), for the relief of Mrs. Bruna Turni and Miss Graziella Turni

93rd Cong., H.R. 3758, Priv. L. No. 49, 87 Stat. 1114 (1973), for the relief of Isabel Eugenia Serrane Macias Ferrier

93rd Cong., S. 89, Priv. L. No. 7, 87 Stat. 1099 (1973), for the relief of Kuay Ten Chang (Kuay Hong Chang)

93rd Cong., S. 428, Priv. L. No. 70, 88 Stat. 2371 (1974), for the relief of Ernest Edward Scofield (Ernesto Espino)

93rd Cong., S. 816 Priv. L. No. 63, 88 Stat. 2369 (1974), for the relief of Mrs. Jozefa Sokolowska Domanski

94th Cong., H.R. 9543, Priv. L. No. 128, 90 Stat. 3007 (1976), for the relief of Eupert Anthony Grant

94th Cong., H.R. 10793, Priv. L. No. 115, 90 Stat. 3001 (1976), for the relief of Afaf Yassine and her children, Najla Yassine, Walid Yassine, Mona Yassine and Maher Yassine

94th Cong., S. 52, Priv. L. No. 51, 90 Stat. 2975, (1976), for the relief of Miss Rosario Y. Quijano, Walter York Quijano, Ramon York Quijano, Tarcisus York Quijano, Denis York Quijano, and Paul York Quijanio

95th Cong., H.R. 1748, Priv. L. No. 159, 92 Stat. 3858 (1978), for the relief of Carmela Scudieri

95th Cong., H.R. 1750, Priv. L. No. 86, 92 Stat. 3829 (1978), for the relief of Anthony Rogers

95th Cong., H.R. 3996, Priv. L. No. 40, 92 Stat. 3807 (1978), for the relief of Mrs. Young Hee Kim Kang, Hee Jae Kang, Hee Jin Kang, Hee Soo Kang

95th Cong., H.R. 4875, Priv. L. No. 103, 92 Stat. 3835 (1978), for the relief of Elizabeth D. Yee Kraus

95th Cong., S. 3109, Priv. L. No. 125, 92 Stat. 3844 (1978), for the relief of Ricardo Rosas Salazar

100th Cong., H.R. 1191, Priv. L. No. 4, 101 Stat. 1975 (1987), for the relief of Jose Maria Vas

Returning Permanent Residents (QPRP)

81st Cong., H.R. 1447, Priv. L. No. 321, 63 Stat. 1199 (1949), for the relief of Ethel Roth

81st Cong., H.R. 7071, Priv. L. No. 790, 64 Stat. A161 (1950), for the relief of Mrs. Masa Iyoki

82nd Cong., H.R. 3152, Priv. L. No. 686, 66 Stat. A92 (1952), for the relief of Mrs. Setsuyo Sumida

83rd Cong., H.R. 2499, Priv. L. No. 693, 68 Stat. A171 (1954), for the relief of Adolfo L. Kalb and Mrs. Eugenia G. Kalb

83rd Cong., S. 2618, Priv. L. No. 999, 68 Stat. A289 (1954), for the relief of Ertogroul Osman

84th Cong., H.R. 4544, Priv. L. No. 456, 69 Stat. A155 (1955), for the relief of Andrew Carrigan

84th Cong., H.R. 6613, Priv. L. No. 360, 69 Stat. A122 (1955), for the relief of Yuji Doi and Mrs. Matsuyo Yamaoka Doi

85th Cong., H.R. 1757, Priv. L. No. 15, 71 Stat. A7 (1957), for the relief of Nicola Marcello

86th Cong., S. 110, Priv. L. No. 37, 73 Stat. A18 (1959), for the relief of Yaeko Inouye

87th Cong., H.R. 1404, Priv. L. No. 409, 76 Stat. 1309 (1962), for the relief of Mrs. Frances Mangiaracina

87th Cong., H.R. 1458, Priv. L. No. 530, 76 Stat. 1350 (1962), for the relief of Lee Dock On

87th Cong., H.R. 2666, Priv. L. No. 243, 75 Stat. 939 (1961), for the relief of Adelina Benedict (nee Rosasco)

88th Cong., S. 1096, Priv. L. No. 154, 77 Stat. 930 (1963), for the relief of Mrs. Susanna Grun (Susanne Roth)

91st Cong., S. 1704, Priv. L. No. 146, 84 Stat. 2127 (1970), for the relief of Lillian Biazzo

93rd Cong., H.R. 1356, Priv. L. No. 21, 87 Stat. 1104 (1973), for the relief of Ann E. Shepherd

95th Cong., H.R. 8192, Priv. L. No. 165, 92 Stat. 3860 (1978), for the relief of Andree Marie Helene McGiffin

WAIVER OF EXCLUSION

Communist Party Membership (WXCP)

78th Cong., H.R. 312, Priv. L. No. 372, 58 Stat. 1021 (1944), for he relief of Freda Utley

82nd Cong., S. 674, Priv. L. No. 221, 65 Stat. 84 (1951), for the relief of Arthur Koestler

83rd Cong., H.R. 5238, Priv. L. No. 109, 67 Stat. A40 (1953), for the relief of Franciszek Jarecki

84th Cong., H.R. 968, Priv. L. No. 149, 69 Stat. A52 (1955), for the relief of Max Kozlowski

84th Cong., H.R. 10984, Priv. L. No. 851, 70 Stat. A174 (1956), for the relief of Nikolai E. Khokhlov

84th Cong., S. 129, Priv. L. No. 74, 69 Stat. A26 (1955), for the relief of Miroslav Slovak

84th Cong., S. 1627, Priv. L. No. 810, 70 Stat. A149 (1956), for the relief of Alexander Orlov and his wife, Maria Orlov

87th Cong., S. 231, Priv. L. No. 155, 75 Stat. 901 (1961), for the relief of Helga G. F. Koehler

Criminal and/or Fraud (WCRF)

74th Cong., S. 3399, Priv. L. No. 425, 49 Stat. 2234 (1936), for the relief of Rosalie Piar Sprecher (nee Rosa Piar)

75th Cong., H.R. 5597, Priv. L. No. 686, 52 Stat. 1382 (1938), for the relief of Luigi Mazza

75th Cong., H.R. 7039, Priv. L. No. 810, 52 Stat. 1434 (1938), for the relief of Paul Hirschmann

75th Cong., H.R. 7297, Priv. L. No. 620, 52 Stat. 1355 (1938), for the relief of Gordon L. Cheasley

75th Cong., H.R. 10136, Priv. L. No. 805, 52 Stat. 1432 (1938), for the relief of John Patrick Toth

76th Cong., S. 796, Priv. L. No. 251, 53 Stat. 1540 (1939), for the relief of Mato, Miljenko, Bozzo, and Augustin Cibilic, or Zibilich

76th Cong., S. 808, Priv. L. No. 184, 53 Stat. 1514 (1939), for the relief of Calliope Minaca Pilavakis

78th Cong., H.R. 480, Priv. L. No. 216, 58 Stat. 956 (1944), for the relief of Francesco P. Mastrilli

80th Cong., H.R. 422, Priv. L. No. 168, 62 Stat. 1308 (1948), for the relief of Francesco and Natalia Picchi

80th Cong., H.R. 4484, Priv. L. No. 338, 62 Stat. 1368 (1948), for the relief of Theordore Loetsch

81st Cong. H.R. 1170, Priv. L. No. 535, 64 Stat. A70 (1950), for the relief of Mrs. John Kaudy (formerly Stella Cappler)

81st Cong., H.R. 1503, Priv. L. No. 1038, 64 Stat. A255 (1950), for the relief of George Washington

81st Cong., H.R. 2602, Priv. L. No. 226, 63 Stat. 1162 (1949), for the relief of John B. Boyle

81st Cong., H.R. 7428, Priv. L. No. 706, 64 Stat. A133 (1950), for the relief of Mrs. Erna Tvedt

81st Cong., S. 118, Priv. L. No. 630, 64 Stat. A105 (1950), for the relief of Clemente Sabin Dopico

81st Cong., S. 356, Priv. L. No. 494, 64 Stat. A59 (1950), for the relief of Hugo Geiger

81st Cong., S. 1551, Priv. L. No. 730, 64 Stat. A142 (1950), for the relief of Jose Augusto Pereira

81st Cong., S. 1552, Priv. L. No. 398, 64 Stat. A21 (1950), for the relief of Ernest E. Heintz

81st Cong., S. 2077, Priv. L. No. 672, 64 Stat. A119 (1950), for the relief of Francisco Gonzalez Perez

82nd Cong., H.R. 714, Priv. L. No. 46, 65 Stat. A19 (1951), for the relief of James A.G. Martindale

82nd Cong., H.R. 1103, Priv. L. No. 238, 65 Stat. A91 (1951), for the relief of Sidney Young Hughes

82nd Cong., H.R. 1791, Priv. L. No. 107, 65 Stat. A42 (1951), for the relief of Joe Tortolini

82nd Cong., H.R. 1836, Priv. L. No. 66(?), 66 Stat. A54 (1952), for the relief of Mrs. Carla Mulligan

82nd Cong., H.R. 2346, Priv. L. No. 659, 66 Stat. A82 (1952), for the relief of Odette Louise Tirman

82nd Cong., H.R. 2455, Priv. L. No. 183, 65 Stat. A70 (1951), for the relief of Mrs. Maryanna Boppel

82nd Cong., H.R. 4396, Priv. L. No. 950, 66 Stat. A188 (1952), for the relief of Elias Papadopoulos

83rd Cong., H.R. 871, Priv. L. No. 177, 67 Stat. A63 (1953), for the relief of Orsola Jacopelli Leggio

83rd Cong., H.R. 954, Priv. L. No. 180, 67 Stat. A64 (1953), for the relief of Edith Smith

83rd Cong., H.R. 1148, Priv. L. No. 324, 68 Stat. A37 (1954), for the relief of Antonino Cangialosi (or Anthony Consola)

83rd Cong., H.R. 1657, Priv. L. No. 410, 68 Stat. A70 (1954), for the relief of Antonio Messina

83rd Cong., H.R. 1673, Priv. L. No. 558, 68 Stat. A128 (1954), for the relief of James I. Smith

83rd Cong., H.R. 2061, Priv. L. No. 889, 68 Stat. A239 (1954), for the relief of Regine du Planty

83rd Cong., H.R. 5354, Priv. L. No. 766, 68 Stat. A194 (1954), for the relief of Liborio Guido Rutilio

83rd Cong., H.R. 5816, Priv. L. No. 761, 68 Stat. A193 (1954), for the relief of Mrs. Caridad Rosa Avila Leyva de Ernest

83rd Cong., H.R. 6955, Priv. L. No. 829, 68 Stat. A215 (1954), for the relief of Margers Nule-Siecenieks

83rd Cong., H.R. 6998, Priv. L. No. 544, 68 Stat. A123 (1954), for the relief of Erna White

83rd Cong., S. 2210, Priv. L. No. 640, 68 Stat. A155 (1954), for the the relief of Frank (Franz) Homolka, Olga Homolka (nee Mandel), Adolf Homolka, Helga Maria Homolka, and Frieda Homolka

83rd Cong., S. 2360, Priv. L. No. 476, 68 Stat. A97 (1954), for the relief of Jacob Vandenbergh

84th Cong., H.R. 973, Priv. L. No. 150, 69 Stat. A52 (1955), for the relief of Mrs. Elizabeth Dowds

84th Cong., H.R. 1185, Priv. L. No. 287, 69 Stat. A99 (1955), for the relief of Jose Domingo Quintanar

84th Cong., H.R. 1203, Priv. L. No. 15, 69 Stat. A7 (1955), for the relief of Ivan Bruno Lomm, also known as Ivan B. Johnson

84th Cong., H.R. 1487, Priv. L. No. 89, 69 Stat. A31 (1955), for the relief of Rosa Marie Phillips

84th Cong., H.R. 1501, Priv. L. No. 46, 69 Stat. A16 (1955), for the relief of Andrea Hernandes Montes Rocha

84th Cong., H.R. 1897, Priv. L. No. 228, 69 Stat. A79 (1955), for the relief of Giuseppe Tumbarello

84th Cong., H.R. 1935, Priv. L. No. 229, 69 Stat A79 (1955), for the relief of Giuseppa Curro Tati

84th Cong., H.R. 2261, Priv. L. No. 22, 69 Stat. A9 (1955), for the relief of Giuseppe Carollo

84th Cong., H.R. 2345, Priv. L. No. 558, 70 Stat. A25 (1956), for the relief of Jean Henri Buchet

84th Cong., H.R. 2788, Priv. L. No. 425, 69 Stat. A145 (1955), for the relief of Miguel Sandoval-Michel (also known as Arturo Rodriguez-Gomez)

84th Cong., H.R. 4147, Priv. L. No. 348, 69 Stat. A119 (1955), for the relief of Angelo DeVito

84th Cong., H.R. 4548, Priv. L. No. 524, 70 Stat. A14 (1956), for the relief of Michele Pica

84th Cong., H.R. 6363, Priv. L. No. 570, 70 Stat. A29 (1956), for the relief of Edward Barnett

84th Cong., H.R. 6617, Priv. L. No. 572, 70 Stat. A29 (1956), for the relief of Boris Kowerda

84th Cong., S. 432, Priv. L. No. 146, 69 Stat. A51 (1955), for the relief of Aniceto Sparagna

85th Cong., H.R. 8014, Priv. L. No. 740, 72 Stat. A200 (1958), for the relief of Edith Dorn

85th Cong., S. 660, Priv. L. No. 253, 71 Stat. A97 (1957), for the relief of Ursula Rosa Pazdro

85th Cong., S. 701, Priv. L. No. 133, 71 Stat. A52 (1957), for the relief of Karl Eigil Engedal Hansen and his wife, Else Viola Agnethe Hansen, and their minor child, Jessie Engedal Hansen

85th Cong., S. 1456, Priv. L. No. 321, 71 Stat. A126 (1957), for the relief of Refugio Guerrero-Monje

86th Cong., H.R. 1422, Priv. L. No. 424, 74 Stat. A76 (1960), for the relief of Alessandro Maraessa

86th Cong., H.R. 2944, Priv. L. No. 432, 74 Stat. A78 (1960), for the relief of Luciano Di Franco

86th Cong., H.R. 2946, Priv. L. No. 200, 73 Stat. A88 (1959), for the relief of Cecil E. Finley

87th Cong., H.R. 3401, Priv. L. No. 279, 75 Stat. 952 (1961), for the relief of Salvatore Cairo

87th Cong., H.R. 3718, Priv. L. No. 249, 75 Stat. 940 (1961), for the relief of Matthias Nock, Jr.

87th Cong., H.R. 9915, Priv. L. No. 528, 76 Stat. 1350 (1962), for the relief of Umberto Brezza

87th Cong., S. 235, Priv. L. No. 308, 76 Stat. 1272 (1962), for the relief of Evagelos Mablekos

88th Cong., H.R. 1174, Priv. L. No. 294, 78 Stat. 1173 (1964), for the relief of Elfriede Unterholzer Sharble

88th Cong., H.R. 1521, Priv. L. No. 183, 78 Stat. 1127 (1964), for the relief of Lororko Lucic

88th Cong., H.R. 2305, Priv. L. No. 134, 77 Stat. 921 (1963), for the relief of Zoltan Friedmann

88th Cong., S. 1999, Priv. L. No. 333, 78 Stat. 1189 (1964), for the relief of Francisco Navarro-Paz

89th Cong., H.R. 1236, Priv. L. No. 11, 79 Stat. 1336 (1965), for the relief of Salvador Munoz-Tostado

89th Cong., H.R. 1414, Priv. L. No. 269, 80 Stat. 1638 (1966), for the relief of Jacobo Temel

89th Cong., H.R. 2752, Priv. L. No. 234, 80 Stat. 1623 (1966), for the relief of Kock Kong Fong

89th Cong., H.R. 3233, Priv. L. No. 283, 80 Stat. 1642 (1966), for the relief of Emanuel G. Topakas

89th Cong., H.R. 3292, Priv. L. No. 70, 79 Stat. 1359 (1965), for the relief of Consuelo Alvarado de Corpus

90th Cong., H.R. 3221, Priv. L. No. 64, 81 Stat. 1005 (1967), for the relief of Dr. Alexander D. Cross

90th Cong., H.R. 5216, Priv. L. No. 138, 81 Stat. 1030 (1967), for the relief of Roberto Martin Del Campo

90th Cong., S. 534, Priv. L. No. 93, 81 Stat. 1016 (1967), for the relief of Setsuko Wilson (nee Hiranaka)

91st Cong., S. 737, Priv. L. No. 187, 84 Stat. 2150 (1970), for the relief of Konrad Ludwig Staudinger

92nd Cong., H.R. 2394, Priv. L. No. 117, 86 Stat. 1549 (1972), for the relief of Antonio Benavides

92nd Cong., H.R. 6907, Priv. L. No. 99, 86 Stat. 1541 (1972), for the relief of Matyas Hunyadi

92nd Cong., H.R. 7641, Priv. L. No. 100, 86 Stat. 1541 (1972), for the relief of Chung Chi Lee

92nd Cong., S. 2270, Priv. L. No. 154, 86 Stat. 1565 (1972), for the relief of Magnus David Forrester

93rd Cong., H.R. 6477, Priv. L. No. 97, 88 Stat. 2382 (1974), for the relief of Lucille de Saint Andre

94th Cong., H.R. 1425, Priv. L. No. 64, 90 Stat. 2981 (1976), for the relief of Juliet Elizabeth Tozzi

94th Cong., H.R. 1645, Priv. L. No. 66, 90 Stat. 2982 (1976), for the relief of Kevin Patrick Saunders

94th Cong., H.R. 2399, Priv. L. No. 69, 90 Stat. 2983 (1976), for the relief of Leonard Alfred Brownrigg

94th Cong., H.R. 8119, Priv. L. No. 121, 90 Stat. 3004 (1976), for the relief of Fernando Alves Macos

94th Cong., H.R. 11890, Priv. L. No. 116, 90 Stat. 3001 (1976), for the relief of Bernard Julian Phillips

95th Cong., H.R. 1396, Priv. L. No. 63, 92 Stat. 3818 (1978), for the relief of Mrs. Sun Pok Winer

95th Cong., H.R. 1422, Priv. L. No. 158, 92 Stat. 3857 (1978), for the relief of Julio Ortiz-Medina

95th Cong., H.R. 1432, Priv. L. No. 31, 92 Stat. 3804 (1978), for the relief of Mrs. Desolina Sciulli

95th Cong., H.R. 1446, Priv. L. No. 64, 92 Stat. 3819 (1978), for the relief of Lester Bruce Priday

95th Cong., H.R. 4401, Priv. L. No. 35, 92 Stat. 3805 (1978), for the relief of Kwi Sok Buckingham (nee Kim)

95th Cong., H.R. 8927, Priv. L. No. 74, 92 Stat. 3822 (1978), for the relief of Monika Grantz

97th Cong., H.R. 783, Priv. L. No. 3, 95 Stat. 1733 (1981), for the relief of Roland Karl Heinz Vogel

100th Cong., S. 391, Priv. L. No. 23, 102 Stat. 4851 (1988), for the relief of Hyong Cha Kim Kay

Draft Dodgers (WXDD)

84th Cong., H.R. 1525, Priv. L. No. 197, 69 Stat. A68 (1955), for the relief of Ardes Albacete Yanez

84th Cong., S. 245, Priv. L. No. 739, 70 Stat. A109 (1956), for the relief of Ahmet Haldun Koca Taskin Ursula and Jadwiga Milarski Goodman

85th Cong., S. 2168, Priv. L. No. 465, 72 Stat. A56 (1958), for the relief of Armas Edvin Jansson-Viik

86th Cong., H.R. 2645, Priv. L. No. 349, 74 Stat. A48 (1960), for the relief of Jesus Cruz-Figueroa

87th Cong., H.R. 2187, Priv. L. No. 485, 76 Stat. 1334 (1962), for the relief of Augustin Ramirez-Trejo

94th Cong., H.R. 1553, Priv. L. No. 17, 89 Stat. 1179 (1975), for the relief of Victor Henrique Carlos Gibson

Health-related (WHEL)

76th Cong., H.R. 4066, Priv. L. No. 588, 54 Stat. 1373 (1940), for the relief of Josefina Alvarado

76th Cong., H.R. 4954, Priv. L. No. 592, 54 Stat. 1375 (1940), for the relief of Rosa Paone

76th Cong., H.R. 5827, Priv. L. No. 366, 54 Stat. 1282 (1940), for the relief of John L. Harder and children, Paul William Harder, Irvin W. Harder, Edna Justina Harder, Elsie Anna Harder, and Elizabeth Harder

76th Cong., H.R. 6888, Priv. L. No. 601, 54 Stat. 1378 (1940), for the relief of Esther Jacobs

81st Cong., H.R. 750, Priv. L. No. 138, 63 Stat. 1128 (1949), for the relief of Lee F. Bertuccioli

81st Cong., H.R. 1079, Priv. L. No. 48, 63 Stat. 1093 (1949), for the relief of Maria Veltri Magnone

81st Cong., H.R. 1275, Priv. L. No. 526, 64 Stat. A70 (1950), for the relief of Anna Helman

81st Cong., S. 2611, Priv. L. No. 502, 64 Stat. A61 (1950), for the relief of Roland Roger Alfred Boccia, also known as Roland Barbera

82nd Cong., H.R. 627, Priv. L. No. 241, 65 Stat. A92 (1951), for the relief of Mrs. Tjitske Bandstra Van Der Velde

82nd Cong., H.R. 1092, Priv. L. No. 869, 66 Stat. A162 (1952), for the relief of Mrs. Mercedes Hernandez Saguar

82nd Cong., H.R. 1968, Priv. L. No. 592, 66 Stat. A60 (1952), for the relief of Senta Ziegler

82nd Cong., H.R. 2180, Priv. L. No. 181, 65 Stat. A69 (1951), for the relief of Mrs. Florence E. Homann and John A. Villas

82nd Cong., S. 1462, Priv. L. No. 467, 66 Stat. A20 (1952), for the relief of Joseph Boris Tchertkoff

83rd Cong., H.R. 4522, Priv. L. No. 816, 68 Stat. A211 (1954), for the relief of Petrus Van Keer

83rd Cong., H.R. 7761, Priv. L. No. 711, 68 Stat. A177 (1954), for the relief of John Lewis Pyles, Jr.

83rd Cong., H.R. 8557, Priv. L. No. 848, 68 Stat. A221 (1954), for the relief of Ezio Bertoni

84th Cong., H.R. 1275, Priv. L. No. 253, 69 Stat. A89 (1955), for the relief of Gennaro Savarese

84th Cong., H.R. 1301, Priv. L. No. 415, 69 Stat. A142 (1955), for the relief of Karlis Abele

84th Cong., H.R. 1667, Priv. L. No. 597, 70 Stat. A41 (1956), for the relief of Lieselotte Boehme

84th Cong., H.R. 2059, Priv. L. No. 303, 69 Stat. A104 (1955),for the relief of Edward Patrick Cloonan

84th Cong., H.R. 2087, Priv. L. No. 52, 69 Stat. A18 (1955), for the relief of Erika Rambauske

84th Cong., H.R. 2949, Priv. L. No. 335, 69 Stat. A114 (1955), for the relief of Jose Armando Quaresma

84th Cong., S. 884, Priv. L. No. 396, 69 Stat. A136 (1955), for the relief of Gabor Lanyi

85th Cong., H.R. 7729, Priv. L. No. 507, 72 Stat. A72 (1958), for the relief of August Widmer

85th Cong., S. 2936, Priv. L. No. 674, 72 Stat. A146 (1958), for the relief of Feofania Bankevitz

86th Cong., H.R. 3534, Priv. L. No. 399, 74 Stat. A65 (1960), for the relief of Epifanio Trupiano

86th Cong., H.R. 6804, Priv. L. No. 438, 74 Stat. A80 (1960), for the relief of Mary Elizabeth Tighe Crespo

86th Cong., S. 2177, Priv. L. No. 321, 74 Stat. A36 (1960), for the relief of Peter J. Waterton

86th Cong., S. 2319, Priv. L. No. 226, 73 Stat. A98 (1959), for the relief of Sergiusz Rudczenko

87th Cong., H.R. 6343, Priv. L. No. 339, 76 Stat. 1283 (1962), for the relief of Mrs. Izabel A. Miguel

87th Cong., H.R. 9669, Priv. L. No. 676, 76 Stat. 1408 (1962), for the relief of Molly Kwauk

87th Cong., S. 3026, Priv. L. No. 565, 76 Stat. 1364 (1962), for the relief of Jeno Nagy

88th Cong., H.R. 9090, Priv. L. No. 250, 78 Stat. 1155 (1964), for the relief of Mrs. Audrey Rossmann

89th Cong., H.R. 1627, Priv. L. No. 66, 79 Stat. 1358 (1965), for the relief of Esterina Ricupero

89th Cong., S. 1111, Priv. L. No. 109, 79 Stat. 1374 (1965), for the relief of Pola Bodenstein

91st Cong., H.R. 3376, Priv. L. No. 30, 83 Stat. 876 (1969), for the relief of Maria da Conceicao Evaristo

92nd Cong., S. 513, Priv. L. No. 88, 86 Stat. 1537 (1972), for the relief of Maria Badalamenti

94th Cong., H.R. 6093, Priv. L. No. 81, 90 Stat. 2988 (1976), for the relief of Maria D'Arpino

95th Cong., H.R. 1420, Priv. L. No. 48, 92 Stat. 3811 (1978), for the relief of Umberto Ruffolo

95th Cong., H.R. 2940, Priv. L. No. 67, 92 Stat. 3820 (1978), for the relief of Daniel Crowley

Illiteracy

81st Cong., H.R. 5375, Priv. L. No. 329, 63 Stat. 1202 (1949), for the relief of Mrs. Hilda De Silva

87th Cong., S. 1786, Priv. L. No. 271, 75 Stat. 949 (1961), for the relief of Heripsime Hovnanian

90th Cong., S. 1652, Priv. L. No. 346, 82 Stat. 1430 (1968), for the relief of Anastasia D. Mpatziani

95th Cong., S. 455, Priv. L. No. 11, 91 Stat. 1653 (1977), for the relief of Ermelinda Rossi

95th Cong., S. 1142, Priv. L. No. 19, 91 Stat. 1656 (1977), for the relief of Kam Lin Cheung

NATURALIZATION

Communist Party Membership (NXCP)

81st Cong., S. 1915, Priv. L. No. 365, 64 Stat. A8 (1950), for the relief of Viktor A. Kravchenko

84th Cong., H.R. 6955, Priv. L. No. 712, 70 Stat. A95 (1956), for the relief of Inna Hekker Grade

86th Cong., H.R. 6954, Priv. L. No. 218, 73 Stat. A95 (1959), for the relief of Frol Martin Simonov

87th Cong., H.R. 6833, Priv. L. No. 492, 76 Stat. 1336 (1962), for the relief of Frantisek Tisler

88th Cong., H.R. 5507, Priv. L. No. 59, 77 Stat. 893 (1963), for the relief of Michal Goleniewski

89th Cong., S. 582, Priv. L. No. 42, 79 Stat. 1347 (1965), for the relief of Aleksandr Kaznacheev

91st Cong., H.R. 3165, Priv. L. No. 51, 83 Stat. 885 (1969), for the relief of Martin H. Loeffler

92nd Cong., H.R. 2076, Priv. L. No. 92, 86 Stat. 1539 (1972), for the relief of Vladimir Rodriguez LaHera

92nd Cong., H.R. 3929, Priv. L. No. 9, 85 Stat. 836 (1971), for the relief of Gheorghe Jucu and Aurelia Jucu

96th Cong., S. 2961, Priv. L. No. 62, 94 Stat. 3599 (1980), for the relief of Viktor Ivanovich Belenko

Confer or Derive Citizenship (NCOD)

62nd Cong., 1912, H.J. Res. 220, Priv. L. 3, 37 Stat. 1346 (1912), for the relief of Eugene Prince

63rd Cong., S. 3419, Priv. L. No. 184, 38 Stat. 1476 (1915), for the relief of George E. Lerrigo

64th Cong., S.J. Res. 208, Priv. L. No. 132, 39 Stat. 1495 (1917), for the relief of Joseph Beech

75th Cong., S. 3064, Priv. L. No. 745, 52 Stat. 1408 (1938), for the relief of George Henry Levins

76th Cong., S. 2427, Priv. L. No. 175, 53 Stat. 1510 (1939), for the relief of John Ullmann, Jr.

78th Cong., H.R. 2016, Priv. L. No. 516, 58 Stat. 1080 (1944), for the relief of William H. Linhart

82nd Cong., S. 2588, Priv. L. No. 657, 66 Stat. A82 (1952), for the relief of Dulcie Ann Steinhardt Sherlock

85th Cong., S. 1782, Priv. L. No. 594, 72 Stat. A116 (1958), for the relief of Carolina M. Gomes

85th Cong., S. 2301, Priv. L. No. 439, 72 Stat. A47 (1958), for the relief of Genevieve M. Scott Bell

85th Cong., S. 2935, Priv. L. No. 631, 72 Stat. A131 (1958), for the relief of Mary Louise Shields Wilkinson

86th Cong., H.R. 5910, Priv. L. No. 210, 73 Stat. A91 (1959), for the relief of Zelda Glick

86th Cong., S. 32, Priv. L. No. 34, 73 Stat. A17 (1959), for the relief of Uwe-Thorsten Scobel

86th Cong., S. 2142, Priv. L. No. 320,74 Stat. A36 (1960), for the relief of George C. McKinney

86th Cong., S. 2554, Priv. L. No. 328, 74 Stat. A39 (1960), for the relief of Leila Finlay Bohin

87th Cong., H.R. 10160, Priv. L. No. 562, 76 Stat. 1363 (1962), for the relief of Mrs. A. R. Lendian

88th Cong., S. 1014, Priv. L. No. 153, 77 Stat. 930 (1963), for the relief of Mrs. Joyce Mark Bouvier

89th Cong., H.R. 11718, Priv. L. No. 277, 80 Stat. 1640 (1966), for the relief of Jack L. Philippot

89th Cong., S. 442, Priv. L. No. 40, 79 Stat. 1347 (1965), for the relief of Carleen Coen

89th Cong., S. 1919, Priv. L. No. 93, 79 Stat. 1366 (1965), for the relief of Laura MacArthur Goditiabois-Deacon

90th Cong., S. 2897, Priv. L. No. 347, 82 Stat. 1430 (1968), for the relief of James T. O'Brien

91st Cong., S. 2863, Priv. L. No. 148, 84 Stat. 2128 (1970), for the relief of Mrs.Cumorah Kennington Romney

92nd Cong., S. 389, Priv. L. No. 35, 85 Stat. 848 (1971), for the relief of Stephen Lance Pender, Patricia Jenifer Pender, and Denese Gene Pender

Draft Dodgers (NXDD)

77th Cong., H.R. 7828, Priv. L. No. 633, 56 Stat. 1259 (1942), for the relief of John Sweeney

81st Cong., S. 2429, Priv. L. No. 402, 64 Stat. A23 (1950), for the relief of Henrique Santos

83rd Cong., S. 2135, Priv. L. No. 665, 68 Stat. A163 (1954), for the relief of Fernando A. Rubio, Jr.

85th Cong., S. 803, Priv L. No. 464, 72 Stat. A56 (1958), for the relief of Claudio Guillen

86th Cong., H.R. 5645, Priv. L. No. 567, 73 Stat. A91 (1959), for the relief of Christopher J. Mulligan

87th Cong., S. 2679, Priv. L. No. 460, 76 Stat. 1326 (1962), for the relief of John Axel Arvidson

English and History and Government (NXEN)

86th Cong., S. 2991, Priv. L. No. 371, 74 Stat. A55 (1960), for the relief of Ah See Lee Chin

87th Cong., H.R. 2156, Priv. L. No. 107, 75 Stat. 886 (1961), for the relief of Mrs. Tui Hing Tow Woo

98th Cong., H.R. 1865, Priv. L. No. 41, 98 Stat. 3432 (1984), for the relief of Nery De Maio

Miscellaneous (NMSC)

25th Cong., 6 Stat. 750 (1839), for the relief of John Campbell White

74th Cong., S. 447, Priv. L. No. 227, 49 Stat. 2145 (1936), for the relief of Rakha Singh

79th Cong., H.R. 1350, Priv. L. No. 460, 60 Stat. 1143 (1946), for the relief of Nora R. Neville

79th Cong., H.R. 3441, Priv. L. No. 695, 60 Stat. 1242 (1946), for the relief of Master Sgt. Gerhard Neumann

80th Cong., H.R. 1652, Priv. L. No. 102, 61 Stat. 1004 (1947), for the relief of Certain United States Army personnel - Yugoslav Fliers

80th Cong., H.R. 1749, Priv. L. No. 305, 62 Stat. 1357 (1948), for the relief of Johannes or John, Julia, Michael, William, and Anna Kostiuk

80th Cong., S. 135, Priv. L. No. 12, 61 Stat. 968 (1947), for the relief of Frank Schindler

81st Cong., H.R. 1866, Priv. L. No. 508, 64 Stat. A63 (1950), for the relief of Honorio Canciller and Nancy Ting Evangelista

81st Cong., H.R. 6442, Priv. L. No. 887, 64 Stat. A201 (1950), for the relief of Mrs. Martha Reid

81st Cong., H.R. 8219, Priv. L. No. 944, 64 Stat. A219 (1950), for the relief of Tadeusz Herka

81st Cong., S. 1506, Priv. L. No. 870, 64 Stat. A194 (1950), for the relief of Andre Lan

81st Cong., S. 2100, Priv. L. No. 366, 64 Stat. A8 (1950), for the relief of Penelope Carolyn Cox

82nd Cong., H.R. 970, Priv. L. No. 256, 65 Stat. A97 (1951), for the relief of Antonios Charalambou

82nd Cong., H.R. 1157, Priv. L. No. 169, 65 Stat. A65 (1951), for the relief of Lum Ying

82nd Cong., H.R. 2718, Priv. L. No. 744, 66 Stat. A111 (1952), for the relief of Enrique M. Orpilla

84th Cong., S. 1044, Priv. L. No. 469, 69 Stat. A159 (1955), for the relief of Edward Naarits

85th Cong., H.R. 3184, Priv. L. No. 212, 71 Stat. A82 (1957), for the relief of Gordon Broderick

87th Cong., S. 217, Priv. L. No. 7, 75 Stat. 853 (1961), for the relief of Alessandro Gellhorn

87th Cong., S. 689, Priv. L. No. 599, 76 Stat. 1377 (1962), for the relief of Karl Heinz Agar

91st Cong., S. 537, Priv. L. No. 11, 83 Stat 870 (1969), for the relief of Noriko Susan Duke (Nakano)

93rd Cong., S. 1852, Priv. L. No. 54, 88 Stat. 2366 (1974), for the relief of Georgina Henrietta Harris

94th Cong., H.R. 1388, Priv. L. No. 2, 89 Stat. 1164 (1975), for the relief of Guadalupe Villegas-Cantu

Posthumous Citizenship (NXPS)

80th Cong., S. 53, Priv. L. No. 51, 61 Stat. 985 (1947), for the relief of Harold Turcean

90th Cong., H.R. 13301, Priv. L. No. 299, 82 Stat. 1021 (1968), for the relief of PFC John R.Aneli

90th Cong., H.R. 15591, Priv. L. No. 263, 82 Stat. 1393 (1968), for the relief of PFC John Patrick Collopy

90th Cong., S. 2759, Priv. L. No. 343, 82 Stat. 1429 (1968), for the relief of S. Sgt.Ivan Claus King

91st Cong., H.R. 1828, Priv. L. No. 22, 83 Stat. 874 (1969), for the relief of James F. Wegener

91st Cong., H.R. 6607, Priv. L. No. 15, 83 Stat. 871 (1969), for the relief of SP4C Klaus Josef Strauss

91st Cong., H.R. 13997, Priv. L. No. 151, 84 Stat. 2128 (1970), for the relief of S. Sgt.Ryuzo Somma

91st Cong., S. 3136, Priv. L. No. 149, 84 Stat. 2128 (1970), for the relief of Guy Andre Blanchette

96th Cong., H.R. 6739, Priv. L. No. 101, 94 Stat. 3628 (1980), for the relief of Leopoldine Marie Schmid

98th Cong., H.R. 960, Priv. L. No. 33, 98 Stat. 3429 (1984), for the relief of Corporal Wladyslaw Staniszewski

Residence (NRES)

80th Cong., H.R. 3742, Priv. L. No. 216, 62 Stat. 1325 (1948), for the relief of Robert Wilhelm Gerling

81st Cong., S. 3238, Priv. L. No. 873, 64 Stat. A195 (1950), for the relief of Dr. Frederick Daniel McDade

82nd Cong., H.R. 890, Priv. L. No. 35, 65 Stat. A16 (1951), for the relief of Athina Mary Onassis

82nd Cong., H.R. 1165, Priv. L. No. 5, 65 Stat. A4 (1951), for the relief of Richard Gregory Rundle, and Valiquette Adele Rundle

82nd Cong., H.R. 2505, Priv. L. No. 423, 66 Stat. A7 (1952), for the relief of Carl Weitlanner

82nd Cong., H.R. 2714, Priv. L. No. 16, 65 Stat. A8 (1951), for the relief of Marcelle Lecomte

82nd Cong., H.R. 3600, Priv. L. No. 792, 66 Stat. A131 (1952), for the relief of Dr. Alexander Symeonidis

82nd Cong., H.R. 4535, Priv. L. No. 603, 66 Stat. A63 (1952), for the relief of Nigel C. S. Salter-Mathieson

82nd Cong., H.R. 6117, Priv. L. No. 761, 66 Stat. A117 (1952), for the relief of Deliana Meulenkamp

83rd Cong., S. 2156, Priv. L. No. 967, 68 Stat. A278 (1954), for the relief of John Enepekides, and his wife, Anna, and his son, George

84th Cong., H.R. 10088, Priv. L. No. 824, 70 Stat. A155 (1956), for the relief of Rupert Waltl

84th Cong., S. 97, Priv. L. No. 534, 70 Stat. A17 (1956), an omnibus relief bill for the relief of Barbara D. Colthurst, Pedro P. Dagamac and Edith Kahler

85th Cong., H.R. 1677, Priv. L. No. 304, 71 Stat. A120 (1957), for for the relief of Gilbert B. Mar

86th Cong., H.R. 6886, Priv. L. No. 217, 73 Stat. A94 (1959), for the relief of Liliana Caprara

86th Cong., H.R. 8156, Priv. L. No. 486, 74 Stat. A100 (1960), for the relief of Jack Kent Cooke

86th Cong., S. 762, Priv. L. No. 358, 74 Stat. A51 (1960), for the relief of Manuel Alves de Carvalho

86th Cong., S. 1915, Priv. L. No. 145, 73 Stat. A63 (1959), for the relief of Chung Ching Wei

86th Cong., S. 2646, Priv. L. No. 363, 74 Stat. A53 (1960), for the relief of Lloyd C. Kimm

86th Cong., S. 2768, Priv. L. No. 365, 74 Stat. A53 (1960), for the relief of Frederick T.C. Yu and his wife, Alice Siao-Fen Chen Yu

86th Cong., S. 3016, Priv. L. No. 372, 74 Stat. A55 (1960), for the the relief of Walter F. Beecroft

87th Cong., H.R. 1394, Priv. L. No. 221, 75 Stat. 932 (1961), for the relief of Laszlo Hamori

87th Cong., H.R. 1395, Priv. L. No. 408, 76 Stat. 1309 (1962), for the relief of Sydney Gruson

87th Cong., H.R. 7582, Priv. L. No. 549, 76 Stat. 1358 (1962), for the relief of Dario Tacquechel

87th Cong., S. 333, Priv. L. No. 158, 75 Stat. 903 (1961), for the relief of Godofredo M. Herzog

87th Cong., S. 438, Priv. L. No. 126, 75 Stat. 892 (1961), for the relief of Mrs. Maria Giovanna Hopkins

87th Cong., S. 1074, Priv. L. No. 481, 76 Stat. 1333 (1962) for the relief of Chao Yao Koh

87th Cong., S. 1234, Priv. L. No. 268, 75 Stat. 948 (1961), for the relief of Max Haleck

87th Cong., S. 1791, Priv. L. No. 317, 76 Stat. 1275 (1962), for the relief of Dr. Tzy-Cheng Peng

87th Cong., S. 2555, Priv. L. No. 670, 76 Stat. 1406 (1962), for the relief of Fong Yee Hin

87th Cong., S. 3267, Priv. L. No. 641, 76 Stat. 1393 (1962), for the for the relief of Gunter Heinz Hillebrand

88th Cong., H.R. 2737, Priv. L. No. 256, 78 Stat. 1157 (1964), for the relief of Pedro Aguinaldo

89th Cong., H.R. 2005, Priv. L. No. 152, 79 Stat. 1392 (1965), for the relief of Miss Gloria Seborg

89th Cong., H.R. 2290, Priv. L. No. 247, 80 Stat. 1627 (1966), for the relief of Charlotte Schulz

89th Cong., H.R. 7453, Priv. L. No. 194, 79 Stat. 1408 (1965), for the relief of Margaret Elizabeth and Frederick Henry Todd

89th Cong., H.R. 10288, Priv. L. No. 398, 80 Stat. 1685 (1966), for the relief of Dr. Antonio B. Santillano

89th Cong., S. 374, Priv. L. No. 169, 79 Stat. 1399 (1965), for the relief of Dr. Guillermo Castrillo (Fernandez)

89th Cong., S. 619, Priv. L. No. 203, 79 Stat. 1413 (1965), for the relief of Nora Isabella Samuelli

89th Cong., S. 826, Priv. L. No. 44, 79 Stat. 1348 (1965), for the relief of Har Gobind Khorana

89th Cong., S. 1084, Priv. L. No. 82, 79 Stat. 1363 (1965), for the relief of Shu Hsien Chang

89th Cong., S. 3189, Priv. L. No. 327, 80 Stat. 1659 (1966), for the relief of Dr. Alonso Portuondo

89th Cong., S. 3222, Priv. L. No. 465, 80 Stat. 1711 (1966), for the relief of Dusko Doder

89th Cong., S. 3272, Priv. L. No. 328, 80 Stat. 1659 (1966), for the relief of Dr. Jacobo Albo Maya

90th Cong., H.R. 2048, Priv. L. No. 18, 81 Stat. 992 (1967), for the relief of William John Masterton and Louis Vincent Nanne

90th Cong., H.R. 5862, Priv. L. No. 57, 81 Stat. 1004 (1967), for the relief of Dr. Juan F.Chaves

90th Cong., S. 164, Priv. L. No. 33, 81 Stat. 996 (1967), for the relief of Dr. Cesar A. Mena

90th Cong. S. 445, Priv. L. No. 139, 81 Stat. 1030 (1967), for the relief of Rosemarie Gauch Neth

90th Cong., S. 747, Priv. L. No. 328, 82 Stat. 1425 (1968), for the relief of Earl C. Chamberlain

90th Cong., S. 1021, Priv. L. No. 114, 81 Stat. 1024 (1967), for the relief of Antonio Luis Navarro

90th Cong., S. 1781, Priv. L. No. 160, 81 Stat. 1037 (1967), for the relief of Kyong Hwan Chang

90th Cong., S. 2720, Priv. L. No. 340, 82 Stat. 1428 (1968), for the relief of Heng Liong Thung

91st Cong., H.R. 5136, Priv. L. No. 20, 83 Stat. 873 (1969), for the relief of George Tilson Weed

91st Cong., S. 85, Priv. L. No. 48, 83 Stat. 884 (1969), for the relief of Dr. Jagir Singh Randhawa

91st Cong., S. 265, Priv. L. No. 53, 83 Stat. 885 (1969), for the relief of John (Giovanni) Denaro

92nd Cong., H.R. 14173, Priv. L. No. 132, 86 Stat. 1555 (1972), for the relief of Walter Eduard Koenig

92nd Cong., S. 306, Priv. L. No. 36, 85 Stat. 849 (1971), for the relief of Eddie Troy Jaynes, Jr., and Rosa Elena Jaynes

92nd Cong., S. 2822, Priv. L. No. 150, 86 Stat. 1563 (1972), for the relief of Alberto Rodriguez

92nd Cong., S. 3583, Priv. L. No. 152, 86 Stat. 1564 (1972), for the relief of Gerald Vincent Bull

93rd Cong., S. 507, Priv. L. No. 62, 88 Stat. 2368 (1974), for the relief of Wilhelm J.R. Maly

93rd Cong., S. 912, Priv. L. No. 64, 88 Stat. 2369 (1974), for the relief of Mahmood Shareef Suleiman

94th Cong., H.R. 2776, Priv. L. No. 44, 90 Stat. 2973 (1976), for the relief of Candido Badua

94th Cong., H.R. 7404, Priv. L. No. 4, 90 Stat. 2989 (1976), for the relief of Christine Donnelly

94th Cong., H.R. 10792, Priv. L. No. 27, 89 Stat. 1189 (1975), for the relief of Jana Hlavaty

96th Cong., H.R. 4013, Priv. L. No. 52, 94 Stat. 3594 (1980), for the relief of Jozef Swiderski

98th Cong., H.R. 3131, Priv. L. No. 13, 98 Stat. 3420 (1984), for the relief of Marina Kunyavsky

98th Cong., S. 1863, Priv. L. No. 7, 98 Stat. 3417 (1984), for the relief of Audun Endestad

98th Cong., S. 2729, Priv. L. No. 15, 98 Stat. 3420 (1984), for the relief of Jean Willhelm Willrich

Retention of Citizenship (NRTN)

80th Cong., S. 83, Priv. L. No. 419, 62 Stat. 1403 (1948), for the relief of Elizabeth Pickering Winn

81st Cong., H.R. 4747, Priv. L. No. 570, 64 Stat. A85 (1950), for the relief of Louise Ahting

81st Cong., S. 905, Priv. L. No. 199, 63 Stat. 1152 (1949), for the relief of John Sewen

82nd Cong., H.R. 1234, Priv. L. No. 522, 66 Stat. A38 (1952), for the relief of Mrs. Selma Cecelia Gahl

82nd Cong., H.R. 4588, Priv. L. No. 953, 66 Stat. A189 (1952), for the relief of Mark Yen Hui

82nd Cong., H.R. 5238, Priv. L. No. 867, 66 Stat. A162 (1952), for the relief of Albert O. Holland and Bergtor Haaland

82nd Cong., H.R. 7833, Priv. L. No. 1023, 66 Stat. A213 (1952), for the relief of Prof. Werner Richter and Prof. Max Horkheimer

82nd Cong., S. 44, Priv. L. No. 2, 65 Stat. A3 (1951), for the relief of John E. Turri and Edward H. Turri

83rd Cong., H.R. 7559, Priv. L. No. 369, 68 Stat. A53 (1954), for the relief of Mrs. Madeleine Alice Aquarone

83rd Cong., S. 2259, Priv. L. No. 902, 68 Stat. A244 (1954), for the relief of Rev. Charles V. Rossini

83rd Cong., S. 2369, Priv. L. No. 533, 68 Stat. A119 (1954), for the relief of Karl Ullstein

85th Cong., S. 2469, Priv. L. No. 771, 72 Stat. A214 (1958), for the relief of Dr. Brant Bonner

85th Cong., S. 3219, Priv. L. No. 729, 72 Stat. A196 (1958), for the relief of Mrs. .Margaret Graham Bonnalie

85th Cong., S. 3221, Priv. L. No. 730, 72 Stat. A196 (1958), for the the relief of Erika Margaretha Zintl Pearce

85th Cong., H.R. 12903, Priv. L. No. 616, 72 Stat. A126 (1958), for the relief of Wolfgang Stresemann

86th Cong., H.R. 1705, Priv. L. No. 125, 73 Stat. A56 (1959), for the relief of Louis J. DeWinter and Simone H. DeWinter

86th Cong., S. 46, Priv. L. No. 36, 73 Stat. A18 (1959), for the relief of Ben Chassin

86th Cong., S. 977, Priv. L. No. 172, 73 Stat. A75 (1959), for the relief of Nasubit Mildred Milkie

86th Cong., S. 1684, Priv. L. No. 102, 73 Stat. A48 (1959), for the relief of Mr. and Mrs. Carl Skogen Woods

86th Cong., S. 3130, Priv. L. No. 352, 74 Stat. A49 (1960), for the relief of Anne-Marie Stehlin

87th Cong., H.R. 4384, Priv. L. No. 253, 75 Stat. 942 (1961), for the relief of Richard Fordham

87th Cong., H.R. 9588, Priv. L. No. 471, 76 Stat. 1329 (1962), for the relief of Claude Homann-Herimberg (nee Wagner)

87th Cong., S. 2865, Priv. L. No. 430, 76 Stat. 1316 (1962), for the relief of Ferdinand A. Hermens

88th Cong., H.R. 2309, Priv. L. No. 38, 77 Stat. 887 (1963), for the relief of Luigi Giuseppe Luraschi

97th Cong., H.R. 1482, Priv. L. No. 24, 96 Stat. 2622 (1982), for the relief of Christina Boltz Sidders

Voluntary Acts of Loss of Citizenship (NVOL)

44th Cong., S. 32, Priv. L. No. 9, 19 Stat. 411 (1877), for the relief of Frederick Hinkel

55th Cong., S. 156, Priv. L. No. 36, 30 Stat. 1496 (1898), for the relief of Nellie Grant Sartoris

64th Cong., S. 8075, Priv. L. No. 196, 39 Stat. 1588 (1917), for the relief of Marguerite Mathilde Slidell D'Erlanger

66th Cong., S.J. Res. 90, Priv. L. No. 1, 41 Stat. 1449 (1919), for the relief of Frances Scoville Mumm

66th Cong., S.J. Res. 134, Priv. L. No. 2, 41 Stat. 1463 (1920), for the relief of Augusta Louise De Haven-Alten

79th Cong., H.R. 5278, Priv. L. No. 845, 60 Stat. 1303 (1946), for the relief of Virginia Harris Casardi

81st Cong., H.R. 711, Priv. L. No. 43, 63 Stat. 1091 (1949), for the relief of Mrs. Margaret Gregg Dilnot

81st Cong., H.R. 7563, Priv. L. No. 1018, 64 Stat. A246 (1950), for the relief of Dr. Nicola Di Palma

81st Cong., S. 1866, Priv. L. No. 864, 64 Stat. A191 (1950), for the for the relief of Mrs. Clayre Louise Forsyth

82nd Cong., H.R. 896, Priv. L. No. 144, 65 Stat. A55 (1951), for the relief of Mrs. Clara Raffloer Droesse

82nd Cong., H.R. 2920, Priv. L. No. 713, 66 Stat. A100 (1952), for the relief of Priscilla Ogden Dickerson Gillson de la Fregonniere

82nd Cong., S. 420, Priv. L. No. 639, 66 Stat. A75 (1952), for the relief of Gloria Wilson

84th Cong., H.R. 1166, Priv. L. No. 12, 69 Stat. A6 (1955), for the relief of Florence Meister

84th Cong., H.R. 1410, Priv. L. No. 720, 70 Stat. A98 (1956), for the relief of Giovanna Scano

84th Cong., H.R. 2072, Priv. L. No. 555, 70 Stat. A24 (1956), for the relief of Julian Nowakowski or William Nowak (Novak)

84th Cong., H.R. 5041, Priv. L. No. 763, 70 Stat. A119 (1956), for for the relief of Mrs. Margaret Dows Thyberg

85th Cong., H.R. 1451, Priv. L. No. 43, 71 Stat. A19 (1957), for the relief of Cecelia Vaccaro

85th Cong., H.R. 7826, Priv. L. No. 623, 72 Stat. A128 (1958), for the relief of Israel Baird Poskanzer

85th Cong., H.R. 8374, Priv. L. No. 310, 71 Stat. A123 (1957), for the relief of Virginia Ray Potts

85th Cong., S. 2989, Priv. L. No. 634, 72 Stat. A132 (1958), for the relief of Salvador Miranda

87th Cong., H.R. 1653, Priv. L. No. 420, 76 Stat. 1312 (1962), for the relief of William Falby

87th Cong., H.R. 6226, Priv. L. No. 299, 76 Stat. 1268 (1962), for for the relief of Arlin David English

94th Cong., S. 1699, Priv. L. No. 52, 90 Stat. 2976 (1976), for the relief of Mrs. Hope Namgyal

VETOES

76th Cong., H.R. 5156, for the relief of Adolph Ernest Helms, July 3, 1940 (H.R. Doc. 868, 3rd Sess.)

76th Cong., H.R. 5640, for the relief of Richard Paul Rehn, August 26, 1940 (H.R. Doc. 935, 3rd Sess.)

76th Cong., H.R. 5641, for the relief of Johann Rudolf Hueneberg, August 26, 1940 (H.R. Doc. 936, 3rd Sess.)

76th Cong., H.R. 6409, for the relief of Motiejus Buzas and Bernice Buzas, his wife, October 10, 1940 (H.R. Doc. 968, 3rd Sess.)

76th Cong., H.R. 7179, for the relief of Louis D. Friedman, October 10, 1940 (H.R. Doc. 975, 3rd Sess.)

76th Cong., H.R. 7563, for the relief of Salomon Georg Kaufmann, Doris Kaufmann, and John Michael Peter Kaufmann, July 3, 1940 (H.R. Doc. 865, 3rd Sess.)

76th Cong., H.R. 9651, for the relief of Meier Langermann, his wife Friederik, and son, Joseph, July 2, 1940 (H. R. Doc. 862, 3rd Sess.)

76th Cong., S. 1384, for the relief of Egon Karl Freiherr Von Mauchenheim and Margarete Von Mauchenheim, May 29, 1940 (S. Doc. 201, 3rd Sess.)

76th Cong., S. 3673, for the relief of Kurt Frings, June 19, 1940 (S. Doc. 248, 3rd Sess.)

76th Cong., S. 4085, for the relief of Max Von Der Porten and wife Charlotte Von Der Porten, January 2, 1941 (*Congressional Record* 86:14012)

77th Cong., S. 381, for the relief of Marcel M. Roman, Clara M. Roman, and Rodica E. Roman, February 17, 1942 (S. Doc. 180, 2nd Sess.)

80th Cong., H.R. 1502, for the relief of Herman Trahn, July 18, 1947 (*Congressional Record* 93:9343)

80th Cong., H.R. 2347, for the relief of Mrs. Akiko Tsukado Miller, April 12, 1948 (H.R. Doc. 609, 2nd Sess.)

80th Cong., H.R. 3061, for the relief of Victor C. Kaminski, April 12, 1948 (H.R. Doc. 607, 2nd Sess.)

80th Cong., H.R. 4199, for the relief of George Haniotis, June 21, 1948, (*Congressional Record* 94:9371)

81st Cong., H.R. 3464, for the relief of John Michael Ancker Rasmussen, August 14, 1950 (H.R. Doc. 683, 2nd Sess.)

81st Cong., H.R. 5016, for the relief of Mrs. Virginia Dalla Rosa Prati and her Minor son, Rolando Dalla Rosa Prati, August 14, 1950 (H.R. Doc. 685, 2nd Sess.)

81st Cong., S. 305, for the relief of Julio Laffitte, August 29, 1950 (S. Doc. 210, 2nd Sess.)

82nd Cong., S. 46, for the relief of Ruth Obre Dubonnet, March 16, 1951 (S. Doc. 15, 1st Sess.)

82nd Cong., S. 1436, for the relief of Mrs. Marie Y. Mueller, October 19, 1951 (*Congressional Record* 97:13534)

83rd Cong., H.R. 692, for the relief of Nina Makeef, also known as Nina Berberova, August 24, 1954 (*Congressional Record* 100:14683)

83rd Cong., S. 153, for the relief of Wilhelm Engelbert, March 17, 1954, (S. Doc. 106, 2nd Sess.)

83rd Cong., S. 154, for the relief of George Pantelas, August 17, 1954 (*Congressional Record* 100:14707)

84th Cong., H.R. 3963, for the relief of Ashot Mnatzakanian and Ophelia Mnatzakanian, March 22, 1956 (*Congressional Record* 102:5696)

84th Cong., S. 143, for the relief of Kurt Glaser, June 3, 1955 (S. Doc. 557, 1st Sess.)

85th Cong., S. 2110, for the relief of Shirley Leeke Kilpatrick, March 31, 1958 (S. Doc. 84, 2nd Sess.)

87th Cong., S. 1934, for the relief of Mrs. Chow Chui Ha, April 16, 1962 (S. Doc. 87, 2nd Sess.)

98th Cong., H.R. 2859, for the relief of John Brima Charles, October 17, 1984 (*Congressional Record,* 130:31086)

Key to Categories

QUOTA (Q)

QIER-Ineligible due to race
QIRA-Immediate relative-Adoption
QIRM-Immediate relative-Miscellaneous
QIRW-Immediate relative-Widow of United States citizen
QMDE-Miscellaneous-Due to deeds
QMDP-Miscellaneous-Displaced Persons Act of 1948
QMGN-Miscellaneous-General
QMOC-Miscellaneous-Occupation
QPRF-Preference
QPRP-Returning Permanent Resident

WAIVERS OF EXCLUSION (W)

WCRF-Criminal and/or fraud
WHEL-Health-related
WXCP-Special exemption-Communist Party Membership
WXDD-Special exemption-Draft Dodger
WXIL-Special exemption-Illiteracy

NATURALIZATION (N)

NCOD-Confer or derive citizenship
NMSC-Miscellaneous
NRES-Residence
NRTN-Retention of citizenship
NVOL-Voluntary acts of loss of citizenship
NXCP-Special exemption-Communist Party Membership
NXDD-Special exemption-Draft Dodger
NXEN-Special exemption-English and History and Government
NXPS-Special exemption-Posthumous citizenship

VETO

Chapter One: What is a Private Bill?

[1]House Committee on the Judiciary, *The History of Private Patent Legislation in the House of Representatives*, 96th Cong., 1st Sess., Committee Print No. 1, Washington, D.C., U.S. Govt. Print. Off., 1979, 1. Quoted from R. Gneist, "The History of the English Constitution" 327 (1891). (Cited as House Committee on the Judiciary, *1979 Private Patent Legislation*)

[2]Ibid., 2.

[3]Ibid. See also *United States v. Realty Co.*, 163 U.S. 427 (1896).

[4]Ibid. (Cited from J.Q. Adams, 8 "*Memoirs*" 479-80 (1876)).

[5]Marc D. Yacker, "Private Bills and Federal Charters," Congressional Research Service, Library of Congress, Rpt. 79-110 Gov., 1979, 4.

[6]Ibid.

[7]"Private Bills in Congress," *Harvard Law Review*, 79:8 (June 1966), 1685.

[8]Yacker, op. cit., 3.

[9]U.S. CONST., amend. I.

[10]*Harvard Law Review*, op. cit., (1966), 1685.

[11]*United States v. Realty Co.*, 163 U.S. 427, 440 (1896), U.S. CONST. art. I, s. 8, cl. 1.

[12]U.S. CONST. art. I, s. 8, cl. 3. *See also* The Passenger Cases: *Smith v. Turner* (48 U.S. 283, 1949) *Henderson v. Mayor of New York* (92 U.S. 259, 1875), *Chy Lung v. Freeman* (92 U.S. 275, 1875).

[13]*United States v. Realty Co.*, 163 U.S. 427, 440 (1896). See also *Pope v. United States*, 323 U.S. 1 (1944), *Paramino Lumber Co. v. Marshall*, 309 U.S. 370 (1940).

[14]*Harvard Law Review* (1966), op. cit., 1684-1688. *See also* "The Constitutionality of Private Acts of Congress," *Yale Law Review*, 49:712 (1940).

[15]Asher C. Hinds, *Hinds' Precedents of the House of Representatives of the United States*, Washington, D.C., U.S. Govt. Print. Off., 1907, IV, 247. Prior to 1968 there had been a statutory definition of what constitutes a private bill, but it was primarily used for printing purposes and was repealed. Yacker, op. cit., 1 (28 Stat. 609).

[16]Precedents have established the following: 1) Private bills which benefit individuals but also include generic authority are classified as public; 2) Private bills which are included among general provisions are classified as public legislation; 3) A private bill amended by the Senate to be a public bill remains private in order to reflect the character of its original consideration. Hinds, op. cit., IV, 249, 250.

[17]House Committee on the Judiciary, *1989 Private Patent Legislation,* op. cit., 7. *See also* Yacker, op. cit., 5.

[18]Priv. L. No. 25-23, 6 Stat. 750 (1839).

[19]*Congressional Record*, April 7, 1971, 117:10143.
[20]Priv. L. No. 97-9, 95 Stat. 1736 (1981) accomp. H.R. 2185.
[21]*Congressional Record*, March 2, 1983, 129:3702.

Chapter Two: Rules Governing Private Bills

[1]Yacker, op. cit., 4. "Private Bills," *Congressional Quarterly Inc.*, (Washington, D.C., Congressional Quarterly Inc., 1982), 350. In the case of the latter, the CQ indicates the number of laws enacted is ten.
[2]*Congressional Record*, April 28, 1977, 123:12619
[3]*Congressional Quarterly*, op. cit., 350.
[4]Act of February 24, 1855 (10 Stat. 612) created a Court of Claims; Act of March 3, 1863 (12 Stat. 765); Act of March 3, 1887 (24 Stat. 505). The laws were later declared unconstitutional, *Glidden v. Zdanok* (370 U.S. 530 (1962)). The Act of October 15, 1966 (80 Stat. 958) revised the process to meet the constitutional questions. *See* Jeffrey M. Glosser, "Congress Reference Cases in the United States Court of Claims: A Historical and Current Perspective," *The American University Law Review* 25:3 (Spring 1976), 595, 604.
[5]*Congressional Quarterly*, op. cit., 350.
[6]54 Stat. 670 (Alien Registration Act of 1940), Act of July 1, 1948 (62 Stat. 1206).
[7]The estimate of the claims bills is based on the total private bills introduced in the 81st Congress, without the immigration bills.
[8]60 Stat. 812 (Act of August 2, 1946)
[9]Lewis Deschler, *Deschler's Precedents of the United States House of Representatives.* 94th Cong., 2nd Sess., H.R. Doc. 661, 7, 326. Act of August 2, 1946 (60 Stat. 812)
[10]Sen. Rep. No. 1011, 79th Cong., 2nd Sess., 24.
[11]*Congressional Record*, July 25, 1946, 92:10039, 10067, 10091.
[12]Wm. Holmes Brown, *Constitution, Jefferson's Manual and Rules of the House of Representatives of the United States*, 98th Congress, 2nd Sess. (H. R. Doc. No. 277), Washington, D.C., U.S. Govt. Print. Ofc., Washington, D.C., 1979. *Deschler's Precedents of the United States House of Representatives*, op. cit. Clarence Cannon, *Cannon's Precedents of the House of Representatives of the United States*, Washington, D.C., U.S. Govt. Print. Off., 1935. *Hinds' Precedents of the House of Representatives of the United States*, op. cit.
[13]*Calendars of the United States House of Representatives*, 100th Congress, Final Edition, Washington, D.C., U.S. Govt. Print. Ofc., 1989.
[14]*Congressional Record*, April 28, 1977, 123:12619
[15]Cannon, op. cit., VII, 46.

[16]Ibid.

[17]Prior to 1911 there were two rules for the date of private bills. Rule XXVI designated Friday as the day for consideration of private bills, and Rule XXIV established the sequence on that day for action. In 1911 the former rule was merged into the new Rule XXIV. From 1826 to 1874 Saturdays were also included for private bill consideration, and during the period 1932 to 1935 private bills were considered on Saturday only. There were three means of dispensing with consideration of private bills during the early years: a majority of the House could request other business (1826-1828, 1880-1885); two-thirds of the House could determine other business was in order (1828-1874); or unless otherwise determined by the full House (1885-1935). *Congressional Record*, April 4, 1911, 54:18. Wm. Holmes Brown, op. cit., 625. Hinds, op. cit., IV, 238-240. Cannon, op. cit., VII, 45, 46.

[18]*Congressional Record*,, April 23, 1932, 75:8812.

[19]Ibid., 8810.

[20]Ibid., 8809.

[21]Ibid., 8811.

[22]*Congressional Record*, March 26, 1935, 79:4483. The rule also required a two-thirds vote to dispense with the call of the calendar as well as eliminated the three day calendar rule prior to consideration.

[23]Ibid., 4488, 4484.

[24]Ibid., 4485.

[25]Ibid., 4486, 4485.

[26]Senate Committee on Immigration, *Deportation of Aliens*, 75th Cong., 1st Sess., Washington, D.C., U.S. Govt. Print. Off., 1937, 71.

[27]*Congressional Record*,, May 4, 1937, 81:4164.

[28]Priv. L. No. 84-572, 70 Stat. A29 (1956). H.R. 1269 reported from House Judiciary Committee February 27, 1951 (H.R. Rep. No. 175, 1st Sess.), Recommitted March 20, 1951. After recommittal, H.R. 1269 was incorporated into an omnibus measure, H.R. 6444 (H.R. Rep. No. 1297, 2nd Sess.), and passed the House (*Congressional Record*, March 18, 1952).

[29]84th Cong., H.J. Res. 457, Priv. L. No. 610, 70 Stat. A46 (1956) and 84th Cong., H.J. Res. 683, 70 Stat. A165 (1956).

[30]Deschler, op. cit., 344.

[31]*Congressional Record*, April 6, 1971, 117:9748.

[32]Ibid.

[33]*Congressional Record*, February 19, 1957, 103:2249; *Congressional Record*, March 19, 1963, 109:4569; *Congressional Record*, March 2, 1965, 111:3914; *Congressional Record*, February 21, 1967, 113:4175; *Congressional Record*, April 6, 1971, 117:9747; *Congressional Record*,

March 13, 1975, 121:6608; *Congressional Record*, April 28, 1977, 123:12619; *Congressional Record*, April 9, 1979, 125:7805; *Congressional Record*, March 4, 1987, 133:4743.

[34]*Congressional Record*, October 19, 1951, 97:A6559.

[35]75th Cong., H.J.Res. 153, H.R. Rep. No. 160, 1st Sess. (1937), Recommitted March 2, 1937.

[36]87th Cong., S. 1793, Sen. Rep. No. 913, 1st Sess. (1961), H.R. Rep. No. 1345, 2nd Sess. (1962), Recommitted February 20, 1962.

[37]90th Cong., H.R. 2278, H.R. Rep. No. 290, 1st Sess. (1967), Recommitted June 20, 1967.

[38]95th Cong., H.R. 10210, H.R. Rep. No. 1002, 2nd Sess., Recommitted July 17, 1978.

[39]95th Cong., H.R. 3085, H.R. Rep. No. 182, 1st Sess., Recommitted October 25, 1977.

[40]100th Cong., H.R. 4363, H.R. Rep. No. 596, 2nd Sess., Recommitted October 4, 1988.

[41]100th Cong., H.R. 2358, H.R. Rep. No. 381, 1st Sess., Recommitted May 3, 1988.

[42]76th Cong., H.R. 358, H.R. Rep. No. 203, 1st Sess., Recommitted April 4, 1939.

[43]77th Cong., H.R. 5539, H.R. Rep. No. 1257, 2nd Sess. (1942), Recommitted December 10, 1941.

[44]99th Cong., H.R. 1756, H.R. Rep. No. 517, 2nd Sess. (1986), Recommitted May 6, 1986.

[45]89th Cong., H.R. 1821, H.R. Rep. No. 468, 1st Sess. (1965), Recommitted September 8, 1965.

[46]89th Cong., H.R. 4032, H.R. Rep. No. 505, 1st Sess. (1947), Recommitted August 3, 1965.

[47]83rd Cong., S. 550, Sen. Rep. No. 535, 1st Sess. (1953), H.R. Rep. No. 1160, 2nd Sess. (1954), Recommitted February 16, 1954.

[48]74th Cong., H.R. 10513, H.R. Rep. No. 3038, 2nd Sess. (1936), Private Calendar No. 1309.

[49]92nd Cong., H.R. 2070, H.R. Rep. No. 105, 1st Sess. (1971), Private Calendar No. 21.

[50]93rd Cong., H.R. 2629, H.R. Rep. No. 491, 1st Sess. (1973), Private Calendar No. 64.

[51]97th Cong., H.R. 2276 and H.R. 2277, H.R. Rep. Nos. 679 and 680, 2nd Sess. (1982), Private Calendar Nos. 50 and 51.

[52]90th Cong., H.R. 14276, H.R. Rep. No. 1655, Private Calendar No. 509 later became law (Priv. L. No. 20, 91st Cong., 83 Stat. 873 (1969)); 91st Cong., H.R. 3436, H.R. Rep. No. 1336, Private Calendar No. 275, later became law (Priv. L. No. 99, 92nd Cong., 86 Stat, 1541 (1972)); and 93rd Cong.,

S. 864, Sen. Rep. No. 917, 2nd Sess. (1974), H.R. Rep. No. 1332, 2nd Sess. (1974), Private Calendar No. 155 became law (94th Cong., Priv. L. No. 17, 89 Stat. 1179 (1975)).

[53]The President Pro-Tempore of the Senate, in the absence of the Vice President of the United States, generally presides over the Senate. However, legislative business is primarily delegated to the Majority Leader.

[54]Floyd M. Riddick, *Senate Procedure, Precedents and Practices,* United States Senate. 93rd Congress, 1st Sess., S. Doc. No. 21, Washington, D.C., U.S. Govt. Print. Off., 183.

[55]*Congressional Record,* Oct. 20, 1969, 115:30528. *See also* Chapter 5 - Controversy.

[56]House Committee on Immigration and Naturalization, *Private Relief Bills Regarding Irregular Admission Documents at Time of Entry,* 74th Cong., 2nd Sess. Ser. No. 74-2-3, Washington, D.C., U.S. Govt. Print. Off., Washington, D.C., 1936.

[57]The Bureau of Immigration was established in the Department of Treasury in 1891 (26 Stat. 1084) and was reorganized several times after that by transfer to the Department of Commerce and Labor (32 Stat. 825, 34 Stat. 596, 35 Stat. 982, 37 Stat. 737), and finally to the Department of Justice in 1940 (54 Stat. 230) reflecting its primary focus at the time. Senate Committee on the Judiciary, *History of the Immigration and Naturalization Service,* Prepared for use of The Select Commission on Immigration and Refugee Policy by the Congressional Research Service, Library of Congress, Committee Print. 96th Cong., 2nd Sess., Washington, D.C., U.S. Govt. Print. Off., 1980, 1, 12, 14, 19, 41, 47.

[58]*Congressional Record,* June 18, 1934, 78:12486.

[59]H.Res. 350, *Congressional Record,*, August 23, 1935, 79:14372, 14374.

[60]Ibid., 14378.

[61]Omnibus bills were introduced from the 75th Congress (1937-1938) to the 78th Congress (1943-1944).

[62]52 Stat. 1249.

[63]Ibid.

[64]Ibid.

[65]*Congressional Record,* June 15, 1938, 83:9475.

[66]Ibid.

[67]There were 36 of those bills which became law.

[68]Act of June 28, 1940 (54 Stat. 670).

[69]*INS v. Chadha,* 462 U.S. 919 (1983).

[70]House Committee on the Judiciary, Minutes, 80th Cong., 1st Sess., February 11, 1947.

[71]Ibid., February 27, 1947. *See also* House Committee on the Judiciary, *Department of Justice Investigation*, 83rd Cong., 1st Sess., Ser. No. 2, Pt. 2, Washington, D.C., U.S. Govt. Print. Ofc. 1953, 2251. (Cited as House Committee on the Judiciary, *1953 Investigation of the Department of Justice*).

[72]National Archives, Files of the House of Representatives, RG 233, "Correspondence H-Z," file 81A F10.3, 53. Letter from Deputy Attorney General Peyton Ford to Subcommittee Chairman Francis E. Walter dated July 26, 1950.

[73]Ibid. Letter from Subcommittee Chairman Francis E. Walter to Commissioner A.R. Mackey dated July 17, 1950 and response from Deputy Attorney General Peyton Ford dated July 26, 1950. file 84A F11.7 23889. Letter from Commissioner J.M. Swing to Committee Chairman Chauncey W. Reed dated August 3, 1954 and response dated August 12, 1954. Letter from Commissioner J.M. Swing to Chairman Emanuel Celler dated July 15, 1955 and response dated July 28, 1955. Freedom of Information Act request response from Alice M. Neary, INS, dated June 21, 1989 (Cited as INS 1989 FOIA). Letter from Chairman Emanuel Celler to Commissioner Raymond F. Farrell dated March 25, 1969 and response dated April 11, 1969. Letter from Chairman Peter W. Rodino, Jr. to Commissioner Leonard F. Chapman dated February 22, 1974 and response dated March 4, 1974. Letter from Chairman Peter W. Rodino, Jr. to Commissioner Alan C. Nelson dated May 6, 1985 and response dated June 11, 1985. Letter from Joseph R. Biden, Jr. to Commissioner Alan C. Nelson dated April 27, 1987 and response dated May 27, 1987.

[74]Senate Committee on the Judiciary, *The Immigration Systems of the United States*, Sen. Rep. No. 1515, 81st Cong., 2nd Sess., Washington, D.C., U.S. Govt. Print. Off., 1950, 608. (Cited as Senate Committee on the Judiciary, *1950 S. 1515 Immigration Systems*). *See also* House Judiciary Committee *1953 Investigation of the Department of Justice*, op. cit., 2231.

[75]*Congressional Record*, June 19, 1948, 94:9085.

[76]House Committee on the Judiciary, Minutes, 80th Cong., 1st Sess., December 16, 1947.

[77]Ibid., 81st Cong., 1st Sess., February 1, 1949.

[78]Senate Committee on the Judiciary, Executive Session XIV, June 13, 1979.

[79]Ibid.

[80]House Committee on the Judiciary, Minutes. 81st Cong., 1st Sess., July 26, 1949. *See also* Chpt. 5 - Controversy.

[81]*New York Herald Tribune*, May 25, 1952, 24.

[82]House Committee on the Judiciary, Minutes. 83rd Cong., 2nd Sess., January 12, 1954.

[83]Ibid. *Congressional Record*, January 21, 1954, 100:610.

[84]House Committee on the Judiciary, *1953 Department of Justice Investigation*, op. cit., 2227.

[85]Ibid. National Archives, Files of the Senate Committee on the Judiciary, RG 46, "Letters 1953-1954 S-Z," file 84A-F11. Letter from Chairman William D. Langer to Commissioner J.M. Swing.

[86]*Congressional Record*, January 21, 1954, 100: 610.

[87]Ibid. House Committee on the Judiciary, Minutes, 83rd Cong., 2nd Sess., January 12, 1954.

[88]House Judiciary Committee, National Archives, file 84A F11.7 23889. "Dear Colleague" from Chairman Chauncey W. Reed, dated August 14, 1954 enclosing letter from Chairman Chauncey W. Reed to Commissioner J.M. Swing dated August 11, 1954 and letter from Commissioner J.M. Swing to Chairman Chauncey W. Reed dated August 3, 1954.

[89]Ibid.

[90]Senate Committee on the Judiciary, National Archives, "Correspondence 1953: Immigration and Nationality Act—I&N Subcommittee Memos," file 83A-F11.

[91]Ibid.

[92]House Committee on the Judiciary, Rules of Procedure, 98th Cong. (1983-1984).

[93]Senate Committee on the Judiciary. Executive Session XIV, June 13, 1979, 9.

[94]*Congressional Record*, February 19, 1957, 103:2249; March 12, 1969, 115:6075; April 7, 1971, 117:10142; March 29, 1973, 119:10160; March 2, 1983, 129:3701; May 13, 1985, 131:11682; May 28, 1987, 113:14049.

[95]House Committee on the Judiciary, Minutes, 84th Cong., 1st Sess., February 8, 1955. The term "extreme hardship" was a requirement until the 92nd Congress (1971-1972) when the criteria was changed to "unusual" hardship" and reverted to "extreme hardship" in the 98th Congress (1983-1984).

[96]Senate Committee on the Judiciary, National Archives, "Letters 1955-1956 Mc-Z," file 84A F11. Letter from Commissioner J.M. Swing to Chairman Harley M. Kilgore dated July 15, 1955 and response dated August 2, 1955.

[97]85th Cong., 1st Sess. Sen. Rep. No. 115 (1957), 2.

[98]House Committee on the Judiciary, Rules of Procedure, 90th Cong. (1967-1968).

[99]Ibid., 91st Cong. (1969-1970)

[100]*Congressional Record*, March 12, 1969, 115:6073.

[101]Ibid.

[102]House Committee on the Judiciary, Rules of Procedure, 91st Cong. (1969-1970). "Rule 4" of the 1954 Rules of Procedure became Rule 6 from the

84th Congress through the 91st Congress (1955-1970). The rule then reverted to Rule 4 of the Rules of Procedure.

[103]*Congressional Record*, April 7, 1971, 117:10143.

[104]*Congressional Record*, September 25, 1973, 119:31381.

[105]Senate Committee on the Judiciary, *Annual Activities Report 1979-1980*, 96th Cong., 2nd Sess., Committee Print. Washington, D.C., U.S. Govt. Print. Ofc., 1980, 69. *See also* Senate Committee on the Judiciary Executive Session XIV, June 13, 1979.

[106]Senate Committee on the Judiciary, Executive Session XIV, June 13, 1979, 9.

[107]Ibid., Executive Session VIII, June 24, 1981.

[108]Ibid.

[109]Dear Colleague from Subcommittee Chairman Alan K. Simpson to Members of the Committee on the Judiciary dated May 18, 1981.

[110]Dear Colleague from Subcommittee Chairman Edward M. Kennedy and Alan K. Simpson, Ranking Minority Member dated February 26, 1987.

[111]*Congressional Record*, July 23, 1981, 127:17036.

[112]Ibid.

[113]84th C., S. 143, Veto Message May 10, 1955 (S. Doc. 557, 1st Sess.)

[114]House Committee on the Judiciary, Rules of Procedure, 98th Congress (1983-1984). *Congressional Record*, March 2, 1983, 129:3701.

[115]Ibid., 3702.

[116]Senate Committee on the Judiciary, National Archives, "Correspondence 1953: Immigration and Nationality Act—I&N Subcommittee Memos," file 83A-F11.

[117]House Committee on the Judiciary, Rules of Procedure and Statement of Policy, 99th Congress (1985-1986).

[118]Ibid., 100th Congress (1987-1988).

[119]Letter to Robert H. Helmick, United States Olympic Committee, from House Immigration Subcommittee Chairman Romano L. Mazzoli and other Subcommittee Members dated April 27, 1987; Letter to Robert H. Helmick from Senate Immigration Subcommittee Chairman Edward M. Kennedy and Alan K. Simpson . *See also* Chapter 5 - Controversy.

[120]House Committee on the Judiciary, *Regulating Powers of Attorney General to Suspend Deportation of Aliens*, 80th Cong., 1st Sess., Ser. No. 5, Washington, D.C., U.S. Govt. Print. Off. 1947, 36. (Cited as House Committee on the Judiciary, *1947 Regulating Powers of Attorney General*).

[121]Ibid., 131.

[122]House Committee on Immigration and Naturalization, *Deportation of Aliens*, 74th Cong., 1st Sess., Washington, D.C., U.S. Govt. Print. Off., 1935, 23.

(Cited as House Committee on Immigration and Naturalization, *1935 Deportation of Aliens*).

[123]Act of June 28, 1940 (54 Stat. 670).

[124]Act of June 27, 1952 (66 Stat. 163).

[125]*Congressional Record,* June 18, 1934, 78:12486.

[126]House Committee on Immigration and Naturalization, *1935 Deportation of Aliens*, op. cit., 23.

[127]Ibid., 25. *Congressional Record,* August 23, 1935, 79:14375.

[128]Ibid., 22.

[129]H.Res. 350, *Congressional Record,* August 23, 1935, 79:14372. H.J. Res. 714, 52 Stat. 1249 (1938)

[130]Act of August 7, 1939 (53 Stat. 1243) advanced the previous registry date of June 3, 1921 (Act of March 2, 1929); Act of June 28, 1940 (54 Stat. 670).

[131]*See* Committee Agreements with the Immigration and Naturalization Service and Rules of Procedure of Immigration Subcommittees of the House and Senate. Also, the Acts of July 1, 1948 (62 Stat. 1206) and June 27, 1952 (66 Stat. 163) provided general relief.

[132]House Committee on the Judiciary, *1947 Regulating Powers of Attorney General,* op. cit., 131.

[133]Immigration and Naturalization Service, *Annual Report,* Fiscal Year ending June 30, 1950, 13.

[134]Ibid., Fiscal Year ending June 30, 1951, 7.

[135]House Committee on the Judiciary, *1953 Department of Justice Investigation,* op. cit., 2227, 2231, 2249.

[136]*Congressional Record,* January 21, 1954, 100:610.

[137]House Committee on the Judiciary, National Archives, file 84A F11.7, 23889. Letter from Chairman Francis E. Walter dated July 13, 1955 to General Wilton B. Persons, Deputy Assistant to the President, The White House, and response dated July 27, 1955 from Wilton B. Persons to Mr. Walter. Letter to Mr. Maxwell M. Rabb, Secretary to the Cabinet, The White House dated July 14, 1955 from Judiciary Committee Chairman Emanuel Celler, and response from Mr. Rabb dated July 30, 1955.

[138]House Committee on the Judiciary, *INS Efficiency Legislation,* 97th Cong., 1st Sess., Ser. No. 3, Washington, D.C., U.S. Govt. Print. Ofc., 1981, 57. (Cited as House Committee on the Judiciary, *1981 INS Efficiency*).

[139]H. R. Rep. No. 2973 on H.R. 6106, 81st Cong., 2nd Sess. (1950), 2.

[140]Sen. Rep. No. 1576 on S. 1347, 81st Cong., 2nd Sess. (1950), 2

[141]H. R. Rep. No. 1650 on H.J. Res. 457, 84th Cong., 2nd Sess. (1956), 3.

[142]Sen. Rep. No. 1955 on S. 918, 81st Cong., 2nd Sess. (1950), 2.

[143]H.R. Rep. No. 1991 on H.R. 2225, 81st Cong., 2nd Sess. (1950).

[144]Sen. Rep. No. 6 on S. 44, 82d Cong., 1st Sess. (1951), 2.

[145]H.R. Rep. No. 851 on H.R. 3818, 82nd Cong., 1st Sess. (1951), 2.

[146]H.R. Rep. No. 748 on H.R. 3504, 82nd Cong., 1st Sess. (1951), 3.

[147]House Committee on the Judiciary, *1981 INS Efficiency*, op. cit., 99.

[148]Ibid., 100.

[149]House Committee on Immigration and Naturalization, *Amendments to the Immigration Laws As Recommended by the Department of Labor and by the Secretary's Ellis Island Committee*), Ser. No. 73-2-2, Washington, D.C., U.S. Govt. Print. Off., 1934, 162. (Cited as House Committee on Immigration and Naturalization, *1934 Ellis Island Committee Recommendations.*

[150]Ibid., 182.

[151]Ibid., 185, 166.

[152]House Committee on the Judiciary, *1947 Regulating Powers of Attorney General*, op. cit., 132.

[153]Ibid., 129.

[154]Ibid., 32.

[155]Report of the President's Commission on Immigration and Naturalization, *Whom We Shall Welcome,* Washington, D.C. U.S. Govt. Print. Off., 216. (Cited as *1953 President's Commission*).

[156]Ibid., 214.

[157]House Committee on the Judiciary, *Immigration*, 89th Cong., 1st Sess., Ser. No. 7. Washington, D.C., U.S. Govt. Print. Off., 1965, 146.

[158]House Committee on the Judiciary, National Archives, file 84A F11.7 23889. Letter from Chairman Francis E. Walter to Attorney General Herbert Brownell, Jr. dated November 14, 1955.

[159]Ibid.

[160]House Committee on the Judiciary, National Archives, Box 84A F11.7 23889. Letter from Deputy Attorney General William P. Rogers to Chairman Francis E. Walter dated November 22, 1955.

[161] Sen. Rep. No. 6 on S. 44, 82nd Cong., 1st Sess., 2 (1951)

[162]House Committee on the Judiciary, National Archives, file 84A F11.7 23889. Letter from Rolland Welch, Director, Visa Office to Chairman Emanuel Celler dated April 11, 1955.

[163]Senate Committee on the Judiciary, National Archives, "Letters 1955-1956 Mc-Z," file 84A-F11. Letter dated October 4, 1955 from Chairman Harvey M. Kilgore to Commissioner J.M. Swing.

[164]Senate Committee on the Judiciary, National Archives, file 84A F11. Letter to Commissioner J.M. Swing from Subcommittee Chairman Francis E. Walter dated June 21, 1956. Letter to Chairman James O. Eastland from Subcommittee Chairman Francis E. Walter dated June 26, 1956, and letter to Chairman James O. Eastland from Commissioner J.M. Swing dated August 7, 1956.

[165]Immigration and Naturalization Service, *Annual Report*, Fiscal Year ending June 30, 1956, 24.

[166]Act of September 11, 1957 (71 Stat. 639).

[167]INS 1989 FOIA. Letter from Subcommittee Chairman Frances E. Walter to Commissioner J.M. Swing dated July 23, 1957.

[168]House Committee on the Judiciary, National Archives, file 87A F10.3, 28125. Letter from David W. Kendall, Special Counsel to the President, to Chairman Emanuel Celler dated October 5, 1959 and response dated February 2, 1960 from Subcommittee Chairman Francis E. Walter to David W. Kendall.

[169]Ibid.

[170]Ibid. Letter from Subcommittee Chairman Francis E. Walter to Chairman James O. Eastland dated July 24, 1962.

[171]Ibid. Letter from Myer Feldman, Deputy Special Counsel to the President to House Judiciary Committee Chairman Emanuel Celler dated July 12, 1963.

[172]INS 1989 FOIA. Letter from House Subcommittee Chairman Francis E. Walter to Commissioner J.M. Swing dated May 31, 1960 and response dated June 7, 1960 from Commissioner J.M. Swing to Subcommittee Chairman Francis E. Walter.

[173]Clarence Berdahl, "The President's Veto of Private Bills," *Political Science Quarterly*, Academy of Political Science, 52:LII No. 4 (1937), 528, 531.

[174]76th Cong., H.R. 7179, Veto Message October 10, 1940 (H.R. Doc. 975, 3rd Sess.).

[175]80th Cong., H.R. 3061, Veto Message April 12, 1948 (H.R. Doc. 607, 2nd Sess.).

[176]81st Cong., H.R. 3464, Veto Message August 14, 1950 (H.R. Doc. 683, 2nd Sess.).

[177]81st Cong., H.R. 5016, Veto Message August 14, 1950 (H.R. Doc. 685, 2nd Sess.).

[178]81st Cong., S. 305, Veto Message August 29, 1950 (S. Doc. 210, 2nd Sess.).

[179]84th Cong., S. 143, Veto Message June 3, 1955 (S. Doc. 557, 1st Sess.).

[180]76th Cong., H.R. 7563, Veto Message July 3, 1940 (H.R. Doc. 865, 3rd Sess.).

[181]80th Cong., H.R. 4199, Pocket Veto, Presented to the President June 21, 1948, *Congressional Record*, 94:9371.

[182]84th Cong., H.R. 3963, Pocket Veto, Presented to the President March 22, 1956, *Congressional Record*, 102:5696.

[183]76th Cong., S. 1384, Veto Message May 29, 1940 (S. Doc. 201, 3rd Sess.).

[184]83rd Cong., S. 153, Veto Message March 17, 1954 (S. Doc. 106, 2nd Sess.).

[185]76th Cong., S. 4085, Pocket Veto, Presented to the President January 2, 1941, *Congressional Record*, 86:14012.

[186]82nd Cong., S. 46, Veto Message March 16, 1951 (S. Doc. 15, 1st Sess.). Subsequently enacted into law, Priv. L. No. 634 (66 Stat. 73, 1952).

[187]80th Cong., H.R. 1502, Pocket Veto, Presented to the President July 18, 1947, *Congressional Record*, 93:9343.

[188]82nd Cong., S. 1436, Pocket Veto, Presented to the President October 19, 1951, *Congressional Record*, 97:13534; Subsequently enacted into law without President's approval, Priv. L. No. 769, 66 Stat. A120 (1952).

[189]83rd Cong., S. 154, Pocket Veto, Presented to the President August 17, 1954, *Congressional Record*, 100:14707. This bill later became law (Priv. L. No. 768, 84th Cong., 70 Stat. A122, 1956)

[190]98th Cong., H.R. 2859, Pocket Veto, Presented to the President October 17, 1984, *Congressional Record*, 130:31086

[191]76th Cong., H.R. 5640, Veto Message August 26, 1940 (H.R. Doc. 935, 3rd Sess.).

[192]76th Cong., H.R. 5641, Veto Message August 26, 1940 (H.R. Doc. 936, 3rd Sess.).

[193]76th Cong., H.R. 6409, Veto Message Oct. 10, 1940 (H.R. Doc. 968, 3rd Sess.).

[194]87th Cong., S. 1934, Veto Message April 16, 1962 (S. Doc. 87, 2nd Sess.).

[195]84th Cong., S. 432, Priv. L. No. 146 (69 Stat. A51, 1955).

[196]82nd Cong., S. 1436, Priv. L. No. 769 (66 Stat. A120, 1952).

[197]82nd Cong., H.R. 896, Priv. L. No. 144 (65 Stat. A55, 1951).

Chapter Three: The Process

[1]There are various drafting measures which the Legislative Counsel may consider. For instance, the waiver of a limited number of provisions of the law which would be applicable, or incorporation of every conceivable obstacle for obtaining immigration status. Legislative Counsels frequently consult with the Committees to determine the best means of drafting the bill to obtain passage. See various precedents for types of bills which have become law. Among those are waiver of draft exclusions, but which prohibit obtaining citizenship; adoption cases which prohibit benefits to family members; narcotics exclusions which require a probationary period; physician cases requiring that the doctor reside in the community a period of time prior to granting final status; retroactive permanent residence in lieu of citizenship; a prohibition on receiving compensation for processing a private bill; and a requirement of a bond in health cases to avoid possible public charge problems.

[2]*See How Our Laws are Made* for sample of private bills and their printing through the legislative process (H.R. Doc. 139, 101st Cong., 2nd Sess., Washington, D.C., U.S. Govt. Printing Office, 1990).

[3]Priv. L. No. 81-357, 64 Stat. A4 (1950) accomp. S.J. Res. 105 on behalf of Sister Elizabeth Kenny of the Sister Kenny Foundation in Minneapolis; Priv. L. No. 99-7, 100 Stat. 4316 (1986), accomp. H.R. 3154 on behalf of a treaty trader, and Priv. L. No. 81-821, 64 Stat. A173 (1950) accomp. H.R. 4604 on behalf of skilled craftsmen.

[4]House Committee on the Judiciary, Rules of Procedure, 99th Congress; Senate Committee on the Judiciary, Rules of Procedure, 97th Congress.

[5]Ibid. Rule 3 in the Senate Rules of Procedure requiring "unusual hardship."

[6]*See* Appendix B for Letters of Agreement.

[7]House Committee on the Judiciary, Rules of Procedure, 99th Congress; Senate Committee on the Judiciary, Rules of Procedure, 97th Congress.

[8]Operating Instructions 107.1, Immigration and Naturalization Service, June 21, 1972, 611. Foreign Affairs Manual, v. 9 - Visas, Appendix D, Pt. IV, Note 2., April 4, 1986 and February 14, 1984.

[9]Immigration and Naturalization Service, *Annual Report*, Fiscal Year ending June 30, 1955, 26. Prior to that time reports were reviewed by the General Counsel's office. (House Committee on the Judiciary, *1953 Department of Justice Investigation*, 2231).

[10]Foreign Affairs Manual, op. cit., Note 2.

[11]House Committee on the Judiciary, Rules of Procedure, 100th Congress.

[12]Priv. L. No. 97-44, 96 Stat. 2631 (1982) accomp. H.R. 828.

[13]*See* Chpt. 2 regarding Committee Agreements.

[14]*See How Our Laws Are Made,* op. cit., for format of House and Senate reports.

[15]Priv. L. No. 396, 87th Cong. (71 Stat. A61, 1962) repealing Priv. L. No. 160, 85th Cong. (66 Stat. 163, 1957); Priv. L. No. 496, 87th Cong. (71 Stat. A55, 1962) amending Priv. L. No. 461, 85th Cong. (66 Stat. 269, 1957).

Chapter Four: Public Bills and Private Legislation

[1]Alistair Cook, *Alistair Cooke's America* (New York: Alfred A. Knopf, 1973), 274. Senate Committee on the Judiciary, *1950 S. 1515*, op. cit., 45.

[2]John Higham, *Send These To Me*. (New York: Atheneum, 1975), 21.

[3]Ibid.

[4]Robert A. Divine, *American Immigration Policy, 1924-1952* (New York: Da Capo Press, 1972, Reprinted from 1957 Yale University Press), 21.

[5]The Burlingame Treaty which provided for the free emigration of Chinese to the United States was approved July 28, 1868 and proclaimed in 1870. It was renegotiated November 17, 1880, ratified July 19, 1881, and proclaimed October 5, 1881 (22 Stat 826) in order to allow the President to regulate but not prohibit immigration of Chinese laborers. The Act of March 3, 1875 (18 Stat. 477) had allowed consular officers to inquire of

the morals of Japanese and Chinese contract laborers, but the first total prohibition occurred with the Act of May 6, 1882 (22 Stat. 58) executing the 1880 treaty which suspended all immigration and prohibited naturalization of Chinese for 10 years. The Act of July 5, 1884 (23 Stat. 115) amended the previous act to include all Chinese ancestry. Amendments in 1888, 1893 and 1894 further refined the law (Act of September 13, 1888 (25 Stat. 476), Act of October 1, 1888 (25 Stat. 504), Act of November 3, 1893 (28 Stat. 7), Act of August 18, 1894 (28 Stat. 390)). The Act of May 5, 1892 (27 Stat. 25) extended the Chinese exclusion and bar to citizenship another 10 years. The Act of April 29, 1902 (32 Stat. 176) extended the act until a new treaty was negotiated. The Act of April 27, 1904 (33 Stat. 428) extended the Chinese prohibitions without limitation until repeal in 1943. The Act of February 5, 1917 (39 Stat. 874) included exclusion of aliens from a designated "barred zone" which extended to virtually all Asians. The Act of May 26, 1924 (43 Stat. 153) incorporated into the Quota Act the inadmissibility of aliens ineligible to citizenship. The Act of December 17, 1943 (57 Stat. 600) allowed a quota for China and naturalization.

[6]The Act of February 20, 1907 (34 Stat. 898) allowing the President to enter into agreements barring immigration gave impetus to President Roosevelt's proclamation March 14, 1907 excluding Japanese and Koreans from entry to the United States. The "Gentleman's Agreement" in 1907 and 1908 between the United States and Japan also limited immigration from that country. The Act of February 5, 1917 (39 Stat. 874) prohibited immigration from the "barred zone" which included Japan and most of Asia. In 1924 Japanese were among those determined to be "ineligible to citizenship" and barred from admission (Act of May 26, 1924 (43 Stat. 153) through 1952 when most exclusions relating to race were repealed (Act of June 27, 1952 (66 Stat. 163)).

[7]Act of February 5, 1917 (39 Stat. 874).

[8]Act of June 27, 1952 (66 Stat. 163).

[9]These exclusions were reinforced with the 1924 Quota Act as countries whose natives were "ineligible to citizenship" (Act of May 26, 1924, 43 Stat. 153) and continued in effect until 1952 (Act of June 27, 1952, 66 Stat. 163) when most prohibitions with respect to race were eliminated, thus allowing immigration from Japan and Korea. The 1952 Act allowed an aggregate 2,000 visas for the Asia Pacific Triangle (previously the so-called "barred zone"). However, the Act added chargeability on behalf of those who had Asian ancestry to the respective quota. The Act of September 26, 1961 (75 Stat. 650) removed the 2,000 limitation. In 1965 (Act of October 3, 1965 (79 Stat. 911)) ancestry was removed. In 1934 the Philippines, upon independence, was granted a quota; and in 1946 both

India and the Philippines were granted immigration and naturalization privileges (Act of March 24, 1934, 48 Stat. 456; Act of July 2, 1946, 60 Stat. 416).

[10]Divine, op cit., 6.

[11]Ibid.

[12]Senate Committee on the Judiciary, *1950 S1515*, op. cit., 56.

[13]Ibid.

[14]Divine, op. cit., 8.

[15]Higham, *Send These To Me*, op. cit., 44.

[16]House Committee on the Judiciary, *Grounds for Exclusion of Aliens Under the Immigration and Nationality Act*, Prepared by Congressional Research Service, Library of Congress. 100th Cong., 2nd Sess., Ser. No. 7. Washington, D.C. U.S. Govt. Print. Off., 1988, 9, 17. (Cited as House Committee on the Judiciary, *1988 Grounds for Exclusion*).

[17]Higham, *Send These To Me*, 47.

[18]Act of May 19, 1921 (42 Stat. 5). The Act expired June 30, 1922 but was extended for two years by the Act of May 11, 1922 (42 Stat. 540).

[19]Higham, *Send These To Me*, op. cit., 46, 53. *See also* Divine, op. cit., 6, 7.

[20]Marion T. Bennett, *American Immigration Policies.* (Washington: Public Affairs Press, 1963), 42.

[21]Higham, *Send These To Me*, op. cit., 57. Bennett, op. cit., 61, 71, 80.

[22]E. P. Hutchinson, *Legislative History of American Immigration Policy* (Philadelphia: University of Pennsylvania Press, 1981), 180.

[23]The 1921 Act (Act of May 19, 1921 (42 Stat. 5)) allowed nonquota admission of children of citizens and preference to wives of United States citizens. The Act of May 26, 1924 (42 Stat. 153) granted nonquota status to wives of United States citizens. The Act of May 29, 1928 (45 Stat. 1009) granted nonquota status to spouses of women through a marriage occurring before June 1, 1928 while spouses of women married after May 31, 1928 were granted preference. Also preference was granted wives of permanent residents. In addition, nonquota status was provided to women who had lost citizenship before September 22, 1922 through marriage to an alien but who were unmarried. The Act of June 13, 1930 (46 Stat. 581) allowed entry of Chinese wives of citizens married before May 26, 1924. The Act of July 3, 1930 (46 Stat. 849) allowed women who married United States veterans to immigrate. Another Act on that date (46 Stat. 854) allowed women who lost citizenship by marriage abroad or residence abroad to immigrate. Spouses of women married before July 1, 1932 were declared nonquota, and those married after July 1, 1932 were granted preference through the Act of July 11, 1932 (47 Stat. 656). The Act of May 19, 1948 (62 Stat. 241) allowed nonquota status to husbands of citizens if the marriage occurred prior to January 1, 1948, and inclusion in

the first preference if married after that date. Various laws extending benefits to spouses of those racially ineligible included the Act of June 13, 1930 (46 Stat. 581) allowing entry of Chinese wives of citizens married before May 26, 1924, the Act of August 9, 1946 granting nonquota status to Chinese wives of citizens (60 Stat. 975), the Act of July 22, 1947 (61 Stat. 401) which amended the GI War Brides Act (Act of December 28, 1945, 59 Stat. 659) to cover those ineligible to citizenship if married prior to August 22, 1947, and the Act of August 19, 1950 (64 Stat. 464) which extended benefits to marriages earlier than six months after enactment, and further extended by six months through the Act of March 19, 1951 (65 Stat. 5). The Act of June 27, 1952 (66 Stat. 163) granted nonquota status to all spouses of citizens.

[24]John Higham, *Strangers in the Land: Patterns of American Nativism,* (New York: 2nd ed., Atheneum, 1981), 313.

[25]Senate Committee on the Judiciary, *1950 S. 1515*, op cit., 60. Quoted from report accomp. H.R. 7995, 68th Cong., 13-14.

[26]Act of May 26, 1924 (43 Stat. 153).

[27]Senate Committee on the Judiciary, *1950 S. 1515*, op. cit., 886, 887.

[28]Ibid., 64.

[29]Hutchinson, op. cit., 194.

[30]The Act of May 29, 1928 (45 Stat. 1009) added wives and unmarried children of permanent residents to the first preference.

[31]Senate Committee on the Judiciary, *U.S. Immigration Law and Policy: 1952-1986*, Prepared by the Library of Congress, Congressional Research Service, Committee Print No. 100, 100th Cong., 1st Sess., Washington, D.C., U.S. Govt. Print. Off., 1988, 23.

[32]Under the Act of 1917 (Act of February 5, 1917 (39 Stat. 874)) Mexican natives entered as contract laborers under exceptions to one of the provisions prohibiting such admissions. The first statutory basis for their entry for purposes of labor was the Act of April 29, 1943 (57 Stat. 70) as a result of an agreement between the United States and Mexico August 4, 1942. That Act was re-enforced by the Act of February 14, 1944 (58 Stat. 11), Act of July 3, 1945 (59 Stat. 361), and the Act of May 26, 1947 (61 Stat. 109). From 1948-1951 laborers entered under the various arrangements allowing exceptions to the contract labor laws. The Act of July 12, 1951 (65 Stat. 119), commonly referred to as PL78, the Bracero program, extended the provisions to December 31, 1953, the Act of August 8, 1953 (67 Stat. 500) for two years, the Act of August 9, 1955 (69 Stat. 615) for 3 1/2 years, the Act of August 27, 1958 (72 Stat. 934) for 2 years, the Act of September 14, 1960 (74 Stat. 1021) for six months, the Act of October 3, 1961 (75 Stat. 761) for 2 years, and the Act of December 13, 1963 (77 Stat. 363)) for one year ending December 31,

1964. The 1952 Act (Act of June 27, 1952 (66 Stat. 163) provided a statutory program for temporary labor (H-2) requiring a test of the United States labor market which was one of the first attempts to resolve the seasonal labor problem.

[33]Act of March 2, 1929 (45 Stat. 1512) covered those who had entered prior to June 3, 1921. The Act of August 7, 1939 (53 Stat. 1243) moved the cut-off date to July 1, 1924 and the Act of August 8, 1958 (72 Stat. 546) advanced the date to June 28, 1940, the date of the Alien Registration Act. The 1965 Act (October 3, 1965, 79 Stat. 911) advanced the date to June 30, 1948. The Act of November 6, 1986 (100 Stat. 3359) moved the date to January 1, 1972.

[34]Hutchinson, op. cit., 563.

[35]The Act of June 28, 1940 (54 Stat. 670). Cases reported to the Congress were required to meet "economic hardship" and disapproval required a resolution by both Houses. The Act of July 1, 1948 (62 Stat. 1206) changed the role of Congress by requiring an affirmative act on approved cases. The Act of June 27, 1952 (66 Stat. 163) required Congressional action on disapproved cases through a one-House veto. Criminal cases, however, required approval by both Houses.

[36]House Committee on Immigration and Naturalization, *1935 Deportation of Aliens*, op. cit., 24.

[37]Act of July 1, 1948 (62 Stat. 1206).

[38]Act of June 27, 1952 (66 Stat. 163). The Act narrowed the qualifiying criteria to "exceptional and extremely unusual hardship," and established five qualifying categories, with residence periods between five and seven years, without regard to date-of-enactment cut-off provisions.

[39]The Act of October 24, 1962 (76 Stat. 1247) reduced the five categories to two broad groups: noncriminal and criminal. It also prohibited crewmen from qualifying. The Act of October 3, 1965 (79 Stat. 911) prohibited benefits on behalf of exchange aliens.

[40]462 U.S. 919.

[41]Bennett, op. cit., 68

[42]Act of December 28, 1945 (59 Stat. 659). Waivers for various exclusion provisions were also included in this law.

[43]Act of July 22, 1947 (61 Stat. 401).

[44]Act of June 29, 1946 (60 Stat. 339). The Act of June 28, 1947 (61 Stat. 190) extended from July 1, 1947 until December 31, 1947 authorization to admit fiancees. Authority for admission until December 31, 1948 was granted in 1948 and other pending cases as of that date were also allowed to be processed in 1949 (Act of March 24, 1948 (62 Stat. 84); Act of April 21, 1949 (63 Stat. 56)). In 1970 permanent provisions for fiancees were

enacted without regard to Armed Forces affiliation (Act of April 7, 1970, 84 Stat. 116).

[45]Act of June 20, 1949 (63 Stat. 208).

[46]"Displaced Persons Act of 1948" (Act of June 25, 1948, 62 Stat. 1009).

[47]Act of August 7, 1953 (67 Stat. 400).

[48]"Displaced Persons Act of 1948" (Act of June 25, 1948, 62 Stat. 1009). The orphan provisions allowed admission of children under age 10 for two years, and certain orphan provisions were extended by the Act of June 16, 1950 (64 Stat. 219) to June 30, 1951, and further extended for certain orphans through June 30, 1952 (Act of June 28, 1951, 65 Stat. 96). The Refugee Relief Act of 1953 (Act of Aug. 7, 1953 (67 Stat. 400)) allowed admission of 4,000 orphans under the age of 10 with a two-petition limitation. The Act of July 29, 1953 allowed admission of 500 orphans (67 Stat. 229). The Act of September 11, 1957 (71 Stat. 639) clarified language relating to orphans under the age of 14, stepchildren, illegitimate children, and provided nonquota status for adopted children under the age of 14 and in legal custody of the natural parents for two years. It allowed the admission of eligible orphans as nonquota immigrants until June 30, 1959. The provisions relating to orphans was extended for two temporary periods expiring in 1961 (Act of September 9, 1959 (73 Stat. 490) extended the period to June 30, 1960; Act of July 14, 1960 (74 Stat. 504) extended the time to June 30, 1961)). The Act of September 9, 1959 (73 Stat. 490) also defined "eligible orphans" and set forth petitioning procedures for eligibility. The Act of September 26, 1961 (75 Stat. 650) placed permanently into the statute adoption requirements.

[49]"Displaced Persons Act," (Act of June 25, 1948, 62 Stat. 1009) allowed admission for a two year period July 1, 1948. The Act of June 16, 1950 (64 Stat. 219) extended it to June 30, 1951. The Act of June 28, 1951 (65 Stat. 96) extended the 1948 Act until December 31, 1951. The Act of September 11, 1957 (71 Stat. 639) removed mortgages under the Displaced Persons Act

[50]Divine, op. cit., 116.

[51]Hutchinson, op. cit., 281.

[52]"The Refugee Relief Act 1953" (Act of August 7, 1953, 67 Stat. 400) was in force 3 1/2 years from August 7, 1953 until December 31, 1956 with extensions to various provisions relating to orphans and others which expired June 30, 1961. The Act of August 31, 1954 (68 Stat. 1044) extended the availability of visas to refugees or relatives from certain other countries. The Act of September 11, 1957 (71 Stat. 639) removed mortgages on quotas imposed under the Displaced Persons Act. The Act of September 22, 1959 (73 Stat. 644) allowed spouses and children admitted under the Refugee Relief Act.

[53]Act of September 11, 1957 (71 Stat. 639). A total of 28,656 nonquota visas were provided. The "Internal Security Act," (Act of September 23, 1950, 64 Stat. 987) granted withholding of deportation in cases involving refugee persecution.

[54]Act of July 14, 1960 (74 Stat. 504), extended by the "Migration and Refugee Assistance Act," Act of June 28, 1962 (76 Stat. 121).

[55]Act of October 3, 1965 (79 Stat. 911).

[56]"The Refugee Relief Act of 1980" (Act of March 17, 1980, 94 Stat. 102) redefined refugee to eliminate reference to Communist dominated countries, accepted the UN definition as well as reduced the two year residence period for adjustment of status to permanent residence to one year, and regularized admission levels.

[57]Act of June 27, 1952 (66 Stat. 163).

[58]Senate Committee on the Judiciary, *1950 S.1515.*

[59]Divine, op. cit., 177.

[60]Ibid., 178.

[61]The 1952 Act simplified the quota formula to 1/6 of 1% of the number of inhabitants in the continental United States in 1920 whose national origin, or ancestry, was attributed to that area. The numbers for each country under this simplified version, however, did not change significantly.

[62]Act of September 22, 1959 (73 Stat. 644) added unmarried sons and daughters of citizens to the second preference, unmarried sons and daughters of permanent residents were added to the third preference family, and the fourth preference was changed to married sons and daughters of United States citizens and visas increased.

[63]The 2,000 limit was repealed by the Act of September 26, 1961 (75 Stat. 650), and ancestry was eliminated as a basis for immigration by the Act of October 3, 1965 (79 Stat. 911).

[64]Pre-examination was established by regulation in 1935 under an informal arrangement between INS and Canadian officials to allow visa processing. The procedures continued until suspended in 1952 when provisions of the Act of June 27, 1952 (66 Stat. 163) allowed limited adjustment of status benefits in the United States. When the new law appeared too stringent, pre-exam was reinstated through regulations from 1955 to 1959. The Act of August 21, 1958 (72 Stat. 699) removed the requirement of lawful status at the time of adjustment, but prohibited benefits to natives of contiguous countries. The Act of July 14 1960 (74 Stat. 504) liberalized eligibility further by simply requiring that the alien had been inspected prior to entry. The Act of October 3, 1965 (79 Stat. 911) denied adjustment of status to natives of the Western Hemisphere because of the many Central American and South Americans who entered for the purpose of immediately taking advantage of such benefits (H.R. Rep. No. 745, 1st

Sess. (1965), 22). The Act of October 20, 1976 (90 Stat. 2703) removed the Western Hemisphere prohibitions but denied privileges for those who engaged in unauthorized employment.

[65]Senate Committee on the Judiciary, *1950 S. 1515*, op. cit., 603.

[66]H.R. Doc. No. 520, 82nd Cong., 2nd Sess., 4.

[67]Act of September 11, 1957 (71 Stat. 639).

[68]Act of August 21, 1958 (72 Stat. 699) granted admission privileges to aliens in the first preference category (skills) who had petitions approved prior to July 1, 1958; the Act of September 22, 1959 (73 Stat. 644) allowed nonquota visas issued to second, third, and fourth preference beneficiaries (relatives) approved before January 1, 1959 and increased the visas available for fourth preference. The Act of September 26, 1961 (75 Stat. 650) allowed similar privileges to second and third preference aliens (relatives) with petitions filed prior to July 1, 1961. The Act of October 24, 1962 (76 Stat. 1247) granted nonquota visas to first preference petitions (skills) filed before April 1, 1962 and fourth preference visas filed prior to January 1, 1962 (family).

[69]Act of September 22, 1959 (73 Stat. 644).

[70]Act of September 26, 1961 (75 Stat. 650).

[71]Act of "Mutual Educational and Cultural Exchange Act of 1961," September 21, 1961 (75 Stat. 527). *See* Exclusions for further information on waivers of this requirement.

[72]The Act of June 30, 1950 (64 Stat. 306) allowed the admission of up to 250 sheepherders chargeable to existing or future quotas. The Act of April 9, 1952 (66 Stat. 50) allowed 500 skilled sheepherders admission. The Act of September 3, 1954 (6 Stat. 1145) allowed an additional 385 special nonquota immigrant visas.

[73]Act of December 13, 1963 (77 Stat. 363).

[74]Act of October 3, 1965 (79 Stat. 911).

[75]Senate Committee on the Judiciary, *United States Immigration Law and Policy: 1952-1986,* op. cit., 51.

[76]Ibid., 56.

[77]Parents of minor citizens, however, received exemption from labor certification, thus priority in visa issuance under the ceiling. The Western Hemisphere system became effective July 1, 1968.

[78]H.R. Rep. No. 745, 89th Cong., 1st Sess. (1965), 48.

[79]Sen. Rep. No. 748, 89th Cong., 1st Sess. (1965), 17.

[80]Act of October 20, 1976 (90 Stat. 2703).

[81]H.R. Rep. No. 1553, 94th Cong., 2nd Sess. (1976), 4.

[82]Act of October 5, 1978 (92 Stat. 907).

[83]H.R. Rep. No. 1206, 95th Cong., 2nd Sess. (1978), 5.

[84]Senate Committee on the Judiciary, *U.S. Immigration Law and Policy: 1952-1986*, op. cit., 24.

[85]Act of April 7, 1970 (84 Stat. 116).

[86]Act of December 16, 1975 (89 Stat. 824).

[87]Act of October 5, 1978 (92 Stat. 917).

[88]Act of October 12, 1976 (90 Stat. 2243). Amendments in 1976 and 1977 (Act of August 1, 1977, 91 Stat. 383) postponed the exam required in 1976 by one year and exempted national or internationally renown physicians.

[89]*See* Exclusions for discussion on waivers of the two-year foreign residence requirement.

[90]*Congressional Record*, July 1, 1976, 122:21915.

[91]"The Refugee Relief Act of 1980" (Act of March 17, 1980, 94 Stat. 102).

[92]Act of November 6, 1986 (100 Stat. 3359).

[93]Act of October 5, 1978 (92 Stat. 907).

[94]Act of December 29, 1981 (95 Stat. 1611).

[95]Act of November 14, 1986 (100 Stat. 3655).

[96]Act of December 29, 1981 (95 Stat. 1611).

[97]Act of October 22, 1982 (96 Stat. 1716). Provisions for Amerasians were further extended in 1987 (101 Stat. 1329).

[98]House Committee on Immigration and Naturalization, *1934 Ellis Island Committee Recommendations*, op. cit., 182.

[99]Ibid., 164.

[100]"The Alien Registration Act of 1940" (Act of June 28, 1940, 54 Stat. 670). In 1983 the Supreme Court declared unconstitutional the one-house veto provisions of suspension of deportation procedures under that Act (*INS v. Chadha,* 462 U.S. 919).

[101]Sen. Rep. No. 1204, 80th Cong., 2nd Sess. (1948), 3.

[102]Ibid.

[103]House Committee on the Judiciary, *1947 Regulating Powers of Attorney General*, op. cit., 133.

[104]Acts of June 27, 1952 (66 Stat. 163), Act of October 24, 1962 (76 Stat. 1247), Act of October 3, 1965 (79 Stat. 911).

[105]Committee on the Judiciary, Joint Hearings, *Revision of Immigration, Naturalization, and Nationality Laws*, 82nd Cong., 1st Sess., Washington, D.C., U.S. Govt. Print. Off., 1951, 352.

[106]*1953 President's Commission*, op. cit., 109.

[107]Ibid., 215.

[108]*Congressional Record*, August 28, 1957, 102:16300.

[109]*Congressional Record*, September 6, 1961, 106:18283.

[110]H.R. Rep. No. 1199, 85th Cong., 1st Sess. (1957), 8.

[111]House Committee on the Judiciary, "Intergovernmental Committee for European Migration and Immigration to the United States," Report of a Special Subcommittee of the Committee on the Judiciary. 84th Cong., 1st Sess., H.R. Rep. No. 1570, Washington, D.C., U.S. Govt. Print. Off., 1955, 32.
[112]Ibid.
[113]H.R. Rep. No. 2258, 85th Cong., 2nd Sess. (1958), 3.
[114]*Congressional Record*, August 19, 1954, 99:15269.
[115]H.R. Rep. No. 67, 85th Cong., 1st Sess. (1957), 2.
[116]Sen. Rep. No. 1905, 85th Cong., 2nd Sess. (1958), 2.
[117]House Committee on the Judiciary, *Immigration*, 88th Cong., 2nd Sess., 1964, Ser. 13, Pt. I, 6.
[118]H.R. Rep. No. 745, 89th Cong., 1st Sess., (1965), 12.
[119]H.R. Rep. No. 462, 93rd Cong., 1st Sess., (1973), 2.
[120]Ibid.
[121]H.R. Rep. No. 1301, 95th Cong., 2nd Sess. (1978), 4.
[122]H.R. Rep. No. 264, 97th Cong., 1st Sess. (1981), 11.
[123]House Committee on the Judiciary, *Foreign Medical Graduates,* 95th Congress, 1st Session, Ser. No. 37, Washington, D.C., U.S. Govt. Print. Off., 1977, 68.
[124]House Committee on the Judiciary, *1981 INS Efficiency*, op. cit., 94.
[125]Ibid., 75.
[126]H.R. Rep. No. 264, 97th Cong., 1st Sess. (1981), 13.
[127]Act of November 6, 1986 (100 Stat. 3359).
[128]Priv. L. No. 77-617, 56 Stat. 1252 (1942) accomp. H.R. 6677.
[129]Priv. L. No. 78-380, 58 Stat. 1024 (1944) accomp. H.R. 2707.
[130]Priv. L. No. 76-98, 53 Stat. 1481 (1939) accomp. S. 1291.
[131]Priv. L. No. 79-818, 60 Stat. 1292 (1946) accomp. H.R. 1402.
[132]Priv. L. No. 76-108, 53 Stat. 1485 (1939) accomp. H.R. 5494.
[133]Priv. L. No. 75-803, 52 Stat. 1432 (1938) accomp. H.R. 9731.
[134]Priv. L. No. 76-329, 54 Stat. 1267 (1940) accomp. H.R. 2948.
[135]Priv. L. No. 76-510, 54 Stat. 1341 (1940) accomp. H.R. 6056.
[136]Priv. L. No. 80-70, 61 Stat. 993 (1947) accomp. H.R. 553.
[137]Priv. L. No. 80-317, 62 Stat. 1360 (1948) accomp. S. 1451.
[138]Priv. L. No. 80-225, 62 Stat. 1328 (1948) accomp. H.R. 1215.
[139]Priv. L. No. 80-144, 62 Stat. 1300 (1948) accomp. S. 84.
[140]Priv. L. No. 80-400, 62 Stat. 1395 (1948) accomp. S. 1409.
[141]Priv. L. No. 80-350, 62 Stat. 1373 (1948) accomp. H.R. 1572.
[142]Priv. L. No. 80-308, 62 Stat. 1357 (1948) accomp. H.R. 3787.
[143]Priv. L. No. 80-393, 62 Stat. 1392 (1948) accomp. H.R. 4047.
[144]Priv. L. No. 80-312, 62 Stat. 1359 (1948) accomp. H.R. 4050.
[145]Priv. L. No. 80-254, 62 Stat. 1338 (1948) accomp. H.R. 4403.

[146]Priv. L. No. 80-342, 62 Stat. 1370 (1948) accomp. S. 2060.
[147]Priv. L. No. 80-330, 62 Stat. 1365 (1948) accomp. H.R. 892.
[148]Priv. L. No. 80-241, 62 Stat. 1334 (1948) accomp. H.R. 1912.
[149]Priv. L. No. 80-296, 62 Stat. 1354 (1948) accomp. H.R. 3880.
[150]Priv. L. No. 80-260, 62 Stat. 1340 (1948) accomp. S. 329.
[151]Priv. L. No. 80-90, 61 Stat. 1000 (1947) accomp. H.R. 3243.
[152]Priv. L. No. 80-290, 62 Stat. 1352 (1948) accomp. S. 1142.
[153]Priv. L. No. 81-434, 64 Stat. A35 (1950) accomp. H.R. 6283.
[154]Priv. L. No. 81-947, 64 Stat. A220 (1950) accomp. S. 2047.
[155]Priv. L. No. 81-350, 63 Stat. 1211 (1949) accomp. H.R. 5354.
[156]Priv. L. No. 81-63, 63 Stat. 1098 (1949) accomp. H.R. 679.
[157]Priv. L. No. 81-403, 64 Stat. A23 (1950) accomp. S. 609.
[158]Priv. L. No. 81-635, 64 Stat. A107 (1950) accomp. S. 2556.
[159]Priv. L. No. 81-310, 63 Stat. 1194 (1949) accomp. H.R. 4306.
[160]Priv. L. No. 81-708, 64 Stat. A133 (1950) accomp. H.R. 7815; Priv. L. No. 81-757, 64 Stat. A150 (1950) accomp. H.R. 8289.
[161]Priv. L. No. 81-64, 63 Stat. 1098 (1949) accomp. H.R. 2360.
[162]Priv. L. No. 81-490, 64 Stat. A57 (1950) accomp. S. 2108.
[163]Priv. L. No. 81-321, 63 Stat. 1199 (1949) accomp. H.R. 1447.
[164]Priv. L. No. 81-790, 64 Stat. A161 (1950) accomp. H.R. 7071.
[165]Priv. L. No. 81-194, 63 Stat. 1150 (1949) accomp. H.R. 2084.
[166]Priv. L. No. 81-898, 64 Stat. A204 (1950) accomp. H.R. 6386.
[167]Priv. L. No. 81-1094, 64 Stat. A276 (1951) accomp. H.R. 8759.
[168]Priv. L. No. 81-1028, 64 Stat. A251 (1950) accomp. H.R. 9082.
[169]Priv. L. No. 81-597, 64 Stat. A94 (1950) accomp. H.R. 714.
[170]Priv. L. No. 81-441, 64 Stat. A38 (1950) accomp. H.R. 2591.
[171]Priv. L. No. 81-981, 64 Stat. A233 (1950) accomp. H.R. 7733.
[172]Priv. L. No. 81-363, 64 Stat. A7 (1950) accomp. S. 753.
[173]Priv. L. No. 81-489, 64 Stat. A57 (1950) accomp. S. 1856.
[174]Priv. L. No. 81-943, 64 Stat. A218 (1950) accomp. H.R. 6804.
[175]Priv. L. No. 81-305, 63 Stat. 1193 (1949) accomp. H.R. 2921.
[176]Priv. L. No. 81-346, 63 Stat. 1209 (1949) accomp. H.R. 4042.
[177]Priv. L. No. 81-976, 64 Stat. A231 (1950) accomp. H.R. 4365.
[178]Priv. L. No. 81-779, 64 Stat. A158 (1950) accomp. H.R. 5947.
[179]Priv. L. No. 81-767, 64 Stat. A153 (1950) accomp. H.R. 3169.
[180]Priv. L. No. 81-13, 63 Stat. 1079 (1949) accomp. S. 27.
[181]Priv. L. No. 81-1031, 64 Stat. A251 (1950) accomp. S. 1192.
[182]Priv. L. No. 81-633, 64 Stat. A106 (1950) accomp. S. 2107.
[183]Priv. L. No. 81-1060, 64 Stat. A262 (1950) accomp. S. 2420.
[184]Priv. L. No. 81-660, 64 Stat. A115 (1950) accomp. S. 2795.
[185]Priv. L. No. 81-1097, 64 Stat. A277 (1951) accomp. S. 2981.
[186]Priv. L. No. 81-1098, 64 Stat. A277 (1951) accomp. S. 3125.

[187]Priv. L. No. 81-1099, 64 Stat. A277 (1951) accomp. S. 3378.
[188]Priv. L. No. 81-821, 64 Stat. A173 (1950) accomp. H.R. 4604.
[189]Priv. L. No. 81-856, 64 Stat. A188 (1950), accomp. S. 2897.
[190]Priv. L. No. 81-1042, 64 Stat. A256 (1950) accomp. H.R. 9144.
[191]Priv. L. No. 81-439, 64 Stat. A37 (1950) accomp. H.R. 1487.
[192]Priv. L. No. 81-795, 64 Stat. A163 (1950) accomp. H.R. 1991.
[193]Priv. L. No. 81-170, 63 Stat. 1141 (1949) accomp. H.R. 2349.
[194]Priv. L. No. 81-282, 63 Stat. 1183 (1949) accomp. H.R. 6006.
[195]Priv. L. No. 81-3, 63 Stat. 1073 (1949) accomp. S. 315.
[196]Priv. L. No. 81-178, 63 Stat. 1144 (1949) accomp. S. 1405.
[197]Priv. L. No. 81-789, 64 Stat. A161 (1950) accomp. H.R. 6758.
[198]Priv. L. No. 81-650, 64 Stat. A112 (1950) accomp. S. 1869.
[199]Priv. L. No. 81-56, 63 Stat. 1096 (1949) accomp. H.R. 1010.
[200]Priv. L. No. 81-577, 64 Stat. A87 (1950) accomp. H.R. 3018.
[201]Priv. L. No. 81-776, 64 Stat. A157 (1950) accomp. H.R. 3330.
[202]Priv. L. No. 81-442, 64 Stat. A38 (1950) accomp. H.R. 3771.
[203]Priv. L. No. 81-894, 64 Stat. A203 (1950) accomp. H.R. 3921.
[204]Priv. L. No. 81-977, 64 Stat. A232 (1950) accomp. H.R. 6106.
[205]Priv. L. No. 81-902, 64 Stat. A206 (1950) accomp. H.R. 7282.
[206]Priv. L. No. 81-847, 64 Stat. A184 (1950) accomp. S. 918.
[207]Priv. L. No. 81-245, 63 Stat. 1169 (1949) accomp. S. 1026.
[208]Priv. L. No. 81-619, 64 Stat. A102 (1950) accomp. S. 1637.
[209]Priv. L. No. 81-653, 64 Stat. A113 (1950) accomp. S. 2682.
[210]Priv. L. No. 81-357, 64 Stat. A4 (1950) accomp. S.J.Res. 105.
[211]Priv. L. No. 82-37, 65 Stat. A16 (1951) accomp. H.R. 898.
[212]Priv. L. No. 82-427, 66 Stat. A9 (1952) accomp. S. 471; Priv. L. No. 82-330, 65 Stat. A123 (1951) accomp. S. 2231.
[213]Priv. L. No. 82-996, 66 Stat. A202 (1952) accomp. H.R. 880.
[214]Priv. L. No. 82-376, 65 Stat. A139 (1951) accomp. S. 118.
[215]Priv. L. No. 82-457, 66 Stat. A17 (1952) accomp. S. 440.
[216]Priv. L. No. 82-658, 66 Stat. A82 (1952) accomp. S. 2770.
[217]Priv. L. No. 82-99, 65 Stat. A39 (1951) accomp. H.R. 616.
[218]Priv. L. No. 82-100, 65 Stat. A39 (1951) accomp. H.R. 715.
[219]Priv. L. No. 82-686, 66 Stat. A92 (1952) accomp. H.R. 3152.
[220]Priv. L. No. 82-289, 65 Stat. A109 (1951 accomp. H.R. 711.
[221]Priv. L. No. 82-302, 65 Stat. A123 (1951) accomp. H.R. 901.
[222]Priv. L. No. 82-563, 66 Stat. A52 (1952) accomp. H.R. 1158.
[223]Priv. L. No. 82-599, 66 Stat. A62 (1952) accomp. H.R. 3524.
[224]Priv. L. No. 82-516, 66 Stat. A36 (1952) accomp. H.R. 5347.
[225]Priv. L. No. 82-562, 66 Stat. A52 (1952) accomp. H.R. 978.
[226]Priv. L. No. 82-676, 66 Stat. A88 (1952) accomp. H.R. 1162.
[227]Priv. L. No. 82-360, 65 Stat. A133 (1951) accomp. H.R. 1236.

[228]Priv. L. No. 82-307, 65 Stat. A114 (1951) accomp. H.R. 1818.
[229]Priv. L. No. 82-934, 66 Stat. A183 (1952) accomp. H.R. 2906.
[230]Priv. L. No. 82-605, 66 Stat. A64 (1952) accomp. H.R. 4788.
[231]Priv. L. No. 82-986, 66 Stat. A198 (1952) accomp. H.R. 7095.
[232]Priv. L. No. 82-215, 65 Stat. A82 (1951) accomp. H.R. 617.
[233]Priv. L. No. 82-32, 65 Stat. A15 (1951) accomp. H.R. 664.
[234]Priv. L. No. 82-164, 65 Stat. A63 (1951) accomp. H.R. 702.
[235]Priv. L. No. 82-341, 65 Stat. A127 (1951) accomp. H.R. 1100.
[236]Priv. L. No. 82-63, 65 Stat. A25 (1951) accomp. H.R. 1150.
[237]Priv. L. No. 82-922, 66 Stat. A179 (1952) accomp. H.R. 1464.
[238]Priv. L. No. 82-923, 66 Stat. A180 (1952) accomp. H.R. 1477.
[239]Priv. L. No. 82-14, 65 Stat. A7 (1951) accomp. H.R. 1479.
[240]Priv. L. No. 82-948, 66 Stat. A187 (1952) accomp. H.R. 4250.
[241]Priv. L. No. 82-176, 65 Stat. A67 (1951) accomp. H.R. 2299.
[242]Priv. L. No. 82-684, 66 Stat. A91 (1951) accomp. H.R. 3124.
[243]Priv. L. No. 82-747, 66 Stat. A112 (1952) accomp. H.R. 3155.
[244]Priv. L. No. 82-296, 65 Stat. A111 (1951) accomp. H.R. 3965.
[245]Priv. L. No. 82-752, 66 Stat. A114 (1952) accomp. H.R. 5208.
[246]Priv. L. No. 82-500, 66 Stat. 31 (1952) accomp. S. 1541.
[247]Priv. L. No. 82-836, 66 Stat. A150 (1952) accomp. S. 1724.
[248]Priv. L. No. 82-955, 66 Stat. A189 (1952) accomp. H.R. 4709.
[249]Priv. L. No. 82-420, 66 Stat. A6 (1952) accomp. H.R. 961.
[250]Priv. L. No. 82-528, 66 Stat. A40 (1952) accomp. H.R. 648.
[251]Priv. L. No. 82-399, 65 Stat. A146 (1951) accomp. H.R. 853.
[252]Priv. L. No. 82-342, 65 Stat. A127 (1951) accomp. H.R. 1252.
[253]Priv. L. No. 82-321, 65 Stat. A120 (1951) accomp. H.R. 1598.
[254]Priv. L. No. 82-25, 65 Stat. A95 (1951) accomp. H.R. 2307.
[255]Priv. L. No. 82-124, 65 Stat. A47 (1951) accomp. H.R. 2310.
[256]Priv. L. No. 82-310, 65 Stat. A116 (1951) accomp. H.R. 2498.
[257]Priv. L. No. 82-95, 65 Stat. A37 (1951) accomp. S. 178.
[258]Priv. L. No. 82-93, 65 Stat. A37 (1951) accomp. S. 364.
[259]Priv. L. No. 82-550, 66 Stat. A47 (1952) accomp. S. 1469.
[260]Priv. L. No. 82-655, 66 Stat. A80 (1952) accomp. S. 2145.
[261]Priv. L. No. 82-30, 65 Stat. A14 (1951) accomp. H.R. 622.
[262]Priv. L. No. 82-745, 66 Stat. A112 (1952) accomp. H.R. 2719.
[263]Priv. L. No. 82-859, 66 Stat. A159 (1952) accomp. S. 1470.
[264]Priv. L. No. 82-386, 65 Stat. A142 (1951) accomp. H.R. 884.
[265]Priv. L. No. 82-777, 66 Stat. A123 (1952) accomp. H.R. 885.
[266]Priv. L. No. 82-81, 65 Stat. A32 (1951) accomp. S. 291.
[267]Priv. L. No. 82-647, 66 Stat. A77 (1952) accomp. S. 1420.
[268]Priv. L. No. 82-737, 66 Stat. A109 (1952) accomp. S. 2566.
[269]Priv. L. No. 83-83, 67 Stat. A31 (1953) accomp. S. 315.

[270]Priv. L. No. 83-986, 68 Stat. A285 (1954) accomp. S. 3145.
[271]Priv. L. No. 83-677, 68 Stat. A166 (1954) accomp. H.R. 1768.
[272]Priv. L. No. 83-650, 68 Stat. A158 (1954) accomp. S. 2504.
[273]Priv. L. No. 83-272, 68 Stat. A17 (1954) accomp. H.R. 711.
[274]Priv. L. No. 83-250, 68 Stat. A10 (1954) accomp. S. 205.
[275]Priv. L. No. 83-475, 68 Stat. A97 (1954) accomp. S. 1955.
[276]Priv. L. No. 83-169, 67 Stat. A60 (1953) accomp. H.R. 3831.
[277]Priv. L. No. 83-651, 68 Stat. A158 (1954) accomp. S. 2512.
[278]Priv. L. No. 83-344, 68 Stat. A44 (1954) accomp. S. 2534.
[279]Priv. L. No. 83-659, 68 Stat. A161 (1954) accomp. S. 3433.
[280]Priv. L. No. 83-693, 68 Stat. A171 (1954) accomp. H.R. 2499.
[281]Priv. L. No. 83-999, 68 Stat. A289 (1954) accomp. S. 2618.
[282]Priv. L. No. 83-404, 68 Stat. A68 (1954) accomp. H.R. 675.
[283]Priv. L. No. 83-50, 67 Stat. A19 (1953) accomp. H.R. 974.
[284]Priv. L. No. 83-62, 67 Stat. A24 (1953) accomp. H.R. 1103.
[285]Priv. L. No. 83-752, 68 Stat. A190 (1954) accomp. H.R. 3855.
[286]Priv. L. No. 83-457, 68 Stat. A92 (1954) accomp. S. 740.
[287]Priv. L. No. 83-296, 68 Stat. A26 (1954) accomp. H.R. 1358.
[288]Priv. L. No. 83-566, 68 Stat. A130 (1954) accomp. S. 278.
[289]Priv. L. No. 83-744, 68 Stat. A188 (1954) accomp. H.R. 2879.
[290]Priv. L. No. 83-807, 68 Stat. A208 (1954) accomp. H.R. 3566.
[291]Priv. L. No. 83-70, 67 Stat. A26 (1953) accomp. H.R. 3678.
[292]Priv. L. No. 83-487, 68 Stat. A101 (1954) accomp. H.R. 4701.
[293]Priv. L. No. 83-121, 67 Stat. A44 (1953) accomp. S. 69.
[294]Priv. L. No. 83-89, 67 Stat. A33 (1953) accomp. S. 1262.
[295]Priv. L. No. 83-509, 68 Stat. A112 (1954) accomp. S. 1382.
[296]Priv. L. No. 83-603, 68 Stat. A142 (1954) accomp. S. 2065.
[297]Priv. L. No. 83-969, 68 Stat. A279 (1954) accomp. S. 2345.
[298]Priv. L. No. 83-168, 67 Stat. A60 (1953) accomp. H.R. 2604.
[299]Priv. L. No. 83-543, 68 Stat. A123 (1954) accomp. H.R. 6650.
[300]Priv. L. No. 83-716, 68 Stat. A179 (1954) accomp. H.R. 8334.
[301]Priv. L. No. 83-456, 68 Stat. A91 (1954) accomp. S. 629.
[302]Priv. L. No. 83-591, 68 Stat. A138 (1954) accomp. S. 855.
[303]Priv. L. No. 83-530, 68 Stat. A119 (1954) accomp. S. 676.
[304]Priv. L. No. 83-621, 68 Stat. A148 (1954) accomp. S. 1212.
[305]Priv. L. No. 83-185, 67 Stat. A65 (1953) accomp. H.R. 1756.
[306]Priv. L. No. 83-110, 67 Stat. A40 (1953) accomp. H.R. 765.
[307]Priv. L. No. 83-728, 68 Stat. A183 (1954) accomp. H.R. 804.
[308]Priv. L. No. 83-537, 68 Stat. A121 (1954) accomp. H.R. 944.
[309]Priv. L. No. 83-330, 68 Stat. A38 (1954) accomp. H.R. 962.
[310]Priv. L. No. 83-297, 68 Stat. A26 (1954) accomp. H.R. 1688.
[311]Priv. L. No. 83-166, 67 Stat. A59 (1953) accomp. H.R. 1695.

[312]Priv. L. No. 83-116, 67 Stat. A42 (1953) accomp. H.R. 1886.
[313]Priv. L. No. 83-810, 68 Stat. A209 (1954) accomp. H.R. 3874.
[314]Priv. L. No. 83-329, 68 Stat. A38 (1954) accomp. H.R. 5085.
[315]Priv. L. No. 83-835, 68 Stat. A217 (1954) accomp. H.R. 7151.
[316]Priv. L. No. 83-125, 67 Stat. A45 (1953) accomp. S. 196.
[317]Priv. L. No. 83-608, 68 Stat. A144 (1954) accomp. S. 233.
[318]Priv. L. No. 83-257, 68 Stat. A12 (1954) accomp. S. 506.
[319]Priv. L. No. 83-258, 68 Stat. A13 (1954) accomp. S. 569.
[320]Priv. L. No. 83-529, 68 Stat. A118 (1954) accomp. S. 579.
[321]Priv. L. No. 83-588, 68 Stat. A137 (1954) accomp. S. 795.
[322]Priv. L. No. 83-473, 68 Stat. A96 (1954) accomp. S. 1682.
[323]Priv. L. No. 84-153, 69 Stat. A53 (1955) accomp. H.R. 995.
[324]Priv. L. No. 84-449, 69 Stat. A153 (1955) accomp. H.R. 2339.
[325]Priv. L. No. 84-483, 69 Stat. A164 (1955) accomp. H.R. 2916.
[326]Priv. L. No. 84-107, 69 Stat. A37 (1955) accomp. H.R. 1081.
[327]Priv. L. No. 84-330, 69 Stat. A113 (1955) accomp. H.R. 1160.
[328]Priv. L. No. 84-418, 69 Stat. A143 (1955) accomp. H.R. 1552.
[329]Priv. L. No. 84-249, 69 Stat. A88 (1955) accomp. H.R. 962.
[330]Priv. L. No. 84-486, 69 Stat. A164 (1955) accomp. H.R. 5546.
[331]Priv. L. No. 84-744, 70 Stat. A111 (1956) accomp. H.R. 877.
[332]Priv. L. No. 84-456, 69 Stat. A155 (1955) accomp. H.R. 4544.
[333]Priv. L. No. 84-360, 69 Stat. A122 (1955) accomp. H.R. 6613.
[334]Priv. L. No. 84-491, 70 Stat. A3 (1956) accomp. H.R. 1022.
[335]Priv. L. No. 84-554, 70 Stat. A24 (1956) accomp. H.R. 2054.
[336]Priv. L. No. 84-598, 70 Stat. A41 (1956) accomp. H.R. 4039.
[337]Priv. L. No. 84-512, 70 Stat. A10 (1956) accomp. H.R. 1193.
[338]Priv. L. No. 84-200, 69 Stat. A69 (1955) accomp. H.R. 3075.
[339]Priv. L. No. 84-446, 69 Stat. A152 (1955) accomp. S. 2088.
[340]Priv. L. No. 84-533, 70 Stat. A17 (1956) accomp. H.R. 1887.
[341]Priv. L. No. 84-307, 69 Stat. A106 (1955) accomp. H.R. 2242.
[342]Priv. L. No. 84-27, 69 Stat. A10 (1955) accomp. H.R. 2354.
[343]Priv. L. No. 84-272, 69 Stat. A95 (1955) accomp. H.R. 2495.
[344]Priv. L. No. 84-583, 70 Stat. A34 (1956) accomp. H.R. 3857.
[345]Priv. L. No. 84-827, 70 Stat. A156 (1956) accomp. H.R. 4152.
[346]Priv. L. No. 84-528, 70 Stat. A15 (1956) accomp. H.R. 5870.
[347]Priv. L. No. 85-317, 71 Stat. A125 (1957) accomp. S. 1175.
[348]Priv. L. No. 85-105, 71 Stat. A42 (1954) accomp. S. 1833.
[349]Priv. L. No. 85-169, 71 Stat. A105 (1957) accomp. H.R. 4854.
[350]Priv. L. No. 85-15, 71 Stat. A7 (1957) accomp. H.R. 1757.
[351]Priv. L. No. 85-271, 71 Stat. A106 (1957) accomp. S. 1290.
[352]Priv. L. No. 85-84, 71 Stat. A36 (1957) accomp. S. 530.
[353]Priv. L. No. 85-394, 72 Stat. A27 (1958) accomp. S. 1578.

[354]Priv. L. No. 85-282, 71 Stat. A109 (1957) accomp. S. 2095.
[355]Priv. L. No. 85-378, 72 Stat. A20 (1958) accomp. S. 1519.
[356]Priv. L. No. 85-513, 72 Stat. A74 (1958) accomp. S. 3060.
[357]Priv. L. No. 85-401, 72 Stat. A30 (1958) accomp. H.R. 8348.
[358]Priv. L. No. 86-142, 73 Stat. A62 (1959) accomp. S. 1557.
[359]Priv. L. No. 86-337, 74 Stat. A42 (1960) accomp. H.R. 4834.
[360]Priv. L. No. 86-57, 73 Stat. A25 (1959) accomp. S. 855.
[361]Priv. L. No. 86-361, 74 Stat. A52 (1960) accomp. S. 2528.
[362]Priv. L. No. 86-394, 74 Stat. A64 (1960) accomp. S. 2566.
[363]Priv. L. No. 86-367, 74 Stat. A54 (1960) accomp. S. 2886.
[364]Priv. L. No. 86-259, 74 Stat. A13 (1960) accomp. H.R. 9444.
[365]Priv. L. No. 86-37, 73 Stat. A18 (1959) accomp. S. 110.
[366]Priv. L. No. 86-122, 73 Stat. A55 (1959) accommp. H.R. 4242.
[367]Priv. L. No. 86-442, 74 Stat. A82 (1960) accomp. H.R. 7551.
[368]Priv. L. No. 87-35, 75 Stat. 862 (1961) accomp. S. 546.
[369]Priv. L. No. 87-417, 76 Stat. 1311 (1962) accomp. S. 2011.
[370]Priv. L. No. 87-73, 75 Stat. 874 (1961) accomp. S. 400.
[371]Priv. L. No. 87-251, 75 Stat. 941 (1961) accomp. H.R. 4028.
[372]Priv. L. No. 87-473, 76 Stat. 1330 (1962) accomp. H.R. 1469.
[373]Priv. L. No. 87-178, 75 Stat. 910 (1961) accomp. S. 570.
[374]Priv. L. No. 87-180, 75 Stat. 910 (1961) accomp. S. 722.
[375]Priv. L. No. 87-323, 76 Stat. 1277 (1962) accomp. S. 2385.
[376]Priv. L. No. 87-409, 76 Stat. 1309 (1962) accomp. H.R. 1404.
[377]Priv. L. No. 87-530, 76 Stat. 1350 (1962) accomp. H.R. 1458.
[378]Priv. L. No. 87-243, 75 Stat. 939 (1961) accomp. H.R. 2666.
[379]Priv. L. No. 87-328, 76 Stat. 1279 (1962) accomp. S. 899.
[380]Priv. L. No. 87-608, 76 Stat. 1381 (1962) accomp. S. 3336.
[381]Priv. L. No. 88-56, 77 Stat. 892 (1963) accomp. H.R. 2287.
[382]Priv. L. No. 88-195, 78 Stat. 1132 (1964) accomp. H.R. 7347.
[383]Priv. L. No. 88-158, 77 Stat. 932 (1963) accomp. H.R. 1560.
[384]Priv. L. No. 88-329, 78 Stat. 1188 (1964) accomp. S. 584.
[385]Priv. L. No. 88-154, 77 Stat. 930 (1963) accomp. S. 1096.
[386]Priv. L. No. 88-50, 77 Stat. 890 (1963) accomp. H.R. 1398.
[387]Priv. L. No. 88-57, 77 Stat. 892 (1963) accomp. H.R. 2444.
[388]Priv. L. No. 88-102, 77 Stat. 909 (1963) accomp. H.R. 2757.
[389]Priv. L. No. 88-177, 78 Stat. 1125 (1964) accomp. H.R. 1182.
[390]Priv. L. No. 89-144, 79 Stat. 1389 (1965) accomp. H.R. 6235.
[391]Priv. L. No. 89-455, 80 Stat. 1708 (1966) accomp. S. 2451.
[392]Priv. L. No. 89-337, 80 Stat. 1662 (1966) accomp. S. 2555
[393]Priv. L. No. 89-178, 79 Stat. 1403 (1965) accomp. H.R. 1393.
[394]Priv. L. No. 89-226, 80 Stat. 1619 (1966) accomp. H.R. 5231.
[395]Priv. L. No. 89-451, 80 Stat. 1706 (1966) accomp. S. 2010.

[396]Priv. L. No. 90-204, 81 Stat. 1050 (1968) accomp. S. 866.
[397]Priv. L. No. 90-121, 81 Stat. 1026 (1967) accomp. S. 1458.
[398]Priv. L. No. 90-339, 82 Stat. 1428 (1968) accomp. S. 2706.
[399]Priv. L. No. 90-42, 81 Stat. 999 (1967) accomp. S. 168.
[400]Priv. L. No. 91-162, 84 Stat. 2132 (1970) accomp. S. 2976.
[401]Priv. L. No. 91-17, 83 Stat. 872 (1969) accomp. H.R. 1939.
[402]Priv. L. No. 91-190, 84 Stat. 2151 (1970) accomp. S. 3620.
[403]Priv. L. No. 91-146, 84 Stat. 2127 (1970) accomp. S. 1704.
[404]Priv. L. No. 91-69, 83 Stat. 891 (1969) accomp. H.R. 6600.
[405]Priv. L. No. 92-14, 85 Stat. 838 (1971) accomp. S. 672.
[406]Priv. L. No. 92-90, 86 Stat. 1538 (1972) accomp. H.R. 1974.
[407]Priv. L. No. 92-129, 86 Stat. 1554 (1972) accomp. S. 2575.
[408]Priv. L. No. 92-42, 85 Stat. 850 (1971) accomp. H.R. 1899.
[409]Priv. L. No. 92-115, 86 Stat. 1548 (1972) accomp. S. 559.
[410]Priv. L. No. 93-12, 87 Stat. 1101 (1973) accomp. H.R. 1366.
[411]Priv. L. No. 93-13, 87 Stat. 1101 (1973) accomp. H.R. 1377.
[412]Priv. L. No. 93-29, 87 Stat. 1107 (1973) accomp. H.R. 3754.
[413]Priv. L. No. 93-49, 87 Stat. 1114 (1973) accomp. H.R. 3758.
[414]Priv. L. No. 93-7, 87 Stat. 1099 (1973) accomp. S. 89
[415]Priv. L. No. 93-70, 88 Stat. 2371 (1974) accomp. S. 428.
[416]Priv. L. No. 93-63, 88 Stat. 2369 (1974) accomp. S. 816.
[417]Priv. L. No. 93-21, 87 Stat. 1104 (1973) accomp. H.R. 1356.
[418]Priv. L. No. 93-22, 87 Stat. 1104 (1973) accomp. H.R. 1367.
[419]Priv. L. No. 94-60, 90 Stat. 2980 (1976) accomp. H.R. 1394; Priv. L. No. 94-61, 90 Stat. 2980 (1976) accomp. H.R. 1395; Priv. L. No. 94-62, 90 Stat. 2980 (1976) accomp. H.R. 1396.
[420]Priv. L. No. 94-73, 90 Stat. 2984 (1976) accomp. H.R. 2565.
[421]Priv. L. No. 94-24, 89 Stat. 1186 (1975) accomp. S. 447.
[422]Priv. L. No. 94-128, 90 Stat. 3007 (1976) accomp. H.R. 9543.
[423]Priv. L. No. 94-115, 90 Stat. 3001 (1976) accomp. H.R. 10793.
[424]Priv. L. No. 94-51, 90 Stat. 2975 (1976) accomp. S. 52.
[425]Priv. L. No. 94-3, 89 Stat. 1165 (1975) accomp. H.R. 1556.
[426]Priv. L. No. 94-111, 90 Stat. 2999 (1976) accomp. H.R. 4583.
[427]Priv. L. No. 95-32, 92 Stat. 3804 (1978) accomp. H.R. 1939.
[428]Priv. L. No. 95-94, 92 Stat. 3832 (1978) accomp. H.R. 2756.
[429]Priv. L. No. 95-5, 91 Stat. 1648 (1977) accomp. H.R. 4246.
[430]Priv. L. No. 95-37, 92 Stat. 3806 (1978) accomp. H.R. 1552.
[431]Priv. L. No. 95-162, 92 Stat. 3859 (1978) accomp. H.R. 2291.
[432]Priv. L. No. 95-17, 91 Stat. 1655 (1977) accomp. H.R. 3461.
[433]Priv. L. No. 95-86, 92 Stat. 3829 (1978) accomp. H.R. 1750.
[434]Priv. L. No. 95-103, 92 Stat. 3835 (1978) accomp. H.R. 4875.
[435]Priv. L. No. 95-125, 92 Stat. 3844 (1978) accomp. S. 3109.

[436]Priv. L. No. 95-159, 92 Stat. 3858 (1978) accomp. H.R. 1748.
[437]Priv. L. No. 95-40, 92 Stat. 3807 (1978) accomp. H.R. 3996.
[438]Priv. L. No. 95-165, 92 Stat. 3860 (1978) accomp. H.R. 8192.
[439]Priv. L. No. 95-131, 92 Stat. 3846 (1978) accomp. H.R. 2256.
[440]Priv. L. No. 96-103, 94 Stat. 3629 (1980) accomp. H.R. 2145.
[441]Priv. L. No. 96-92, 94 Stat. 3625 (1980) accomp. H.R. 2433.
[442]Priv. L. No. 96-95, 94 Stat. 3626 (1980) accomp. H.R. 3138.
[443]Priv. L. No. 96-60, 94 Stat. 3598 (1980) accomp. S. 215.
[444]Priv. L. No. 96-99, 94 Stat. 3628 (1980) accomp. S. 1772.
[445]Priv. L. No. 96-42, 93 Stat. 1406 (1979) accomp. H.R. 1619.
[446]Priv. L. No. 96-50, 94 Stat. 3593 (1980) accomp. H.R. 1829.
[447]Priv. L. No. 96-63, 94 Stat. 3599 (1980) accomp. S. 707.
[448]Priv. L. No. 97-34, 96 Stat. 2627 (1982) accomp. H.R. 684.
[449]Priv. L. No. 97-17, 96 Stat. 2619 (1982) accomp. H.R. 1681.
[450]Priv. L. No. 97-7, 95 Stat. 1735 (1981) accomp. H.R. 1785.
[451]Priv. L. No. 97-36, 96 Stat. 2627 (1982) accomp. H.R. 1826.
[452]Priv. L. No. 97-4, 95 Stat. 1734 (1981) accomp. H.R. 1469.
[453]Priv. L. No. 97-44, 96 Stat. 2631 (1982) accomp. H.R. 828.
[454]Priv. L. No. 97-26, 96 Stat. 2623 (1982) accomp. S. 167.
[455]Priv. L. No. 98-28, 98 Stat. 3426 (1984) accomp. H.R. 1236.
[456]Priv. L. No. 98-27, 98 Stat. 3426 (1984) accomp. H.R. 1150.
[457]Priv. L. No. 98-25, 98 Stat. 3425 (1984) accomp. S. 1060.
[458] Priv. L. No. 99-5, 100 Stat. 4314 (1986) accomp. H.R. 483.
[459]Priv. L. No. 99-2, 100 Stat. 4313 (1986), accomp. H.R. 737.
[460]Priv. L. No. 99-9, 100 Stat. 4316 (1986), accomp. H.R. 3154.
[461]Priv. L. No. 99-19,100 Stat. 4321 (1986), accomp. H.R. 5016.
[462]Priv. L. No. 100-38, 102 Stat. 4861 (1988), accomp. H.R. 2109.
[463]Priv. L. No. 100-35, 102 Stat. 4859 (1988), accomp. S. 2637.
[464]Priv. L. No. 100-4, 101 Stat. 1975 (1987), accomp. H.R. 1191.
[465]Priv. L. No. 100-48, November 16, 1988 accomp. S. 1842.
[466]Hutchinson, op. cit., 388.
[467]Ibid., 404.
[468]Ibid., 406.
[469]18 Stat. 477.
[470]House Committee on the Judiciary, *1988 Grounds for Exclusion*, op cit., 6.
[471]Ibid.
[472]Ibid., 6 (Quoted from *Congressional Record*, December 7, 1874, 3:4).
[473]Ibid., 7.
[474]Act of August 3, 1882 (22 Stat. 214).
[475]House Committee on the Judiciary, *1988 Grounds for Exclusion*, op. cit., 7.
[476]The Passenger Cases *(Smith v. Turner)*, 48 U.S. 282 (1849); *Henderson v. Mayor of City of New York*, 92 U.S. 259 (1875.

[477]Hutchinson, op. cit., 412.
[478]22 Stat. 58.
[479]Higham, *Send These to Me*, op. cit., 35, 36.
[480]57 Stat. 600.
[481]Act of February 26, 1885 (23 Stat. 332).
[482]House Committee on the Judiciary, *1988 Grounds for Exclusion*, op. cit., 8.
[483]Ibid., 9.
[484]Ibid.
[485]Act of March 3, 1891 (26 Stat. 1084).
[486]House Committee on the Judiciary, *1988 Grounds for Exclusion*, op. cit., 10.
[487]Ibid., 10-11.
[488]Ibid., 13. (Quoted from Higham, *Strangers in the Land*, 111)
[489]Act of March 3, 1903 (32 Stat. 1213).
[490]House Committee on the Judiciary, *1988 Grounds for Exclusion*, op. cit., 13.
[491]Ibid. (Quoted from H.R. Rep. No. 982, 57th Congress, 1st Sess., March 18, 1902, 3).
[492]Ibid.
[493]Ibid.
[494]34 Stat. 898.
[495]House Committee on the Judiciary, *1988 Grounds for Exclusion*, op. cit., 14.
[496]Ibid. (Quoted from *Congressional Record*,, December 7, 1903, 38:3).
[497]39 Stat. 874.
[498]House Committee on the Judiciary, *1988 Grounds for Exclusion*, op. cit., 16-17.
[499]Ibid., 17. (Quoted from *Congressional Record*, February 3, 1915, 52:2973).
[500]Ibid. (Quoted from *Congressional Record*, August 17, 1916, 53:12773).
[501]Ibid., 21 (Quoted from H. R. Rep. No. 95, 64th Cong., 1st Sess. (1916), 2).
[502]Ibid. (Quoted from Sen. Rep. No. 352, 64th Cong., 1st Sess. (1916), 5).
[503]Ibid., 22.
[504]Act of October 16, 1918 (40 Stat. 1012).
[505]Act of June 5, 1920 (41 Stat. 1008). House Committee on the Judiciary, *1988 Grounds Exclusion*, op. cit., 22.
[506]43 Stat. 153.
[507]House Committee on the Judiciary, *1988 Grounds for Exclusion*, op. cit., 23. (Quoted from H.R. Rep. No. 350, 68th Cong., 1st Sess. (1924), 6).
[508]Act of March 4, 1929 (45 Stat. 1551).
[509]Act of May 14, 1937 (50 Stat. 164); "Alien Registration Act," (Act of June 28, 1940, 54 Stat. 670).
[510]307 U.S. 22, 29 (1939). See also House Committee on the Judiciary, *1988 Grounds for Exclusion*, op. cit., 25.
[511]Act of June 20, 1941 (55 Stat. 252); Act of May 25, 1948 (62 Stat. 268).
[512]64 Stat. 987.

[513]Act of March 28, 1951 (65 Stat. 28).

[514]Act of September 27, 1944 (58 Stat. 746)

[515]Act of June 25, 1948 (62 Stat. 1009).

[516]Act of June 27, 1952 (66 Stat. 163).

[517]House Committee on the Judiciary, *1988 Grounds for Exclusion*, op. cit., 27 (Quoted from *Congressional Record*, June 27, 1952, 98:8254)

[518]Exclusion based on drug offenses were later expanded with the Act of July 18, 1956 (70 Stat. 567) relating to possession of drugs, the Act of July 14, 1960 (74 Stat. 504) specifically relating to marijuana, the Act of October 27, 1986 (100 Stat. 3207) and the Act of December 22, 1987 (101 Stat. 1331) relating to other Controlled Substances.

[519]House Committee on the Judiciary, *1988 Grounds of Exclusion*, op. cit., 74-75 (Quoted from Sen. Rep. No. 1137, 82nd Cong., 2nd Sess., 1952, 9; H. R. Rep. No. 1365, 83rd Cong., 2nd Sess., 1952, 46, 47).

[520]Act of September 3, 1954 (68 Stat. 1145) and Act of September 26, 1961 (75 Stat. 650) and Act of October 12, 1984 (98 Stat. 1837) which repealed the provisions with substitute language for ease of administration. House Committee on the Judiciary, *1988 Grounds for Exclusion*, op. cit., 98, 99)

[521]Act of September 11, 1957 (71 Stat. 639).

[522]House Committee on the Judiciary, *1988 Grounds for Exclusion*, op. cit., 76. Act of September 1, 1959 (73 Stat. 490); Act of September 26, 1961 (75 Stat. 650).

[523]Act of January 27, 1948 (62 Stat. 6). That Act amended the Act of August 1, 1946 (60 Stat. 754) providing for limited exchange programs (Fulbright Amendment). The Act of June 4, 1956 (70 Stat. 241) provided a two year foreign residence requirement barring admission as a permanent resident or change to another temporary visa. A waiver was allowed where the Attorney General found admission to be in the public interest. The Act of September 21, 1961 (75 Stat. 527) added a hardship waiver and designated "J" as the new visa category for exchange visitors. The Act of April 7, 1970 (84 Stat. 116) provided waivers based on persecution or "no objection" letters from the home government. It also allowed residence in a "cooperating country" and established a "skills" list for each country participating in exchanges. In 1976 (Act of October 12, 1976, 90 Stat. 2243) foreign medical graduates were prohibited from obtaining waivers based on no objection from their home government.

[524]Act of June 4, 1956 (70 Stat. 241).

[525]"Mutual Educational and Cultural Exchange Act," (Act of September 21, 1961, 75 Stat. 527).

[526]79 Stat. 911.

[527]House Committee on the Judiciary, *1988 Grounds for Exclusion*, op. cit., 77.

[528]Act of December 29, 1981 (95 Stat. 1611).

[529] "Immigration Marriage Fraud Amendments of 1986," Act of November 10, 1986 (100 Stat. 3537).

[530] House and Senate Committees of the Judiciary, Joint Hearings, *Revision of Immigration, Naturalization, and Nationality Laws,* op. cit., 480. See also *Congressional Record,* February 19, 1951, 97:1370.

[531] House Committee on the Judiciary, *1988 Grounds for Exclusion*, op. cit., 98 (Quoted from *Congressional Record.*, Aug. 20, 1954, 100:15490-15491).

[532] Act of June 4, 1956 (70 Stat. 241).

[533] Sen. Doc. No. 47, 84th Cong., 1st Sess. (1955), Relief of Kurt Glaser-Veto Message, 3.

[534] House Committee on the Judiciary, "Immigration Aspects of the International Educational Exchange Program," H.R. Rep. No. 721, 87th Cong., 1st Sess. (1961), 31, 86.

[535] Ibid, 84-87. (Quoting from a Speech of Mr. Francis E. Walter in the House of Representatives February 5, 1959).

[536] H.R. Rep. No. 1199, 85th Cong., 1st Sess. (1957), 11-12.

[537] House Committee on the Judiciary, *Immigration*, 89th Cong., 1st Sess., Ser. 7, Washington, D.C., U.S. Print. Off., 1965, 145.

[538] Ibid., 147.

[539] H.R. Rep. No. 1199, 85th Cong., 1st Sess. (1957), 11.

[540] *Congressional Record,* August 21, 1957, 103:15492.

[541] House Committee on the Judiciary, *Immigration*, Ser. No. 9, Washington, D.C., U.S. Govt. Print. Ofc., 1970, 7.

[542] "Mutual Educational and Cultural Exchange Act," (Act of September 21, 1961, 75 Stat. 527).

[543] H.R. Rep. No. 264, 97th Cong., 1st Sess. (1981), 12.

[544] Ibid.

[545] Priv. L. No. 74-425, 49 Stat. 2234 (1936) accomp. S. 3399.

[546] Priv. L. No. 76-588, 54 Stat. 1373 (1940) accomp. H.R. 4066.

[547] Priv. L. No. 76-592, 54 Stat. 1375 (1940) accomp. H.R. 4954.

[548] Priv. L. No. 76-366, 54 Stat. 1282 (1940) accomp. H.R. 5827.

[549] Priv. L. No. 76-601, 54 Stat. 1378 (1940) accomp. H.R. 6888.

[550] Priv. L. No. 75-686, 52 Stat. 1382 (1938) accomp. H.R. 5597.

[551] Priv. L. No. 75-810, 52 Stat. 1434 (1938) accomp. H.R. 7039.

[552] Priv. L. No. 75-620, 52 Stat. 1355 (1938) accomp. H.R. 7297.

[553] Priv. L. No. 75-805, 52 Stat. 1432 (1938) accomp. H.R. 10136.

[554] Priv. L. No. 76-251, 53 Stat. 1540 (1939) accomp. S. 796.

[555] Priv. L. No. 76-184, 53 Stat. 1514 (1939) accomp. S. 808.

[556] Priv. L. No. 78-216, 58 Stat. 956 (1944) accomp. H.R. 480.

[557] Priv. L. No. 78-372, 58 Stat. 1021 (1944) accomp. H.R. 312.

[558] Priv. L. No. 80-168, 62 Stat. 1308 (1948) accomp. H.R. 422.

[559] Priv. L. No. 80-338, 62 Stat. 1368 (1948) accomp. H.R. 4484.

[560]Priv. L. No. 81-138, 63 Stat. 1128 (1949) accomp. H.R. 750.
[561]Priv. L. No. 81-48, 63 Stat. 1093 (1949) accomp. H.R. 1079.
[562]Priv. L. No. 81-526, 64 Stat. A70 (1950) accomp. H.R. 1275.
[563]Priv. L. No. 81-502, 64 Stat. A61, (1950) accomp. S. 2611.
[564]Priv. L. No. 81-535, 64 Stat. A70 (1950) accomp. H.R. 1170; Priv. L. No. 81-706, 64 Stat. A133 (1950) accomp. H.R. 7428.
[565]Priv. L. No. 81-226, 63 Stat. 1162 (1949) accomp. H.R. 2602.
[566]Priv. L. No. 81-494, 64 Stat. A59 (1950) accomp. S. 356.
[567]Priv. L. No. 81-672, 64 Stat. A119 (1950) accomp. S. 2077.
[568]Priv. L. No. 81-1038, 64 Stat. A255 (1950) accomp. H.R. 1503.
[569]Priv. L. No. 81-398, 64 Stat. A21 (1950) accomp. S. 1552.
[570]Priv. L. No. 81-630, 64 Stat. A105 (1950) accomp. S. 118.
[571]Priv. L. No. 81-730, 64 Stat. A142 (1950) accomp. S. 1551.
[572]Priv. L. No. 81-329, 63 Stat. 1202 (1949) accomp. H.R. 5375.
[573]Priv. L. No. 82-241, 65 Stat. A92 (1951) accomp. H.R. 627.
[574]Priv. L. No. 82-869, 66 Stat. A162 (1952) accomp. H.R. 1092.
[575]Priv. L. No. 82-181, 65 Stat. A69 (1951) accomp. H.R. 2180.
[576]Priv. L. No. 82-592, 66 Stat. A60 (1952) accomp. H.R. 1968.
[577]Priv. L. No. 82-467, 66 Stat. A20 (1952) accomp. S. 1462.
[578]Priv. L. No. 82-46, 65 Stat. A19 (1951) accomp. H.R. 714.
[579]Priv. L. No. 82-567,66 Stat. A54 (1952) accomp. H.R. 1836.
[580]Priv. L. No. 82-659, 66 Stat. A82 (1952) accomp. H.R. 2346.
[581]Priv. L. No. 82-238, 65 Stat. A91 (1951) accomp. H.R. 1103.
[582]Priv. L. No. 82-107,65 Stat. A42 (1951) accomp. H.R. 1791.
[583]Priv. L. No. 82-183, 65 Stat. A70 (1951) accomp. H.R. 2455.
[584]Priv. L. No. 82-950, 66 Stat. A188 (1952) accomp. H.R. 4396.
[585]Priv. L. No. 82-221, 65 Stat. A84 (1951) accomp. S. 674.
[586]Priv. L. No. 83-816, 68 Stat. A211 (1954) accomp. H.R. 4522.
[587]Priv. L. No. 83-848, 68 Stat. A221 (1954) accomp. H.R. 8557.
[588]Priv. L. No. 83-711, 68 Stat. A177 (1954) accomp. H.R. 7761.
[589]Priv. L. No. 83-177, 67 Stat. A63 (1953) accomp. H.R. 871.
[590]Priv. L. No. 83-180, 67 Stat. A64 (1953) accomp. H.R. 954.
[591]Priv. L. No. 83-558, 68 Stat. A128 (1954) accomp. H.R. 1673.
[592]Priv. L. No. 83-410, 68 Stat. A70 (1954) accomp. H.R. 1657.
[593]Priv. L. No. 83-766, 68 Stat. A194 (1954) accomp. H.R. 5354.
[594]Priv. L. No. 83-761, 68 Stat. A193 (1954) accomp. H.R. 5816.
[595]Priv. L. No. 83-829, 68 Stat. A215 (1954) accomp. H.R. 6955.
[596]Priv. L. No. 83-544, 68 Stat. A123 (1954) accomp. H.R. 6998.
[597]Priv. L. No. 83-324, 68 Stat. A37 (1954) accomp. H.R. 1148.
[598]Priv. L. No. 83-640, 68 Stat. A155 (1954) accomp. S. 2210.
[599]Priv. L. No. 83-476,68 Stat. A97 (1954) accomp. S. 2360.
[600]Priv. L. No. 83-889, 68 Stat. A239 (1954) accomp. H.R. 2061.

[601]Priv. L. No. 83-109, 67 Stat. A40 (1953), accomp. H.R. 5238.
[602]Priv. L. No. 84-52, 69 Stat. A18 (1955) accomp. H.R. 2087.
[603]Priv. L. No. 84-396, 69 Stat. A136 (1955) accomp. S. 884.
[604]Priv. L. No. 84-253, 69 Stat. A89 (1955) accomp. H.R. 1275.
[605]Priv. L. No. 84-415, 69 Stat. A142 (1955) accomp. H.R. 1301.
[606]Priv. L. No. 84-597, 70 Stat. A41 (1956) accomp. H.R. 1667.
[607]Priv. L. No. 84-303, 69 Stat. A104 (1955) accomp. H.R. 2059.
[608]Priv. L. No. 84-335, 69 Stat. A114 (1955) accomp. H.R. 2949.
[609]Priv. L. No. 84-228, 69 Stat. A79 (1955) accomp. H.R. 1897.
[610]Priv. L. No. 84-229, 69 Stat. A79 (1955) accomp. H.R. 1935.
[611]Priv. L. No. 84-22, 69 Stat. A9 (1955) accomp. H.R. 2261.
[612]Priv. L. No. 84-89, 69 Stat. A31 (1955) accomp. H.R. 1487.
[613]Priv. L. No. 84-348,69 Stat. A119 (1955) accomp. H.R. 4147; Priv. L. No. 84-524, 70 Stat. A14 (1956) accomp. H.R. 4548.
[614]Priv. L. No. 84-570, 70 Stat. A29 (1956) accomp. H.R. 6363.
[615]Priv. L. No. 84-150, 69 Stat. A52 (1955) accomp. H.R. 973.
[616]Priv. L. No. 84-15, 69 Stat. A7 (1955) accomp. H.R. 1203.
[617]Priv. L. No. 84-558, 70 Stat. A25 (1956) accomp. H.R. 2345.
[618]Priv. L. No. 84-425, 69 Stat. A145 (1955) accomp. H.R. 2788.
[619]Priv. L. No. 84-287, 69 Stat. A99 (1955) accomp. H.R. 1185.
[620]Priv. L. No. 84-46, 69 Stat. A16 (1955) accomp. H.R. 1501.
[621]Priv. L. No. 84-146, 69 Stat. A51 (1955) accomp. S. 432.
[622]Priv. L. No. 84-739, 70 Stat. A109 (1956) accomp. S. 245.
[623]Priv. L. No. 84-197, 69 Stat. A68 (1955) accomp. H.R. 1525.
[624]Priv. L. No. 84-149, 69 Stat. A52 (1955) accomp. H.R. 968.
[625]Priv. L. No. 84-851, 70 Stat. A174 (1956) accomp. H.R. 10984.
[626]Priv. L. No. 84-74, 69 Stat. A26 (1955) accomp. S. 129.
[627]Priv. L. No. 84-810, 70 Stat. A149 (1956) accomp. S. 1627.
[628]Priv. L. No. 85-507, 72 Stat. A72 (1958) accomp. H.R. 7729.
[629]Priv. L. No. 85-674, 72 Stat. A146 (1958) accomp. S. 2936.
[630]Priv. L. No. 85-740, 72 Stat. A200 (1958) accomp. H.R. 8014.
[631]Priv. L. No. 85-253, 71 Stat. A97 (1957) accomp. S. 660.
[632]Priv. L. No. 85-133, 71 Stat. A52 (1957) accomp. S. 701.
[633]Priv. L. No. 85-321, 71 Stat. A126 (1957) accomp. S. 1456.
[634]Priv. L. No. 85-465, 72 Stat. A56 (1958) accomp. S. 2168.
[635]Priv. L. No. 86-399, 74 Stat. A65 (1960) accomp. H.R. 3534.
[636]Priv. L. No. 86-438, 74 Stat. A80 (1960) accomp. H.R. 6804.
[637]Priv. L. No. 86-321, 74 Stat. A36 (1960) accomp. S. 2177.
[638]Priv. L. No. 86-226, 73 Stat. A98 (1959) accomp. S. 2319.
[639]Priv. L. No. 86-424, 74 Stat. A76 (1960) accomp. H.R. 1422.
[640]Priv. L. No. 86-432, 74 Stat. A78 (1960) accomp. H.R. 2944.
[641]Priv. L. No. 86-200, 73 Stat. A88 (1959) accomp. H.R. 2946.

[642] Priv. L. No. 86-349,74 Stat. A48 (1960) accomp. H.R. 2645.
[643] Priv. L. No. 87-339, 76 Stat. 1283 (1962) accomp. H.R. 6343.
[644] Priv. L. No. 87-676, 76 Stat. 1408 (1962) accomp. H.R. 9669.
[645] Priv. L. No. 87-565, 76 Stat. 1364 (1962) accomp. S. 3026.
[646] Priv. L. No. 87-279, 75 Stat. 952 (1961) accomp. H.R. 3401.
[647] Priv. L. No. 87-249, 75 Stat. 940 (1961) accomp. H.R. 3718.
[648] Priv. L. No. 87-528, 76 Stat. 1350 (1962) accomp. H.R. 9915.
[649] Priv. L. No. 87-308, 76 Stat. 1272 (1962) accomp. S. 235.
[650] Priv. L. No. 87-155, 75 Stat. 901 (1961) accomp. S. 231.
[651] Priv. L. No. 87-485, 76 Stat. 1334 (1962) accomp. H.R. 2187.
[652] Priv. L. No. 87-271, 75 Stat. 949 (1961) accomp. S. 1786.
[653] Priv. L. No. 88-250, 78 Stat. 1155 (1964) accomp. H.R. 9090.
[654] Priv. L. No. 88-294, 78 Stat. 1173 (1964) accomp. H.R. 1174.
[655] Priv. L. No. 88-183, 78 Stat. 1127 (1964) accomp. H.R. 1521.
[656] Priv. L. No. 88-134, 77 Stat. 921 (1963) accomp. H.R. 2305.
[657] Priv. L. No. 88-333, 78 Stat. 1189 (1964) accomp. S. 1999.
[658] Priv. L. No. 89-66, 79 Stat. 1358 (1965) accomp. H.R. 1627.
[659] Priv. L. No. 89-109, 79 Stat. 1374 (1965) accomp. S. 1111.
[660] Priv. L. No. 89-11, 79 Stat. 1336 (1965) accomp. H.R. 1236.
[661] Priv. L. No. 89-269, 80 Stat. 1638 (1966) accomp. H.R. 1414.
[662] Priv. L. No. 89-283, 80 Stat. 1642 (1966) accomp. H.R. 3233.
[663] Priv. L. No. 89-70, 79 Stat. 1359 (1965) accomp. H.R. 3292.
[664] Priv. L. No. 89-234, 80 Stat. 1623 (1966) accomp. H.R. 2752.
[665] Priv. L. No. 90-64, 81 Stat. 1005 (1967) accomp. H.R. 3221.
[666] Priv. L. No. 90-138, 81 Stat. 1030 (1967) accomp. H.R. 5216.
[667] Priv. L. No. 90-93, 81 Stat. 1016 (1967) accomp. S. 534.
[668] Priv. L. No. 90-346, 82 Stat. 1430 (1968) accomp. S. 1652.
[669] Priv. L. No. 91-30, 83 Stat. 876 (1969) accomp. H.R. 3376.
[670] Priv. L. No. 91-187, 84 Stat. 2150 (1970) accomp. S. 737.
[671] Priv. L. No. 92-88, 86 Stat. 1537 (1972) accomp. S. 513.
[672] Priv. L. No. 92-99, 86 Stat. 1541 (1972) accomp. H.R. 6907.
[673] Priv. L. No. 92-154, 86 Stat. 1565 (1972) accomp. S. 2270.
[674] Priv. L. No. 92-100, 86 Stat. 1541 (1972) accomp. H.R. 7641.
[675] Priv. L. No. 92-117, 86 Stat. 1549 (1972) accomp. H.R. 2394.
[676] Priv. L. No. 93-97, 88 Stat. 2382 (1974) accomp. H.R. 6477.
[677] Priv. L. No. 94-81, 90 Stat. 2988 (1976) accomp. H.R. 6093.
[678] Priv. L. No. 94-64, 90 Stat. 2981 (1976) accomp. H.R. 1425.
[679] Priv. L. No. 94-66, 90 Stat. 2982 (1976) accomp. H.R. 1645.
[680] Priv. L. No. 94-69. 90 Stat. 2983 (1976) accomp. H.R. 2399.
[681] Priv. L. No. 94-116, 90 Stat. 3001 (1976) accomp. H.R. 11890.
[682] Priv. L. No. 94-121, 90 Stat. 3004 (1976) accomp. H.R. 8119.
[683] Priv. L. No. 94-17, 89 Stat. 1179 (1975) accomp. H.R. 1553.

684 Priv. L. No. 95-48, 92 Stat. 3811 (1978) accomp. H.R. 1420.
685 Priv. L. No. 95-67, 92 Stat. 3820 (1978) accomp. H.R. 2940.
686 Priv. L. No. 95-63, 92 Stat. 3818 (1978) accomp. H.R. 1396.
687 Priv. L. No. 95-64, 92 Stat. 3819 (1978) accomp. H.R. 1446; Priv. L. No. 95-35, 92 Stat. 3805 (1978) accomp. H.R. 4401.
688 Priv. L. No. 95-74, 92 Stat. 3822 (1978) accomp. H.R. 8927.
689 Priv. L. No. 95-158, 92 Stat. 3857 (1978) accomp. H.R. 1422.
690 Priv. L. No. 95-31, 92 Stat. 3804 (1978) accomp. H.R. 1432.
691 Priv. L. No. 95-11, 91 Stat. 1653 (1977) accomp. S. 455.
692 Priv. L. No. 95-19, 91 Stat. 1656 (1977) accomp. S. 1142.
693 Priv. L. No. 97-3, 95 Stat. 1733 (1981) accomp. H.R. 783.
694 Priv. L. No. 100-23, 102 Stat. 4851 (1988) accomp. S. 391.
695 Priv. L. No. 100-36, 102 Stat. 4859 (1988) accomp. S. 1919.
696 Gordon and Rosenfield (1990), op. cit., 12-7, 8, 13-3, 12-9.
697 The Fourteenth Amendment provided that "All persons born or naturalized in the United States, and subject to the jurisdiction thereof, are citizens of the United States and of the State wherein they reside." U.S. CONST., amend. XIV, s.1.
698 Bancroft Treaties, in existence since 1868, held that naturalization was a means of effecting expatriation. Gordon and Rosenfield, op. cit., p. 11-20.
699 Senate Committee on the Judiciary, *1950 S. 1515*, op. cit., 43.
700 Charles Gordon, "The Citizen and the State: Power of Congress to Expatriate American Citizens," *The Georgetown Law Journal*, 53:318, 322.
701 Senate Committee on the Judiciary, *1950 S. 1515*, op. cit. 43.
702 Ibid.
703 Hutchinson, op. cit., 11.
704 Michael T. Hertz, "Limits to the Naturalization Power," *The Georgetown Law Journal*, 64:5, May 1976, 1009. (Quoted from G. Hunt, *The Writings of James Madison*, 226-27 (1900).
705 Gordon and Rosenfield (1990), op. cit., 12-3.
706 U.S. CONST., art. 1, s. 8, cl. 4.
707 Act of March 16, 1790 (1 Stat. 103).
708 Gordon and Rosenfield (1990), op. cit., 13-5. (Quoted from 1 *Annals of Congress* 1121 (1790)).
709 Ibid., 13-5.
710 Ibid., 13-19. Act of May 24, 1934 (48 Stat. 797).
711 Act of January 29, 1795 (1 Stat. 414).
712 Hutchinson, 12.
713 Act of June 18, 1798 (1 Stat. 566).
714 Hutchinson, op. cit., 12. Act of June 25, 1798 (1 Stat. 570), Act of July 6, 1798 (1 Stat. 577).

[715]Ibid., 17. Act of April 14, 1802 (2 Stat 153).

[716]Act of February 10, 1855 (10 Stat. 604). Gordon and Rosenfield (1990), op. cit., 18-4.

[717]Ibid., 15-39.

[718]Ibid., 18-3.

[719]Act of March 2, 1907 (34 Stat. 1228).

[720]Act of September 22, 1922 (42 Stat. 1021), the so-called Cable Act, prohibited discrimination due to sex and provided only one year residence in lieu of the 5 year requirement prior to submission of an application for citizenship.

[721]Act of April 9, 1866 (14 Stat. 27).

[722]U.S. CONST., amend. XIV, s. 1.

[723]Act of July 14, 1870 (16 Stat. 250).

[724]Hutchinson, op. cit., 57, 58.

[725]Ibid., 56.

[726]Ibid.

[727]Ibid., 63.

[728]Act of May 6, 1882 (22 Stat. 58).

[729]Gordon and Rosenfield (1990), op. cit., 14-9.

[730]Ibid.

[731]Ibid., 14-8.

[732]34 Stat. 596.

[733]Act of March 2, 1907 (34 Stat. 1228); Gordon and Rosenfield (1990), op. cit., 13-28.

[734]Act of September 22, 1922 (42 Stat. 1021).

[735]*Schneider v. Rusk*, 377 U.S. 163 (1964) held unconstitutional loss of citizenship through residence abroad; *Afroyim v. Rusk*, 387 U.S. 253 (1967) held that citizenship could only be lost through voluntary acts; *Vance v. Terrazas*, 444 U.S. 252 (1980) remanded to determine whether the Government can prove intention to surrender United States citizenship. Act of October 10, 1978 (92 Stat. 1046), Act of November 14, 1986 (100 Stat. 3655).

[736]House Committee on Immigration and Naturalization. *To Revise and Codify the Nationality Laws of the United States into a Comprehensive Nationality Code*, Washington, D.C: U.S. Govt. Print. Off., 1945, 420. (Cited as *1940 Revision of Nationality Code*) (Quoted from For. Rel. 1873, I. 256; 3 Moore, Digest of International Law 282)

[737]Gordon and Rosenfield (1990) op. cit., 17-46, 58. Act of May 9, 1918 (40 Stat. 542) amending the Act of June 29, 1906 (Armed Forces) and amending the Act of June 7, 1872 (17 Stat. 268) (Seamen).

[738]Act of May 26, 1924 (43 Stat. 153).

[739]Act of May 6, 1882 (22 Stat. 58) and Act of February 5, 1917 (39 Stat. 874).

740 Act of June 27, 1952 (66 Stat. 163).
741 Act of May 24, 1934 (48 Stat. 797).
742 Gordon and Rosenfield, op. cit., 11-19, 13-40, 13-29.
743 Senate Committee on the Judiciary, *1950 S. 1515*, op. cit., 703.
744 June 25, 1936 (49 Stat. 1925).
745 Act of June 25, 1936 (49 Stat. 1917).
746 Act of August 9, 1939 (53 Stat. 1273). Gordon and Rosenfield (1990), op. cit., 15-26.
747 Act of October 14, 1940 (54 Stat. 1137).
748 House Committee on the Judiciary, *1940 Revision of Nationality Code*, op. cit., 607. (Quoted from June 1, 1938 Letter to the President from Secretary of State, Attorney General, and Secretary of Labor).
749 Gordon and Rosenfield (1990), op. cit., 13-21 (Quoted from S. Rep. 2150, 76th C., 3rd Sess., 4).
750 House Committee on the Judiciary, *1940 Revision of Nationality Laws*, op. cit., 608 (Quoted from June 1, 1938 Letter to the President from Secretary of State, Attorney General, and Department of Labor).
751 Gordon and Rosenfield, op. cit., 13-30, 13-37.
752 *1950 S. 1515*, op. cit., 707.
753 Gordon and Rosenfield (1990), op. cit., 13-45, 13-46.
754 Those married after September 21, 1922 and before May 24, 1934; 2) Those married before 1934 had a one year residence requirement; 3) Those married after 1934 had a three year residence requirement.
755 Senate Committee on the Judiciary, *1950 S. 1515*, op. cit., 699.
756 Gordon and Rosenfield, op. cit., 20-84, 76, 85, 87.
757 House Committee on the Judiciary, *1940 Revision of Nationality Laws*, op. cit., 608 (Quoted from June 1, 1938 Letter to President from Secretary of State, Attorney General, and Department of Labor).
758 *Afroyim v. Rusk* (387 U.S. 253 (1967)); *Schneider v. Rusk* (377 U.S. 163 (1964)); Act of October 10, 1978 (92 Stat. 1046), Act of November 14, 1986 (100 Stat. 3655).
759 Act of December 17, 1943 (57 Stat. 600). Senate Committee on the Judiciary, *1950 S. 1515*, op. cit., 369.
760 Act of July 2, 1946 (60 Stat. 416).
761 Act of July 31, 1946 (60 Stat. 721). Gordon and Rosenfield, 1990, op. cit., 13-22.
762 Act of March 27, 1942 (56 Stat. 182); Act of June 1, 1948 (62 Stat. 281). Gordon and Rosenfield, 1990, op. cit., 17-46.
763 Act of April 2, 1942 (56 Stat. 198), Gordon and Rosenfield (1990), op. cit., 17-66.
764 Act of June 24, 1948 (62 Stat. 604).
765 Act of August 16, 1951 (65 Stat. 191); Act of July 20, 1954 (68 Stat. 495).

[766]Act of September 23, 1950 (64 Stat. 987).
[767]Higham, op. cit., *Send These To Me*, 60.
[768]H.R. Doc. 702, 81st Cong., 2nd Sess., 2.
[769]Act of June 27, 1952 (66 Stat. 163).
[770]Senate Committee on the Judiciary, *1950 S. 1515*, op. cit., 697, 710.
[771]Ibid.
[772]Gordon and Rosenfield, op. cit., 13-48, 31, 37. Previously, the 1940 Act provided that retention requirements had to be met between the ages of 13 and 21 and residence in the United States established before the age of 16.
[773]Senate Committee on the Judiciary, *1950 S. 1515*, op. cit., 698.
[774]Ibid., 711.
[775]Ibid., 705. Gordon and Rosenfield (1990), op. cit., 17-20.
[776]71 Stat. 639.
[777]Act of August 20, 1958 (72 Stat. 687).
[778]Act of December 18, 1967 (81 Stat. 661).
[779]Act of September 21, 1961 (75 Stat. 684).
[780]Act of October 24, 1968 (82 Stat. 1344).
[781]Act of June 29, 1968 (82 Stat. 279).
[782]Act of March 16, 1956 (70 Stat. 50).
[783]Act of November 6, 1966 (80 Stat. 1322). Gordon and Rosenfield (1990), op. cit., 13-25.
[784]Act of October 27, 1972 (86 Stat. 1289).
[785]Act of October 10, 1978 (92 Stat. 1046), Act of November 14, 1986 (100 Stat. 3655).
[786]401 U.S. 815.
[787]H. R. Rep. No. 1493, 95th Cong., 2nd Sess., 4.
[788]Act of November 14, 1986 (100 Stat. 3655).
[789]Act of August 4, 1959 (73 Stat. 274).
[790]356 U.S. 86.
[791]377 U.S. 167.
[792]387 U.S. 253.
[793]Act of November 14, 1986 (100 Stat. 3655).
[794]Act of November 2, 1966 (80 Stat. 1161).
[795]Act of November 2, 1978 (92 Stat. 2474).
[796] "Internal Security Act of 1950" (Act of September 23, 1950, 64 Stat. 987).
[797]Act of October 5, 1978 (92 Stat. 917).
[798]Act of December 29, 1981 (95 Stat. 1611).
[799]Act of December 4, 1985 (99 Stat. 1002).
[800]Act of November 14, 1986 (100 Stat. 3655).
[801]House Committee on the Judiciary, Rules of Procedure, 100th Congress.
[802]Act of August 16, 1951 (65 Stat. 191).
[803]Act of July 20, 1954 (68 Stat. 495).

[804]*Schneider v. Rusk* (377 U.S. 163).
[805]Act of October 10, 1978 (92 Stat. 1046), Act of November 14, 1986 (100 Stat. 3655).
[806]Act of November 2, 1966 (80 Stat. 1161).
[807]Act of October 27, 1972 (86 Stat. 1289).
[808]Act of October 10, 1978 (92 Stat. 1046), Act of November 14, 1986 (100 Stat. 3655).
[809]Act of November 14, 1986 (100 Stat. 3655).
[810]House Committee on the Judiciary, Rules of Procedure, 100th Congress.
[811]*Schneider v. Rusk* (377 U.S. 163).
[812]House Committee on Immigration and Naturalization, *Citizenship of Wives of Americans in the Foreign Service*, 68th Cong., 1st Sess., Washington, D.C., U.S. Govt. Print. Off., 1924, 12.
[813]Senate Committee on Immigration, *American Citizenship Rights of Women*, 72nd Cong., 2nd Sess., Washington, D.C., U.S. Govt. Print. Ofc. 1933, 25.
[814]Act of May 24, 1934 (48 Stat. 797).
[815]Act of March 2, 1907 (34 Stat. 1228).
[816]Act of October 14, 1940 (54 Stat. 1137).
[817]Act of August 16, 1951 (65 Stat. 191; Act of July 20, 1954 (68 Stat. 495).
[818]House Committee on the Judiciary, *1951 Revision of Immigration, Naturalization, and Nationality Laws*, op. cit., 249.
[819]Act of August 4, 1959 (73 Stat. 274).
[820]377 U.S. 167.
[821]387 U.S. 253.
[822]Act of June 27, 1952 (66 Stat. 163).
[823]Acts of March 16, 1956 (70 Stat. 50); Act of November 6, 1966 (80 Stat. 1322); Act of October 27, 1972 (86 Stat. 1289); Act of November 2, 1978 (92 Stat. 2474).
[824]Act of June 27, 1952 (66 Stat. 163)
[825]Act of December 4, 1985 (99 Stat. 1002).
[826]H.R. Rep. No. 373, 99th Cong., 1st Sess., 22.
[827]H.R. Rep. No. 1978, 89th Cong., 1st Sess., 8.
[828]Act of October 10, 1978 (92 Stat. 1046), Act of November 14, 1986 (100 Stat. 3655).
[829]Act of November 14, 1986 (100 Stat. 3655).
[830]Act of November 2, 1978 (92 Stat. 2474).
[831]Priv. L. No. 25-23, 6 Stat. 750 (1839).
[832]Priv. L. No. 44-9, 19 Stat. 411 (1877) accomp. S.Res. 32.
[833]Priv. L. No. 55-36, 30 Stat. 1496 (1898) accomp. S.Res.156.
[834]Priv. L. No. 64-196, 39 Stat. 1588 (1917) accomp. S. 8075.
[835]Priv. L. No. 66-1, 41 Stat. 1449 (1919) accomp. S.J. Res. 90.

[836]Priv. L. No. 66-2, 41 Stat. 1463 (1920) accomp. S.J. Res. 134.
[837]Priv. L. No. 79-845, 60 Stat. 1303 (1946) accomp. H.R. 5278.
[838]Priv. L. No. 62-3, 37 Stat. 1346 (1912) accomp. H.J.Res. 200.
[839]Priv. L. No. 63-184, 38 Stat. 1476 (1915) accomp. S. 3419.
[840]Priv. L. No. 64-132, 39 Stat. 1495 (1917) accomp. S.J. Res. 208.
[841]Priv. L. No. 75-745, 52 Stat. 1408 (1938) accomp. S. 3064.
[842]Priv. L. No. 76-175, 53 Stat. 1510 (1939) accomp. S. 2427.
[843]Priv. L. No. 78-516, 58 Stat. 1080 (1944) accomp. H.R. 2016.
[844]Priv. L. No. 77-633, 56 Stat. 1259 (1942) accomp. H.R. 7828.
[845]Priv. L. No. 74-227, 49 Stat 2145 (1936) accomp. S. 447.
[846]Priv. L. No. 79-460, 60 Stat. 1143 (1946) accomp. H.R. 1350.
[847]Priv. L. No. 79-695, 60 Stat. 1242 (1946) accomp. H.R. 3441.
[848]Priv. L. No. 80-419, 62 Stat. 1403 (1948) accomp. S. 83.
[849]Priv. L. No. 80-216, 62 Stat. 1325 (1948) accomp. H.R. 3742.
[850]Priv. L. No. 80-51, 61 Stat. 985 (1947) accomp. S. 53.
[851]Priv. L. No. 80-102, 61 Stat. 1004 (1947) accomp. H.R. 1652.
[852]Priv. L. No. 80-12, 61 Stat. 968 (1947) accomp. S. 135.
[853]Priv. L. No. 80-305, 62 Stat. 1357 (1948) accomp. H.R. 1749.
[854]Priv. L. No. 81-43, 63 Stat. 1091 (1949) accomp. H.R. 711.
[855]Priv. L. No. 81-864, 64 Stat. A191 (1950) accomp. S. 1866.
[856]Priv. L. No. 81-1018, 64 Stat. A246 (1950) accomp. H.R. 7563.
[857]Priv. L. No. 81-570, 64 Stat. A85 (1950) accomp. H.R. 4747.
[858]Priv. L. No. 81-199, 63 Stat. 1152 (1949) accomp. S. 905.
[859]Priv. L. No. 81-873, 64 Stat. A195 (1950) accomp. S. 3238.
[860]Priv. L. No. 81-365, 64 Stat. A8 (1950) accomp. S. 1915.
[861]Priv. L. No. 81-402, 64 Stat. A23 (1950) accomp. S. 2429.
[862]Priv. L. No. 81-944, 64 Stat. A219 (1950), accomp. H.R. 8219.
[863]Priv. L. No. 81-366, 64 Stat. A8 (1950) accomp. S. 2100.
[864]Priv. L. No. 81-870, 64 Stat. A194 (1950) accomp. S. 1506.
[865]Priv. L. No. 81-887, 64 Stat. A201 (1950) accomp. H.R. 6442.
[866]Priv. L. No. 81-508, 64 Stat. A63 (1950) accomp. H.R. 1866.
[867]Priv. L. No. 82-713, 66 Stat. A100 (1952) accomp. H.R. 2920
[868]Priv. L. No. 82-639, 66 Stat. A75 (1952) accomp. S. 420.
[869]Priv. L. No. 82-144, 65 Stat. A55 (1951) accomp. H.R. 896.
[870]Priv. L. No. 82-657, 66 Stat. A82 (1952) accomp. S. 2588.
[871]Priv. L. No. 82-588, 66 Stat. A59 (1952) accomp. H.R. 3271.
[872]Priv. L. No. 82-937, 66 Stat. A184 (1952) accomp. H.R. 3280.
[873]Priv. L. No. 82-867, 66 Stat. A162 (1952) accomp. H.R. 5238.
[874]Priv. L. No. 82-1023, 66 Stat. 213 (1952) accomp. H.R. 7833.
[875]Priv. L. No. 82-2, 65 Stat. A3 (1951) accomp. S. 44.
[876]Priv. L. No. 82-522, 66 Stat. A38 (1952) accomp. H.R. 1234.
[877]Priv. L. No. 82-953, 66 Stat. A189 (1952) accomp. H.R. 4588.

[878]Priv. L. No. 82-5, 65 Stat. A4 (1951) accomp. H.R. 1165.

[879]Priv. L. No. 82-423, 66 Stat. A7 (1952) accomp. H.R. 2505; Priv. L. No. 82-16, 65 Stat. A8 (1951) accomp. H. R. 2714.

[880]Priv. L. No. 82-603, 66 Stat. A63 (1952) accomp. H.R. 4535; Priv. L. No. 82-761, 66 Stat. A117 (1952) accomp. H.R. 6117.

[881]Priv. L. No. 82-35, 65 Stat. A16 (1951) accomp. H.R. 890.

[882]Priv. L. No. 82-792, 66 Stat. A131 (1952) accomp. H.R. 3600.

[883]Priv. L. No. 82-256, 65 Stat. A97 (1951) accomp. H.R. 970.

[884]Priv. L. No. 82-744, 66 Stat. A111 (1952) accomp. H.R. 2718.

[885]Priv. L. No. 82-169, 65 Stat. A65 (1951) accomp. H.R. 1157.

[886]Priv. L. No. 83-369, 68 Stat. A53 (1954) accomp. H.R. 7559.

[887]Priv. L. No. 83-902, 68 Stat. A244 (1954) accomp. S. 2259.

[888]Priv. L. No. 83-533, 68 Stat. A119 (1954) accomp. S. 2369.

[889]Priv. L. No. 83-967, 68 Stat. A278 (1954) accomp. S. 2156.

[890]Priv. L. No. 83-665, 68 Stat. A163 (1954) accomp. S. 2135.

[891]Priv. L. No. 84-12, 69 Stat. A6 (1955) accomp. H.R. 1166.

[892]Priv. L. No. 84-763, 70 Stat. A119 (1956) accomp. H.R. 5041.

[893]Priv. L. No. 84-720, 70 Stat. A98 (1956) accomp. H.R. 1410.

[894]Priv. L. No. 84-555, 70 Stat. A24 (1956) accomp. H.R. 2072.

[895]Priv. L. No. 84-534, 70 Stat. A17 (1956) accomp. S. 97.

[896]Priv. L. No. 84-824, 70 Stat. A155 (1956) accomp. H.R. 10088.

[897]Priv. L. No. 84-469, 69 Stat. A159 (1955) accomp. S. 1044.

[898]Priv. L. No. 85-310, 71 Stat. A123 (1957) accomp. H.R. 8374.

[899]Priv. L. No. 85-634, 72 Stat. A132 (1958) accomp. S. 2989.

[900]Priv. L. No. 85-43, 71 Stat. A19 (1957) accomp. H.R. 1451.

[901]Priv. L. No. 85-623, 72 Stat. A128 (1958) accomp. H.R. 7826.

[902]Priv. L. No. 85-439, 72 Stat. A47 (1958) accomp. S. 2301; Priv. L. No. 85-631, 72 Stat. A131 (1958) accomp. S. 2935.

[903]Priv. L. No. 85-594, 72 Stat. A116 (1958) accomp. S. 1782.

[904]Priv. L. No. 85-771, 72 Stat. A214 (1958) accomp. S. 2469.

[905]Priv. L. No. 85-616, 72 Stat. A126 (1958) accomp. H.R. 12903.

[906]Priv. L. No. 85-729, 72 Stat. A196 (1958) accomp. S. 3219.

[907]Priv. L. No. 85-730, 72 Stat. A196 (1958) accomp. S. 3221.

[908]Priv. L. No. 85-304, 71 Stat. A120 (1957) accomp. H.R. 1677.

[909]Priv. L. No. 85-464, 72 Stat. A56 (1958) accomp. S. 803.

[910]Priv. L. No. 85-212, 71 Stat. A82 (1957) accomp. H.R. 3184.

[911]Priv. L. No. 86-210, 73 Stat. A91 (1959) accomp. H.R. 5910.

[912]Priv. L. No. 86-320, 74 Stat. A36 (1960) accomp. S. 2142.

[913]Priv. L. No. 86-328, 74 Stat. A39 (1960) accomp. S. 2554.

[914]Priv. L. No. 86-34, 73 Stat. A17 (1959) accomp. S. 32.

[915]Priv. L. No. 86-125, 73 Stat. A56 (1959) accomp. H.R. 1705.

[916]Priv. L. No. 86-36, 73 Stat. A18 (1959) accomp. S. 46.

[917]Priv. L. No. 86-102, 73 Stat. A48 (1959) accomp. S. 1684.
[918]Priv. L. No. 86-352, 74 Stat. A49 (1960) accomp. S. 3130.
[919]Priv. L. No. 86-172, 73 Stat. A75 (1959) accomp. S. 977.
[920]Priv. L. No. 86-372, 74 Stat. A55 (1960) accomp. S. 3016; Priv. L. No. 86-365, 74 Stat. A53 (1960), accomp. S. 2768.
[921]Priv. L. No. 86-358, 74 Stat. A51 (1960) accomp. S. 762.
[922]Priv. L. No. 86-217, 73 Stat. A94 (1959) accomp. H.R. 6886.
[923]Priv. L. No. 86-145, 73 Stat. A63 (1959) accomp. S. 1915.
[924]Priv. L. No. 86-363, 74 Stat. A53 (1960) accomp. S. 2646.
[925]Priv. L. No. 86-486, 74 Stat. A100 (1960) accomp. H.R. 8156.
[926]Priv. L. No. 86-209, 73 Stat. A91 (1959) accomp. H.R. 5645.
[927]Priv. L. No. 86-218, 73 Stat. A95 (1959) accomp. H.R. 6954.
[928]Priv. L. No. 86-371, 74 Stat. A55 (1960) accomp. S. 2991.
[929]Priv. L. No. 87-299, 76 Stat. 1268 (1962) accomp. H.R. 6226.
[930]Priv. L. No. 87-420, 76 Stat. 1312 (1962) accomp. H.R. 1653.
[931]Priv. L. No. 87-562, 76 Stat. 1363 (1962) accomp. H.R. 10160.
[932]Priv. L. No. 87-471, 76 Stat. 1329 (1962) accomp. H.R. 9588; Priv. L. No. 87-430, 76 Stat. 1316 (1962) accomp. S. 2865.
[933]Priv. L. No. 87-253, 75 Stat. 942 (1961) accomp. H.R. 4384.
[934]Priv. L. No. 87-221, 75 Stat. 932 (1961) accomp. H.R. 1394; Priv. L. No. 87-408, 76 Stat. 1309 (1962) accomp. H.R. 1395.
[935]Priv. L. 87-126, 75 Stat. 892 (1961) accomp. S. 438.
[936]Priv. L. No. 87-549, 76 Stat. 1358 (1962) accomp. H.R. 7582.
[937]Priv. L. No. 87-158, 75 Stat. 903 (1961) accomp. S. 333.
[938]Priv. L. No. 87-268, 75 Stat. 948 (1961) accomp. S. 1234.
[939]Priv. L. No. 87-670, 76 Stat. 1406 (1962) accomp. S. 2555.
[940]Priv. L. No. 87-641, 76 Stat. 1393 (1962) accomp. S. 3267.
[941]Priv. L. No. 87-481, 76 Stat. 1333 (1962) accomp. S. 1074.
[942]Priv. L. No. 87-317, 76 Stat. 1275 (1962) accomp. S. 1791.
[943]Priv. L. No. 87-460, 76 Stat. 1326 (1962) accomp. S. 2679.
[944]Priv. L. No. 87-492, 76 Stat. 1336 (1962) accomp. H.R. 6833.
[945]Priv. L. No. 87-107, 75 Stat. 886 (1961) accomp. H.R. 2156.
[946]Priv. L. No. 87-7, 75 Stat. 853 (1961) accomp. S. 217.
[947]Priv. L. No. 87-599, 76 Stat. 1377 (1962) accomp. S. 689.
[948]377 U.S. 163.
[949]Priv. L. No. 88-153, 77 Stat. 930 (1963) accomp. S. 1014.
[950]Priv. L. No. 88-38, 77 Stat. 887 (1963) accomp. H.R. 2309.
[951]Priv. L. No. 88-256, 78 Stat. 1157 (1964) accomp. H.R. 2737.
[952]Priv. L. No. 88-59, 77 Stat. 893 (1963) accomp. H.R. 5507.
[953]Priv. L. No. 89-277, 80 Stat. 1640 (1966) accomp. H.R. 11718.
[954]Priv. L. No. 89-93, 79 Stat. 1366 (1965) accomp. S. 1919.
[955]Priv. L. No. 89-40, 79 Stat. 1347 (1965) accomp. S. 442.

[956]Priv. L. No. 89-194, 79 Stat. 1408 (1965) accomp. H.R. 7453.
[957]Priv. L. No. 89-398, 80 Stat. 1685 (1966) accomp. H.R. 10288.
[958]Priv. L. No. 89-169, 79 Stat. 1399 (1965) accomp. S. 374.
[959]Priv. L. No. 89-44, 79 Stat. 1348 (1965) accomp. S. 826.
[960]Priv. L. No. 89-82, 79 Stat. 1363 (1965) accomp. S. 1084.
[961]Priv. L. No. 89-328, 80 Stat. 1659 (1966) accomp. S. 3272; Priv. L. No. 89-327, 80 Stat. 1659 (1966) accomp. S. 3189.
[962]Priv. L. No. 89-465, 80 Stat. 1711 (1966) accomp. S. 3222.
[963]Priv. L. No. 89-152, 79 Stat. 1392 (1965) accomp. H.R. 2005; Priv. L. No. 89-247, 80 Stat. 1627 (1966) accomp. H.R. 2290.
[964]Priv. L. No. 89-203, 79 Stat. 1413 (1965) accomp. S. 619.
[965]Priv. L. No. 89-42, 79 Stat. 1347 (1965) accomp. S. 582.
[966]387 U.S. 253.
[967]Priv. L. No. 90-347, 82 Stat. 1430 (1968) accomp. S. 2897.
[968]Priv. L. No. 90-114, 81 Stat. 1024 (1967) accomp. S. 1021.
[969]Priv. L. No. 90-340, 82 Stat. 1428 (1968) accomp. S. 2720.
[970]Priv. L. No. 90-139, 81 Stat. 1030 (1967) accomp. S. 445.
[971]Priv. L. No. 90-160, 81 Stat. 1037 (1967) accomp. S. 1781.
[972]Priv. L. No. 90-18, 81 Stat. 992 (1967) accomp. H.R. 2048.
[973]Priv. L. No. 90-57, 81 Stat. 1004 (1967) accomp. H.R. 5862.
[974]Priv. L. No. 90-33, 81 Stat. 996 (1967) accomp. S. 164; Priv. L. No. 90-328, 82 Stat. 1425 (1968) accomp. S. 747.
[975]Priv. L. No. 90-299, 82 Stat. 1021 (1968) accomp. H.R. 13301; Priv. L. No. 90-263, 82 Stat. 1393 (1968) accomp. H.R. 15591; Priv. L. No. 90-343, 82 Stat. 1429 (1968) accomp. S. 2759.
[976]Priv. L. No. 91-148, 84 Stat. 2128 (1970) accomp. S. 2863.
[977]Priv. L. No. 91-20, 83 Stat. 873 (1969) accomp. H.R. 5136.
[978]Priv. L. No. 91-48, 83 Stat. 884 (1969) accomp. S. 85.
[979]Priv. L. No. 91-53, 83 Stat. 885 (1969) accomp. S. 265.
[980]Priv. L. No. 91-51, 83 Stat. 885 (1969) accomp. H.R. 3165.
[981]Priv. L. No. 91-149, 84 Stat. 2128 (1970) accomp. S. 3136; Priv. L. No. 91-15, 83 Stat. 871 (1969) accomp. H.R. 6607; Priv. L. No. 91-22, 83 Stat. 874 (1969) accomp. H.R. 1828; Priv. L. No. 91-151, 84 Stat. 2128 (1970) accomp. H.R. 13997.
[982]Priv. L. No. 91-11, 83 Stat. 870 (1969) accomp. S. 537.
[983]Priv. L. No. 92-35, 85 Stat. 848 (1971) accomp. S. 389.
[984]Priv. L. No. 92-132, 86 Stat. 1555 (1972) accomp. H.R. 14173; Priv. L. No. 150, 86 Stat. 1563 (1972) accomp. S. 2822; Priv. L. No. 92-152, 86 Stat. 1564 (1972) accomp. S. 3583.
[985]Priv. L. No. 92-36, 85 Stat. 849 (1971) accomp. S. 306.
[986]Priv. L. No. 92-92, 86 Stat. 1539 (1972) accomp. H.R. 2076.
[987]Priv. L. No. 92-9, 85 Stat. 836 (1971) accomp. H.R. 3929.

[988]Priv. L. No. 93-62, 88 Stat. 2368 (1974) accomp. S. 507.
[989]Priv. L. No. 93-64, 88 Stat. 2369 (1974) accomp. S. 912.
[990]Priv. L. No. 93-54, 88 Stat. 2366 (1974) accomp. S. 1852.
[991]Priv. L. No. 94-52, 90 Stat. 2976 (1976) accomp. S. 1699.
[992]Priv. L. No. 94-27, 89 Stat. 1189 (1975) accomp. H.R. 10792.
[993]Priv. L. No. 94-44, 90 Stat. 2973 (1976) accomp. H.R. 2776.
[994]Priv. L. No. 94-4, 90 Stat. 2989 (1976) accomp. H.R. 7404.
[995]Priv. L. No. 94-2, 89 Stat. 1164 (1975) accomp. H.R. 1388.
[996]Priv. L. No. 96-52, 94 Stat. 3594 (1980) accomp. H.R. 4013.
[997]Priv. L. No. 96-101, 94 Stat. 3628 (1980) accomp. H.R. 6739.
[998]Priv. L. No. 97-24, 96 Stat. 2622 (1982) accomp. H.R. 1482.
[999]*See* Chpt. 5 - Controversy.
[1000]Priv. L. No. 98-13, 98 Stat. 3420 (1984) accomp. H.R. 3131; Priv. L. No. 98-7, 98 Stat. 3417 (1984) accomp. S. 1863; Priv. L. No. 15, 98 Stat. 3420 (1984) accomp. S. 2729.
[1001]Priv. L. No. 98-33, 98 Stat. 3429 (1984) accomp. H.R. 960.
[1002]Priv. L. No. 98-41, 98 Stat. 3432 (1984) accomp. H.R. 1865.

Chapter Five: Controversy

[1]"World Racket Smuggles Aliens into U.S. @ $100-$1,500 Apiece," *New York Herald Tribune*, May 25, 1952, 1, 24; May 26, 1952, 8; and May 27, 1952, 14, 24.
[2]House Committee on the Judiciary, *1953 Department of Justice Investigation*, op. cit., 2227.
[3]Select Committee on Standards and Conduct, *U.S. Senate on the Investigation of the Introduction of Private Immigration Bills in the Senate for Chinese Crewmen*, 90th and 91st Congresses, Sen. Rep. No. 911, 91st Cong., 2nd Sess., 1970.
[4]Ibid., 2.
[5]Ibid., 1-3.
[6]*Congressional Record*,, October 20, 1969, 115:30528. Letter from Sen. Mike Mansfield, Majority Leader and Sen. Hugh Scott, Minority Leader, to Secretary of the Senate Francis R. Valeo dated October 1, 1969.
[7]House Committee on the Judiciary, *Court Proceedings and Actions of Vital Interest to the Congress*, Current to March 1, 1981. Committee Print No. 11, 97th Cong., 1st Sess., Washington, D.C., U.S. Govt. Print. Off., 1981,. 71, 80.
[8]Yacker, op. cit., 19.
[9]House Committee on the Judiciary, *Court Proceedings and Actions of Vital Interest to the Congress, Current to September 1, 1983*. Committee Print

No. 7, 98th Cong., 1st Sess., Washington, D.C., U.S. Govt. Print. Off., 1984, 25.

[10]*Congressional Record*, October 2, 1980, 126:28966.

[11]Ibid., 28954.

[12]Chairman Emanuel Celler (D-NY) 81st Congress through 92nd Congress (1949-1972) except the 83rd Cong. (1953-1954) when Chauncey W. Reed (R-ILL) was Chairman; Peter W. Rodino, Jr. (D-NJ) 93rd Congress through 100th Congress (1973-1988).

[13]*New York Herald Tribune*, op. cit., May 25, 1952, 24.

[14]House bills 5,972.

[15]*Congressional Record*, April 7, 1971, 117:10142.

[16]House bills 2,085

[17]Peter W. Rodino, Jr. (D-NJ) 92nd Congress (1971-72); Joshua Eilberg (D-PA) 93rd through 95th Congress (1973-1978), Elizabeth Holtzman (D-NY) 96th Congress (1979-80), Romano L. Mazzoli (D-KY) 97th Congress through 100th Congress (1981-1988).

[18]*Congressional Record*, July 23, 1981, 127:17036. House Committee on the Judiciary, Rules of Procedure, 97th and 98th Congresss (1981-1984).

[19]1957 through 1978 (85th Congress through 95th Congress)

[20]P.L. 97-276 (96 Stat. 1186, 1203, 1982). Sec. 155. *Congressional Record*, September 29, 1982, 128:25715.

[21]*Congressional Record*, October 1, 1982, 128:27291.

[22]Ibid.

[23]101 Stat. 1329 (1987)

[24]"Obey Helps Marshfield Surgeon Battle Fight to Stay in the U.S.," *The Milwaukee Journal*, Jan. 14, 1988, 3D.

[25]92 Stat. 2474 (1978).

[26]H.R. Rep. No. 1683, 95th Cong., 2nd Sess. (1978), 3.

[27]Ibid., 1.

[28]Priv. L. No. 91-114, 84 Stat. 2112 (1970).

[29]Priv. L. 98-53, 98 Stat. 3437 (1984).

[30]P.L. 88-6 (77 Stat. 5, 1963) on behalf of Winston Churchill granting honorary citizenship; P.L. 97-54 (95 Stat. 574, 1981) on behalf of Raoul Wallenberg granting honorary citizenship. P.L. 98-516, granting honorary citizenship on behalf of William and Hannah Callowhill Penn (98 Stat. 2423, 1984); P.L. 95-466, restoring citizenship on behalf of Jefferson F. Davis (92 Stat. 1304, 1978); P.L. 94-67, restoring citizenship on behalf of Robert E. Lee (89 Stat. 380, 1975).

[31]Priv. L. No. 86-189 (73 Stat. A84, 1959); Priv. L. No. 91-9 (83 Stat. 869, 1969); Priv. L. No. 91-22 (83 Stat. 874, 1969) and Priv. L. No. 98-33 (98 Stat. 3429, 1984). All beneficiaries who were veterans of Vietnam and granted posthumous citizenship.

[32]House Committee on the Judiciary, Minutes, 83rd Cong., 2nd Sess., August 5, 1954.

[33]*Congressional Record*, August 25, 1959, 105:16924.

[34]*Congressional Record*, December 13, 1980, 126:34146.

[35]Ibid.

[36]*Congressional Record*, December 20, 1982, 128:32891.

[37]Ibid., 32892.

[38]Ibid., 32893.

[39]Ibid.

[40]*Congressional Record*, February 29, 1960, 106:3830.

[41]H.R. Rep. No. 1002, 95th Cong., 2nd Sess. (1978), 7.

[42]Ibid., 8, 9.

[43]Audun Endestad, (Priv. L. No. 98-7, 98 Stat. 3417, 1984), placed 18; Jean Willrich (Priv. L. No. 98-15, 98 Stat. 3420, 1984), scored one goal; Maria Kunyavsky (Priv. L. No. 98-13, 98 Stat. 3420, 1984) did not make the team.

[44]Letter to Robert H. Helmick, President, U.S. Olympic Committee from Subcommittee Chairman Romano L. Mazzoli and Hon. Patrick L. Swindall, and Members of the Subcommittee on Immigration, Refugees, and International Law, Committee on the Judiciary, U.S. House of Representatives, April 27, 1987, and response from Robert H. Helmick dated December 14, 1987. Letter to Robert H. Helmick, President, U.S. Olympic Committee from Senate Immigration Subcommittee Chairman Edward M. Kennedy and Alan K. Simpson.

[45]Priv. L. 100-8, 102 Stat. 4843 (1988). Ms. McFarlane placed 14, 6 and 2 in several events during the 1988 Olympic Games.

[46]House Committee on the Judiciary, Meeting of Subcommittee on Immigration, Refugees, and International Law on Olympic Cases, April 21, 1988.

[47]Ibid., Statement of U.S. Olympic Committee.

[48]Ibid.

[49]H.R. Rep. No. 596, 100th Cong., 2nd Sess. (1988), 3,4.

[50]H.R. Rep. No. 597, 100th Cong., 2nd Sess. (1988), 3,4.

[51]H.R. Rep. No. 598, 100th Cong., 2nd Sess. (1988), 3-5.

[52]House Committee on the Judiciary, Subcommittee on Immigration, Refugees, and International Law, Meeting on Olympic Cases.

[53]Ibid., 12.

[54]*Congressional Record*, May 17, 1988, 134:11257.

[55]Ibid.

[56]October 4, 1988.

[57]Associated Press Wire No. 1145, "Lendl-Immigration," April 10, 1988 (Permission for use dated November 19, 1996).

[58]"Needed: A Ban on U.S. Imports," *The Philadelphia Inquirer*, April 24, 1988.

[59]Ibid., May 20, 1988.

[60]"Citizen Ivan? The Reasons to Rush It Are Wrong," *The New York Times*, June 19, 1988, S7.

[61]P.L. 97-54, 95 Stat. 971 (1981).

[62]H. R. Rep. No. 152, Pt. 2, 97th Cong., 1st Sess. (1981), 3.

[63]House Committee on the Judiciary, *Honorary U.S. Citizenship for Raoul Wallenberg*, 97th Cong., 1st Sess., Ser. No. 5, Washington, D.C., U.S. Govt. Print. Off., 1981, 8.

[64]Ibid., 13.

[65]H.R. Rept. 152, 97th Cong., Pt. 2, 1st Sess. (1981), 1, 12.

[66]Ibid., 9.

[67]Ibid., 10.

[68]Priv. L. 98-33, 98 Stat. 3429 (1984).

[69]*Congressional Record*, September 24, 1984, 130:26573.

[70]Ibid., 26575.

[71]Ibid.

[72]House Committee on the Judiciary, *Siberian Seven*, 97th Cong., 2nd Sess., Ser. No. 80, Washington, D.C., U.S. Govt. Print. Off., 1983, 7.

[73]House Committee on the Judiciary, Meeting of the Committee, August 27, 1980, 53-55. Priv. L. No. 96-63, 94 Stat. 3599 (1980)

[74]Sen. Rep. No. 2031, 76th Cong., 3rd Sess., Pt. 2, 2.

[75]H.R. Rep. No. 2200, 76th Cong., 3rd Sess., 2. House passed resolution June 13, 1940, *Congressional Record*, 86:8214.

[76]H.R. Rep. No. 2200, 76th Cong., 3rd Sess. (1940), 1.

[77]Sen. Rep. No. 2031, 76th Cong., 3rd Sess. (1940), 1, 10.

Statistical Notes

1. **Statistical Analysis on Private Bills Introduced and Enacted** - There has always been some controversy about the varied statistics provided by INS and the House and Senate Committees on the number of private bills introduced and those which are enacted into law. This book primarily relies on records of INS for the number of bills introduced because the records of the House and Senate Committees cannot be reconciled. For instance, Committee totals often include suspension of deportation cases. Also, the records sometimes include all "referred" bills (bills which have been introduced as well as those which have been passed by the House or Senate) which inflates the number of introduced bills. In the case of laws, this book uses statistics which I have accumulated based on the legislative reports on each law enacted. The major difference between INS and my records on enacted bills are during the Congresses when omnibus measures were enacted. In these cases, the statistics in this book are higher because they identify each bill which is included in an omnibus measure. In other cases, there are a few discrepancies where the book has included private laws which were included in public legislation as well as private laws which may appear to be public in nature (American University of Beirut).
2. **Categories of Private Bills for Precedent and Statistical Basis**-In determining which category a particular private law is placed, the primary purpose of the benefit is used as the guide. For instance, in the quota area where aliens were ineligible to immigrate based on race, this was a provision involving quotas, exclusion, and citizenship. I have included these bills in the quota category since ineligibility due to race was primarily aimed at immigration from certain countries and was the first obstacle to immigrating before consideration of exclusionary grounds or citizenship. This is also the case for fiancee cases which also waived exclusionary grounds. The primary purpose in most cases related to alleviating low quotas, therefore, those cases were placed in the quota category.

   In addition, in the quota area of adoption which included single adoption, two-petition adoption cases, and age limitations, I have placed all adoption in one group since in this area and others such as preference, it is difficult to always determine the particular provision of law for which the private bill was needed to overcome. This is also the case in the occupational categories where it was sometimes unclear whether country oversubscription (low quota) was the obstacle, or the lack of visas available for a particular preference category which limited immigration. In addition, in some cases, the occupation as well as familial relationship appeared to be the reason for enactment. When the law was not clear in these types of cases, the category of "miscellaneous-general" was designated for statistical purposes.

   Also, in the quota area where private laws were enacted based on deeds, or national interest, those cases were identified as such. But in some cases, there was a conflict between whether the primary motivating factor was the deeds, the particular occupation, or provisions of the Displaced Persons Act. In cases when the Displaced Persons Act was specifically identified, they were placed in that category. When the specific provision of law was not clear, the case was placed in "miscellaneous-due to deeds" or "miscellaneous-general" category.

In the waiver area, such as medical cases, there were several occasions when illiteracy was based on a health condition. In such cases, the category was determined to be health-related. But when it was clear the major reason for waiver of the exclusion was illiteracy, that ground of exclusion was chosen as the category.

In the citizenship area, when a law waived a ground of exclusion as well as a naturalization provision, I have placed the bill in the naturalization category since that is the ultimate relief granted. This is the same case in the private laws which provided retroactive permanent residence such as those involving Cuban nationals. These cases were primarily aimed to waive the naturalization statutes by providing the requisite residence period; therefore, they were placed in that category. In the cases of derivative citizenship, when it was not clear whether citizenship transmission, the inability to confer or derive, or retention was the obstacle to be overcome by private law, I discerned the primary purpose of the bill.

3. **Permanent residence Versus Specific Provision of Law** - In many cases, private laws were enacted which granted full permanent residence. These laws did not specifically identify a particular ground of quota, exclusion, or naturalization provision which was to be overcome. In those cases, I relied on the legislative history or the most important provision of the law which the private bill addressed. This was the same case when handling the laws which canceled deportation.
4. **Group Bills, Nonimmigrant Bills, and Miscellaneous Bills** - There were some occasions when private laws were enacted for a group of individuals not considered an omnibus measure. For instance, a bill which allowed 653 Mennonites to obtain permanent residence. In other cases, such as Sister Kenny of the Kenny Foundation of the Mayo Clinic, the bill granted temporary status. In these and other cases which were not clearly defined for a particular category, they were placed in the quota group as "miscellaneous-general" because ultimately it was the quota (or permanent residence) which was an obstacle to entry, and the uniqueness prevented them from being incorporated into a specific subcategory. Also, in the case of omnibus bills, I have separated each bill within the omnibus measure for statistical purposes.

Glossary

Adjustment of status - A provision of the immigration law which allows aliens who are in the United States to adjust their temporary status to permanent status while in the country. The forerunner of this provision is the pre-examination process.

Agreements with INS - In 1947 the Committees on the Judiciary of the House and the Senate entered into agreements with INS regarding when a stay of deportation in relationship to a private immigration bill would be effective. These agreements are confirmed in each Congress.

Barred zone - A geographic area noted in the Act of 1917 which encompassed most of Asia (parts of China, all of India, Burma, Siam, the Malay States, a part of Russia, part of Arabia, and part of Afghanistan).

Beneficiary - A person who benefits from a particular provision of law.

Chain relatives - The relatives of persons who have immigrated to the United States. For instance, if the spouse of a United States citizen has immigrated, upon obtaining United States citizenship she could then file a petition for the immigration of her parents and brothers and sisters. After their admission as immigrants and subsequent citizenship, they could then petition for other relatives.

Dear Colleague - A letter to colleagues of the House or the Senate from a Member of Congress advocating a particular position, or informing colleagues of certain information.

Eugenics - The study of genetics at the turn of the 19th century espousing intelligence based on race.

Foreign medical graduate (FMG) - Physicians who have graduated from medical school abroad and subsequently enter the United States for clinical training.

Grandfather - The provision in a new law which allows certain activities which occurred prior to the new law to be exempt from its provisions. In most cases, this occurs when the new law is more restrictive in nature.

Immediate relative - The parent, spouse, or child of a United States citizen whose visa is issued outside the overall immigration ceilings. This was formerly identified as "nonquota" visas.

Indefinitely postpone - In the Senate, this results in final action and defeat of a private bill.

Ineligible to citizenship - Under early immigration laws and Supreme Court decisions, Chinese, Japanese, and other Asians were not allowed to immigrate or become citizens. These stemmed from the Chinese Agreements and the Gentleman's Agreement by President Theodore Roosevelt as well as amendments to the immigration law.

Jus soli - Citizenship derived based on country of birth.

Jus sanguinis - Citizenship derived based on parentage.

Legalization - Provisions which allow illegal aliens who entered the United States prior to a certain date to become legal permanent residents.

Moral turpitude - A ground of exclusion relating to offenses which seriously challenge societal norms such as theft and most other crimes.

Mortgaging of visas - Allocating visas for oversubscribed countries to future yearly allotments of visas, such as in the Displaced Persons Act of 1948.

Nonimmigrant - A status allowing an alien temporary admission to the United States; that is, admission which is not as a permanent immigrant.

Nonpreference - A channel of immigration to the United States prior to 1978 under which aliens registered who did not have the required relative or skills for the particular preferences.

Nonquota - A category of immigration usually reserved for close relatives of United States citizens and permanent residents, such as the spouse or child. In 1965 this category was identified as "immediate relatives." This also means that this group is not charged to a country quota.

Omnibus - A bill which has been recommitted by the House of Representatives to its originating Committee, or a bill which includes a number of beneficiaries with similar benefits.

Oversubscribed - With respect to the National Origins Act, a country where the number of aliens registered for immigration exceeded its quota was oversubscribed. In later years, a country which had aliens registered exceeding the per country ceiling was also oversubscribed.

Parole - An immigration procedure which allows the Attorney General to bring into the United States an alien without the required documentation. This procedure, however, does not provide any permanent status.

Pass over without prejudice - In the House of Representatives, an Official Objector who has requested that a bill which is on the Private Calendar remain on the Calendar. This means it is not passed until the objector allows it to be considered.

Pre-examination - Prior to 1952, aliens who entered the United States were not allowed to change from a temporary status to permanent residence status. The pre-examination process allowed these aliens to be screened for visa requirements before going to Canada for a visa interview. At that time, a permanent visa could be issued for re-entry to the United States.

Preference - A priority for the admission of aliens to the United States. For instance, the highest preferences since 1965 have been reserved for close relatives of United States citizens or permanent residents, and other preferences relate to skills and other relatives.

Public charge - A provision of the law which excludes an alien due to the possibility that the alien may incur expenses such as institutionalization at public expense.

Quota - Prior to 1965, this was the ceiling established for each country under the National Origins Quota Act of 1921 and 1924. It was based on the nationality of the aliens from a particular country already in the United States.

Registry - The act of registering for permanent residence based on a certain date of entry into the country, whether legal or illegal

Reports from Committees (Legislative report) - Legislative reports on each bill approved by a Committee in Congress are prepared by the Committee. These reports contain a summary of the facts of the legislation, reports from the Executive Branch, and other pertinent information. They are printed as public documents prior to a bill being considered by the House or the Senate.

Report from INS (Request for report) - In the Immigration Subcommittee, after a waiver of Rule 4, a report is requested from the INS which interviews the beneficiary and checks FBI records. The report is requested under the signature of the Chairman of the Judiciary Committee, and stays deportation. In the case of an alien outside the United States, the request for report process is streamlined and also is forwarded to the Department of State. After the report is completed by the Executive Branch, it is submitted to the Committee on Judiciary and forwarded to the Subcommittee. The INS report is also included in the legislative report for the processing of the bill.

Rule 4 - A Rule of Procedure, based on an INS Agreement with the Judiciary Committees, relating to whether the Immigration Subcommittee will request a report from the INS for an alien in the United States, which would thus stay deportation until final action by the Subcommittee and full Committee. In the Senate Immigration Subcommittee, this rule has been designated Rule 3.

Sponsor - Member of Congress who introduces a bill.

Suspension of deportation - A particular provision of law which allows aliens illegally in the country to become permanent residents if they establish a certain period of residence and good moral character.

Table - Final action on a private immigration bill which is defeated in the House.

Bibliography

Berdahl, Clarence A. "The President's Veto of Private Bills." *Political Science Quarterly*, LII:4 , New York: Columbia University, 1937.

Bennett, Marion T. *American Immigration Policies.* Washington: Public Affairs Press, 1936.

Bennett, Marion. "Private Claims and Congressional Reference Cases." *Jag. L. Review*, 9:6, 1967.

Congressional Record and Annals of Congress, 1810-1988.

"The Constitutionality of Private Acts of Congress." *Yale Law Journal*, 49:712-723. New Haven: Yale Law Journal Company, 1940.

Cook, Alistair. *Alistair Cooke's America.* New York: Alfred A. Knopf, 1973.

Department of State, "Foreign Affairs Manual." 9 - Visas. Appendix D. Pt. IV, 1984, 1986.

Divine, Robert A. *American Immigration Policy, 1924-1952.* New York: Da Capo Press, 1972.

Gordon, Charles and Harry Rosenfield. *Immigration Law and Procedure.* Rev. ed., New York: Matthew Bender, 1, 1982, 4, 1990.

Gordon, Charles. "The Citizen and the State: Power of Congress to Expatriate American Citizens." *The Georgetown Law Journal*, 53, 1965.

Harper, Elizabeth J. *Immigration Laws of the United States.* 3rd ed. Indianapolis: Bobbs-Merrill Co., Inc., 1975.

Hertz, Michael T. "Limits to the Naturalization Power." *The Georgetown Law Journal*, 64:5, 1976.

Higham, John. *Strangers in the Land: Patterns of American Nativism.* 2nd ed. New York: Atheneum, 1981.

———. *Send These To Me.* New York: Atheneum, 1975.

Hutchinson, E. P. *Legislative History of American Immigration Policy.* Philadelphia: University of Pennsylvania Press, 1981.

Immigration and Naturalization Service. *Annual Report.* Fiscal Years Ending 1950, 1951, 1955, and 1956.

———. "Operating Instructions." 107.1, 1972.

———. Freedom of Information Act (FOIA) Request, Response from Alice M. Neary, dated June 21, 1989.

National Archives. House. Committee on the Judiciary. RG 233. Senate. Committee on the Judiciary. RG46.

"Private Bills." *Congressional Quarterly, Inc.*, Washington, 1982.

"Private Bills in Congress." *Harvard Law Review*, 79, 1966.

U.S. Congress. House. "Calendars of the United States House of Representatives."

———. *Cannon's Precedents of the House of Representatives of the United States.* Washington: U.S. Govt. Print. Off., VII, 1935.

———. *Constitution, Jefferson's Manual and Rules of the House of Representatives of the United States*. Wm. Holmes Brown. 98th Cong., 2nd Sess. (H. R. Doc. 277). Washington: U.S. Govt. Print. Off., 1986.

———. *Deschler's Precedents of the United States House of Representatives*, Lewis Deschler. 94th Cong., 2nd Sess., (H.R. Doc. 661). Washington: U.S. Govt. Print. Off., VI, 86th Cong.-97th Cong.

———. *Hinds' Precedents of the House of Representatives of the United States*. Asher C. Hinds. Washington: U.S. Govt. Print. Off., IV, 1907.

———. Committee on Immigration and Naturalization. *Amendments to the Immigration Laws As Recommended by the Department of Labor and by the Secretary's Ellis Island Committee*. Ser. 2-2. Washington: U.S. Govt. Print. Off., 1934.

———. *American Citizenship Rights of Women*. 72nd Cong., 2nd Sess. Washington: U.S. Govt. Print. Off., 1933.

———. *Citizenship of Wives of Americans in the Foreign Service*. 68th Cong., 1st Sess., Washington: U.S. Govt. Print. Off., 1924.

———. *Deportation of Aliens*. Hearings. 74th Cong., 1st Sess. Ser. No. 1-5. Washington: U.S. Govt. Print. Off., 1935.

———. *Naturalization of Individuals by Special Acts of Congress*. 67th Cong., 1st Sess. Washington: U.S. Govt. Print. Off., 1921.

———. *Private Relief Bills Regarding Irregular Admission Documents at Time of Entry*. 74th Cong., 2nd Sess. Ser. No. 2-3. Washington: U.S. Govt. Print. Off., 1936.

———. Committee on the Judiciary. "Calendar of Legislation." 1948-1988.

———. "Court Proceedings and Actions of Vital Interest to the Congress, Current to September 1, 1983. Committee Print No. 7, 98th Cong., 1st Sess. Washington: U.S. Govt. Print. Off., 1984.

———. "Court Proceeding and Actions of Vital Interest to the Congress, Current to March 1, 1981. Committee Print No. 11. 97th Cong., 1st Sess. Washington: U.S. Govt. Print. Off., 1981.

———. *Foreign Medical Graduates*. 95th Cong., 1st Sess. Washington: U.S. Govt. Print. Off., 1977.

———. "Grounds for Exclusion of Aliens Under the Immigration and Nationality Act." Prepared by Congressional Research Service. Library of Congress. Washington: U.S. Govt. Print. Off., 1988.

———. "The History of Private Patent Legislation in the House of Representatives." Prepared by Congressional Research Service. Library of Congress. 96th Cong., 1st Sess. Committee Print No. 1. Washington: U.S. Govt. Print. Off., 1979.

———. *Honorary U.S. Citizenship for Raoul Wallenberg*. 97th Cong., 1st Sess. Ser. No. 5. Washington, U.S. Govt. Print. Off., 1981.

———. "How Our Laws Are Made." H. R. Doc. 139. 101st Cong., 2nd Sess. Washington: U.S. Govt. Printing Off., 1990.

———. *Immigration*. 88th Cong., 2nd Sess. Pt. I, Ser. No. 13. Washington: U.S. Govt. Print. Off., 1964.

———. *Immigration.* 89th Cong., 1st Sess. Ser. No. 7. Washington: U.S. Govt. Print. Off., 1965.

———. *Immigration.* 91st Cong., 1st Sess. Ser. No. 9. Washington: U.S. Govt. Print. Off., 1970.

———. "Immigration Aspects of the International Educational Exchange Program," H.R. Rep. No. 721, 87th Cong., 1st Sess. Washington: U.S. Govt. Print. Off., 1961.

———. *INS Efficiency Legislation.* 97th Cong., 1st Sess. Washington: U.S. Govt. Print. Off., 1981.

———. "Intergovernmental Committee for European Migration and Immigration to the U.S." 84th C., 1st Sess., H.R. Rep. No. 1570. Washington: U.S. Govt. Print. Off., 1955.

———. *Investigation of the Department of Justice.* 83rd Cong., 1st Sess. Pt. 2. Washington: U.S. Govt. Print. Off., 1953.

———. Minutes. 1947-1988.

———. *Regulating Powers of Attorney General to Suspend Deportation of Aliens.* 80th Cong., 1st Sess. Washington: U.S. Govt. Print. Off., 1947.

———. *To Revise and Codify the Nationality Laws of the United States into a Comprehensive Nationality Code.* Washington: U.S. Govt. Print. Off., 1945.

———. "Rules of Procedure." 1954-1988.

———. *Siberian Seven.* 97th Cong., 2nd Sess., Ser. No. 80. Washington: U.S. Govt. Print Off., 1983.

———. Senate. "Senate Procedure, Precedents and Practices." Floyd M. Riddick. 93rd Cong., 1st Sess., Sen. Doc. No. 21. Washington, U.S. Govt. Print. Off.

———. Select Committee on Standards and Conduct. *Investigation of the Introduction of Private Immigration Bills in the Senate for Chinese Crewmen.* 90th and 91st Congresses. Sen. Rep. No. 911.

———. "Presidential Vetoes, 1789-1976." Washington: U.S. Govt. Print. Off., 1978.

———. Committee on Immigration. *Deportation of Aliens.* 75th Cong., 1st Sess. Washington: U.S. Govt. Print. Off., 1937.

———. *Deportation of Criminals, Preservation of Family Units, Permit Noncriminal Aliens to Legalize Their Status*, 74th Cong., 2nd Sess. Washington: U.S. Govt. Print. Off., 1936.

———. Committee on the Judiciary. "Annual Activities Report 1979-1980." 96th Cong., 2nd Sess. Committee Print. Washington, U.S. Govt. Print. Ofc., 1980.

———. "Calendar of Legislation." 1948-1988.

———. "The Immigration and Naturalization Systems of the United States." 81st Cong., 2nd Sess., Sen. Rep. No. 1515. Washington: U.S. Govt. Print. Off., 1950.

———. "Rules of Procedure." 1981.

———. "U.S. Immigration Law and Policy: 1952-1986." Prepared by Library of Congress. Congressional Research Office. 100th Cong., 1st Sess. Committee Print No. 100. Washington: U.S. Govt. Print. Off., 1988.

———. Senate and House. Joint Hearings before the Subcommittee of the Judiciary. *Revision of Immigration, Naturalization, and Nationality Laws*, 82nd Cong., 1st Sess. Washington: U.S. Govt. Print. Off., 1951.

U.S. President's Commission on Immigration and Naturalization. *Whom We Shall Welcome*. Washington: U.S. Govt. Print. Off., 1953.

Yacker, Marc D. "Private Bills and Federal Charters," Library of Congress. Report 79-110 JK 1000B, 1979.

Index